Operation Bagration, 23 June–29 August 1944 – The Rout of the German Forces in Belorussia covers the Red Army's Belorussian strategic operation, the linchpin of the ten major Soviet offensive efforts launched that year to clear the country of the invader. During the course of this operation the German position along the western strategic direction was destroyed, which paved the way for an advance into Poland and Germany. The success of this operation also set the stage for the Red Army's subsequent advance into the Baltic and south-eastern Europe.

Like most works generated by the General Staff, the Belorussian study divides the operation into two parts: preparation and conduct. The first deals with the massive efforts by the First Baltic and First, Second and Third Belorussian fronts to accumulate the men and materiel to break through the German defences in the swampy and forested terrain of Belorussia. This section contains valuable information on the overall correlation of forces, equipment and troop densities along the breakthrough sectors and Soviet plans for supplying the offensive, as well as detailed information regarding the employment of the various combat arms. The second part deals with the actual conduct of the several *front* operations that made up the overall effort. This section covers the initial breakthrough battles and the encirclement of the Vitebsk and Bobruisk garrisons, followed by the capture of Minsk and the encirclement of sizeable German forces east of the city.

The narrative then continues with the the follow-on operations to cut off German forces in the Baltic States and to seize crossings over the Vistula River in eastern Poland. Compiled and written by professional staff officers, this study provides a detailed look at the conduct of one of the major operations of the Second World War. This latest work, along with other studies in this series, offers another insight into the Red Army's conduct of the war at the operational-strategic level.

Richard W. Harrison earned his undergraduate and master's degrees from Georgetown University, where he specialized in Russian area studies. In 1994 he earned his doctorate in War Studies from King's College London. He also was an exchange student in the former Soviet Union and spent several years living and working in post-communist Russia.

Dr. Harrison has worked for the US Department of Defense as an investigator in Russia, dealing with cases involving POWs and MIAs. He has also taught Russian history and military history at college and university level, most recently at the US Military Academy at West Point.

Harrison is the author of two books dealing with the Red Army's theoretical development during the interwar period: *The Russian Way of War: Operational Art, 1904–1940* (2001), and *Architect of Soviet Victory in World War II: The Life and Theories of G.S. Isserson* (2010). He has also authored a number of articles on topics in Soviet military history. He is currently working on a history of the Red Army's high commands during World War II and afterwards.

Dr. Harrison currently lives with his family near Carlisle, Pennsylvania.

OPERATION BAGRATION, 23 JUNE–29 AUGUST 1944

THE ROUT OF THE GERMAN FORCES IN BELORUSSIA

OPERATION BAGRATION, 23 JUNE–29 AUGUST 1944

The Rout of the German Forces in Belorussia

Soviet General Staff

Edited and translated by Richard W. Harrison

Helion & Company

Published in cooperation with the Association of the United States Army

Helion & Company Limited
26 Willow Road
Solihull
West Midlands
B91 1UE
England
Tel. 0121 705 3393
Fax 0121 711 4075
Email: info@helion.co.uk
Website: www.helion.co.uk
Twitter: @helionbooks
Visit our blog http://blog.helion.co.uk/

Published by Helion & Company 2016, in cooperation with the Association of the United
States Army

Designed and typeset by Mach 3 Solutions Ltd (www.mach3solutions.co.uk)
Cover designed by Paul Hewitt, Battlefield Design (www.battlefield-design.co.uk)
Printed by Lightning Source Limited, Milton Keynes, Buckinghamshire

Text and maps © Association of the United States Army. English edition translated and
edited by Richard W. Harrison. Maps drawn by David Rennie.

ISBN 978-1-911096-59-7

British Library Cataloguing-in-Publication Data.
A catalogue record for this book is available from the British Library.

For details of other military history titles published by Helion & Company Limited contact
the above address, or visit our website: http://www.helion.co.uk.

We always welcome receiving book proposals from prospective authors.

Contents

List of Maps

List of Tables

Preface to the English-Language Edition

This translation of the Soviet General Staff Academy's study of the Belorussian offensive operation of 1944 contains a number of terms that may not be readily understandable to the casual reader in military history. Therefore, I have adopted a number of conventions designed to ease this task. For example, a *front* is a Soviet wartime military organization roughly corresponding to an American army group. Throughout the narrative the reader will encounter such names as the First Belorussian Front and Second Belorussian frons, and the First Baltic Front, etc. To avoid confusion with the more commonly understood meaning of the term front (i.e., the front line); italics will be used to denote an unnamed *front*. Similar German formations (i.e., Army Group Center) are also spelled out in full.

Due to their large number and frequent appearance, I have chosen to designate Soviet armies using the shortened form (i.e., 48th Army). German or Axis armies, on the other hand, are spelled out in full (Third Panzer Army). In the same vein, Soviet corps are designated by Arabic numerals (103rd Rifle Corps), while German and other Axis units are denoted by Roman numerals (e.g., LVI Panzer Corps). Smaller units (divisions, brigades, etc.) on both sides are denoted by Arabic numerals only (29th Rifle Division, 24th Infantry Division, etc.).

Given the large number of units involved in the operation, I have adopted certain other conventions in order to better distinguish them. For example, Soviet armored units are called tank corps, brigades, etc., while the corresponding German units are denoted by the popular term *panzer*. Likewise, Soviet infantry units are designated by the term rifle, while the corresponding German units are simply referred to as infantry.

Many of the place names in this study are hyphenated, such as Brest-Litovsk. In these cases, the names are separated by a single hyphen, which is to distinguish them from the recitation of a particular line of individual locales, often countered in such works, such as Moscow—Smolensk—Minsk. In the latter case, the individual villages and towns are separated by two hyphens.

The work subscribes to no particular transliteration scheme, because no entirely satisfactory one exists. I have adopted a mixed system that uses the Latin letters ya and yu to denote their Cyrillic counterparts, as opposed to the ia and iu employed by the Library of Congress, which tends to distort proper pronunciation. Conversely, I have retained the Library of Congress's ii ending (i.e., Rokossovskii), as opposed to the commonly-used y ending. I have also retained the apostrophe to denote the Cyrillic soft sign.

The original work contains a number of footnotes inserted by the authors, in order to explain this or that technical question. These have been retained as endnotes and have been supplemented by a number of appropriately identified editorial notes, which have been inserted as an explanatory guide for a number of terms that might not be readily understandable to the foreign reader.

Elsewhere, I have taken some small liberties as regards the book's overall organization, although there is nothing here that deviates in a major way from the original. These liberties primarily involve leaving out some maps, copies of orders, and tables, the inclusion of which would have made the final product too long. On the other hand, I do not take issue with some of the claims made in the text, and any errors or interpretations should be disputed after examining the relevant documents in the two countries' military archives. Nor have I attempted to make the language more "literary," and have striven throughout to preserve the military-bureaucratic flavor of the original.

Volume 1

The Preparation for the Belorussian Operation of 1944

Preface to the Russian edition

This military-historical work was prepared by an author's collective at the General Staff Academy of the USSR Armed Forces and is dedicated to the research of the multi-*front* operation carried out by the Soviet Army in Belorussia in the summer of 1944.

In creating this monograph, archival documents from the *fronts*, armies and formations, materials from the military-historical section of the General Staff's Military-Scientific Directorate, and various academies, as well as individual printed works—books, brochures and journal articles, were used.

The entire multi-*front* Belorussian operation, which consists of ten *front* operations, is examined as a complete whole. This work consists of two volumes. The first volume is divided into two parts.

The first part describes the international military-political situation by the summer of 1944, the situation on the Soviet-German front by the start of the operation, and the plan of the *Stavka*[1] of the Supreme High Command for conducting the operation, and the tasks laid down by the *Stavka* to the *fronts*, long-range aviation and the partisans are shown. This part concludes with an explanation of the measures taken by the *Stavka* of the Supreme High Command for preparing for and supplying the operation.

The second part examines the preparation of the operation in the *fronts* and armies, and then lays out the planning of the *front* and army operations, highlights the problems of the organization, the combat employment of different combat arms, the operational, engineering, party-political, materiel and medical support, troop control, communications, and operational preparation, as well as regrouping of forces, their concentration and occupation of their jumping-off positions by the start of the operation.

The second volume lays out the course of combat operations according to the stages of the multi-*front* operation, and also sums up the overall conclusions of the Belorussian by a group of *fronts* and conclusions for military art.

The work was written by a collective of authors, consisting of: Major General (retired, deceased) V.N. Asafov (combat operations of the Second Belorussian Front); senior lecturer and candidate of military sciences Colonel A.D. Bagreev (combat operations by the First Belorussian Front's left wing, conclusions on military art, and the finishing touches on several chapters on the combat operations of the First Baltic and Second and Third Belorussian fronts); candidate of military sciences and senior lecturer Major General S.S. Bronevskii (combat operations by the Third Belorussian Front); candidate of military sciences and senior lecturer, Major General F.R. Zhemaitis (retired, deceased) (introduction, the preparation and conduct of the Belorussian operation by a group of *fronts*); Major General A.K. Makar'ev (retired) (combat operations of the First Baltic Front); Major General P.N. Rubtsov (retired) (employment of the combat arms and services of the armed forces, operational support), and; Major General (retired) Yu.I. Sokolov (combat operations by the right flank of the First Belorussian Front, combat operations of the *fronts* in August 1944, and an operational summary).

---

1   Editor's note. The *Stavka* of the Supreme Commander-in-Chief (*Stavka Verkhovnogo Glavnokomanduyush-chego*) was the highest Soviet military body during the Second World War. It was formed on 23 June 1941.

Aside from this, the following individuals took part in working up the material for different sections of the work: Major General I.F. Ivanov (retired), candidate of military sciences Major General G.K. Kublanov, Colonel M.D. Malitskii (retired), candidate of military sciences Colonel M.N. Minakov, candidate of military sciences and associate professor Major General M.F. Sochilov, candidate of military sciences and associate professor Lieutenant General A.V. Sukhomlin, candidate of military sciences and associate professor Colonel Ye.S. Chalik (retired), and Major General of Artillery V.P. Chistyakov (retired).

The overall editing of this work was carried out by candidate of military sciences and associate professor Colonel A.D. Bagreev.

The work's elaboration and editing was supervised by associated professor Lieutenant General V.G. Poznyak.

Introduction

The multi-*front* Belorussian operation, which was conducted by the Soviet Army in the summer of 1944, was one of the largest operations of the Great Patriotic War. As a result of this operation the German-Fascist troops of Army Group Center were smashed, and our troops: a) completely liberated the Belorussian Soviet Republic; b) reached the Vistula River and liberated a significant part of allied Poland; c) reached the Neman River and liberated a large part of the Lithuanian Soviet Republic, and; d) forced the Neman River and reached the border of East Prussia.

Four *fronts* took part in the Belorussian offensive operation of 1944—the First Baltic, Third, Second and First Belorussian fronts, and Long-Range Aviation. This operation was organized and conducted by the *Stavka* of the Supreme High Command, the representatives of which exercised control on the ground of the operation's preparation and organized the *fronts'* cooperation.

The successful operations of these four *fronts* had a significant influence on changing the situation along the entire Soviet-German front and facilitated the assumption of the offensive by the Leningrad, Third and Second Baltic fronts in the north, as well as the First and then the Fourth Ukrainian fronts in the south. In this manner, the Belorussian operation, in the final analysis, grew into a large operation by nine Soviet *fronts* in the area from the Baltic Sea to the Carpathian Mountains.

According to the kind of combat operations, one may divide the multi-*front* Belorussian operation into two stages.

During the operation's first stage (23 June- 4 July) Soviet troops carried out the task of encircling and destroying the major forces of Army Group Center, liberated the capital of Soviet Belorussia—Minsk, and began to pursue the remains of the enemy's defeated forces. Four *front* operations were carried out during this stage of the operation.

1. The First Baltic Front's Vitebsk—Polotsk offensive operation (23 June-4 July). In this operation, the *front's* forces, while cooperating with the Third Belorussian Front, encircled the enemy's Vitebsk group of forces in the tactical defense zone and in the course of five days eliminated it. While developing the offensive in the operational depth along the Polotsk and Lepel' axes, by 4 July the *front's* forces had overcome the enemy's army and rear defensive sectors and, having inflicted a defeat on his reserves being brought up from the depth, reached the line Dvinsk (Daugavpils)—Lake Naroch', having advanced in this manner up to 180 kilometers in 12 days.

2. The Third Belorussian Front's Vitebsk—Minsk offensive operation (23 June-4 July 1944). In this operation, the *front*, while cooperating with the First Baltic Front, routed and captured the enemy's Vitebsk group of forces, broke through his defense along the main—Minsk—axis and, while pursuing his forces, forced a major water barrier—the Berezina River—on the march. Having routed the Orsha and Borisov groups of forces and having overcome the rear sectors of the enemy's defense on the march and defeating the enemy's arriving reserves, the *front* continued its headlong offensive toward Minsk, and on 3 July took the city and took part in the encirclement of a 100,000-man enemy force east of Minsk. In 12 days of attacking the *front* advanced to a depth of 280-300 kilometers.

3. The Second Belorussian Front's Mogilev—Minsk offensive operation (23 June-13 July 1944). In this operation the Second Belorussian Front operated along an auxiliary axis, but carried out important tasks. It broke through the enemy's defense, forced the Dnepr River, took the city of Mogilev, forced the Berezina River and, together with the Third and First Belorussian fronts, encircled a 100,000-man enemy group of forces east of Minsk. The task of eliminating this group of forces was entrusted to the Second Belorussian Front, which carried out this task by the close of 13 July 1944.

4. The First Belorussian Front's Bobruisk—Slutsk offensive operation (24 June-4 July 1944). In this operation the *front's* forces encircled and destroyed the enemy's Bobruisk group of forces, took part in the liberation of Minsk and the encirclement of the enemy group of forces east of Minsk, and captured the major towns of Zhlobin, Bobruisk and Slutsk, captured on the march the enemy's rear defensive sectors and, having advanced 230 kilometers, reached the Naliboki Forest and the town of Baranovichi.

The following factors had great significance for the successful conduct of the first stage of the multi-*front* Belorussian offensive operation:

a) the defeat of the right-flank groups of forces of the enemy's Army Group Center and the arrival of the *fronts'* forces in the enemy's operational depth (during the first stages of the Vitebsk—Polotsk, Vitebsk—Minsk and Bobruisk—Slutsk operations);
b) the encirclement of Army Group Center's main forces in the area east of Minsk (at the concluding stage of the Vitebsk—Minsk, Mogilev—Minsk and Bobruisk—Slutsk operations).

Our mobile forces, aviation and the Belorussian partisans played a large role in the course of some operations.

During the operation's second stage (from 5 July through 2 August 1944) the Soviet armies pursued the retreating enemy forces, defeated his strategic reserves, reached the border of East Prussia, seized bridgeheads across the Vistula River, and went over to the defensive along these lines.

During the second stage five *front* operations were conducted.

1. The First Baltic Front's Dvinsk—Siauliai offensive operation (5 July-1 August 1944). In this operation the *front's* forces first defeated the Dvinsk and then the Panezevys—Siauliai groups of enemy forces, liberated the city of Dvinsk (Daugavpils), Siauliai and, having overcome the entire operational zone of the enemy's defense, reached the shore of the Gulf of Riga.

2. The Third Belorussian Front's Vilnius—Kaunas offensive operation (5-31 July 1944). The *front's* forces, having advanced another 300 kilometers, liberated the capital of the Lithuanian Soviet Socialist Republic—Vilnius—and the second city of Lithuania—Kaunas—and reached the Neman River along a broad front and seized bridgeheads along its western bank.

3. The Second Belorussian Front's Bialystok offensive operation (5-27 July 1944) concluded successfully with the capture of the city of Bialystok. During the course of this operation the *front's* forces, having broken through the entire depth of the enemy's defense and pursuing the enemy, advanced 270 kilometers.

4. The Baranovichi—Slonim offensive operation by the right wing of the First Belorussian Front (5-16 July 1944). In this operation the *front's* forces, having broken through the enemy's defense and pursuing him, defeated the enemy's arriving reserves, advanced to a depth of 200 kilometers,

defeated the Baranovichi—Slonim enemy group of forces, and liberated the towns of Baranovichi, Slonim, Pruzhany, and others.

5. The First Belorussian Front's Brest—Siedlce offensive operation (17 July-2 August 1944).[1] In this operation the *front's* forces, having broken through the enemy's defense and defeated his operational and strategic reserves, advanced another 260 kilometers, liberated the cities of Brest, Siedlce and Lublin, reached the Vistula River in the area south of Warsaw, forced the river and established bridgeheads in the areas of Magnuszew and Pulawy.

All of these consecutive *front* operations had great significance for the development of the success achieved during the first stage of the multi-*front* Belorussian operation to a great depth, and at high speed for that time.

In strategic cooperation with the above-enumerated operations, offensive operations were also conducted along other axes: the Second Baltic Front's Rezhitska—Dvinsk (Rezekne—Daugavpils); the Third Baltic Front's Pskov—Ostrov operation; the Leningrad Front's Narva operation, and the Second Baltic Front's Madona operation. As a result of these operations, individual groups of forces from the German-Fascist Army Group North were defeated and part of the Baltic States liberated.

The strength and power of the Soviet Army in the summer of 1944 had increased so much that the Soviet Supreme High Command could almost simultaneously, along with the Belorussian operation, conduct the L'vov—Sandomierz operation, which was directed at the defeat of the German-Fascist Army Group North Ukraine and the complete liberation of Western Ukraine and the southeastern part of Poland. This operation, conducted by the forces of the First Ukrainian Front, and then by the forces of the reconstituted Fourth Ukrainian Front, was closely linked with the operations being conducted by Soviet forces in Belorussia.

From 3-29 August the First Baltic, Third, Second, and First Belorussian fronts repulsed enemy counterblows and carried out local offensive operations for improving their operational situation. Military operations took place in a situation of growing enemy resistance, for which reasons the rate of advance on some axes did not exceed 50-100 kilometers.

The scope of the multi-*front* Belorussian operation was significantly greater than even such large-scale operations of the Great Patriotic War as Stalingrad, Orel, or Belgorod—Khar'kov. 88 divisions took part in the Stalingrad multi-*front* operation, along with 15,500 guns and mortars, 900 tanks, and 1,349 planes.[2] In the Orel operation (part of the Battle of Kursk) 65 divisions took part in the first echelon, along with 18,400 guns and mortars, 2,361 tanks and self-propelled guns, and more than 3,000 planes.[3] In the Belorussian operation 160 divisions, more than 45,000 guns and mortars, more than 6,000 tanks and self-propelled guns, and around 8,000 planes (including more than 1,000 planes from Long-Range Aviation) took part.[4]

If one takes into account the fact that the L'vov—Sandomierz operation and a number of other operations were taking place at the same time, then it is not difficult to understand the enormous scope of the Soviet forces' strategic offensive.

Typical of the Belorussian operation, as was the case for many other offensive operations during 1944, was not only the great scope, but also the forces' broad maneuver, the decisiveness, daring and originality of the plan, and the ability of find new forms and methods of fighting. The problems

---

1   This operation is also referred to in Soviet historical literature as the Brest--Lublin or the Lublin—Brest operation.
2   *Operatsii Sovetskikh Vooruzhennykh Sil v Velikoi Otechestvennoi Voine*. Moscow: Voennoe Izdatel'stvo, 1958, vol. 2, p. 42.
3   *Ibid*, pp. 256-57.
4   *Ibid*, vol. 3, p. 292.

of coordinating the *fronts* were especially precisely worked out, thanks to which we managed to quickly encircle and destroy the enemy.

A distinguishing feature of the Belorussian operation was the broad participation of the partisan masses, who actively aided the Soviet troops throughout the entire operation. The partisan movement played a major role in defeating the enemy group of forces in Belorussia. Suffice it to say that by 1 May 1944 there were 449,310 partisans here.[5] The partisans' actions were closely linked with the troops' operations. For example, the partisans took part in the creation of the exterior and interior encirclement fronts of the enemy's group of forces east of Minsk, captured crossings, prepared column routes for the attacking Soviet forces, carried out reconnaissance, hindered the withdrawal of the German-Fascist formations and units, the removal of valuable property, and the removal of Soviet civilians.

In terms of the profundity and boldness of the design, the scope, number of forces and means involved, the thoroughness of preparation, and its masterful conduct, the Belorussian operation is one of the classic multi-*front* operations of the Great Patriotic War.

The victory in Belorussia had a great influence on events in Western Europe. All the reserves that the German-Fascist command still had at its disposal were transferred to the Soviet-German front, while in the West the Germans had to make do with whatever forces they had at hand. This enabled the Anglo-American forces, which had landed in northern France, to solidly consolidate on its shore and prepare an offensive for the purpose of capturing all French and Belgian territory.

The instructiveness of the Soviet forces' operations in the Belorussian operation consists in the fact that they give an example of conducting an operation for the encirclement and destruction of large enemy groups of forces in the shortest time possible.

---

5   D.F. Naumov, *Rol' Belorusskikh Partizan v Pyatom Udare 1944 Goda.* Author's dissertation abstract. Frunze Military Academy, 1953, p. 10.

Part 1

The Military-Political Situation by the Summer of 1944, the Plan for the Belorussian Operation and the *Stavka* of the Supreme High Command's Measures for Preparing the Operation

1

The Situation at the Beginning of the Belorussian Operation of 1944

The International Military-Political Situation

By the summer of 1944 the international military-political situation was being determined most of all by the historic victories of the Soviet armed forces during the preceding periods of the Great Patriotic War, as well as in the first half of 1944. These victories had been achieved thanks to the bravery and self-sacrifice of the entire Soviet people, who were giving all their spiritual and physical strength to the struggle with the German-Fascist occupiers, and who were led by the Communist Party of the Soviet Union, which had aroused the Soviet people for the sacred struggle against German fascism—the most aggressive force of world imperialism. The superiority of the Soviet social and state structure, the unity and heroic labor of the entire Soviet people, the immortal feats of the Soviet soldiers at the front, the superiority of Soviet military science, and the purposeful leadership of the Communist Party of the entire life and activity of our country were the most important factors in determining our final victory.

However, the outstanding victories gained by the Soviet army by the summer of 1944 did not yet mean that the enemy had been completely defeated. The nearer the Soviet armed forces came to the borders of Fascist Germany, the more desperate the resistance of the enemy forces became. The fascist command still had sufficiently large forces for this and the Soviet army faced a gigantic exertion of force in order to bring the war to a victorious conclusion.

The Soviet army's enormous successes showed the world that the Soviet Union could independently complete the defeat of the German-Fascist troops and liberate the peoples of Europe from the fascist yoke. This forced the USA and England, following a long delay, to open, at last, the second front in Western Europe, which was done in the summer of 1944. Fascist Germany, for the first time since the beginning of the war, found itself squeezed between two fronts.

As early as September 1943, fascist Italy—Germany's main ally in Europe—had been removed from the war. This was the result of defeats inflicted on the Italian-Fascist forces on the Soviet-German front, as well as in the area of the Mediterranean Sea. The removal of Italy from the war signified the beginning of the downfall of the fascist bloc.

The Soviet-German front continued to remain the most important one even after the landing by US and English armed forces in Normandy. However, the second front in Europe had a certain significance from the point of view of bringing closer the end of the war. Following the opening of the second front the process of disintegration became even stronger. It became clear that the fascist bloc, squeezed between two fronts, could not resist for long.

The Soviet forces, having begun their offensive in Belorussia, pinned down the main German-Fascist forces and, in this way, helped the Anglo-American forces to expand their beachhead in northern France and carry out wide-ranging offensive operations from it. As a result of the Soviet armed forces' successful offensive, the German-Fascist command could not only not remove a single division from the eastern front for repelling the Anglo-American landing, but was forced to use its available reserves to plug the breach that had appeared on the main Minsk—Warsaw direction.

The victory of the Soviet armed forces and the events in Western and Southern Europe exacerbated the internal political situation not only in Germany, but throughout the entire fascist bloc.

By the summer of 1944 fascist Germany's economic situation had worsened. Enormous human losses on the Soviet-German front were made good only by the total mobilization of those skilled workers engaged in manufacturing, in the transportation sphere, and in agriculture. The manpower shortage led to breakdowns in the production of weapons and ammunition (particularly beginning in the second part of 1944). Millions of foreign workers, which had been forcibly shipped to Germany, could not (and did not want to) replace the cadre workers mobilized into the army. Germany's agriculture also went into decline. Fascist Germany experienced a severe shortage of food, forage and raw materials. The state budget deficit grew. In 1943 the state debt rose to 250 billion marks.[1] All of this led to a sharp worsening in morale in both the army and the country's population.

The systematic strikes by Anglo-American aviation against the country's most important centers also facilitated, to a certain degree, the worsening of Germany's situation.

Fascist Germany's economic and political ties with neutral states were seriously undermined. Under the influence of the Soviet army's victories, many neutral countries began to restrict their trade with the fascist states and avoid political ties with them.

The situation among Germany's satellites was no better. The defeat of the Romanian forces at Stalingrad and in succeeding operations had led to a situation in which the Romanian monarchical government, led by Antonescu,[2] could no longer actively support fascist Germany, because the Romanian people began to more and more decisively come out against such a policy. Under pressure from the popular masses, Antonescu was forced to declare that in the future Romanian troops would be employed only for the defense of their own territory.

In Bulgaria the partisan movement had assumed a broad scope and had set itself the task of liberating Bulgaria from the fascist yoke. In the summer of 1944 the number of partisans exceeded 40,000 men. Under the influence of the Soviet army's victories and the growth of the partisan movement, the Bulgarian czarist government was forced to begin negotiations with Anglo-American circles for a separate peace.

The situation in Hungary at the beginning of 1944 was so tense, in connection with the defeat of Hungarian troops on the territory of the Soviet Union, that the German-Fascist command was forced to occupy Hungary in March 1944.

The situation of Germany's last satellite—Finland—was the most difficult. Following the Soviet forces' offensive in Karelia, Finland was on the verge of a military catastrophe.

The situation in the German-occupied European countries had become sharply exacerbated by the summer of 1944.

In France the power of the Resistance, led by communists, had broadly expanded its struggle for the complete expulsion of the occupiers, for national independence and for democratic changes in the country. In the summer of 1944 these forces numbered about 400,000 fighters.[3]

Following the Anglo-American landing in France the French patriots became more active and they began to destroy enemy garrisons. By the end of June and beginning of July 1944 they had

---

1   N.I. Somin, *Vtoraya Mirovaya Voina (1939-1945 gg.).* Moscow, 1954, p. 49.

2   Editor's note. Ion Victor Antonescu (1882-1946) joined the Romanian army in 1904 and served in the Second Balkan War and the First World War. During the interwar period he rose rapidly through the ranks and became defense minister. He early on associated himself with the Iron Guard and came to power in a 1940 coup. He aligned Romania with Nazi Germany and took his country into war against the Soviet Union. Antonescu was deposed in August 1944 and arrested. He was later tried and executed.

3   *Vtoraya Mirovaya Voina 1939-1945 gg. Voenno-Istoricheskii Ocherk.* Moscow: Voenizdat, 1958, p. 642.

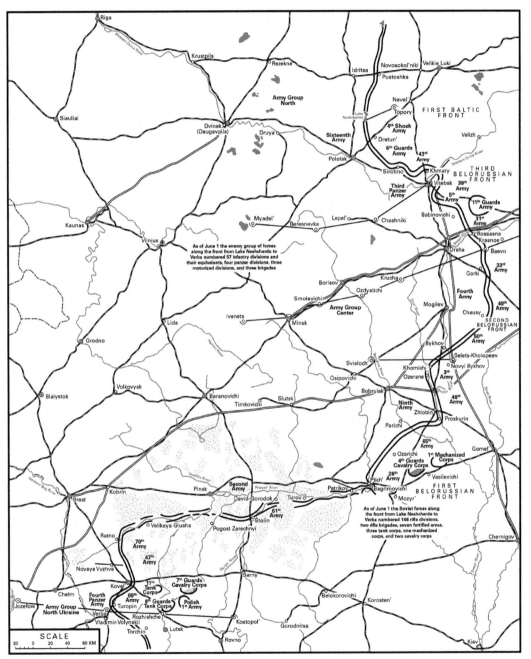

Map 1 The Situation, 1 June 1944.

liberated 24 large French towns and had completed their preparations for an armed rising in the French capital of Paris.

In Czechoslovakia, as in France, the communists headed the national-liberation struggle of the popular masses against the fascist occupiers. This struggle took on such broad contours that it grew into an uprising that broke out in August 1944 in Slovakia.

The Yugoslav People's Liberation Army, which numbered up to 300,000 fighters in its ranks, was also struggling against the fascist occupiers.

The small but brave Albanian people were also waging a very heroic struggle against the occupiers and had created their own national liberation army, which in the summer of 1944 numbered up to 70,000 members.

In Greece, which had been occupied by the fascist states throughout the Second World War, the partisan war also did not cease. In 1944 this war became particularly widespread in connection with the approach of the Soviet army to the Balkans.

In Poland, with the formation on 21 July 1944 of the Polish Committee of National Liberation, which was the first government of the new Poland, the Polish people acquired a strong centralized leadership, which facilitated the further growth of the struggle against the occupiers.

There was also a national-liberation movement in such countries as Belgium, Denmark, Holland, and Norway. The enemy in these countries was forced to maintain significant occupation forces.

Thus the national-liberation movement in all the enslaved countries in 1944 was developing at a rapid pace and was becoming an important factor in world events.

As of 10 June 1944 the German-Fascist command disposed of 374 divisions and 23 independent brigades. Of these, 325 divisions and five brigades were German, while the satellites had 49 divisions and 18 brigades. These forces were deployed as follows: 228 divisions and 23 brigades on the Soviet-German front, of which 179 divisions and five brigades were German, while the satellites had 49 divisions and 18 brigades; 60 German-Fascist divisions in France, Belgium and Holland; 26 German-Fascist divisions in Italy; 17 German-Fascist divisions in Norway and Denmark; 19 German-Fascist divisions in Yugoslavia, Albania and Greece, and; the German High Command disposed of 24 divisions in its reserve in Germany, Austria, Poland, and Hungary.[4]

This data shows quite conclusively that by the summer of 1944 the Soviet-German front remained, as before, the most important front of the Second World War. Here were located more than half of the fascist bloc's forces in Europe. Along with this, the resistance movement in the occupied countries also drew off significant enemy forces and kept the German-Fascist command from freely transferring them.

By the summer of 1944 Fascist Germany's Far Eastern ally—imperialist Japan—was also in a difficult situation.

In 1944 Anglo-American forces continued their offensive operations in the Pacific area, launching their main attack in the central part of the ocean, with the goal of occupying the primary air and sea bases of the Japanese first line of defense. In the beginning of 1944 American forces occupied the majority of the Marshall Islands and in the summer began operations to occupy the Mariana and Caroline islands. On 15 June 1944, before the beginning of the Belorussian operation, the American armed forces captured the island of Saipan in the Mariana Islands, which was located 1,350 miles from Tokyo. This enabled the American air force to begin systematic raids on the Japanese home islands from airfields located on the Marianas.

In Burma the Japanese forces, which were waging defensive actions against the Anglo-Indian and Chinese-American forces, were forced in the first half of 1944 to abandon the northern part of the country.

---

4   *Ibid*, p. 571.

A difficult situation for the Japanese also arose in China in 1944. The Japanese command, foreseeing the possible loss of its maritime communications with the South Seas and Southeast Asia, undertook a number of offensive operations on the mainland against the Kuomintang forces for the purpose of creating a corridor connecting the central and southern parts of China. This secured the land communications between Japan and the southern Chinese ports and through them with the South Seas. As a result of the traitorous policies of the Chiang-Kai-shek[5] clique, the Japanese troops managed to seize a significant part of central China in the first half of 1944 and capture such an important locale as the city of Zhengzhou. However, the Chinese Eighth and New Fourth National Liberation armies, which began active operations in the beginning of 1944 and which pinned down up to 60 percent of the enemy forces located in China at this time, created the greatest difficulties for the Japanese imperialists. The leading role in these armies belonged to the heroic Chinese Communist Party, which inspired the Chinese people to struggle against the interventionists. The conduct of military operations over the years against large Japanese forces in China was a major contribution to the overall struggle of the freedom-loving peoples against imperialism and its most aggressive force—fascism.

In 1944 the national-liberation struggle became especially broad in the Japanese-occupied countries of Southeast Asia.

All of this taken together led to a situation whereby in the spring of 1944 the Japanese General Staff adopted War Plan "Sho-Go," according to which the main Japanese strategic defensive line in the Pacific ran through the islands of the South Seas, the Philippines, Taiwan (Formosa), the Ryukyu Islands, and the Japanese home islands. According to this plan, the main Japanese task was to hold the metropolitan area, the area of the South Seas, and the captured territories on the Asian mainland. Simultaneously, the Japanese militarists were forced to change their policy and, together with this, their strategy *vis a vis* the Soviet Union. Having renounced their strategic offensive plan for seizing the Soviet Far East, which had been prepared in 1941-42, in 1944 they began working on a new defensive plan.

For the Soviet Union, 1944 was a year of a new expansion of our military economy and the growth of our industry, agriculture, transport, and cultural construction.

The production of ferrous metals in 1944 grew, compared to 1943, almost by a third, while the smelting of iron grew by 31 percent, steel by 29 percent, the production of rolled iron by 28 percent, coal production by 31 percent, and the production of electrical energy by 21 percent.[6] The volume of production in the eastern part of the country increased 1.5 times in 1944 in comparison with the previous year.[7]

The pace of constructing industrial enterprises in the east significantly surpassed the pace of construction in peacetime. The country's eastern areas became the basis of our military economy, while industry in the Urals accounted for up to 40 percent of all military production.[8]

Thanks to the wise leadership of the Communist Party of the Soviet Union and the Soviet government, industry, agriculture and transportation were quickly being restored in those areas of

---

5   Editor's note. Chiang Kai-shek (1887-1975) joined in the army in 1906 and later took part in the Chinese revolution of 1911. He then joined Sun Yat-sen's Kuomintang and, following the latter's death, soon became head of the Nationalist movement. For twenty years he fought domestic communists and the Japanese until his defeat by the Chinese Communists in 1949. He and his Nationalist government escaped to Taiwan.

6   Ye.I. Soldatenko, *Trudovoi Podvig Sovetskogo Naroda v Velikoi Otechestvennoi Voine*. Gospolitizdat, 1954, pp. 50-51.

7   *Ibid*, pp. 50-51.

8   *Ibid*, pp. 50-51.

the country liberated from the enemy. The gross output of industry in the liberated areas increased almost three times in 1944, compared to 1943.[9]

The output of weapons and ammunition in 1944 reached such a level that the Soviet Union left behind not only fascist Germany, but also, according to a number of indices, even such countries as Great Britain and the USA. Soviet military industry in 1944 produced two times more tanks, self-propelled guns and armored cars than Germany, 1.5 times more than the USA, and six times more than Great Britain; two times more aircraft than Germany or Great Britain; four times as many guns of all calibers than Germany, 2.5 times more than the USA, and six times more than Great Britain.[10]

In 1944 the Soviet army was fully supplied with shells. In that year 240 million shells, bombs and mines were produced, as well as 7.4 billion small-arms rounds, which enabled us to support the Soviet troops' combat activities with fire of all types better than before.

In 1944 Soviet transport honorably coped with the tasks facing it. The railroads carried twice as much freight that year as in the first year of the war. The railroads' turnover of goods in 1944 rose 22 percent compared with the previous year. The railroads' work in the liberated areas was quickly organized.

Agriculture also achieved great successes. From 1943 through 1944 the amount of land under cultivation grew by almost 16 million hectares. Despite the war, the number of cattle, sheep, goats, and pigs grew. Thanks to the help of the entire country, agriculture was quickly restored in the liberated areas. Labor productivity in agriculture in 1944 grew 1.5 times compared to the prewar level.

Thus the situation by the summer of 1944 had become significantly more favorable for the Soviet Union, even in comparison with the previous year. Although late, nonetheless the enormous forces of all the main states of the antifascist coalition were now in motion. The second front in Western Europe was now a fact. The growing power of the Soviet Union instilled complete confidence in the favorable outcome of the war in the immediate future.

The victorious offensive operations by the Soviet armed forces, which had continued almost uninterruptedly since November 1942, had by the spring of 1944 led to a radical change in the military-political situation. The rapid end of the Second World War was already apparent. It was clear to the entire world that the bloc of fascist powers could not change the course of the war in its favor.

The German-Fascist command, lacking sufficient reserves, was determined to drag out the war and achieve a separate peace with the USA and Great Britain. In connection with this, despite enormous losses in the spring of 1944, as well as the fact that the overall correlation of forces on the Soviet-German front was not in Germany's favor, the German command continued to wage military operations, while striving to delay and bleed the Soviet forces.

The Situation on the Soviet-German Front

The Soviet armed forces were assigned the following tasks in 1944: the complete liberation of the Soviet country from the German-Fascist occupiers, reaching the state borders in the west and carrying military operations onto the enemy's territory. These tasks were to be resolved by means of consecutively defeating the enemy's main strategic groups of forces along the entire Soviet-German front.

---

9   *Ibid*, p. 53.
10 *Ibid*, p. 55.

In 1944 the Soviet army conducted an almost uninterrupted offensive. In the first half of 1944 it conducted operations to defeat the enemy's flank groups of forces operating on the Soviet-German front.

The first such operation—the operation to lift the blockade of Leningrad—was conducted in January-February 1944 against the German-Fascist Army Group North. As a result of the offensive, the northern strategic flank of the German-Fascist armies was defeated, all of Leningrad Oblast' was liberated, and the blockade of Leningrad completely lifted. Favorable conditions were created for launching new and powerful attacks against the enemy in the future along the Karelian Isthmus, in the Baltic States, and in Belorussia.

There then followed a series of consecutive offensive operations on the Ukrainian right bank in January-April 1944, against Army Group South. As a result of this offensive, the southern strategic flank of the German-Fascist armies was defeated and the Ukrainian right bank was liberated. Our forces reached the state borders of Romania and Czechoslovakia along a 400-kilometer front and transferred combat operations onto Romanian territory. With the arrival of the Soviet armed forces at the Carpathians, the defense of the German-Fascist forces was cut into two isolated parts: one was based on southeastern Poland, with the other on Romania. An enormous jumping-off bridgehead had been created, which could support the possible launching of new attacks both toward Belorussia, as well as the Black Sea coast, the Balkans and the Crimea.

Following this, an offensive operation was conducted to liberate the Crimea. This operation was successfully carried out in April-May 1944.

In June 1944 an offensive operation by Soviet land and naval forces began in Karelia, for the purpose of defeating the German-Finnish forces operating in this area, liberating the greater part of Soviet Karelia, the Kirov Railroad, the White Sea-Baltic Canal, and supporting the right flank of the Soviet forces along the southern shore of the Gulf of Finland.

As a result of all these operations, favorable conditions were created for defeating the German-Fascist Army Group Center in Belorussia.

The defeat of the enemy around Leningrad and in Karelia resulted in the complete breakdown of the Finnish armed forces and rendered them incapable of further active participation in the war on the side of fascist Germany.

Our offensive operations on the Ukrainian right bank and in the Crimea placed not only Romania, but fascist Germany's other Balkan allies, before a military catastrophe.

The Soviet army's successes in the first half of 1944 showed that the Soviet Union was capable, relying on its own forces alone, of finally defeating fascist Germany and liberating all of Europe from the Hitlerite yoke.

As a result of the Soviet army's victories in the first half of 1944, by the middle of June the line of the Soviet-German front had radically changed. The line ran almost along the border of Soviet Karelia as far as Vyborg, from Narva and Pskov, south. At Polotsk the front turned to the southeast, rounded Vitebsk from the north, east and south, and then ran east of Orsha and Mogilev, turned to the southwest in the direction of Zhlobin and Mozyr', and then to the west in the direction of Kovel', rounding it from the north, east and south. At Kovel' the front sharply turned to the south, ran east of L'vov, west of Chernovtsy, north of Iassi and Kishinev, and then ran to the southeast to the lower course of the Dnestr River.

By the middle of 1944 two spacious salients (bulges) had formed on the Soviet-German front. One was in Ukraine, to the south of the Pripyat'' River, where the forces of the First and Second Ukrainian fronts had cut deeply into the enemy's defense, occupying a flanking position *vis a vis* army groups Center and North Ukraine. The other was in Belorussia, where Army Group Center was defending a front deep into our position (the so-called "Belorussian balcony"). This created a situation whereby Army Group Center's strategic front was outflanked by Soviet *fronts* to the north and south.

The strategic initiative was solidly in the hands of the Soviet army and the Soviet Supreme High Command, while planning operations for the summer of 1944, could freely choose among the types of strategic actions and directions of the main attack.

The German-Fascist command attached great importance to the retention of Belorussia, due to the fact that this bridgehead covered the shortest route to Germany's important political-administrative centers and economic areas, particularly East Prussia, and was the center of the entire German-Fascist defense on the Soviet-German front. On the other hand, the liberation of Belorussia by Soviet forces meant the shifting of the war to German territory and the creation of the prerequisites for attacks against forces operating in the Baltic States and in Ukraine, and could, on the whole, lead to significant changes in the strategic situation in favor of the Soviet troops.

The German-Fascist command, in evaluating the strategic situation of the Soviet armed forces, believed that in the summer of 1944 the Soviet army's main attack would fall south of the Pripyat" River, while in Belorussia only supporting actions could be expected. Thus by the summer of 1944 the German-Fascist command maintained a large part of its forces (particularly mobile units) along the southern wing of the Soviet-German front.

This was the German-Fascist command's latest miscalculation in evaluating the forces, type and direction of the Soviet forces' activities.

The Hitlerite command, issuing from such an evaluation of the situation, had created by the summer of 1944 the following group of its forces on the Soviet-German front.

In the north, in the area of Murmansk Oblast', Karelia, and the Karelian Isthmus, the Twentieth German-Fascist Mountain Army and the Finnish army were defending, consisting of 22 infantry and one *panzer* division, and nine infantry divisions and one cavalry brigade.

In the Baltic States, on a front from Narva to Polotsk, Army Group North ("Group Narva," Eighteenth and Sixteenth armies) was defending, numbering 34-35 divisions. The army group's actions were supported by the First Air Fleet.

In Belorussia, against the First Baltic, Third, Second, and First Belorussian fronts, Army Group Center (Third Panzer, Fourth, Ninth and Second field armies) was operating along a front from Polotsk to the Pripyat' River. This was a powerful enemy army group, numbering 48-49 divisions, whose operations were supported by the Sixth Air Fleet.

Western Ukraine and Romania were defended by two army groups—North Ukraine and South Ukraine, consisting of 77 infantry, 13 panzer, two motorized, and two cavalry divisions. The main forces of the Eighth and Fourth air fleets supported their operations.

The German-Fascist command on the eastern front had in its reserve only five divisions (one infantry, two panzer, one motorized, and one cavalry) and one brigade (motorized).

Fascist Germany's air force on the Soviet-German front in June 1944 numbered more than 2,500 aircraft.

By the beginning of the Belorussian operation, the forces of the German-Fascist Army Group North in the Baltic States and Army Group Center in Belorussia were supported by the Sixth Air Fleet (First and Fourth air divisions, the "Posen" and "Ost" air areas, and the Second Anti-Aircraft Corps), which accounted for about 56 percent of all the military air forces on the Soviet-German front.

Thus if we discount the German-Fascist troops operating in Finland, the maneuver of which was difficult for the fascist command to carry out, then the greater part of the entire number of German-Fascist divisions, including 70 percent of all the panzer and motorized divisions, were located south of the Pripyat' River.

On the whole, the situation on the Soviet-German front was favorable to the further development of offensive operations by Soviet troops.

Features of the Most Important Operational Directions in Belorussia

The situation that had arisen in Belorussia by the summer of 1944, as well as the physical-geographical conditions of the area of military activities, the grouping of the sides' forces, and other data determined the following five most important operational directions in the Belorussian operation of 1944.

The Polotsk—Svencionys operational direction leads in a western direction from the Nevel'—Gorodok—Velizh area, to the important locales of Polotsk, Lepel' and Svencionys. This direction is limited to the north by the line Nevel'—Daugavpils, and to the south by the line Velizh—Vitebsk—Begoml'—Vilnius. The axis of the direction is the line Gorodok—Lepel'—Svencionys. The overall depth of the direction from the front line to the line Daugavpils—Svencionys—Vilnius is about 200 kilometers, and its width is 100-120 kilometers.

The operational direction's significance is that it enabled us to launch an attack along the northern flank of Army Group Center's main forces and liberate such important targets as Polotsk, Lepel', Vitebsk, Daugavpils, and Vilnius.

The troops' combat operations along this operational direction developed over broken terrain. The large number of lakes within this direction and the wooded and swampy areas of the upper reaches of the Berezina and Western Dvina rivers made it easier for the enemy to wage defensive actions and significantly restricted the maneuver of our attacking forces.

The direction's natural borders were the Western Dvina and Berezina rivers (in their upper reaches).

Within the direction were the Vitebsk—Polotsk—Daugavpils through railroad line and the Vitebsk—Lepel' paved road.

The Orsha—Minsk operational direction led from the Vitebsk—Krasnoe—Smolensk area through Borisov to the capital of Belorussia—Minsk. The direction is bounded on the north by the Polotsk—Svencionys operational direction and on the south by the line Krasnoe—Minsk. The direction's axis was the line Orsha—Borisov—Minsk. The direction's overall depth from the front line to the line Molodechno—Minsk is about 200-22- kilometers, while its width is 80-90 kilometers.

The operational direction's significance was that it led to the Belorussian capital—Minsk, and included within its boundaries such important targets as Vitebsk, Orsha and Borisov. An attack along this direction would hit the center of Army Group Center.

The troops' combat activities along this direction developed over slightly broken terrain, which does not present serious natural obstacles for the conduct of large-scale operations involving all the combat arms.

The direction's natural borders were the Dnepr and Berezina rivers and the wooded and swampy areas of the Berezina River north of Borisov.

Within the direction was the Smolensk—Minsk through railroad and the Smolensk—Minsk paved road.

The Mogilev—Minsk operational direction was bordered to the north by the southern boundary of the Orsha—Minsk operational direction, and to the south by the line Gaishin—Pukhovichi. The direction's axis was the line Mogilev—Berezino—Minsk. The direction's overall depth from the front line to Minsk was 220-240 kilometers, with a width of 100-120 kilometers.

The operational direction's significance is, that in moving from the front Baevo—Slavgorod, it constituted the shortest route to Minsk and included such an important locale as the town of Mogilev, and threatened the enemy with a breakthrough of his defense along the central direction.

Combat operations along this direction would develop in wooded and swampy terrain, which would limit their maneuver to a significant degree. The direction's natural borders were the Dnepr, Drut' and Berezina rivers, along with their swampy valleys.

The direction's road net is limited. Here there was only the Mogilev—Minsk paved road.

The Mogilev—Minsk operational direction was secondary *vis a vis* the Orsha—Minsk and Bobruisk—Slutsk directions.

The Bobruisk—Slutsk operational direction, proceeding from the line Komarichi—Zhlobin—Kobyl'shchina, led to such important towns as Bobruisk, Minsk and Slutsk.

The direction was bordered on the north by the southern boundary of the Mogilev—Minsk direction, and on the south by the Pripyat' River. The direction's axis was the road Zhlobin—Bobruisk—Slutsk.

The direction's overall depth from the front line to Slutsk was 150-170 kilometers, and its width 120-150 kilometers.

The operational direction's significance was that it made it possible to outflank the enemy's main forces in Belorussia and included such important towns as Bobruisk and Slutsk.

Combat operations developed over broken and wooded-swampy terrain, which limited the troops' maneuver to a significant degree, as well as cooperation with forces operating along the Kovel'—Lublin operational direction.

The direction's natural borders were the Berezina and Ptich' rivers, along their lower courses.

The direction's road net was limited. The most important was the Bobruisk—Slutsk paved road.

The Kovel'—Lublin operational direction ran to the northwest from the Kamen'-Kashirskii—Kovel'—Sokal'—Sarny area to the important towns of Lublin, Brest and Siedlce, and then on to Warsaw. The direction was bordered on the north by the Pripyat' River, Brest and the Western Bug River, and on the southwest by Sokal', Lublin and the Vistula River. The direction's axis was the line Kovel'—Lublin. The direction's overall depth from the front line as far as Lublin was about 120-150 kilometers, while its width was about 100 kilometers.

The operational direction's significance was that it included such important targets as Lublin and Siedlce and led to the Polish capital of Warsaw.

Combat operations developed over broken terrain that did not inhibit broad maneuver. The direction's natural boundary was the Western Bug River.

The direction's road network was well developed. There were two through rail lines—Kovel'—Brest—Siedlce—Warsaw, and Kovel'—Lublin—Warsaw, and two paved roads, Kovel'—Brest—Warsaw, and Kovel'—Lublin—Warsaw.

These five operational directions were, on the whole, accessible to operations by all the combat arms and enabled us to carry out a large-scale multi-*front* offensive operation directed at defeating the enemy's powerful Army Group Center.

The Sides' Situation and Condition

The Engineering Preparation of the Belorussian Bridgehead and the Character of the Enemy's Defense

The enemy, taking advantage of the extremely favorable terrain conditions, employed his troops, construction organizations, prisoners of war, and the local population to construct defensive lines in Belorussia, beginning in 1941. This construction was especially intensive in the spring of 1944.

The engineering outfitting of the terrain was most developed along the Polotsk—Minsk, Orsha—Minsk, Mogilev—Minsk, and Bobruisk—Minsk operational directions, which led from the front line to road junctions, large towns and other important targets.

Taking into account the great significance of defending Belorussia, which covered the highly important East Prussian and Warsaw directions, the German-Fascist command issued an order in the first half of March 1944, calling for the construction of the Vitebsk, Orsha, Mogilev and Bobruisk defensive areas.

Along the northeastern and eastern borders of the Belorussian salient the enemy had prepared his main "Panther" defensive line, which consisted along the main directions of several defensive zones, based upon the strong fortifications of the Polotsk and Vitebsk areas; then this line ran to the south and ended with the fortifications southeast of Orsha. This line had been most powerfully prepared along the Orsha—Minsk direction for covering the areas along the Moscow—Minsk railroad and paved road.

The so-called Dnepr defensive system was the continuation of the "Panther" defensive line south of Orsha, which stretched as far as Zhlobin and consisted of several defensive zones, based upon the Mogilev and Bobruisk defensive centers of resistance.

The enemy had in his operational depth a number of defensive zones, which cut the most important directions and covered the crossing over the main water obstacles.

The army defensive zone (the position of the army reserves) was built along the entire front and was based on such important centers of resistance as Polotsk, Beshenkovichi, Bogushevsk, Orsha, Mogilev, and Bobruisk.

The enemy was building a rear defensive zone in the operational depth along the Berezina River, which cuts through the entire territory of Belorussia,. Having christened this the "Catastrophe" zone, he evidently did not plan to retreat to it.

There were two more rear defensive zones to the west of the Berezina River. The first such zone ran along the line Svencionys—Baranovichi and then to the south. It had been in existence since the time of the First World War and was run down. The enemy, evidently, did not place great hopes on it.

The second zone was located even further to the west, along the East Prussian border. In its depth, this zone merged with the old permanent fortifications in East Prussia itself.

Along the Warsaw direction, to the west of the Berezina River, there was an intermediary defensive zone along the Ptich' River. This zone did not represent a serious obstacle, as it was outfitted only with intermittent trenches.

Such was the enemy's overall system of fortifications on Belorussian territory before the beginning of the Belorussian operation.

The Character of the Enemy's Defense Along the Polotsk—Svencionys Operational Direction

The enemy had in the tactical zone along this direction two previously prepared defensive zones.

The depth of the main zone (the "main battlefield") varied from three to four kilometers and, along certain axes, reached five to six kilometers.

The engineering preparation of the main zone was not homogenous, and the most well prepared sectors were along the Polotsk and Vitebsk directions, where the enemy expected our attacks.

The engineer outfitting was most durable in certain strong points and defensive centers. In places these strong points and defensive junctions were connected with each other by trenches. Anti-tank and anti-personnel obstacles, such as mines and fortifications, were not constructed before the front line of defense, but in the depth, mainly along roads and in narrow areas between the lakes.

The city of Vitebsk was an important center in the enemy defensive system along this direction. Rail lines and roads ran through Vitebsk to the Baltic States. The German-Fascist command considered Vitebsk the "key" and "shield" of the Baltic States. Vitebsk's engineer outfitting consisted of two defensive zones on the approaches to the city, while the city itself had been well configured for defense. The overall defensive depth, including the city, reached as much as 15 kilometers.

The second defensive zone (the "corps reserves' position") along both the Polotsk and Vitebsk directions was not contiguous. It ran 5-10 kilometers from the front line of the first defensive position. It was 2-3 kilometers deep and consisted of one position.

All the large inhabited locales in the tactical zone were prepared for defense and were included, as were the strong points, in the overall defensive system.

An army and two intermediate defensive zones were outfitted in the operational zone along the Polotsk and Vitebsk directions.

The army defensive zone (the "position of the army reserves") along the Polotsk direction was prepared 20-30 kilometers from the forward edge of the main defensive zone. The forward edge of this zone ran through Polotsk and then along the western bank of the Western Dvina River. The engineer outfitting here was not well developed. The town of Polotsk was configured for perimeter defense. Along the Vitebsk direction the army defensive zone ran 30-50 kilometers west of Vitebsk, but was weakly prepared in the engineering sense, consisting of two positions, outfitted with broken trenches.

Nor were intermediate defensive zones well developed. The town of Lepel', located in the operational depth, was configured for perimeter defense.

The overall depth of the terrain's engineer outfitting in the enemy's defense along the Vitebsk direction reached up to 150 kilometers (as far back as the "Catastrophe" rear defensive position).

The Character of the Enemy's Defense Along the Orsha—Minsk Operational Direction

The German-Fascist command devoted a lot of attention to the engineer outfitting of the terrain along the Orsha—Minsk direction, which cut the Moscow—Minsk highway.

Main and second defensive zones were prepared in the tactical zone to the east of Orsha.

The main defensive zone (the "main battlefield") was 1.5-3 kilometers deep and, in the engineering sense, was outfitted with 2-3 trenches. In the area adjacent to the Moscow—Minsk highway, the number of trenches had been raised to five.

A second defensive zone had been prepared at a remove of 7-15 kilometers from the forward edge of the first zone (the position of the corps reserves). This zone also had a single position, outfitted with 1-2 trenches. In the sector where the second defensive position covered the Moscow—Minsk highway, the number of trenches reached 3-4. In the important sectors of the main and second zones, armored hoods had been set up, as well as prefabricated reinforced concrete firing structures.

An intermediate position had been prepared ten kilometers east of Orsha.

Anti-tank and anti-personnel mines were most dense in the area of the Moscow—Minsk highway.

Between Vitebsk and Orsha, along the Bogushevsk axis, the terrain was wooded and swampy, with a large number of lakes and river barriers. The enemy did not calculate on the possibility of large troop formations and equipment being employed here, and thus along this direction the main and second defensive zones were relatively weakly developed.

Army, intermediate and rear defensive zones were outfitted in the operational zone.

The army defensive zone (the position of the army reserves), which included the towns of Bogushevsk and Orsha, had been prepared along the western bank of the Dnepr River. Its remove from the forward edge of the main defensive zone reached 25-30 kilometers. The engineer preparation of this zone was not homogenous. The most heavily prepared positions were along the Moscow—Minsk highway, where four trench lines had been dug.

The town of Orsha, which was a major junction for roads and crossings across the Dnepr River, was configured for perimeter defense.

The intermediate defensive zone, which ran along the western bank of the Drut' River, cut the Moscow—Minsk highway. Its engineer outfitting consisted of the preparation of separate strong points.

The rear defensive zone ("Catastrophe"), which ran along the western bank of the Berezina River, included the town of Borisov, which had been prepared for perimeter defense and which consisted of a single position and had 1-2 continuous trenches along the main axes.

Along the Moscow—Minsk highway, besides Borisov, Minsk had been prepared for all-round defense, as a very important rail and road junction.

The overall depth of the engineering preparation of the defense as far back as Minsk along the Moscow—Minsk highway reached 300 kilometers.

The Character of the Enemy's Defense Along the Mogilev—Minsk Operational Direction

Main and second defensive zones were outfitted in the tactical zone to a depth of 20 kilometers.

The depth of the main defensive zone (the "main battlefield") reached 4-5 kilometers. Its engineer outfitting was uneven. Along the main axes the number of trenches reached up to 5-7, of which the first two were continuous, with the rest intermittent.

The second defensive zone (the "position of the corps reserves") ran at a remove from the forward edge of the first zone of up to 10-15 kilometers and had only one intermittent trench.

Army, intermediate and rear defensive zones had been prepared in the operational zone.

The army defensive zone (the "position of the army reserves") ran along the western bank of the Dnepr at a distance of 40-50 kilometers from the forward edge of the main defensive zone. From the engineering point of view, it was outfitted with two lines of trenches. A number of towns and large inhabited locales, which covered the important crossings over the Dnepr River, formed part of this zone's defensive system.

The town of Mogilev, which covered the crossings over the Dnepr River, was a large rail and road junction and had been prepared for all-round defense.

The enemy had an intermediate defensive zone In the operational depth along the Drut' River, and along the Berezina River a rear defensive zone ("Catastrophe"), which cut the Mogilev—Minsk paved road.

The overall depth of the previously prepared engineering defense along the Mogilev axis reached as much as 140 kilometers.

The Character of the Enemy's Defense Along the Bobruisk—Slutsk Operational Direction

Main and second defensive zones had been prepared in the tactical zone.

The depth of the main defensive zone (the "main battlefield") reached six kilometers and, in places, eight. The zone was most highly developed in the engineering sense. It had 3-4 and, in places, 5-7 trench lines, with a large number of communications trenches.

Obstacles, as well as fortification outfitting, were highly developed along the Rogachev—Bobruisk and Zhlobin—Bobruisk paved roads.

The second defensive zone (the position of the corps reserves) ran at a distance of 15-20 kilometers from the forward edge of the main defensive zone. It consisted of a single position and was outfitted with 1-2 lines of trenches.

Large inhabited locales, located in the tactical defensive zone, had been prepared for defense (for example, the town of Zhlobin).

Army and rear defensive zones had been prepared in the operational zone.

The army defensive zone (the position of the army reserves) ran at a distance of 25-40 kilometers from the forward edge of the main zone. Located at a distance of 15-20 kilometers from Bobruisk, it served as the outer defensive line for the town.

In the engineering sense, the army defensive zone was outfitted with 2-3 lines of trenches.

A rear defensive zone ("Catastrophe") had been outfitted along the western bank of the Berezina River. This zone was up to 50 kilometers from the forward edge of the main defensive zone and had 1-2 lines of trenches.

The town of Bobruisk, which was an important communications junction and a center for crossings over the Berezina River, was extremely important to the enemy's defensive system. As a large center of resistance, it was well developed in the engineering sense.

30 kilometers west of Bobruisk, along the western bank of the Ptich' River, there was an intermediate defensive zone, outfitting with individual strong points, which covered the crossings along the main routes.

Thus the enemy along the Bobruisk direction had a prepared defensive in the engineer sense, which reached up to 80 kilometers and more in depth. It was most developed up to a depth of 50 kilometers, (as far as Bobruisk). Along this stretch, the enemy, by skillfully using the terrain's natural features, had previously outfitted a series of defensive zones with a developed system of trenches and obstacles.

In the southern part of Belorussia, along the Pripyat' River and its tributaries, there were undeveloped positions facing to the south. Large inhabited locales and the town of Pinsk, which were located along this direction, had been prepared by the enemy for defense.

The Character of the Enemy's Defense Along the Kovel'—Lublin Operational Direction

Two defensive zones had been prepared in the tactical zone. The main zone's main center of resistance was the town of Kovel' (140 kilometers southwest of Pinsk), which had been heavily fortified in the engineering sense.

A second defensive zone was being prepared west of Kovel', at a distance of 4-15 kilometers from the forward edge of the main defensive zone.

Army and rear defensive zones had been prepared in the operational zone.

The army defensive zone (the position of the army reserves) ran along the western bank of the Western Bug River, at a distance of 50-70 kilometers from the forward edge of the main defensive zone. The defense along the western bank of the river consisted of centers of resistance, which were connected by a system of trenches.

The city and fortress of Brest (160 kilometers southwest of Pinsk) covered the approaches to the Western Bug River along the main route of the Warsaw highway and had been transformed into a powerful fortified area, which included three defensive zones.

A rear defensive zone having strategic significance, had been under construction for some time along the western bank of the Vistula River.

The overall depth of the enemy's defense along this direction was 170-250 kilometers.

Overall Conclusions Regarding the Engineering Preparation of the Belorussian Bridgehead and the Character of the Enemy's Defense

Over the course of a considerable time, and especially since the beginning of 1944, the enemy had been building a defensive system in Belorussia, which was well prepared in the engineering sense.

The favorable terrain conditions (up to a third of Belorussian territory is covered with forests, and there are a large number of lakes and rivers) facilitated the strengthening of the defense to a significant degree.

The presence of large rivers, swamps and large wooded areas facilitated the creation of a system of anti-tank obstacles.

Taking into account the terrain conditions, and seeking to retain Belorussia in its hands at any cost, the German-Fascist command built its defense, for the most part, along the main operational directions that covered the approaches to East Prussia and the routes to the west along the most important Warsaw—Berlin direction.

By the beginning of the Soviet forces' offensive in the summer of 1944, the enemy had managed to prepare in the engineering sense defensive lines with an overall depth of 150-200 kilometers along the main directions.

The engineering works were most highly developed in the tactical defensive zone.

In the operational depth the enemy was not able to fully develop the designated defensive zones. Their engineering outfitting was limited to 1-2 trenches and individual strong points.

Large inhabited locales and towns served as defensive centers and covered the crossings over rivers and were astride the most important roads. Such inhabited locales, as a rule, were being prepared for perimeter defense.

Switch positions in the depth of the tactical defense, particularly in the operational depth, were not highly developed.

The greatest engineering work had been done in the main defensive zone, where up to 2-3 positions had been outfitted to a depth of 4-6 kilometers and the overall number of trenches varied from three to seven.

A system of engineering anti-tank and anti-personnel obstacles was widely employed in the tactical zone. Of the anti-tank obstacles, mines and wood and earth obstacles, ditches, cuttings in the forests and barriers in the towns were most widely employed.

Of the anti-personnel obstacles, mines, wooden and earth and all sorts of barriers using barbed wire were employed.

The enemy was preparing his main resistance in the tactical defensive zone. In case of a breakthrough by Soviet forces along a particular direction, the enemy counted on delaying them along natural water or forest and swamp barriers.

The enemy's defensive, in the engineering sense, was most prepared along the Orsha—Minsk (along the Minsk highway) and Bobruisk—Slutsk directions.

The German-Fascist Forces' Grouping and Condition

The territory of Belorussia was defended by the enemy's Army Group Center (commanded by Field Marshal Busch), consisting of the Third Panzer, Fourth, Ninth and Second armies. The army group headquarters was in Minsk. To the right, units of Army Group Northern Ukraine's Fourth Panzer Army were defending, and to the left, Army Group North's Sixteenth Army.

Formations from the Sixteenth Army (four infantry, one security and one training field division) were defending a 60-kilometer front northeast and east of Polotsk, covering the Polotsk—Svencionys direction.

The Third Panzer Army (seven infantry, two *Luftwaffe* field and one security divisions, and two divisional combat groups) was defending a 150-kilometer front along a line east of Polotsk and Bogushevsk, covering the southern part of the Polotsk—Svencionys and northern part of the Orsha—Minsk directions.

The Fourth Army (eight infantry, one security and two motorized divisions) was defending a 225-kilometer front along the line Bogushevsk—Bykhov, covering the Orsha—Minsk and Mogilev—Minsk directions.

The Ninth Army (eight infantry and one security divisions) was defending a 220-kilometer front from excluding Bykhov to the Pripyat' River, which covered the Bobruisk—Slutsk direction, and had concentrated its main forces here.

The Second Army (two infantry, one light infantry, three Hungarian reserve divisions, one cavalry, and one security divisions, three divisional combat groups, and three brigades) was defending along a 320-kilometer front along the Pripyat' River as south as far as Kovel' (140 kilometers southwest of Pinsk), covering the Kovel'—Lublin direction.

The LVI Panzer Corps and other formations (four infantry and two panzer divisions, and one brigade) from Army Group North Ukraine's Fourth Panzer Army, were defending in the Kovel' area and to the south.

The reserve of the commander of Army Group Center consisted of seven divisions (two infantry, one panzer, four security, and one training), a large part of which was engaged in constructing defensive works in the rear, guarded communications and fighting the partisans.

In all, by the beginning of the Belorussian operation, Army Group Center, along with formations from Army Group North's Sixteenth Army and Army Group North Ukraine's Fourth Panzer Army, consisted of 65 divisions and combat groups and three brigades.

Besides this, there were 43 independent regiments, six independent batteries of assault artillery, and five independent panzer battalions as part of Army Group Center.

The German-Fascist aviation's main forces were located 100-150 kilometers from the front line. Fighters were mostly deployed at the forward airfields.

In all, by the beginning of the operation, all intelligence sources had uncovered the following numbers of enemy aircraft (see table 1).

Among the planes in the German-Fascist air park were a number of models that were already outdated by this time: the Focke-Wulf 190[11] (these were sometimes used as assault aircraft), Me-109,[12] Me-110[13] (night fighters) fighter aircraft, the Ju-87,[14] Ju-88[15] and Heinkel-111[16] bombers, and the Henschel-126[17] and Focke-Wulf 189[18] reconnaissance aircraft.

---

11 Editor's note. The FW-190 was a single-engine fighter plane used by the Germans from 1941 to the end of the war. A later model had a maximum speed of 685 km/hr and a range of 800 kilometers. It was armed with two 13mm machine guns and two 20mm cannons, and could carry a single 500 kilogram bomb.

12 Editor's note. The Messerschmitt Bf 109 was a single-engine fighter plane that first appeared in 1937 and was the workhorse of the Luftwaffe's fighter wing during World War II. A later model had a crew of one and a maximum speed of 640 km/hr and a range of 850 kilometers. It was armed with two 13mm machine guns and one 20mm cannon and could carry a single 250 kilogram bomb.

13 Editor's note. The Messerschmitt Bf 110 was a twin-engine heavy fither that firist appeared in 1937. A later model had a crew of two, a maximum speed of 595 km/hr and a range of 900 kilometers. It was armed with two 20mm cannons and five 7.92mm machine guns.

14 Editor's note. The Ju-87, popularly known as the "Stuka," was a single-engine dive bomber that appeared in 1936. On model had a crew of two, a maximum speed of 600 km/hr and a range of 500 kilometers. It was armed with three 7.92mm machine guns and could carry one 250 kilogram bomb and four 50 kilogram bombs.

15 Editor's note. The Ju-88 was a twin-engine combat aircraft that appeared in 1939. One model carried a crew of four, with a maximum speed of 510 km/hr and a range of 2,430 kilometers. It was armed with five 7.92mm machine guns and could carry up to 3,000 kilograms of bombs.

16 Editor's note. The Heinkel-111 was a twin-engine bomber that appeared in 1935. One model had a crew of five, a maximum speed of 440 km/hr and a range of 2,300 kilometers. It was armed with up to seven 7.92mm machine guns, a 13mm machine gun and one 20mm cannon, and could carry up to 3,600 kilograms of bombs.

17 Editor's note. The Henschel-126 was a German two-seat reconnaissance plane which first appeared in 1937. It had a crew of two, a maximu speed of 356 km/hr and a maximum range of 998 kilometers. It was armed with two 7.92mm machine guns and could carry up to 150 kilograms of bombs.

18 Editor's note. The Focke-Wulf 189 was a twin-engine German reconnaissance plane which first appeared in

In examining the grouping of the German-Fascist troops, one should note the following:

1. The enemy had created the greatest operational densities along the Orsha—Minsk Minsk and Bobruisk—Slutsk directions.

    In all cases, the main forces were concentrated so as to retain the tactical defensive zone, particularly in the areas of the Vitebsk and Bobruisk salients, as well as in the center, along the Mogilev—Minsk direction. Not only were the corps reserves located in the tactical zone, but, as a rule, the army ones as well.
2. The location of the enemy's forces in the tactical depth was characterized by their single-echelon formation. As concerns the operational zone, comparatively small operational reserves were located here.
3. By the beginning of our offensive, the enemy's infantry divisions had already been placed on a new organization for 1944. The basic principles of this organization came down to a reduction in the size of the infantry division (12,703 men instead of 16,855), with a simultaneous attempt to increase its firepower by means of new anti-tank and anti-aircraft weaponry (new 88mm anti-tank guns were being introduced, along with improved 20mm self-propelled anti-aircraft guns) and an increase in the number of heavy mortars.

Table 1. The Number of Aircraft in the German-Fascist Air Park

Type of Aircraft	Against Which *Front*				Total	
	1st Baltic	3rd Belorussian	2nd Belorussian	1st Belorussian	Aircraft	%
Fighters	130	50	60	160	400	28
Bombers	104	148	152	396	800	58
Reconnaissance	70	42	30	58	200	14
Total	304	240	242	614	1,400[1]	100

Note
1. *Operatsii Sovetskikh Vooruzhennykh Sil v Velikoi Otechestvennoi Voine, 1941-1945 gg.* Military-Historical Directorate of the USSR Armed Forces General Staff, 1958, vol. 3, p. 287.

The 1944 infantry division, while retaining its three-regiment organization, had only six infantry battalions instead of nine, one artillery regiment consisting of four batteries (of which one was a heavy 150mm howitzer battalion), a fusilier battalion, an anti-tank battalion (12 75mm and 88mm anti-tank guns and 12 20mm anti-aircraft guns), a battalion of assault artillery, a sapper battalion, and a communications battalion.

The necessity of reorganizing the German infantry divisions was brought about, most of all, by the colossal personnel losses and the exhaustion of Germany's human resources in connection with the growing power of the Soviet army's crushing blows.

4. The German-Fascist troops' political-moral condition by the summer of 1944 had sharply changed for the worse. Their combat capability had been reduced. To replace the cadre contingent, soldiers and officers were arriving in the army who had been conscripted as part of the "total"

1938. It had a crew of three, a maximum speed of 356 km/hr and a maximum range of 670 kilometers. It was armed with four 7.92mm machine guns and could carry up to 200 kilograms of bombs.

mobilization and who lacked experience and sufficient combat training. The German-Fascist forces were beginning to more and more understand that there could be no thought of success-fully concluding the war in the east.

The actions of the heroic Belorussian partisans, who had opened a ruthless struggle against the occupiers in the rear, also influenced the moral condition of the German-Fascist troops in Belorussia.

The collapse of one after the other of all the Hitlerites' strategic plans had led the fascist army to a state of deep crisis, from which it could no longer extricate itself. By the summer of 1944 the Hitlerite command could no longer elaborate any active plans capable of changing the course of the war on the Soviet-German front. Active operations, under present conditions, could only result in the further destruction of the German-Fascist divisions and bring the final catastrophe closer. Disorder and discord in the upper echelons of the Hitlerite leadership had begun. A part of the High Command understood the hopelessness of fascist Germany's situation and had reached the conclusion that it was necessary, by removing Hitler, to ease the conduct of separate negotiations with the governments of the USA and England. This group, which included well-known repre-sentatives of the fascist generalitet, hoped that by concluding a separate peace with the USA and England they could secure their rear in the West, in order to concentrate all its forces against the Soviet Union, to withstand the Soviet Army's pressure and achieve an acceptable peace.

The disorder in the upper ranks of the Hitlerite leadership led to a situation that by the summer of 1944 the German-Fascist army essentially lacked any clear plans for its further activities.

The Soviet Forces' Grouping and Condition

By the summer of 1944 the *Stavka* of the Supreme High Command had deployed on the territory of Belorussia four *fronts*: the First Baltic, Third, Second and First Belorussian (see table 2).

The First Baltic Front (6th Guards, 4th Shock and 43rd combined-arms armies, and the 3rd Air Army) was defending a 160-kilometer front along the line Neshcherdo—Koitovo. The forces of the Second Baltic Front were defending to the right.

The Third Belorussian Front (39th, 5th and 31st combined-arms armies, and the 1st Air Army) covered the Minsk—Smolensk direction along a 130-kilometer front, with the front line along the line Konchani—excluding Baevo. By the beginning of the operation the *front* had been reinforced by the arrival of the 11th Guards and 5th Guards Tank armies.

According to the plan by the *Stavka* of the Supreme High Command, this *front* was slated to launch the main attack.

The Second Belorussian Front (33rd, 49th and 50th combined-arms armies, and the 4th Air Army) was improving its defensive lines during April and May along the Mogilev direction, along a 160-kilometer front. The front line here ran along the line from Baevo to Selets and Kholopaev.

The First Belorussian Front was defending along a line running through Rogachev and Zhlobin to the mouth of the Ptich' River, and then to the west along the Pripyat' River, and then to the south as far as Kovel' (140 kilometers southwest of Pinsk), and then south as far as Verba (south of Kovel'). The length of the front reached 700 kilometers.

Along the Bobruisk axis, to the north of the Pripyat' River, laid the *front's* right wing—3rd, 48th and 65th combined-arms armies, and the 16th Air Army. The 28th Army, newly arrived from the *Stavka* reserve, was moved up to the first echelon before the beginning of the operation and occupied a defensive sector to the left of the 65th Army. The overall width of the First Belorussian Front's right wing was 240 kilometers.

Along the southern bank of the Pripyat' River, along a 360-kilometer front, were the forces of the 61st Army. Further to the south of the Pripyat' River, as far as the *front's* left boundary, the 70th, 47th and 69th armies were defending, behind which in the second echelon and reserve there were concentrated the Polish 1st, 8th Guards and 2nd Tank armies. However, the concentration of all these forces had not been completed by the start of the Belorussian operation. Besides this, the *front* included the headquarters of the 6th Air Army. This headquarters was slated for uniting a number of air formations and supporting the operations of the First Belorussian Front's left wing.

Table 2. The *Fronts'* Combat and Numerical Composition by the Start of the 1944 Belorussian Operation

Formations and Units, Personnel and Equipment	1st Baltic	3rd Belorussian	2nd Belorussian	1st Belorussian (right wing)[1]	Total
Combined-Arms Armies	3	4	3	4	14
Tank Armies	–	1	–	–	1
Rifle Corps	8	11	7	14	40
Tank Corps	1	3	–	2	6[2]
Mechanized Corps	–	1	–	1	2
Cavalry Corps	–	1	–	1	2
Rifle Divisions	24+1 rifle bde	33	22	39+1 rifle bde	118+2 rifle bdes
Cavalry Divisions	–	3	–	3	6
Fortified Areas	1	1	1	4	7
Battalions	216	277	204	384	1,081
Personnel (Combat)	222,706	371,653	198,452	418,541	1,211,352
Guns and Mortars (76mm and higher)	4,926	7,134	3,989	8,314	24,363
Guns (45mm and 57mm)	778	1,175	833	1,444	4,230
Anti-Aircraft Guns	420	792	329	762	2,303
Tanks and Self-Propelled Guns	687	1,810	276	1,297	4,070
Planes	902	1,864	528	2,033	5,327[3]

Notes
1 For the combat and strength of the First Belorussian Front, see part 3 of this work.
2 Of these, four were independent.
3 Aside from this, 1,007 aircraft from Long-Range Aviation took part in the operation.

The forces of the First Ukrainian Front were defending to the left of the First Belorussian Front.

The Soviet forces' successes in the operations of 1944 depended to a great deal on the fact that by this time the Soviet army had grown, not only quantitatively, but qualitatively as well and was the world's most forward and combat-capable army. Reinforcements arrived better trained, equipment was arriving in significantly greater quantities, and its quality had become better.

In 1944 the combined-arms armies were, as a rule, composed of three rifle corps. The combined-arms formations' firepower had increased significantly. The number of guns and mortars in a rifle division had increased almost two times in the three years of the war (from 142 to 252). The overall weight of a salvo by all a rifle divisions' guns and mortars had increased from 1.1 tons in 1943 to 1.58 tons in 1944. All of the division's artillery had been mechanized. The division had 218 motor vehicles. The lift capability of the division's transport had increased from 382 tons to 706 tons.

The overall weight of a corps' artillery salvo exceeded five tons, as opposed to 3.3 tons in 1943.

In 1944 the number of large formations from the High Command Artillery Reserve had increased significantly. In May 1944 army gun artillery regiments had been reformed into army gun artillery brigades, consisting of 48 guns. Light artillery brigades, consisting of three regiments, had been introduced into the tank armies' organization, and light artillery regiments into the tank corps' organization. The number of anti-tank brigades in the High Command reserve continuously increased.

All the artillery formations began to receive large numbers of new 57mm, 85mm and 100mm guns, 160mm mortars, and M-31[19] rocket artillery vehicles.

In 1944 the armored forces developed further. Independent guards heavy tank brigades were created, each of which consisted of three heavy tank regiments. Independent guards tank breakthrough regiments were reformed into independent heavy tank regiments, outfitted with IS[20] heavy tanks. We began to create independent heavy, medium and light self-propelled gun brigades. The number of tanks in independent tank brigades increased to 65, as opposed to 53 in 1943. Independent tank breakthrough regiments got new IS tanks to replace their older KV[21] tanks. Heavy tank brigades, consisting of three regiments were created, as were self-propelled gun brigades: heavy ones consisting of 65 SAU-152s,[22] medium ones consisting of 65 SAU-100s,[23] and light ones consisting of 60 SAU-76s.[24] The overall number of armored units in a tank army increased organizationally: up to 620 tanks and 189 self-propelled guns.

In the air force new aircraft models began to arrive—Il-10s,[25] La-7s,[26] Yak-9s,[27] and others. The maximum speeds of many planes reached 600-700 kilometers per hour, with a practical ceiling of 11 kilometers, and a maximum range of up to 800-1,000 kilometers. The combat composition of the *fronts'* air armies increased and usually consisted of no less than 1,000-1,200 planes, a figure which began to reach as high as 2,500-3,000 planes along the most important directions.

Our cadre's military skills rose significantly. Officers and generals had mastered the art of leading troops and had learned to skillfully organize and conduct a battle in both offensive and defensive operations. Troop control had improved considerably, which enabled the *Stavka* of the Supreme High Command to quickly concentrate enormous masses of men along the necessary directions and to inflict powerful and surprise attacks against the enemy.

---

19 Editor's note. The M-31 was a 300mm heavy model rocket used in Soviet multiple rocket units. These were organized into guards mortar units.

20 Editor's note. This was a series of Soviet heavy tanks that first appeared in 1943 and named after Joseph Stalin (Iosif Stalin). These included the IS-2 and IS-3, which weighed 46 and 46.5 tons respectively, and carried a crew of four. Both models were armed with a 122-mm gun and two 12.7mm machine guns.

21 Editor's note. The KV series was named after the former Soviet defense minister Kliment Voroshilov and first appeared in 1939. This series included the KV-1, which was armed with a 76.2mm gun, the KV-2, which was armed with a 152-mm howitzer, and the later KV-85, which was armed with an 85mm gun. This series was later replaced by the heavier IS models.

22 Editor's note. The SAU-152 was a Soviet self-propelled gun mounted on an IS heavy tank chassis. It weighed 47 tons and had a crew of five. It was armed with a 152mm howitzer.

23 Editor's note. The SAU-100 was a Soviet self-propelled gun mounted on a T-34/85 medium tank chassis. It weighed 31.6 tons and had a crew of four. It was armed with a 100mm gun.

24 Editor's note. The SAU-76 was a Soviet self-propelled gun mounted on a T-70 light tank chassis. It weighed 11.2 tons and had a crew of four. It was armed with a 76.2mm gun.

25 Editor's note. The Il-10 was a single-engine Soviet ground attack aircraft that appeared in 1944. It had a crew of two, a maximum speed of 551 km/hr and a range of 800 kilometers. It was armed with two 23mm cannons and one 20mm cannon, or one 12.7mm machine gun, four rockets, and could carry up to 500 kilograms of bombs.

26 Editor's note. The La-7 was a single-engine Soviet fighter which first appeared in 1944. It had a crew of one, a maximum speed of 661 km/hr and a range of 665 kilometers. It was armed with two or three 20mm cannons and could carry up to 200 kilograms of bombs.

27 Editor's note. The Yak-9 was a single-engine Soviet fighter which first appeared in 1942. One model had a crew of one, a maximum speed of 591 km/hr and a range of 1,360 kilometers. It was armed with one 20mm cannon and one 12.7mm machine gun.

The troops had learned to break through the enemy's defense, to energetically develop the success in depth, and to carry out deep maneuver to encircle and destroy both small and large enemy groups of forces.

All of these indices of the Soviet army's growth and power manifested themselves in the Belorussian operation—the largest offensive operation of 1944.

The Belorussian Partisans

By the summer of 1944 there were 14 partisan formations in Belorussia, uniting 148 brigades and 53 independent detachments. The overall number of partisans in these formations and brigades reached 218,830 people. Besides this, there were 18,570 scouts and 9,060 messengers who did not form part of these brigades and detachments. The Belorussian partisans also disposed of a sizable reserve. As of 1 May 1944 there were 449,310 partisans overall.[28]

The Belorussian partisans' main basing areas were the wooded areas and swampy sectors in the Lepel', Senno, Pogosta, Begomlya, Chervenya areas, and the Nalibokskaya, Lepechan and Belovezh woods, Ushachei, and other areas; that is, those areas less accessible to active offensive operations by the enemy's mechanized and tank forces. The conditions in these areas facilitated the creation and concealment for a prolonged period of the necessary supplies of ammunition and food, as well as the construction of living quarters, etc.

For the purpose of the firm leadership of the partisan movement, detachments, brigades and formations were subordinated to groups of the Belorussian headquarters of the partisan movement (BShDP), attached to the *fronts*.

The Correlation of Forces

By the start of the operation along a front from Lake Neshcherdo to Verba (150 kilometers south-west of Pinsk), a force consisting of the First Baltic and the Third, Second and First Belorussian fronts numbered 160 rifle divisions, nine rifle brigades and fortified areas, ten tank corps, two mechanized corps, and four cavalry corps. Among the combat troops in this group were about 31,300 guns and mortars 76mm and higher (aside from anti-aircraft artillery), more than 5,200 tanks and self-propelled guns, 5,675 planes from the *fronts'* air armies, and 1,007 planes from Long-Range Aviation.

In all, taking into account the reserves of the *Stavka* of the High Command arriving in the second half of June and the beginning of July, more than 2.5 million men were to take part in the operation on the Soviet side, more than 45,000 guns and mortars of all calibers, more than 6,000 tanks and self-propelled guns, about 8,000 planes, including those from long-range aviation.[29]

During the operation's first stage, the *fronts'* forces did not operate throughout the entire area indicated above, but only along the front from Lake Neshcherdo to the mouth of the Ptich' River, along which our forces numbered 124 rifle and cavalry divisions, nine rifle brigades and fortified areas, and eight tank and mechanized corps.[30]

The overall correlation of forces along this front before the start of the Belorussian operation of 1944 is shown by the following data (following the completion of regroupings).

---

28 Change to Naumov, D.F., *Rol' Belorusskikh Partizan v Pyatom Udare 1944 g.* Frunze Military Academy, 1953, pp. 10-11.
29 *Operatsii Sovetskikh*, vol. 3, p. 292.
30 *Ibid*, p. 292.

Table 3. The Correlation of Forces as of 23 June 1944[31]

Forces	Enemy	Soviet[1]	Correlation
Divisions (rifle, infantry, security, air, and cavalry)	43-44	124	1:3
Number of Troops	426,168	1,211,352	1:2.8
Guns and Mortars	9,635 (of which 2,822 were anti-tank)	28,593 (of which 4,230 were 45mm and 57mm)	1:2.9
Tanks and Self-Propelled Guns	932	4,070	1:4.3

Note

1 Not counting *front* and army rear, the troops of the First Belorussian Front's left wing, and the personnel of the air armies.

It should be taken into account that by the beginning of the Belorussian operation the average strength of the majority of the German-Fascist divisions varied from 7,000 to 9,000 men. The enemy's independent divisions numbered 16,000 men (the Fourth Army's 78th Assault Division). The average strength of our divisions did not exceed 5,400-6,600 men. In the First Baltic Front this figure reached 6,100 men, 6,600 in the Third Belorussian Front, 6,400 in the Second Belorussian Front, and 5,400 in the First Belorussian Front (right wing).

The greatest number of our men and materiel was concentrated in the zones of the Third and First Belorussian fronts.

The Soviet forces enjoyed a quantitative and qualitative superiority in equipment and armaments.

The correlation of air power by the start of the Belorussian operation, in the sector from Lake Neshcherdo to the Ptich' River, was as follows: (see table 4)

From the table it is clear that as a result of corresponding measures by the Soviet High Command, significant air superiority was achieved over the enemy's planes (4.5:1).

It should be noted that Soviet fighters (Yak-1,[32] Yak-7,[33] Yak-7b,[34] Yak-9, and La-5,[35] according to their armament and speed indices, were superior to the German Me-109 and Focke-Wulf 190 fighters. The Pe-2[36] bombers were slightly inferior in their bomb load to the German Ju-88 and Heinkel-111 bombers, although they were superior in speed and armament. As for assault aircraft, the Germans were completely lacking in specialized assault aircraft.

From all of this it follows that the Soviet air force enjoyed a significant quantitative and qualitative superiority over the enemy's air force.

---

31 *Ibid*, pp. 292-93.

32 Editor's note. The Yak-1 was a single-engine Soviet fighter that first saw service in 1940. It had a crew of one, a maximum speed of 592 km/hr and a range of 700 kilometers. It was armed with one 20mm cannon and two 7.62mm machine guns.

33 Editor's note. The Yak-7 was a single-engine fighter that first entered service in 1942. One model had a crew of one, a maximum speed of 495 km/hr and a range of 643 kilometers. It was armed with one 20mm cannon and two 7.62 machine guns.

34 Editor's note. The Yak-7b was a single-engine Soviet fighter that entered service in 1942. It had a crew of one and a maximum speed of 570 km/hr. It was armed with one 20mm cannon and two 12.7mm machine guns.

35 Editor's note. The La-5 was a single-engine Soviet fighter that entered service in 1942. One model carried a crew of one, with a maximum speed of 648 km/hr and a range of 765 kilometers. It was armed with two 20mm cannon and could carry up to 200 kilograms of bombs.

36 Editor's note. The Pe-2 was a twin-engine Soviet medium bomber that first entered service in 1941. One model had a crew of three, a maximum speed of 580 km/hr and a range of 1,160 kilometers. It was armed with four 7.62mm machine gunsand could carry up to 1,600 kilograms of bombs.

The presence of the sides' reserves is important for understanding the correlation of forces. The Germans' Army Group Center disposed of very small reserves and, moreover, the majority of reserves had been drawn into fighting the Belorussian partisans, while the Soviet forces had powerful reserves, which played a major role in the course of the operation.

Thus the overall correlation of forces in Belorussia before the start of the Belorussian operation of 1944 was in favor of the Soviet armed forces, both on the ground and in the air, which enabled us to achieve and even greater superiority over the enemy along the directions of the main attack.

The superiority in men and materiel created in Belorussia over the German-Fascist armed forces, as well as the growing skill of our command cadres and the high political-moral condition of the Soviet forces, guaranteed the achievement of major operational and strategic results.

On the whole, the Belorussian operation of 1944 was prepared and carried out in a situation favorable for the Soviet forces, which enabled us to assign and achieve decisive results in the operation.

Table 4. The Correlation of Air Power

Aircraft Types	The *Fronts'* Air Armies[1]				Long-Range Aviation	Total	Enemy Air	Correlation
	3rd AA	1st AA	4th AA	16th AA				
Fighters	403	767	196	952	–	2,318	400	5.7:1
Assault Aircraft	368	547	193	636	–	1,744	–	
Bombers:								
Daylight	–	392	–	263	–	655	–	3.5:1[2]
Night	79	81	121	150	–	431	800	4.7:1[2]
Long-Range	–	–	–	–	1,007	1,007	–	
Reconnaissance and Fire Correctors	52	77	18	32	–	179	200	1:1.1
Total	902	1,864	528	2,033	1,007	6,334	1,400	4.5:1

Notes
1 Not counting the 6th Air Army, which by the beginning of the operation was still being formed, in the sector along the left wing of the First Belorussian Front (south of the Pripyat' River).
2 The numerator indicates the correlation with Long-Range Aviation, and the denominator without it.

2

The Plan of the Belorussian Operation and Measures by the *Stavka of the Supreme* High Command for its Preparation

The Plan of the *Stavka* of the Supreme High Command

The favorable conditions that had arisen by the summer of 1944 and the overall military-political situation along the Soviet-German front enabled the *Stavka* of the Supreme High Command to assign the Soviet armed forces in the second half of the year the task of completely liberating our territory from the enemy, to defeat his main groups of forces, and carry the war onto the enemy's territory.

The plan of the Belorussian operation, which from the beginning carried the code name of "Bagration," had been laid out in the latter half of May in the form of a memorandum by the chief of the General Staff, General A.I. Antonov.[1] According to the latter, operation Bagration's goal was to "… eliminate the salient in the area Vitebsk—Bobruisk—Minsk and to reach the front Disna—Molodechno—Stolbtsy—Starobino."[2]

The overall depth of the operation was planned at 250 kilometers, while it was to last 45-50 days. In order to achieve the operation's assigned goal, the General Staff proposed allotting the following forces: 77 rifle divisions, three tank corps, one mechanized corps, and one cavalry corps. Besides this, it was planned to have a reserve of 32 rifle divisions.[3]

In the process of preparing operation Bagration, the initial plan was subjected to changes and additions, which in the final analysis were reflected in the directives of the *Stavka* of the Supreme High Command.

In its final variant, the goal of the Belorussian offensive operation of 1944 was the defeat of the German-Fascist Army Group Center, the liberation of the Belorussian Soviet Socialist Republic, and the creation of favorable conditions for the subsequent defeat of the enemy's forces in the Baltic States and in Western Ukraine. It was planned to achieve this goal by means of the consecutive and simultaneous resolution of a series of large-scale operational tasks.

---

1 Editor's note. Aleksei Innokent'evich Antonov (1896-1962) served as a junior officer in the Russian imperial army during the First World War. He joined the Red Army in 1918 and took part in the civil war. During the Great Patriotic War he served in various front-line staff assignments, before being appointed chief of the General Staff's operational directorate in 1942 and deputy chief of staff the following year. Antonov was appointed chief of the General Staff in 1945, although he held that post for less than a year. Following the war, Antonov commanded a military district and served as chief of staff of the Warsaw Pact forces.
2 *Operatsii Sovetskikh*, vol. 3, p. 288.
3 *Ibid*, p. 288.

The plan of the multi-*front* Belorussian operation called for a simultaneous offensive by Soviet forces along the Polotsk—Svencionys, Orsha—Minsk, Mogilev—Minsk, and Bobruisk—Slutsk directions, the encirclement and destruction of the enemy's groups of forces in the areas of Vitebsk and Bobruisk, the development of the attacks along converging axes toward Minsk, and the encirclement and destruction of the main enemy group of forces.

In order to defeat Army Group Center, the *Stavka* of the Supreme High Command decided to employ the forces of the First Baltic, and the Third, Second and First Belorussian fronts.

The plan called for the following:

a) the forces of the First Baltic and Third Belorussian fronts were to, first of all, defeat the Vitebsk—Orsha—Lepel' group of forces, while the First Belorussian Front's right wing, in conjunction with the Dnepr Flotilla, was to defeat the enemy's Bobruisk group of forces, while tying down the enemy along the Mogilev direction with the forces of the Second Belorussian Front;

b) following the defeat of the enemy's flank groups of forces, to develop the attack by the Third, Second and First Belorussian fronts along converging axes toward Minsk, for the purpose of encircling and destroying the main forces of Army Group Center east of Minsk.

The Belorussian partisans were to facilitate the realization of this plan through active operations.

The First Baltic Front was to develop its success along the Svencionys direction, in order to deeply outflank the southern flank of Army Group North and to secure the Belorussian fronts from the north.

The beginning of the offensive was set for 23-24 June 1944.

Because the main forces of Army Group Center were to be defeated as a result of these actions, a situation would subsequently arise that made it possible for all four *fronts* to develop their attacks to the west toward the borders of East Prussia and the Neman, Narew and Vistula rivers. During the operation, the left wing of the First Belorussian Front would prepare to go over to the offensive (from 15 July 1944) along the Warsaw direction, in conjunction with the right flank of the First Ukrainian Front, which was supposed to begin offensive operations, according to the plan for the L'vov—Sandomierz operation, approximately 20 days following the beginning of the Belorussian operation.

Thus according to this plan, the multi-*front* Belorussian operation was to encircle and destroy the enemy's opposing group of forces by launching powerful frontal attacks along several axes, followed by the development of the attacks in depth, along converging axes, in order to get into the flanks and rear of the main enemy group of forces in the operational depth. The *fronts'* initial assignments covered only a comparatively shallow depth. The *fronts* received directives for the subsequent development of the offensive from the *Stavka* of the Supreme High Command during the course of the operation.

It was planned to carry out the breakthrough of the enemy's defense simultaneously along six sectors, in a line from Vitebsk to Bobruisk, against an overall length of front of more than 600 kilometers. Of the six breakthrough sectors, four were designated along the flanks of Army Group Center in the areas of Vitebsk and Bobruisk, and two in the center—in the areas of the Minsk highway and Mogilev.

Following the breakthrough of the enemy's tactical defense in the areas of Vitebsk and Bobruisk, it was planned to commit large-scale mobile forces into the breach, so that by launching an impetuous attack along converging axes, to split the enemy front and then destroy his groups of forces in detail. Proceeding from this, the *Stavka* of the Supreme High Command attached special importance to the defeat of the enemy's flank groups of forces located in the areas of Vitebsk and Bobruisk. The efforts of the three Belorussian fronts would then be directed toward encircling and

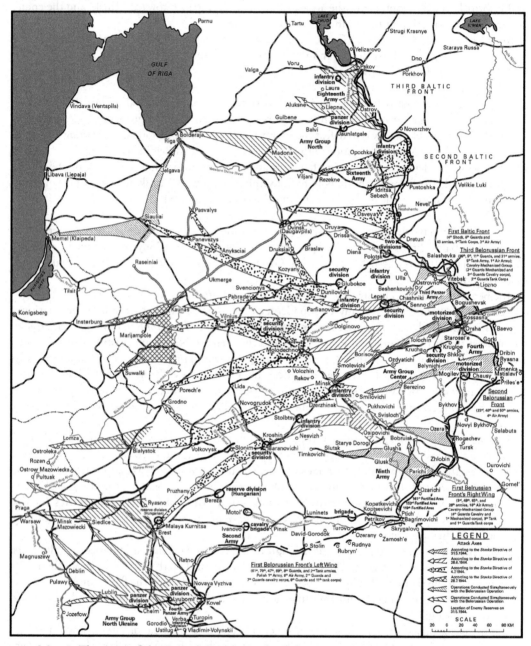

Map 2 The Axes of the Fronts' Attacks in the Belorussian Operation, According to the Directives of the *Stavka* of the Supreme High Command.

destroying Army Group Center's main forces along the main, Minsk, direction and to liberate the capital of Belorussia—Minsk.

Subsequently, in connection with the commitment of the strategic reserves and the offensive by the First Belorussian Front's left wing, there would arise the possibility of developing the offensive along two directions—the East Prussian and Warsaw directions.

The Tasks of the *Fronts*, Long-Range Aviation and Partisans

In accordance with the plan for the multi-*front* Belorussian offensive operation, the *Stavka* of the Supreme High Command's directives at the end of May 1944 laid out the following tasks for the *fronts*, Long-Range Aviation and the partisans:

The First Baltic Front, in conjunction with the right wing of the Third Belorussian Front, was to defeat the Vitebsk—Lepel' enemy group of forces and reach the southern bank of the Western Dvina River in the Chashniki—Lepel' area, for which the forces of the 6th Guards and 43rd armies were to break through the enemy's defense in the area southwest of Gorodok, launching the main attack in the direction of Beshenkovichi.

The immediate objective was to force the Western Dvina River and seize the Beshenkovichi area. A part of these forces, in conjunction with the right wing of the Third Belorussian Front, was to defeat the enemy's Vitebsk group of forces and capture the city of Vitebsk.

The offensive was to be subsequently developed in the general direction of Lepel' and Svencionys, securely guarding the *front's* main group of forces from the Polotsk direction.

The Third Belorussian Front, in conjunction with the left wing of the First Baltic and the Second Belorussian fronts, was to defeat the Vitebsk—Orsha enemy group of forces and reach the Berezina River, and was to break through the enemy front by launching two attacks:

a) the first attack would be launched by the forces of the 39th and 5th armies, from the area west of Liozno, in the general direction of Bogushevsk and Senno; a part of this group of forces would attack to the northwest, enveloping Vitebsk from the southwest, for the purpose of defeating the enemy's Vitebsk group of forces and capturing Vitebsk in conjunction with the left wing of the First Baltic Front;

b) the second attack would be launched by the forces of the 11th Guards and 31st armies along the Minsk highway in the general direction of Borisov; part of this group of forces would capture the town of Orsha by an attack from the north.

The *front's* immediate objective, following the defeat of the Vitebsk—Orsha group of forces, was to capture the line Senno—Orsha. The *front* was to subsequently develop the offensive on Borisov and, in conjunction with the Second Belorussian Front, to defeat the enemy's Borisov group of forces and reach the western bank of the Berezina River in the Borisov area.

The *front* was authorized to employ its mobile forces for developing the success, following the breakthrough of the defense's tactical zone, in the general direction of Borisov.

The Second Belorussian Front, in conjunction with the left wing of the Third Belorussian Front and the right wing of the First Belorussian Front, was to defeat the enemy's Mogilev group of forces and reach the Berezina River.

In order to achieve this goal, the *front* was to launch its main attack with the forces of no less than 10-12 rifle divisions from the area Dribin—Dednya—Ryasna in the general direction of Mogilev and Belynichi.

The *front's* immediate task was to reach the Dnepr River and seize a bridgehead on its western bank.

It was subsequently to force the Dnepr River with its main forces, to capture Mogilev and then develop the offensive in the general direction of Berezino and Smilovichi.

The First Belorussian Front was to defeat the enemy's Bobruisk group of forces and reach the Pukhovichi—Slutsk—Osipovichi area with its right wing's main forces, for which it was to break through the enemy's defense by launching two attacks:

a)   the first attack would be launched by the forces of the 3rd and 48th armies from the Rogachev area in the general direction of Bobruisk and Osipovichi;

b)   the second attack would be launched by the forces of the 65th and 28th armies from the area of the lower course of the Berezina River in the general direction of Starye Dorogi and Slutsk.

The *front's* immediate task was to defeat the enemy's Bobruisk group of forces and capture the Bobruisk—Glusha—Glusk area; part of its forces along the right flank would assist the Second Belorussian Front in defeating the enemy's Mogilev group of forces.

The *front* would subsequently develop the offensive for the purpose of reaching the area Pukhovichi—Slutsk—Osipovichi.

The *front's* mobile forces would be used to develop the success following the breakthrough of the tactical defense zone.

Before the start of the operation, Long-Range Aviation was to assist in retaining air superiority by suppressing the enemy's air strength based on airfields in the areas of Orsha, Mogilev, Bobruisk, and Minsk; during the night preceding the attack, Long-Range Aviation was to take part in the operation's air preparation and launch attacks against defensive installations, strong points, and enemy forces, according to the *front* plans; during the operation, Long-Range Aviation was to foil maneuver by the enemy's reserves by launching systematic attacks against railroad junctions and to be ready for operations against individual large enemy groups of forces during the operation.

The partisans were assigned the following tasks.[4]

To maximally increase the gathering of reconnaissance data about the enemy's forces in Belorussia; to identify his defensive lines in the operational depth and the degree of their readiness and; to determine the railroads' capacity and the type of freights being carried.

The partisans were to destroy the enemy's communications and disorganize his transport and communications equipment; to disrupt in the rear the enemy's regular deliveries along rail, highway and dirt roads, thus depriving the enemy of the ability to bring up men, materiel and ammunition from the deep rear to the front, or to carry out regroupings of men and materiel during the operation, or to carry out a planned withdrawal to a previously-prepared defensive line in the depth.

The partisans, by strengthening the attacks against the enemy rear, against his garrisons, headquarters and offices, were to tie down Army Group Center's reserves. By maintaining their hold on predetermined areas and lines, the partisans were to take part in creating internal and external encirclement fronts around the main forces of the German-Fascist Army Group Center, in conjunction with the other *fronts'* forces.

The partisans, by retaining the most favorable lines and areas until the arrival of the Soviet army's units, were to assist them in capturing these lines on the march. By seizing crossings over the Berezina and other rivers, they were to assist the *fronts'* forces in quickly forcing water barriers in the depth of the enemy's defense.

By taking part in the parallel pursuit of the enemy, the partisans were to exhaust the enemy's retreating units, destroy his personnel, and force him to abandon his equipment and supplies.

---

4   Naumov, *Rol' Belorusskikh*, pp. 13-15.

Partisans were to be chosen as guides and be subordinated to the commanders of the attacking forward units, in order to carry out deep outflanking movements against the enemy's forces.

Through joint operations with the Soviet army's regular units, the partisans were to surround the enemy, capture inhabited locales, towns and other important targets.

The partisans were to save the local population from being sent into slavery, to liberate the population and prisoners of war from concentration camps, and to fight against the enemy's saboteurs, trying to destroy industrial concerns and inhabited areas.

In analyzing the tasks assigned to the *fronts'* forces, Long-Range Aviation, and the partisans, one can make the following conclusions.

The *Stavka* of the Supreme High Command, in assigning these tasks, proceeded from the idea that the overall goal—the defeat of the German-Fascist Army Group Center—could be achieved by the joint actions of all the services of the armed forces. Each *front* could carry out its assigned task only if it operated in close conjunction with the neighboring *fronts*, Long-Range Aviation and the partisans. On the other hand, the achievement of the overall goal was impossible without the fulfillment of its tasks by each formation taking part in the operation.

The main and decisive role in the operation was assigned to the forces of the four *fronts*, in the interests of which Long-Range Aviation and the partisans operated. It should be noted, in particular, that the tasks assigned to the partisans could be achieved only in conditions of the operational or tactical cooperation of the partisan formations with the *fronts'* forces, under the leadership of the latter.

The operation was to begin along a front from Lake Neshcherdo to the mouth of the Ptich' River, with a breakthrough of the enemy's defense along six sectors of the front. Missions were initially assigned to the forces of all the *fronts* to a depth of 80-160 kilometers. It was planned to assign missions for the *fronts'* offensive to the west of the Berezina River and Osipovichi during the course of the offensive, taking into account the specific situation and the *fronts'* fulfillment of the previously assigned tasks.

On the whole, the plan by the *Stavka* of the Supreme High Command and the tasks assigned to the *fronts*, Long-Range Aviation and the partisans fully corresponded to the real correlation of forces and demanded of the commanders at all levels and the troops the manifestation of a high level of military skill in the interests of achieving a common strategic and operational goal.

Measures by the *Stavka* of the Supreme High Command for Preparing the Operation

In preparing the multi-*front* Belorussian operation along the most important strategic direction, the *Stavka* of the Supreme High Command carried out, beginning in the spring of 1944, a series of important measures, without which the large-scale offensive activities in Belorussia, as foreseen by the plan, would have been impossible.

Measures were planned and carried out for reinforcing the *fronts* with men and military equipment, for organizing cooperation between the *fronts* and groups of *fronts*, for the operational-strategic and materiel-technical support of the operation. Simultaneous with this went the preparation for restoring the organs of political and economic power in the liberated areas and for rendering help to the Polish people.

Strengthening the most important directions with men and equipment was carried out by reinforcing the *fronts* with *Stavka* reserves, as well as changing the width of the operational formations' attack fronts.

By changing the boundary line between the Second and First Baltic fronts, the *Stavka* of the Supreme High Command narrowed the First Baltic Front's sector from 214 to 160 kilometers. This measure enabled the commander of the First Baltic Front to regroup the 6th Guards Army to the axis of the main attack. The 11th Guards Army, which had been part of the First Baltic Front, was transferred to the Third Belorussian Front, and to replace it the 103rd Rifle Corps (29th and 270th rifle divisions) was transferred from the *Stavka* reserve. Besides this, the First Baltic Front received from the *Stavka* reserve the 1st Tank Corps, three tank regiments, a flamethrower tank regiment, and a regiment of minesweeper tanks. The *Stavka* also transferred from its air reserve the 11th Air Corps and the 332nd Assault Air Division.

The Third Belorussian Front, which was to launch one of the decisive attacks, had been significantly reinforced by the start of the operation by *Stavka* reserves. The *front* was reinforced with the 11th Guards Army, which had been taken from the First Baltic Front, while the *Stavka* transferred the 5th Guards Tank Army, the 2nd Guards Tatsinskaya Tank Corps, the 3rd Guards Mechanized Corps, and the 3rd Guards Cavalry Corps from its reserve. Besides this, the *front* had attached to it powerful means of reinforcement: 15 artillery brigades, three breakthrough artillery divisions, one gun division, two independent special and high-powered artillery batteries, one division of rocket artillery, three fighter air corps, an assault air corps, three assault engineering brigades, four engineering-sapper brigades, and a pontoon-bridge brigade.

The right wing of the First Belorussian Front, which to launch one of the decisive attacks in the Bobruisk area, was reinforced with the 28th Army from the *Stavka* reserve, as well as the 1st and 9th Guards tank, 1st Mechanized, and the 4th Guards Cavalry corps, an artillery corps, five cannon-artillery brigades, two howitzer brigades, a mortar brigade, an assault air corps, a mixed air corps, two independent tank regiments, eight independent self-propelled artillery regiments, an armored train battalion, an assault engineering-sapper brigade, an engineering brigade, and two pontoon-bridge battalions.

Besides this, the First Belorussian Front's left wing (south of the Pripyat' River) was to be reinforced by the beginning of the operation along this direction by the 8th Guards, Polish 1st and the 2nd Tank armies, the 2nd and 7th guards cavalry, and 11th Tank corps, as well as a significant number of special units. The 6th Air Army, which was to support the operations of the *front's* left wing, was being significantly reinforced.

Overall, the *Stavka* of the Supreme High Command, during the period of the operation's preparation, transferred to the *fronts* an additional 25 rifle divisions, eight tank and mechanized corps, two cavalry corps, an artillery corps, five artillery divisions, 23 artillery and mortar brigades, two independent artillery battalions, five air corps, three air divisions, and many other units and formations.[5]

All of this enabled the *fronts* and armies to create high operational densities along the axes of the main attacks, to guarantee the breakthrough of the enemy's defensive lines, and to develop the success in the operational depth.

The multi-*front* operation in Belorussia was planned and carried out in strategic cooperation with a group of *fronts* operating along other strategic directions. The offensive operations in the Leningrad area and the Karelian Isthmus, and then along the Ukrainian right bank and in the Crimea, led to the defeat of the enemy's strategic groups of forces along the flanks of the Soviet-German front, the tying down of significant enemy reserves and created the necessary conditions for launching a powerful against the German-Fascist Army Group Center. In its turn, the victory in Belorussia created the necessary conditions for realizing broad offensive operations in the Baltic States, Western Ukraine, and along other directions.

Within the confines of the multi-*front* Belorussian offensive operation, we can observe the cooperation between the *fronts*, precisely organized by the *Stavka*, which consisted of a clear definition of the operation's strategic design, the place and role of each *front* in it, and the coordination of the

---

5   Not counting the men and materiel transferred during the operation.

main attacks, by the cooperating *fronts*, according to time and direction, for the purpose of encircling and the subsequent destruction of the enemy's opposing groups of forces. The encirclement and defeat of the Vitebsk and Bobruisk enemy groups of forces by the First Baltic, Third and First Belorussian fronts were connected by the Second Belorussian Front's blow in the center.

The cooperation among the *fronts* was subsequently expressed in the combination of parallel pursuit by the forces of the Third and First Belorussian fronts and the frontal pursuit by the Second Belorussian Front, for the purpose of encircling the enemy's Minsk group of forces. At the same time, the First Baltic Front was to carry out the important task of securing the main group of forces against attacks from the north.

One of the measures facilitating precise cooperation between the *fronts* was the dispatch by the *Stavka* of the Supreme High Command of its representatives, who coordinated the activities of the *fronts* in the interests of the better conduct of the overall operational design.

In preparing a large-scale offensive operation in Belorussia, directed at defeating Army Group Center, the *Stavka* simultaneously took measures to prevent possible counterblows by army groups North and North Ukraine, by which means the actions of the *fronts* carrying out the main task in Belorussia were secured. In connection with this, the First Baltic Front, according to the *Stavka* plan, was to carry out a double task. On the one hand, it was to assist the attack by the Belorussian fronts, while on the other, while advancing on Svencionys, it would cover the operations of these *fronts* and tie down the actions of Army Group North.

From the south the offensive of the Belorussian fronts would be covered by the wooded and swampy valley of the Pripyat' River. Besides this, the *Stavka* ordered the commander of the First Ukrainian Front to attack toward Baranovichi with part of his forces, so as to secure the activities of the Belorussian fronts along the Minsk direction, and then, upon the arrival of the *front's* right-flank armies at the Western Bug River, to launch a powerful attack with the *front's* left-wing forces against the enemy's group of forces defending along the Kovel'—Lublin direction.

Aside from these specific measures for securing the operation, the *Stavka* was preparing the adjoining *fronts* for offensive operations along the neighboring strategic directions. The Second Baltic Front was preparing for an offensive against Army Group North, and the First Ukrainian Front was preparing an offensive along the L'vov direction against Army Group North Ukraine.

The *Stavka* of the Supreme High Command also carried out important measures for confusing the enemy as to the direction of the attacks being prepared by the Soviet forces. For the purpose of concealing the gathering major offensive operation in Belorussia, a large-scale false concentration by the armies of the Third Ukrainian Front along the Kishinev direction was carried out at the end of May and the beginning of June 1944. For this same purpose the concentration of the greater part of our Long-Range Aviation was carried out to Ukrainian airfields. These and a number of other measures led to a condition in which the enemy was not able to uncover our plans and believed that only supporting operations by Soviet troops were possible in Belorussia in the summer of 1944 and that the main attack would be launched in the south.

All the measures for preparing the operation were carried out so skillfully and secretly that the enemy only began to show nervousness during the final days, although he never succeeded in uncovering the full picture of the forthcoming offensive in Belorussia.

During the course of preparing the Belorussian operation, the *Stavka* of the High Command reserve, aside from the 11th Guards Army and the 28th Army and 9th Tank Corps, which arrived at the end of May to the Third and First Belorussian fronts, respectively, large amounts of men and materiel were additionally allocated to the *fronts*. For example, the First Baltic Front was reinforced with the 1st Tank Corps; the Third Belorussian Front received the 5th Guards Tank Army, the 2nd Guards Tank, 3rd Guards Mechanized, and 3rd Guards Cavalry corps; the Second Belorussian Front received the 81st Rifle Corps, and; the 1st Guards Tank Corps arrived to strengthen the right wing of the First Belorussian Front, and the 8th Guards and 2nd Tank armies[6] and the 2nd Guards Cavalry Corps the *front's* left wing.[7]

By the start of the operation the *fronts* had also been reinforced with a significant number of independent tank and self-propelled artillery regiments and brigades, artillery, mortar and engineering formations and units, as well as a large number of reinforcements and equipment.

Simultaneously with the reinforcement of the group of ground forces, the *fronts'* air armies were reinforced by 11 air corps and five air divisions, totaling 2,978 aircraft. Simultaneous with the arrival of the air formations, the air armies received a significant number of aircraft to make up the losses in the air formations. Aside from reinforcing the First Baltic, Third, Second and First Belorussian fronts, the *Stavka* allocated from its reserve the 2nd Guards and 51st armies, as well as a number of various formations and units to the western theater of military activities.[8]

The operation's increased scale and the employment of a large amount of military equipment demanded the significantly greater delivery of all types of military cargoes than was previously the case. During the preparation for the offensive operation in Belorussia, the *fronts* received an enormous amount of various types of supplies, including more than 11,000 cars of ammunition, 110,000 rifles, 59,000 automatic rifles, 2,083 guns of various calibers, and much other military equipment.

Enormous amounts of equipment were released for conducting the operation. During the operation's preparation phase, it was planned to deliver from the country's rear to the four *fronts* about 400 trains of ammunition along, of which it was planned to expend on the operation's first day two combat loads of ammunition, which in terms of weight was about 140,000 tons, or 160 trains.[9]

All the *Stavka's* measures for the *fronts'* materiel-technical supply led to a situation whereby before the start of the offensive in Belorussia all the armies had 12-20 days' rations, 3.4-4.2 fuel refills, and 2.2-4 combat loads of ammunition.

The Soviet army's rear organs faced particularly complex and difficult tasks in supplying the troops with everything necessary during the course of the advance, particularly while pursuing the enemy. In order to resolve this task, the rear organs planned to employ, first of all, automobile transport, having created an automobile transport reserve in each *front*. It should be noted that as early as 1943 the *Stavka* of the Supreme High Command radically changed the system of delivering ammunition, food, fuel, and other types of supplies to the troops. This measure came down to a system whereby the troops themselves did not deliver everything they needed from the army and *front* depots, but just the opposite—the army and *front* transport organs delivered all necessities to the troops. This measure exerted a great influence on the successful outcome of all the operations of 1944, particularly the Belorussian operation.

The presence of strong and numerous party organizations and a mighty popular partisan movement facilitated that rapid restoration of the organs of Soviet power in the liberated areas of Belorussia.

By the summer of 1944 there were nine underground oblast' committees and 174 city district committees of the Belorussian Communist Party operating in the enemy rear in Belorussia.[10]

The Communist Party of Belorussia, which had carried out its heroic labor, by the summer of 1944, actually controlled about 60 percent of the territory occupied by the enemy.[11] At this time

---

6   The 8th Guards and 2nd Tank armies were subordinated to the First Belorussian Front (left wing) by a *Stavka* directive of 13 June 1944.

7   The 2nd Guards Cavalry Corps arrived at the First Belorussian Front's left wing on 7 July 1944.

8   *Operatsii Sovetskikh*, vol. 3, p. 291.

9   *Ibid*, p. 292.

10   Naumov, *Rol' Belorusskikh*, pp. 45-46.

11   Soldatenko, *Trudovoi*, p. 230.

the Belorussian communists were putting out 162 newspapers, which served not only the partisan detachments, but the entire population of Belorussia.[12]

The presence of a combat-capable communist party and a massive partisan army, which numbered in its ranks about 450,000 people, created favorable conditions for the rapid restoration of the organs of Soviet power on the entire territory liberated from the enemy.

The restoration of the economy in the areas liberated from the enemy was one of the most important measures of the Communist Party and the Soviet government. Trains from all corners of the Soviet Union moved to the liberated areas with equipment, construction materials, food, and livestock. For example, Soviet Kirgiziya sent 20,000 horses, 10,000 head of cattle, 100,000 sheep and goats to the liberated areas during the war. The Kazakh SSR in 1944 alone allocated 318,000 head of livestock for the liberated areas.[13]

No less assistance was provided by the other republics, oblasts and provinces of the Soviet Union.

On the basis of instructions by the *Stavka* of the Supreme High Command, the *fronts* rendered a great amount of assistance to the Belorussian people to rapidly restore industry and agriculture. For example, the First Belorussian Front transferred to the Belorussian economy a significant amount of trucks, tractors, horses, carts, harness gear, medicines, food for children's services, and fuel and lubricants. Concrete assistance was rendered in the matter of restoring industrial enterprises, communal buildings, and bridges, etc. The *front's* military council required all units and *front* departments, without upsetting operations, to render all-round assistance to agriculture.[14]

By the summer of 1944 the situation on the Soviet-German front had changed so much that the question now arose of liberating Poland, which had been occupied by the Hitlerites.

As early as 1943 the Union of Polish Patriots had been formed on Soviet territory, which in May of that year had begun forming the Polish 1st Division, named after Tadeusz Kosciuszko.[15] This division became the core of the Polish army in the USSR, which took an active part in the struggle against fascist Germany. The *Stavka* of the Supreme High Command and Soviet government rendered all-round assistance to the newly-reborn Polish army, supplying it with weapons, food, and equipment and established normal conditions for its military training.

All citizens of Polish descent, located on the territory of the Soviet Union and expressing a desire to serve in the Polish army, were immediately transferred to the disposal of the Polish command.

On the other side of the front, the Polish Worker's Party, which had arisen as early as 1942 and which was now in the deep underground, began to simultaneously form the People's Army in the rear of the fascist troops on the territory of Poland, Western Belorussia and Western Ukraine. The People's Army's partisan detachments carried out an active struggle with the Hitlerite aggressors and during the course of the first six months of 1944 alone wrecked 127 German trains, destroyed 36 railroad stations, killed 1,335 German soldiers, 77 officers, and destroyed 14 planes, etc.

On 1 January 1944 the Polish National Council was established in the underground. On 21 July, when Soviet troops were forcing the Western Bug River, the Polish National Council, at its underground meeting in Lublin, adopted a decree creating the Polish National Liberation Committee. This committee took upon itself the functions of a provisional government for the

---

12 Naumov, *Rol' Belorusskikh*, p. 9.

13 Soldatenko, *Trudovoi*, p. 239.

14 Antipenko, N.A. *Organizatsiia i Rabota Tyla 1-go Belorusskogo Fronta v Operatsiiakh po Razgromu Nemetsko-Fashistkikh Voisk v Belorussii*. Moscow: Voennoe Izdatel'stvo, 1955, p. 11.

15 Editor's note. Andrzej Tadeusz Bonawentura Kosciuszko (1746-1817) was born in Poland and later moved to France. He took part in the Revolutionary War in America and then returned to Poland. He led an unsuccessful uprising against Russia in 1794, which led to the third partition the following year and the disappearance of an independent Poland. He died in exile in Switzerland.

Polish Republic. The *Stavka* of the Supreme High Command of Soviet forces used all means at its disposal to render assistance to the Polish people and the provisional government. Thanks to this assistance, the strength of the new Poland steadily grew, both on the territory of the Soviet Union and in the enemy rear. The Soviet army's assistance to the Polish people became noticeable as early as the Belorussian operation, particularly in the operations of the First Belorussian Front, and the Polish 1st Army, which had been formed on the territory of the USSR, participated actively.

Conclusions to Part 1

In preparing the Belorussian operation of 1944, the *Stavka* of the Supreme High Command made an all-round accounting of the character of the enemy's defense, his grouping of men and materiel, and the German-Fascist command's possible plans.

The myth, put about by the Hitlerite propaganda, that the armed forces of the fascist bloc had created "impenetrable defensive walls" on the eastern front was overturned by Soviet forces as early as the summer and fall of 1943, and then again during the winter campaign of 1944. On the basis of the experience acquired in conducting offensive operations against previously constructed and enemy-occupied defensive zones, the correct conclusion was made that in Belorussia the Soviet forces, given the necessary preparation, would be able to overcome the enemy's resistance and open up this decisive direction for launching a blow against fascist Germany. However, it's necessary to note that the prolonged and stubborn fighting that occurred along the Belorussian direction (near Vitebsk, Orsha and other sectors) in the first half of 1944 created an impression that the enemy here had a particularly stout defense, the overcoming of which would require great efforts on the part of the Soviet forces and take up considerable time. This, evidently, explains why in the *Stavka* directives the tasks assigned to the *fronts*, both initial and subsequent, were initially to a comparatively small depth.

In preparing the Belorussian operation, the *Stavka* of the Supreme High Command took into account the grouping of the enemy's men and materiel not only in Belorussia, but along the entire Soviet-German front. It was known that the enemy's main mobile forces were located along the southern wing of the Soviet-German front and that the enemy's main strategic reserves were designated for this area. Taking this into account, the Soviet Supreme High Command had reason to believe that during the first stage of the Belorussian operation the enemy would not be able to throw any large reserve groups of forces against our troops, because he would require a significant amount of time to regroup his forces to Belorussia from the other directions. This would give the Soviet forces freedom of action, at least for the operation's first stage, that is, during the defeat of the enemy's main forces in his tactical and operational depth.

Following the defeat of the German-Fascist forces in 1943 at Kursk and the severe defeats he suffered during the winter campaign of 1944, the Hitlerite command could no longer organize a large-scale offensive directed at changing the course of the war on the Soviet-German front. The strategic initiative was completely in the hands of the Soviet army. This could not but influence the character of the offensive operation being prepared in Belorussia, as the Soviet army had the unrestricted opportunity of choosing the direction of its main attacks and transferring troops from one direction to another.

The time for the start of the offensive in Belorussia, which was chosen by the *Stavka*, was favorable for the Soviet armed forces from three points of view. First of all, the enemy was still under the impression of the major defeats inflicted on him during the course of our first offensive operations of 1944. He had not yet been able to restore his reserves and raise his forces' morale, which had been shaken by the continuous failures. Secondly, the summertime was the most favorable for conducting a major offensive operation on the territory of Belorussia, which was covered with a multiplicity of wooded and swampy sectors, rivers and streams.

The operational directions chosen by the *Stavka* of the Supreme High Command enabled us to turn Army Group Center's flanks and isolate it from the other enemy groups of forces located to the north and south; they led by the shortest route to such important political and strategic centers as the capital of the Belorussian SSR—Minsk, the capital of the Lithuanian SSR—Vilnius, and the capital of Poland—Warsaw, as well as to the border of East Prussia, which would enable us to carry the war onto enemy territory.

The offensive by Soviet forces along five operational directions would enable us to break up the enemy's defense along a broad front, disperse his forces, and mislead him as to the direction of the main attacks. On the other hand, such a method of conducting an offensive would make it easier for our forces to maneuver men and materiel.

The plan of the *Stavka* of the Supreme High Command precisely expressed the idea of concentrating forces along the Minsk direction, and it was characteristic that these forces had to be concentrated not before the operation, but during its course, upon our forces reaching the enemy's operational depth. Upon breaking through the enemy's defense along a broad front, the three Belorussian fronts were to subsequently attack along converging axes toward Minsk, for the purpose of encircling and destroying the main forces of Army Group Center in the area to the east of the city.

In analyzing the contents of the tasks laid down by the *Stavka* of the Supreme High Command to the *fronts*, the following characteristic features should be noted: the immediate tasks were laid down to the *fronts* to a depth of 30-40 kilometers, and subsequent tasks to a depth of 80-150 kilometers; it was precisely pointed out which groups of enemy forces should be defeated and by which methods (by means of the three *fronts'* close cooperation); the methods of employing the *fronts'* mobile forces were defined, proceeding from the operation's overall goal, and; they sought to secure the entire multi-*front* offensive operation, as a whole, particularly the flanks of the shock groups of forces.

The successful achievement of the operation's goals, as laid down by the *Stavka*, predetermined not only the defeat of the central group of the German-Fascist armies and the closely-linked liberation of the Belorussian and Lithuanian peoples, but also a number of other important tasks. Fascist Germany would be deprived of the last large agricultural and raw materials base on Soviet territory, which it barbarously exploited to support its tottering economic situation. The defeat of Army Group Center would signify the creation of favorable strategic prerequisites for subsequent attacks against Army Group North in the Baltic States, and against Army Group North Ukraine. The arrival of our armies at the western borders of the USSR would signify the creation of the necessary prerequisites for an invasion of East Prussia. The liberation of Poland would potentially secure the arrival of Soviet forces along the Berlin strategic direction.

On the whole, the successful realization of these tasks signified the further change of the political and strategic situation in our favor, not only in Belorussia, but along the entire Soviet-German front.

The operation's plan conformed to its goals; it drawing it up, the specific features of the situation were taken into account.

The form of conducting operations, called for by the plan, corresponded to the features and strengths of the enemy's defense, the configuration of the front line, as well as the overall character of the terrain, which required the rapid overcoming of the wooded and swampy spaces between the rivers along comparatively narrow axes, and preempting the enemy's arrival in the more accessible terrain west of the Berezina River. A decisive and active form of conducting operations should guarantee the following: a) the splitting of the enemy's strategic defensive front by the forces of four *fronts*, along with the simultaneous encirclement and destruction of the Vitebsk and Bobruisk enemy groups of forces, while the encirclement itself of these groups of forces was to be carried out in the north by attacks along converging axes by the First Baltic and Third Belorussian fronts, and in the south along converging axes by the right wing of the First Belorussian Front; b) the combination of the parallel pursuit of the enemy by the Third and First Belorussian fronts' mobile formations, with a frontal pursuit by the forces of the Second Belorussian Front in the general direction of Minsk; c) the encirclement of the main forces of the enemy's Army Group Center in the operational depth, with their simultaneous destruction; attacks against the enemy would be launched along converging axes, and; d) the creation of favorable conditions for the arrival of our troops at the western borders of the USSR.

As early as the planning, the scope of the Belorussian operation exceeded many previous multi-*front* operations of the Great Patriotic War, according to a number of indices. On our side 124 divisions, containing more than 1.2 million soldiers, were to take part in the first stage alone. On the enemy's side, over 420,000 men and officers would take part in this stage. The operation was planned along a front reaching 690 kilometers in width, which required the particularly precise organization of the *fronts'* cooperation.[1] Although during the first stage an advance was called for only 40-150 kilometers in depth, overall, the operation could achieve higher rates by developing the success in the operational depth. The rates of the planned advance were average for 1944 and did not exceed 10-15 kilometers per day, although in reality they could be significantly surpassed.

On the whole, the plan by the *Stavka* of the Supreme High Command for carrying out the Belorussian operation called for the defeat of the enemy's main forces along a most important strategic direction and the creation of conditions for carrying the war onto German territory.

The preciseness of the *Stavka* plan, the clarity and specific nature of the tasks assigned to the *fronts* facilitated the brilliant realization of this major offensive operation of the Great Patriotic War.

---

1   Not counting the First Belorussian Front's left wing.

Part 2

Operational Preparation at the *Front* Level

By the start of the Belorussian operation, all four participating *fronts* were in an almost identical situation. Having gone over to the defensive at the end of March 1944, they had the opportunity over the course of three months to study the opposing enemy's group of forces and his defensive system.

In the second half of May the *front* commanders received preliminary instructions from the *Stavka* of the Supreme High Command for conducting the Belorussian operation. Somewhat later, at the end of May, the *Stavka* issued directives to the *fronts* on preparing their operations. Thus the preparation for the operation began at the end of May. This continued until 22-23 June; that is, nearly a month.

The *front* operations were prepared as a part of a single multi-*front* operation, conducted under the leadership of the *Stavka* of the Supreme High Command. Thus a great deal of attention was devoted to the problems of cooperation between the *fronts*.

The First Baltic Front prepared the Vitebsk—Polotsk offensive operation, which was directed at defeating the Vitebsk—Lepel' and Polotsk German-Fascist groups of forces.

The Third Belorussian Front, which occupied a jumping-off position in the area of the so-called "Smolensk gates," between the large water barriers of the Western Dvina and Dnepr rivers, prepared the large-scale Vitebsk—Minsk offensive operation for the purpose of defeating the enemy's forces along one of the decisive directions leading to the capital of Belorussia—Minsk. According to the *Stavka's* instructions, the *front* prepared a breakthrough of the enemy's defense along two sectors, separated from each other by more than 30 kilometers.

The Second Belorussian Front, according to the *Stavka* plan, prepared the Mogilev—Minsk offensive operation, which occupied an auxiliary position in the system of the multi-*front* operation.

The First Belorussian Front prepared two independent operations along two axes. The first or Bobruisk—Slutsk offensive operation was prepared on the *front's* right flank for breaking through the enemy's defense along the Bobruisk direction, followed by a development of the success toward Minsk and Slutsk. The second, or Brest—Siedlce offensive operation (in the plan, it was called the Kovel' operation) was prepared along the *front's* left wing, at first for capturing the Kovel' salient and developing the success toward Baranovichi and Brest, followed by a change of the main attack's axis toward Siedlce. It is interesting that the left-wing forces, according to the operational plan, were to go over to the offensive approximately during the second stage of the multi-*front* operation in Belorussia.

Thus from the end of May 1944 four *fronts* took part in preparing the Belorussian operation and were designated for defeating Army Group Center—one of the most powerful German-Fascist groups of forces on the Soviet-German front.

3

Decisions of the *Front* and Army Commanders

The Decisions of the Commander of the First Baltic Front and the Commanders of the Front's Armies

The Situation in the First Baltic Front's Operational Zone by the Beginning of the Operation

The First Baltic Front (formerly the Kalinin Front) as early as the fall of 1943 had arrived at the approaches to the city of Vitebsk, where during the winter of 1943-44 it conducted independent operations to improve its situation. As a result of such operations, the *front* managed to outflank the Vitebsk area from the north and northwest and advance to the near approaches to Polotsk.

By the beginning of June 1944 the troops of the First Baltic Front (6th Guards, 4th Shock and 43rd armies) were defending along the line: Lake Berezno (50 kilometers north of Lake Neshcherdo)—Lake Neshcherdo—Lake Chervyatko—Gurki—Koitovo (12 kilometers northeast of Vitebsk).

In accordance with a coded telegram from the *Stavka* of the Supreme High Command (No. 11568), from 2400 on 5 June 1944, the 54-kilometer wide defensive zone north of Porech'e, which was occupied by the 6th Guards Army, was to be transferred to the Second Baltic Front.

The 6th Guards Army, following its relief by formations of the Second Baltic Front, was to be moved into the *front* reserve for the purpose of subsequently being employed along the axis of the main attack, along the boundary between the 4th Shock and 43rd armies.

In the grouping of Soviet forces along the central sector of the Soviet-German front, the First Baltic Front was designated for operations along the important Polotsk—Vitebsk direction, which was favorable for launching an attack along the boundary between two German-Fascist army groups—North and Center.

To the right of the First Baltic Front the Second Baltic Front was defending along the Riga direction. To the left the Third Belorussian, the right flank of which outflanked the Vitebsk area from the southeast and south, was preparing for going over to the offensive.

The systematic preparation of the offensive operation began in the headquarters of the First Baltic Front on 29 May 1944. Thus the *front* had 25 days (through 22 June) for planning the offensive operation.

Defending against the First Baltic Front were formations from Army Group North's Sixteenth Army, and Army Group Center's Third Panzer Army (IX and LIII army Corps).

The enemy in the *front's* area had been preparing defensive lines since November 1943 and, using the favorable terrain conditions, had created a deeply echeloned defense.[1]

---

1 A description of the defense is contained in the first part of this work.

In all, parts of 11 German-Fascist divisions and combat groups were defending in the area immediately opposite the First Baltic Front, of which four divisions (24th Infantry and the 281st, 391st and 201st security divisions) were in the second echelons and reserves of the corps, armies and the army group). Besides this, up to 11 independent security regiments and up to 40 independent battalions of various types were operating in the operational depth.

The security formations and units were occupied, as a rule, with fighting against the partisans, although this did not exclude the possibility of their being used against the First Baltic Front's attacking forces. For example, the Third Panzer Army's combat log for 17 June 1944 contains a notation that the commander of the 201st Security Division had been issued a telegraphic order in which it was stated: "In the event of a large enemy offensive, the security forces must be employed at the front."

In all, opposite the First Baltic Front there were 11 divisions, 728 field guns, 823 mortars, 622 anti-tank weapons, and 130 tanks and self-propelled guns.

The disposition of the enemy's forces along the various axes was as follows:

The Polotsk axis. Along the 38-kilometer Chernoe—Lake Chervyatka—Rovnoe sector the enemy had three infantry divisions, of which two (87th and 205th) were in the first echelon and one (24th) was in reserve. Besides this, another three divisions (281st, 391st and 201st security divisions) could be employed.

The Vitebsk axis. Along the 36-kilometer Rovnoe—Chisti sector, where the German-Fascist command did not foresee a large-scale offensive by the First Baltic Front, there was one infantry division (252nd) in the first echelon and up to two battalions from Corps Group "D."

In the immediate depth of this sector there were no enemy troops, although the German-Fascist command could employ the 24th Infantry and the 201st and 1st and 391st security divisions.

Along the 45-kilometer excluding Chisti—Staroe Selo—excluding Koitovo sector the enemy had Corps Group "D", the 246th Infantry and 4th *Luftwaffe* Field divisions in the first echelon. The enemy could also employ the 201st Security Division, which located in the Lepel' area, from its reserves along this axis.

The First Baltic Front command, disposing of complete data, and having carefully studied the grouping of enemy forces and his defensive system, arrived at the conclusion that "… an offensive directly along the Polotsk and Vitebsk axes may encounter strong enemy resistance, based on a multi-zonal defensive system. The greatest results can be achieved by an offensive along a broad front between the towns of Polotsk and Vitebsk, with the main attack landing between the boundary of the enemy's Sixteenth and Third Panzer armies in the general direction of Lovzha and Beshenkovichi, bypassing the enemy's group of forces from the west."[2]

By the start of the offensive operation (21 June 1944) the First Baltic Front consisted of three armies, which included the headquarters of eight rifle and one tank corps, 24 rifle divisions, one rifle brigade, and powerful reinforcements (see table 5). In all, the front numbered 687 tanks and self-propelled guns, 4,926 guns and mortars greater than 76mm, and 778 anti-tank guns.

The *front* had a single-echelon formation. The *front* commander had a single rifle division (154th) in reserve and, as the *front's* mobile group, the 1st Tank Corps.

The correlation of forces and the operational densities in the *front's* attack zone at the start of the operation are shown in table 6.

From table 6 it is clear that the First Baltic Front was superior to the enemy, especially in tanks and planes. This superiority was overwhelming along the axis of the main attack, particularly at

---

2   Archival section of the Ministry of Defense's Directorate of Affairs, opis' no. 20488. From the report by the commander of the First Baltic Front General Bagramyan on his ideas about the plan for the Vitebsk operation to the Supreme Commander-in-Chief.

the beginning of the operation up to the commitment of the nearest enemy reserves (24th Infantry and 201st Security divisions) into the battle, which were located at a distance of 40-80 kilometers from the forward edge of the defense.

Along the axis of our main attack, the enemy could also employ the 391st Security Division, which was located in the Glubokoe area; but this division, which was 125 kilometers from the forward edge of the defense, could be committed into the battle only in the operational depth. It should be noted that the enemy's security divisions, which were fighting the Belorussian partisans, were widely scattered and it would require a certain time to gather them together.

Table 5. The First Baltic Front's Strength at the Start of the Belorussian Operation (as of 20 June 1944)

Name	4th Shock Army	6th Guards Army
Rifle Formations	83rd Rifle Corps (119th, 332nd, 360th rifle divs),	2nd Gds Rifle Corps (9th, 46th, 116th rifle divs),
	16th Lithuanian Rifle Div, 101st Rifle Bde	22nd Gds Rifle Corps (51st, 47th rifle divs, 90th Gds Rifle Div) 23rd Gds Rifle Corps (51st, 67th, 71st gds rifle divs) 103rd Rifle Corps (29th, 270th rifle divs)
Artillery Reinforcements	46th Anti-Aircraft Div, 1623rd Anti-Aircraft Rgt, 99th Gds Mortar Rgt	21st Breakthrough Artillery Div, 26th, 27th cannon artillery bdes (8th Cannon Artillery Div), 4th Cannon Artillery Bde, 64th, 283rd howitzer rgts, 38th Corps Artillery Rgt, 45th Anti-Tank Artillery Bde, 39th Anti-Aircraft Artillery Div, 1625th Anti-Aircraft Artillery Rgt, 408th Mortar Rgt, 22nd Gds Mortar Rgt
Armored and Mechanized Forces	One tank battalion, 171st Self-Propelled Artillery Rgt	34th Gds and 143rd tank brigades, 2nd Gds Heavy Tank Rgt, 119th and 47th tank rgts (flamethrower and mine clearing), 333rd and 335th gds self-propelled artillery rgts
Engineering Troops	2nd Engineer-Sapper Bde	29th Engineer-Sapper Bde, 10th Assault Engineer-Sapper Bde, 37th, 91st, 106th pontoon-bridge bns
Chemical Troops	35th Flamethrower Battalion	
Aviation		

Name	43rd Army	*Front* Formations and Units	3rd Air Army
Rifle Formations	1st Rifle Corps (179th, 357th, 306th rifle divs), 60th Rifle Corps (334th, 235th, 156th rifle divs), 92nd Rifle Corps (204th, 145th rifle divs, 155th Fortified Area)	145th Rifle Div	
Artillery Reinforcements	37th Gds, 28th cannon artillery rgts (8th Cannon Artillery Div), 480th, 1224th, 376th howitzer rgts, 17th Anti-Tank Artillery Bde, 17th Anti-Aircraft Artillery Div, 1626th Anti-Aircraft Artillery Rgt, 221st Independent Anti-Aircrft Artillery Rgt, 31st Mortar Bde, 39th, 34th gds mortar rgts	183rd, 622nd independent anti-aircraft artillery divs, 26th Gds Mortar Rgt, 2nd Gds Mortar Div	

Name	43rd Army	*Front* Formations and Units	3rd Air Army
Armored and Mechanized Forces	39th, 10th tank bdes, 105th Tank Rgt., 337th, 1203rd heavy self-propelled artillery rgts	1st Tank Corps (159th, 89th, 117th tank bdes, 44th Motorized Rifle Bde, 55th Howitzer Artillery Bde, 1437th Artillery Rgt, 26th Gds Mortar Rgt, 108th Motar Rgt, 1487th, 1720th anti-aircraft artillery rgts, 1514th Self-Propelled Artillery Rgt, 376th Howitzer, Rgt, 4th, 6th gds. engineering bns, 86th Motorcycle Rgt), 46th Motorized Bde, 272nd Amphibious Automobile Bn	
Engineering Troops	28th Engineer-Sapper Bde, 5th Assault Engineer-Sapper Bde	5th Gds Motorized Engineering Bde, 37th Independent Engineer-Sapper Bn with canine mine detectors, 9th Pontoon Bde, 21st Defense Construction Directorate, 4th Front Defensive Structures Directorate	
Chemical Troops	44th Flamethrower Bn		
Aviation			11th Fighter Corps (190th, 5th Gds fighter divs), 211th, 332nd, 335th, assault air divs, 259th Fighter Div, 6th Gds Assault Air Rgt, 314th Night Bomber Div, 11th Reconnaissance Rgt, 206th Fire Correction Reconnaissance Air Div

Table 6. The Correlation of Forces and Operational Densities along the First Baltic Front's Attack Zone, 22 June 1944

Men and Materiel	Correlation of Forces[1]			Operational Densities per Kilometer of Front			
	Soviet	German	Correlation	The Entire Front (160 km)		Axis of the Main Attack (25 km)	
				Soviet	German	Soviet	German
Men (combat)	222,706	133,500	1.7:1	–	–	–	–
	168,908	55,500	3:1	–	–	–	–
Divisions (rifle and infantry)	24	11	2.2:1	.15	.07	.76	.14
	19[2]	3.5[3]	4.7:1				
Battalions (rifle and infantry)	229	66	3.5:1	1.4	.4	6.7	1.04
	168	26	6.5:1				
Machine Guns (light and heavy)	8,432	7,433	1.1:1	52.7	46.5	248.5	134.5
	6,212	3,362	2:1				

Men and Materiel	Correlation of Forces[1]			Operational Densities per Kilometer of Front			
	Soviet	German	Correlation	The Entire Front (160 km)		Axis of the Main Attack (25 km)	
				Soviet	German	Soviet	German
Guns and Mortars (all calibers)	5,704 3,768	2,306 970	2.4:1 3.8:1	48.1	14.4	151	39
Tanks and Self-Propelled Guns	687 535	130 90	5.1:1 6:1	42.9	.8	25.5	3.6
Aircraft	902	335	2.8:1				

Notes
1 The numerator shows the overall correlation of forces, and the denominator the correlation along the axis of the main attack.
2 Here the 1st Tank Corps' mechanized brigade and motorized rifle brigade are counted as one division.
3 Counting the 24th Infantry and 201st Security divisions, which were in the second echelon.

On the first day of the First Baltic Front's offensive the enemy could only oppose his 252nd Infantry Division, two battalions from Corps Group "D" and, in the best case, the 24th Infantry Division, located in an area five kilometers northeast of Polotsk; that is, 2.5 divisions. This created an even more favorable correlation of forces for us.

On the whole, the situation in the *front's* attack zone was favorable for the unfolding of successful offensive operations.

The Front Commander's Decision

General I.Kh. Bagramyan,[3] the commander of the First Baltic Front, made the decision to break through the enemy's front with the neighboring flanks of the 6th Guards and 43rd armies along the 25-kilometer Volotovki—Toshnik sector; upon committing the *front's* mobile group—the 1st Tank Corps—into the breach and launching the main attack in the direction of Sirotino and Beshenkovichi, to force the Western Dvina River and seize the Beshenkovichi area; with part of its forces the *front* was to operate in conjunction with the right wing of the Third Belorussian Front and destroy the enemy's Vitebsk group of force and capture the city of Vitebsk; by firmly securing the *front's* main group of forces from the Polotsk area, the *front* was to attack toward Lepel' and on the 10-11 day of the operation reach the line Zelenyi Gorodok—Krulevshchizna (northwest of Lepel').[4]

The *front* had a single-echelon operational formation in its jumping-off point, with a single rifle division (154th) in reserve, along with the *front's* mobile group—the 1st Tank Corps. The operation was planned in detail as far as the line Kovalevshchina—Chashniki, at a depth of 65-70 kilometers, with a length of seven days and an average rate of advance of ten kilometers per day.

---

3 Editor's note. Ivan Khristoforovich Bagramyan (1897-1982) served as a junior officer in the Russian imperial army during World War I. He joined the Red Army in 1920 and served in a number of command, staff and teaching posts during the interwar period. During the Great Patriotic War he served chiefly in staff positions at the *front* level, before making the jump to army commander. He later commanded the First Baltic Front and the Samland operational group in East Prussia at the end of the war. Following the war, Bagramyan commanded a military district and held a number of positions within the central military apparatus.
4 *Sbornik Materialov po Izucheniyu Opyta Voiny*, no. 18 (1945), p. 17.

The *front's* armies and independent formations were given the following tasks:

The 6th Guards Army,[5] in launching the main attack along its left flank, was to break through the enemy's defense along the 18-kilometer Volotovki—excluding Novaya Igumenshchina and, upon defeating the Sirotino enemy group of forces, was to reach the line Zavodka—Gubitsa with its main forces by the end of the operation's first day.

With the arrival of the army's units at the line Mazurina—Lovzha, the army was to secure the commitment of the main forces of the *front's* mobile group—the 1st Tank Corps—into the breach from this line in the general direction of Beshenkovichi.

Subsequently, by energetically developing the offensive by the army's main forces in the general direction of Beshenkovichi and Chashniki, the army was to force the Western Dvina River and reach the front Ulla—Svecha—Dubrovki. Simultaneously, part of the right-flank corps' forces, in conjunction with its neighbor on the right—the 4th Shock Army's 360th Rifle Division—was to defeat the enemy's opposing group of forces and, with the corps' main forces, capture and firmly consolidate the Obol' area, covering the army's flank against attacks from the Polotsk area.

The 43rd Army, in launching its main attack with its right-flank forces in the direction of Shumilino, was to break through the enemy's defense along the 7-kilometers Novaya Igumenshchina—excluding Toshnik sector and, having defeated the enemy's Shumilino group of forces, reach the line Il'nitsy—Ol'khoviki by the end of the first day.

Upon the arrival of the army's units in the Shumilino area, it was to secure the 46th Mechanized Brigade's (1st Tank Corps) commitment into the breach in the direction of Plyushchevka and Krivoe Selo.

Subsequently, the army, by rolling up the enemy's defense with its left-flank corps, was to reach and firmly consolidate along the line of the Western Dvina River and, with its main forces, developing the offensive to the south and bypassing Lake Budovishche from the west, was to force the Western Dvina River in the Mil'kovichi area and capture the line Krivoe Selo—Chernogost'e.

The 1st Tank Corps—the *front's* mobile group—upon the arrival of the 6th Guards and 43rd armies' units in the Shumilino area, was to be committed along the front Mazurina—Shumilino and, attacking in the general direction of Beshenkovichi, to force the Western Dvina River and capture a bridgehead on its left bank in the Beshenkovichi area. Subsequently, by cutting off the Vitebsk group of forces' route of retreat, the corps was to be ready to attack to the southwest in the general direction of Lepel'.

The 4th Shock Army, while securely defending the Polotsk axis with its main forces along the front Pal'kovo—Glistinets, was to capture the Rovnoe area with its left-flank 360th Rifle Division and the 119th Rifle Division's 421st Rifle Regiment. Subsequently, in conjunction with its neighbor to the left—the 6th Guards Army's 22nd Guards Rifle Corps—it was to destroy the enemy group of forces southwest of Starinovichi and reach the line Lipniki—Pagory—Rassolai and firmly secure it.

The *front's* reserve—the 154th Rifle Division—was to concentrate in the Koz'yany area.

This decision is evidence of the *front* commander's desire to not only break through the enemy's tactical defense with his first attack, but also to overcome the German-Fascist forces' army defensive zone and force a large water barrier—the Western Dvina River. After carrying out this assignment, the *front's* main forces, having reached the line Zelenyi Gorodok—Krulevshchizna (northwest and west of Lepel') were to face northwest and prepare for operations against Army Group North, in this way breaking its connection with Army Group Center. This decision by

---

5   The army, having turned over its previous sector to the forces of the Second Baltic Front, was by the begin-ning of the operation regrouping to a new sector within the First Baltic Front and was designated for employ-ment in the first echelon.

the *front* commander completely corresponded to the plan by the *Stavka* of the Supreme High Command, which sought to isolate from its neighbors Army Group Center, which was the main target of the entire Belorussian operation.

With the arrival of its forces in the Krulevshchizna area, the First Baltic Front would reach the enemy's rear defensive position ("Catastrophe"), which would signify the defeat of the German-Fascist forces not only in the tactical, but in the operational zone as well.

The Army Commanders' Decisions

The decision by the commander of the 6th Guards Army fully repeated the task assigned to the army by the *front*.

The operational configuration called for two echelons, with two corps—22nd and 23rd guards—in the first, and two—103rd and 2nd Guards—in the second.

The corps were given the following tasks:

The 22nd Guards Rifle Corps was to break through the enemy's defense along the front Shun'ki—Byvalino and, launching an attack in the general direction of Spasskoe, defeat the opposing enemy group of forces; by the end of the first day the corps was to reach the line Starosel'e—Cheremka—Spasskoe—Zaluzh'e. The corps would subsequently develop the offensive, with its main forces, in the direction of Obol', covering the army's flank against enemy attacks from the Polotsk area. The corps was to be ready along the line Tverdunovka—Zaluzh'e to secure the commitment of the formations of the *front's* mobile group—the 1st Tank Corps.

The 23rd Guards Rifle Corps was to break through the enemy's defense along the front Byvalino—excluding Novaya Igumenshchina; by a headlong drive in the direction of Dobrino, it was to defeat the opposing enemy group of forces by the end of the first day and cut the highway and Polotsk—Vitebsk railroad and, with its main forces, capture the line Verbali—Gubitsa. The corps was to subsequently attack toward Zheludova and Pyatigorsk. The corps was to be ready to along the line excluding Mazhurina—Gubitsa to secure the commitment of the formations of the *front's* mobile group—the 1st Tank Corps.

The 103rd Rifle Corps was to be ready to commit all its forces on the morning of the offensive's second day in the direction of Latkova and Ulla and to force the Western Dvina River along the Ulla—Bol'shie Shet'ki sector and capture a bridgehead on its opposite bank.

The 2nd Guards Rifle Corps, following behind the 23rd Guards Rifle Corps, was to be ready to be committed into the battle from behind its left flank, for an attack in the direction of Lyubichi and Beshenkovichi.

The commander of the 43rd Army decided, while securely defending the front Zherebichi—Voroshilovo—Koitovo (east of Kozlov), to break through the enemy's front with a shock group, consisting of six rifle divisions and two tank brigades, supported by artillery and *front* aviation, along the front Medvedi—the woods southeast of Zabolotniki and, launching its main attack in the general direction of Shumilino and Kutino, to destroy the enemy's units in the Shumilino area and, by the end of the second day to reach the front Novoe Selo—Grineva—Novki. Forward detachments would seize crossings over the Western Dvina River along the Sharylino—Vyazhishche sector, and in the Komli area. The army was to have a single-echelon formation.

In accordance with the operational plan, the army commander assigned his corps the following tasks:

The 1st Rifle Corps was to break through the enemy's defense along the front Medvedi—excluding Kozonogovo. The immediate objective was to take Shumilino and, by the end of the day to reach the line Belyai—Lazuki with the main forces.

The 60th Rifle Corps was to break through the enemy's defense along the front Kozonogovo—the woods northeast of Zabolotniki. The immediate objective was to capture the line

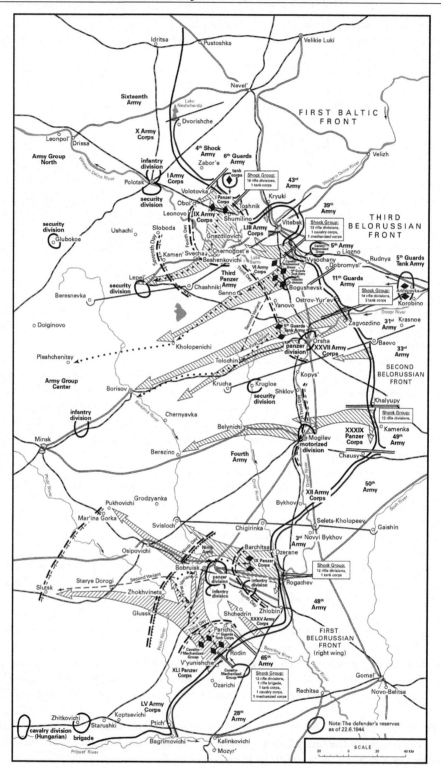

Map 3 The Decision by the Commanders of the First Baltic, Third, Second and First Belorussian Fronts for the Conduct of the Vitebsk—Orsha, Mogilev and Bobruisk Operations.

Zasinniki—Zavyaz'e and, by the end of the day to reach the line Lazuki—Yazvino with its main forces.

The 92nd Rifle Corps was to defend the front excluding Chisti—Koitovo (east of Kozlovo) and be ready to launch an attack in the direction of the village of Staroe Selo.

The commander of the 4th Army decided to defend his assigned area with the forces of the 83rd Rifle Corps, with the mission of preventing an enemy breakthrough of the forward edge of the defense; he would break through the enemy's defense with the 360th Rifle Division, including reinforcements, in the Rovnoe area and reach the line Lipniki—Pagory—Rassolai—Fedosovka, for the purpose of securing contact with his neighbor to the left. The army's operational formation would be in a single echelon.

The 16th Rifle Division was concentrating in the reserve in the Dretun' area.

In accordance with the army commanders' decisions, the combat formations of almost all the corps of the first operational echelon were arrayed in a single echelon, while the divisions were deployed in 1-2 echelons.

Brief Conclusions on the Decisions of the Front Commander and the Army Commanders

By his decision, the commander of the First Baltic Front sought to exactly carry out the plan of the *Stavka* of the Supreme High Command. Following the breakthrough of the enemy defense, the *front's* forces were to carry out two missions. The 6th Guards Army and 1st Tank Corps, attacking to the northwest, west and southwest, were to broaden and deepen the breakthrough, wedging themselves into the boundary between the enemy army groups North and Center. This attack was primarily designated for disrupting coordination between these enemy groups of forces, to isolate Army Group Center, and in this way facilitate its defeat by the forces of the Belorussian fronts. The 43rd Army, while attacking to the south and southeast directions, was to resolve the *front's* task—to destroy, along with the Third Belorussian Front's 39th Army, the enemy's Vitebsk group of forces. The 6th Guards and 43rd armies were to establish operational cooperation, which was to express itself by the fact that the 6th Guards Army, attacking on a broad front, would create an external encirclement front around the enemy's Vitebsk group of forces, while the 43rd Army, in its turn, by attacking to the south and southeast, was to secure the 6th Guards Army from a possible counterblow by the enemy's Vitebsk group of forces.

The direction of the main attack was chosen successfully. The enemy, while expecting an attack by Soviet forces along the Polotsk and Vitebsk directions, did not pay much attention to the Sirotino—Beshenkovichi axis, thanks to which the Soviet forces managed to achieve operational surprise here. This is confirmed by the fact that the enemy did not only fail to reinforce this axis, but, quite the opposite, he moved his 95th Infantry Division from the Beshenkovichi are to the Mashkany area on 19 June; that is, in the Third Belorussian Front's operational area.

The breakthrough sector, compared to those of the First and Third Belorussian fronts, which disposed of considerably larger forces, was planned to be wider (25 kilometers), which was reflected in the operational densities. However, it should be noted that the army commanders, taking into account the character of the highly broken terrain, concentrated their forces along the axes of their main attacks and, in this way achieved an overwhelming superiority over the enemy. For example, the commander of the 6th Guards Army used his tanks (204 machines) not along his entire designated 18-kilometer breakthrough zone, but only along the Mazury—Sirotino sector—that is; along a sector only ten kilometers in width.

On the whole, it should be noted that the First Baltic Front had everything it needed to successfully carry out its assigned tasks.

The decisions by the army commanders also corresponded to the plan and decision of the *front* commander.

The operational formation of the armies corresponded to the men and materiel present. The 6th Guards Army, which had four corps, arrayed them in two echelons. In the first echelon were two corps (22nd and 23rd), and in the second—another two corps (103rd and 2nd Guards). The 43rd Army, which had only three corps and, besides, was defending a broad front, arrayed its corps in a single echelon. The 4th Shock Army had the same formation.

The insufficient depth of the formation at the operational level was compensated by the deep formation of the combat formations. For example, while the 6th Guards Army's first-echelon corps were arrayed in a single echelon, the 43rd Army's corps were arrayed in two.

It was planned to employ the 6th Guards Army's second echelon to develop the success in the operational depth. The army commander planned to commit his 103rd Rifle Corps into the battle on the second day of the operation, following the breakthrough of the enemy's second defensive zone, in order to seize a bridgehead on the western bank of the Western Dvina River. It was planned to commit the army's 2nd Guards Rifle Corps, which was also located in the second echelon, into the battle in order to capture the Beshenkovichi area, that is; for breaking through the enemy's army defensive zone.

The First Baltic Front's mobile group was to be committed into the breach before the army's second echelons at a depth of 10-12 kilometers and was designated for completing the breakthrough of the tactical defensive zone and the subsequent development of the success in the operational depth.

On the whole, the decisions by the *front* commander and that of the army commanders corresponded to the situation that had arisen and to the assigned objectives, as well as the level of military art reached at the time.

The Decisions of the Commander of the Third Belorussian Front and the Commanders of the *Front's* Armies

The Situation in the Third Belorussian Front's Operational Zone by the Beginning of the Operation

In the beginning of 1944 the Third Belorussian Front (formerly the Kalinin Front) was defending in Belorussia, covering the Minsk—Smolensk operational direction (the "Smolensk Gates"). Before 1 June the *front* consisted of the 39th, 5th and 31st combined-arms armies and the 1st Air Army. In the first part of June the Third Belorussian Front was reinforced with the following: the 11th Guards Army from the First Baltic Front, the 5th Guards Tank Army, 2nd Guards Tatsinskaya Tank, 3rd Guards Mechanized, and 3rd Guards Cavalry corps from the reserve of the *Stavka* of the Supreme High Command.

By the beginning of June 1944 the Third Belorussian Front was defending along the line Konchani—Belynovichi—the woods two kilometers west of Vorona—Brodki—1st Vinokorno—the eastern bank of lakes Zelenskoe and Sitnyanskoe—Novoe Selo—Zastenok Yur'ev—Kovshichi. The Soviet forces had reached this line as as early as 1943 as the result of the fall-winter operations by the Western and Kalinin fronts. Certain refinements were made during the course of the Western Front's spring operations (February-March, 1944), the goal of which was the capture of Vitebsk and Orsha.

The Second Belorussian Front was defending to the left.

Upon receiving the *Stavka* of the Supreme High Command's directive on 31 May 1944, the *front* began preparing the Vitebsk—Minsk operation and completed this work by 22 June 1944.

By the beginning of the operation, the Third Belorussian Front was opposed by formations from the enemy's Third Panzer and Fourth armies.

The Third Panzer Army (IX, LIII and VI army corps) was a tank army in name only and consisted of seven infantry, two *Luftwaffe* field and one security divisions. The army covered the Vilnius direction, with its main group of forces in the Vitebsk area. The divisions of the LIII and VI army corps were defending opposite the Third Belorussian Front. The army's headquarters was in Beshenkovichi.

The Fourth Army (XXVII and XII army and XXXIX Panzer corps) consisted of eight infantry, two motorized and one security divisions). The army was covering the Minsk direction, with its main forces in the areas of Orsha and Mogilev. The XXVII Army Corps was defending opposite the Third Belorussian Front.

By 23 June 1944 the enemy had deployed six infantry and one motorized divisions in the tactical defensive zone against the *front's* forces, along a 140-kilometer front.

The nearest reserves were concentrated as follows: the 95th Infantry Division in the area to the northwest of Bogushevsk; the 14th Infantry Division, along with the 667th Assault Gun Battalion in the area northwest of Orsha.

Aside from this, three security divisions, which were being used against the Soviet partisans and defending communications and other rear targets, were deployed to the west as far as the line Vilnius—Baranovichi.

The enemy also had opposite the *front* by the start of the operation 12 independent security and police regiments and up to 34 various independent battalions (special, police, etc.), which were operating against Soviet partisans in the area between the Western Dvina River and the Dnepr River, and between the line Orsha—Minsk.

The enemy, attaching very great importance to the retention of the main defensive zone (the "main battlefield"), reinforced his first-echelon troops with a large number of specialized units from the High Command Reserve.

Each infantry division occupied a 12-15 kilometer defensive front, while certain divisions, which were defending areas with inaccessible sectors, had defensive fronts of 20-25 kilometers.

The enemy's tactical defensive densities are shown in table 7.

It can be seen from this table that the enemy had his greatest tactical densities along the Vitebsk and Orsha directions.

The enemy's tactical reserves were deployed, as a rule, in the areas of the command posts of those commanders to whom they were subordinated. A regiment usually had up to a reinforced company in reserve, while a division had no less than a reinforced battalion, and a corps from two infantry battalions to an infantry regiment, reinforced with a battalion of tanks and a battalion of assault guns. It was also planned to employ sapper and other specialized units and subunits as an overall reserve.

Thus by the start of the operation the enemy's forces occupied only the tactical defensive zone, while the enemy's nearby reserves had not occupied beforehand their defensive zones, which had been prepared in the depth; the security divisions were tied down with fighting the partisans.

The deployment of the German-Fascist troops enabled our armies, upon breaking through the enemy's tactical defensive zone with powerful and concentrated attacks and, defeating his main groups of forces facing the *front* here, to subsequently develop the operation in depth and to preempt the enemy in occupying his defensive zones in depth and to defeat his reserves in detail, as they came up.

Table 7. The Enemy's Tactical Densities per Kilometer of Front

	Infantry Battalions	Guns	Tanks and Assault Guns
Vitebsk Direction			
6th Air-Infantry and 206th Infantry divisions	0.4-0.5	13	4
197th Infantry Division	0.3	10	–
Bogushevsk Direction			
299th Infantry Division	0.4-0.5	16	6-7
256th Infantry Division	0.25	6	–
Orsha Direction			
78th Assault Infantry Division (along the highway)	0.5	up to 20	8-9
25th Infantry Division	0.2	10	–

Table 8. The Third Belorussian Front's Strength at the Start of the Belorussian Operation (as of 23 June 1944)

Name	39th Army	5th Army	11th Gds Army
Rifle and Cavalry Formations	5th Gds Rifle Corps (17th, 19th, 91st gds rifle divs, 251st Rifle Div), 84th Rifle Corps (158th, 164th, 262nd rifle divs)	72nd Rifle Corps (215th, 63rd, 277th rifle divs), 65th Rifle Corps (371st, 97th, 144th rifle divs), 45th Rifle Corps (159th, 338th, 184th rifle divs)	8th Gds Rifle Corps (5th, 26th, 83rd gds rifle divs), 16th Gds Rifle Corps (1st, 11th, 31st gds rifle divs), 36th Gds Rifle Corps (16th, 18th, 84th gds rifle divs, 152nd Fortified Area)
Artillery Reinforcement	139th Cannon Artillery Bde, 1481st Anti-Aircraft Rgt, 54th Gds Mortar Rgt	3rd Gds Breakthrough Artillery Div (99th Howitzer Bde, 22nd Cannon Artillery Bde, 43rd Mortar Bde, 7th, 8th light howitzer bdes, 119th High Powered Howitzer Bde), 16th Gds Anti-Tank Artillery Bde, 326th, 95th gds mortar rgts, 33rd Anti-Aircraft Artillery Div, 1480th Anti-Aircraft Artillery Rgt	20th and 2nd Gds breakthrough artillery divs. (5th Breakthrough Artillery Corps), 4th Cannon Artillery Div, 7th Gds Mortar Bn, 149th Cannon Artillery Bde, 1st Gds Anti-Tank Artillery Bde, 117th High-Powered Howitzer Bde, 226th, 402nd, 406th, 316th, 245th high caliber artillery divs, 1093rd, 523rd, 1165th corps artillery rgts 38th Gds Corps Corps Artillery Rgt, 42nd, 67th, 317th guards mortar rgts, 48th, and 34th anti-aircraft artillery divs, 1281st Anti-Aircraft Artillery Rgt
Armored and Mechanized Forces	28th Gds Tank Bde, 735th, 957th self-propelled artillery rgts	153rd, 2nd Gds tank bdes, 1st Flamethrower Tank Rgt, 1st Minesweeper Tank Rgt, 343rd, 954th, 395th, 337th 122nd, 953rd self-propelled artillery rgts	2nd Gds Tank Corps, 120thIndependent Tank Bde, 35th, 63rd gds heavy tank rgts, 148th, 517th flamethrower and minesweeping tank rgts, 1435th, 345th, 348th heavy self-propelled artillery rgts, 9 self-propelled artillery bns
Engineer Troops	32nd Engineer-Sapper Bde	4th Assault Engineer-Sapper Bde, 63rd Engineer-Sapper Bde	66th Engineer-Sapper Bde, 2nd Assault Engineer-Sapper Bde
Chemical Troops		513th Flamethrower Rgt	517th Flamethrower Rgt
Aviation			

Name	31st Army	5th Gds Tank Army	*Front* Formations and Units	1st Air Army
Rifle and Cavalry Formations	71st Rifle Corps (38th, 192nd, 331st rifle divs), 113th Rifle Corps (62nd, 174th rifle divs), 36th Rifle Corps (220th, 173rd, 352nd rifle divs)		3rd Gds Cavalry Corps (5th, 6th, 32nd gds cavalry divs.	
Artillery Reinforcements	140th and 15th cannon artillery bdes, 43rd Anti-Tank Artillery Bde, 392nd, 570th corps artillery rgts, 74th Gds Mortar Rgt, 66th Anti-Aircraft Artillery Div, 1275th Anti-Aircraft Artillery Rgt, 525th Independent Anti-Aircraft Artillery Div, 9th Gds Mortar Bde, 83rd Gds. Howitzer Rgt	76th Gds Mortar Rgt	6th, 20th anti-aircraft artillery divs, 24th, 64th, 500th independent anti-aircraft artillery divs	
Armored and Mechanized Forces	213th Independent Tank Bde, 1445th, 959th, 926th self-propelled artillery rgts, 958th Heavy Self-Propelled Artillery Rgt	29th Tank Corps (25th, 31st, 32nd tank bdes); 3rd Gds Tank Corps (3rd, 18th, 19th gds tank bdes) 75th Motorcyle Bn, 107th Gds Motorcycle Bn, 1st Gds Motorcycle Rgt, 14th Gds Tank Rgt, 64th Gds Mortar Div, 1464th, 1223rd, 376th gds, 1436th, 2498th self-propelled artillery rgts	3rd Gds. Mechanized Corps (7th, 8th, 9th gds mechanized bdes)	
Engineer Troops	31st Engineer-Sapper Bde		3rd Assault Engineer Bde, 8th Pontoon Bde, 13th Engineer-Sapper Bde, 52nd Miltary Field Construction Directorate, 5th Front Defensive Structures Directorate	
Chemical Troops	14th, 15th fougasse flamethrower bns			

Name	31st Army	5th Gds Tank Army	*Front* Formations and Units	1st Air Army
Aviation				1st Gds, 3rd fighter air corps, 3rd Assault Air Corps, 1st Gds Bomber Corps, 240th, 303rd, 1st Gds, 311th, 9th, 3rd, 6th Gds bomber divs, 213th Night Bomber Div, 10th Reconnaissance Rgt, 117th Target Correction Reconnaissance Rgt

By the start of the Vitebsk—Minsk operation, the combat composition of the Third Belorussian Front, by a decision of the *Stavka* of the Supreme High Command, had been considerably strengthened by means of concentrating new armies, formations and units from all the combat arms, as well as by bringing up reinforcements and a large amount of different military equipment by rail and automobile transport.

The *front*, before the start of the operation, consisted of four combined-arms armies (39th, 5th, 11th Guards, and 31st), which numbered between them 33 rifle divisions, one tank army (5th Guards), the First Air Army, and many units and formations of specialized arms (see table 8). The *front* had 1,810 tanks and self-propelled guns—more than all the other *fronts*. The Third Belorussian Front was significantly superior to the First Baltic and Second Belorussian fronts in the number of guns and mortars and was inferior in this regard only to the First Belorussian Front. The Third Belorussian Front had the most powerful mobile forces designated for commitment into the breach (the 5th Guards Tank Army and a cavalry-mechanized group).

The *front*'s rifle divisions had been significantly reinforced, although only 21 divisions had been brought up to 7,000 men, while the remaining 12 divisions had a strength of between 4,500 and 6,500 men in each. The number of men and junior commanders in the companies had been raised to 85-102 men.

The correlation of forces and the operational densities in the *front*'s attack zone by the beginning of the operation are shown in table 9.

It is clear from the table that the Third Belorussian Front outnumbered the enemy in men 2.2 times, and 1.7-7.7 times in combat equipment. Such an overall superiority in the conditions of 1944 was considered completely sufficient for carrying out a *front* offensive operation and for creating an even greater superiority of men and materiel along the axes of the main attack.

On the whole, the situation along the front was favorable to successfully breaking through the enemy's defense and developing the success at high speeds.

The Front *Commander's Decision*

The plan of the commander of the Third Belorussian Front, Colonel General I.D. Chernyakhovskii,[6] for the Vitebsk—Minsk operation called for the defeat of the opposing enemy group of forces and

---

6   Editor's note. Ivan Danilovich Chernyakhovskii (1906-45) joined the Red Army in 1924 and served in various command capacities before the war. During the Great Patriotic War he advanced from the command of a division to that of a corps and army, and in 1944 was appointed to command the Third Belorussian Front. He

reaching the Berezina River and creating the conditions for a subsequent offensive in the general direction of Minsk.

The *front* commander decided to launch two attacks: the first, from the area west of Liozno in the direction of Bogushevsk, Senno, and Lukoml'; the second, from the area to the northeast of Dubrovno, along the Minsk highway in the direction of Tolochin and Borisov, to split the Vitebsk—Orsha group of enemy forces and, in conjunction with the left wing of the First Baltic Front and the Second Belorussian Front, defeat it in detail, preventing the enemy's retreat behind the Berezina River. All of the *front's* combined-arms armies were to be deployed in a single echelon. In order to carry out the operational plan, it was necessary to create a northern group of forces, consisting of the 39th and 5th armies and the *front's* cavalry-mechanized group, and a southern group, consisting of the 11th Guards Army and the 2nd Tank Corps, the 31st Army and the 5th Guards Tank Army. The *front's* main efforts were to be concentrated along the axis of the southern group's efforts.

Table 9. The Correlation of Forces and Operational Densities along the Third Belorussian Front's Attack Zone, 22 June 1944

Men and Materiel	Correlation of Forces[1]			Operational Densities per Kilometer of Front			
				The Entire Front (140 km)		Axis of the Main Attack (37 km)	
	Soviet	German	Correlation	Soviet	German	Soviet	German
Men	371,653	167,648	2.2:1				
	225,042	103,848	2.2:1				
Divisions (rifle, Infantry)	33	14	2.5:1	0.2	0.1	0.7	0.2
	27	7	3.8:1				
Battalions (rifle, Infantry)	277	118	2.3:1	2.0	1.5	6.0	1.6
	224	58	3.8:1				
Machine Guns (light, heavy)	13,214	7,505	1.7:1	94.4	53.6	200.5	141.5
	7,418	5,235	1.4:1				
Guns and Mortars (all calibers)	8,309	2,569	3.2:1	59.3	18.3	156	58
	5,764	2,160	2.3:1				
Tanks and Self-Propelled Guns	1,810	316	5.7:1	29.2	2.2	34.5	3.7
	1,466	138	10.5:1				
Aircraft	1,864	240	7.7:1	–	–	–	–

Note
1 The numerator shows the overall correlation of forces, while the denominator shows the correlation along the axis of the main attack.

The forces of the 39th and 5th armies were to break through the enemy's defense along the 18-kilometer Karpovichi—Vysochany sector and, while developing the 39th Army's offensive toward Gnezdilovichi, and the 5th Army and the cavalry-mechanized group toward Bogushevsk, to defeat the opposing enemy, and encircling the enemy's Vitebsk group of forces in conjunction with the First Baltic Front's left wing.

was killed during the East Prussian operation in February 1945.

The *front's* cavalry-mechanized group, consisting of the 3rd Guards Cavalry and the 3rd Guards Mechanized corps, was to be committed on the morning of the operation's second day from the line of the Luchesa River, in the 5th Army's sector, in the direction of Bogushevsk, Senno, Lukoml', and Pleshchenitsy.

Subsequently, the 39th Army, in conjunction with the First Baltic Front, was to complete the destruction of the enemy's Vitebsk group of forces; the 5th Army and the cavalry-mechanized group, in conjunction with the 11th Guards Army, was to develop the offensive to the Berezina River, in the direction of Senno, Lukoml' and Moiseevshchina.

The 11th Guards Army, along with the 2nd Tank Corps and the 31st Army, was to break through the enemy's defense along the 19-kilometer Ostrov—Yur'ev—excluding Zagvazdino sector and, launching an attack along the these armies' neighboring flanks in the general direction of Tolochin and Borisov, defeat the enemy's Orsha group of forces and capture Orsha. The 11th Guards Army, bypassing Orsha from the north, was to assist the 31st Army in capturing this very important enemy strong point.

From the area of Orsha the southern group of forces, having the 5th Guards Tank Army ahead of it, was to energetically develop the offensive toward Borisov.

It was planned to commit the 5th Guards Tank Army into the battle following the break-through of the enemy's entire tactical defensive depth by the first-echelon armies according to one of the following variants: the first—along the Orsha direction and the highway in the 11th Guards Army's sector in the general direction of Borisov, approximately on the morning of the operation's third day; the second—in the 5th Army's sector in the general direction of Rechki, Bogushevsk and Smolyany, followed by the tank army's reaching the highway in the Ozertsy area (five kilometers east of Tolochin), also for developing the attack on Borisov.

The *front's* immediate task was to defeat the enemy's Vitebsk—Orsha group of forces by taking the towns of Orsha and Vitebsk and reaching the line Lake Sarro—Yanovo—Baran'—Chernoe on the operation's third day.

The *front's* subsequent task was to defeat the enemy's Borisov group of forces and reach with its main forces, no later than the operation's tenth day, the Berezina River and forcing it with mobile formations for the purpose of further developing the operation on Minsk.

On the whole, the plan of the commander of the Third Belorussian Front for the Vitebsk—Minsk operation is an example of when a *front*, in order to carry out the operational breakthrough of the enemy's defense, simultaneously launches two concentrated attacks and, in conjunction with a neighboring *front*, encircles and destroys the enemy group of forces along one of its flanks, in this case, the right flank in the Vitebsk area.

The *front* operation was planned to a depth of 150-60 kilometers. The armies were to receive their assignments throughout the entire depth of the *front* operation. The depth of an army's immediate tasks reached 35-40 kilometers, with three days allotted for their achievement.

In order to carry out their immediate tasks, the combined-arms armies were operationally arrayed in a single echelon, which was conditioned by the absence of sufficiently strong reserves in the depth of the enemy's defense. The rifle corps were to break through the enemy's defense along 2.5-5-kilometer sectors and were arrayed in one or two echelons.

The breakthrough front along the two sectors totaled 37 kilometers.

In accordance with the decision elaborated above, the commander of the Third Belorussian Front assigned his armies the following tasks:

The 39th Army was to launch an attack, with the forces of five rifle divisions and reinforcements, in the general direction of Zamostoch'e, Pesochna and Gnezdilovichi and, in conjunction with the First Baltic Front's left wing, defeat the enemy's Vitebsk group of forces and take Vitebsk.

The army's immediate task was to break through the enemy's defense along the sector Karpovichi—Kuzmentsy. It was to link up with the left wing of the First Baltic Front's forces in the area north of Ostrovno and thus encircle the enemy's Vitebsk group of forces.

Subsequently, while developing the offensive on Beshenkovichi with part of its forces, the main forces werer to destroy the encircled enemy and capture the city of Vitebsk.

The 5th Army was to launch an attack, with the forces of eight rifle divisions and reinforcements, in the direction of Bogushevsk, Senno, Lukoml', and Moiseevshchina and, in conjunction with the 11th Guards Army, defeat the enemy's Bogushevsk—Orsha group of forces, preventing it from falling back to the west.

The army's immediate objective was to break through the enemy's defense along the Podniv'e—Vysochany sector and by the end of the operation's third day capture the line excluding Lake Lipno—Novaya Obol'—Yanovo.

After forcing the Luchesa River, approximately on the morning of the operation's second day, the army was to secure the commitment of the *front*'s cavalry-mechanized group in the direction of Bogushevsk and Senno.

The army's subsequent objective was to develop, in conjunction with the cavalry-mechanized group and the 11th Guards Army, an energetic offensive in the direction of Senno, Lukoml' and Moiseevshchina and, by the end of the operation's tenth day, to reach the Berezina River with its main forces near Lake Palik and to the north.

In order to broaden the breakthrough and roll up the enemy's defense in the southern direction, one of the army's rifle divisions was to attack toward Babinovichi, in order to meet up with the forces of the 11th Guards Army's 152nd Fortified Area.

The 11th Guards Army was to launch an attack, with nine rifle divisions and reinforcements, along the front Settlement No.7—Kirieva in the direction of Tolochin and Borisov and, in conjunction with the 5th and 31st armies, defeat the enemy's Orsha group of forces and prevent it from retreating to the west.

The army's immediate objective was to break through the enemy's defense along the Ostrov Yur'ev—Kirieva sector and, in conjunction with the 5th and 31st armies, defeat the enemy's Orsha group of forces and capture, by the close of the operation's third day, the line excluding Yanovo—Molotan'—Lamachin.

Upon arriving at the line Kurovshchina—Moshkovo, the 2nd Guards Tank Corps would be committed, for the purpose of attacking from the area to the west of Orsha on Starosel'e and, by the end of the operation's fourth day, to capture Starosel'e.

The army was to be ready, from the morning of the operation's third day, to secure the commitment of the 5th Guards Tank Army, attacking toward Borisov, into the breach.

The army's subsequent objective was to, by employing the 5th Guards Tank Army's success, to develop an energetic offensive toward Borisov and, in conjunction with the 5th and 31st armies, reach the line of the Berezina River in the area of Borisov and to the north, by the close of the operation's tenth day.

In order to widen the breach and roll up the enemy's defense to the north, units of the 152nd Fortified Area were to attack toward Babinovichi, toward the 5th Army's formations. With the arrival of the main group of forces to the north of Orsha, one rifle division was to launch an attack toward Baran' and Novosel'e from the Moshkovo area, in order to assist the 31st Army in taking Orsha from the north.

The 31st Army was to attack, with five rifle divisions and reinforcements, in the direction of Dubrovno and Orsha along both banks of the Dnepr River and, in conjunction with the 11th Guards Army, defeat the enemy's Orsha group of forces and prevent it from retreating to the west.

The army's immediate objective was to break through the enemy' defense along the sector excluding Kirieva—excluding Zagvazdino and, by the end of the operation's first day, take

Dubrovno; by the end of the operation's third day it was to take Orsha and reach the line excluding Lomachin—Cherven'—Chernoe.

The army's subsequent objective, in conjunction with the 11th Guards Army, was to develop the offensive with its main forces on Vorontsevichi and Vydritsa.

The army, along its auxiliary axis, was to attack with the forces of the 113th Rifle Corps in the direction of Krasnaya Sloboda, Negotina and Borodino and, by rolling up the defense from the south, in conjunction with the Second Belorussian Front's 33rd Army, prevent the enemy's withdrawal behind the Dnepr.

On the night of the operation's second day, the *front's* cavalry-mechanized group, upon the 5th Army's infantry taking the line of the Luchesa River, was to be ready to move into the breach and develop an energetic offensive toward Bogushevsk, Senno, Kholopenichi, and Pleshchenitsy. By the end of the operation's second day, the group's main forces were to reach the Bogushevsk area. By the end of the operation's third day, the 3rd Guards Mechanized Corps' main forces were to take the Senno area, while the 3rd Guards Cavalry Corps was to take Rechki, Morgoitsy, Veino, and Nemoita.

No later than the operation's fifth day, the cavalry-mechanized group was to capture crossings over the Berezina River along the Begoml'—Zembin sector.

Securing the commitment of the cavalry-mechanized group was, by a decision by the *front* commander, to be entrusted to the commander of the 5th Army.

According to the first variant, the 5th Guards Tank Army, having entered the breach in the 11th Guards Army's sector from the line Kurovshchina—Mezhevo—Korovo—excluding Khorobrovo, was to develop the offensive along the Minsk highway and, upon defeating the enemy's reserves, was to take the town of Borisov, force the Berezina River in this area and seize bridgeheads on its western bank. According to the second variant, the 5th Guards Tank Army was to be ready to enter the breach in the 5th Army's sector along the Yazykovo—Vysochany—excluding Babinovichi sector and by the end of the first day following its commitment was to capture the Tolochin area. The army was to subsequently take the town of Borisov and the crossings over the Berezina River in that area.

The Third Belorussian Front was to be ready to attack by the morning of 22 June. The hour of attack was to be determined by a separate order.

The Army Commanders' Decisions

The commander of the 39th Army decided to launch his main attack with the forces of the 5th Guards Rifle Corps and reinforcements, and two rifle divisions from the army reserve, along the front Makarova—Yazykovo in the general direction of Sharki, Zamostoch'e, Pesochna, Ostrovno and, upon breaking through the enemy's defense along the sector excluding Perevoz—excluding Savchenki, prevent the enemy's Vitebsk group of forces from retreating and, upon encircling it, destroy it in close conjunction with the First Baltic Front's 43rd Army.

In the army's remaining 40-kilometer sector, two rifle divisions from the 84th Rifle Corps were to defend their sectors. Simultaneous with an attack by the 5th Guards Rifle Corps, two rifle regiments of the 84th Rifle Corps' 262nd Rifle Division were to attack in the direction of Trubachi.

The army's immediate objective was to defeat the opposing enemy, to force the Luchesa River on the march along the front Perevoz—the mouth of the Sukhodrovka River, and by the end of the operation's first day capture the line Poddublyane—Pushkari—Stupishche—Zamostoch'e—excluding Savchenki, having seized the Vitebsk—Orsha railroad.

The army was to attack in single-echelon formation.

The troops were given the following assignments:

The 84th Rifle Corps was to actively defend its sector; on the left flank the corps' 262nd Rifle Division, simultaneously with the 5th Guards Rifle Corps, was to break through the enemy's defense north of the line Bondino—Mosino and take Starinki. The corps was to subsequently attack toward Trubachi, outflanking the Vitebsk group of forces from the south and southwest.

The 5th Rifle Corps was to break through the enemy's defense along the sector excluding Perevoz—excluding Savchenki, launching its main attack in the direction of Sharki and Zamostoch'e. The corps was to force the Luchesa River from the march along the front excluding Perevoz—the mouth of the Sukhodrovka River. By the end of the day it was to seize the line Borisovka—the railroad bridge over the Chernichenka River, thus cutting the Vitebsk—Orsha railroad. On the second day the corps was to develop its main attack toward Pecochna.

The 164th and 251st rifle divisions made up the army's general reserve.

The commander of the 5th Army decided to launch his main attack with the forces of his 72nd and 65th rifle corps, along with reinforcements, plus two of the second-echelon 45th Rifle Corps' rifle divisions, in the general direction of Bogushevsk and Senno and, in conjunction with the *front's* cavalry-mechanized group and the 11th Army, defeat the enemy's Bogushevsk—Orsha group of forces and prevent it from withdrawing to the west.

Simultaneously, two regiments of the 45th Rifle Corps' 159th Rifle Division were to launch a supporting attack in the direction of Osetki and Makeevo, with the objective of, in conjunction with the 11th Guards Army's 152nd Fortified Area, destroying the enemy in the Osetki—Makeevo—Sleptsy area.

The army had a two-echelon operational formation.

It was planned to commit the army's second echelon—the two-division 45th Rifle Corps—into the battle to develop the success in the general direction of Bogushevsk and Senno.

The army's immediate task was to break through the enemy's defense along the 15-kilometer sector Podniv'e—excluding Osetki and, having defeated the opposing enemy, to force the Luchesa River on the march; by the end of the operation's first day, it was to take the line Noviki—Verkhnee Aleksandrovo—Nizhnee Aleksandrovo—Astapenki—Lake Streshno—Murashki. On the morning of the operation's second day it was to secure the commitment of the *front's* cavalry-mechanized group into the breach from a bridgehead over the western bank of the Luchesa River along the Luchkovskoe—Malye Kalinovichi sector.

The troops received the following assignments:

The 72nd Rifle Corps was to break through the enemy's defense along the Podniv'e—Buraki sector and, launching the main attack with its left flank, by the end of the battle's first day capture the line Noviki—Astapenki, having forced the Luchesa River on the march. The corps was to support the commitment of the 3rd Guards Mechanized Corps' right-flank units into the breach on the western bank of the Luchesa River on the morning of the offensive's second day. The corps would subsequently develop the offensive in the direction of Savinichi.

The 65th Rifle Corps was to break through the enemy's defense along the sector excluding Buraki—excluding Osetki and, launching its main attack with its right flank in the direction of Bogushevsk, by the end of the offensive's first day capture the line excluding Astapenki—Murashki, having forced the Luchesa River on the march. The corps would secure the commitment of the 3rd Mechanized Corps' left-flank units into the breach, as well as those of the 3rd Guards Cavalry Corps, on the western bank of the Luchesa River on the morning of the operation's second day.

The corps would subsequently develop the offensive toward Bogushevsk and Senno.

The 45th Rifle Corps would be in readiness to attack with its main forces in the general direction of Senno, and part of them on Makeevo.

The commander of the 11th Guards Army decided to launch his main attack with the forces of the 16th, 8th and 36th Guards rifle corps and the 2nd Guards Tank corps, with reinforcements, in the general direction along the Minsk highway and, in conjunction with the 5th and 31st armies, defeat the enemy's Orsha group of forces and prevent it front falling back to the west.

The enemy's defense along the 10.5-kilometer Ostrov Yur'ev—Kirieva sector was to be pierced by the forces of the 16th, 8th and 36th Guards rifle corps, with four rifle divisions arrayed in these corps' first echelons along the breakthrough sector.

Simultaneously, the corps would launch a supporting attack with the forces of the 152nd Fortified Area in the direction of Samostoika, Ukraishche, toward the 5th Army's 159th Rifle Division.

The army's rifle corps, were to attack in a single echelon.

The army's immediate objective was to break through the enemy's defense along the Ostrov Yur'ev—Kirieva sector, and having committed the army's mobile group—the 2nd Guards Tank Corps—defeat the opposing enemy (78th Infantry Assault Division), and by the end of the operation's first day seize the line of the Orshitsa River with units of the 2nd Guards Tank Corps.

Subsequently, by developing the main attack along the Minsk highway, the army was to attack to the north with part of its forces and, in conjunction with the 5th Army, encircle the enemy's units in the woods north of the highway; by the end of the operation's fifth day the army was to seize the line Veino settlement—Videnichi—Zabolot'e, thus securing the left flank of the army's shock group against possible enemy counterblows from the Orsha direction.

The army, with the arrival of the 2nd Guards Tank Corps at the line of the Adrov River, was to be in readiness to turn to the southeast for an attack on Starosel'e and allow for the passage of the 5th Guards Tank Army in the direction of Tolochin and Borisov.

The troops were given the following assignments:

The 16th Rifle Corps was to break through the enemy's defense along the sectors excluding Lake Sitnyanskoe—Rudnya and excluding the woods north of Ostrov Yur'ev—excluding Osintroi and, launching its main attack in the direction of Starye Kholmy, seize the line Sitna—Kholmy. The corps was to subsequently develop the offensive to the west and northwest and by the end of the second day, in conjunction with the 5th Army, complete the encirclement of the enemy in the woods to the north of the Minsk highway.

The 8th Guards Rifle Corps was to break through the enemy's defense along the Osintroi—Slepin sector and, launching its main attack in the direction of Zabezhnitsa, seize the line excluding Brokhovskie—height 172.3 (two kilometers west of Zabezhnitsa). The corps would subsequently develop the offensive toward Selekta.

The 36th Guards Rifle Corps was to break through the enemy's defense along the sector excluding Slepin—Kirieva and, launching its main attack in the direction of Shalashino, seize the line excluding marker 172.3—excluding Makarovo. Subsequently, having secured the commitment of the 2nd Guards Tank Corps into the breach along the Zabezhnitsa—Bokhotovo line, the corps would develop the offensive toward Barsuki.

The 2nd Guards Tank Corps, having entered the breach along the line Zabezhnitsa—Shalashino—Bokhotovo, was to attack along the Minsk highway. It was to defeat the enemy's arriving reserves and by the end of the offensive's first day seize the line Obukhovo—Barsuki, securing behind it the crossings over the Orshitsa River in this area.

The commander of the 31st Army decided to launch his main attack with the forces of the 71st and 36th rifle corps, including reinforcements, along the front excluding Kirieva—Zastenok Yur'ev in the general direction of Dubrovno and Orsha along both banks of the Dnepr River and, in conjunction with the 11th Guards Army and, having defeated the enemy's Orsha group of forces, capture the town of Orsha.

The enemy's defense along the 39-kilometer sector excluding Kirieva—height 215.2 was to be pierced by the forces of the 71st and 36th rifle corps (five rifle divisions), which had four rifle divisions in their first echelon.

Simultaneously, while covering itself with part of the 13th Rifle Corps' forces along the front Vokolakova—Kovshichi, the corps' 174th Rifle Division was to launch a supporting attack along the sector excluding Zastenok Yur'ev—Kolkolakova in the direction of Negotina and Svatoshitsa.

The army's immediate task was to break through the enemy's defense along the sector excluding Kirieva—height 215.2 and, having defeated the opposing enemy (the 25th Motorized Division), by the end of the operation's first day capture the enemy's large strong point of Dubrovno, reaching the line Makarovo—Dubrovno—Negotina—Pet'ki. Subsequently, the 71st and 36th rifle corps would launch converging attacks from the northwest and south in order to capture Orsha; by the end of the operation's third or fourth day, the army's main forces were to take the line Lamachin—Balbasovo—Bol'shoe Zamosh'e.

The army was to attack in a single-echelon formation.

The troops were assigned the following tasks:

The 71st Rifle Corps was to break through the enemy's defense along the sector excluding Kirieva—Dnepr River and, launching its main attack along the left flank, by the end of the battle's second day capture the line excluding Barsuki—Kobelyaki.

The 36th Rifle Corps was to break through the enemy's defense along the sector Dnepr River—height 215.2 and, launching its main attack with along the right flank, by the end of the offensive's second day capture the line Pashino—Bol'shoe Bakhovo.

The 113th Rifle Corps was to break through the enemy's defense along the sector excluding height 215.2—Krasnaya Sloboda; while securing the army's main group of forces against enemy counterblows from the south, the corps was to launch an attack at Negotina and by the end of the offensive's first day capture the line Negotina—Pet'ki. The corps was to subsequently attack toward Svatoshitsa.

The 173rd Rifle Division was assigned to the army reserve.

In his decision, the commander of the 5th Guards Tank Army laid out in detail the order in which the assignment must be carried only according to the first variant, by which is was planned that during the breakthrough of the enemy's defense by the 11th Guards Army, the 5th Guards Tank Army's main forces would remain in their waiting area: Poteenki—Gusino—excluding Arkhipovka, in readiness on the night of the operation's second day to move to their jumping-off point: Sharuty—Red'ki—Novaya Zemlya. It was planned to occupy the jumping-off area with the army's main forces upon the 11th Guards Army's infantry reaching the line of the Vitebsk—Orsha road.

It was planned to organize the army's operational formation in one echelon: to the right the 29th Tank Corps, and to the left the 3rd Guards Tank Corps.

A forward detachment was allotted from each tank corps.

The troops were assigned the following objectives:

The 29th Tank Corps was to enter the breach along the line Kurovshchina—Neshevo and with its main forces attack in the direction of Ostrov Yur'ev and Obchuga (25 kilometers northwest of Tolochin); by the end of the operation's fourth day it was to reach the area south and southeast of Ridomlya. The corps was to subsequently capture Borisov and a bridgehead on the western bank of the Berezina River.

The 3rd Tank Corps was to enter the breach along the line Korovo—Korobrovo and with its main forces attack along the Minsk highway. By the end of the operation's fourth day the corps was to reach the Tolochin area. The corps was to subsequently capture Novo-Borisov and a bridgehead on the western bank of the Berezina River.

The commander of the cavalry-mechanized group decided to commit the 3rd Guards Cavalry and 3rd Guards Mechanized corps into the break from the line of the Luchesa River, in the 5th Army's zone, on the morning of the operation's second day, in the direction of Bogushevsk, Senno and Lukoml'; by the end of the operation's sixth day, the corps would force the Berezina River in the Voloka—Ploshchenitsy—Zembin area and seize a bridgehead on its western bank.

Brief Conclusions on the Decisions of the Front Commander and the Army Commanders

The Third Belorussian Front's headquarters, thanks to the good organization of all kinds of intelligence, correctly evaluated the opposing enemy. All the German divisions in the first line were exactly identified and the army and *front* staffs knew their combat strength with sufficient accuracy. The enemy's immediate operational reserves—the 95th and 14th infantry divisions—were also known, although their deployment areas had not yet been specified as of 23 June 1944. Our intelligence and the partisans uncovered the German-Fascist forces' deeper operational reserves, particularly their security divisions along the Minsk and Vilnius directions.

Concrete instructions from the *Stavka* of the Supreme High Command determined the character of the Third Belorussian Front's Vitebsk—Minsk offensive operation. In accordance with the *Stavka* plan, the commander of the Third Belorussian Front organized the breakthrough of the enemy's defense along two sectors, 30 kilometers apart from each other. According to the commander's decision, two groups of forces were to be created, having everything necessary both for breaking through the enemy's tactical defense zone and for developing the success in his operational depth. Each group of forces contained mobile forces, which were designated for developing the tactical success into an operational one.

In the commander's plan for the *front's* forces, the idea of the rapid advance of the *front's* forces to a great depth in the enemy's defense was clearly expressed, along with the consequent defeat of the enemy's opposing groups of forces. The 39th Army was designated for the defeat of the Vitebsk group of forces, and the 31st Army for the defeat of the Orsha group of forces. The 5th and 11th Guards armies and the mobile forces were to only assist the 39th and 31st armies in defeating the opposing enemy groups of forces, having as their chief task the rapid achievement of the Berezina River.

In their decisions, the army commanders fully carried out the *front* commander's plan, but planned their army operations only to a depth of 45-65 kilometers. The 39th Army's operation was planned to a greater depth, as the commander planned not only the encirclement, but the destruction of the enemy's Vitebsk group of forces. The 5th Army commander assigned tasks to his corps for the operation's first three days; these objectives indicated only the corps' assigned goals by day, the directions of the main attacks and measures for securing the commitment of the *front's* mobile group into the breach. In the plan and objectives for the corps there were not specific instructions as to the destruction of the enemy's group of forces and combating his reserves.

In his decision, the commander of the 11th Guards Army formulated objectives not only for breaking through the enemy's defense, but also for the encirclement and destruction of the opposing enemy groups of forces. The operation was planned for five days, to a depth of up to 65 kilometers.

The commander of the 31st Army built his entire operation around the capture of the main target—the town of Orsha, which was the enemy's major strong point. The army commander's plan expressed the idea of encircling the enemy in Orsha. The operation was planned for four days to a depth of 45-50 kilometers.

In the *front* commander's decision, a great deal of attention was devoted to the commitment of the *front's* mobile forces into the breach. The cavalry-mechanized group was to be committed into the breach at a depth of 10-12 kilometers following the forcing of the Luchesa River by the 5th Army. The commitment sector did not exceed 10-12 kilometers, and then was to increase to 30 kilometers. Two variants were foreseen for the commitment of the 5th Guards Tank Army into the breach; however, the army commander planned in detail to commit the army into the breach only according to the first variant.

The troops were operationally deployed in one or two echelons. For example, the 5th Army had the two-division 45th Rifle Corps in its second echelon; the first-echelon corps were also deployed in two echelons. In the 11th Guards Army all the corps were in the first echelon, with their divisions in two-echelon formation.

It was planned to employ the mobile troops, second echelons and reserves, depending on the concrete situation. For example, the commander of the 39th Army planned to employ his two reserve rifle divisions for developing the success along the flanks and to secure his flanks. The commander of the 5th Army ordered the 45th Rifle Corps, which was in the army's second echelon, to be ready to develop the success in the direction of Bogushevsk and Senno. The *front's* mobile groups were to be committed into the breach after overcoming the enemy's tactical defensive zone.

On the whole, it was planned to employ the main forces of the Third Belorussian Front's northern group of forces to maneuver in the enemy's defensive depth, for the purpose of breaking through the enemy's main defensive belts in the tactical and operational zones. Part of the shock group's forces was to maneuver toward the flank for encircling the enemy's Vitebsk group of forces.

After breaking through the enemy's tactical defense zone, the Third Belorussian Front's southern shock group (11th Guards and 31st armies) was to carry out a flanking maneuver for the purpose of encircling the enemy's Orsha group of forces and seizing his extremely strong Orsha fortified area. The 31st Army planned to bypass the Orsha fortified area from the north and south, with a simultaneous attack on it from the east. According to the plan, as early as the operation's third day, the 31st Army was to create an internal encirclement front around Orsha and begin to destroy the enemy. The 11th Guards Army, following its arrival in the area north of Orsha, was to continue attacking to the west with its main forces, while attacking with part of its forces directly south, for the purpose of assisting the 31st Army in taking the town of Orsha. According to the 11th Guards Army commander's plan, these forces were to create an external front and prevent the enemy's Orsha group of forces from retreating to the west. According to the operational plan, the 2nd Guards Tank Corps would be committed into the breach on the operation's first day, after overcoming the enemy's tactical defense zone. On the operation's second day it was to reach the area west of Orsha.

In this fashion, it was planned to realize the close cooperation of two armies in the Orsha area, in order to encircle and destroy the enemy's Orsha group of forces.

On the whole, in both the decision of the *front* and army commanders the basic idea of the *Stavka* of the Supreme High Command was to be precisely carried out—to quickly break through the enemy's defense, to defeat the opposing enemy groups of forces and develop an energetic offensive in the depth of the enemy's operational defense, using, foremost, the mobile forces. One must admit that this plan basically corresponded to the concrete situation and the *front's* objective. However, in preparing the operation, the strength of the enemy defense along the Minsk highway was insufficiently considered. The commitment of the 5th Guards Tank Army was without foundation prepared only according to one variant—along the sector where the enemy's strongest fortifications were located.

The Decisions of the Commander of the Second Belorussian Front and the Commanders of the Front's Armies

The Situation in the Second Belorussian Front's Operational Zone by the Beginning of the Operation

The Second Belorussian Front had been defending its sector for some time, from the autumn of 1943. In the first half of 1944 Soviet forces carried out local offensive operations along this direction, in order to improve their position, but did not led to any significant changes in the front line.

By the beginning of June the Second Belorussian Front was defending along the line Baevo—Lenino—Dribin—the eastern bank of the Pronya River—Ust'e—Selets—Kholopeev.

The *front* was faced by the enemy's Fourth Army, which covered the Mogilev—Minsk direction. The command of this army concentrated its main attention on defending the tactical zone, believing that an offensive by Soviet forces would be carried out by insignificant forces and with limited aims, and would smash itself against the main defensive zone (the "main battlefield"), which had a strong system of defensive structures.

Of the ten divisions making up the Fourth Army (organized into three corps headquarters—XXVII and XII army and XXXIX Panzer), seven were defending opposite the Second Belorussian Front. Aside from these, there were formations and units from the High Command Reserve.

Units of the 260th, 110th, 337th, 12th, and 31st infantry divisions and the 18th Motorized Division occupied the enemy's tactical defense zone, as well as two regiments from the 267th and one regiment from the 57th infantry divisions. Tactical reserves, with a strength of between an infantry battalion up to an infantry regiment, were deployed 5-10 kilometers from the forward edge of the defense.

The troops were arrayed in a single echelon and supported by small reserves. Within the corps the divisions, as a rule, were arrayed in a single echelon.

The enemy did not have any artillery or tank units in the operational depth opposite the Second Belorussian Front, with the exception of the divisions' authorized units.

The movement of formations and units to the Fourth Army's sector from other armies was considered unlikely, because powerful attacks were planned by the forces of the Third and First Belorussian fronts along these armies' sectors.

The German-Fascist command devoted a great deal of attention to guarding communications, fearing the many partisan detachments active in the rear. One security division (286th) and 17 security and field replacement regiments, and up to 30 reserve battalions, were engaged in guard duty and in constructing defensive lines in the Fourth Army's rear.

The enemy's forces were improving their defensive structures on the front line along the Pronya River and carrying out defensive work along the Resta River and the western bank of the Dnepr River. Particularly intensive bulking up of the defense and defensive structures was noted along the Mogilev direction.

The Second Belorussian Front, before the start of the offensive, consisted of three combined-arms (33rd, 49th and 50th) armies and one air army (4th). The combined-arms armies at first had six rifle corps, but in the beginning of June the 84th Rifle Corps, which had been transferred to the 49th Army, arrived to strengthen the *front*. In all, the *front* numbered 22 rifle divisions and one fortified area (see table 10 for the *front's* strength).

The correlation of forces in the *front's* sector by the start of the operation is shown in table 11.

It can be seen from table 11 that the Second Belorussian Front did not have a sufficient overall superiority over the enemy. Only along the direction of the main attack did it achieve a superiority of 2:1 in men and 3.8:1 in guns and mortars.

However, if one considers that the Second Belorussian Front was operating between the Third and First Belorussian fronts, which were to launch the decisive attacks against the enemy, then even given the existing correlation of forces, it had a good chance of successfully conducting the offensive operation.

The Front Commander's Decision

In accordance with the *Stavka* directive, the commander of the Second Belorussian Front, Colonel General Zakharov,[7] made the decision, while stolidly defending along the *front's* right and left wings, to break through the enemy defense in the center of his line; to launch the main attack from the Dribin—Dednya—Ryasna area in the general direction of Mogilev and Belynichi, for the purpose of reaching the Dnepr River and seizing a bridgehead on its western bank. The *front* would subsequently employ its main forces to force the Dnepr River and capture the town of Mogilev and develop the offensive in the general direction of Berezino and Smilovichi. In breaking through the enemy's defense, it was planned to launch the main attack in the direction of Zatony, Shestaki, Vasilevichi, Ozer'e, and Barsuki. The forcing of the Pronya River and the breakthrough were to be carried out along the 12-kilometer sector excluding Khalyupy—Staryi Perevoz.

Table 10. The Second Belorussian Front's Strength at the Start of the Belorussian Operation (24 June 1944)

Name	33rd Army	49th Army
Rifle Formations	344th Rifle Div, 70th Rifle Div, 154th Fortified Area	69th Rifle Corps (222nd, 42nd rifle divs), 84th Rifle Corps (32nd, 95th, 153rd rifle divs), 70th Rifle Corps (290th, 199th, 49th rifle divs), 62nd Rifle Corps (369th, 330th, 64th rifle divs)
Artillery Reinforcements		55th, 49th, 56th, 1231st, 331st, 16th, 85th, 81st howitzer artillery rgts, 544th Mortar Rgt, 77th, 29th, 100th, 307th, 325th gds mortar rgts, 4th Gds Mortar Bde, 5th, 27th, 13th anti-tank artillery bdes, 31st Heavy Howitzer Bde, 32nd Heavy Howitzer Bde, 19th Mortar Bde, 144th, 143rd, 142nd cannon artillery bdes, 517th, 41st, 557th corps artillery rgts, 2nd Corps Artillery Bde, 322nd Heavy Artillery Div, 1479th Anti-Aircraft Artillery Rgt, 47th and 49th anti-aircraft artillery divs
Armored and Mechanized Forces	6th Independent Chemical	42nd, 43rd, 23rd gds tank bdes, 233rd Independent Tank Rgt, 334th, 342nd gds heavy self-propelled artillery rgts, 1197th, 1196th, 1902nd and 722nd self-propelled artillery rgts
Engineer Troops	8th Electrical Bn, 209th Engineer-Sapper Bn (34th Engineer-Sapper Bde), 143rd Motorized Engineer Bn (33rd Motorized Engineer Bde)	34th Engineer-Sapper Bde (140th, 42nd, 345th engineer-sapper bns), (34th bns, 9th, 87th, 92nd, 122nd independent pontoon bns, 1st Gds Assault-Sapper Bde
Chemical Troops		66th Independent Chemical Bn
Aviation		

---

7   Editor's note. Georgii Fedorovich Zakharov (1897-1957) joined the imperial Russian army in 1915 and the Red Army in 1919. During the Great Patriotic War he commanded armies and fronts. Following the war, he commanded a number of military districts.

Name	50th Army	*Front* Formations and Units	4th Air Army
Rifle Formations	38th Rifle Corps (385th, 110th rifle divs), 19th Rifle Corps (380th, 324th, 362nd rifle divs), 121st Rifle Corps (139th, 238th rifle divs)	157th Rifle Div, 307th Rifle Div	
Artillery Reinforcements	1099th Corps Artillery Rgt 4th Anti-Tank Artillery Bde	225th, 341st, 734th, 1268th, 1270th, 1482nd and 1709th anti-aircraft artillery rgts, 4th, 490th and 614th independent anti-aircraft divs	
Armored and Mechanized Forces	1819th and 1830th self-propelled artillery rgts	256th Tank Bde, 1434th Self-Propelled Artillery Rgt	
Engineer Troops	50th Engineer-Sapper Bde	33rd Motorized Engineer Bde, 20th Defense Construction Directorate, five independent special companies	
Chemical Troops	16th Independent Flamethrower Bn	5th Independent Chemical Bn	
Aviation			213th Gds and 233rd assault air divs, 229th and 309th fighter divs, 25th Night Bomber Div, 164th Independent Reconnaissance Rgt

Table 11. The Correlation of Forces and Operational Densities along the Second Belorussian Front's Attack Zone, 22 June 1944

Men and Materiel	Correlation of Forces[1]			Operational Densities per Kilometer of Front			
	Soviet	German	Correlation	The Entire Front (156 km)		Axis of the Main Attack (12.5 km)	
				Soviet	German	Soviet	German
Men (combat)	198,452 68,500	114,000 34,200	1.4:1 2:1				
Divisions (rifle, infantry)	22 12	9.5 3	2:1 4:1	0.14	0.06	1.2	0.2
Battalions (rifle, infantry)	204 112	74 18-27	3:1 4-6:1	1.3	0.5	9.0	0.4
Machine Guns (light and heavy)	5,750 2,533	4,947 1,245	1.2:1 2:1	36.8	31.7	202.5	99.6
Guns and Mortars	4,822 2,168	2,207 580	2.1:1 3.8:1	30.8	14.1	181	46.4
Tanks and Self-Propelled Guns	276 227	120 120	2.4:1 1.8:1	1.7	0.7	30.0	9.6
Aircraft	528	240	2.1:1				

Note

1 The numerator shows the overall correlation of forces, while the denominator shows the correlation along the axis of the main attack.

For launching the main attack, the commander of the Second Belorussian Front decided to allocate 13 rifle divisions, reinforced with artillery and tanks.

The armies were given the following objectives:

The 49th Army was to launch its main attack along the front excluding Khalyupy—Staryi Perevoz in the direction of Zatony, Shestaki, Vasilevichi, Ozer'e, and Barsuki. The army's immediate objective was to force the Pronya River, defeat the opposing enemy and, by the end of the operation's first day to reach the Basya River with the shock group's main forces along the sector Chernevka—Popovka and seize a bridgehead on the western bank with its mobile detachments. A reconnaissance in force was planned during the artillery preparation, for which a single rifle company was to be allotted from each first-echelon rifle regiment, with the mission of identifying the enemy's fire system and securing the seizure of a bridgehead on the western bank of the Pronya River. The left-flank corps was to attack from the Radomlya area in the direction of Raduchi and Bol'shie Amkhinichi, with the task of rolling up the position of the enemy's Chausy group of forces. The right-flank corps was to secure the shock group's right flank from the direction of Gorki and Orsha. By the end of the operation's third day it was to reach the front Bel'—Zakhody—Mostok. Particular attention should be paid to securing the flanks of the shock group from the direction of Orsha and Mogilev.

The subsequent task of the *front's* shock group was to force the Dnepr River and by the end of the operation's fifth day reach with its main forces the line Vysokoe—Staraya Vodva—Sen'kovo and, attacking from this line, seize Mogilev by an attack from the north and northwest.

The 49th Army, in order to successfully carry out the assigned objectives, was reinforced by the arrival of new formations and units, as well as forces from the 33rd and 50th armies. By the beginning of the operation the army had 50 percent of all divisions, 60 percent of all artillery, and up to 80 percent of the *front's* tanks.[8]

The operational plan called for the creation of a *front* mobile group under the command of Lieutenant General Tyurin, consisting of the 157th Rifle Division, 13th Anti-Tank Artillery Brigade, the 23rd and 256th tank brigades, the 1434th Self-Propelled Artillery Regiment, the 1st Guards Engineer-Sapper Brigade, and the 87th Independent Mechanized Pontoon Battalion, with a staff from the *front's* field headquarters. The mobile group had the objective, once the 49th Army reached the Basya River, of vigorously leaping forward to the Dnepr River, forcing it, and by the operation's third day capture the line Vysokoe—Staraya—Vodva—Sen'kovo and hold it until the arrival of the 49th Army's main forces. In the areas of Bel' and Mostok a strong covering force would be left to prevent any enemy attacks from the direction of Orsha and Mogilev.

The 33rd Army was to securely hold its line: on the right flank, in conjunction with the Third Belorussian Front's 31st Army, it was to prepare an attack with a single rifle division along the front Baevo—Lenino in the general direction of Yurkovo, Sava and Mikhailovichi. The offensive was to begin on the receipt of a special order. On the army's left flank, part of its forces was to secure the 49th Army's right flank. All of the army's forces were to be ready to go over to the offensive to the west.

The 50th Army, consisting of three rifle corps, was to securely retain its present line and be ready to in the general direction of Kutnya and Lykovo.

By 16 June 1944 it was planned to remove a rifle corps (three rifle divisions) into the army reserve. It was planned to commit this corps into the breach in the 49th Army's sector, for operations in toward Chausy or Blagovichi.

---

8 *Operatsii*, vol. 3, p. 298.

The Army Commanders' Decisions

The 49th Army commander decided, by launching the main attack in the direction of Zatony and Ozer'e, to break through the enemy's defense, defeat his opposing group of forces and capture the line of the Basya River; he would subsequently defeat the enemy's operational reserves east of the Dnepr River and reach the eastern bank of the Dnepr River with his forward detachments. The Dnepr River would then be forced and Mogilev taken. The army had a single-echelon operational formation.

The army's formations were given the following assignments—to break through the enemy's defense along the following sectors: 69th Rifle Corps—excluding Khalyupy—excluding Kareby; 81st Rifle Corps—Kareby—excluding Zatony; 70th Rifle Corps—the fork in the road one kilometer east of Zalozh'e—Budino settlement; 62nd Rifle Corps—excluding Budino settlement—excluding Staryi Perevoz.

The corps' immediate objective was to break through the enemy's defense along the front Slasteny—Raduchi and reach the line Staryi Pribuzh—Suslovka—Kolesyanka; they were to subsequently reach the line Novyi Pribuzh—Chernevka and then move south along the eastern bank of the Basya river as far as Sushchevskaya Sloboda.

Upon carrying out these objectives, the 81st and 70th rifle corps were to launch the main attack in the direction of Shestaki and Ozer'e.

It was planned to employ mobile detachments to pursue the enemy, to clear out the eastern bank of the Dnepr River, and to seize a bridgehead on its western bank.

It was planned to secure the flanks of the army's shock group in the following manner:

a)   the 69th and 62nd corps' divisions were to occupy and securely defend the lines Zhevan'—Krivel', facing north, and Blagovichi—Lyubuzh, facing south;
b)   the 70th and 81st rifle corps were to hold a division each in their second echelons, in readiness for operating along the flanks.

As previously planned, the 81st and 70th rifle corps were to subsequently launch the main attack in the direction of Nizhnie Prudki and Sen'kovo, bypassing Mogilev from the west.

The commander of the 33rd Army decided to securely maintain his present line and to prepare an attack by two of the 334th Rifle Division's rifle regiments along the front Baevo—Lenino in the general direction of Yurkovo and Sava, and then toward Mikhailovichi.

The commander of the 50th Army decided to securely defend his present line and simultaneously prepare a local operation for eliminating the enemy's Chausy group of forces in conjunction with the 49th Army.

Two variations of this operation were drawn up.

According to the first, or "southern" variation, the 38th and 19th rifle corps were to continue to wage an active defense, while the 121st Rifle Corps would launch, with part of its forces, an attack along the front Antonovka—Golovenchitsy in the direction of Golovenchitsy, Ostreni and Udovsk; the success would subsequently be developed in the direction of Garbovichi and Lykovo. By the end of the fifth day, the army's units would arrive at the eastern bank of the Dnepr River and seize crossings over it.

For developing the 121st Rifle Corps' success, on the morning of the second day forces of the 38th Rifle Corps would launch an attack in the direction of Novoselki, Lyubavino and Voinily.

According to the second, or "northern" variation, the 121st Rifle Corps would be committed into the breach along the 49th Army's sector and would attack in the direction of Sushchi, Blagovichi and Udovsk. Simultaneously, the 38th Rifle Corps would launch a supporting attack in the direction of Golovenchitsy, Ostreni and Otrazh'e. The army would subsequently develop the offensive in the direction of Blagovichi and Lykovo and, by the end of the sixth day, reach the eastern bank of the Dnepr River and seize bridgeheads along its western bank.

Brief Conclusions on the Decisions of the Front Commander and the Army Commanders

The fulfillment of the objective by the commander of the Second Belorussian Front was eased by the fact that he had to organize a breakthrough of the enemy's defense along one sector. Nonetheless, only by decisively concentrating his forces along the axis of the main attack did he manage to create the necessary densities and achieve a superiority over the enemy. Along the 12.5-kilometer breakthrough front were concentrated 12 rifle divisions, nine howitzer artillery regiments, three corps artillery regiments, two howitzer brigades, three anti-tank artillery brigades, a mechanized brigade, and other reinforcements.

A salient point of the *front* commander's decision was the creation of an improvised *front* mobile group, consisting of a rifle division, two tank brigades, an anti-tank brigade, a self-propelled artillery regiment, and an engineering-sapper brigade, which was made necessary by the absence of a sufficient number of mobile forces with the *front*.

The *front* commander actually made all the decisions for the commander of the 49th Army and planned the army operation day by day right up to the capture of Mogilev.

The 49th Army was to break through the enemy's tactical defense zone with a frontal attack, after which it was to outflank Mogilev from the north and, in conjunction with the First Belorussian Front, destroy the enemy's Mogilev group of forces.

The corps' combat formations were organized into 2-3 echelons, which enabled us to successively increase the strength of the attack, to successfully force the water barriers and to bypass Mogilev.

It was planned to commit the *front's* mobile group into the breach after overcoming the second defensive zone, which was located along the Basya River. The mobile group was to lunge forward and reach the Dnepr River and force it, and by the end of the operation's third day seize a broad bridgehead on the river's western bank. The 50th Army's second echelon—the 121st Rifle Corps—was to be committed into the breach in the 49th Army's sector and was to be employed along that army's left flank for rolling up the enemy's defense and widening the breakthrough.

The 33rd and 50th armies would support the 49th Army's actions and were to take advantage of its success.

On the whole, the decisions of the *front* and army commanders corresponded to the specific situation and the real correlation of forces along the direction of the supporting operations of a group of *fronts*. The insufficient number of men and materiel and the absence of a success develop echelon forced us to, at first, wage offensive operations actually only in one army's sector to a comparatively small depth.

The Decisions of the Commander of the First Belorussian Front and the Commanders of the *Front's* Armies

The Situation in the First Belorussian Front's Operational Zone by the Beginning of the Operation

By the start of the preparation for the Belorussian operation (the end of May 1944) the *front's* forces were defending along the line Yanovo—Rogachev—excluding Proskurin—V'yunishche—Skrygalovo, to the west along the Pripyat' River as far as—excluding Ratno (southwest of Pinsk), and from this point south through Kovel' as far as Verba.

Opposite the First Belorussian Front the German-Fascist forces of Army Group Center—Ninth and Second armies were defending, as well as part of Fourth Army, and an army corps from Army Group North Ukraine's Fourth Panzer Army. In all, up to 26 infantry divisions (including security and training divisions), up to two panzer divisions, two brigades (cavalry and special designation), and an infantry regiment were facing the *front*.

Of these forces, 22 infantry (including light and security divisions), a single panzer division and both brigades were defending in the armies' first echelons. The enemy's operational reserves consisted of five divisions (707th Security Division, 390th Field Training Division, 52nd Security Division, and the Hungarian 5th and 23rd reserve divisions), were located, for the most part, in the deep rear and were fighting the Belorussian partisans. The 20th Panzer Division, which was deployed in the First Belorussian Front's operational zone, formed part of the reserve of the commander of Army Group Center.

A denser operational formation had been created by the enemy along the Bobruisk and Kovel' directions.

In the multi-*front* operation for defeating the German-Fascist forces in Belorussia, only the right-wing forces of the First Belorussian Front, which were located to the north of the Pripyat' River, initially took part in the operation's first stage—that is; the 3rd, 48th and 65th armies, as well as the 28th Army, which had arrived from the reserve of the *Stavka* of the High Command.

By the beginning of the operation (24 June 1944), in the area to the north of the Pripyat' River, the *front's* right wing was opposed by the Ninth German-Fascist Army (XXXV and LV army and XLI Panzer corps) and part of the Fourth Army to the north; in all, ten infantry divisions (134th, 296th, 6th, 383rd, 45th, 36th, 35th, 129th, 292nd, and 797th), one panzer division (20th), an infantry regiment from the SS "Nord" Division, and 12 independent battalions of various types, along with reinforcements. All these forces, with the exception of the 707th Security Division, were located in the armies' first operational echelons.

The enemy's defense was built on the basis of a highly developed system of continuous trenches and communications trenches, in close combination with strong points and centers of resistance in the inhabited locales and along tactically important sectors of terrain. Moreover, the peculiarities of the wooded and swampy terrain were also employed and taken into account.

The enemy's Ninth Army, occupying the southeastern part of the tip of the Belorussian salient, covered the Bobruisk—Minsk direction as the shortest route to Minsk from the southeast and the approaches to the Slutsk—Baranovichi direction.

The Ninth Army had a greater density of forces along two axes—Bobruisk and Glusk. Along the most important Bobruisk axis—along the 35-kilometer Rekta—Luchin sector—the main group of the Ninth Army's forces had been concentrated, consisting of three infantry and one panzer divisions (of these, the panzer division and an infantry division were deployed in the reserve). Along the Glusk axis—along the 55-kilometer Zdudichi—Tramets sector—up to four infantry divisions had been deployed in the corps' first echelons.

The disposition of the enemy's forces in the tactical zone was characterized by the single-echelon formation of all the army corps and the majority of the infantry divisions, as well as the location of the army reserves in this zone (up to six infantry regiments).

By 23 June 1944 the German-Fascist command had reinforced its forces north of the Pripyat' River, had thickened its combat formations along the Soviet forces' probable offensive axes, created operational reserves in the Bobruisk area, strengthened measures to consolidate and maintain the important Bobruisk center of resistance, sharply increased its air activity, and completed the reorganization of its infantry divisions. In particular, the following measures were carried out: the 20th Panzer Division was regrouped from around Kovel' to an area 10-12 kilometers east of Bobruisk (by 21 June 1944); the 707th Security Division had been brought up to the area 3-4 kilometers south of Bobruisk (by 15 June 1944); the infantry regiment from the SS "Nord" Division had been transferred to Osipovichi; the 390th Training Division had been regrouped to the area 3-5 kilometers northeast of Minsk; in the Pinsk area the Hungarian I Cavalry Corps, which had heretofore not been noticed in the *front's* area, had concentrated.

If in May and the first part of June, the main efforts of air and ground intelligence, as well as the enemy's bomber efforts, had concentrated 80 percent of their efforts along the *front's* left wing, then beginning from 10 June this activity sharply increased along the Rogachev and Parichi axes. For example, the enemy air force launched up to 30 raids along our rail communications in these areas, in which 707 planes took part and dropped 3,328 high-explosive and 1,599 incendiary bombs and 70 mines.

By the start of the operation's preparation (the end of May 1944) the First Belorussian Front had along its right wing (from Khomichi to the Pripyat' River) three combined-arms armies (3rd, 48th and 65th), one air army (16th) and the Dnepr River Flotilla.

In order to carry out the operation, the forces of the *front's* shock groups were significantly reinforced by *Stavka* reserves and partially by regrouping within the *front* itself. For example, during the 1-23 June period the *Stavka* reserve transferred to the *front* for its right wing shock group the following forces: 28th Army, 4th Guards Cavalry Corps, 1st Guards and 9th tank corps, and many other air, artillery, engineering, and other units and formations. From 15 June the 8th Guards Army (4th, 28th and 29th rifle corps and other units) and the 2nd Tank Army (3rd and 16th tank corps, 11th Guards Tank Brigade, and other units) began to arrive at the *front* and concentrate along its left wing south of the Pripyat' River.

The following forces arrived from the *front* reserve, as a result of an internal regrouping to strengthen the *front's* right wing: a rifle division, a self-propelled artillery brigade, two independent tank regiments, a battalion of armored trains, an artillery division, a cannon-artillery brigade, three guards mortar brigades, eight guards mortar regiments, three anti-tank artillery brigades, an anti-tank artillery regiment, four anti-aircraft artillery divisions, an anti-aircraft artillery regiment, two engineer-sapper brigades, a motorized pontoon-bridge battalion, and from the left wing—three guards mortar regiments.

In this way, by the start of the operation the overall strength of the *front's* right wing had been significantly reinforced and consisted of four combined-arms armies, a cavalry corps, two tank corps, a mechanized corps, 14 artillery divisions, seven artillery brigades, a self-propelled artillery brigade, 26 tank and self-propelled artillery regiments, five air corps, 11 independent air divisions, and a river flotilla (two brigades) (see table 12).

Table 12. The First Belorussian Front's Strength at the Start of the Belorussian Operation (24 June 1944)

Name	3rd Army	48th Army
Rifle and Cavalry Formations	35th Rifle Corps (250th, 323rd, 348th rifle divs), 40th Rifle Corps (129th, 169th rifle divs), 41st Rifle Corps (108th, 120th, 269th rifle divs), 46th Rifle Corps (72nd, 413th rifle divs), 80th Rifle Corps (283rd, 5th, 186th rifle divs)	42nd Rifle Corps (399th, 170th, 137th rifle divs), 29th Rifle Corps (217th, 102nd, 194th rifle divs, 115th Fortified Area), 53rd Rifle Corps (73rd, 17th, 96th rifle divs)

Name	3rd Army	48th Army
Artillery Reinforcements	44th Cannon Artillery Bde, 122nd and 124th high-power howitzer bdes, 41st, 44th anti-tank artillery bdes, 1071st, 1311th, 120th anti-tank artillery rgts, 133rd Mortar Rgt, 16th Gds Mortar Bde, 5th Gds Mortar Div, 35th Gds Mortar Bde, 37th, 56th, 94th, 313th gds mortar rgts, 28th Anti-Aircraft Artillery Div, 235th Anti-Aircraft Artillery Rgt, 13th Independent Anti-Aircraft Div	22nd Breakthrough Artiley Div, 68th Cannon Artillery Bde, 1st Anti-Tank Artillery Bde, 684th Guards Mortar Rgt, 295th Corps Artillery Rgt, 143rd Mortar Rgt, 530th Anti-Tank Artillery Rgt, 143rd Mortar Rgt, 530th Anti-Tank Artillery Rgt, 31st, 13th anti-aircraft artillery divs, 461st Anti-Aircfaft Artillery Rgt, 27th Independent Anti-Aircraft Artillery Div
Armored and Mechanized Forces	9th Tank Corps, 36th, 193rd, 223rd tank rgts, 340th Gds Heavy Self-Propelled Artillery Rgt, five self-propelled artillery rgts, one flame-thrower tank rgt, one minesweeper tank rgt, one self-propelled artillery bde	42nd Heavy Tank Rgt, 231st Tank Rgt, three self-propelled artillery rgts, one heavy self-propelled artillery rgt
Engineer Troops	1st Gds and 2nd engineer-sapper bdes, 7th Pontoon Bde, 48th Pontoon Bn	10th Engineer-Sapper Bde, 8th Assault Engineer-Sapper Bde
Chemical Troops	510th Flamethrower Rgt	
Aviation		

Name	65th Army	28th Army
Rifle and Cavalry Formations	18th Rifle Corps (69th, 37th gds, 15th rifle divs), 105th Rifle Corps (193rd, 75th gds, 354th rifle divs), 44th Gds, 356th rifle divs, 115th Rifle Bde	3rd Gds Rifle Corps (54th, 96th, 50th gds rifle divs), 20th Rifle Corps (55th, 48th gds, 20th rifle divs), 128th Rifle Corps (52nd, 130th, 61st rifle divs, 161st, 119th, 153rd fortified areas)
Artillery Reinforcements	26th Breakthrough Artillery Div, 30th Gds, 157th, and 147th cannon artillery bdes, 3rd Gds Anti-Tank Artillery Bde, 315th, 317th independent large-caliber artillery divs, 22nd, 23rd gds mortar bdes, 5th Gds Mortar Div, 43rd, 92nd, 311th gds mortar rgts, 3rd Gds Anti-Aircraft Artillery Div, 4th Corps Artillery Bde, 377th Corps Artillery Rgt, 286th, 475th mortar rgts, 543rd, 584th anti-tank artillery rgts, 607th Anti-Aircraft Artillery Rgt, 31st Independent Ant-Aircraft Artillery Div	4th Breakthrough Artillery Corps (5th and 12th artillery divs, 1st, 62nd, 316th Gds mortar rgts, 12th Anti-Aircraft Div, 3rd Corps Artillery Bde, 1091st Corps Artillery Rgt, 479th Mortar Rgt, 220nd Gds Anti-Tank Artillery Rgt, 1284th Anti-Aircraft Artillery Rgt, 615th Independent Anti-Aircraft Artillery Div
Armored and Mechanized Forces	1st Gds Tank Corps (15th, 16th, 17th gds tank bdes, 1st Gds. Motorized Rifle Bde), 251st Tank Rgt, 345th, 354th self-propelled artillery rgts, two heavy self-propelled artillery rgts	30th Gds Heavy Tank Rgt, 347th Heavy Self-Propelled Artillery Rgt, one tank rgt, three self-propelled artillery rgts, one flame-thrower tank rgt, one minesweeper tank rgt
Chemical Troops		516th Flamethrower Rgt
Aviation		

Name	*Front* Formations and Units	16th Air Army
Rifle and Cavalry Formations	4th Gds Cavalry Corps (9th, 10th, 30th cavalry divs), 1st Gds Mechanized Corps (19th, 35th, 37th motorized rifle bdes)	
Artillery Reinforcements	2nd Gds Anti-Aircraft Artillery Div (with the cavalry-mechanized group)	
Armored and Mechanized Forces	219th Tank Bde, 75th, 1822nd self-propelled artillery rgts (with the 1st Gds Mechanized Corps), 4th Gds Cavalry Corps (151st, 128th, 134th tank rgts), 1715th Self-Propelled Artillery Rgt	
Engineer Troops	36th, 57th engineer-sapper bdes, ten independent assault engineer-sapper bns, 9th Gds Independent Engineer-Sapper Bn, one motorized engineer bde, 6th, 8th independent engineer-sapper bn with canines, 27th Defense Construction Directorate	
Chemical Troops		
Aviation		6th Fighter Corps, 4th Assault Air Corps, 8th Fighter Corps, 3rd Bomber Corps, 6th Mixed Air Corps, 286th, 282nd, 1st Gds, 283rd fighter divs, 2nd, 299th, 300th assault air divs, 271st Night Bomber Div

The correlation of forces and their densities in the operational zone of the *front's* right-wing shock group are shown in table 13.

From the table it can be seen that the command of the First Belorussian Front had managed to create an overwhelming superiority of men and materiel and significant densities on the right wing, which would secure the breakthrough of the enemy's defense throughout its entire depth.

By the start of the operation the shock group on the *front's* left wing had only begun to be created (for a fuller description of this activity, see the work's third part).

On the whole, the situation along the First Belorussian Front was favorable to the conduct of large-scale offensive operations from the areas north and south of the Pripyat' River (the Poles'ye area).

The Front *Commander's Decision*

The *front* commander, General K.K. Rokossovskii,[9] by taking advantage of the favorable operational situation of our forces along the Bobruisk—Minsk direction, and securing his flanks, planned to launch powerful attacks with two groups of forces along the *front's* right wing along narrow sectors from the areas north of Rogachev and south of Parichi, in order to break through the enemy's defense and, developing the attack along converging axes toward Bobruisk, seize the

---

9 Editor's note. Konstantin Konstantinovich Rokossovskii (1896-1968) served in the Russian imperial army and joined the Red Army in 1918. Rokossovskii was arrested in 1937, but managed to survive and return to the army in 1940. During the Great Patriotic War he commanded a mechanized corps and an army, as well as several *fronts*, including the Second Belorussian Front from late 1944. Following the war, Rokossovskii commanded the northern group of Soviet forces and served several years a Polish defense minister. Upon his return to the USSR, he commanded a military district and held posts in the central military apparatus.

large-scale Bobruisk center of resistance, to encircle and destroy the enemy's Bobruisk group of forces and, reach the areas of Pukhovichi and Slutsk with his main forces.

The *front's* main task was to encircle and defeat the enemy's Bobruisk group of forces, take the areas of Bobruisk, Glusha and Glusk, and with part of its right-wing forces assist the Second Belorussian Front.

The subsequent task was to develop the offensive along the Bobruisk—Minsk and the Bobruisk—Slutsk directions for the purpose of reaching the area of Pukhovichi and Slutsk.

In order to carry out these tasks, the first shock group of the *front's* right-wing forces (3rd and 48th armies), upon going over to the offensive from the area north of Rogachev, was to break through the enemy's defense along the 15-kilometer Ozerane—Kolosy sector and develop the offensive in the general direction of Bobruisk and Pukhovichi. The right wing's second shock group (65th and 28th armies), while launching an attack from the area south of Parichi, was to break through the enemy's defense along the Radin—V'yunishche sector (14 kilometers south of Radin) and develop the offensive along the Romanishche—Glusha and Romanishche—Glusk axes.

The *front's* cavalry-mechanized group, which was to be committed in the left shock group's sector south of Parichi, was to develop the offensive toward V'yunishche and Gorodok and then, depending on the situation, toward Osipovichi or Starye Dorogi and Slutsk.

Table 13. The Correlation of Forces and Operational Densities along the First Belorussian Front's Attack Zone, 22 June 1944

Men and Materiel	Correlation of Forces[1]			Operational Densities per Kilometer of Front			
	Soviet	German	Correlation	The Entire Front (240 km)		Axis of the Main Attack (29 km)	
				Soviet	German	Soviet	German
Men (combat)	418,541	130,920	3.3:1				
	304,800						
Divisions	39	14	2.7:1	0.16	0.06	1.0	0.15
(Rifle, Infantry)	30	4.7	5.5:1				
Battalions	384	112	3.5:1	1.6	0.5	8.3	1.4
(Rifle, Infantry)	242	41	6:1				
Machine Guns	16,035	5,137	3.1:1	67	21.4	329.0	68.0
(Light and Heavy)	9,544	1,969	4.5:1				
Guns and Mortars	9,758	2,533	3.8:1	40.6	10.6	204.4	32.1
(all calibers)	5,929	931	6.3:1				
Tanks and Self-Propelled Guns	1,297	366	3.5:1	5.4	1.5	44.7	12.6
	1,297	352	3.6:1				
Aircraft	2,033	600-685	3.4:1				

Note

1 The numerator shows the overall correlation of forces, while the denominator shows the correlation along the axis of the main attack.

The *front's* right-wing armies were assigned the following tasks:

The 3rd Army, was to securely defend the right-flank Yanovo—Khomichi sector with one rifle corps, an anti-tank artillery brigade, and a self-propelled artillery regiment, securing the army's right flank, while part of its forces were to be ready to render assistance to the 50th Army's attacking forces. The army's main forces, along with all the reinforcements, in close conjunction with the

48th Army's right wing, were to break through the enemy's defense along the 8-kilometer front excluding Ozerane—excluding Kostyashevo and, having committed the 9th Tank Corps into the breach, were to develop the main attack with its left flank in the general direction of Filippkovichi, Staraya Sharoevshchina and Bobruisk.

Subsequently, upon reaching the Ol'sa and Berezina rivers, part of the army's forces was to securely consolidate along the line Yanovo—Khomichi—Vilenki—Novoselki—Rudnya—Zarech'e—Ol'sa River, while the left flank would continue the offensive in the general direction of Svisloch'.

The 48th Army was to launch an attack with the forces of two right-wing rifle corps, in conjunction with the 3rd Army's left wing, along the 7-kilometer Kostyashevo—Kolosy sector. Upon forcing the Drut' River, the army's main forces would develop the success in the direction of Repki, Turki and Bobruisk and, by launching an attack from the south, southwest and west, take Bobruisk, while a part of its forces would launch an attack toward the south and roll up the enemy's forces along the western bank of the Dnepr River. Along the army's left flank and center, our forces would employ fire from all weapons and, through the actions of separate detachments, pin down the enemy and, once his retreat had begun, go over to the offensive in the general direction of Shchedrin and Stasevka, in order to prevent the enemy from organizing a defense along the intermediate lines.

Subsequently, upon taking Bobruisk, the army's entire force would develop the success in the general direction of Osipovichi and Pukhovichi.

In this manner, the 3rd and 48th armies, by launching powerful attacks along their adjoining flanks, were to break through the enemy's 15-kilometer front along the line excluding Ozerane—Kolosy and, developing the success in the general direction of Bobruisk, defeat the enemy's XXXV Army Corps and 20th Panzer Division, encircling and destroying their remnants in the Bobruisk area.

By the end of the offensive's ninth day, this group of forces was to take Bobruisk and the line Novoselki—eastern bank of the Ol'sa River to the Berezina River—Krasnoe—Bogushevka.

The 65th Army's main forces, in close conjunction with the 28th Army's right wing and the Dnepr River Flotilla, while securing its attack from the right, was to break through the enemy's defense along the 6-kilometer Radin—Korma sector; commit the 1st Guards Tank Corps into the breach and, developing the attack in the general direction of Gomza, Kruki, Makarovichi, and Glusha and cut all the enemy's communications leading to Bobruisk from the west.

Upon the army's reaching the line Bogushevka—Glusha—Gorodishche—Krapivna, its main forces would develop the attack in the general direction of Glusha, Daraganovo and Krinka.

The 28th Army, in close coordination with the 65th Army's left-flank units, while securing itself from the south, was to break through the enemy's defense along the 8-kilometer sector excluding Korma—height 140.6 and develop the offensive toward Glusk. Upon the army's main forces reaching the line Tsegel'nya—Glusk—Novo-Andreevka, they were to attack toward Starye Dorogi.

By the end of the offensive's ninth day, the shock group, consisting of the 65th and 28th armies, was to take the line Bogushevka—Gorodishche—Zholvinets—Glusk—Novo-Andreevka—Zael'nitsa—Lyaskovichi—Bubnovka—the eastern bank of the Ptich' River as far as Kapatkevichi.

In order to develop the success in the direction of Glush, with the arrival of the 65th and 28th armies at the Sekirichi—Goduny line, the cavalry-mechanized group, consisting of the 4th Guards Cavalry and 1st Mechanized corps, would be committed into the breach along the boundary of these armies. The cavalry-mechanized group was to reach the area V'yunishche—Ozemlya—Chernye Brody by the end of the first day of combat and its powerful forward detachments were to seize crossings across the Ptich' River in the Poblin area and, by the end of the third day capture the area Glusha—Makovichi—Knyshi; it was to subsequently be ready to develop the offensive toward Osipovichi or Starye Dorogi and Slutsk.

The Dnepr River Flotilla was to support the 65th Army's right-flank units' offensive by fire and maneuver along the Berezina River and support the crossing of the 48th Army's units across the Berezina River.

According to the *front* commander's decision, all four combined-arms armies on the right wing were to attack in the first echelon. The 3rd and 65th armies were ordered to have an operational formation in two echelons, while the 48th and 28th armies were to have theirs in a single echelon.

The offensive operation by the *front's* right wing was planned to a depth of up to 130 kilometers.

Simultaneous with the adoption of the decision on conducting the operation by the right wing, the commander of the First Belorussian Front set forth tasks for the forces of the *front's* left wing. During the course of June, they were to pin down the enemy forces along their front through active operations by comparatively small forces and prevent their transfer to the Minsk direction. Along with this, the forces of the *front's* left wing were ordered to prepare for going over to the offensive approximately from the middle of July 1944 along the northwestern (toward Baranovichi and Brest) and western (toward Kovel' and Lublin) directions.

The Army Commanders' Decisions

The commander of the 3rd Army decided that while securely defending the line excluding Yanovo—Khomichi on the army's right flank, with part of his forces, the army's main forces, in close coordination with the 48th Army, was to launch the main attack on the left flank along the sector excluding Ozerane—the mouth of the Dobritsa River in the general direction of Novoselki, Filippkovichi, Staraya Sharoevshchina, and a supporting attack with part of his forces from the area east of Letobich in the direction of Lipki, Dubrovki, and Nemki. The army was to have an operational formation in two echelons.

In accordance with this decision, the breakthrough of the enemy's defense along the axis of the main attack was to be carried out by two reinforced rifle corps (35th and 41st), and upon their arrival at the line of the Drobitsa River the success would be developed by the army's mobile group (9th Tank Corps) and the army's second echelon (46th Rifle Corps), with the objective of defeating the opposing enemy and assisting the 48th Army in taking Bobruisk, and the 50th Army in developing the offensive to the west.

Along the supporting attack's axis the breakthrough would be carried out by two of the 80th Rifle Corps' division in conjunction with the army's main group of forces, tasked with destroying the opposing enemy and securing the main attack from the north and northwest.

The sector excluding Yanovo—Khomichi was securely defended by the divisions of the 40th Rifle Corps and the 80th Rifle Corps' 283rd Rifle Division. The 40th Rifle Corps had its main forces along the right flank, for the purpose of preventing a breakthrough by the enemy's tanks in the direction of Novyi Bykhov

By the close of the offensive's seventh day, the army, in conjunction with the 48th Army's right-flank units, was to seize the line Chigirinka—Kobylyanka—Barki—Klichev—Batsevichi—Orlino—Lake Orlinskoe—the eastern bank of the Berezina River.

Subsequently, the army, having consolidated along the line Dnepr River—Chigirinka—Klichev—Ol'sa River, with its front facing to the north, was to concentrate its main forces on developing the offensive in the general direction of Svisloch', with the task of taking that town and cutting the Mogilev—Bobruisk railroad, and in this way creating favorable conditions for forcing the Berezina River and assisting the 48th Army in taking Bobruisk.

On the basis of this decision, the formations were given the following tasks:

The 40th Rifle Corps was to securely defend the line excluding Yanovo—excluding Guta Romanyazhskaya and, with its main group of forces along its right flank, to prevent the enemy from breaking through in the direction of Novyi Bykhov.

The 80th Rifle Corps, while securely defending the line Guta Romanyazhskaya—Khomichi, was to launch its main attack from the area east of Litobich in the direction of Nemki and, destroying the enemy, by the end of the offensive's first day, capture the line Podsely—marker 155; part of the corps' forces, operating along the southwestern axis, was to capture Ozerane along with the 35th Rifle Corps' right-flank units. The corps was to subsequently take the line Chigirinka—Kobylyanka and, going over to the defensive, secure the army's right flank from the north.

The 35th Rifle Corps, in conjunction with the 41st Rifle Corps, was to break through the enemy's defense along the front excluding Ozerane—Rogovo. Launching the main attack with its left flank in the direction of Dobritsa, by the end of the offensive's first day the corps was to take the line Osovnik—Dobritsa, thus securing the commitment of the 9th Tank and 46th Rifle corps into the fighting. A part of the corps' forces, along with the 80th Rifle Corps' 186th Rifle Division, was to take Ozerane. The corps would subsequently reach the line excluding Kobylyanka—excluding Klichev.

The 41st Rifle Corps, in conjunction with the 35th Rifle Corps, was to break through the enemy's defense along the front excluding Konoplitsa—the mouth of the Dobritsa River, and, bypassing the Verichev and Tikhinichi centers of resistance from the north and south, launch its main attack in the direction of Staraya Sharoevshchina. While destroying the opposing enemy units, by the end of the first day the corps was to take the line Krasnaya Gorka—Novyi Put', thus securing the commitment of the 9th Tank and 46th Rifle corps into the battle. The corps would subsequently reach the front Klichev—Novye Dvoryanovichi.

With the arrival of the 35th and 41st rifle corps at the line of the Dobritsa River the 9th Tank Corps—the army's mobile group—was to develop the offensive in the direction of Zhilichi and Staraya Sharoevshchina, and by the end of the offensive's second day take the Dvoryanovichi area and subsequently seize the crossings over the Berezina River near Stasevka, preventing the withdrawal of the enemy's Rogachev—Zhlobin group of forces behind this water barrier.

With the arrival of the forward units of the 35th and 41st rifle corps at the line of the Dobritsa River, the 46th Rifle Corps—the army's second echelon—was to attack in the direction from Ozerane to Dobysno.

In this fashion, the 3rd Army commander, having five rifle corps at his disposal, decided to break through the enemy's defense with three corps along two axes—a main one and an auxiliary one. One corps was left in the army's second echelon and was designated for developing the success in the depth of the enemy's defense. The 3rd Army's form of operational maneuver was a frontal attack followed by its development in the depth and in the direction of the right flank.

The army operation was planned as far as the Ol'sa River to a depth of 60-65 kilometers. The troops were to cover this distance over the course of seven days, with an average daily rate of advance of 9-10 kilometers. In his decision, the 3rd Army commander indicated a wider offensive sector than was called for by the *front* commander's decision. The sector indicated by the *front* commander by the close of the seventh day did not exceed 23 kilometers, and the army commander increased this sector to 42 kilometers. The depth of the breakthrough was also increased by nearly 20 kilometers. Such changes, later confirmed by the *front* commander, were explained by the fact that the army was operating along the *front's* right wing, lacking close contact with the Second Belorussian Front.

The 3rd Army had a single two-division rifle corps in its second echelon. The rifle corps arrayed their combat orders in a single echelon, while the rifle divisions arrayed theirs in two echelons, with the exception of the 5th and 269th rifle divisions, which were organized in single-echelon formation.

The commander of the 48th Army decided to make his main attack with the forces of the 42nd and 29th rifle corps, which had been reinforced with artillery and tanks, along the 7-kilometer Kostyashevo—Kolosy sector, in the direction of Repki, Turki and Bobruisk, break through the enemy defense and, developing the success, reach the rear of the enemy's Zhlobin group of forces (6th, 383rd and 45th infantry divisions), cut it off from the crossings over the Berezina River and then, together with the 65th Army, encircle and destroy it between the Ola and Berezina rivers. Simultaneous with this, the army would seize crossings south of Bobruisk along the sector Domanovo—Stasevka and, with an attack from the south, seize Bobruisk. The army would have a single-echelon operational formation.

Subsequently, all the army's forces would develop the success in the general direction of Osipovichi and Pukhovichi.

In order to secure the operations by the army's main group of forces from the south, four independent machine gun-artillery battalions from the 115th Fortified Area, together with one assault company, were to roll up the enemy's forces along the western bank of the Dnepr River along the sector Rogachev—Zhlobin.

On the operation's second day, a supporting attack by two of the 73rd Rifle Division's rifle regiments was to take place along the Proskurin—Savin sector in the direction of the southwestern outskirts of Zhlobin, and with the forces of two of the 53rd Rifle Corps' rifle divisions (17th and 96th) along the Gryada—Lake Selitse sector in the direction of Shchedrin.

In accordance with this decision, the army's formations were given the following tasks:

The 42nd Rifle Corps was to break through the enemy's front along a 1-kilometer front north of the line Kostyashevo—excluding Kolosy and develop the offensive in the general direction of Koshary, with the task of seizing bridgeheads along the western bank of the Dobysna River with its forward detachments by the end of the second day.

The 29th Rifle Corps was to break through the enemy's defense in the Kolosy area and attack in the general direction of Liski, with the task of seizing Ostrov with its forward detachments by the end of the second day.

The 53rd Rifle Division was to prevent the enemy from removing forces from the sector Proskurin—Lake Selishche, for which it was to create shock groups on the corps's flanks. The corps was to be ready on the morning of the offensive's second day to make a supporting attack: on the right flank—in the direction of Korma, and on the left flank—in the direction of Shchedrin, with the task of taking Zhlobin by the end of the fourth day.

The 115th Fortified Area, with the task of securing the army's main group of forces from the south, was to roll up the enemy's forces defending along the western bank of the Dnepr River and, by the end of the operation's second day, occupy the line Min'kov—Luchin. Along the remainder of its sector, the corps, defending with all kinds of fire, was to destroy the enemy's personnel; should the enemy be observed withdrawing, the unit was to force the Dnepr River and by successively occupying lines in the depth of the defense, secure the flank of the army's main group of forces.

Thus the commander of the 48th Army built his army operation in exact conformity with the instructions of the *front* commander. The army's form of operational maneuver was a frontal attack along a narrow 7-kilometer sector, with a subsequent development of the success in depth in the direction of the left flank, for the purpose of rolling up the enemy's defense. The operation was planned to a depth of 80-85 kilometers and for a duration of nine days, with an average daily rate of advance of 9-10 kilometers.

The army had a single-echelon operational formation. Those corps making the main attack were formed into two echelons, while the corps operating along the supporting axis had a single-echelon formation. The majority of the rifle divisions were arrayed in a single echelon, while the 17th and

96th rifle divisions had a two-echelon formation. Besides this, the 19th Rifle Corps and a few divisions had their own reserves.

The commander of the 65th Army decided to make his main attack with the forces of the 18th Rifle Corps and the greater part of his reinforcements on his left flank along the 6-kilometer Radin—Petrovichi sector, in the direction of Chernin, Gomza and Kruki, and a secondary attack with the left flank of the 105th Rifle Corps along the neighboring sector marker 139.1—Radin in the direction of Selishche, and Peschanaya Rudnya, with the objective of breaking through the defense's fortified zone, destroying the opposing enemy and, together with the 28th Army, by developing the success along the northwestern axis in the direction of Glusha, reach the enemy's communications west of Bobruisk and, in conjunction with the 48th Army and the Dnepr River Flotilla, defeat the Bobruisk—Parichi enemy group of forces. The army was to subsequently develop the success in the general direction of Glusha, Doroganovo and Krinka. The army was to have a single-echelon operational formation, with the army's mobile group consisting of a single tank corps.

In accordance with this decision the corps were given the following tasks:

The 105th Rifle Corps was to break through the enemy's defense along the sector marker 139.1—Radin and, making its main attack on the left flank in the direction of Peschanaya Rudnya, by the end of the day occupy the line Selishche—excluding Chernin. Taking advantage of the 1st Tank Corps' success, by the end of the offensive's third day the corps was to defeat the enemy's Parichi group of forces and occupy the Parichi area. Subsequently, along with the 18th Rifle Corps, the corps was to develop the offensive to the northwest and cut all of the enemy's communications leading from Bobruisk to the southwest and west.

The 18th Rifle Corps was to break through the enemy's defense along the line Radin—Petrovichi and, making the main attack with its right flank in the direction of Kruki, by the end of the day occupy the line Chernin—Sekirichi, thus securing the commitment of the 1st Guards Tank Corps into the breach from the line Rakovichi—Nikolaevka in the direction of Moiseevka. Employing the 1st Guards Tank Corps' success, by the end of the offensive's second day, the corps was to reach the line Gubnoe—Romanishche. The corps was to subsequently develop the offensive to the northwestern on Glusha as far as the line of the Ptich' River.

The 1st Guards Tank Corps, along with the 44th Guards Rifle Division, was to enter the breach in the 18th Rifle Corps' sector from the line Rakovichi—Nikolaevka and, operating in the direction of Moiseevka, develop the success of the 18th and 105th rifle corps. By the close of the operation's second day, the corps was to reach the area Moiseevka—Mekhovo—Gorodets and, along with the 105th Rifle Corps, defeat the enemy's Parichi group of forces and assist the corps in taking the Parichi area.

The corps was to subsequently develop the offensive on Bobruisk. The corps was to occupy its jumping-off position for the commitment into the breach by the end of the offensive's first day.

The 356th Rifle Division and the 115th Rifle Brigade were in the army reserve.

Thus the commander of the 65th Army organized a frontal attack along his left flank in a sector only six kilometers wide. Following the breakthrough of the forward edge of the enemy's defense, the success would be developed both in depth and breadth in the direction of the right flank. The army operation was initially planned to a depth of 65-75 kilometers and slated to last nine days, with an average daily rate of advance of 7-9 kilometers. This reduced rate of the army's advance was later increased and raised to a planned 10-15 kilometers per day.

The 65th Army had both its rifle corps in a single echelon. Behind them was deployed the 1st Guards Tank Corps, which was designated for commitment into the breach and developing the success in the operational depth. The rifle corps' combat orders were arrayed in a single- (18th Rifle Corps) and double-echelon (105th Rifle Corps) formation.

The commander of the 28th Army decided to make his main attack with his right flank, employing the forces of the 3rd Guards and 20th rifle corps along the 9-kilometer Chernyavka—marker 140.6 sector in the direction of Starishchi and Zelenkovichi, and a supporting attack with the forces of the 128th Rifle Corps and the 161st Fortified Area along the 4-kilometer sector Mostki—Yurki in the direction of Grab'e, with the task of destroying the units of the 35th and 129th infantry divisions and by the end of the offensive's first day occupy the line excluding Zales'e—Mikul'-Gorodok—Podosinniki, and by the end of the third day occupy the line Protasy—Istopki—Zubarevskaya Buda—Smolovitsa—Grab'e—Mushichi—Zarizh'e. The army's main forces would subsequently reach the line of the Ptich' River, seize crossings along the Poblin—Bubnovka sector and develop the attack in the general direction of Glusk and Starye Dorogi.

On the army's left wing along the sector Mezhelishche—Zagreblya—Klepan', and then along the eastern bank of the Ptich' River as far as the Pripyat' River, the army would continue to securely defend its line with the forces of the 153rd and 119th fortified areas.

The army was to have a single-echelon operational formation.

Thus the 28th Army was to carry out a breakthrough by means of a frontal attack along a narrow sector on its right flank, followed by a development of the success in depth, combined with a secure defense of the fortified areas along the rest of the front. The breakthrough sector along the axis of the main attack was about nine kilometers in width, that is, nearly 10 percent of the army's entire sector. The operation was planned to a length of nine days, with an advance into the depth of the enemy's defense of 44-54 kilometers, and an average daily rate of advance of 5-6 kilometers.

In accordance with this decision, the army's formations were given the following assignments:

The 3rd Guards Rifle Corps was to break through the enemy's defense along the Korma—Gorokhovishche sector and, making its main attack along the center in the direction of marker 142, by the end of the first day it was to reach the line excluding Zales'e—excluding marker 142. Taking advantage of the cavalry-mechanized group's success, the corps was to subsequently develop the offensive with its right flank in the direction of Istopki and on the battle's third day occupy the line Protasy—Zubarevskaya Buda.

The 20th Rifle Corps was to break through the enemy's defense along the sector excluding Gorokhovishchi—marker 140.6 sector and, making its main attack along the right flank in the direction of the Stalin Collective Farm, it was to occupy the line excluding marker 142—Mikul'-Gorodok by the end of the battle's first day. The corps was to subsequently develop the offensive in the direction of Ozemlya, and with the commitment of the cavalry-mechanized group into the breach along the line Gustaya Dubrava—Lyuban', it was to widen the breach with its two left-flank divisions toward the west and southwest and on the battle's third day occupy the line excluding Zubarevskaya Buda—Smolovitsa.

The 128th Rifle Corps was to break through the enemy's defense along the Mostki—Yurki sector and, making its main attack in the direction of Grab'e, by the end of the battle's first day occupy the western bank of the Tremlya River. The corps would subsequently develop the offensive in the direction of Bubnovka.

The 161st Fortified Area, which was operationally subordinated to the commander of the 128th Rifle Corps, was to cover the corps' left flank, and as its rifle divisions advanced, would consolidate their gains.

Thus the 28th Army was to break through the enemy's defense along a 9-kilometer front, having a single-echelon operational formation, although its formations would have deep combat formations. The entire operation's depth would reach 50-60 kilometers. The time indicated by the *front* commander for reaching the assigned lines enabled the commander of the 28th Army to plan the pace of the offensive's advance, which was not to exceed 6-8 kilometers per day. The real correlation of forces would give us the opportunity to attack at a faster pace.

Brief Conclusions on the Decisions of the Front Commander and the Army Commanders

The First Belorussian Front command possessed sufficiently complete information about the location of the enemy's forces, the character of their defense, and the enemy's plans and intentions. The enemy's main groups of forces had been uncovered, his most important defensive lines revealed, and the German-Fascist forces' defensive system determined, not only in the tactical zone, but in the operational depth as well. However, there were nonetheless significant shortcomings, testifying to the insufficiently exacting work of several intelligence sections. For example, according to the situation on 1 June 1944, it was believed that the 3rd Army faced the 260th Infantry Division in the first line, although by that time it had been relieved by the 57th Infantry Division, which had arrived from the Orsha area and that its main forces were already around Orsha. It was believed that the 20th Panzer Division was deployed in an area 20 kilometers northeast of Bobruisk, with one of its mechanized regiments along the front line near Ozerane; actually, the mechanized regiment had been relieved as early as 16 May, and the entire division had been transferred by rail to the Kholm—Selitse—Krasnostav area (100 kilometers west of Kovel'), were it was concentrating on 19 May. It was believed that the 216th Infantry Division was deployed near Konkovichi opposite the 61st Army, when it was actually the 102nd Infantry Division. It was believed that the 57th Security Regiment was occupying the sector from the Styr' River to the west (opposite the boundary between the 61st and 70th armies), when actually the area was held by part of Colonel Wulf's cavalry brigade. The presence of the 52nd Special Designation Security Division in the Baranovichi area was completely overlooked.

The same shortcomings in studying the enemy should be noted as of 23 June. The reinforcement of Army Group Center with the Hungarian I Cavalry Corps, which had been concentrated in the Pinsk—Luninets area and to the south, had not been established; the Ninth Army's reinforcement by the 707th Infantry Division, which had concentrated in the area 3-4 kilometers south of Bobruisk was not established; nor was the return of the 20th Panzer Division from the Kovel' area to the area 8-10 kilometers east of Bobruisk (20 June), and; finally, the shortening of the 393rd Infantry Division's front by six kilometers, and that of the XLI Panzer Corps by 25 kilometers was not picked up.

The plan and decision by the commander of the First Belorussian Front were worked out in accordance with the plan of the *Stavka* of the Supreme High Command, which had assigned the *front* the task of defeating, first of all, the enemy's Bobruisk group of forces and creating favorable conditions for subsequent operations in the operational depth of the enemy's defense.

In his decision, the commander of the First Belorussian Front precisely directed the efforts of all four armies and mobile forces toward the defeat of the enemy's Bobruisk group of forces, first of all. This goal would be achieved by breaking through the enemy's defense immediately along two sectors, by committing the mobile forces into the breach along these sectors, and by the active outflanking actions of all the troops against the Bobruisk fortified area.

A characteristic of the operation was that the *front* offensive operation would initially begin along an approximately 140-150-kilometer sector, which, following the breakthrough of the enemy's defense, would gradually narrow and not exceed 80 kilometers in the Bobruisk area; that is, it would contract almost in half. This was explained by the straightening of the front line following the elimination of the Bobruisk salient.

Four combined-arms armies and the powerful forces of the mobile groups, attacking along converging axes, would encircle the enemy's Bobruisk group of forces in a thick ring and create favorable conditions for its rapid defeat.

The number of troops along the First Belorussian Front's right wing alone exceeded that of the entire Third Belorussian Front, with the exception of tanks, of which there were almost 600 less in the First Belorussian Front. Evidently the latter circumstance was a result of the fact that the commander of the First Belorussian Front laid out narrower breakthrough sectors for his armies than did the commander of the Third Belorussian Front.

The decisions by the First Belorussian Front's army commanders, on the whole, corresponded to the spirit and demands of the *front* commander's plan. The efforts of all four armies were directed at the rapid encirclement and destruction of the enemy's Bobruisk group of forces.

All four armies of the First Belorussian Front's right wing, which were holding a front of about 240 kilometers, were to break through the enemy's defense along sectors amounting to 29 kilometers overall, that is; 12 percent of the overall front, or 20 percent of the offensive sector.

The operational formation of the First Belorussian Front's armies was in one or two echelons. Deep combat orders were created for the formations using a single-echelon formation. Such a deep formation was to secure the successful development of the offensive into the depth of the enemy's defense and enable us to augment the force of the attack, particularly when fighting the enemy's reserves.

The *front's* cavalry-mechanized group was to be committed into the breach in the 28th Army's sector, once the army had advanced to a depth of up to ten kilometers. A 20-kilometer commitment sector had been foreseen, which would enable us to simultaneously commit both corps. Artillery and engineering support for the cavalry-mechanized group's commitment into the breach was entrusted to the 28th Army.

On the whole, it should be noted that the decision of the First Belorussian Front's commander, and those of the *front's* army commanders, corresponded to the concrete situation and the demands by the *Stavka* of the Supreme High Command.

The forms of operational maneuver employed by the First Belorussian Front were characterized by the following features.

The First Belorussian Front planned to make frontal attacks with its four armies along two sectors and counted on quickly breaking through the tactical defensive zone and committing mobile forces into the breach, which would energetically develop the success into the depth, and outflanking Bobruisk from the north and south.

The commander of the 3rd Army planned to commit his mobile group (9th Tank Corps) into the breach after breaking through the enemy's tactical defense zone, for the purpose of attacking directly toward Bobruisk, in which area he was to arrive by the end of the operation's third day.

The *front's* mobile group would also be committed into the breach upon overcoming the enemy's tactical defense zone, and it was to seize crossings over the Ptich' River on the operation's first day; by the end of the operation's third day it was to reach the Glusha area, forming the external encirclement front around the enemy's Bobruisk group of forces from the west.

Thus following the breakthrough of the tactical zone, two army mobile groups sped directly toward Bobruisk, creating an internal encirclement front around the enemy's entire Bobruisk group of forces, while the *front's* mobile group would arrive west of Bobruisk, creating an external encirclement front.

The combined-arms armies would continue their offensive behind the mobile forces, and while the *front's* first right-wing shock group (3rd and 48th armies) maneuvered to encircle the enemy's entire Bobruisk group of forces, the right wing's second shock group (65th and 28th armies) would secure the 3rd and 48th armies' maneuver by attacking to the northwest and, in turn cutting off the enemy's routes of retreat from the Bobruisk area to the west.

4

The Planning of the Front and Army Operations

Characteristics of Planning the *Front* Operations

The offensive operations in all the *fronts* were planned in a comparatively quiet situation, because the *fronts* were defending and the enemy did not evince any kind of activity. However, it should be noted that the planning in all the *fronts* was conducted under the impression of the difficult and predominantly unsuccessful fighting that took place in Belorussia in the spring of 1944, in which the enemy displayed extreme stubbornness and prevented us from breaking through his main defensive lines. The fighting was particularly stubborn around Vitebsk, along the Orsha axis, and in the Kovel' area.

Having begun the planning for the new offensive operations, the *front* and army headquarters expected no less amount of enemy resistance at this time, as a result of which excessive caution crept into planning questions: the Soviet army's high degree of morale uplift was not taken into account and the further growth of our troops' technical outfitting, which, to a significant degree, facilitated the rapid and decisive breakthrough of the German-Fascist troops' defense. During the course of the offensive, significantly amendments were made to both the decisions made by the commanders of the *fronts* and armies, as well as the plans drawn up by their staffs.

The scope of the *front* operations under review was determined only during the course of the offensive. The *front* staffs planned in detail beforehand only the immediate task laid down by the *Stavka* of the Supreme High Command, and the subsequent objective only in part. Evidently, the *front* commanders received only a general orientation as regards the subsequent offensive from the line of the Berezina River.

The First Baltic Front command planned its operation in three stages, as far as the line Kovalevshchina—Chashniki.

The first stage involved the breakthrough of the enemy's main defensive zone and the arrival of the *front's* shock group to the line Zavadka—Ol'khoviki, to a depth of 9-10 kilometers, with one day set aside for this. The arrival of the shock group's forces on the offensive's first day at a depth of 9-10 kilometers would create the conditions for the commitment of the 1st Tank Corps into the breach, which was to develop the tactical breakthrough into an operational one.

The second stage was the forcing of the Western Dvina River and the destruction, in conjunction with the Third Belorussian Front's right wing (39th Army) of the enemy's Vitebsk group of forces and the arrival to the line Podory—Repinshchina—Dukovshchina—Kosarevshchizna—Dubrovki—Chernogor'e—Novki, to a depth of 23-32 kilometers, lasting three days. The rate of advance, as in the first stage, was planned at 9-11 kilometers.

The third stage was the forcing of the Ulla River and the arrival of the *front's* shock group to the line Kovalevshchina—Pilatovshchina—Kamen'—Chashniki, to a depth of 25-30 kilometers in three days' time.

The second and third stages were planned to a depth of up to 65 kilometers, with the successive expansion of the breakthrough front, while the strength of the attack was to increase by the commitment of the second echelons. The chief task was to launch a single overall attack in the direction of Beshenkovichi and Chashniki; simultaneously, a part of the *front's* forces, in conjunction with the Third Belorussian Front, was to encircle and destroy the enemy's Vitebsk group of forces and firmly secure itself against attack from the Polotsk area.

The Third Belorussian Front's operational plan called for seizing bridgeheads along the western bank of the Berezina River by the forces of the cavalry-mechanized group and the 5th Guards Tank Army on the operation's sixth day and the entire western bank of the Berezina River along the *front's* attack zone by the *front's* main forces (5th, 11th Guards and 31st armies) by the operation's eleventh day. The operations of the *front's* forces, within the bounds of the indicated operation, were planned to a depth of 160 kilometers, and were to last 11 days, with an average daily rate of advance of 12-15 kilometers for the infantry, and 30-35 kilometers for the mobile forces.

The *front's* immediate task was laid out in accordance with the demands of the *Stavka* directive and consisted of defeating the opposing enemy by means of breaking through the entire depth of his tactical defense and the arrival of the *front's* forces at the line Lake Sarro—Senno—Smolyany—Baran' (ten kilometers northwest of Orsha) on the operation's third day; the cavalry-mechanized group would occupy the Senno area.

A feature of the operation was the planning of the *front's* efforts for every day of the operation, from the first through the eleventh day of the offensive. The operation's first three days, or its first stage, were planned in greater detail, with instructions on the employment of the men and materiel attached to the armies and their interaction with each other and the air force. For the remaining days, or the operation's second stage, the armies were instructed only as to the general direction of their main forces' offensive and the deadline for reaching the Berezina River.

The commander of the Second Belorussian Front decided to carry out his objectives with the reinforced 49th Army alone. He not only laid out exhaustive tasks to this army, but also planned its operations by day. In five days the army was to cover a distance of 50-65 kilometers, with an average daily rate of advance of 10-13 kilometers.

The First Belorussian Front compiled its plan for the Belorussian offensive operation, in which the tasks were formulated for two stages.

The first stage involved the defeat of the enemy's Bobruisk group of forces. This stage's length was defined as nine days, with a planned depth of 60-70 kilometers and an average rate of advance of 7-8 kilometers per day.

The second stage involved the development of the success by the two shock groups in the following directions: a) Osipovichi and Pukhovichi, with a turn by part of the 3rd Army from the Svisloch' area along the western bank of the Berezina River toward Berezino; b) Starye Dorogi and Slutsk; the duration of the second stage was not defined.

If one takes the objective of the line Pukhovichi—Slutsk, then the depth of the entire Bobruisk operation would reach a planned 130-40 kilometers.

Characteristics of Planning the Army Operations

A great deal of uniformity was achieved in planning the army operations in the *fronts*. As a rule, the army operations were planned by stages and days, with a detailed explication of objectives for the first stage, or for the first day or two of the operation.

In the First Baltic Front the attacking armies planned their operations in the following manner.

It was planned to carry out the offensive by the 6th Guards Army in two stages:

The first stage encompassed the attack and breakthrough of the main defensive zone and the arrival of the army's main forces to the line Starosel'e—Zavodka—Verbali—Gubitsa. This stage was to last one day and be carried to a depth of 11 kilometers.

The second stage encompassed the commitment into the breach of the *front* mobile group, the development of the offensive in depth, with the forcing of the Western Dvina River and the arrival of our troops at the line Fed'kovo—Ulla—Bubishche—Makarovichi—Dubrovki. This stage was to last two days and be conducted to a depth of 25-35 kilometers.

According to the army's offensive plan, the operations of the rifle corps were planned for all three days, with a detailed explication of their tasks for each day of the operation.

It was planned to conduct the 43rd Army's offensive in three stages.

The first stage involved the breakthrough of the enemy's main defensive zone along the front Medvedi—Zabolotniki and the arrival of the army's main forces to the line Belyan—Ryabushkovo—Koshali—Yazvino. This stage was to last one day and be conducted to a depth of 7-9 kilometers.

The second stage involved the overcoming of the enemy's second defensive line and the arrival of the army's main forces at the line Novoe Selo—Grineva, and then along the Western Dvina River as far as Novki. By the end of this stage the divisions' forward detachments were to seize bridgeheads on the southern bank of the Western Dvina River along the Sharylino—Vyazhishche sector and in the Komli area. This stage was to last one day and be waged to a depth of 10-12 kilometers.

The third stage involved forcing the Western Dvina River, consolidating the seized bridgeheads, and taking, in conjunction with the Third Belorussian Front's 39th Army, the major road intersection of Ostrovno. This stage was to last one day and be conducted to a depth of 12-20 kilometers. In planning the third stage, the plan foresaw extending its length to two days, should the enemy's 95th Infantry Division occupy a defense along the southern bank of the Western Dvina River.

The planning of the army operations in the Third Belorussian Front was approximately the same.

In the 39th Army the operation was planned in two stages, while the troops' activities within each stage were also planned by days.

The operation's first stage included the breakthrough of the enemy's defense throughout the entire tactical depth, the defeat of his opposing group of forces and our arrival to the line Trubachi—Zarudnitsa—Pesochna—excluding Moshkany. This stage was to last two days, with a depth of 16-18 kilometers.

The operation's second stage involved completing the encirclement of the enemy's Vitebsk group of forces and our arrival at the Western Dvina River; the defeat of the enemy and the capture of Vitebsk, with our simultaneous arrival to the line Beshenkovichi—Novoe Ranchishche—Shalamy. This stage would last three days and be conducted to a depth of 32-40 kilometers.

The operation's overall depth was set at 50-55 kilometers, with a duration of five days.

The planned rate of advance for the first day was up to 6-8 kilometers, and 10-15 kilometers for the following days. The operation's daily rate of advance was set at ten kilometers.

The actions of the 5th Army were planned for each day of the operation, while the rifle corps' tasks were for three days. The fourth day was planned in approximate terms, and the plan noted only the arrival of the troops to a line by the end of the day and the army's grouping of forces by corps. The commitment of the 45th Rifle Corps was planned approximately for the morning of the third or fourth day of the operation in the general direction of Senno. The overall depth of the 5th Army's planned combat activities, from the jumping-off point to the line Borkuny—Senno—Andreichiki, was 55 kilometers, while these were to last four days. The army's planned average daily rate of advance was 13-14 kilometers, while the greatest advance (16 kilometers) was planned during the course of the operation's first day, when the enemy's developed defense had to be broken through along the front line and the Luchesa River forced. In connection with this, it is necessary to emphasize that the operational plan low-balled the troops' possible rate of advance during the operation's second and third days (it was planned to advance ten kilometers per day) and did not take into account that on the morning of the second day the cavalry-mechanized group would be attacking in the 5th Army's sector.

The 11th Guards Army's operation was planned in two stages, while the actions of the troops in each stage were also planned by day.

The operation's first stage involved the breakthrough of the enemy's defense throughout the entire tactical depth, with the encirclement by part of the army's right-wing forces of the enemy group of forces in the woods north of the Minsk highway; the commitment of the 2nd Guards Tank Corps and the arrival of the army's main forces to the line excluding Dobrino—Chepelina—Obukhovo—Baretski. By the end of the second day the 2nd Guards Tank Corps was to occupy the area of Belobrod'e. This stage's length was planned at two days, with a depth of 20-25 kilometers.

The operation's second stage involved the vigorous and unceasing pursuit of the enemy in the general direction of Tolochin, with the simultaneous securing of the army's left flank against possible enemy counterblows from the south, and the arrival of the army's forces to the line Veino settlement—Videnichi—Zabolot'e. Simultaneously, on the army's right flank the destruction of the enemy's surrounded units south of Bogushevsk, in conjunction with the 5th Army, would be completed. This stage was to last three days and be conducted to a depth of 40-45 kilometers.

The army's operational plan for the second stage called for it to be ready to attack, with the forces of two rifle divisions (26th and 84th), around Orsha from the west in the direction of Baran', in order to assist the 31st Army in taking Orsha, and the 2nd Guards Tank Corps' turn from the line of the Adrov River in the direction of Starosel'e.

The 152nd Fortified Area was to be regrouped to the 11th Guards Army's left flank on the operation's fourth day in order to secure it from the Orsha area.

It is necessary to note that the 11th Guards Army's operational plan did not foresee any kinds of measures for securing the commitment of the 5th Guards Tank Army into the breach, which constitutes its major shortcoming.

The overall depth of the 31st Army's planned operations, from the jumping-off point to the line Lomachin—Balbasovo—Bol'shoe Zamosh'e, was 45-50 kilometers, with a duration of four days. The troops' activities were planned by day, while the corps' combat tasks were laid out for two days (in detail for the first day). The operation's third and fourth days were planned very approximately, and then only on a map.

It was planned to take Orsha in the course of the operation's third or fourth day. The daily rate of advance was set at 11-12 kilometers.

In the Second Belorussian Front's 49th Army the offensive operation was planned by stages, in accordance with the *front* commander's instructions. During the first stage the army was to carry out those tasks laid down by the *front* commander for the first day, while during the second stage the tasks laid down for the operation's second and third days, and during the third stage—for the operation's fourth and fifth days.

The *front's* 33rd Army, which was continuing to defend, foresaw making only a local attack with a single division along a subsidiary axis.

The commander of the 50th Army drew up two variations for his force, which, however, were planned only in general terms.

In the First Belorussian Front's attacking armies the army operations were planned with the greatest detail.

In the 3rd Army the operation's conduct was planned in three stages.

The first stage, which was scheduled to last four days, foresaw the breakthrough of the enemy's entire tactical defense, the destruction of his arriving operational reserves and the army's arrival at the Ola River. The planned depth of advance into the enemy's defensive depth was 30-35 kilometers, with an average daily rate of advance of 8-9 kilometers.

The second stage was to last three days and foresaw the breakthrough of the enemy's intermediate line along the Ola River, the arrival of the army's main group of forces to the line Chigirinka—Barki—Batsevichi—Orlino—Lake Orlinskoe—the eastern bank of the Berezina River, the consolidation of this line and the seizure of crossings over the Berezina River. This stage's depth was planned at 30 kilometers, with a daily rate of advance of 9-10 kilometers.

The third stage was to last two days and was planned in general terms. This stage involved the capture of Svisloch' and, having cut the Mogilev—Bobruisk railroad, the creation of favorable conditions for forcing the Berezina River. This stage would be conducted to a depth of 15-20 kilometers, at an average daily rate of advance of 7.5-10 kilometers.

In the 48th Army it was planned to conduct the operation in three stages.

The first stage, planned for four days, foresaw the breakthrough of the entire tactical defense zone, the destruction of the opposing enemy and his arriving reserves, the army's arrival to the line Mikhalevo—Uznoga—Mikulichi—Starye Ovsimovichi—Kovrin—Pristan'—Korma—Nivy, and preventing the enemy's Zhlobin group of forces from exiting from the woods southwest of Korma. The stage's depth was set at 32-35 kilometers, with an average daily rate of advance of 8-9 kilometers.

The three-day second stage called for the breakthrough of the enemy's intermediate defensive line along the western bank of the Ola River, the army's pursuit and arrival at the line Titovka—Domanovo—Kobylichi—Mel'niki, and the forcing of the Berezina River. The stage's depth was set at 25 kilometers, with an average daily rate of advance of 8-9 kilometers.

The two-day third stage called for the development of the offensive's success, the capture of Bobruisk and the army's arrival to the line of the Volchanka River. The stage's depth was set at 22 kilometers, and the average daily rate of advance at 11 kilometers.

In the 65th Army the operation was initially planned in three stages, with low rates of advance. On orders by the *Stavka* of the Supreme High Command, the operation was planned again, although this new plan was not laid out in documentary form and was not even reflected in the journal of combat activities. The altered decision was preserved only on maps under the code name "Usk" ("quickened offensive"), but it was communicated to all the corps commanders and actually put into practice.

According to the altered decision, the forces' tasks were refined:

By the end of the first day, the army was to occupy the line Pogantsy—Lipniki—Peschanaya Rudnya—Knyshevichi—Slobodka—Romanishche, while the 1st Guards Tank Corps was to enter the breach and arrive in the Moiseevka—Mekhovo—Gorodets area (an assignment that was originally to be carried out by the army by the end of the second day). The previously planned offensive pace of 5-6 kilometers was increased to 9-15 kilometers per day;

By the close of the operation's second day the army was to capture Parichi and the line Parichi—Belitsa—Prudishche—Kruki—excluding Protasy (the third day's line in the initial plan);

By the close of the third day the army was to reach the line Slobodka—Makarovichi—Kryukovshchina, with an increased rate of advance of 16-20 kilometers, while the 1st Guards Tank Corps was to reach the area to the west of Bobruisk;

By the close of the operation's fourth and fifth days the army was to occupy the line Bogushevka—Glusha—Gorodishche, and then along the eastern bank of the Pripyat' River, with a rate of advance of 14-22 kilometers, or 7-11 kilometers per day.

The 28th Army's offensive operation was planned in detail only for the first three days. However, upon studying the *front* directive, the army plan and the map with the army commander's decision, one may conclude that three operational stages were planned, excluding a preparatory one.

The first stage was to last two days and included the breakthrough of the entire tactical defense zone, the destruction of the opposing enemy forces, the army's arrival to the line Romanishche—Goduny—Ivanishchevichi, and securing the commitment of the *front's* cavalry-mechanized group into the breach. The offensive's depth was set at 12-15 kilometers, with an average daily rate of advance of 6-8 kilometers.

The operation's second stage was to last five days and called for the development of the offensive in the direction of Zelenkovichi, employing the success of the cavalry-mechanized group, the destruction of the enemy's arriving reserves, the arrival of the army's main forces to the line of the Ptich' River, and the seizure of bridgeheads along the sector Poblin—the mouth of the Oresa River. This stage's depth was set at 25-27 kilometers, and the average daily rate of advance at 5-6 kilometers.

The operation's third stage was to last two days and included the breakthrough of the enemy's defensive line along the Ptich' River, followed by the forcing of the latter, the development of the further offensive in the direction of Glusk and the army's arrival at the line Glusk—Bubnovka. This stage's depth was set at 13-16 kilometers, with an average daily rate of advance of 6-8 kilometers.

Thus all the army operations were planned in two or three stages. The operation's first stage was developed in a more detailed (by days) way.

Planning the Distribution of Men and Materiel Throughout the Entire Depth of the *Front* and Army Operations

All four *fronts* carrying out the Belorussian operation deployed their combined-arms armies in their jumping-off positions in a single echelon. Each army had an attack zone and resolved its assigned task within the bounds of the *front* operation.

The *front* commanders, in order to augment the force of the attack in the depth of the enemy's defense, disposed of only mobile groups, air armies, and reserves of technical equipment. Only the commanders of the First Baltic and Second Belorussian fronts retained a rifle division apiece in the form of a *front* reserve.

All of the *front* commanders created their own *front* mobile groups, which were designated for developing the success following the breakthrough of the enemy's tactical defense zone. Tank armies, cavalry and mechanized corps made up these groups, as well as, in part, tank corps, although the majority of the latter was allotted for the creation of army mobile groups.

The *front* mobile groups included up to half of the tanks and self-propelled guns available to the *fronts*. For example, of the First Baltic Front's 535 tanks and self-propelled guns operating along the main axis, 297 were in the mobile group. The Third Belorussian Front had a total of 1,810 tanks and self-propelled guns, of which the mobile groups (the tank army, a cavalry and a mechanized corps) had 1,098. The Second Belorussian Front had 276 tanks and self-propelled guns, of which 76 were allotted to the mobile group. The First Belorussian Front had a cavalry and a mechanized corps as the *front* mobile group; of the *front's* 1,297 tanks and self-propelled guns, the mobile group had 777.

Of the four independent tank corps within the *fronts*, only one was used in a *front* mobile group, while the remainder were transferred to the armies and made up their army mobile groups.

Front artillery groups were not created.

The combined-arms armies were the chief link in resolving the task of breaking through the enemy's defense and defeating his groups of forces and developing the success in depth, which had been powerfully reinforced by the *front* and the *Stavka* of the Supreme High Command.

The combined-arms armies varied in strength—from several divisions to five rifle corps. The armies, which were slated to make the main attacks, were considerably larger and had been powerfully reinforced. Of 14 combined-arms armies within all four *fronts*, 11 armies participated in launching the main attacks, while only three armies made supporting attacks and supported the operations of the shock groups.[1]

The majority of armies operating along the *fronts'* main attack axes had a deep operational formation (six of 11 armies). Those armies that had a single-echelon operational formation usually made their rifle corps' combat formations in two echelons, having, as a rule, no less than two rifle divisions in these corps' second echelons. In those armies where the corps were arrayed in a single echelon, reserves of one or two rifle divisions were created. On the whole, of 118 rifle divisions within the *fronts*, 74 of them were in the first echelons, and 44 in the armies' second and third echelons, as well as in the army and *front* commanders' reserve.

The troops' deep formation at the army-corps and corps-division level guaranteed the augmentation of their efforts while breaking through the tactical, and then, the operational depth of the enemy's defense. The chief means of developing the success at the *front* level were the mobile groups.

Planning for the Maneuver of Men and Materiel

Following the frontal attack and the breakthrough of the main zone, and then the entire tactical zone of the enemy's defense, the complex maneuver of men and materiel was planned in all the *fronts* and armies for the most rapid defeat of the opposing enemy groups of forces, the seizure of rear defensive zones and the forcing of water barriers. This maneuver was to be carried out primarily by the *fronts'* and armies mobile groups, by the corps' and armies' second and third echelons, and by the reserves of the corps, army and *front* commanders.

For example, in the First Baltic Front the mobile group (1st Tank Corps) was designated for commitment into the breach, rapidly advancing in the operational depth of the enemy's defense and the seizure of bridgeheads over the Western Dvina River in the Beshenkovichi area. The mobile group was to achieve this by the end of the operation's second day.

In the Third Belorussian Front two *front* mobile groups were created: the first of these, consisting of the 3rd Guards Cavalry and the 3rd Guards Mechanized corps, received orders to capture the crossings over the Obolyanka River by the end of the operation's third day, and the crossings over the Berezina River by the end of the fifth day; the second, consisting of the 5th Guards Tank Army, was designated to rapidly advance in the depth of the enemy's operational defense, to capture crossings over the Bobr River and force the Berezina River in the Borisov area.

In the Second Belorussian Front the mobile group was to develop the success of the first echelons formations and by the end of the operation's third day capture the crossings over the Dnepr River.

Thus the mobile groups in these *fronts* were to carry out a rapid maneuver in the depths of the enemy's operational defense for the purpose of forcing large water obstacles and seizing bridgeheads on their western banks.

In the First Belorussian Front it was planned to employ the *front's* right-wing mobile group not only for seizing water obstacles, but also for encircling the enemy's Bobruisk group of forces and subsequently developing the success to the west.

The army mobile groups were mainly designated for aiding the rifle corps in breaking through the enemy's tactical defense zone, and for seizing important objectives and crossings over water obstacles. For example, the 2nd Tank Corps, which formed the 11th Guards Army's mobile group, was to maneuver along the Minsk highway for the purpose of quickly cutting the Vitebsk—Orsha paved road and forcing the Orshitsa River. The 9th Tank Corps, which formed the 3rd Army's mobile group, had the task of quickly seizing the crossings, at first over the Ola River, and then

---

1   This figure includes only the right-wing armies in the First Belorussian Front.

the crossings over the Berezina River by the end of the operation's third day. The 1st Tank Corps, which formed the 65th Army's mobile group, was to first assist in destroying the enemy's Parichi group of forces, and then in encircling the Bobruisk group of forces.

The combined-arms armies' second echelons and reserves were designated for mainly carrying out the following types of maneuver, after breaking through the enemy's defense: a) developing the success in the operational depth and seizing the enemy's rear defensive lines; this task was to be carried out by the 6th Guards Army's 103rd and 2nd Guards rifle corps, the 5th Army's 45th Rifle Corps, the 3rd Army's 46th Rifle Corps, and the 65th Army's 356th Rifle Division and 115th Rifle Brigade; b) strengthening the first echelon's forces and securing the flank; this was the task, for example, of the 39th Army's second-echelon divisions; c) reinforcing the armies' mobile groups following their commitment into the breach; the 65th Army's 44th Rifle Division had such a task, as well as one division of the 6th Guards Army's 2nd Guards Rifle Corps; d) the development of the success in a neighboring army's sector, which was making the main attack; the 50th Army's 121st Rifle Corps had such a task.

All of these examples testify to the variety of means of employing mobile groups and second echelons, which had been developed up to that time by Soviet forces and planned for employment in the course of the Belorussian operation.

Planning the Organization of Interaction Throughout the Operation's Entire Depth

In the decisions of the *front* and army commanders a significant amount of attention was given to questions of organizing cooperation between the *fronts* and armies, although it is necessary to note that complete precision in working these out was not achieved.

For example, the decisions of the commanders of the First Baltic and Third Belorussian fronts and the working out of questions of cooperation between the 43rd and 39th armies in encircling the enemy's Vitebsk group of forces was not fully realized. In his decision, the commander of the Third Belorussian Front assigned the 39th Army the task of attacking toward Ostrovno and in this area look for a link-up with the 43rd Army, while at the same time the commander of the First Baltic Front did not only not instruct his 43rd Army regarding the link-up area with the 39th Army, but actually directed it 15-20 kilometers west of this point. If one compares the decisions by the commanders of the 43rd and 39th armies, it immediately becomes obvious that sufficient linkage between the two armies' operations was lacking. Both armies, upon carrying out their objectives, would not be facing the enemy, but each other, which could have led to a great deal of confusion. In the decisions by the *front* and army commanders there is not even a mention of how the two armies should operate after encircling the enemy's Vitebsk group of forces.

In the decisions of the commanders of the First Baltic and Third Belorussian fronts there are no instructions as to coordinating the two *fronts'* operations while attacking in the operational depth of the enemy's defense.

Cooperation between the Third and Second Belorussian fronts was foreseen only during the operation's first stage. The commander of the Second Belorussian Front ordered the 33rd Army to prepare a single-division attack along the front Baevo—Lenino in the general direction of Yurkovo, Sava and Mikhailovichi, in order to cooperate with the Third Belorussian Front's 31st Army.

The idea of cooperation between the Second and First Belorussian fronts is mentioned in the *front* and army commanders' decisions only in general terms. The commander of the First Belorussian Front ordered the 3rd Army to assist the 2nd Belorussian Front's 50th Army with part of its right-flank forces, although the commander of the 3rd Army did not assign any active tasks to his right-flank corps.

The problems of working out questions of cooperation between the *fronts'* armies were worked out with the same lack of detail.

The commander of the First Baltic Front ordered the commander of the 6th Guards Army to organize the cooperation of his right-flank corps with the 4th Shock Army for destroying the enemy in the Starinovichi area, although the army commander allotted insufficient forces for this task.

The questions of cooperation between armies were most fully resolved in the Third Belorussian Front. The *front* commander ordered the commander of the 5th Army to attack with a single rifle division (159th) toward Babinovichi toward the 11th Guards Army's 152nd Fortified Area. The commander of the 5th Army allotted two of the division's regiments to carry out this task. The 11th Guards Army commander received orders that upon the arrival of the army's main forces in the area to the north of Orsha, he should attack with a single rifle division from the Moshkovo area toward Baran' and Novosel'e, and in this way assist the 31st Army in taking Orsha. The army commander allotted for this task not one division, but two (26th and 84th guards). Besides this, he turned the 2nd Guards Tank Corps from the line of the Adrov River toward Starosel'e, for the purpose of assisting the 31st Army in taking Orsha. The commander of the 39th Army designated one rifle division (251st), which had been left in the army's second echelon, for cooperating with the neighboring 5th Army.

Questions of cooperation between the 5th Guards Tank and 5th armies proved to be insufficiently worked out, because the tank army was preparing for commitment into the battle not in the 5th Army's sector, but in that of the 11th Guards Army, according to the first variation.

On the whole, cooperation in the *fronts* and armies was supposed to secure coordinated actions for defeating the enemy. However, there were still a lot of shortcomings, which testified to our undervaluing the significance of cooperation by individual commanders and their staffs.

5

Planning the Employment of Artillery, Armored Forces and Aviation

Planning the Combat Employment of Artillery

In connection with the forthcoming breakthrough of the enemy's prepared defense, as well as for guaranteeing our troops' high rates of advance, both during the course of breaking through the defense, as well as the development of the success, the First Baltic, Third, Second, and First Belorussian fronts were reinforced by the following units from the Supreme High Command's artillery reserves: ten artillery divisions, three guards mortar divisions, 17 anti-aircraft artillery divisions, 35 independent artillery brigades, five mortar and guards mortar brigades, and also a large number of artillery, mortar and anti-aircraft artillery units (see table 14).

From table 15 one can see that our forces had more than 28,500 guns and mortars against 9,635 of the enemy. Thus our overall superiority in artillery over the enemy was 2.9:1. Such a significant overall superiority enabled us to create artillery densities along the decisive axes that would guarantee an overwhelming superiority of the enemy's artillery (see table 16).

In connection with such a high complement of artillery, there arose before the command and staffs of the *fronts* and armies, as well as before the corresponding artillery commanders and their staffs, a most responsible task, connected with the concentration of the Supreme High Command reserve's artillery that was arriving at the *fronts*, as well as by internal *front* artillery regroupings to the sectors of the *fronts'* main groups of forces, as well as with the artillery's arrival in the areas of the firing positions and its deployment among the combat formations.

One may judge as to the enormity of this mission by the following data. The First Belorussian Front received by railroad alone more than 67 operational trainloads with artillery (up to 40 regiments). Eight railroad stations were designated for unloading these trains. After unloading the artillery was moved up to a distance of up to 200 kilometers to its concentration area. Artillery units and formation with automobile transport covered this distance on their own. For those units and formations employing tractor transport, the unloading areas were moved forward closer to the concentration areas, so that these formations and units would have to travel as short a distance as possible. Up to 69 artillery regiments (the 4th Breakthrough Artillery Corps, 22nd Breakthrough Artillery Division, the 44th and 68th cannon artillery brigades, 1091st Cannon Artillery Regiment, 35th Mortar Brigade, 1st, 3rd and 44th anti-tank artillery brigades, and the 1071st Anti-Tank Artillery Regiment were regrouped from the *front's* left to right wing to the 3rd, 48th, 65th, and 28th armies' sectors).

Table 14. Supreme High Command Reserve Artillery Formations and Units within the *Fronts* by the Start of the Belorussian Operation

Artillery Formations and Units	1st Baltic Front[1]	3rd Belorussian Front[2]	2nd Belorussian Front[3]	1st Belorussian Front[4]
Breakthrough Artillery Divisions	21st	5th Breakthrough Artillery Corps (2nd Gds, 20th, 3rd Gds)	–	4th Breakthrough Artillery Corps (5th, 12th), 22nd, 26th
Cannon Artillery Divisions	8th	4th Gds	–	–
Cannon Artillery Brigades	4th	15th Gds, 139th, 140th, 149th	142nd, 143rd, 144th	30th Gds, 44th, 68th, 147th, 157th
Corps Artillery Brigades	–	–	2nd	3rd, 4th
High-Caliber Howitzer Brigades	–	117th, 119th	32nd	122nd, 124th
Heavy Howitzer Brigades	–	–	31st	–
Corps Artillery Regiments (cannon artillery regiments)	38th	392nd, 523rd, 570th, 1093rd 1165th, 38th Gds,	41st, 517th, 557th, 1099th	295th, 377th, 1091st
Howitzer Regiments	64th, 283rd, 480th, 376th, 1224th	83rd Gds	16th, 49th, 55th, 56th, 81st, 85th, 331st, 472nd, 1231st	–
High Caliber and Heavy Artillery Divisions	–	226th, 245th, 316th, 402nd, 406th	322nd	315th, 317th
Mortar Brigades	31st	–	19th	35th
Mortar Regiments	408th	–	540th, 544th	133rd, 143rd, 286th, 475th, 479th
Anti-Tank Artillery Brigades	17th, 45th	1st Gds, 16th Gds, 43rd	4th, 5th, 13th, 27th	1st, 3rd Gds, 41st, 44th
Anti-Tank Artillery Regiments	–	–	–	120th, 530th, 543rd, 584th, 220th Gds, 1071st, 1311th
Guards Mortar Divisions	2nd Gds	7th Gds	–	5th Gds (16th, 22nd, 23rd gds mortar bdes)
Guards Mortar Brigades	–	9th Gds	4th Gds	–
Guards Mortar Regiments	39th, 99th, 22nd, 26th, 34th	42nd, 54th, 67th, 74th, 76th, 95th, 317th, 326th	77th, 29th, 100th, 307th, 325th	1st Gds, 6th, 37th, 43rd, 56th, 62nd, 84th, 92nd, 94th, 311th, 313th, 316th
Anti-Aircraft Artillery Divisions	17th, 39th, 16th	6th, 20th, 33rd, 34th, 48th, 66th	47th, 49th	2nd Gds, 3rd Gds, 12th, 13th, 28th, 31st
Anti-Aircraft Artillery Regiments	1623rd, 1625th, 1626th	1275th, 1281st, 1480th, 1481st	225th, 341st, 734th, 1268th, 1270th, 1479th, 1482nd, 1709th	235th, 461st, 607th, 1284th

Artillery Formations and Units	1st Baltic Front[1]	3rd Belorussian Front[2]	2nd Belorussian Front[3]	1st Belorussian Front[4]
Independent Anti-Aircraft Artillery Divisions	183rd, 221st, 622nd	64th, 24th, 500th, 525th	4th, 490th, 614th	13th, 27th, 31st, 615th

Notes

1 Includes the following newly-arrived units from the Supreme High Command reserve: 4th Cannon-Artillery Brigade, 45th Anti-Tank Artillery Brigade, 2nd Guards Mortar Division (20th and 26th guards mortar brigades), 22nd and 26th guards mortar regiments, 39th and 46th anti-aircraft artillery divisions.

2 Includes the following newly-arrived units from the Supreme High Command reserve: 5th Breakthrough Artillery Corps (2nd and 20th guards breakthrough artillery divisions), 117th and 119th high-powered howitzer brigades, 316th, 245th, 226th, 402nd, and 406th high-caliber artillery divisions.

3 Includes the following newly-arrived units from the Supreme High Command reserve: 32nd High-Powered Howitzer Brigade, 2nd Corps Artillery Brigade, 4th Guards Mortar Brigade, 5th and 27th anti-tank artillery brigades.

4 Includes the following newly-arrived units from the Supreme High Command reserve: 26th Breakthrough Artillery Division, 157th Cannon-Artillery Brigade, 122nd and 124th heavy caliber howitzer brigades, 30th, Guards Cannon Artillery Brigade, 3rd and 4th corps artillery brigades, 315th and 317th high-powered artillery divisions, 12th Breakthrough Artillery Division (4th Breakthrough Artillery Corps).

Table 15. The Amount of Artillery and Mortars Transferred to the First Baltic, Third, Second and Third Belorussian Fronts for Carrying out the Belorussian Operation

	The Correlation of Artillery Forces Soviet Forces			
Fronts	Field Guns	Anti-Tank Guns & Regimental Artillery[1]	82- and 120-mm Mortars	Total Guns & Mortars
1st Baltic	2,555	778 303	2,068	5,704
3rd Belorussian	3,249	1,175 383	3,502	8,309
2nd Belorussian	1,996	833 175	1,818	4,822
1st Belorussian (right wing)	3,880	1,444 498	3,936	9,758
Total	10,328	4,230 2,711	11,324	28,593[2]

Notes

1 Anti-tank weapons are in the numerator, and regimental artillery in the denominator.

2 24,363, not counting 45mm and 57mm guns.

	The Correlation of Artillery Forces Soviet Forces		
Front	Rocket-Propelled Artillery Launchers	Overall Frontage (in kilometers)	Guns, Mortars and Rocket Launchers (per kilometer of front)
1st Baltic	647	160	39.6
3rd Belorussian	648	130	68.9
2nd Belorussian	243	160	31.4
1st Belorussian (right wing)	739	240	43.7
Total	2,277	690	44.7

The Correlation of Artillery Forces
Enemy Forces

Fronts	Guns	Mortars & Rocket Launchers[2]	Total[1]	Per Kilometer of Front	Correlation
1st Baltic	1,483	823	2,306	14.4	2.4:1
3rd Belorussian	1,572	997 116	2,569	19.7	3.2:1
2nd Belorussian	1,537	670	2,207	13.7	2.1:1
1st Belorussian	1,605	948 16	2,553	10.6	3.8:1
Total	6,197	3,438 132	9,635	13.9	2.9:1

Notes
1 Not counting rocket launchers.
2 The numerator shows the number of guns and mortars, while the denominator shows the number of rocket launchers.

Table 16. Artillery Densities Along the Breakthrough Sectors of the *Fronts'* Main Groups of Forces. The Correlation of Forces Along the Breakthrough Sectors

Fronts	Soviet Forces				Enemy Forces	
	Guns & Mortars (not counting anti-tank)	Breakthrough Sector (in kilometers)	Density per Kilometer[1] (Breakthrough Sector)	Total Guns & Mortars	Density per Kilometer	Correlation
1st Baltic	3,768	25	151	970	39	3.8:1
3rd Belorussian	5,764	37	156	2,160	58	2.7:1
2nd Belorussian	2,168	12	181	580	46.4	3.8:1
1st Belorussian (right wing)	5,929	29	204.4	931	32.1	6.3:1
Total	17,629	103	134.5 162.6	2,986	29	5.6:1

Note
1 The numerator is without cannon and anti-tank artillery, while the denominator is with cannon and anti-tank artillery.

According to the First Baltic Front's plan the 21st Breakthrough Artillery Division (consisting of six brigades), the 31st Mortar Brigade, 408th Mortar Regiment, and the 17th and 39th anti-aircraft artillery divisions were to be regrouped. Aside from this, the following units were to arrive from the High Command Artillery Reserve to reinforce the *front*: 2nd Guards Mortar Division, (20th and 26th guards mortar brigades), 4th Cannon Artillery Brigade, 45th Anti-Tank Artillery Brigade, 22nd and 26th guards mortar regiments, and the 39th and 46th anti-aircraft artillery divisions. In general, besides the divisions' authorized artillery, a total of up to 85 independent artillery battalions, regiments and brigades were concentrated along the 25-kilometer breakthrough sector.

The artillery's regrouping within the *fronts* was carried out, as a rule, according to general regrouping plans, which had been drawn up by the *fronts'* staffs. The artillery's movement was usually carried out at night, while observing all masking measures.

In the First Baltic Front artillery from the west and northwest of Nevel' was transferred to the 6th Guards and 43rd armies' sectors during 2-9 June. Interarmy regroupings, the artillery's arrival to the positional areas and the artillery's deployment into combat orders were completed on 21 June. All the artillery formations and units arrived at their new concentration areas in a timely manner, without interference from the enemy and without losses.

In the Third Belorussian Front the *front* regrouping was completed during 1-11 June. The arrival of the artillery in the areas of the firing positions and its deployment into combat orders was carried out at night in all the *front's* armies and was completed by 18 June.

In the Second Belorussian Front the artillery units and formations regrouped from the 33rd and 50th armies to the 49th Army. In all, nine brigades and 11 artillery regiments were subject to regrouping. The intrafront regrouping of artillery was completed in time, during 8-16 June, in an organized manner and without losses. Only a few independent formations, which were arriving by railroad, were delayed a bit. The occupation of the firing positions and the artillery's deployment into its combat orders were carried out during 16-22 June.

In the First Belorussian Front the artillery's intrafront regrouping began on 2 June and was completed on time, on 19 June. The regrouping was carried out in an organized fashion and without losses. In the concentration areas strict order and masking discipline were observed.

The forward movement of the arriving artillery units and formations from the High Command Artillery Reserve was also carried out, as a rule, at night and with the observation of all masking measures. However, as the result of the great overloading of the rail transport, some units arrived late. This circumstance forced us to move the late-arriving units to their concentration areas during the day.

The artillery's arrival at its firing positions was carried out during 14-22 June. By 22 June all the artillery along the *front's* right-wing had been deployed.

Thus the regrouping, concentration and deployment of all four *fronts'* artillery acquired an enormous scope. This grandiose work was mainly carried out within the established deadlines, secretly, without enemy interference, and without losses. The engineer outfitting of the artillery's firing positions was carried out, as a rule, during the units' tenure in the concentration areas or in the pre-position areas. During this time topographical work to pin down the firing positions was carried out.

The timeliness and secrecy of the artillery's regrouping and deployment guaranteed its readiness by the scheduled time and facilitated offensive surprise.

The distribution of the reinforcement artillery at the disposal of the *fronts* was carried out in accordance with the operational decisions by the *front* commanders. The armies of the *fronts'* main groups of forces received such an amount of artillery reinforcement that enabled them to create an overwhelming superiority over the enemy along the decisive axes (see table 17).

In the First Baltic Front 73 percent of the *front's* guns and mortars were concentrated along the breakthrough sector. Thanks to this, we managed to bring the average artillery density—not counting anti-tank artillery—up to 151 guns and mortars per kilometer along the 25-kilometer breakthrough sector. The average density in the 6th Guards Army reached 167.7 guns and mortars per kilometer of front along the breakthrough sector. In the 43rd Army the artillery density reached 176 guns and mortars along the army's 7-kilometer breakthrough sector.

In the Third Belorussian Front 65 percent of all the *front's* artillery was concentrated along the breakthrough sector. This enabled us to raise the average artillery density along the breakthrough sectors to 156 guns and mortars per kilometer of front. The greatest artillery density was in the 11th Guards Army, where it was 212 guns and mortars per kilometer of front. Along the sectors of the armies' corps group's main attacks the artillery densities reached a maximum of 276-306 guns and mortars per kilometer of front in the 5th Army's 72nd and 65th rifle corps.

In the Second Belorussian Front the average artillery densities along the breakthrough sector reached 181 guns and mortars per kilometer of front. In some of the 49th Army's corps the artillery densities along the axes of the main attacks reached a maximum of 184-192 guns and mortars per kilometer of front. 50 percent of all the *front's* artillery was concentrated along the breakthrough sector.

Table 17. The Distribution of Artillery Reinforcements Among the Armies of the First Baltic, Third, Second and First Belorussian Fronts' Shock Groups

First Baltic Front			Third Belorussian Front		
6th Guards Army	**43rd Army**	**39th Army**	**5th Army**	**11th Guards Army**	**31st Army**
21st Breakthrough Artillery Div	28th Cannon Artillery Bde (8th Cannon Artillery Div)	54th Gds Mortar Rgt	4th Gds Cannon Artillery Div	5th Breakthrough Artillery Corps (2nd Gds and 20th breakthrough artillery divs, 7th Gds Mortar Div)	83rd Gds Howitzer Rgt, 392nd and 570th corps artillery rgts
26th and 27th cannon artillery bdes (8th Cannon Artillery Div)	31st Mortar Bde		3rd Gds Breakthrough Artillery Div	117th High-Caliber Howitzer Bde	43rd Anti-Tank Artillery Bde
4th Cannon Artillery Bde	376th, 480th, 1224th howitzer rgts		119th High-Caliber Howitzer Bde	523rd, 1093rd, 1165th corps artillery rgts	14th Gds Cannon Artillery Bde, 4th Gds Cannon Artillery Div
64th and 283rd howitzer rgts	17th Anti-Tank Artillery Bde		16th Gds Anti-Tank Artillery Bde	226th, 245th, 316th, 402nd, and 406th high-power artillery divs	
38th Gds Corps Artillery Rgt	17th Mortar Bde, 2nd Gds Mortar Div		9th Gds Mortar Bde	1st Gds Anti-Tank Artillery Bde	
408th Mortar Rgt	34th and 39th gds mortar rgts		95th and 326th gds mortar rgts	42nd, 317th and 67th Gds mortar rgts	
45th Anti-Tank Artillery Rgt					

Second Belorussian Front		First Belorussian Front		
49th Army	**3rd Army**	**48th Army**	**65th Army**	**28th Army**
142nd, 143rd and 144th cannon artillery rgts	122nd and 124th high-caliber artillery bdes	22nd Breakthrough Artillery Div	26th Breakthrough Artillery Div	4th Breakthrough Artillery Corps
31st Heavy Howitzer Bde	35th Gds Mortar Bde	6th and 84th gds mortar rgts	30th Gds, 147th and 157th cannon artillery bdes	377th Cannon Artillery Rgt

Second Belorussian Front		First Belorussian Front		
49th Army	**3rd Army**	**48th Army**	**65th Army**	**28th Army**
32nd Gds Heavy Howitzer Bde	295th and 1091st cannon artillery rgts	68th Cannon Artillery Bde	315th and 317th high caliber artillery divs	62nd and 316th gds mortar rgts
19th Mortar Bde	120th, 1071st and 1311th anti-tank artillery rgts		4th Corps Artillery Bde	3rd Corps Artillery Bde
2nd Corps Artillery Bde	286th Mortar Rgt		22nd and 23rd gds mortar bdes, 5th Gds Mortar Div	
41st, 517th and 557th corps artillery rgts	41st and 44th anti-tank artillery bdes		3rd Gds Anti-Tank Artillery Bde	
16th, 49th, 55th, 56th, 81st, 85th, 331st, 1231st, and 472nd howitzer rgts	16th Gds Mortar Bde, 5th Gds Mortar Div		43rd, 92nd and 311th gds mortar rgts	
540th and 544th mortar rgts	37th, 56th, 94th, and 313th Gds mortar rgts			
322nd High-Power Artillery Div	44th Cannon Artillery Bde			
5th, 13th and 27th anti-tank artillery bdes, 4th Gds Mortar Bde, 29th, 77th, 100th, 307th, and 325th				
325th gds mortar rgts				

In the First Belorussian Front the right-wing armies had concentrated 60 percent of all their artillery along their breakthrough sectors. This enabled us to create the following artillery densities: 182 guns and mortars along the northern sector, and 220.7 guns and mortars along the southern sector, for an average of 204.4 guns and mortars along the breakthrough sectors.

Thus from 50 to 78 percent of the artillery available to the *fronts* was concentrated along the breakthrough sectors of the *fronts'* main groups of forces. The artillery densities along the *fronts'* breakthrough sectors helped to achieve an overwhelming superiority over the enemy and were sufficient for the successful breakthrough of the enemy's previously-prepared defense.

The artillery grouping within the *fronts* is shown in table 18.

Table 18. Artillery Dispositions

First Baltic Front

There were created in both armies of the *front's* main group of forces army, corps, divisional, and regimental artillery groups.

In the 6th Guards Army the army long-range artillery group consisted of the 4th Cannon-Artillery Brigade, the 8th Cannon-Artillery Division's 26th and 27th cannon-artillery brigades, and the 21st Breakthrough Artillery Division's 64th Cannon-Artillery Brigade.

In the 43rd Army, besides the army long-range artillery group (the 8th Breakthrough Artillery Division's 37th Army Cannon-Artillery Brigade and 28th Cannon-Artillery Brigade), an army group of guards mortars (17th Mortar Brigade) was created as well.

The corps artillery groups consisted of units of howitzer and anti-tank artillery, as well as of guards mortar and mortar units. The strength of the corps artillery groups varied from five to 12 battalions.

In each rifle division of the armies' first-echelon corps, breakthrough artillery groups were created. On the average, they consisted of one or two artillery regiments and either anti-tank artillery or guards mortar elements. However, several of these groups were too weak. For example, the artillery groups of the 22nd Guards Rifle Corps' 51st Rifle Division and the 60th Rifle Corps 235th Rifle Division had only one anti-tank artillery regiment each; the 1st Rifle Corps' 306th and 179th rifle divisions disposed of one or two battalions from guards mortar regiments, while the 60th Rifle Corps' 234th Rifle Division did not have an artillery group.

The rifle regiments' infantry-support artillery groups were created, consisting of from one to 4-5 battalions. Besides this, each rifle battalion had an artillery or mortar battalion attached to it.

Third Belorussian Front

In the greater part of the *front's* armies army artillery groups and infantry support groups were created in the rifle regiments, while the corps and divisions did not have artillery groups.

For example, in the 39th Army an army artillery group (139th Army Cannon-Artillery Brigade) was created. The remaining artillery was employed for organizing infantry-support groups in the rifle regiments. Due to a shortage of artillery in the corps and divisions, no artillery groups were created there.

In the 5th Army several army artillery groups were created: a long-range group (4th Breakthrough Artillery Division, the 3rd Guards Breakthrough Artillery Division's 22nd Guards Cannon-Artillery Brigade, and the 15th Army Cannon-Artillery Brigade); a destruction group (the 3rd Guards Breakthrough Artillery Division's 107th Cannon-Artillery Brigade, and the 119th High-Power Howitzer Brigade); a breakthrough group (the 3rd Guards Breakthrough Artillery Division's 99th Heavy Howitzer Brigade, 8th Guards Howitzer Brigade, 7th Guards Light Artillery Brigade, and the 43rd Mortar Brigade), and; a rocket-propelled artillery group (9th Guards Mortar Brigade, the 95th and 326th guards mortar regiments). Corps and divisional artillery groups were not created in the 5th Army.

The actual corps groups were the subgroups of the army breakthrough artillery group, which were predominantly controlled by the corps artillery commanders.

The rifle regiments' infantry-support artillery groups were created at the expense of the 184th and 338th rifle divisions' authorized artillery, and the 16th Guards Anti-Tank Artillery Brigade.

In the 31st Army an army artillery group (the 392nd Breakthrough Artillery Corps' 14th Guards and 140th army cannon artillery brigades) was created. Corps and divisional artillery groups were not created. There were infantry-support artillery groups in the rifle regiments.

In the 11th Guards Army an army artillery group (the 2nd Guards Breakthrough Artillery Division's 16th Guards and 114th cannon artillery brigades, the 20th Breakthrough Artillery Division's 53rd Cannon-Artillery Brigade, the 149th Army Cannon-Artillery Brigade, the 523rd, 1093rd and 1165th corps artillery regiments, and the 402nd and 406th high-power artillery divisions), as well an army group of guards mortars (the 7th Guards Mortar Division's 11th and 24th mortar brigades, and the 67th, 42nd and 317th guards mortar regiments). Corps breakthrough artillery groups, which were divided into subgroups according to the number of first-echelon divisions, were created in the rifle corps. Powerful infantry-support groups, with subgroups for the rifle battalions and rifle regiments, were created. On the average, the strength of the subgroups was as follows: two battalions for a battalion, an artillery regiment for a regiment. 185 guns, ranging from 45mm to 203mm, were deployed along the breakthrough sector for firing over open sight, in order to destroy targets along the enemy's forward defense line.

Second Belorussian Front

The following army artillery groups were created in the 49th Army: long-range, destruction, and rocket-propelled artillery.

The long-range army artillery group included the 142nd, 143rd and 144th cannon-artillery brigades, the 2nd Corps Artillery Brigade, the 41st, 517th and 557th corps artillery regiments. The groups were divided into two subgroups—the 81st and 70th rifle corps.

The army's destruction artillery group consisted of the 32nd High-Power Artillery Brigade and the 332nd Large-Caliber Artillery Division.

The army rocket-propelled artillery group consisted of the 4th Guards Mortar Brigade, the 29th, 100th, 307th and the 325th guards mortar regiments. The group was divided into subgroups—the 81st, 70th and 62nd rifle corps.

Corps artillery groups were created in the rifle corps, which mainly included howitzer reinforcement units and anti-tank artillery. The strength of the corps artillery groups varied from two to seven battalions.

The divisional artillery groups in the rifle divisions consisted of these divisions' authorized artillery regiments and anti-tank artillery. In some cases, howitzer reinforcement artillery was included in these groups.

Regimental artillery groups were very weak. These consisted of only those guns mounted for firing over open sights and the rifle battalions' authorized 82mm mortars.

First Belorussian Front

Several army artillery groups were created in all the armies.

For example, the following army artillery groups were created: a long-range army artillery group (44th Cannon-Artillery Brigade, 295th and 1091st cannon-artillery regiments); an army destruction artillery group (122nd and 124th heavy-caliber howitzer brigades), and; an army group of guards mortars (16th Guards Mortar Brigade, the 37th, 56th, 94th and 313th guards mortar regiments).

In the 65th Army the following also existed: a long-range army artillery group (30th Guards, and the 147th and 157th cannon-artillery brigades); an army artillery destruction group (315th and 317th high-caliber artillery divisions), and; an army group of guards mortars (43rd, 92nd and 311th guards mortar regiments).

In the 28th Army there was a long-range army artillery group (24th and 41st cannon-artillery regiments); and army destruction artillery group (100th and 104th high-powered howitzer brigades, and the 4th Artillery Corps' 26th and 89th heavy howitzer brigades), and; an army breakthrough artillery group, consisting of the 4th Breakthrough Artillery Corps, except those brigades which formed a part of the preceding groups. Groups of guards mortars were not created in the army.

In the 48th Army there were only two army artillery groups—a long-range group (68th Cannon-Artillery Brigade), and a group of guards mortars (6th and 84th guards mortar regiments).

In the 65th Army's 18th Rifle Corps—the 26th Breakthrough Artillery Division's 56th Cannon-Artillery Brigade, and the 4th Corps Artillery Brigade; in the 28th Army's 123rd Rifle Corps—the 3rd Corps Artillery Brigade and the 377th Cannon-Artillery Regiment. Breakthrough artillery groups were also created in the 48th Army's 42nd Rifle Corps, using weapons from the 22nd Breakthrough Artillery Division.

In all the armies' rifle divisions there were created, as a rule, infantry-support artillery groups according to the number of first-echelon regiments, by using the divisions' authorized artillery. These groups, while they were considered divisional groups, were actually regimental artillery groups. In some cases, divisional groups were created for firing over open sights, which were divided into subgroups according to the number of first-echelon regiments.

In those rifle regiments where there were no divisional groups, artillery groups were usually created from the authorized mortars and from a group of guns deployed for firing over open sights. In general, depending on the number of identified targets, from 15 to 20 guns were allotted for firing over open sights per kilometer of the breakthrough sector.

At the center of the artillery grouping in the First Baltic, Third, Second and First Belorussian fronts' armies, corps and divisions, as can be seen, lay the idea of turning over the artillery to the commanders of the rifle corps, divisions, regiments, and battalions, with the help of which they could exert an influence on the course of the battle by their formations, units and subunits. The artillery groups created in the armies, corps, divisions, and regiments, although they had the old name of long-range, destruction, breakthrough, and infantry-support, in terms of their strength, employment and means of control, in many ways approached general designation groups. However, questions of the number of artillery groups, the duration of their existence, and their qualitative composition had not yet been fully resolved.

Characteristic of the artillery's grouping in the Third and First Belorussian fronts was the fact that the artillery groups (long-range, destruction, breakthrough, and guards mortar) were powerful and numerous, while the regimental infantry support groups were very weak. As concerns the corps and divisional artillery groups, in a number of armies they were either very weak or were not created at all.

The artillery grouping in the armies of the First Baltic and Second Belorussian fronts was more expedient, although divisional and regimental groups were weak here.

The planning of the artillery's employment in the *fronts* was carried out in the following fashion (see table 19).

In the First Baltic Front the *front's* artillery staff drew up three documents: a plan for the operation's artillery support; instructions for the artillery's support of the operation, and; a schedule for the artillery offensive.

In these documents, the commander of the *front's* artillery established the duration of the artillery preparation at two hours and 15 minutes (one hour and 30 minutes for destruction and 45 minutes for suppression), and infantry and tank support through a rolling barrage in conjunction with the consecutive concentration of fire—30 minutes. The first fire onslaught against the enemy's batteries was planned for ten minutes after the beginning of the artillery preparation. Following the fire onslaught of 50 minutes, the fire observation by volleys was planned. During the course of the destruction period's following 20 minutes the mortars would continue to carry out their previous task, while the guns allotted for firing over open sights, opened passages in the barbed wire obstacles, destroying machine guns, individual rifle trenches, anti-tank weapons, and observation posts to a depth of up to one kilometer. The infantry-support artillery groups and breakthrough groups would suppress the enemy's firing weapons and defensive structures to a depth of 1-4 kilometers. When the guns allotted for firing over open sights opened fire, the long-range artillery groups would carry out a second against the enemy's batteries.

Table 19. The Organization of the Artillery Offensive in the *Fronts*, According to the Plans Drawn Up by the Start of the Belorussian Operation

Front, Date	Artillery Preparation (in minutes)							
	10	20	30	40	50	60	70	80
1st Baltic, 23 June 1944	Two hours and 15 mins of artillery preparation Destruction-90 mins							
3rd Belorussian, 23 June 1944	Two hours and 20 minutes of artillery preparation Fire Onslaught, 5 mins Destruction—90 mins							
2nd Belorussian, 23 June 1944	Two hours of artillery preparation Onslaught Fire–10 mins Destruction—65 mins Fire Onslaught—5 mins False Shift of Fire—10 mins							
1st Belorussian (3rd and 48th armies), 24 June	Two hours and 20 minutes of artillery preparation Fire Onslaught, 15 mins Destruction—90 mins							

Front, Date	Artillery Preparation (in minutes)							
	90	100	110	120	130	140	150	Artillery Support for the Attack
1st Baltic, 23 June 1944		Suppression Period –45 mins						Rolling Barrage with Successive Concentration of Fire
	Against Targets on the Front Line	Against Targets in the second trench to a depth of 2 km	Against Targets on the Front Line to a Depth of 2 km					Rolling Barrage with Successive Concentration of Fire
3rd Belorussian, 23 June 1944		Suppression —45 mins						Rolling Barrage with Successive Concentration of Fire
2nd Belorussian, 23 June 1944		Suppression and Destruction						Rolling Barrage with Successive Concentration of Fire
	Fire Onslaught— 5 mins	Deliberate Fire	Fire Onslaught-10 mins					
	Successive Fire Onslaught							
1st Belorussian (3rd and 48th armies), 24 June 1944	Fire Onslaught— 20 mins with a density of 25%	50%	75%	100%				Fire Onslaught with Consecutive Concentration of Fire

In the first five minutes of the suppression period, all of the artillery and mortars, with the exception of the long-range groups' artillery, were to conduct observation fire against the enemy's weapons and personnel in the first and second trenches. Long-range groups were to carry out fire observation against the enemy's batteries. M-13[1] rocket-propelled artillery launchers were to launch salvos against strong points along the front line. During the next ten minutes the shifting of the entire artillery's fire was planned to the second trench to a depth of up to two kilometers. During the final 30 minutes of the suppression period all of the artillery and mortars, except for the artillery in the long-range groups, were supposed to conduct observation fire against the first and second trenches and the most important targets in the depth up to two kilometers. The long-range groups' artillery, once the infantry's movement from their jumping-off point into the attack has begun, was to then suppress the enemy's personnel and weapons to a depth of up to two kilometers.

The support for the attack by a rolling barrage was called for up to the infantry's seizing the second line of trenches, in the course of 30 minutes. The long-range artillery group, once the attack

---

1 Editor's note. The M-13 was a 132mm rocket used in Soviet multiple rocket artillery units. These were grouped together as guards mortar units.

had begun, was to carry out a fire onslaught against the enemy's batteries, after which it was to carry out fire observation by battery volleys.

On the whole, the planning of the artillery offensive by the staff of the *front's* artillery was carried out in a timely and correct fashion.

However, there were shortcomings. For example, the schedule for the artillery offensive required the conduct of destructive fire with 82mm and 120mm mortars, in order to destroy enemy personnel in the trenches and communications trenches. This could make it difficult to correct the artillery's destructive fire and lower its effectiveness, especially in the final 20 minutes, when the guns were firing over open sights.

The first fire onslaught against the enemy's batteries was planned for just ten minutes after the start of the artillery preparation. This was dangerous, because the enemy could use this time and open fire with his own artillery with impunity and inflict heavy losses on our forces occupying their jumping-off positions for the offensive.

During the suppression period the fire onslaughts were not allotted according to time. The suppression of the enemy's fire system, mainly to a depth of only two kilometers, cannot be viewed as sufficient.

The support of the attack by a fire onslaught was planned to a very shallow depth.

Besides this, it should be noted that in planning the expenditure of ammunition for the artillery preparation, the *front's* artillery staff by no means took full advantage of the artillery's capabilities allowed for by the technical regime of fire.

The 6th Guards Army's artillery staff drew up a plan for the artillery support for the commitment of the 1st Tank Corps—the *front's* mobile group—into the breach. In accordance with the plan, fire sectors along six lines were prepared to a depth of ten kilometers, counting from the commitment line. Artillery officers were allotted to the tank corps for summoning and correcting the artillery's fire. Three battalions from the army long-range artillery group (one battalion apiece from the 4th, 26th and 27th cannon-artillery brigades) were brought in to support the 1st Tank Corps' commitment into the breach. The decision to bring in the army's long-range artillery group for this purpose should be viewed as expedient. However, the allotment of three battalions from three different brigades made control more difficult and hampered the organization of cooperation.

In the Third Belorussian Front, in the *front's* artillery staff, two planning documents were drawn up: instructions on planning the *front's* artillery offensive, and the schedule for the artillery offensive.

The duration of the artillery preparation was established at two hours and 20 minutes, of which five minutes were set aside for a fire onslaught against the enemy's personnel and weapons throughout the entire tactical defensive depth, against his headquarters, communications centers, artillery and mortar batteries; 90 minutes for the destruction period, during the course of which control of adjustment fire was planned.

During the first 70 minutes of this period the infantry-support and breakthrough artillery groups were to seek to destroy the enemy's trenches, communications trenches, and earth and timber pillboxes. Army long-range artillery groups had the task of suppressing the enemy's active batteries and carrying out the fire observation of the remainder, and destroying the enemy's durable defensive structures. In the following 20 minutes the guns, set aside for firing over open sights were to open up, which besides their tasks of destroying were designated for making gaps in the barbed-wire entanglements. The army long-range artillery groups were to carry out the repeat suppression of the enemy's batteries. M-13 rocket-propelled artillery platforms had the task of suppressing the enemy's active mortar and rocket-propelled batteries.

The artillery preparation was to conclude with the suppression of the enemy's front line and immediate depth by deliberate fire. During this period the mortars and guns, allotted for firing over open sights, as well as the infantry-support and breakthrough artillery groups were to suppress the enemy's personnel in the trenches, communications trenches and shelters along the front line to a depth of 200-500 meters. Army artillery groups had the task of suppressing with their fire the most important enemy targets. From minus five minutes to plus five minutes these groups would shift their fire among the enemy's batteries for the purpose of suppressing them before the beginning and at the start of the attack. Rocket-propelled mortars had the task, from minus 20 to minus five minutes to suppress the enemy's personnel through a fire onslaught in his main strong points.

The attack's artillery support was planned during the course of an hour by a barrage in conjunction with a rolling concentration of fire to a depth of 1.5-2 kilometers. The artillery support was to be carried out by the fire of mortars and guns deployed for firing over open sights, and by infantry-support and breakthrough artillery groups. Army long-range artillery groups had the task of suppressing the enemy's active batteries.

The duration of the artillery's accompanying fire during the fighting in the depth of the enemy's defense, according to time, was not determined, and the artillery's tasks for this period were laid down in general terms.

In the 5th Army a plan for supporting the commitment of the *front's* mobile group into the breach was drawn up. Special artillery groups were to be created for supporting the commitment of the 3rd Guards Mechanized and 3rd Guards Cavalry corps into the breach.

Table 20. Artillery Support for the Commitment of the Third Belorussian Front's Mobile Group into the Breach

Formation	Change to Artillery Support for the Commitment of the Third Belorussian Front's Mobile Group into the Breach
3rd Guards Mechanized Corps	1 cannon-artillery bde
	2 light artillery rgts
	1 howitzer rgt
3rd Guards Cavalry Corps	1 cannon-artillery bde
	2 howitzer rgts

In the plan for supporting the commitment of the *front's* mobile group into the breach, concrete tasks were assigned to the artillery, and an artillery firing chart was drawn up. Besides this, the plan pointed out the line of commitment, the routes the mobile group would take in being committed into the breach, the areas of firing positions of the artillery supporting the commitment, and also the order and timetable for occupying the firing positions.

In the Second Belorussian Front the *front's* artillery staff drew up two planning documents: instructions on planning and conducting the artillery offensive and a schedule for the 49th Army's artillery preparation.

The duration of the artillery preparation was established at two hours. It was planned to begin the artillery preparation with a 10-minute artillery fire onslaught, with a half of its density along the entire depth of the enemy's defense. It was planned to conduct a fire onslaught against the enemy's artillery and mortar batteries, beginning with the start of the artillery preparation, for a period of five minutes. A period of destruction would then ensue for a period of 65 minutes. During the final 15 minutes of the destruction period those guns deployed for firing over open sights were to participate. Then for five minutes it was planned to launch a fire onslaught against the enemy's first and second trenches and communications trenches. After the fire onslaught a false shift of fire was to take place against the third and fourth trenches for ten minutes. During this time the army artillery group was to fire against headquarters, communications centers and the enemy reserves.

50 percent of the artillery was to take part in the shift of fire, while the remaining artillery was to be ready to open fire on the front line.

Then the artillery was to carry out a fire onslaught for five minutes against the enemy's first and second trenches, his artillery and mortar batteries and observation posts.

Following this fire onslaught, deliberate fire was to be waged for 15 minutes against the first fire onslaught's targets, and the guns allotted for firing over open sights were to fire on the enemy's firing points, which had been discovered after the false shift of fire.

The artillery preparation was to conclude with a 10-minute fire onslaught against the first and second trenches until our infantry's arrival.

Support for the attack was planned to the depth of the fourth trench by a barrage and then by the successive concentration of fire.

In the First Belorussian Front the *front* artillery staff drew up the following planning documents: instructions on employing the artillery in an offensive operation, and instructions on organizing and conducting a double rolling barrage, and a schedule for the artillery preparation.

The duration of the artillery preparation was established at two hours and five minutes. The artillery preparation was to begin with a 15-minute fire onslaught along the enemy's entire defense. Then for 90 minutes the destruction of revealed targets and the suppression of the enemy's artillery and mortar batteries were to take place. The artillery preparation would conclude with a 20-minute fire onslaught against the front line and the tactical depth of the enemy's defense, with a varying density of fire: in the first five minutes the fire density was set at 25 percent, in the course of the second five minutes—at 50 percent, in the course of the third five minutes—at 75 percent, and, in the last five minutes—at 100 percent.

In the armies plans for supporting the commitment of the *front's* mobile groups into the breach were drawn up.

Table 21. Artillery Support for the Commitment of the First Belorussian Front's Commitment of its Mobile Groups into the Breach

Mobile Group	Artillery Designated for Supporting the Mobile Group's Commitment into the Breach
1st Don Tank Corps	2 cannon-artillery bdes
	1 anti-tank artillery bde
The *front's* cavalry-mechanized group	2 cannon-artillery bdes
	6 cannon-artillery rgts
	1 howitzer rgt
	2 light artillery rgts
	2 mortar rgts

In order to support the commitment of the mobile groups into the breach, the assigned artillery prepared a concentrated fire: in the 65th Army against the sectors on three lines to an overall depth of up to three kilometers; in the 28th Army against the sectors along several lines to an overall depth of up to five kilometers.

In the army artillery staffs the expenditure of ammunition on the artillery preparation was planned significantly lower than the norms allowed for by the fire's technical regime. Only 50 percent of the artillery's fire capabilities were used.

The artillery's coordination with the infantry and tanks was mainly organized by means of the joint work of the artillery commanders with the combined-arms and tanks commanders on the ground. During the preparatory period the tasks of the artillery, infantry and tanks in subunits,

units, combined-arms formations and operational field forces were nailed down by means of joint reconnaissance. During this period the responsible parties on the ground cleared up the following: the objective, zone (axis) of the formation's (unit's, subunit's) offensive; the objects of the infantry's and tanks' attacks and the artillery's task in supporting these efforts; targets to be suppressed by the artillery and aviation during the offensive; the order in which these tasks were to be performed by the artillery; the order and means of communications, as well as cooperation signals.

The combined-arms formations, as well as units and elements, received charts of targets from the artillery groups, units and elements supporting them. This circumstance, to a significant degree, eased mutual orientation and the laying out of tasks for the artillery.

Control of the artillery was centralized and was to be carried out through the command and observation post and through the headquarters.

The commanders of the *fronts'* artillery, due to the absence of wire communications at their disposal, had wire communications with the commanders of the armies' artillery and their headquarters: in the Third Belorussian Front—along the combined-arms lines, and in the First Belorussian Front—partially along combined-arms lines and partially along lines established by the commanders of the armies' artillery. Aside from this, the artillery commanders in the Third and First Belorussian fronts had communications with the commanders of the armies' artillery and the artillery commanders of the reinforcement formations through the assistance of communications officers. Radio communications for the commanders of the *fronts'* artillery was organized independently.

Communications in the First Baltic and Second Belorussian fronts was organized according to this same plan, as well as in the rifle corps and divisions.

Despite the existing shortcomings, chiefly in the availability of communications equipment, artillery control at all levels was organized correctly. Thus the commanders of the artillery formations (units) and artillery groups could successfully carry out the centralized direction of fire and maneuver their artillery not only during the preparatory phase, but in the course of the operation.

The availability of ammunition by the start of the operation, on the whole, enabled us to resolve the assigned tasks, but their uneven distribution was not always conditioned by the concrete demands of the situation (see table 22).

Table 22. The *Fronts'* Provisioning with Ammunition by the Start of the Operation (In Combat Loads)

Ammunition	1st Baltic	3rd Belorussian	2nd Belorussian[1]	1st Belorussian[2]
82mm mortar	4.1	2.6	3.1	2.8
120mm mortar	5.4	3.9	2.6	3.3
76mm gun (regimental artillery)	3.4	3.0	2.8	2.5
76mm gun (divisional artillery)	3.0	2.8	2.2	2.5
122mm howitzer	5.3	3.2	2.4	2.5
122mm gun	5.0	3.0	2.6	3.8
152mm howitzer	6.1	8.3	4.3	7.7
152mm gun-howitzer	5.1	3.4	2.2	3.8
203mm howitzer	7.0	3.0	–	6.9

Notes
1 In the 49th Army.
2 In the *front's* right-wing armies.

By the start of the operation the ammunition supply in the First Baltic Front more than covered the demands of the operation's first and second stages. Shell delivery in the armies was planned at 0.2 combat loads a day from the second through the eighth day of the operation.

In the Third Belorussian Front the provisioning of the armies of the *front's* main groups with shells was, in general, sufficient, although uneven (39th and 31st armies).

The provision of shells in the Second Belorussian Front was quite sufficient.

The provision of shells was sufficient, although uneven, within the armies of the First Belorussian Front's main groups.

Thus the principle of massing along the axis of the main blow lay at the basis of employing the artillery. Of the overall amount of the *fronts'* artillery the following numbers were concentrated along the breakthrough sectors: in the First Baltic Front—78 percent, in the Third Belorussian Front—65 percent, in the Second Belorussian Front—50 percent, and, in the First Belorussian Front—60 percent. Thus high artillery densities were to be created along the main axes, which would ensure the suppression of the enemy's defense in a short time.

The largest artillery regroupings during the operation's preparatory period took place in the *fronts*. In the armies the movement of artillery was carried out over comparatively short distances. The artillery's regrouping and concentration was carried out quickly (8-16 days). The regrouping's secrecy and the concentration of enormous masses of artillery was one of the most important factors that facilitated the achievement of operational surprise.

The documents that planned the artillery's activities in the operation were usually "instructions for employing artillery" and a "schedule for the artillery offensive." In the first document the timetables and order for carrying out a number of preparatory measures were indicated, and initial data were also given for planning the artillery offensive. The schedule of the artillery offensive (see table 19) guaranteed the unity of the organization and duration of the artillery preparation, the unity of means of supporting the attack, and the overall character of the artillery's activities in the depth of the enemy's defense.

In the operation under review, it is worth nothing that the artillery preparation was nearly the same in its duration in the various *fronts*, but there were significant differences in its organization. In the First and Second Belorussian fronts the artillery preparation began with fire onslaughts, after which the fire onslaughts alternated with periods of deliberate fire. In the Third Belorussian Front the artillery preparation began with a fire onslaught and was then followed by deliberate fire. In the First Baltic Front, during the period of the artillery preparation, fire onslaughts were employed on for suppressing the enemy's artillery and mortars, and only fire for destruction was conducted against his defense, or deliberate fire for suppression purposes.

Such a variety in the planning of the artillery preparation was conditioned not only by differences in the situation's conditions in the sector of one or the other *front*, but to a significant degree by the lack of unity in views on the role of fire onslaughts during the artillery preparation.

Among the shortcomings in planning the artillery's employment that should be noted are: the insufficient depth of the planned suppression of the enemy's defense during the artillery preparation (Third Belorussian Front), the absence of plans for artillery reconnaissance in the *fronts*, and the not always precise issuing of concrete tasks to the armies' artillery staffs for reconnaissance.

It should be noted that the expenditure of shells during the artillery preparation in all the *fronts* was planned at a lower rate than that allowed for by the fire regime. This is explained by the fact that during the artillery preparation deliberate fire was mostly conducted, which is why the artillery could not take advantage of its full range of possibilities (see table 23).

In the First Belorussian Front, for the first time in the Great Patriotic War a double rolling barrage was planned on an operational scale for supporting the infantry and tank attack in conjunction with consecutive concentrations of fire.

The problem of artillery support for the *fronts*' mobile groups' commitment into the breach was not fully resolved. In the given operation concrete plans for the artillery support of the mobile groups into the breach were compiled in the headquarters of those armies, in the sectors of which it was planned to commit these groups. The *fronts*' artillery staffs limited themselves to issuing general instructions as to who was assigned this task and they sometimes defined what kind of artillery weapons should be employed to strengthen the *front's* mobile group.

Table 23. The Percentage of Artillery Capabilities Employed in the First Baltic and First Belorussian Fronts During the Artillery Preparation

Guns	1st Baltic Front, 23 June 1944) (6th Guards and 48th armies)			1st Belorussian Front (24 June 1944) (3rd Army)		
	Planned Expenditure	Possible Expenditure	% of Expenditure to Possible Norm	Planned Expenditure	Possible Expenditure	% of Expenditure to Possible Norm
76mm (regimental artillery)	110	340	32	72	340	21
76mm (divisional artillery)	80	210	38	154	210	73
122mm	75	160	47	88	160	55
152mm gun-howitzer	36	85	42	76	85	89
203mm	35	50	70	34	50	68

Guns	1st Belorussian Front (24 June 1944)					
	48th Army			65th Army		
	Planned Expenditure	Possible Expenditure	% of Expenditure to Possible Norm	Planned Expenditure	Possible Expenditure	% of Expenditure to Possible Norm
76mm (regimental artillery)	–	–	–	170	340	50
76mm (divisional artillery)	180	210	86	140	210	66
122mm	130	160	81	88	160	55
152mm gun-howitzer	100	85	117	40	85	47
203mm	–	–	–	50	50	100

| Guns | 1st Belorussian Front (24 June 1944) | | |
| | (28th Army) | | |
	Planned Expenditure	Possible Expenditure	% of Expenditure to Possible Norm
76mm (regimental artillery)	70	340	21
76mm (divisional artillery)	125	210	59
122mm	110	160	69
152mm gun-howitzer	63	85	75
203mm	50	50	100

Planning the Combat Employment of Armored and Mechanized Forces

By the start of the Belorussian operation the First Baltic, Third, Second and First Belorussian fronts included as the *fronts'* and armies' mobile groups the following: one tank army consisting of two tank corps, two cavalry-mechanized groups, each consisting of a mechanized and a cavalry corps, and four independent tank corps.[2] Aside from this, among the armies of the above-enumerated *fronts*, the following units were included in the capacity of tank and self-propelled artillery groups for infantry support: 13 independent tank brigades, one independent self-propelled artillery brigade, 23 independent tank regiments, 46 independent self-propelled artillery regiments, and nine independent self-propelled artillery battalions (see table 24).

In all, by the start of the Belorussian operation there were a hitherto unsurpassed number of combat vehicles in the four *fronts*, namely 4,070 tanks and self-propelled artillery pieces. Among this amount were 2,560 combat tanks and 1,510 self-propelled artillery pieces. During the course of the operation, the overall number of tanks and self-propelled artillery pieces rose to more than 6,000.[3]

The German-Fascist troops occupying the Belorussian salient had 932 combat vehicles (tanks and assault guns).

Thus our forces began the Belorussian operation, having more than a four-to-one superiority over the enemy in tanks and self-propelled guns.

The overall superiority in the *fronts* in tanks and self-propelled guns over the enemy is shown by the following data (table 25).

Table 24. Armored and Mechanized Forces as Part of the *Fronts* at the Start of the Belorussian Operation

1st Baltic Front	3rd Belorussian Front	2nd Belorussian Front	1st Belorussian Front
1st Tank Corps 46th Mechanized Bde, 272nd Amphibious Car Bn (36 amphibious cars)	5th Guards Tank Army Cavalry-Mechanized Group—3rd Gds Mechanized Corps and 3rd Gds Cavalry Corps 2nd Gds Tank Corps—11th Gds Army's mobile group	4 tank bdes 1 tank rgt 9 heavy self-propelled gun and self-propelled gun rgts	9th Tank Corps—3rd Army's mobile group; 1st Gds Tank Corps—65th Army's mobile group; Cavalry-Mechanized Group—1st Mechanized Corps, 4th Gds Cavalry Corps—the *front's* mobile group

2   In the First Belorussian Front only the mobile groups of the *front's* right wing are included.
3   In January 1944 the First, Second and Third Ukrainian fronts' armored and mechanized forces had 3,072 combat vehicles.

1st Baltic Front	3rd Belorussian Front	2nd Belorussian Front	1st Belorussian Front
Infantry-Support Tanks: 6th Gds Army—2 tank bdes, 1 heavy tank rgt, 2 heavy self-propelled gun rgts, 1 flamethrower tank rgt, 1 tank minesweeper rgt	Infantry-Support Tanks: 39th Army—1 tank bde, 2 self-propelled gun rgts; 5th Army—2 tank bdes, 6 self-propelled gun rgts, 1 tank flame-thrower rgt, 1 tank minesweeper rgt	Of these: 49th Army—2 tank bdes, 1 tank rgt, 4 self-propelled gun rgts, 2 heavy self-propelled gun rgts	Infantry-Support Tanks: 3rd Army—3 tank rgts, 1 heavy self-propelled gun rgt, 5 self-propelled gun rgts, 1 flame-thrower tank rgt, 1 tank mine-sweeper rgt, 1 self-propelled gun bde
43rd Army—2 tank bdes, 1 tank rgt, 2 heavy self-propelled gun rgts	11th Gds Army—1 tank bde, 2 heavy tank rgts, 3 heavy self-propelled gun rgts, 9 self-propelled gun battalions, 1 heavy flamethrower tank rgt, 1 tank minesweeper rgt	*Front* Mobile Group 2 tank bdes, 1 self-propelled gun rgt 50th Army—2 self-propelled gun rgts, 42 self-propelled guns	48th Army—1 tank rgt, 1 heavy tank rgt, 3 self-propelled gun rgts, 1 heavy self-propelled gun rgt
4th Shock Army—1 tank bn		Total for the *front*—205 tanks and 71 self-propelled guns	
Total Infantry-Support Tanks in *Front*: 236 tanks and 234 self-propelled guns Total Combat Vehicles—319	31st Army—1 tank bde, 1 heavy self-propelled gun rgt, 3 self-propelled gun rgts	Total Combat Vehicles—	65th Army—1 tank rgt, 2 heavy self-propelled gun rgts, 2 self-propelled gun rgts
	Total Infantry-Support Tanks in *Front*: 276 tanks and 436 self-propelled guns		28th Army—1 tank rgt, 1 heavy tank rgt, 3 self-propelled gun rgts, 1 heavy self-propelled gun rgt, 1 flamethrower tank rgt, 1 independent minesweeper tank rgt
In the *Front* Mobile Group: 235 tanks and 62 self-propelled guns Total Combat Vehicles—297	Total Combat Vehicles—751 In the Mobile Group— 886 tanks and 212 self-propelled guns		

1st Baltic Front	3rd Belorussian Front	2nd Belorussian Front	1st Belorussian Front
Total in *Front*: 491 tanks and 296 self-propelled guns	Total Combat Vehicles—1,098		In the Mobile Group—630 tanks and 147 self-propelled guns Total Combat Vehicles—777
687 total combat vehicles and 43 specialized vehicles	1,162 tanks and 648 self-propelled guns 1,810 combat vehicles and 86 specialized vehicles		Total Infantry-Support Tanks in the *Front*— 172 tanks and 342 self-propelled guns Total in the *Front*—802 tanks and 495 self-propelled guns 1,297 total combat vehicles and 72 specialized vehicles
	Total combat vehicles—1,810, and 86 specialized vehicles		616 total combat vehicles and 72 specialized vehicles

Table 25. The Correlation of Tank and Self-Propelled Gun Forces

Front	Tanks and Self-Propelled Guns[1]	Enemy Tank and Assault Guns	Correlation
1st Baltic	687	130	About 5.1:1
	43		
3rd Belorussian	1,810	316	5.7:1
	86		
2nd Belorussian	276	120	2.4:1
1st Belorussian (right wing)	1,297	366	3.6:1
	72		
Total	4,070	932	4.3:1
	201		

Note
1 The combat vehicles are in the numerator, and the specialized tanks (minesweeper and flamethrower) in the denominator.

Almost all the tank and mechanized corps, which formed the *fronts'* and armies' mobile groups, as well as a large part of the formations and units comprising the tank and self-propelled infantry-support groups, were included in the Third and First Belorussian fronts. Thus, of eight tank and mechanized corps brought in to participate in the Belorussian operation, seven were in the Third and First Belorussian fronts. Of the overall number of 4,070 tanks and self-propelled guns that were in the four *fronts*, 3,107, or 76 percent of the combat vehicles were inthe Third and First Belorussian fronts.

Of these two *fronts*, the larger number of tank and mechanized formations and units, in their turn, were subordinated to the Third Belorussian Front. The *front* included four tank and mechanized corps (50 percent), 1,810 combat vehicles, or 44.4 percent of the tanks and self-propelled guns comprising the total number of combat vehicles in all four *fronts*. The First Belorussian Front, correspondingly, accounted for 37.5 percent of the tank and mechanized corps and 31.8 percent of the combat vehicles.

From this it follows that the densities of tanks and self-propelled guns were higher and the correlation of forces in the main groups' operational sectors was more favorable in the First, and particularly in the Third Belorussian fronts. In the 11th Guards Army the density of direct infantry-support tanks and self-propelled guns reached 36 combat vehicles per kilometer of front, although this was not the case along the army's entire breakthrough sector, but just along those parts, where due to terrain conditions, tank and self-propelled guns could be employed. In the *front's* remaining armies the direct infantry-support tank and self-propelled gun densities varied from 15.5 to 22 combat vehicles per kilometer along the breakthrough sector, or along those parts where combat vehicles could be employed (31st Army). In the First Belorussian Front the greatest density of direct infantry-support tanks and self-propelled guns—26 combat vehicles per kilometer of front along the breakthrough sector—was reached in the 48th Army.

The densities of tanks and self-propelled guns rose significantly in the offensive zones of those armies, where it was planned to commit the armies' and *fronts'* mobile groups into the breach. For example, in the First Baltic Front's 6th Guards Army the density of direct infantry-support tanks and self-propelled guns was to reach nine combat vehicles per kilometer of front along the entire breakthrough sector, and along the part where it proved possible to commit combat vehicles due to the terrain conditions, the density of tanks and self-propelled guns was to rise to 16.1 vehicles per kilometer of front. By taking into account the commitment of the *front's* mobile group—1st Tank Corps—into the breach, the density of tanks and self-propelled guns along the breakthrough sector would increase to 25.5 combat vehicles per kilometer of front. In the Third Belorussian Front's 11th Guards Army the densities of the tanks and self-propelled guns was to grow in connection with the commitment of the army's mobile group—2nd Guards Tank Corps—to 51.6 combat vehicles per kilometer of front along the breakthrough sector. In the same *front's* 5th Army, in connection with the commitment of the *front's* mobile group—the cavalry-mechanized group—into the breach, the density of tanks and self-propelled guns would increase to 47.7 vehicles per kilometer of front along the breakthrough sector.

In the First Belorussian Front's armies, in the sectors in which the armies' mobile groups were to be committed, the densities of tanks and self-propelled guns were to grow as follows: in the 3rd Army up to 42; in the 65th Army up to 60 combat vehicles.

If one also takes into account the planned commitment of the *fronts'* mobile groups into the breach: the 5th Guards Tank Army in the Third Belorussian Front's 11th Guards or the 5th armies' zones; the cavalry-mechanized group along the boundary between Belorussian Front's 65th and 28th armies, then the densities of tanks and self-propelled guns increase as follows:

in the 5th Army from 47.7 to 93 combat vehicles;
in the 11th Guards Army from 51.6 to 101.5 combat vehicles, and;
in the zone of the southern group of forces of the First Belorussian Front's right wing—65th and 28th armies—from 16 to 51 combat vehicles.

Such high densities along the axes of the *fronts'* main attacks were planned for the first time in the Great Patriotic War.

However, it was not only the quantitative growth of tanks and self-propelled guns that was characteristic of the operation, but also their qualitative growth. In the *fronts*, heavy tanks and heavy self-propelled guns comprised 6.5-15.5 percent of the overall number of tanks and self-propelled guns. In some armies the share of heavy combat vehicles reach 30 percent (11th and 6th guards armies), and even 40 percent (65th Army). At the same time, one should also keep in mind that our heavy IS-2[4] tanks, with a powerful 122mm gun, were the most powerful of all the tanks that took part in the Second World War. ISU-122[5] heavy self-propelled guns were created on the basis of the IS-2 and armed with the same kind of 122mm gun. Thus, given the overall favorable correlation of forces in tanks and self-propelled guns, the inclusion of new combat vehicles in our combat formations, although in small amounts, could not but have the most favorable influence on the success of our attacking troops' combat activities.

The armored and mechanized forces began to arrive to reinforce the First Baltic, Third and First Belorussian fronts from the middle of May (see table 26). The 5th Guards Tank Army's tank corps were the last to concentrate on 22 June.

67 percent of the independent tank regiments and 50 percent of the independent self-propelled artillery regiments designated for operating within the tank and self-propelled gun infantry-support groups, and 100 percent of the tank and mechanized corps, slated for operations within the *fronts'* and armies' mobile groups, arrived at the *fronts* from the Supreme High Command reserve.

---

4   Editor's note. The IS-2 was a Soviet heavy tank which entered service in 1944. One model weighed 46 tons and had a crew of four. It was armed with a 122mm gun and two 12.7mm machine guns.
5   Editor's note. The ISU was a Soviet self-propelled gun mounted on a SAU-152 chassis, which entered service in 1944. It weighed 45.5 tons and had a crew of four or five. It was armed with a 122mm gun and a 12.7mm machine gun.

The majority of the tank, mechanized and self-propelled artillery formations and units disposed of limited time for preparing for the operation. Of eight tank and mechanized corps, six had from two to six days to prepare, and only two corps had more than six days.

All the work connected with preparing the armored and mechanized forces for the forthcoming operation was conducted in a sufficiently organized manner, while especial attention was devoted to observing deception measures. Trains unloading were brought up only at night-time. Concentration areas were chosen not closer than 30-70 kilometers from the sectors where it was planned to employ the arriving formations and units. Only a restricted circle of people were informed of the arrival of new units and formations. All correspondence on these questions, even in code, was forbidden. All vehicle movement during the preparatory period for the operation was carried out only at night, with switched-off lights.

Intermediate position areas were chosen at a distance of 10-15 kilometers from the front line. The stay of units and formations in these areas, as a rule, was limited to 2-4 days. The departure areas for the tank and mechanized corps were chosen 5-7 kilometers from the front line. The departure positions for the units and formations designated for operations within the tank and self-propelled direct infantry-support groups were deployed 1-3 kilometers from the front line. Arrivals in these areas and positions were carried out only the night before the offensive.

Table 26. The Concentration of the First Baltic, Third, Second and First[6] Belorussian Fronts' Armored and Mechanized Forces

Fronts	Formations and Units Slated for Tank and Self-Propelled Gun Infantry-Support Groups	Formations and Units That Arrived at the *Front* the Supreme High Command and Were Slated for Tank and Self-Propelled Gun Infantry-Support Groups	Tank and Mechanized Formations that Arrived at the *Front* and Were Slated for Employment in the Mobile Groups
1st Baltic	1 tank bde 1 motorized bde 2 tank rgts 1 self-propelled artillery rgt 1 tank bn	Arrived at the beginning of June by rail: 3 heavy self-propelled artillery rgts 1 flamethrower tank rgt 1 minesweeper tank rgt a battalion of amphibious cars	1st Tank Corps from the Supreme High Command reserve
3rd Belorussian	5 tank bdes 4 self-propelled artillery rgts	Arriving from the middle of May to 22 June to reinforce the *front*: 2 heavy tank rgts 6 heavy self-propelled artillery rgts 5 self-propelled artillery rgts 2 flamethrower tank rgts 2 minesweeper tank rgts	5th Gds Tank Army (2nd Gds and 29th tank corps 2nd Gds Tank and 3rd Gds Mechanized corps from the Supreme High Command reserve
2nd Belorussian	4 tank bdes 1 tank rgt 2 heavy self-propelled artillery rgts 7 self-propelled artillery rgts	–	–
1st Belorussian	5 tank rgts 10 self-propelled artillery rgts	8 self-propelled artillery rgts 4 tank rgts 2 flamethrower tank rgts 2 minesweeper tank rgts	9th Tank, 1st Gds Tank and 1st Mechanized corps from the Supreme High Command reserve

6 In the First Belorussian Front, only the *front's* right-wing armies, formations and units are counted.

The masking of the concentration areas was checked from the air by reconnaissance flights and photography.

All of these measures guaranteed the achievement of surprise.

It was planned to employ the armored and mechanized forces in the following manner.

It was planned to employ the direct infantry-support tanks and self-propelled guns in the combat formations of the combined-arms formations in a multi-echelon formation. The tank minesweepers were to attack ahead, and behind them the tanks of the independent tank brigades and independent tank regiments and the self-propelled guns of the heavy self-propelled artillery regiments, along with the rifle divisions' first-echelon rifle units and elements being supported by them. The flamethrower tank regiments and light self-propelled artillery regiments were to attack with the rifle divisions' second echelons. It was planned to use the mobile groups in the following manner (see table 27).

In the Third Belorussian Front the mobile groups, which were designated for developing the success, were to be committed consecutively on the second (cavalry-mechanized group) and third (5th Guards Tank Army) days of the operation.

In the First Belorussian Front it was planned to commit into the southern group's attack zone along the *front's* right wing on the operation's first day the 1st Guards Tank Corps and behind it on the same day the cavalry-mechanized group.

Thanks to such an employment of the mobile groups, the operational density of the tanks and self-propelled guns per kilometer along the main blow increased significantly. Besides this, the consecutive commitment of the armies and *fronts'* mobile groups into the breach enabled the army and *front* commanders and the High Command to augment their efforts during the operation and in this way guarantee the operation's development at high speeds and to a great depth.

The First Belorussian Front's operational plan foresaw a two-sided envelopment of the enemy's Bobruisk group of forces by the forces of the 9th and 1st Guards tank corps, for the purpose of encircling and destroying it in conjunction with the combined-arms armies. It was planned, by an attack by General Pliev's[7] cavalry-mechanized group in the direction of Glusha, to isolate the encircled group of forces from the possible arrival of the enemy's reserves from the west. This employment of several mobile groups in an encirclement operation against a large enemy group of forces would enable us to simultaneously create both an internal and an external encirclement front. At the same time, by the time the tank corps completed the encirclement of the enemy, the cavalry-mechanized group was to already be 15-20 kilometers west of the tank corps, which was to ease the *front's* subsequent actions in eliminating the encircled enemy group of forces.

If in the given example the armies' and *front's* mobile groups were directed at simultaneously creating internal and external encirclement fronts around the enemy's Bobruisk group of forces, then while encircling the enemy's Vitebsk group of forces, which was located in the tactical defensive zone at a short distance from the front line, the mobile groups of the First Baltic and Third Belorussian fronts were directed at creating an external front. Only rifle formations, reinforced with direct infantry-support tanks, were directed toward the internal encirclement front.

It was planned to commit the army mobile groups and the *front* mobile groups, in strength up to a corps, along 2-3 routes, and *front* groups larger than a corps along four routes. The width of the commitment sector varied : for army mobile groups—from six to eight kilometers, and for *front* mobile groups—from eight to 20 kilometers.

---

7   Issa Aleksandrovich Pliev (1903-79) joined the Red Army in 1922. During the Greeat Patriotic War he commanded a cavalry division, cavalry corps and a cavalry-mechanized group in both Europe and Asia. Following the war, he commanded armies and military districts, as well as Soviet forces in Cuba during the Cuban Missile Crisis.

Table 27. The Order of the *Fronts'* and Armies' Mobile Groups' Commitment into the Breach and Their Objectives

Fronts	Mobile Group	Mobile Group Strength	Sectors and Times for Commitment	Departure Area (lines)
1st Baltic	*Front* mobile group	1st Tank Corps 46th Mechanized Bde	Boundary of 6th Gds and 43rd armies, the morning of the operation's second day	Commitment line: 7 km in width, 10 km from the front line
3rd Belorussian	*Front* mobile group	Gen. Oslikovskii's[1] cavalry-mechanized Group (3rd Gds Mechanized and 3rd Gds Cavalry corps)	In 5th Army's zone on the morning of the operation's second day	Departure area: 6 km from the front line Commitment line: 8 km in width, 10 km from the front line
	11th Gds Army's mobile group	2nd Gds Tank Corps	In 11th Gds Army's zone on the operation's second day	Departure area: 5 km from the front line Two commitment lines were planned: 1) along the 71st and 36th rifle corps' 6-km sector, 10 km from the front line 2) along the 16th Gds Rifle Corps' sector, in the event of the left-flank corps' attack's lack of success
	Front mobile group	5th Gds Tank Army (3rd Gds and 29th tank corps)	According to two variations: 1) in the 11th Gds Army's zone; 2) in the 5th Army's zone on the operation's third day	Intermediate areas, according to both variations, were outfitted 8-10 km from the front line. The group's arrival in one or the other intermediate area was slated for the morning of the second or third day of the operation
1st Belorussian	3rd Army's mobile Group	9th Tank Corps	In the 3rd Army's zone, along the sectors of the 80th, 35th, or 41st rifle corps. The main variation was that of the 35th Rifle Corps on the operation's second day	Commitment line: at a depth of 10 from the front line km
	65th Army's mobile	1st Gds Tank Corps group	In the 65th Army's zone along the 18th Rifle Corps' sector on the operation's first day	Commitment line: at a depth of 2-3 km from the front line
	Front mobile group	Gen. Pliev's Cavalry-Mechanized Group (1st Mechanized and 4th Gds Cavalry corps)	Along the boundary of the 65th and 28th armies on the first day of the operation	The width of the commitment sector was 20 km

Note

1 Editor's note. Nikolai Sergeevich Oslikovskii (1900-71) joined the Red Army in 1919 and fought in the civil war. During the Great Patriotic War he commanded a cavalry division, cavalry corps and a cavalry-mechanized group. Following the war, Oslikovskii commanded a cavalry division and a cavalry school before retiring in 1953.

Fronts	Formation in Entering the Breach, Securing the Commitment	Planned Depths and Rates of Advance
1st Baltic	It was planned to commit the corps into the breakthrough along three routes, in a two-echelon formation. Aviation support for the commitment into the breach and beyond to be provided by the 5th Fighter Division, 11th Fighter Corps, and the 335th Assault Air Division. Artillery and engineer support according to the plan by the headquarters of the 6th Gds Army. Artillery support—three artillery battalions, one each from three cannon-artillery brigades of the 6th Gds Army's long-range artillery group. The artillery fire was prepared by sectors along six lines, with an overall depth of up to 10 km. Engineering support—2 engineering-sapper bdes, 1 engineer-sapper bn, 2 mine-engineer bns, 2 pontoon bns, and 1 bn of amphibious cars	To enter the breach in the enemy's defense to a depth of up to 12-15 km (with the forces of 6th and 43rd armies). The depth of the corps' combat actions is 30 km, with an advance of 10 km per day.
3rd Belorussian	The cavalry-mechanized group's commitment was planned in single-echelon formation: to the right—3rd Gds Mechanized Corps; to the left—3rd Gds Cavalry Corps along four routes. The aviation support for the commitment into the breach—213th Night Bomber Div, 3rd Fighter Corps, 3rd Assault Air Corps, 1st Gds Bomber Corps, then the 265th Fighter Div, 3rd Fighter Corps, 311th Assault Air Corps, 3rd Bomber Div	To enter the breach on the morning of the second day of the operation, after the breakthrough by the 5th Army of the enemy's tactical defensive zone. The depth of advance is 150 km, and the rate of attack is 37.5 km per day
	Artillery and engineer support according to the plan by the 5th Army headquarters The corps' commitment into the breach was planned in a two-echelon formation along two routes: tanks bdes in the first echelon, and a tank and and motorized rifle bdes. Aviation support for the commitment and subsequent operations—2nd Fighter Corps and 3rd Assault Air Corps Artillery and engineer support is according to the plan of the 11th Gds Army's headquarters	To enter the breach, formed by the first-echelon's formations. The depth of advance is 160 km, with a speed of 32 km per day
3rd Belorussian	It was planned to commit the army into the breach in single-echelon formation: 29th Tank Corps along the right flank, and 3rd Gds Tank Corps along the left flank. The corps were to be in a double-echelon formation. Aviation support—2nd Fighter Corps, 3rd Assault Air Corps, 1st Gds Bomber Corps. Artillery and engineer support is according to the plans of the 11th Gds and 5th armies' headquarters.	To enter the breach made by the 11th Gds Army according to the first variation, and the 5th Army, according to the second. The depth of the advance is to be as far as the Berezina River in the Borisov area.
1st Belorussian	It was planned to commit the corps into the breach in a two-echelon formation. Aviation support of the commitment into the breach and subsequent actions—286th Fighter Div, 4th Assault Air Corps' 195th Assault Air Div. Artillery and engineer support is according to the plan of 3rd Army headquarters.	To enter the breach in the 3rd Army's attack zone. The depth of advance is 60 km, at a rate of 20 km per day.
	It was planned to commit the corps into the breach in a two-echelon formation, with the main group of forces along the enveloping left flank: 3 bdes in the first echelon, and one in the second.	To enter the breach in the 65th Army attack zone. The depth of the advance is 75 km, with a rate of advance of 25 km per day.

Fronts	Formation in Entering the Breach, Securing the Commitment	Planned Depths and Rates of Advance
	Aviation support for the commitment into the breach, and subsequent actions—2 fighter regiments from the 8th Fighter Corps, 2nd Gds Assault Air Div.	
	It was planned to commit the cavalry-mechanized group into the breach in single-echelon formation: 1st Mechanized Corps to the right and 4th Gds Cavalry Corps to the left.	To enter the breach along the boundary of 65th and 28th armies. The depth of advance is 60-70 km, with a rate of advance of 20-25 km per day.
	Aviation support for the commitment and subsequent actions—8th Fighter Corps and 299th Assault Air Div. Artillery and engineer support is according to the plan by 28th Army headquarters.	

The commanders of the corresponding armies were the organizers of the commitment of the army mobile groups. Securing the commitment of the *front's* mobile groups into the breach was entrusted to the commander of one of the combined-arms armies (as appointed by the *front*) and the commander of the air army.

On the whole, the Belorussian operation was prepared in conditions of our threefold superiority in tanks and self-propelled guns over the enemy.

The high number of direct infantry-support tanks and self-propelled guns, including heavy ones, as well as the appearance of specialized tanks, enabled us to create beforehand groups of direct infantry support in the rifle divisions' second echelons, which, as a rule, had not been the case before. As a result, it became possible to augment the efforts of the tanks and self-propelled guns in committing the second echelons into the battle.

The Third and First Belorussian fronts disposed of a large number of army and *front* mobile groups. This circumstance enabled us to commit the mobile groups consecutively and thus augment efforts from the depth along the decisive direction.

The possibility of augmenting efforts from the depth enabled us to complete the breakthrough of the enemy's tactical defense with the forces of the rifle formations, supported by direct infantry-support tanks and self-propelled guns, in conjunction with the armies' mobile groups. Thanks to this, the *fronts'* mobile groups could irrupt into the enemy's operational depth without expending their strength on completing the breakthrough of his tactical defensive zone.

Thus, disposing of a significant number of mobile groups, the *front* commanders could count on achieving decisive results in the operations.

Planning the Combat Employment of Aviation

By the beginning of the Belorussian operation air superiority was on our side. This circumstance was most favorably reflected in the actions of our aviation.

In all, four air armies of *front* aviation took an immediate part in the operation's first stage (First Baltic Front's 3rd Air Army; Third Belorussian Front's 1st Air Army; Second Belorussian Front's 4th Air Army, and; First Belorussian Front's 16th Air Army), and one air army from Long-Range Aviation.[8]

---

8   Aside from this, the First Belorussian Front disposed of the 6th Air Army, which supported the *front's* left-wing forces south of the Pripyat' River.

For 10-15 days before the start of the operation the air armies of the First and Third Belorussian fronts received nearly 2,500 extra combat aircraft from the reserve of the Supreme High Command (see table 28).

The overall number of *front* aviation aircraft rose 73 percent and by the beginning of the operation amounted to (see table 29):

Counting the 1,007 aircraft from Long-Range Aviation, which took part in the operation, our superiority over the enemy in bomber and assault aviation was 4.7:1 and overall 4.5:1.

In the individual *fronts* our aviation superiority over the enemy was as follows: 3:1 in the First Baltic Front; 7.7:1 in the Third Belorussian Front; 2:1 in the Second Belorussian Front, and; 3.3:1 in the First Belorussian Front (right wing).

Thus the enemy could counter our aviation, numbering more than 5,300 planes belonging to *front* air and, with the addition of Long-Range Aviation—more than 6,300 aircraft—with only 1,400 aircraft forming the Sixth Air Fleet. This was the case despite the fact that the German-Fascist command concentrated along the given front up to 60 percent of all its aircraft operating on the Soviet-German front. Of the enemy's air group, the greatest number of planes was deployed opposite the First Baltic and First Belorussian fronts.

In evaluating the enemy's air basing (see table 30), it should be noted that the main mass of his planes was deployed on airfields located at a remove of more than 100-150 kilometers from the front line, because of the danger of Soviet air attacks against them. Only fighter aviation was based on the forward airfields.

The existing system of such major permanent airfield centers as Dvinsk, Vitebsk, Orsha, Mogilev, Kovel', Minsk, Borisov, and others enabled us to accommodate up to 2,000 planes, which eased the enemy's aviation maneuver.

By the start of the operation, the airfield network at the disposal of our air force was characterized by the following (see table 30).

Table 28. The Number of Planes Arriving as Reinforcements for the 1st and 16th Air Armies

Air Armies	Air Corps	Independent Air Divisions	Aircraft			
			Fighters	Assault Planes	Bombers	Total
1st	4	4	864	280	369	1,513
16th	5	–	480	270	190	940

Table 29. The Number of Aircraft in the *Fronts*

Air Armies	3rd	1st	4th	16th
	1 fighter corps	3 fighter corps	2 fighter divs	2 fighter corps
	1 fighter div	1 assault air corps	2 assault air divs	1 assault air corps
	3 assault air divs	1 bomber corps	1 night bomber div	1 mixed air corps
	1 night bomber div	2 fighter divs	1 reconnaissance rgt	1 bomber corps
	1 assault air rgt	2 assault air divs		4 fighter divs
	1 reconnaissance rgt	2 bomber divs		3 assault air divs
		2 night bomber divs		2 night bomber divs
		1 fighter rgt		1 fighter rgt
		2 reconnaissance rgts		2 reconnaissance rgts

Air Armies	3rd	1st	4th	16th
Types of Aircraft				
Fighter	403	767	196	952
Assault	368	547	193	636
Bomber (daylight)	–	392	–	263
Bomber (night)	79	81	121	150
Reconnaissance	52	77	18	32
Total	902	1,864	528	2,033

Types of Aircraft	Long-Range Aviation	Total *Front* Aviation[1]	Total Enemy Aircraft	Correlation
Fighter	–	2,318	400	5.7:1
Assault	–	1,744		
Bomber (daylight)	1,007	655	800 (this figure includes all bombers)	3.5:1
				4.7:1[2]
Bomber (night)	–	431		
Reconnaissance	–	179	200	1:1.1
Total	1,007	5,327	1400	3.8:1
				4.5:1[2]

Notes

1 Not counting the 6th Air Army.

2 The numerator includes *front* aviation only, while the denominator also includes Long-Range Aviation.

Table 30. The Airfield Network's Capacity in the First Baltic, Third, Second and First Belorussian Fronts' Sectors

Air Army	Number of Airfields & Landing Strips	Average Distance of Airfields and Landing Strips from the Front Line (in km)	Maximum Possible Number of Aircraft that could be based on these Airfields and Landing Strips
3rd	16	15-80	about 1,000
1st	35	25-100	above 2,000
4th	46	25-75	about 2,000
16th	30	10-140	above 2,000
Total	127		up to 7,000

This airfield network guaranteed the basing not only of the available aviation, but also of the air corps and air divisions for the Supreme High Command reserve, which were arriving to reinforce the *fronts'* aviation, as well as the maneuver of our aviation along the front and in depth.

Initially, only a small number of planes, necessary for carrying out reconnaissance and covering certain areas, were concentrated on the forward airfields at a distance of 15-30 kilometers from the front line. The main mass of aircraft was deployed on airfields located in the depth.

For the purpose of masking the aviation's concentration, the air corps and divisions arriving to reinforce the 1st and 16th air armies were deployed on rear airfields at a distance of 60-100 kilometers from the front line.

The rebasing of the main mass of aircraft to the forward airfields was carried out 1-3 days before the start of the operation.

Before the start of the Belorussian operation both sides' aviation was not particularly active. This can be explained, on the one hand, by the fact that the ground forces were not active, and also by the unfavorable weather.

In preparing for the forthcoming operation, our air formations carried out reconnaissance of the enemy for the purpose of pinpointing his defensive system, his groups of forces, the location of his reserves and the grouping of his aircraft on their airfields; they sought to prevent the enemy's rail shipments by destroying his trains at the stations and stages; they fought the enemy's reconnaissance aircraft and bombers that appeared over the locations of our troops; they launched periodic raids against the enemy's troop and equipment concentrations on the battlefield, based on the orders of the command of the armies and *fronts*. For carrying out these tasks, the commanders of the air armies allotted a small amount of planes based on forward airfields.

The main tasks assigned by the *front* commanders to the air armies came down to the following:

a) to secure from the air the troops' concentration and regrouping, and their occupation of their jumping-off positions;
b) to facilitate the armies of the *fronts'* main groups during their breaking trough of the enemy's tactical defense, and in subsequent actions by suppressing the enemy's combat formations and resistance centers, preventing the arrival of his reserves to the battlefield, as well as by directly accompanying the attacking troops' combat formations;
c) to cover the commitment of the *fronts'* mobile groups into the breach and their subsequent activities in the operational depth, and;
d) to carry out non-stop reconnaissance of the enemy throughout the entire depth of the operation.

The specific tasks assigned by the *front* commanders to the air army commanders are shown in table 31.

Table 31. Aviation Objectives, Assigned by the *Front* Commanders

To the Commander of the First Baltic Front's 3rd Air Army
To cover the 6th Guards and 43rd armies' shock groups, as well as the 1st Tank Corps in its jumping-off position and during the offensive.
To suppress the enemy's combat formations and centers of resistance, in conjunction with the ground forces, in the 6th Guards and 43rd armies' attack sectors.
To prevent the arrival of the enemy's reserves.
To support the commitment of the 1st Tank Corps into the breach and to assist its advance.

To the Commander of the Third Belorussian Front's 1st Air Army
To achieve air superiority and to support the regrouping and concentration of the *front's* forces.
To assist the shock group's armies in breaking through the enemy's tactical defensive zone.
To concentrate the main aviation efforts along the Orsha axis in the interests of the 11th Guards and 5th Guards Tank armies, and with the remainder of its forces to support the 5th Army and the cavalry-mechanized group; to create a powerful air reserve of no less than one assault air and one fighter divisions.
To isolate the operations area against the arrival of the enemy's reserves.
To support the commitment into the breach and the subsequent combat activities of the cavalry-mechanized group, the 5th Guards Tank Army, and the 2nd Guards Tatsinskaya Tank Corps.
To carry out aerial reconnaissance throughout the entire depth of the operation.

To the Commander of the Second Belorussian Front's 4th Air Army

To cover the 49th Army's shock group from the air.

To assist the 49th Army's breakthrough of the enemy's main defensive zone by suppressing his artillery and personnel.

To destroy the enemy's arriving reserves.

To support the mobile group's combat activities.

To carry out aerial reconnaissance as far as the line of the Dnepr River.

To the Commander of the First Belorussian Front's 16th Air Army

Upon the beginning of the operation and throughout its conduct, to secure air superiority: along the Bobruisk axis—with the forces of the 6th Fighter Corps, and along the Glusk axis—with the forces of the 8th Fighter Corps.

All the forces of the 6th Fighter, 4th Assault Air, 3rd Bomber, and 6th Mixed Air corps, the 286th, 282nd and 1st Guards fighter divisions are to support the offensive by the 3rd and 48th armies; the actions of the 2nd Guards and 300th Assault Air and 28th Fighter divisions, and the 8th Fighter Corps are to support the 65th Army's offensive; the actions of the 299th Assault Air Division and two regiments of the 8th Fighter Corps are to support the 28th Army's offensive.

From the second half of the operation's first day, the 4th Assault Air Corps (minus two assault air regiments) and the 286th Fighter Division are to be operationally subordinated to the commander of the 3rd Army; two regiments from the 4th Assault Air Corps, along with their fighter cover, are to be operationally subordinated to the commander of the 48th Army; the 2nd Guards Assault Air Division, with two fighter regiments from the 283rd Fighter Division are to be operationally subordinated to the commander of the 65th Army, and; the 299th Assault Air Division, with two of the 8th Fighter Corps' fighter regiments, are to be operationally subordinated to the commander of the 28th Army.

With the commitment of the tank corps into the breach, the army commanders are to support their activities with the attached air units.

Air support for the cavalry-mechanized group during its commitment into the breach and activities in the rear is to be entrusted to the commander of the 16th Air Army, who is to allot an assault air division and two regiments of fighters for direct support of the group's activities, and who is to organize its cover from the air with the forces of the 8th Fighter Corps.

As the table shows, the aviation's assigned objectives were most fully formulated by the commander of the First Belorussian Front. As regards the formulation of those tasks assigned by the commanders of the Third and Second Belorussian fronts, these cannot be viewed as sufficient. It was hardly worth assigning the 1st Air Army the objective of gaining air superiority for the purpose of only covering the regrouping and concentration of the *front's* forces. The air army should have covered from the air not only the regrouping and concentration of the *front's* forces, but also their activities throughout the course of the operation. The 1st Air Army was supposed to support the *front's* main groups of forces both in breaking through the enemy's tactical defensive zone, as well as their subsequent activities to the end of the operation. The 4th Air Army's objective of assisting the 49th Army in breaking through only the main defensive zone was obviously insufficient. The 16th Air Army should have been assigned the task of achieving air superiority not only from the beginning of the operation, but during the preparatory period as well. The army should also have been ordered to allot not one assault air division for directly supporting the operations of the cavalry-mechanized group, but larger air forces.

On the basis of the tasks assigned by the *front* commanders, decisions were made by the commanders of the air armies (see table 32).

Table 32. The Decisions of the Air Army Commanders

The Commander of the 3rd Air Army

1. Coverage of the *front's* shock group is to be carried out by the forces of the 11th Fighter Corps and the 259th Fighter Division:

a) While in the jumping-off position—by means of patrolling the combat zone, and also by means of covering the closest airfields.

b) During the operation—the 6th Gds Army is to be covered by the 5th Guards Fighter Division, and the 43rd Army by the 259th Fighter Division. These same fighter divisions are also entrusted with supporting the combat activities of our assault air units in these armies' attack zones.

2. Assistance to the combined-arms armies in breaking through the enemy's defense is to be carried out by means of a preliminary (nighttime) air preparation and the air support of the offensive during the breakthrough.

a) The preliminary aviation preparation is to be carried out by successive raids by single planes from the 314th Night Bomber Division throughout the night before the 6th Guards and 43rd armies' attack. 450 sorties are planned.

b) Aviation support for the offensive: the 6th Guards Army will be supported by the forces of the 211th and 335th assault air divisions, the 6th Independent Assault Air Regiment, and the 259th Fighter Division (201 *shturmoviks*,[1] 217 fighters); the 43rd Army will be supported by the forces of the 332nd Assault Air and 190th Fighter divisions (120 *shturmoviks*, 60 fighters).

   Method—echeloned raids by groups of 6-8 *shturmoviks*, with fighter cover, for the purpose of suppressing the enemy's artillery and mortars and his strong points, and to foil counterattacks by his infantry and tanks. Aviation is to support the 43rd Army in its advance in the defensive depth.

3. Support for the commitment of the 1st Tank Corps into the breach and its subsequent activities in depth is to be carried out by switching the 11th Fighter Corps to covering against enemy air attacks, and by suppressing the enemy's artillery and tanks in the commitment zone and along the flanks with the forces of the 335th Assault Air Division.

4. To prevent the arrival of the enemy's reserves. To combat the enemy's attempts to destroy the railroads.

5. Cooperation with the combined-arms armies is to be carried out according to the principle of support. Cooperation within the air army is to be realized as follows: the 335th and 211th assault air divisions with the 259th Fighter Division; the 332nd Assault Air Division with the 11th Fighter Corps' 190th Fighter Division.

6. The air reserve consists of 40 fighters (a single fighter regiment) from the 180th Fighter Division.

Note

1 Editor's note. This was the popular name for the Il-2 assault airplane.

The Commander of the 1st Air Army

1. Achievement of air superiority, as well as the covering of the groups of forces, the concentration and offensive by the *front*), is to be carried out through the active operations by fighter aviation, and the blocking and bombing of the enemy's airfields.

   The 1st Guards Fighter Corps is to destroy the enemy's aircraft on the far approaches for the purpose of covering the 11th Guards, 31st and 5th Guards Tank armies, and the 2nd Tatsinskaya Tank Corps. 470 sorties are planned.

   The 3rd Fighter Corps is to destroy the enemy's air on the far approaches for the purpose of covering the 39th and 5th armies. 450 sorties are planned.

   One division of the 1st Guards Bomber Corps, and the 6th and 3rd guards bomber divisions, are to suppress and block the enemy's aviation on their airfields. 258 sorties are planned.

   The 2nd Fighter Corps is to support the 1st Guards bomber and 3rd Assault Air corps.

   The "Normandy" Fighter Regiment[1] is to be held in reserve for augmenting efforts in air battles and in carrying out free hunting.

2. Assisting the combined-arms armies in breaking through the enemy's defense is to be carried out by the preliminary and direct aviation preparation of the attack, as well as through the aviation support (accompaniment) of the offensive.

a) The preliminary aviation preparation is to be carried out from 2300 to 0230 hours on the night before the attack. The 6th Guards Bomber and 213th Night Bomber divisions are to suppress the enemy's fire system and demoralize his enemy's personnel (in the 11th Guards Army's attack zone). Simultaneously, the noise of the planes' motors is to mask the advance of our tanks to their jumping-off positions for the attack.

b) Direct aviation support:

In the 5th Army's zone, 20 minutes before the start of the attack, the 3rd Guards Bomber and 311th Assault Air divisions, covered by the 303rd Fighter Division, are to suppress the enemy's fire system, personnel and command and control. 97 sorties of bomber and assault air aviation are planned and 48 sorties by fighter aviation.

In the 11th Guards Army's zone, 15-30 minutes before the attack, the 1st Guards Bomber and the 3rd Assault Air corps, and the 6th Guards Bomber Division, covered by the 2nd Fighter Corps, are to suppress the enemy's centers of resistance, disrupt his troop control, and destroy his artillery. 231 sorties by bombers are planned, 122 sorties by assault air, and 170 sorties by fighters. In all, 523 sorties.

In the 31st Army's zone, 15 minutes before the beginning of the attack, the 6th Guards Bomber Division, covered by the 240th Fighter Division, is to suppress the enemy's strong points. 27 bomber and 12 fighter sorties are planned.

c) Aviation support is to be carried out by continuously accompanying the attacking troops in the course of 2-3 hours and suppressing the enemy's artillery and personnel in certain areas, both independently, and on orders from the combined-arms commanders.

The 311th Assault Air and 303rd Fighter divisions were to operate in the 39th and 5th armies' attack zones; the 3rd Assault Air and 2nd Fighter corps are to operate in the 11th Guards Army's attack zone, as well as the 1st Guards Assault Air and 240th Fighter divisions.

Bomber aviation was is to be directed at launching concentrated blows against the enemy's centers of resistance along the following defensive lines:

The 3rd and 1st guards bomber divisions in the 5th Army's zone;

The 1st Guards Bomber Corps in the 11th Guards Army's zone.

Within the three armies' zones 488 assault air sorties, 270 bomber sorties, and 332 fighter sorties were planned, for a total of 1090 sorties.

3. The following measures are to be taken to support the commitment into the depth and the subsequent activities of the *front's* mobile formations in the operational depth:
On the night before the cavalry-mechanized group's commitment into the breach, the 213th Night Bomber Division is to:
interfere with the approach of the enemy's reserves, exhaust his personnel and complicate his troop movements, drop illuminating bombs for the purpose of orienting the cavalry-mechanized group's (3rd Guards Mechanized and 3rd Guards Cavalry corps) night activities.
60 sorties are planned.
The 3rd Assault Air and 1st Guards Bomber corps are to assist the 5th Army in forcing the Luchesa River and seizing bridgeheads.
The subsequent support of the cavalry-mechanized group is to be carried out by the forces of the 311th Assault Air and 3rd Guards Bomber divisions, as well as the 3rd Fighter Corps' 265th Fighter Division.
Supporting the 2nd Guards Tatsinskaya Tank Corps' commitment into the breach and beyond is to be carried out by the forces of the 3rd Assault Air and 2nd Fighter corps, with 370 planned assault air sorties, and 170 sorties by the fighters.
Support for the 5th Guards Tank Army's commitment into the breach is to be carried out by the forces of the 3rd Assault Air, 1st Guards Bomber and 2nd Fighter corps. During the first two days 800 assault air sorties are planned and 600 by the bombers.

4. The 1st Guards Bomber Corps, 1st Guards and 311th assault air divisions, and the 213th Night Bomber Division are to be employed for combating the enemy's reserves along the Vitebsk and Orsha directions.

5. Cooperation within the air army:
The 3rd Guards Bomber and 311th Assault Air divisions are to cooperate with the 303rd Fighter Division;
The 1st Guards Bomber and 3rd Assault Air corps are to cooperate with the 2nd Fighter Corps;
The 6th Guards Bomber and 1st Guards Assault Air divisions are to cooperate with the 240th Fighter Division.

6. The reserve is to consist of the bomber formations following their first attacks.

Note

1 Editor's note. The Normandy-Neman fighter squadron (later a regiment) was a unit of French pilots who fought with the Red Army from 1943 to the end of the war.

The Commander of the 4th Air Army

1.   Covering the 49th Army is to be carried out by the forces of the 309th Fighter Division, from 0300 to 2230, by means of non-stop patrolling (during the first hour of the offensive patrols, consisting of 16 planes, and during the following hours, patrols of eight planes).
      With the troops' advance, the combat zone moves to the west by the decision of the division commander. Patrols are to be relieved in the air.
      The augmentation of efforts is to be carried out by three patrol groups, with six planes in each.

2.   Support for the 49th Army's breakthrough of the enemy's defense is to be carried out by preliminary air preparation and the aviation support for the offensive.

a)   preliminary air preparation is to be carried out by the forces of the 325th Night Bomber Division from 2300 on the night before the offensive, for the purpose of suppressing the enemy's artillery and personnel. 510 sorties are planned.

b)   aviation support for the 69th and 81st rifle corps' offensive is to be carried out by the forces of the 233rd Assault Air Division, with the forces of the 230th Assault Air Division supporting the 70th and 62nd rifle corps.

      During the first two hours the aviation's main efforts were to be directed at destroying the enemy's artillery, firing points and personnel in the main defensive zone; subsequently, from 2.5 hours after the start of the attack, to the end of the day, the aviation would directly accompany the infantry.

      The first attack, which was to last for two hours and five minutes, was to be carried out in 160 assault air and 80 fighter sorties.

      In the second and third attacks, from 2.5 hours after the start of the offensive to the end of the day, the *shturmoviks* would be directed for the direct support of specific rifle corps.

3.   In order to support the *front's* mobile group, which was to be committed in the 49th Army's attack zone, it was planned to redirect two of the 233rd Assault Air Division's regiments.

4.   The fight against the enemy's tactical reserves would be carried out by 16 *shturmoviks* and 16 fighters, which were at the direct disposal of the commander of the air army.

5.   Cooperation within the air army:
      The 233rd Assault Air Division was to cooperate with the 309th Fighter Division;
      The 230th Assault Air Division was to cooperate with the 229th Fighter Division.

To The Commander of the 16th Air Army

1.   The achievement of air superiority is to be gained through the active operations of fighters, covering our troops, battling the enemy's aerial reconnaissance, and blocking and bombing his nearby airfields.

a)   the 6th Fighter Corps is to achieve air superiority along the Bobruisk axis, for the purpose of preventing the enemy's bombing raids against the 3rd and 48th armies and supporting the activities of our *shturmoviks* and bombers over the battlefield. This is to be achieved by non-stop patrolling by three four-plane groups at various altitudes along the likely routes of the enemy's aircraft flights at a depth of 30-40 kilometers from the front line, as well as fighter patrols over the airfields.

b)   the 8th Fighter Corps is to achieve air superiority along the Glusk axis, for the purpose of preventing the enemy's aviation from bombing the 65th and 28th armies and supporting the operations of the 2nd Guards, 299th and 300th assault air divisions. The corps is to cover the 1st Guards Tank Corps' commitment into the breach and beyond, and then that of General Pliev's cavalry-mechanized group.

c)   the 271st Night Bomber Division is to bomb the enemy's aircraft on their airfields during several nights. The enemy's air reconnaissance is to be combated by the fighter corps in those zones set aside for them, by employing radar sites, patrol pairs and fighter wings.

2.   Support for the combined-arms armies in breaking through the enemy's defense is to be carried out through a preliminary aviation support and air support for the offensive.

a)   preliminary air preparation is to be carried out by the forces of the 271st Night Bomber Division in the 48th Army's attack zone on the night of 23-24 June, for the purpose of suppressing the enemy's artillery and personnel. 270 sorties are planned. The forces of the 292nd Night Bomber Division are to suppress the enemy's men and materiel in the 65th and 28th armies' attack zones. 250 sorties are planned.

b)   the aviation support for the offensive:
By the 3rd and 48th armies is to be carried out by the forces of the 6th Mixed, 4th Assault Air and 3rd Bomber corps, covered by the 1st Guards, 282nd and 286th fighter divisions. These forces were to launch five concentrated raids (from 120-170 planes in each) during two and a half hours, for the purpose of suppressing the enemy's personnel and weapons in his strong points and centers of resistance. 300 fighter, 235 assault air and 280 bomber sorties are planned, for a total of 815 sorties. When the 6th Fighter Corps' 185 sorties are added, the total is 1,000 sorties.
The aviation support for the 65th and 28th armies is to be carried out by the forces of the 2nd Guards, 299th and 300th assault air divisions, covered by the 283rd Fighter Division and two of the 8th Fighter Corps' fighter regiments. These forces were to launch three concentrated raids (from 96-150 planes in each) in the course of three hours after the attack, for the purpose of suppressing the enemy's artillery, personnel and centers of resistance. 350 assault air and 190 fighter sorties were planned. When the 8th Fighter Corps' 175 sorties are added, the total is 715 sorties.
Following the air attacks along the *front's* right wing the 4th Assault Air Corps (minus two assault air regiments) and the 286th Fighter Division were to be operationally subordinated to the commander of the 3rd Army in order to carry out air support for the offensive, as well as for supporting the 9th Tank Corps' commitment into the breach; two of the 4th Assault Air Corps' assault air regiments, along with their fighter cover, are to be operationally subordinated to the commander of the 48th Army; on the left wing, following the launching of the first raids, the 2nd Guards Assault Air Division, along with two fighter regiments from the 283rd Fighter Division, are to be operationally subordinated to the commander of the 65th Army, with the 299th Assault Air Division and two fighter regiments from the 8th Fighter Corps subordinated to the commander of the 28th Army.
Following the launching of the first raids, bomber aviation's formations, as well as the 300th Assault Air Division, are to be transferred to the air army commander's reserve for launching raids, depending on the situation, in the attack zones of the 3rd and 48th, or the 65th and 28th armies.

3.   Support for the commitment into the breach and subsequent operations in depth are to be entrusted to:
The 4th Assault Air Corps' 195th Assault Air Division is to support the 9th Tank Corps, and the 2nd Guards Assault Air Division and two fighter regiments from the 8th Fighter Corps are to support the 1st Guards Tank Corps.

4.   Cooperation within the air army:
The 3rd Bomber Corps is to cooperate with the 282nd Fighter Division;
The 6th Mixed Corps is to cooperate with the 1st Guards Fighter Division;
The 4th Assault Air Corps is to cooperate with the 286th Fighter Division;
The 2nd Guards and 300th assault air divisions are to cooperate with the 283rd Fighter Division, and;
The 299th Assault Air Division is to cooperate with two of the 8th Fighter Corps' fighter regiments.
In analyzing these decisions, one can make the following conclusions:

The organization of troop coverage from the air. In the commanders' decisions the most powerful air armies—1st and 16th—were called upon to carry out the main task—the achievement of air superiority as those measures most reliably supporting the offensive operation's success. It was also planned to employ the entire complex of possible combat measures by the aviation, which would support the successful resolution of the given objective. The commanders of the 3rd and 4th air armies, as regards covering the forces of the First Baltic and Second Belorussian fronts from the air, assigned their air armies more limited objectives.

In laying out the tasks for fighter aviation in covering the troops from the air, a difference in the methods of dividing up the zones of combat activity for the fighter corps and divisions may be observed. For example, in the Third Belorussian Front the combat zones were cut off from the front line toward the enemy, while not embracing the jumping-off area for the offensive. In the First Belorussian Front, the combat zones of the 16th Air Army's 6th and 8th fighter corps included both the area of the enemy's line, as well as the jumping-off area for our forces' offensive. The latter method of dividing the combat zones for the fighter formations was the more expedient.

Direct air preparation was planned only in the Third Belorussian Front. In the remaining *fronts*, only the preliminary air preparation and aviation support were planned. In the First Baltic and Second Belorussian fronts the absence of a direct air preparation may be explained by the shortage of aviation, and the simultaneous organization of direct air preparation and the aviation support in these *fronts* involved a dispersion of air assets. Thus the commanders of the First Baltic and Second Belorussian fronts concentrated their entire aviation efforts on air support. The preparation of the attack was entrusted to the artillery. As regards the First Belorussian Front, one must assume that the *front* commander, considering the high artillery densities for the artillery preparation and the conduct of the preliminary air preparation with the forces of both *front* aviation and Long-Range Aviation, also decided to concentrate the aviation's main efforts on air support and planned to carry this out with large densities. In the First Belorussian Front 2,050 sorties were planned for the aviation support period. In the Third Belorussian Front 707 sorties were planned for direct aviation preparation, with 1,090 sorties for aviation support, for a total of 1,797 sorties, that is, 250 sorties less than in the First Belorussian Front for aviation support.

The decision by the commander of the 16th Air Army did not foresee operations against the enemy's reserves.

The strength of the air armies, particularly the 1st and 16th, enabled us to create powerful aviation groups for supporting high rates of attack by the *fronts'* main groups of forces. The distribution of the efforts of the *fronts'* air armies, as well as the planned air densities, is characterized by the following data (see table 33).

There were no such air densities in the Soviet forces' previous operations, such as were created in the Belorussian operation. Our aviation's air densities in the Belorussian operation exceeded by 2-3 times the aviation densities achieved by our air force in the Stalingrad and Belgorod—Khar'kov operations, in the operations along the Ukrainian left bank, and in others.

These aviation densities will rise even more if we take into account the actions of Long-Range Aviation in the operations of the Belorussian *fronts*. Before the start of the operation, Long-Range Aviation was to suppress the enemy's air power on the airfields in the following areas: Orsha, Minsk, Bobruisk, Baranovichi, Pinsk, Luninets, Brest, and Bialystok. It was planned to launch the first raid on the night of 13 June with the forces of the 2nd, 5th, 6th, 7th, and 8th bomber corps; repeat attacks, based on intelligence data, were to be launched on 14 and 15 June. The main targets of these raids were the enemy's planes, landing strips, structures and air unit personnel (see table 34).

Besides this, on the night before the operation's first day, Long-Range Aviation was to carry out a nighttime air preparation in the *fronts'* attack zones along the main attack sectors, for the purpose of destroying the enemy's artillery, defensive structures and personal, as well as morally suppressing his forces:

a)　in the Third Belorussian Front's zone, the air force would launch raids on the night of 22-23 June against the enemy's personnel in the area of Budy, Chertki and Zhabyki (20 kilometers northeast of Orsha) in support of the 11th Guards Army, with the forces of the 3rd Guards and 7th bomber corps, with a density of 30-40 tons of bombs.

b)　in the Second Belorussian Front's zone, the air force would launch raids on the night of 22-23 June against the enemy's forces in the second and third trench lines, and against his artillery in the area of Zastenki, Zalozh'e (east of Mogilev) in support of the 49th Army, with the forces of the 2nd Guards, 5th and 6th bomber corps, with a bomb density of 50-60 tons.

c)　in the First Belorussian Front's zone, the air force would launch raids on the night of 23-24 June against the enemy's troops and defensive structures in the following areas: Verichev, Tikhinichi, Gomza, Vazhny, and Chirnin in support of the 48th and 65th armies, with the forces of the 5th and 6th bomber corps, with a bomb density of 25-30 tons.

Simultaneously with the conduct of the nighttime air preparation, Long-Range Aviation was to blockade the enemy's nearby airfields.

In the course of the operation's first stage, and subsequently, Long-Range Aviation was to carry out the following: disrupt the work of the enemy's rail communications by launching raids against his rail junctions and stations at Polotsk, Obol', Borisov, Osipovichi, Minsk, and Luninets; to launch raids against individual groups of enemy forces, by order of the *front* commanders.

Table 33. The Distribution of the Efforts of the *Fronts'* Air Armies

Air Armies	Groups Being Supported	Air Formations		Aircraft		
		Air Corps	Independent Air Divs	Fighters	*Shturmoviks*	Bombers
3rd	6th Gds Army	1 fighter corps	1 assault air div 2 fighter divs 1 night bomber div	217	201	72
	43rd Army		1 assault air div 1 fighter div	116	120	–
1st	5th and 39th armies	1 fighter corps	1 assault air div 1 bomber div 1 night bomber div	176	93	149
	11th Gds and 31st armies	2 fighter corps 1 assault air corps 1 bomber corps	1 assault air div 1 night bomber div	424	353	242
	Reserve		2 fighter divs 1 assault air div 1 bomber div	187	101	82
4th	49th Army		2 fighter divs 2 assault air divs 1 night bomber div	196	193	121
16th	3rd and 48th armies	1 fighter corps 1 assault air corps 1 bomber corps 1 mixed air corps	3 fighter divs 1 night bomber div	592	250	348
	65th and 28th armies	1 fighter corps	2 fighter divs 2 assault air divs 1 night bomber div	360	386	65

Air Armies	Group Being Supported	Aircraft Total	Width of the Breakthrough Sector Along the Main Axis (in kms)	Number of Planes Per Kilometer Along the Breakthrough Sector of the Main Axis
3rd	6th Gds Army	490		
	43rd Army	236	25	29
1st	5th and 39th armies	418	17.5	24/25[1]
	11th Gds and 31st	1,019	19.5	52/63[2]
	Reserve	370		
4th	49th Army	510	12.5	40
16th	3rd and 48th armies	1,190	15	83
	65th and 28th armies	811	14	58

Note
1 The numerator shows the density without the reserve, while the denominator shows the density including the reserve.
2 The numerator shows the density without the reserve, while the denominator shows the density including the reserve.

Table 34. Long-Range Aviation Strikes Against Enemy Airfield Centers, 13-18 June 1944

Targets	Time of Attack	Air Formations	Number of Sorties	Bomb Tonnage
Bialystok	nights of 12-13 and 14-15 June	3rd Bomber Corps	90	93.3
Brest	night of 13-14 June	3rd Bomber Corps	79	93.7
Baranovichi	night of 12-13 June	2nd Bomber Corps	81	91.2
	night of 14-15 June	1st Bomber Corps	62	69.4
	nights of 14-15 and 17-18 June	4th Bomber Corps	138	142.7
	night of 17-18 June			
Minsk	nights of 13-14 and 17-18 June	2nd Bomber Corps	157	160.4
	Nights of 13-14 and 17-18 June	1st Bomber Corps	148	157.85
Pinsk	nights of 12-13, 13-14 and 17-18 June	5th Bomber Corps	165	163.85
Luninets	night of 12-13 June	6th Bomber Corps	87	89.3
	night of 14-15 June	5th Bomber Corps	55	56.3
Bobruisk	night of 12-13 June	7th Bomber Corps	106	115
Orsha	night of 13-14 June	8th Bomber Corps	70	79.5
	night of 13-14 June	6th Bomber Corps	30	47.85

In this manner, Long-Range Aviation's role in the preparation and conduct of the Belorussian operation was quite significant.

The greatest degree of air activity was planned in the First Belorussian and First Baltic fronts, with the least in the Third Belorussian Front. If the First Belorussian Front planned 3.3 sorties per aircraft, the figure in the First Baltic Front was 2.7, with 2.4 sorties in the Second Belorussian Front, while only 1.7 sorties per plane were planned in the Third Belorussian Front.

Besides this, it is worthy of attention that in the Third and Second Belorussian fronts the degree of air activity for fighter aviation on the operation's first day was planned to be at a lower level than assault air and bomber aviation. Such planning could only be possible in conditions of our aviation's undisputed air superiority; otherwise it could lead to excessive losses in assault air planes and bombers. In the plans for employing the air force, the character of the aviation's tasks and the distribution of its forces for cooperating with the ground forces were laid out in sufficient detail. On the basis of these plans, the air corps and independent air divisions were issued instructions in a timely manner as to the kind of operational field forces and combined-arms formations they would be cooperating with. This enabled the air formations' commanders and staffs to communicate beforehand with the commanders and staffs of the corresponding armies and corps to draw up a plan for coordination.

In the plans drawn up by the air armies' staffs the aviation's combat activity was reflected in time and place only for the operation's first day. Only general tasks were assigned for the subsequent days, which enabled us to orient the air formations as to the type and intensity of the forthcoming combat activities.

The plans were supplemented with the necessary documents, detailing the order of carrying out the combat assignments, as well as the order for their combat and materiel-technical support.

Excerpts from the plans for the combat employment of the air force were communicated in time to the executors, which ensured that the latter would have sufficient time for the training of their air units. For example, an order by the 1st Air Army command, indicating to the air formations their concrete assignments for the operation's first day, was issued on 20 June 1944, that is, three days before the beginning of the operation; by the 16th Air Army command on 17 June; that is, seven days before the start of the operation. Simultaneously with the excerpt from the order to the commanders of the 16th Air Army's formations, maps of the target areas were passed out, so that the flight crews had time to study them in detail.

During the preparatory period, on the basis of instructions by the *front* and air army commanders, the commanders of the combined-arms armies, along with the commanders of the air formations slated to support them, drew up planning cooperation tables, which laid out the tasks of the ground forces, the operation's stages, the air force's tasks, the number and types of planes, the number of sorties for carrying out the assigned objectives, and maps of the targets, and also defined more precisely the location of command posts in the jumping-off position and during the operation. Besides this, the air formation commanders were drawn into taking part in operational games, which were carried out in the armies of the *fronts'* main groups of forces under the leadership of the *front* commanders.

Exercises were also conducted and measures adopted, directed at supporting maneuver by the air formations during the course of the operation. The problem of the rapid and unimpeded rebasing of such a large number of aircraft in the air armies in the wake of the troops advancing at such high rates of speed and the creation of airfield conditions that would ensure normal combat activity (uninterrupted technical servicing, the availability of oils and lubricants and ammunition, etc.) assumed great significance in the Belorussian operation.

In planning their airfield maneuver, the commanders and staffs of the air armies did not foresee that the operation would develop to such a great depth and the rebasing of the air formations was planned, for the most part, to a depth of 150-200 kilometers. In the 1st and 16th air armies the organization of airfield maneuver was decentralized, that is, the entire responsibility for the timely and uninterrupted aircraft rebasing was entrusted to the commanders of the air basing areas. Such an organization of rebasing led to a situation in which in certain cases the air formations were not able to shift bases in a timely manner, due to the new airfields' lack of readiness, or they could not sustain the necessary combat intensity because of a shortage of oils, lubricants and ammunition at the new airfields. This problem was somewhat better resolved within the 4th Air Army, where the air army commander was personally in charge of rebasing his planes, and who had at his disposal an operational group of airfield specialists and several reserve airfield service battalions.

The air armies formed from subunits of the airfield service battalions forward airfield commands, consisting of 20-25 men on two trucks, for preparing airfields on territory seized from the enemy. The task of each command consisted of reconnoitering and, in the course of 2-3 days, with the aid of troops and the local population, preparing 3-4 airfields to which 3-4 fighter or assault aircraft regiments could be rebased.

Thus the availability of time enabled the commanders of the air armies, the commanders of the air formations and their staffs to carry out, without haste, the necessary organizational measures that would ensure the independent preparation of air formations and units for the forthcoming operation, in all respects, and enabled us to lay a secure basis for the cooperation of the air formations and units with the operational field forces and combined-arms formations of the *fronts'* main groups that they would be supporting.

Of course, these foundations of the aviation's cooperating with the ground forces could only be realized under conditions of the corresponding organization of the command and control of the air formations by the air armies.

The commanders of the air armies organized the control of their air formations from their command posts, which were located either near the command posts of the *front* commanders (1st and 3rd air armies), or near the command posts of the army commanders who were to launch the main attack (16th Air Army).

All the air army commanders exercised centralized control. The exception was the 16th Air Army, where according to the *front* commander's instructions, it was planned to subordinate the assault aircraft formations to the army commanders on the operation's first day.

In the 1st and 16th armies, as noted earlier, two large air groups each were created. In the 1st Air Army one group of air formations was directly controlled by the commander of the 1st Guards Bomber Corps, while the second group of air formations was controlled initially by the deputy army commander, and then by the commander of the 3rd Fighter Corps. The commander of the 1st Air Army had direct radio communications with the commanders of these air groups.

In the 16th Air Army the army commander directly controlled one air group, but through the army headquarter's communications center, where the chief of staff was; the deputy commander of the air army directly controlled the other air group.

A similar organization of control was called for by the presence of a large number of air formations in the air armies, as well as the necessity of supporting two main groups of forces in the Third and First Belorussian fronts.

Control of fighter aviation was to be exercised by the commanders of the fighter corps from their command posts, which by the start of the operation had been organized from 2-3 kilometers from the front line along the attack axes of the *fronts'* main groups.

The equipping of the staffs of the air armies', air formations' and air units' staffs with a large number of long-range detection radio stations ("Redout"), and air guidance radio stations, and the establishment of direct telephone and telegraph ("ST" apparatus) communications between the command posts of the air army commanders and the air corps commanders, and between their divisions' airfields ensured the security and constancy of control and increased the likelihood of detecting the air enemy in time.

On the whole, the Soviet air force's air superiority and its good preparation for the operation supported the aviation's and ground forces' bold maneuver, the launching of powerful attacks against the enemy, and the achievement of decisive results.

6

Operational Support

Great significance in the *fronts* and armies was attached to the operation's operational support.

Particular attention was devoted to intelligence of all sorts.

Intelligence was given the assignment of exactly determining the breakthrough sectors; the contours of the forward edge of the enemy's defense; what men and materiel the enemy was using to defend each sector; the strong points and centers of resistance; the presence of permanent structures, steel covers and shelters for the enemy's personnel; the enemy's subunit, unit and formation boundaries; the enemy's fire system; the enemy's system of minefields and artificial obstacles; the location of the enemy's command and observation posts, and; and whether or not our tanks and artillery could pass through the terrain.

Besides this, intelligence was to continue refining the data on the enemy's overall group of forces in the *fronts'* sectors, on his ability to maneuver his reserves, on the development and character of his operational defensive system, and on his aviation basing.

Land intelligence worked quite hard. A highly-developed system of observation posts, combined-arms as well as artillery and engineering, enabled us to conduct continuous observation of the enemy and eavesdrop on his calls. For example, in the Second Belorussian Front 979 observation posts were constructed, of which eight were army posts, 12 were corps, 17 were divisional, 24 were regimental, 41 were battalion, 830 were artillery, and 47 were engineering.

During the preparatory period for the operation in the First Belorussian Front, 400 daytime and nighttime reconnaissance searches were conducted, as well as a large number of engineering searches. As a result of troop intelligence's work, 18 prisoners were taken in the First Baltic Front's sector, 20 in that of the Second Belorussian Front, and 84 in the First Belorussian Front's sector, as well as important documents and weapons, while a large number of diversionary acts were carried out.

All of this enabled us to uncover the enemy's group of forces in the first line, with accuracy down to the regimental level, and down to individual battalions along the armies' main attack sectors, as well as unit boundaries, the approaches to the front line, the trench system, the types of obstacles, the location of minefields, the enemy's system of artillery, mortar and machine gun fire, and the location and strength of the enemy's reserves in the depth of his tactical defense.

Radio intelligence managed to precisely establish the location of many enemy army, corps and division headquarters. In particular, the First Baltic Front's radio intelligence managed to establish the headquarters of the Sixteenth Army in Luza and that of the Third Panzer Army in Beshenkovichi; that of the X Army Corps in Rudnya, the I Army Corps in Borovukha, that of the IX Army Corps in Ulla, and that of the LIII Army Corps in Vitebsk. All of this radio intelligence data was confirmed in the course of the operation.

Air reconnaissance uncovered the enemy's defensive system and photographed the attack zones of the *fronts'* main groups. In particular, units of the First Baltic Front's reconnaissance aviation photographed an area of 48,000 square kilometers, including the sector of the *front's* main group. As a result of photo interpretation, up to 300 batteries, 400 wood and earthen pillboxes, 700 machine gun nests, and 600 overhead coverings were uncovered. The 16th Air Army's reconnaissance aviation carried out the complete photographic reconnaissance of the enemy's fortifications along the Bobruisk axis. The resulting intelligence material yielded information regarding the depth of the enemy's defense, the character of his defensive structures, the conditions of the crossings, and the location of enemy reserves. Besides this, our aviation uncovered the enemy's airfield system and this information was updated every day.

The partisans passed on detailed information to the headquarters of the First Belorussian Front regarding the defensive structures and the defensive system of Bobruisk.

All the intelligence data on the enemy was systematized and analyzed in the armies' and *fronts'* headquarters. As a result, the *front* headquarters compiled intelligence charts, from which the *fronts'* topographical sections prepared maps containing the following detailed information: the enemy's group of forces, his fire system down to and including light machine guns, and his engineering structures. The 1:25,000 and 1:50,000 scale maps were delivered to the units in sufficient number and in a timely manner.

Thus by the beginning of the operation the *front* and army headquarters possessed sufficiently complete data as to the disposition of the enemy's forces, his defensive system, his fire system, the enemy's engineering outfitting of his defensive lines, as well as the character of the terrain in the main groups' attack sectors.

Operational concealment was carried out in the following manner.

In order to fool the enemy as to our intentions, the Red Army General Staff assigned to the Third Ukrainian Front the objective of demonstrating the concentration of its armies for an offensive along the Kishinev direction (false concentration). This measure, which was conducted from the end of May and throughout June, played a certain role.

No large-scale false measures were carried out in the Third Belorussian Front to fool the enemy. This was explained by the fact that the *front's* narrow sector (140 kilometers) and the creation of two main groups of forces in two areas did not allow for misleading the enemy by revealing to him false troop concentrations of operational significance. For this reason we showed the enemy only false targets of tactical significance. In the First Belorussian Front, the commander of the 48th Army imitated the creation of the main group of forces along his left flank. In the Second Belorussian Front we imitated the creation of a large group of forces in the 33rd Army's sector.

Aside from special measures of operational concealment, the daily concealment of all troop movements and actions was carried out, as well as that of the headquarters.

In order to avoid giving away military secrets, a very limited circle of responsible officers was allowed to become familiar with higher command operational documents relating to the preparations for the operation.

Offensive assignments were delivered in written form to the corps five days—and to the divisions three days—before the start of the offensive. Prior to this, only oral instructions were given.

Requisition requests made by the chiefs of the combat arms and services to the Defense Commissariat's central directorates were carried out only by the *fronts'* headquarters through the Red Army General Staff.

The existing regime of waging fire was preserved. The registration of artillery and mortar batteries was carried out according to a strictly established order, which was to guarantee the secrecy of the artillery's grouping along the main axes.

The radio networks' work regime was also maintained as before. The radio stations of newly arriving units and formations, or those being regrouped, were not allowed to work. From 2400 on 18 June the radio networks of the Red Army General Staff observed radio silence.

The conduct of conversations about ongoing measures along wire communications, particularly open ones, was forbidden, and strict control was established over communications centers.

No less strict measures were carried out by the *fronts*, in order to hide from the enemy the concentration and deployment of the *fronts'* main groups of forces.

In May and June intensified work for strengthening and developing the defensive lines along the entire front was carried out, and along the First Belorussian Front's right wing. Under the cover of this work, which was being carried out to a great depth, we prepared jumping-off areas for the offensive by the *fronts'* main groups of forces. Trenches were dug, as were communications trenches, as well as false trenches and the erection of artificial obstacles. A number of sectors were lined with barbed wire or small stakes, and signs reading "mines" were hung up (mines were not laid along the false sectors).

The concentration of forces to the front and the regroupings of the *fronts'* forces were carried out by observing concealment measures. Written orders for the march were issued as far down as the headquarters of the rifle divisions, and for one day. Written orders were not issued at all in the tank and mechanized corps arriving from the Supreme High Command reserve,. The movement of men and materiel was carried out only at night. The movement of the tank troops' formations and units, as well as that of self-propelled artillery, was carried out by echelon, in battalion columns at night, with dimmed headlights.

The troops' crossing over bridges was carried out only at night, while floating bridges were taken up during the daytime.

When enemy aircraft appeared over a column, the troops would change direction and begin marching in the opposite direction.

In bivouac and day's rest, and in new concentration areas, men and materiel were stationed predominantly outside inhabited locales, dispersed, and carefully screened from the air. Massed anti-aircraft fire against single aircraft and the rank and file's socializing with the local population was forbidden. Bathing and washing clothes in rivers and lakes in open areas were forbidden.

Officers from higher headquarters were appointed to carry out the thorough daily control over the observance of concealment measures and order on the march, and while resting and in the concentration areas. Besides this, officers from the *front* and army headquarters, as well as the *Stavka*, exercised control over concealment from airplanes, and by means of air observation and photography.

The unloading of trains was carried out only at night. As they disembarked, units and subunits were led off to areas hidden from air observation and thoroughly concealed. However, we did not always manage to conceal our concentration, as was the case, for example, in the Third Belorussian Front's 11th Guards Army.

All of the newly-arriving units and formations subordinated to the first-echelon combined-arms armies were forbidden, pending special permission by the *front* staff, to carry out reconnaissance against the enemy. Reconnaissance was carried out by the units and formations which had earlier occupied the front line.

The conduct of reconnaissance was permitted only to small groups and only while wearing rifle troops' uniforms. Reconnaissance was conducted along a broad front, including passive sectors.

Cross-country flights and the landing of arriving air formations and units, as well as the rebasing of aviation to other airfields, were carried out in a dispersed manner, in small groups. The aircraft were concealed as they landed. New air units were allowed to carry out training flights in a zone not closer than 25 kilometers to the front line.

In May 1944, in accordance with a decree by the *Stavka* of the Supreme High Command, the removal of the civilian population from the front zone to a depth of 25 kilometers was completely carried out.

For the fight against enemy agents being dropped in our rear in Red Army uniforms, the Third Belorussian Front established special rules regulating the movement of individual servicemen in the army and *front* rear.

The First Belorussian Front practiced the imitation of tank and gun movements from the front to the rear.

The task of securing the boundaries and flanks of the armies, corps and divisions was carried out by battalions, specially selected for this purpose from the infantry-support artillery groups, and partially from the army artillery groups' subgroups, as well as by mobile obstacle detachments (for example, in the Second Belorussian Front).

Aside from this, the boundaries and flanks were secured by the corresponding location of reserves of all types, as well as by the echeloned movement order of the subunits and units.

Anti-tank defense consisted of allotting artillery anti-tank reserves and mobile obstacle detachments by the *fronts*, armies, corps and divisions. The *front's* anti-tank artillery reserve consisted of 1-2 anti-tank artillery brigades; the army's of 1-2 anti-tank artillery regiments, a self-propelled artillery regiment, and a flamethrower battalion; the *front* and army mobile obstacle detachments consisted of an engineer-sapper battalion. Both of these units were assigned deployment lines.

Anti-aircraft defense was organized in a situation favorable to the Soviet troops, when by the beginning of the Belorussian operation we enjoyed air superiority.

The basis of the *fronts'* planning for anti-aircraft defense was the principle of concentrating the efforts of the anti-aircraft artillery and fighter aviation on covering the troops making up the *fronts'* main groups of forces.

The distribution of anti-aircraft weapons and densities of anti-aircraft artillery are shown in tables 35, 36, 37, and 38.

Table 35. The Distribution of Anti-Aircraft Weapons Among the *Fronts* by the Start of the Belorussian Operation

Fronts	Anti-Aircraft Artillery Weapons	Medium-Caliber Anti-Aircraft Artillery	Small-Caliber Anti-Aircraft Artillery	Anti-Aircraft Machine Guns
1st Baltic	*Front* weapons	80	337	361
	National Air Defense weapons	87	74	149
	Total	167	411	510
3rd Belorussian	*Front* weapons	128	664	615
	National Air Defense weapons	160	84	232
	Total	288	748	847
2nd Belorussian	*Front* weapons	32	297	–
1st Belorussian	*Front* weapons	189	573	897
	National Air Defense weapons	388	411	477
	Total	577	984	1,374

Table 36. The Distribution of Anti-Craft Artillery Formations and Units Among the Armies by the Start of the Belorussian Operation

Fronts	Armies	Anti-Aircraft Units Attached to the Armies and Mobile Groups
1st Baltic	6th Guards	39th and 46th anti-aircraft artillery divs (minus one anti-aircraft regiment), 1526th Anti-Aircraft Artillery Rgt (medium caliber), 183rd Independent Anti-Aircraft Artillery Bn
	43rd	17th Anti-Aircraft Artillery Div, 246th Anti-Aircraft Artillery Rgt, 221st Independent Anti-Aircraft Artillery Bn

Fronts	Armies	Anti-Aircraft Units Attached to the Armies and Mobile Groups
	4th Shock	617th Anti-Aircraft Artillery Rgt (46th Anti-Aircraft Artillery Div), 622nd Independent Anti-Aircraft Artillery Bn
3rd Belorussian	39th	20th Anti-Aircraft Artillery Div
	5th	33rd Anti-Aircraft Artillery Div, 1480th Anti-Aircraft Artillery Rgt
	11th Guards	34th and 48th anti-aircraft artillery divs
	31st	66th Anti-Aircraft Artillery Div
2nd Belorussian	49th	47th and 49th anti-aircraft artillery divs
	33rd	–
	50th	–
1st Belorussian	3rd	28th Anti-Aircraft Artillery Div
	48th	13th Anti-Aircraft Artillery Div
	65th	3rd Gds Anti-Aircraft Artillery Div
	28th	12th Anti-Aircraft Artillery Div
	Cavalry-Mechanized Group	2nd Gds Anti-Aircraft Artillery Div

Table 37. The Distribution of Anti-Aircraft Weapons for Covering Troops and Rear-Area Targets (Counting National Air Defense Weapons)[1]

Fronts	Total *Front* and National Air Defense Anti-Aircraft Weapons			Allotted to Covering the Troops		
	Medium-Caliber Weapons	Small-Caliber Weapons	Anti-Aircraft Machine Guns	Medium-Caliber Weapons	Small-Caliber Weapons	Anti-Aircraft Machine Guns
1st Baltic	170/100	411/100	510/100	71/42	307/75	280/57
3rd Belorussian	288/100	748/100	847/100	80/30	388/55	320/38
1st Belorussian[2]	577/100	984/100	1,374/100	64/35[3]	366/38[3]	298/33[3]
				93/16	546/41	423/30

Notes

1 The numerator shows the number and the denominator the percentage.

2 Of the overall number of anti-aircraft weapons allotted for covering the troops, 29 medium-caliber and 180 small-caliber weapons, and 125 anti-aircraft machine guns were in the *front's* left-wing armies. The overwhelming number of anti-aircraft artillery weapons, which were defending rear area targets, were located along the *front's* right wing.

3 The figures above the line refer to troop cover on the *front's* right wing, while the figures under the line refer to troop cover on both wings.

Fronts	Allotted for Covering Rear Area Targets		
	Medium-Caliber Weapons	Small-Caliber Weapons	Anti-Aircraft Machine Guns
1st Baltic	99/58	104/25	230/43
3rd Belorussian	208/38	360/45	527/62
1st Belorussian	484/84	618/62	951/70

Table 38. Anti-Aircraft Artillery Densities by *Front* by the Start of the Belorussian Operation

Fronts	Number of Anti-Aircraft Artillery Weapons Deployed for Troop Cover Along the *Front's* Entire Sector		Width of Attack Sector (in km)	Average Density of Anti-Aircraft Artillery per km of Front	
	Medium-Caliber Weapons	Small-Caliber Weapons		Medium-Caliber Weapons	Small-Caliber Weapons
1st Baltic	71	307	160	0.5	about 2
3rd Belorussian	80	388	140	0.5	about 3
2nd Belorussian	32	208	172	0.1	1.2
1st Belorussian (right wing)	64	366	240	0.25	1.5

The principle of the close cooperation of two anti-aircraft systems lay at the basis of employing anti-aircraft weapons: that of National Air Defense and that of *front* anti-aircraft defense, and within the latter the principle of close cooperation between the anti-aircraft weapons and fighter aviation. The order of cooperation between the anti-aircraft weapons in the *fronts'* anti-aircraft defense system was concretely expressed in the following: The First Baltic Front's anti-aircraft artillery groups were to cooperate with the 3rd Air Army's 11th Fighter Corps and the 259th Fighter Division; the Third Belorussian Front's anti-aircraft artillery groups were to cooperate with the 1st Air Army's 1st Guards and 3rd fighter corps; the Second Belorussian Front's anti-aircraft artillery groups were to cooperate with the 4th Air Army's 309th Fighter Division, and; the First Belorussian Front's anti-aircraft artillery groups were to cooperate with the 16th Air Army's 6th and 8th fighter divisions.

As a rule, besides the *fronts'* anti-aircraft weapons, units of National Air Defense were added for covering the *fronts'* rear targets. For example, the First Baltic Front was reinforced for this purpose by the 2nd National Air Defense Corps. And despite this, the number of anti-aircraft weapons for simultaneously covering all the targets in the *fronts'* areas was insufficient. Because of this, the broad maneuver of anti-aircraft artillery weapons was planned and carried out for the purpose of concentrating them in order to cover the most important targets (for example, for covering a railroad station while disembarking troops).

With the deployment of the troops into their combat formations, the main mass of anti-aircraft artillery weapons was shifted to covering the first-echelon troops. Cover was planned according to stages in the armies' and *fronts'* operations.

Significant numbers of weapons were allotted for the organization of continuous anti-aircraft artillery and aviation cover of the mobile groups. For example, the Third Belorussian Front's cavalry-mechanized group and 5th Guards Tank Army were to be reinforced by no less than one anti-aircraft artillery division and covered from the air by the forces of up to one fighter division to one fighter corps each.

Of the overall number of anti-aircraft artillery weapons allotted for covering the troops, a large part was designated for the armies playing the decisive role in the *fronts'* operations. For example, in the First Baltic Front the 6th Guards and 43rd armies received 83 percent of the medium-caliber weapons, 67 percent of the small-caliber weapons, and 56 percent of the anti-aircraft machine guns. In the Third Belorussian Front the following weapons were allotted for covering the 5th and 11th Guards armies: 60 percent of the medium-caliber weapons, about 62 percent of the small-caliber weapons, and 60 percent of the anti-aircraft machine guns. In the Second Belorussian

Front 100 percent of the medium-caliber weapons and 84 percent of the medium caliber weapons were allotted for covering the 49th Army.

In the armies, the anti-aircraft artillery weapons were, as a rule, used for covering the troops, as the rear-area targets were covered, in the majority of cases, by *front* weapons. The anti-aircraft artillery weapons were unified in anti-aircraft artillery groups. The number of anti-aircraft artillery groups was determined depending on the army's supply of anti-aircraft artillery weapons and on the number of objects to be covered.

Control of the anti-aircraft artillery was centralized. All the anti-aircraft artillery groups were subordinated to the deputy army commander for anti-aircraft artillery.

Thus anti-aircraft artillery support and coverage of the troops and rear targets from the air in the operation, by *fronts* and armies, corresponded to the operational plans and the situation. Anti-aircraft artillery cover was planned on the basis of the close cooperation of the anti-aircraft artillery with aviation. Anti-aircraft artillery weapons were employed *en masse* for covering the *fronts'* main groups of forces and the armies. The distribution of anti-aircraft artillery weapons was carried out in accordance with the importance of the targets to be protected from the air. All of this made it easier to repel the enemy's air raids and facilitated the overall success of the offensive operation.

Anti-chemical defense was expressed in the organization of the observation and chemical reconnaissance of the enemy, in deploying degasification posts in the rifle divisions and regiments, as well as in supplying the troops with gas masks, and cloaks and packets against mustard gas.

For example, by the start of the offensive 72 meteorological and chemical observation posts and sections for chemical defense and reconnaissance had been organized in the Second Belorussian Front. These posts were primarily located among the observation posts of the rifle regiment and division commanders. In the army and *front* rear chemical observation was carried out by posts of the rear units and installations, by control posts and examination posts.

On the whole, the systematic and rigorously carried out measures by the *fronts* for the operational support of the operation during the preparatory period enabled us to unmask the enemy's group of forces, his fire system, and the character of his engineering outfitting of the defense, as well as to achieve operational surprise, although we did not manage to completely hide the forthcoming offensive from the enemy. As early as the first half of June, the enemy opposite the forces of the First and Third Belorussian fronts knew about the preparations for our forces' offensive. However, the operation's large scale proved unexpected for him.

7

Engineering Support

A great deal of attention was devoted to the operation's engineering support, which was conditioned by the wooded and swampy character of the terrain and the necessity of overcoming the enemy's prepared defense, as well as a large number of water obstacles.

By the start of the operation all the *fronts* had been significantly reinforced by engineer-sapper formations and units. Overall, within the First Baltic, Third, Second and First Belorussian fronts, there numbered 39 different engineer, engineer-sapper and pontoon-bridge brigades, eight engineer-tank and flamethrower tank regiments, 29 independent pontoon-bridge and special engineer battalions, as well as a significant number of engineer-construction and road units and formations. The *fronts* were reinforced with the following Supreme High Command formations and units (see table 39).

The engineering troops were assigned the following tasks: to carry out non-stop engineering reconnaissance for the purpose of uncovering the enemy's defensive system and his engineering measures; to outfit jumping-off areas for the offensive for the *fronts'* main groups of forces; to carry out road and bridge work; to create mobile obstacle detachments and to support the troops with engineering obstacles; to carry out concealment measures, and; to support the forthcoming river crossings.

In order to get information about the enemy, all means and methods of engineering reconnaissance were employed. For example, the engineering reconnaissance of the front line was carried out by observation, with the aid of engineering posts (for example, 120 engineering observation posts were organized along the First Belorussian Front's 214-kilometer front), through independent nighttime searches, as well as by including the engineering groups in the combined-arms reconnaissance groups. The depth of the defense was reconnoitered by sending engineering groups into the enemy rear (in the Second Belorussian Front five such groups were dispatched into the enemy's rear and ten in the First Belorussian Front). The necessary information was also obtained through interrogating prisoners, as well as through the partisans and aerial photo reconnaissance.

As a result of generalizing all the intelligence data, we managed to discover the engineering outfitting system in the enemy's defense, to unearth the location of minefields, barbed wire obstacles, the enemy's defensive structures, and also to specify the character of the terrain, roads and river obstacles in the rear of the enemy's defense.

On the basis of all this data, detailed charts of the defensive structures, obstacles and river sectors and maps of passable terrain were drawn up on a 1:10,000 and 1:50,000 scale, 1:20,000 and 1:50,000 scale, which were supplied to the troops in sufficient quantity.

Movement off the roads was extremely difficult in the wooded and swampy terrain, and the poorly developed road network could not meet the demand for communications routes necessary for concentrating, regrouping and deploying large masses of troops, outfitted with a great deal of modern military equipment, in a limited time. Thus road and bridge work occupied a great part of the overall sum of engineering measures during the preparatory period.

Table 39. The Strength of the *Fronts'* Engineering Troops by the Start of the Belorussian Operation (Not Counting Troop Sappers)

1st Baltic Front	3rd Belorussian Front	2nd Belorussian Front	1st Belorussian Front
2nd, 28th and 29th army engineer-sapper bdes (12 bns)	2nd, 3rd and 4th assault engineer-sapper bdes (15 bns)	1st Gds Assault Engineer-Sapper Bde (5 bns)	2nd, 10th, 14th, 35th, 36th, and 57th engineer-sapper bdes (21 bns)
5th and 10th assault engineer-sapper bdes (10 bns)	8th Pontoon Bde (5 bns)	33rd Motorized Engineer Bde (3 bns), 11th, 34th and 50th engineer-sapper bdes (12 bns)	1st Gds Engineer-Sapper Bde (4 bns), an independent assault engineer-sapper bde (10 bns)
5th Gds Motorized Engineer Bde (3 bns)	13th, 31st, 32nd, 63rd, and 66th engineer-sapper bdes (20 bns)	9th, 87th, 92nd, and 122nd independent pontoon bns	9th Gds Independent Engineer-Sapper Bn, a motorized engineer bde (3 bns)
9th Pontoon Bde (5 bns)	52nd Supreme High Command Defense Construction Directorate	20th Defense Construction Directorate (8 bns)	6th and 8th independent sapper bns with dog mine detectors
37th, 91st, 94th, and 106th pontoon bns	5th Front Defense Construction Directorate	8 electric bns	27th Defense Construction Directorate (6 bns)
21st Supreme High Command Defense Construction Directtorate (3 bns in each)		5 independent special companies (1 bn)	8th Assault Engineer-Sapper Bde (5 bns)
4th Front Directorate for Special Construction (3 bns)			7th Pontoon Bde (5 bns)
37th Independent Sapper Bn (with dog mine detectors)			48th Pontoon Bn

We had to check a large number of existing roads and cross-country routes of march for mines, to lay down new roads and cross-country routes of march, repair, improve and strengthen existing roads and bridges.

In the wooded and swampy terrain conditions, the necessity arose to strengthen the roadbeds with materials at hand, primarily materials from the woods. In order to give the reader an idea of the volume of road and bridge work according to the experience of one of the *fronts*, it is sufficient to examine table 40.

In the First Baltic Front, in the 20 days preceding the operation 275 kilometers of roads were built and restored, and another 820 kilometers repaired. Bridges were built on these roads with an overall length of 1,800 meters. The roads were built on the calculation of one per first-echelon rifle division and two per rifle corps and army.

In the First Belorussian Front, by the beginning of the operation four army routes had been built in the 3rd Army's sector, from the front line to the Dnepr River.

Such a large volume of road and bridge work, carried out in a short time period, required a very large work force and much equipment. For example, in the First Baltic Front 6,000 sappers were brought in for road work and, in the course of 12 days 4,700 men were employed daily in the 6th Guards Army's sector from the troops of the army's second echelon. Equipment was represented by 380 vehicles, 22 transports, nine graders, five diesel pile drivers, and a number of other machines.

In order to cover the roads, about 45,000 cubic meters of lumber and about 17,000 cubic meters of gravel and sand had to be hauled out. Such an amount of material could be simultaneously lifted by 5,000 3-ton vehicles. In the First Belorussian Front six of nine engineering brigades and 14 independent battalions of engineering and road construction troops were used for road and bridge work.

Table 40. The Volume of Road and Bridge Work Carried out by the Third Belorussian Front

Types of Work	39th Army	5th Army	11th Gds Army	31st Army	Total
Roads checked for mines (in kms)	120	75	293	150	638
Bridges cleared of mines	9	2	–	5	16
Roads repaired (in kms)	7	15	305	8	335
Cross-country routes of march laid down (in kms)	14	12	1.5	2	29.5
Roads built with a brushwood and corduroy bedding	4	11	8	7	30
New bridges built (units/linear meters)	47/330	63/1,200	36/280	11/159	157/1,969
Repaired and strengthened bridges (units/linear meters)	84/213	219/815	15/150	30/315	348/1,493

The road network's timely preparation enabled us to carry out the concentration, regrouping and deployment of the *fronts'* main groups of forces in the time set forth in the operational plan.

During the preparatory period the *fronts'* forces carried out additional fortification works on a large scale for preparing the jumping-off areas for the offensive by the first and follow-on echelons. These works consisted, for the most part, in adapting and developing the existing system of trenches and communications trenches, primarily in the jumping-off areas of the first-echelon divisions (the main defensive zone) for the purpose of securing the secret occupation of the jumping-off position for the offensive and the secret deployment of troops and a large amount of equipment in the jumping-off position, as well as to create conditions favorable to the troops going over to the attack.

Besides this, the system of indicated engineering measures also had the goal of strengthening the defense along the secondary axes, so that these axes could be defended with as few troops as possible.

During the course of the preceding battles, the *fronts'* forces had gone over to the defensive along some sectors at a distance of 1,000-1,200 meters from the enemy's front line. It was namely because of this that measures had to be adopted along these sectors that would reduce the distance required for the attack by 150-300 meters by moving up the forward trenches by that amount.

In the First Baltic Front the *front's* forces dug up to 230 kilometers of trenches and communications trenches during the preparatory period.

One may judge the volume of the fortification works by the Third Belorussian Front's 39th Army, where 26 kilometers of trenches and 22 kilometers of communications trenches were dug along the 6-kilometer breakthrough sector, which yielded eight kilometers of trenches and communications trenches per kilometer of front, which corresponded to 3-4 trench lines.

In the Second Belorussian Front the first-echelon divisions' jumping-off area along the main attack sector had been outfitted by the start of the operation to a depth of seven kilometers with 5-6 trench lines. The artillery and tanks had been well camouflaged and had main and reserve positions, shelters for the rank and file and munitions. In each rifle division, the company, battalion and regimental commanders had outfitted observation posts in the first line of trenches. The main group of forces' corps and division commanders had outfitted observation posts at a distance of

200-500 meters from the front line. 183 observation posts had been outfitted for the combined-arms and artillery commanders along the axis of the main attack.

The front line had been thickly covered with mines and other kinds of engineering obstacles. On may get an idea of the work done on the basis of the following table.

Table 41. The Condition of the Engineer Outfitting of the Second and First Belorussian Fronts' Jumping-Off Areas

Types of Structures	Unit of Measure	2nd Belorussian Front		1st Belorussian Front
		As of 23/4/44	As of 23/6/44	As of 23/6/44
Trenches	kms	419	2,487.5	635
Communications trenches	kms	102	912.5	181
Wooden and earth pillboxes	units	–	542	23
Machine gun platforms	units	2,799	27,840	6,923
Artillery trenches	units	1,018	6,984	1,324
Mortar trenches	units	920	6,110	960
Trenches for anti-tank rifles	units	725	5,380	1,028
Shelters	units	2,600	10,670	2,813
Command-observation posts	units	394	2,714	690

So as to conceal the operation's preparation from the enemy, as well as to ensure the concealment of the locations of the operational echelons and the troops' combat formations, fortification works for developing the trench system were carried out, as a rule, on a broad front.

In preparing the jumping-off areas for the offensive, we had to carry out a great volume of work for the complete mine clearing of the terrain.

For example, in the First Baltic Front this work had to be done in the Nevel'—Dretun'—Gorodok triangle, where a significant number of mines had been laid during the fall and winter battles of 1943-44. Two engineer brigades cleared the mines, and in the period from April through 12 June they checked and cleared 4,000 square kilometers of mines. During this time (55 days) more than 120,000 different mines were removed and neutralized.

Similar work was carried out by the engineer troops along the other *fronts*.

In the 10-20 days before the start of the operation the engineer troops began to remove our minefields in the defensive depth and, in 3-4 days began partially removing our minefields and making passages in the minefields laid out in front of the forward edge of the defense. Passages were made for the infantry, both in the barbed wire obstacles and in the minefields, 10-20 meters wide, and 20-40 meters for the tanks. Passages were made on a calculation of six passages per battalion for the infantry and one passage for a tank battalion, and 6-8 passages for a tank brigade.

In the Second Belorussian Front 225 passages were made for the infantry and 38 for the tanks; in the First Belorussian Front there were six passages per battalion. In the Third Belorussian Front a single, solid 120-meter passage was made for tanks in the 39th Army, and a single, solid 300-meter passage in the 11th Guards Army. 6,500 anti-tank and anti-personnel mines were removed from the Second Belorussian Front, and about 21,000 in the First Belorussian Front. Clearing passages in the enemy's minefields and obstacles was carried out in two or even one nights before the attack. 193 passages were made in the night before the attack In the First Belorussian Front, while 34,450 anti-tank and anti-personnel mines were removed, as well as 132 other kinds of mines, and 76 booby traps.

During the course of the operation the main groups of forces of some fronts (the word fronts should be italicized) had to force several water obstacles. For example, the First Baltic Front's main group of forces had to force the Western Dvina River, those of the Third Belorussian Front the Berezina River, those of the Second Belorussian Front the Pronya, Dnepr, Drut', and Berezina rivers, and those of the First Belorussian Front the Drut', Berezina, Svisloch', and Ptich' rivers. At the same time, the Second and, partially, the First Belorussian fronts began the operation by forcing rivers, while the First Baltic Front had the Western Dvina River only 15-30 kilometers from the front line. Only in the Third Belorussian Front's sector was the Berezina River 150 kilometers removed from the front line.

The necessity of forcing large water obstacles, with wide and swampy valleys, in the offensive zones of the *fronts'* main groups of forces obliged the *front* commands to adopt a number of timely measures directed toward securing the operation's successful development. Thus significant attention was devoted to the preparation of crossing parks, crossing equipment, and equipment for overcoming flooded sectors in the overall sum of measures for the engineer support of the operation.

The *fronts'* supply of the most important crossing equipment is shown in the following table.

Table 42. The *Fronts'* Provision with Organic Bridge and Crossings Parks

Crossing Equipment	*Front* Supply			
	1st Baltic	3rd Belorussian	2nd Belorussian	1st Belorussian
Heavy Bridge Train parks	–	–	–	1
Division Bridge Parks	–	–	2	2
Bow Half-Pontoon parks	5	2⅔	1	5
Division Light Pontoon Parks	4[1]	2	–	–
"V" parks	–	–	1	1
Light Inflatable Pontoon parks	7	6	–	1
Parks on A-3 boats	–	11	–	13
Small Inflatable Boats	50	–	–	601
A-3 boats	21	–	–	402
Collapsible Landing Boats	200	–	30	532
Diving suits	600	–	–	–
Lifejackets	220	–	–	–
Wooden Sapper Boats	–	–	100	–
Iolshin sacks	1,300	–	–	–
Flotation Equipment	–	–	14	–

Note
1 Of these, three were prepared by pontoon troops.

The First Baltic Front's provisioning with pontoon troops and crossing equipment enabled it to throw up to seven bridges over the Western Dvina River. This enabled us to have two bridges per first-echelon rifle corps, of which one had a capacity of 30 tons, and the other 16 tons.

Besides this, during the preparatory period the engineer troops prepared 450 linear meters of parts for low-water 60-ton bridges.

The limited amount of organic crossing equipment forced the Third Belorussian Front's engineer troops to prepare beforehand a large number of wooden low-water bridge parts and assault bridges, which may be seen in the following table.

In addition its the organic equipment, the Second Belorussian Front's engineer forces prepared 72 assault bridges, based on a calculation of 18-22 bridges for a first-echelon rifle division. Parts for 32 wooden low-water bridges were prepared for crossing tanks and artillery. The overall length of these bridges was 860 meters.

In the First Belorussian Front, in connection with the shortage of organic crossing equipment, the engineering troops also had to build low-water wooden bridges and prepare assault bridges. In all, 51 assault bridges, with an overall length of about 1,000 meters, were built. In all, by the start of the offensive, 42 bridges had been laid down or prepared for laying across the Drut' and Dnepr rivers at the start of the offensive.

Table 43. The Preparation of Parts for Low-Water and Assault Bridges in the Third Belorussian Front

Equipment Name	39th Army	5th Army	11th Guards Army	31st Army	Total
Parts for a 60-ton bridge (units/linear meters)	1/80	4/160	7/560	3/60	15/860
Parts for a 30-ton bridge (units/linear meters)	1/88	2/80	–	6/120	9/288
Parts for a 16-ton bridge (units/linear meters)	2/90	–	–	2/120	4/210
Parts for a 9-ton bridge (units/ linear meters)	1/45	–	–	–	1/45
Assault bridges (units/linear meters)	15/600	120/2,400	290/5,800	20/400	445/9,200

For overcoming swamps during the offensive, the following had been prepared beforehand from available material: 376 travois for the artillery, 234 travois for the heavy machine guns, 1,144 brushwood mats, and 1,924 fittings for shoes to help the soldiers cross swampy areas.

River barriers were one of the targets of engineer reconnaissance. For example, in the First Baltic Front the Polotsk—Staroe Selo sector of the Western Dvina River was reconnoitered. In the Second Belorussian Front the engineer troops reconnoitered 18 active bridges over the Dnepr River. In the First Belorussian Front the reconnaissance of the river lines went as far as the Ptich' River.

All of these measures were carried out in a timely manner and, to a significant degree, facilitated the breakthrough of the enemy's defense along with the forcing of a large number of river lines, as well as overcoming swampy terrain.

By the beginning of the operation the disposition of the engineer troops in the armies and formations subordinated to the *fronts* was as follows (see table 44).

Aside from this, part of the engineer formations and units were located in the *front* groups of engineering troops, in the reserve and in the *front's* mobile obstacle detachments. For example, in the First Baltic Front there remained in the *front* commander's disposal: a motorized engineer brigade, four pontoon battalions, a battalion with dog mine detectors, a defense construction directorae (three battalions), a *front* defense construction directorate (three battalions), and other engineer units, for a total of 52 calculated sapper companies. Of the overall number of 48 engineer and pontoon battalions (not counting troop sappers), there were 45 battalions, that is, 95 percent of the engineer troops were concentrated along the main axis.

In the Third Belorussian Front 51 calculated sapper companies were tasked with carrying out the *front's* engineering measures; in the Second Belorussian Front—60, and in the First Belorussian Front—46 calculated sapper companies, or one engineer-sapper brigade, two pontoon battalions, one electrical battalion, one special mining battalion, two military-construction detachments, two mine removal battalions with dogs, or, in all, 12 battalions. Of 58 calculated engineer battalions that the First Belorussian Front's right wing disposed of (not counting troop sappers), 51 calculated engineer battalions, or 90 percent of the engineering troops, were employed along the main axis.

Mobile obstacle detachments were created in all the operational field forces and combined-arms formations.

By the start of the operation the troops were provisioned with the main obstacle equipment. For example, in the First Baltic Front there were 44 tons of anti-tank and 78 tons of anti-personnel mines.

Table 44. The Distribution of Engineer Troops by Army

1st Baltic Front		3rd Belorussian Front		2nd Belorussian Front		1st Belorussian Front	
Armies and Formations	Engineer Units and formations	Armies	Engineer Units and formations	Armies	Engineer Units and formations	Armies	Engineer Units and formations
4th Shock	army engineer-sapper bde	39th	army engineer-sapper bde	49th	army engineer-sapper bde, 4 pontoon bns	3rd	2 engineer-sapper bdes pontoon bde, pontoon bn
6th Guards	army engineer-sapper bde, assault engineer-sapper bde, 3 pontoon bns	5th	army engineer-sapper bde, assault engineer-sapper bde	33rd	army engineer-sapper bde, electrical bn, motorized engineer bn	48th	army engineer-sapper bde, assault engineer-sapper bde
43rd	army engineer-sapper bde, assault engineer-sapper bde	11th Gds	army engineer-sapper bde, assault engineer-sapper bde	50th	army engineer-sapper bde	65th	army engineer-sapper bde
1st Tank Corps	2 engineer bns	31st	army engineer-sapper bde			28th	army engineer-sapper bde

The density of the engineering troops in the Belorussian operation may be determined by the following table.

Table 45. The Density of Engineering Troops by the Start of the Operation

Fronts	Width of Breakthrough Sector (in kms)	Calculated Sapper Companies	
		Main Attack Axis (total)	Per Kilometer of Breakthrough Sector
1st Baltic	25	200	8
3rd Belorussian	37	265 (not counting (5th Guards Tank Army)	7.2
2nd Belorussian	12	156	13
1st Belorussian (right wing)	29	320	11
Total	103	941	9.1

On the whole, the concentration of the engineering forces main efforts and the creation of high densities of engineering troops along the axes of the *fronts'* main attacks, the large-scale and successful work of all the combat arms in preparing the jumping-off areas for the offensive, the thorough training of the troops for the breakthrough of the enemy's previously-prepared defense under conditions where roads were lacking and in a wooded and swampy terrain, and the training of the troops to overcome large river obstacles, facilitated the successful breakthrough of the enemy's defense and the development of the operation at a high rate of speed.

8

Party-Political Support

The basic goal of party-political work in the preparatory period before the Belorussian operation consisted on mobilizing the moral and physical forces of the *fronts'* forces toward carrying out the combat tasks assigned by the Supreme High Command.

This could be achieved by means of explaining the goals and character of the Great Patriotic War to the *fronts'* rank and file, and the objectives of the people and the Soviet army in achieving victory over the enemy, and by means of inculcating the rank and file in a spirit of burning hatred for the enemy, by inculcating bravery, valor and courage in the troops and a feeling of personal responsibility for the liberation of their Soviet motherland from the German occupiers, and in connection with this, by raising the combat training, strengthening military discipline, and increasing vigilance and raising the troops' combat readiness.

For the successful resolution of such a grandiose goal for the moral-political and combat preparation of the *fronts'* forces, it was necessary, first of all, to train the command and party-political cadres, as well as the political organs, party and *Komsomol*[1] organizations for intensive party-political work.

Operational preparation by the *fronts'* political directorates began with a check of the party-political work in the armies and divisions. At this time the party-political workers were thoroughly checked, all the way down to the regimental level, from the point of view of their work and political qualities. As a result of this work, part of the party-political workers in the armies and divisions were replaced by more qualified ones. All the vacant posts were filled. Political worker reserves were created in the armies' political sections.

The review also showed that party organizations were absent in many rifle companies. For example, following the intensive fighting in the winter of 1943-44, as a result of the heavy losses, the number of party organizations, mainly at the company level, fell significantly. For example, in January 1944 there were no party organizations at all in 1,224 companies and their equivalents in the First Belorussian Front. The same situation was observed in the Third Belorussian Front's forces. As late as May 1944 it was established that some chiefs of the divisions' political sections and the regiments' party bureaus were not taking any kind of measures for restoring and creating party organizations in the First and Third Belorussian fronts' rifle and machine gun company party organizations.

Thus in the operation's preparatory period the units' political organs' and political apparatuses' most important task was the restoration and creation of full-blooded and cohesive and actively working party and *Komsomol* organizations in each company and equivalent subunit.

This task was successfully resolved, most of all, by selection and induction into the party and *Komsomol* soldiers who had distinguished themselves in battle, and by transferring communists from the rear units and subunits, and, finally, through the arrival of communists and *Komsomol* members returning as reinforcements after recovering in the hospitals and medical battalions.

---

1   Editor's note. The *Komsomol* stood for the *Kommunisticheskii Soyuz Molodezhi* (Communist Youth Union), the youth auxiliary of the Communist Party.

The main source for adding to and restoring the party and *Komsomol* organizations was the induction of new members, which was understandable. During the years of the Great Patriotic War the Communist Party's authority rose in particular. The Soviet army's soldiers, the workers, collective farmers and representatives of the intelligentsia saw in the party their tested leader, organizer and inspirer. They were deeply interested in expanding and strengthening the party's ranks and voluntarily entrusted themselves to the party's leadership. From this the drive of the best people in the years of the Great Patriotic War, in the years of harsh trials, to join the ranks of the Communist Party is understandable.

However, some of the *fronts'* political organs and party organizations at first committed grave violations of the principle of individual selection in accepting people into the party. There were instances when party organizations inducted into the party everyone who submitted an application, without the necessary checking of their political and work qualities. As a result, people were sometimes accepted into the party who were not worthy of bearing the high calling of party member. Some party organizations, in inducting people into the party, incorrectly extended the decree by the Communist Party Central Committee on the induction of soldiers, who had particularly distinguished themselves in the fighting, to all military personnel.

At the same time, in a number of units and formations there were instances of an incorrect approach to an evaluation of the reinforcements from the liberated areas. Not all political organs carried out the main political administration's demand to hand out party documents to newly inducted party members in the course of five days.

As a result of the measures adopted, the work of the party organs, party organizations and party commissions on inducting people into the party improved significantly. Party organizations and party bureaus began to treat more seriously the selection of the best soldiers into the party and began to really verify and study the work and political qualities of those joining the party.

By the start of the operation the party and *Komsomol* stratum grew significantly in the *fronts'* units and formations, and the number of party organizations increased, as can be seen in the following table.

In the rifle divisions of the Third Belorussian Front's 5th Army the party element accounted for 18 percent to 22 percent of the entire rank and file. For example, on 21 June 1944 the 277th Rifle Division included 898 Communist Party members and 479 candidate members, or 20.2 percent of the overall number of the division's rank and file.

Before the June offensive of 1944 the party organizations made up an enormous force in the *fronts'* armies. For example, in the Third Belorussian Front's 5th Army there were 597 primary party organizations, 1,000 company and company-equivalent organizations, which included 13,178 party members and 6,353 candidate members, for a total of 19,531 members. In the First Belorussian Front's 28th Army on 1 June 1944 there were 505 primary and 701 company and equivalent party organizations, in which there were 10,572 party members and 5,804 candidate members, or a total of 16,376 men. In the First Belorussian Front's 3rd Army on 21 June 1944 there were 915 primary and 1,441 company and equivalent party organizations.

In the majority of the First, Second and Third Belorussian fronts' formations the company party organizations had 5-10 communists apiece, while the *Komsomol* element in the formations' companies comprised 10-20 members each.

Within the companies the communists and *Komsomol* members were positioned so as to ensure the party's influence on the rank and file of each section and crew. We tried to create a higher party-*Komsomol* element in the subunits and crews servicing group and automatic weapons, and in reconnaissance subunits.

Besides this, particularly thorough work was carried out in securing the party's influence in the ranks of the attacking subunits, assault detachments and groups. The communists and *Komsomol* members were deployed in such a way that they could inspire the troops by their personal example.

Thanks to this, the first attacking ranks' combat actions were distinguished by risk-taking, bravery, initiative, and vigor.

Long before the offensive, the communists and *Komsomol* members trained themselves for the role of leader, both in the political and military sense. During the preparatory period each communist in an attacking line had a complete opportunity to study his non-party comrades from all sides and to prepare them to make the attack successful through their joint efforts. During the combat training period they were an example of insistent work for improving their combat skills and, in battle, through their bravery and fearlessness they inspired the troops of the attacking line.

Table 46. The Party and *Komsomol* Element in the Formations of the First Belorussian Front's 28th Army by the Start of the Operation

Formation	% of Communists and *Komsomol* Members among Officers	Among Enlisted Personnel and NCOs		Overall % of Communists and *Komsomol* Members
		% of Communists	% of *Komsomol*	
50th Gds Rifle Div	68.4	14	16	34.4
54th Gds Rifle Div	51.0	13	9	25.3
48th Gds Rifle Div	76.7	14	12	31.4
20th Gds Rifle Div	43.0	22	13	39.4
56th Gds Rifle Div	77.1	24	11	40.1
In the remaining formations	59.0-65.0	NA	NA	23.0-26.0

The creation and strengthening of full-blooded party and *Komsomol* organizations and the correct deployment of communists and *Komsomol* members in subunits created the necessary base for the unfolding of party-political work during both the preparatory period, as well as during the course of the operation.

The tasks of organizationally strengthening the company and equivalent party and *Komsomol* organizations required the thorough selection of the companies' party and *Komsomol* organizers. The political organs carried out, in this regard, a great deal of work. New cadres, made up of the best sergeants and soldiers, with combat experience, were moved up for leadership positions in the company and equivalent subunit party organizations. Because these cadres lacked the necessary theoretical training and experience of organizing party work in a combat setting, they were taught this work in the units.

The training of party workers was conducted primarily at seminars and meetings, which were systematically conducted in the divisional political sections and in the regiments. The main content of the seminars and meetings was studying the experience of the practical work of the party organizers and party organizations in preparing for the offensive and during the offensive.

One can get an idea of the volume of work done, if only by materials. In the rifle regiments of the 28th Army's 50th Guards Division, 64 communists were selected and confirmed by the companies' party organizers. In June the 5th Army' party section dispatched to the formations 98 company party organizers, who had undergone a two-month preparation according to the *front* political directorate's program. Besides this, in the formations' political sections 126 party organizers were trained and dispatched to the companies. A party company reserve was created in all the *fronts'* armies and formations for rapidly replacing company party workers in case of their removal from the ranks during the offensive. The deputy unit commanders for political affairs and the divisional political sections were directly responsible for selecting candidates for the combat organizer reserve. Candidates were selected from among those rank and file and NCO party members with the greatest training and combat experience, primarily from the service and rear subunits and units, from those recovering in the medical battalions and hospitals, and by advancing rank and file party members in the rifle companies.

The selection and training of party and *Komsomol* company organizers was organized in accordance with the Main Political Directorate's directive no. 010, of 7 September 1943, which obliged the chiefs of the armies' and formations' political sections to have a reserve of company party organizers of no less than 8-10 men in a formation, and 20-25 in an army. However, practice showed that the reserve of party organizers, which had been created in the amount called for by the Main Political Directorate's directive no. 010, was insufficient, and that it was necessary to increase the amount by approximately two times. Thus some political organs increased their reserve of company party organizers, on their own initiative, to 30 men to a division.

The constant concern over the selection of authoritative communists with combat experience as company party organizers, and the non-stop work with them for the purpose of teaching them the theory and practice of party work had a decisive influence on strengthening company party organizations.

During the Great Patriotic War the Central Committee of our Communist Party paid particular attention to the ideological-political conditioning of the political workers' military knowledge, which was only natural. The political apparatus's work was a very important factor in determining, to a significant degree, the moral strength and combat capability of the Soviet army's units and formations. Thus the political workers' training for the upcoming battles occupied a central place at all levels of the command and political organs. The Main Political Directorate's directive no. 010 of 7 September 1943 noted:

> The education of new cadres of party workers, who have arrived to take up the leadership of party organizations, should be considered one of the political organs' main tasks. Meetings and seminars of party organizers and their assistants should be systematically conducted in the party organs, with questions of party construction, the practice of party work, and questions of ongoing policy, put forward there.

Work with the cadres of the party-political apparatus called for: ideological-theoretical training, military training, and the raising of work qualities on the basis of studying and generalizing the progressive experience of organizing party-political work in a combat situation.

The forms of preparing all levels of the party-political apparatus were as follows: meetings, gatherings, seminars, theoretical discussions, independent work, and studying the practice of organizing party-political work in a combat situation by means of rendering daily assistance on the spot.

In order to judge what questions were studied and discussed at these meetings, gatherings and seminars for political workers, we can cite a few examples.

For example, at a meeting of the chiefs of the corps and divisions in the First Belorussian Front's 3rd Army, the following were discussed: a) the reports by the political section chiefs "On the Course of Studying and Carrying out the Supreme Commander-in-Chief's order no. 70"; b) the report by the chief of the army's intelligence section, "Information on the Enemy Facing Us, and on Events Along the Soviet Army's Fronts"; c) instructions by the member of the army's military council on training units for the offensive battle. Such questions were raised at a meeting of the chiefs of the political sections of the artillery divisions and brigades, of the engineering brigades, and of the deputy commanders for political affairs of army regiments and units.

The political section of the First Belorussian Front's 28th Army conducted a three-day meeting (22-25 May 1944) of deputy regimental commanders for political affairs, during which they heard 16 lectures and reports, including "Teachings about the Party," "The Supreme

Commander-in-Chief's orders nos. 16 and 70—A Program for the Final Defeat of the German-Fascist Aggressors," "Fundamentals of Combat Activities in Wooded and Swampy Terrain," "The Essence of Cooperation Between the Combat Arms in the Offensive Battle," "The Strengthening of Unity of Command in the Soviet Army," and; "Questions of Intraparty Agitation Work."

At a ten-day meeting of party organizers of primary party organizations, which was conducted by the same army's political section on 21 June, lectures and reports on political questions, party-political and organizational-political work were heard and discussed

In May seminars for the regimental party organizers were conducted in the 28th Army's rifle corps, in which the following topics were heard and discussed: "The Responsibilities of the Regimental Party Organizer for Organizing Party-Political Work During the Preparatory Period for the Offensive Battles, During the Battle and Afterwards"; "The Company Party Organization—the Commander's Support and Assistant"; "The Party Organizer's Work to Create and Teach the Party Activists"; "The Party's Growth and Educational Work with Young Communists," and; "On Studying the Main Political Directorate's directives nos. 188 and 64, and order no. 134."

In May and June in the political section of the Third Belorussian Front's 5th Army two-and three-day seminars for the chiefs of political organs, the assistant regimental commanders for political affairs, the regimental party and *Komsomol* organizers, and the agitators for the divisions' and regiments' political sections, were conducted. The main content of the seminars' work were questions connected with the practice of organizing party-political work for training the rank and file for offensive battles. The army commander, members of the military council, and the chief of the army's political section, took part in the seminars' conduct.

On 8 June a conference of chiefs of the corps' and divisions' political sections was conducted in the army's political section to discuss the political organs' tasks for preparing the troops for offensive battles.

During 10-12 June meetings in corps, divisions and regiments were conducted for the workers of the corps and divisional political sections and the regimental apparatus. At these meetings the commanders and chiefs of the formations' political sections, unit commanders and their deputies for political affairs laid down specific tasks before the political workers for the combat and political training of units and formations for the forthcoming battles.

In all of the army's formations in May there were carried out two-day seminars for the deputy battalion and artillery battalion commanders for political affairs on the following themes: "Tasks on the Combat Improvement of the Rank and File and Cementing the Elements Together," and "The Exchange of Experience of Practical Work for Training the Rank and File for the Offensive"; seminars for the party organizers of the battalion and artillery battalion primary party organizations, on the following themes: "The Party Organizations' Work for Supporting the Fulfillment of the Tasks for the Rank and File's Combat Improvement"; "Induction into the Party and the Creation of Full-Blooded Company Party Organizations," and; "The Practice of Leading Company Party Organizations"; seminars for the *Komsomol* organizers for the primary organizations on the following themes: "Tasks for Educating the *Komsomol* Members in a Spirit of Offensive Enthusiasm," and "The Growth of *Komsomol* Organizations and their Work in Educating Newly-Inducted Members."

In order to successfully train the troops in the moral-political sense and support their combat training for the forthcoming operation, the political workers had to not only insistently acquire Marxist-Leninist theory, but also deeply study military affairs, weaponry, equipment, instructions, and manuals.

For this purpose, the training of the political works was organized and which was carried out, as a rule, along with the command element in a system of commander's training, in accordance with Defense Commissariat order no. 0144.

The political workers' systematic military training favorably influenced the improvement in the quality of the party-political work among the troops. Party-political work was becoming more directed, specific and more closely linked to the tasks being resolved by the subunits, units and formations.

A no less important activity by the political organs during the preparatory period was the work on selecting and training a reserve of organic political organs, party organizers and company *Komsomol* organizers.

The *front* political directorates and army political sections worked to create and train a reserve of organic political workers. The deputy unit commanders for political affairs and the division political sections were in charge of selecting candidates for the company party organizer reserve.

The reserve of company party organizers was usually concentrated and instructed within the division's training company, and sometimes in groups of those recovering from their injuries, and at the army level—in a reserve regiment.

The basic form of training a reserve of company party organizations in the division's training companies was five- and ten-day seminars. In order to reinforce the knowledge gained at these seminars, the future party organizers were dispatched for on-site training to the units where they were to be sent for preparing party meetings, for drawing up plans for party work, and for talking with the soldiers and sergeants.

The training of a reserve of party organizers in the army's political sections was more extended than in the divisions. In all, up to 600 study hours were devoted to training, which lasted during the course of two months. Of this number of hours, more than 200 were devoted to party-political work, up to 300 hours to combat training, and up to 70 hours to independent work, as in the First Belorussian Front's 3rd Army.

The *fronts'* political directorates exercised continuous control over the training of reserve of company party organizers and eliminated shortcomings in this important work in a timely manner. For example, we managed to get rid of the shortcomings in time in the selection and training of the company party organizers in the units of the First Belorussian Front, where there were incidents when some political organs created a reserve of party organizers, but did not work with it; in a number of units and formations, from the moment the company party organizers were appointed, all manner of work with them ceased; insufficient attention was devoted to questions of vigilance and strengthening discipline in the programs. Aside from this, in the 3rd Army's reserve regiment there were unearthed such shortcomings in the training of company party organizers such as the low quality of lectures, a severe shortage of teachers, and the necessary literature.

The *Komsomol* organizations were a reliable support and help for the command, the political organs and the party organizations in the moral-political and combat training of the *fronts'* troops. A large number of *Komsomol* activists, with a small amount of experience, were brought in to head up the *Komsomol* work after the winter battles of 1943-44. This circumstance required the political organs and party organizations to devote a great deal of attention to the ideological education of the *Komsomol* activists.

Work in the field of training and educating the *Komsomol* cadres was carried out along the same lines as that of the party cadres. The most widespread forms of training were seminars, gatherings, and meetings of the *Komsomol* activists. In the seminars the *Komsomol* activists raised their ideological-political level, studied the history of the Communist Party, Marxist-Leninist theory, the practice and experience of *Komsomol* work in a military situation, learned to generalize and analyze its work, and organize it in a specific and directed fashion.

Particular attention was given to the training of company party organizers, as the majority of them had no experience in *Komsomol* work. Lectures were read to the company party organizers on general political themes, on the themes of intra-*Komsomol* work, and about the *Komsomol's* role in the Great Patriotic War.

Besides independent work, seminars, gatherings, and meetings, and the study of Marxist-Leninist theory by *Komsomol* officers were conducted in a system of commander training, by rank and file and NCO *Komsomol* members in the second-echelon units during political lessons; the *Komsomol* members were exposed to political conversations along the front line.

Meetings and gatherings were important for training the *Komsomol* activists in a combat situation.

At these meetings they discussed the activists' tasks for assisting the commanders in supporting a high quality of combat training, in strengthening discipline, in ensuring the troops' combat readiness, and in inculcating vigilance, etc.

During the period of training the *fronts*' troops for the operation, the command element, political organs and party organizations devoted serious attention to the moral-political training of the officer element. Lessons on Marxist-Leninist training with the officer element were included in the plans and schedules for combat training and were carried out according to a special program. The main method was independent work in the work of the officer element in raising its ideological-theoretical level. To aid in the matter of the officers' Marxist-Leninist education, lectures and reports were read, while consultations and theoretical discussions were conducted.

For the purpose of strengthening unity of command and instilling in the officers, particularly young ones, habits of educating subordinates, as well as for the purpose of increasing their responsibility for the condition of educational work and the political-moral condition of their subordinate subunits and units, a special course of lectures was carried out. This course included lectures about Soviet patriotism, the history and theory of military art, and the traditions of the Soviet army. Besides this, in the First Belorussian Front the course included such specific themes as "The Moral Aspect of the Soviet Officer," "How to Organize Educational Work in the Subunit," "The Officer—the Educator of his Subordinates," and "On the Forms and Methods of Political-Educational Work in the Subunit."

Military and military-historical propaganda, which had as its goal to help in understanding military experience, occupied a large place in the educational work with the officer element. For this purpose, lectures were read, reports given, and seminars and meetings conducted for the exchange of experience.

Much attention was devoted to teaching the officers—particularly at the battalion-company-platoon level—to lead political work in their subunit in a combat situation. This was due to the fact that by that time the institute of deputy company commanders for political affairs had been abolished, in connection with which the commanders now had responsibility for the organization and conduct of political work with their subunits' rank and file. Full-time seminars for platoon and company commanders were organized in all units, and battalions in the formations. At each seminar several reports were usually assigned on general political questions and questions of organizing political-educational work in the subunit. Besides this, the units' political organs and political apparatuses rendered practical assistance to the commander and party organizations in the organization of educational work with the officer element. Many subunit commanders acquired experience in leading the subunits' political work and, relying on the party and *Komsomol* organizations, achieved positive results in educating the rank and file.

However, by the start of the operation the political organs and political organizations had not succeeded in creating a situation whereby all the subunit and unit commanders had correctly defined their place in the leadership of political work. Some of these still stood apart from the leadership of the rank and file's education, did not plan their political work, and themselves took insufficient part in educational work. A number of company commanders placed this work completely on the company party organizers.

In working with the officer element, a great deal of attention was devoted to working with the staff officers. The political organs directed the activities of the staffs' party organizations toward raising the ideological-theoretical training of the staff officers, toward the broadening of their military knowledge, toward the inculcation of vigilance and a feeling of responsibility for their task, and for the raising of the culture of staff work.

The success of the sections' and crews' combat activities depends, first of all, on the political-moral condition, combat training, resourcefulness, organizational abilities, bravery, and discipline of the sergeants—the commanders of the sections and crews. Thus in the preparatory period before the operation, serious attention was devoted to the selection and the moral-political and combat training of the NCO component. The basic form of political education for the NCOs was political lessons according to the schedule of combat and political training.

Aside from this, such forms of work were employed as reports, discussions and meetings. The subunit, unit and formation commanders, the high-ranking officers and political workers read reports for the sergeants about the role of the NCOs in teaching and educating the soldiers, in strengthening troop discipline, and in controlling the sections in the battle. For the sergeants, lectures were read about the international situation, about the combat oath, and on the inculcation of Soviet patriotism. For the purpose of exchanging experience, addresses were organized in the gatherings and meetings of the most trained and experienced sergeants—the war's veterans.

The popularization of the best sergeants' combat experience was carried out through divisional, army and *front* leaflets and newspapers, as well as booklets.

The political organs rendered daily assistance to the commanders and political apparatus of the units in organizing political-educational work with the NCOs and linked it with the tasks being resolved by the subunit, unit and formation in each given period of the operation's preparation.

The totality of measures for the moral-political training of the party-political and command cadres for restoring and strengthening the company party and *Komsomol* organizations, for educating and teaching the party and *Komsomol* activists and communists, had the purpose of preparing cadres capable of leading and supporting the leadership of the moral-political and combat training of the *fronts'* entire rank and file and NCO complement for conducting the Belorussian operation.

One of the most important means for the moral-political training of the *fronts'* rank and file for the operation and, most importantly, the rank and file and NCOs, was mass agitation work. The content of the mass agitation work during this period was determined by the tasks arising from the party's and government's decisions and the specific combat tasks being carried out by the formations and units.

The propaganda of the military oath, questions of strengthening discipline, unity of command, order, organizational abilities, vigilance, and the improvement of combat training occupied a large place in the mass agitation work among the rank and file. Simultaneously, subjects for mass agitation work were such questions as the manual's requirements for waging battle in a wooded and swampy area, the system and tactics of the enemy's defense, and popularizing the feats of the Great Patriotic War's heroes.

The overwhelming mass of the elements' agitators, who consisted primarily of communists and *Komsomol* members drawn from the rank and file and NCO ranks and who were constantly in the subunits combat formations, carried out constant agitation work. In all the elements (platoon, gun crews and tank crews) agitators were selected and a reserve created from among the most well prepared communists and *Komsomol* members.

One of the most efficacious and flexible forms of mass agitation work was political information, which was usually carried out in the first-echelon in each platoon and section, and in the second echelon—within the subunit. Meetings and soldiers' meetings had a particular place in mass agitation work in a combat setting, when the situation allowed. These forms of work were usually dedicated to the most important overall political questions and most important events in the life of the subunit, units and formation (studying the orders of the Supreme Commander-in-Chief, the appeals by the military councils, the awarding of medals, and the awarding of honorary designations, etc.).

Visual agitation was an important component part of mass-agitation work. In the covers, Lenin tents, dugouts, and communications trenches in the first echelon there were hung the latest editions of newspapers with announcements by the Soviet Information Bureau, and materials on the Hitlerites' atrocities on occupied Soviet territory.

Printed agitation and propaganda was extremely important in the cause of preparing the *fronts'* forces for the operation. In a front-line setting, newspapers, magazines, brochures, leaflets, pamphlets, and books simultaneously embraced hundreds of thousands of soldiers, sergeants and officers.

The timely provision of the subunits and units with a sufficient number of newspapers and magazines and the organization of work with the newspapers were very important component parts of agitation and propaganda work in conditions at the front. The political organs devoted particular attention so that the newspapers didn't lie around the headquarters and offices and were, instead, delivered as quickly as possible to the subunits on the front line.

One of the important tasks of mass-agitation work was the task of educating Soviet soldiers in a spirit of combat traditions, love for one's unit and combat banner. For the propaganda of combat traditions among the troops, such forms and methods of party-political work as political lessons, lectures, reports, conversations, army print, visual aids, and movies were employed. Other forms of party-political work were also employed, for example: meetings, soldiers' meetings, *Komsomol* meetings, and the solemn observance of memorable dates (the anniversary of the unit's or formation's creation, etc.), meetings with heroes of the Soviet Union, with cavaliers of the "Glory" order, with war veterans and decorated soldiers.

One of the most important questions in the political support of operational training was work to inculcate the high political vigilance of the rank and file to keep the forthcoming offensive a secret.

The necessity of daily work for raising vigilance was dictated by the fact that amongst the reinforcements called up from the liberated areas of Belorussia and western Ukraine, German-Fascist intelligence agents could filter in.

Besides this, the necessity of raising political vigilance was conditioned by the fact that as a result of the Soviet army's non-stop successes along the Great Patriotic War's fronts, some military personnel began to show signs of complacency and carelessness and underestimating the enemy' power and perfidy. Thus the political organs and political workers did not weaken their attention on educating the rank and file in a spirit of political vigilance, and the new methods of sabotage, spying and diversionary activity by the enemy and his agents were explained to the units' and formations' rank and file.

Questions of educating the rank and file in a spirit of high political vigilance and the ability to keep military secrets were discussed at meetings of the units' and formations' party and *Komsomol* activists, at party and *Komsomol* meetings, and at sessions of the party and *Komsomol* bureaus.

In the units and formations a check was carried out as to the correctness of preserving party and service documents and the necessary measures were taken to get rid of the existing shortcomings.

Questions of political vigilance and preserving military secrets were constantly highlighted on the pages of the army press.

The commanders, political organs and political workers conducted a great deal of work for the political support of the secrecy of the troops' regroupings and concentrations.

A most important task of the commanders, political organs, party and *Komsomol* organizations during the preparatory period was the all-round strengthening of troop discipline and order in the units and subunits. The commanders, political organs and party organizations, by insistently trying to raise the subunits' and units' combat effectiveness, viewed the strengthening of troop discipline as one of the main questions of agitation-propaganda and all party-political work. And this was no accident. A mass of new recruits, which consisted primarily of people called up from the areas liberated from the Germans, was pouring into the combat subunits. Besides this, as early as the beginning of regular combat training during the preparatory period, there were negative phenomena in a number of the *fronts'* units and formations in the organization of lessons, accidents, and incidents of a serious disruption of troop discipline. In this regard, so-called noncombat losses due to the careless handling of weapons were particularly dangerous.

The political organs, political workers and party organizations helped the officers master the methods of educating their subordinates, to skillfully combine high demands with concern for the materiel-daily conditions of the soldiers, and for their political and military education. The explained the role and importance of the commander in battle to the new recruits, told about the commanders' combat history and that of their subunits, units and formations and inculcated within them love, respect and a belief in their combat commander, a readiness to carry out his orders, and to defend him in battle at the cost of one's own life. The commanders and political workers explained to the rank and file the just goals of the Great Patriotic War, the essence and significance of troop discipline, inculcated in their soldiers a clear understanding of their military duty, fealty to the military oath, and a readiness to defend the Motherland without sparing one's blood and even life. The commanders, political organs and political workers, while organizing educational work with the new recruits, relied on veteran soldiers—participants in the battles for Stalingrad, Orel and the Dnepr. Communists and *Komsomol* members, by personal example of high discipline and a truthful word, influenced the mass of troops, fought for the strengthening of the commander's authority, for firm discipline, order and a sense of organization.

Of great significance in the matter of strengthening the political-moral condition and the combat capabilities of the *fronts'* forces was the concern of the commanders, political organs and political workers for the materiel and daily conditions and health of the soldiers.

During the operation's preparatory period the *fronts'* political directorates and the armies' and formations' political sections paid serious attention to the conduct of educational work among girls and women serving in the *fronts'* forces and to the improvement of their living conditions.

The political support for the troops' training was the main task of the political organs, political workers, and party and *Komsomol* organizations in the *fronts'* forces. At the basis of this work lay the task of communicating to the consciousness of the entire rank and file the demand by the Supreme High Command of the necessity of improving one's combat training, raising one's combat skills, and for mobilizing the entire rank and file for carrying out these demands. The party and the Soviet government constantly demanded from the Soviet army that it tirelessly improve its combat training and study and skillfully employ the war's experience.

The political workers, being constantly in the subunits, at field and tactical exercises, were constantly influencing the subunits' and units' rank and file through the party and *Komsomol* activists, communists and *Komsomol* members.

Questions about the leading role of communists and *Komsomol* members in combat training were discussed at party and *Komsomol* meetings.

A great deal of party-political work was carried out, particularly in connection with reviews of the battalions' (artillery battalions') and regiments' combat readiness for the offensive, which were conducted by the army and corps commanders in the first part of June 1944.

The planned and focused everyday moral-political training of the *fronts'* forces was closely linked to the combat tasks and supported the constant rise of the troops' moral-combat spirit and offensive *elan*, and their high state of combat readiness.

The basis of this entire huge amount of work was the following organizational-party measures:

a)   the restoration and strengthening of full-blooded and actively operating party and *Komsomol* organizations in the companies and equivalent combat subunits, the transformation of these organizations into a firm support for the commanders and political organs in their work for the political and military education of the rank and file of the *fronts'* forces and for providing for political influence on each soldier;

b)   the correct selection, deployment, education and teaching of the party-political cadres;

c)   the correct deployment of party and *Komsomol* forces in the subunits and their necessary concentration along the decisive sectors.

The progressive and leading role of the communists and the *Komsomol* members' example in combat and political training were the basis for the success of all the work in the field of political and combat training of the *fronts'* troops for the operation.

9

Materiel and Medical Support

The operational sector of the four *fronts* slated to take part in the Belorussian operation was 1,150 kilometers in length, of which the First Baltic Front's was 160 kilometers, the Third Belorussian Front's was 130 kilometers, the Second Belorussian Front's was 160 kilometers, and the First Belorussian Front's was 700 kilometers, of which the right-wing armies covered 240 kilometers.

The given sector's boundary line ran from the rear through the following locales: Rzhev, Vyaz'ma, Kirov, Pochep, and Konotop. The boundary lines on the left and right corresponded to the operational boundaries.

The size of the *fronts'* rear areas varied from 220 to 650 kilometers in depth.

The First Baltic Front's rear area ran along the line Nevel'—Velizh and was divided into two parts: an eastern and a western one. The eastern part represented a wooded and swampy area, with a very small number of dirt roads and a total absence of roads with a stone surface, which made the rear's work harder. The western part was characterized by a small number of forests and swamps, a large number of inhabited points and dirt roads, some of them with a stone surface. Thanks to this, in the western part of the rear sector sufficiently good conditions existed for the work of the troop and operational rears' work.

The main communications route in the *front's* rear sector was the Rzhev—Velikie Luki—Nevel' railroad, which had a capacity of 12 pairs of trains per day.

Nevel' was a rail and road junction in the rear sector, from which ran the Nevel'—Velikie Luki—Rzhev, Nevel'—Vitebsk, and Nevel'—Polotsk railroads, with a capacity of six pairs of trains per day and the Nevel'—Vitebsk and Nevel'—Polotsk dirt roads.

The *front's* regulating station was located at the Staraya Toropa station. A section of the regulating station had been moved up to Nevel' station.

The *front* depots were deployed along the entire depth of the *front's* rear sector, and along the Rzhev—Velikie Luki—Nevel' railroad they were grouped in the areas of the Staraya Toropa and Nevel' stations.

The *front's* armies were based in the following manner:

Table 47. The Basing of the First Baltic Front's Armies

Armies	Railroad Section	Supply Stations	Detraining Station
4th Shock	Nevel'—Dretun'	Klyastitsa, Alesha,	Dretun'
6th Gds	Nevel'—Dretun'	Novokhvansk	Bychikha
43rd	Nevel'—Gorodok	Gorodok	

The depth of the supplies' echelonment did not exceed 80-90 kilometers; the army bases were located at a distance of 40-45 kilometers from the first echelon of the *front* depots.

During the preparatory period the movement of the rear units and establishments nearer to the front line took place.

Part of the functions of the *front's* regulating station from Staraya Toropa station was moved to Nevel' station (the readdressing of the transports, the formation of trains for the armies, etc.). *Front* depots—artillery, oils and lubricants, and food—were distributed along the line of the army bases.

Sections of the 43rd and 6th Guards armies' army bases had been moved up directly to the troops.

The direction of the dirt road supply routes, both for the *front* and the armies, coincided with the direction of the railroads. Thus, running parallel to the railroads, the main *front* and army dirt roads provided for supply reliability.

The Third Belorussian Front's rear area disposed of a poor network of railroads and surfaced roads. However, the direction of the rail lines created sufficiently favorable conditions for basing the armies and the delivery of materiel and equipment along the railroad directly to the troops.

Only a single railroad ran across the territory of the *front's* rear area—Vyaz'ma—Smolensk. From Smolensk this railroad branched in two directions: Smolensk—Vitebsk and Smolensk—Orsha.

Aside from this, yet another railroad—Yel'nya—Smolensk—ran in the *front's* rear area through the Second Belorussian Front's area.

For the railroad sectors and *fronts*, see table 48.

The overall capacity of the *front's* railroads, which were handling supplies from the rear, was as follows: 32 pairs of trains per day as far as Smolensk station, and 20 pairs of trains from Smolensk west.

Table 48. The Third Belorussian Front's Railroad Sectors

Railroad Sectors	Daily Capacity in Pairs of Trains
Vyaz'ma—Smolensk	20
Smolensk—Gusino	12
Gusino—Krasnoe	8
Smolensk—Liozno	12
Yel'nya—Smolensk	12

During the preparatory period the restoration of the rail lines went on non-stop, and by the start of the operation the railroads had been brought up right to the front line.

The *front's* regulating station was located at Smolensk station, while its sectors were located at Vyaz'ma and Rudnya stations. The *front's* main materiel supplies were located in the area of Krasnoe and Smolensk stations.

The *front's* armies were based in the following manner (see table 49):

Table 49. The Basing of the Third Belorussian Front's Armies

Operational	Railroad Sector	Supply Station	Detraining Station
39th Army	Smolensk—Krynki (north of Vysochany)	Liozno	Krynki (north of Vysochany)
5th Army	Smolensk—Krynki (north of Vysochany)	Zaol'sha (southeast of Liozno)	Vydreya
31st Army	Velino—Shukhovtsy	Velino	Krasnoe
11th Guards Army	Velino—Shukhovtsy	Katyn' (east of Velino)	Gusino
5th Guards Tank Army	Velino—Shukhovtsy	Shukhovtsy	–

Operational	Railroad Sector	Supply Station	Detraining Station
Cavalry-Mechanized Group (3rd Gds Cavalry Corps and 3rd Guards Mechanized Corps)	Smolensk—Krynki (north of Vysochany)	Rudnya	Krynki (north of Vysochany)

The army supply stations were based from 15-30 kilometers from the divisional depots and made it possible to concentrate the necessary materiel means for the operation in a short time.

The following railroads ran through the Second Belorussian Front's rear area:

Table 50. Railroads in the Second Belorussian Front's Rear Area

Railroad Sectors	Daily Capacity in Pairs of Trains
Kirov—Roslavl'—Krichev—Veremeiki	12
Krichev—Temnyi Les	12
Krichev—Klimovichi	10

The capacity of the *front's* railroads as far as Krichev was 12 pairs of trains per day, and from Krichev station to the west—24 pairs of trains, with ten pairs to the south. A major shortcoming of the *front's* rail network was the fact that all the rail lines came together at two junctions: Roslavl' and Krichev.

The *front's* regulating station was located at Roslavl' station. A section of the regulating station had been moved up to Krichev.

The *front's* main materiel supplies were located in the areas of Roslavl' and Krichev stations, while Krichev station was viewed as the *front's* forward base, located immediately near the army bases.

By the start of the preparatory period, the armies were based as follows:

Table 51. The Basing of the Second Belorussian Front's Armies

Armies	Railroad Section	Supply Stations	Unloading Station
33rd	Krichev—Temnyi Les	Khodosy	Temnyi Les
49th	Krichev—Veremeiki	Osovets	Veremeiki
50th	Krichev—Kostyukovichi	Klimovichi	–

An army base had been organized for the 50th Army in Slavgorod (Proposik) on the ground with the following army depots: artillery, fuel, oils and lubricants, food, and engineer equipment. In the Khotishche area (20 kilometers west of Slavgorod) a section of the army base, with artillery, oils and lubricants, and food, had been brought up. At the beginning of the preparatory period additional measures had been adopted to define the rear's organization in accordance with the operational plan and the troops' regrouping. For example, by the start of the operation the 50th Army had been rebased to the Krichev—Dranikha railroad (20 kilometers west of Veremeiki). In the area of the Peremozhniki passing track (12 kilometers west of Veremeiki) and the stage between Veremeiki and Peremozhniki, a section of the army base had been deployed with depots for artillery, oils and lubricants, and food for supplying the forces of the army's right wing. The left-wing forces were supplied from the section of the army base, which had been deployed in the Rabovichi area (12 kilometers northwest of Slavgorod).

The Temnyi Les station had been set aside as a detraining station for the 33rd and 49th armies.

Thus the army supplies, which were located along the railroad, were 70-90 kilometers from the line of the divisional depots, while those located on the ground in Slavgorod (Propoisk) and Rabovichi were 20-35 kilometers from the line of the divisional depots.

With the arrival of the troops at the Dnepr River, it was planned to move the *front* regulating station to Krichev station, and the forward sections of the *front* depots to Khodosy and Veremeiki.

The First Belorussian Front was based on the railroad lines: a) Pochep—Gomel'—Zhlobin; b) Bakhmach—Gomel'—Kalinkovichi, and; c) Korosten'—Sarny—Kovel'.

The overall capacity of the *front's* rail lines was equal to 48 pairs of trains per day, including the Pochep—Gomel' line—18 pairs, Bakhmach—Gomel'—18 pairs, and Korosten'—Sarny—12 pairs.

In connection with the fact that the *front's* left wing included the overwhelming number of its forces, their basing on the poorly developed Korosten'—Sarny rail line was extremely difficult. Thus the First Belorussian Front command made the decision to speed up the restoration in any way possible the Chernigov—Ovruch—Belokorovichi rail sector and increase the capacity along the Korosten'—Sarny section to 24 pairs of trains per day. Besides this, it was also necessary to speed up the restoration of the rail bridge near the Shatsilki (about 40 kilometers south of Zhlobin) passing track, because the 48th and 65th armies were based on the Kalinkovichi—Shatsilki sector.

The *front* regulating stations were located at the Novobelitsa (east of Gomel') and Korosten' stations. The overall distance of the Novobelitsa station was 100 kilometers from the front and did not make it sufficiently convenient or safe for stationing *front* rear units and establishments at the *front's* regulating station, and thus a significant part of the establishments, particularly medical ones, had to be stationed east of Novobelitsa.

The main materiel supplies and rear establishments were stationed at the following: a) artillery depots for the *front's* right-wing forces—Novobelitsa, and food depots in Novobelitsa and Kalinkovichi; depots for oils and lubricants in Narodichi; b) for the *front's* left-wing forces—in the Sarny and Kivertsy areas. A maneuver materiel reserve was stationed in the areas of Korosten' and Ovruch.

The forces of the *front's* right wing were based on the following railroads: a) Pochep—Gomel'—Kalinkovichi; b) Bakhmach—Gomel'—Zhlobin.

As far as their carrying capacity is concerned, the railroads provided for the *front's* needs, although a weak point of the basing system was that all the railroads along which the *front's* right-wing forces were supplied ran through one junction—Gomel'.

The overall carrying capacity of these railroad sectors as far as Gomel' was the equivalent of 40 pairs of trains, and from Gomel' to the west—20 pairs of trains. Besides this, the *front* could employ another ten pairs of trains along the Korosten'—Kalinkovichi—Zhlobin rail line for supplying its right-wing forces.

By the start of the preparatory period the railroads had been restored along the Gomel'—Bobruisk line and along the Gomel'—Luninets line as far as the front line. Besides this, the Kalinkovichi—Zhlobin lateral railroad ran in the troop rear and made the delivery of everything necessary significantly easier.

Thus the army bases were located 40-100 kilometers from the front line, and the detraining stations at a remove of 10-35 kilometers. The 3rd Army, whose army base was located 120 kilometers, and its detraining station 40-50 kilometers from the front line, was in an especially difficult situation. Thus the *front* command ordered that an artillery depot be moved up along this line. Under these conditions, it was especially important that the Zhlobin rail junction be quickly restored during the offensive.

Table 52. The Basing of the First Belorussian Front's Armies

Armies	Railroad Section	Supply Stations	Detraining Station
3rd	Gomel'—Zhlobin	Kostyukovka (northwest Of Gomel')	Saltanovka
48th	Gomel'—Zhlobin	Buda-Koshelevo	Shatsilki
65th	Gomel'—Kalinkovichi	Babichi (west of Krynki)	Kholodniki, Gorochichi, Zherd'
28th	Gomel'—Kalinkovichi	Vasilevichi	Kalinkovichi, Kotsury, Gorochichi

In order to support the work of the Gomel' rail junction, bypasses were built around the junction by order of the *front's* military council. Besides this, the Chernigov—Ovruch—Belokorovichi line was restored and put into action for hauling cargoes intended for the *front's* left-wing forces.

Bypasses were also built around the Kalinkovichi, Sarny and Rovno junctions.

The carrying capacity of the Korosten'—Sarny—excluding Kovel' railroad was raised to 24 pairs of trains per day, and that of the Chernigov—Ovruch—Belokorovichi line to 12 pairs of trains per day.

In this fashion, the outline of the railroad network and its carrying capacity supported the accumulation and stationing of materiel supplies in the *fronts'* rear areas within the established deadlines and in the necessary amounts, as well as the favorable basing of the *fronts'* armies, with the exception of the First Belorussian Front's 3rd Army.

As an unfavorable aspect of the *fronts'* rear organization, there is the circumstance that in the *fronts'* rear areas all the railroads, running from the rear, came together in rail junctions located near the front. Among these are Nevel' in the First Baltic Front's sector, Smolensk in the Third Belorussian Front's sector, Krichev in the Second Belorussian Front's sector, and Gomel' in the First Belorussian Front's sector. Thus only the extremely favorable air situation saved our forces from serious difficulties in organizing the *fronts'* rear work.

The dirt roads in the *fronts'* sectors were characterized by the following.

Dirt roads with a hard surface were a rarity in the First Baltic Front's sector. Of seven *front* and three army roads, only two *front* roads had a hard surface.

Having railroads along both flanks and within the army and even troop rear, the *front* could significantly shorten the length of its dirt roads.

Each army had 1-2 dirt roads with an overall length of 204 kilometers.

Out of an overall length of 711 kilometers of dirt roads in the *front*, there were only 120 kilometers of surfaced roads.

The number of dirt roads with a hard surface in the Third Belorussian Front's rear area was also obviously insufficient, especially in the army and troop rear areas. From east to west only one surface road—the Minsk highway—ran in the *front's* rear area. From Smolensk this road branched out in two directions: Smolensk—Vitebsk and Smolensk—Orsha—Borisov.

The overall length of the *front's* dirt roads totaled 732 kilometers, of which 352 were part of the armies' dirt road system. Each army had 3-5 dirt roads (39th Army—52 kilometers, 5th Army—81 kilometers, 11th Guards Army—132 kilometers, and the 31st Army—87 kilometers).

Two surfaced roads ran through the Second Belorussian Front's rear area: Brest and Bryansk—Smolensk. Each army had from three to five dirt roads with an overall length of 249 kilometers (33rd Army—81 kilometers, 49th Army—74 kilometers, and 50th Army—94 kilometers).

The First Belorussian Front serviced and exploited roads with a total length of 313 kilometers. The length of the army dirt roads was 263 kilometers, of which 55 kilometers were surfaced (33rd Army—122 kilometers, of which 55 were surfaced, 48th Army—76 kilometers, 65th Army—25 kilometers, and 28th Army—40 kilometers). Of an overall length of 576 kilometers for the dirt roads, 185 kilometers were surfaced.

The condition of the dirt roads and their servicing is shown in the following table (see table 53).

Thus the network of dirt roads completely satisfied the *fronts'* and armies' requirements as regards their length, but the quality of the dirt road network, as a whole, could not satisfy these requirements, as the figure that characterizes the share of the surfaced roads, both as a whole and in the *fronts*, eloquently notes. The majority of army roads were improved earthen roads with a wooden floor in those places that were especially difficult to traverse. The roads ran through swampy terrain and in rainy weather were hard for automobile transport to pass through. The First Belorussian Front's 65th and 28th armies experienced the greatest difficulties with roads.

During the preparatory period the *fronts'* railroads worked with a high degree of intensity.

If you count each train as consisting of 35 cars, then for the period 1-22 June 812 trains arrived at the Third Belorussian Front. This means that in the course of this period 37 trains arrived for unloading each day, given the railroads' carrying capacity of 32 pairs of trains per day as far as Smolensk. During the period 1-30 June about 40 trains per day passed over the railroads of the First Belorussian Front's right wing, given the railroads' carrying capacity of 40 pairs of trains per day as far as Gomel'.

Table 53. The Length of the Dirt Roads in the *Fronts*

Fronts	Length of Dirt Roads (in kilometers)			Of These Were Surfaced	
	Serviced by			in kilometers	in %
	Front	Army	Total		
First Baltic	507	204	711	120	17
Third Belorussian	380	352	732	380	about 52
Second Belorussian	398	249	647	256	about 40
First Belorussian	313	263	576	185	32
Total	1,598	1,068	2,666	941	about 32

Table 54. The Work of the *Fronts'* Railroads in June 1944

Front	Period	Rail Cars		Including				
		Arriving	With Ammunition	With Weapons	With Fuel, Oils and Lubricants	With Food and Forage	With Operational Cargoes	With Other Cargoes
3rd Belorussian,	1-22 June	28,415	2,345	–	572	1,217	21,414	2,867
2nd Belorussian	1-25 June	2,741	1,080	–	578	893	–	190
1st Belorussian	1-30 June	41,368	4,292	836	1,891	1,679	29,811	1,859
Total		72,524	7,717	836	3,041	3,789	51,225	4,916

An analysis of the table shows that in the Third Belorussian Front, of 28,415 cars arriving from in the *front's* sector from the country's rear, 21,414, or 75 percent, were responsible for operational deliveries and only 7,001, or 25 percent, were carrying supply cargoes.

There was something similar in the First Belorussian Front. There operational shipments comprised 72 percent of the deliveries, and supply cargoes 28 percent. Ammunition deliveries were first in total tonnage among the supply deliveries, followed by food and forage and, finally, oils and lubricants.

Thus the three *fronts* required 72,524 rail cars for delivering troops and materiel, or 72,524 divided by 35 equals 2,072 trains. If one considers the First Baltic Front's requirements, then the overall number of rail cars and trains increases further.

The First Baltic Front received 2.2 *front* combat loads of ammunition (by the beginning of the preparatory period the *front* disposed of two combat loads, which rose to 4.2 combat loads by the start of the operation). For this, approximately 1,685 rail cars were required (the weight of a combat load was 12,256 tons × 2.2 combat loads = 26,962 tons, which divided by 16 equals 1,685). In order to deliver 3-4 refills of fuel, oils and lubricants, an amount which was to be delivered as a minimum to cover expenditures and accumulate reserves, 560-745 tank cars were needed. 1,200 rail cars were needed for delivering weapons and other cargoes. Approximately another 1,025 rail cars were required to deliver 20 days' food rations by rail to the *front*.

Thus in the preparatory period of the given operation, it proved necessary to deliver 77,000 rail cars to the four *fronts*.

Of this number, up to 26,000 rail cars were occupied with delivering supplies.

Thus by the start of the operation, if all four *fronts* received approximately 25,769 rail cars, of these more than 9,402 cars carried supplies, 5,814 carried food and forage, and 3,601-3,786 carried fuel, oils and lubricants.[1]

An enormous amount of work with supply and operational deliveries was carried out by the *fronts'* automobile transport. For example, from 1-22 June the Third Belorussian Front's auto transport (the *front* reserve's 10th Automobile Brigade) carried 64,282 tons of freight, of which 35,087 tons, or 55 percent, consisted of supplies and 29,195 tons, or 45 percent, consisted of cargoes other than supplies. Thus each day, on the average, about 3,000 tons of freight were delivered, of which 1,600 tons were of supplies.

During just the 8-18 June period the First Belorussian Front's auto transport transported 15,774 tons of supply cargoes, or 1,434 tons daily.

During 20-25 June period the Second Belorussian Front''s auto transport carried 5,011 tons of supplies, or 835 tons daily.

Table 55. The Arrival of Rail Cars With Freight at the *Fronts*

Fronts	Of Which					
	Ammunition	Weapons	Fuel, Oils and Lubricants	Food and Forage	Other Cargoes	Rail Cars Engaged in Operational Deliveries
3rd, 2nd and 1st Belorussian Fronts	7,717	836	3,041	4,789	4,916	51,225
1st Baltic	1,685	200	560-745	1,025	1,000	No data
All four *Fronts*	9,402	1,036	3,601-3,786	5,814	5,916	51,225

The *fronts'* degree of materiel provision by the start of the operation can be seen from the following data (table 56):

---

1   If one takes into account the First Belorussian Front's left-wing armies, then the overall number of rail cars arrived will grow and the number of cars with ammunition will be close to 11,000.

Table 56. The *Fronts'* Materiel Provision by the Start of the Operation

Types of Materiel Supply	1st Baltic	3rd Belorussian	2nd Belorussian	1st Belorussian (right wing)
Ammunition in *Front* Combat Loads	4.2	2.2	3.0	4.0
Fuels, Oils and Lubricants in *Front* Refills				
B-78	9.2	6.2	10.4	12.5[1]
B-70	–	19.0	20.7	15.7
Auto Fuel	4.1	3.4	2.5	4.1
Diesel Fuel	7.6	6.3	6.4	7.1
Food in Daily Rations				
Bread	16.4	39.0[2]	21.5	22.4
Groats	21.5	34.1	34.1	
Meat	22.3	9.0	33.8	16.7
Fats	33.1	12.0	20.0	21.0
Sugar	40.4	22.7	17.2	8.8

Note
1 Aviation fuel is not included in the calculation.
2 Editor's note. This figure includes both bread and groats.

By the start of the operation, the situation was as follows. In the First Baltic Front the level of provision was close to the norms foreseen by the operational plan.

In the Third Belorussian Front, in connection with the huge scope of the operational deliveries, by the start of the operation the supplies had not yet reached the norms planned by the *front*. Particularly insufficient were the supplies of ammunition and auto fuel and, in the armies, with the exception of the 39th Army, of diesel fuel.

The Second Belorussian Front's main group of forces—the 49th Army—was provisioned with ammunition according to norms, while the level of provision in the 33rd and 50th armies was 50-60 percent of the norm. The armies' supply of auto fuel, diesel fuel, and B-70 auto fuel was insufficient. The *front's* supply of food was satisfactory.

The First Belorussian Front's plan for accumulating materiel was fulfilled almost completely, with only an insufficiency in supply for some kinds of ammunition and auto fuel.

Thus for all the *fronts* the uninterrupted delivery of materiel cargoes, particularly of ones in which there were already shortages, from the depth, both by rail and by dirt road, acquired particular importance. From this point on the question of restoring railroads and roads from the moment of the troops' attack and of employing the *fronts'* auto transport for delivering materiel to the troops during the offensive was to be the center of attention.

The following measures for restoring the railroads were to be carried out.

In the First Baltic Front it was planned to restore the Nevel'—Vitebsk, Vitebsk—Polotsk and Nevel'—Polotsk railroads, and then the Krynki—Vitebsk sector (along the front line southeast of Vitebsk). For carrying out restoration work on the railroads, the *front* disposed of the directorate of military-restoration work No. 7, with the 6th and 7th railroad brigades.

For restoring the railroads, the Third Belorussian Front disposed of the 1st and 26th railroad brigades. During the offensive the *front* planned to restore the following railroads: a) Shukhovtsy—Orsha—Borisov, 174 kilometers; b) Orsha—Lepel', 132 kilometers; c) Orsha—Vitebsk, 83 kilometers, and; d) the Orsha railroad junction.

The restoration was planned at a rate of 8-8.5 kilometers per day.

In view of the obvious shortage of men and materiel for restoring all of the planned sectors, it was decided to request the People's Commissariat for Transportation to urgently second a railroad brigade to the Military Restoration Work Directorate-4, two lead repair trains, two forward repair trains, and two bridge trains, with a strength of 8,000 men, and the delivery of 100 kilometers of track with fastenings.

The question was also raised of allowing Military Restoration Work Directorate-4 to employ 5,000 people from the local population for the duration of the restoration work.

The rear chief made the decision to allot from the *front's* inventory 100 motor vehicles, 15 tractors, two horse-drawn transportation companies, and the necessary amount of fuel for the restoration work.

In the Second Belorussian Front it was planned to restore two railroads: a) first the Veremeiki—Chausy—Mogilev line, at a rate of five kilometers per day, and; b) secondly, the line Temnyi Les—Zubry (northwest of Gorki), at a rate of eight kilometers per day.

Such railroad restoration rates, given the presence of two rail brigades and the corresponding preliminary preparation, were quite realistic.

The commander of the First Belorussian Front confirmed the plan for restoring the railroad from Shatsilki toward Zhlobin and Bobruisk, and then west as far as Brest, and it was next decided to restore the route from Kalinkovichi to the west as far as Brest.

Even before the start of the operation, the railroad restoration units were concentrated along the Shatsilki—Zhlobin axis. It should be noted that the *front* disposed of an extremely limited number of restoration units. By the start of the operation the *front* disposed of three railroad brigades, but one of them was working under People's Commissariat of Communication's orders in the deep rear, while a second was still undergoing formation. In this manner, the *front* disposed of only one full-bodied railroad brigade on which practically all the restoration work would lie. Of course, given these conditions it was not possible to count on a high rate of restoration work.

On the whole, the First and Third Belorussian fronts were the least well equipped with a work force and the necessary equipment for restoring the railroads.

The restoration of the dirt roads was organized along the following lines.

The road units of the *front* reserve were concentrated along the main axes in direct proximity to the front line for supporting the rapid restoration of the dirt roads in the wake of the attacking troops. All the road units were tasked to lay in store boards and plates for the restoration of bridges and the building of tread roads, as well as bridge-construction material for laying down crossings during the troops' advance to the west.

By 23 June the main road units of the Third Belorussian Front's reserve had been concentrated along the Moscow—Smolensk—Minsk highway.

Bridging materials for the restoration of bridges had been brought up and concentrated at depots at the Liozno, Gusino and Krasnoe stations.

The *front's* road directorate compiled beforehand a coordinated plan with the chief of the engineering troops, entitled "Prospects for the Road Support of the Third Belorussian Front's Offensive Operation."

The forces of the First Belorussian Front's right wing, once they went over to the offensive, would have the opportunity to use the Warsaw or Brest-Litovsk highway. As a result of the natural qualities of the theater of military activities, the road units' main task was the construction and restoration of bridges and other artificial structures, which had been destroyed by the enemy. Thus immediately before the start of the operation, all the *front* and army road construction, bridge construction and road exploitation units were brought up to the front line and deployed in the areas of Rogachev, Zhlobin and Shatsilki.

Immediately before the start of the operation, all the army military-automobile roads began to be serviced by *front* units, and the army road units were thus freed up for moving in the troops' wake.

A large part of the *fronts'* armies had road construction and road exploitation units.

Reconnaissance groups, consisting of a restoration command, a section of mine layers, and a subunit from the road-command service, with previously prepared road signs and indicators, were formed by the road sections and were ready to advance in the attackers' wake.

The automobile transport's condition and capabilities are characterized by the following data (tables 57, 58, 59):

During the preparatory period, automobile transport delivered a large amount of different types of cargoes to the troops.

The following daily delivery norms were at the basis of planning of automobile deliveries: 0.1 combat loads, 0.25-0.3 refills of oils and lubricants, and a day's ration of food.

By the start of the operation all the automobile units had been relocated to the main roads, moved closer to the supply bases; repair bases were stationed and flying teams deployed, which had been organized within the repair bases, in a corresponding manner.

Table 57. The Strength of the *Fronts'* Automobile Parks

Fronts	Front and Army Transport	Number of Trucks	% of Readiness	Carrying Capacity
First Baltic	*Front*	no data	78	3,100
	Army	no data	84	about 1,200
Third Belorussian	*Front*	2,253	90	5,000
	Army	824	93	1,500
Second Belorussian	*Front*	1,958	97	3,850
	Army	762	87	1,400
First Belorussian	*Front*	2,700	91	7,500
	Army	997	85	2,100

Table 58. The Number of Cargoes Delivered to the Troops During the Preparatory Period (in tons)

Front	Ammunition	Fuel, Oils and Lubricants	Food and Forage	Other Cargoes	Total
First Baltic	No data				
Third Belorussian	13,954	2,933	18,200	29,195	64,282
Second Belorussian	1,115	–	1,561	2,335	5,011
First Belorussian	No data				15,783[1]

Note
1 This figure includes the totals for the 3rd Army—3,684 tons; 48th Army—2,799 tons, and; the 65th Army—3,359 tons; 3,061 tons at the *front* depots, and; 2,880 tons in units subordinated to the *front*.

Table 59. Weight of a Combat Load, Refill and Daily Ration in the _Fronts_

Fronts	Weight of a Combat Load and 0.1 of a combat load	Weight of a Single Refill of Oils and Lubricants, and 0.25-0.30 of a Refill	A Day's Food Ration Load, Refill and Daily Ration	Overall Weight of Combat Weight of a Daily Transport Norm
First Baltic	12,250	3,000	800	16,050
				2,750-3,000
	1,200	750-1,000		
Third Belorussian	20,200	5,400	1,700	27,300
				5,100-5,500
	2,000	1,400-1,800		
Second Belorussian	9,500	1,600	800	11,900
				2,150-2,250
	950	400-500		
First Belorussian	16,000	4,000	500	20,500
				3,100-3,400
	1,600	1,000-1,300		

Medical Support

In planning such a large-scale operation as the multi-_front_ Belorussian operation of 1944, one of the most important questions in preparing for it was that of medical support.

The organization and placement of the hospital base, its utilized capacity and capabilities in the _fronts_ before the start of the operation are shown in table 60.

The First Baltic Front's _front_ hospitals were arrayed in two echelons, with a hospital reserve set aside. The armies' hospital bases were also arrayed in two echelons.

The Third Belorussian Front had a total of 39,925 beds in its forward hospital groups in the area Smolensk—Liozno—Gusino, of which 9,747 were occupied by the sick and wounded. The _front_ did not manage to free up all its forward hospital groups because of the operational deliveries: the permanent and temporary trains, standing on the approaches, were not allowed to pass.

Upon the start of the operation, the evacuation of the 39th and 5th armies' wounded was to be directed to the _front_ hospital group in Liozno, and those from the 5th Guards Tank, 11th Guards and 31st armies to the forward _front_ hospital in Gusino.

The army hospital bases were chiefly located in the areas of the supply stations. Each army had from three to six reduced-establishment surgical field mobile hospitals as a reserve. In order to strengthen the army hospital bases, the _front_ reserve allotted the following: three surgical field mobile hospitals for the 5th Army; one surgical field mobile hospital for the 39th Army, and; two surgical field mobile hospitals for the 31st Army.

In the Second Belorussian Front the army hospital bases were located as follows: 33rd Army—in the area of Temnyi Les station, with 4,500 beds; 49th Army—in the area of Veremeiki station, with 7,600 beds, and; 50th Army—in the area of Slavgorod (Propoisk), with 6,600 beds. In this way the army hospital bases were moved up to a distance of 10-15 kilometers from the front line.

For the evacuation of the wounded, the _front_ had five temporary military-medical trains, with a capacity of 22,500 men, and 13 medical evacuation installations, with a capacity of 4,350 men.

Of the hospital groups located in Kaluga and Spas Demensk, two hospitals for the lightly wounded and three receiving evacuation hospitals were moved to the Krichev area for the purpose of strengthening the evacuation posts that were to support the offensive. In the Osovets—Khodosy—Veremeiki area a group of reduced-establishment hospitals was concentrated, consisting of two hospitals for the lightly wounded, a field evacuation post, and five surgical evacuation hospitals. This group had as its task to advance in the wake of the attacking forces and, deploying in the areas of the greatest concentration of wounded, to free up the army evacuation establishments.

Table 60. The Disposition and Operating Capacity of the Hospital Base in the *Fronts* and Armies by the Start of the Belorussian Operation of 1944

Front	*Front* Hospital Bases	Army Hospital Bases	Number of Authorized Beds	Number of Wounded Being Treated
First Baltic	Kalinin		17,625	
	Rzhev, Nevel'		19,652	
	Bychikha		2,300	
	Total		39,577	
		4th Shock Army	8,800	
		6th Gds Army	9,610	
		43rd Army	8,300	
	Total		26,710	
	Front total		66,287	
Third Belorussian	Vyaz'ma		3,697	3,753
	Gzhatsk		5,100	6,231
	Smolensk		21,450	5,088
	Gusino		7,600	1,634
	Liozno		10,875	3,025
	Total		48,772	19,731
		39th Army	6,800	
		5th Army	6,300	
		11th Gds Army	6,900	
		31st Army	6,100	
	Total		26,100	
	Front total		74,872	
Second Belorussian	Total		40,650	1,668
	Total		18,700	688
	Front total		59,350	2,336
First Belorussian	Klintsy, Buda		3,000	
	Koshelevo (198th Medical Evacuation Station)		24,700	
	Gomel'	(14th Medical Evacuation Station)	43,300	
	Total		71,000	
		3rd Army	8,600	3,010
		48th Army	7,600	2,050
		65th Army	6,000	2,340
		28th Army	8,100	405
		Total	30,300	7,805
	Front total (right wing)		101,300	7,806

In the First Belorussian Front the armies' hospital assets were located, as a rule, in two echelons—first-line hospitals and hospital bases. For example, in the 65th Army the echelonment of the medical-sanitary establishments was carried out in the following manner: the medical-sanitary battalions were located 6-8 kilometers from the front line, while in the first line of hospitals there were two surgical field mobile hospitals with reduced establishments; the army hospital bases was located 16-18 kilometers from the front line and consisted of three surgical field mobile hospitals, one evacuation post, one hospital for the lightly wounded, one therapeutic and one hospital for infections. Medical transport was distributed in the following manner: the army had 33 motor vehicles; the medical-sanitary battalions had 55, and the field evacuation station 12. A surgical field mobile hospital was set aside for supporting the cavalry-mechanized group.

As a result of increased evacuation, by the start of the operation the 3rd Army had 65 percent of its beds free, the 48th Army had 73 percent, the 65th Army had 61 percent, the 28th Army had 95 percent of its beds free, and the *front* hospital groups had the following: 198th Medical-Evacuation Station had 40 percent and the 14th Medical-Evacuation Station had 80 percent.

Of the existing 20 temporary military-sanitary trains and nine emergency sanitary stations in the *front*, 12 temporary military-sanitary trains and one emergency sanitary station were located along the right flank, with capacity for 5,735 men.

On the whole, the *front* and army auto transport assets could simultaneously evacuate about 1,200 men.

On the whole, the rear of the four *fronts* that were to take part in the Belorussian operation, carried out a great deal of work for the materiel supply of the troops, which enabled us to began and conduct a large-scale offensive operation. However, in order to successfully complete it, the additional delivery of the most important kinds of materiel and equipment support was required during the course of the operation.

10

The Organization of Control and Communications

In preparing the Belorussian operation, we made use of the very rich experience in troop control, which had accumulated during the entire preceding period of the Great Patriotic War.

Troop control in preparing the offensive operations of the *fronts* was carried out by means of the personal contact of the *front* commanders with the army commanders and the commanders of those formations subordinated to the *front*; by issuing individual operational directives and combat orders to the troops; by bringing the *front's* and the armies' headquarters closer to the troops and by exercising daily control by the higher-ranking commanders and headquarters over the timely preparation of the troops for the offensive.

Long before receiving the directive from the *Stavka* of the Supreme High Command for conducting the operation, the commanders of the First and Third Belorussian fronts had been oriented by the *Stavka* as to the forthcoming operation and thus had the opportunity, observing strict secrecy, to carry out a number of preliminary measures beforehand for preparing the operation. Thanks to such an orientation in the First Belorussian Front, for example, preliminary ideas and even preliminary plans for the *front's* Bobruisk and Kovel' operations were drawn up.

During the operation's preparation, following the *front's* receipt of the *Stavka* directive, the issuing of orders to the armies was carried out in the following manner. In the beginning, these tasks were assigned orally on the map by the *front* commander personally, and preliminary orders were also issued to the troops, after which local operational directives were issued. The latter were issued at the following times: in the First Belorussian Front the armies received the directives on 8 June and the cavalry-mechanized group on 12 June; in the Third Belorussian Front the armies received their orders only on 20 June. In the First Belorussian Front the troops received their tasks in written form as follows: the corps five days before the start of the offensive, and the divisions three days before. Approximately the same order of issuing assignments to the troops was followed in the other *fronts*.

The work on planning the operation lasted 7-8 days in the *fronts* and 7-9 days in the armies.

For controlling and rendering assistance in planning and preparing the operation, generals and officers from the *fronts'* headquarters were dispatched to the lower headquarters and eliminated shortcomings on the spot and informed the *front* commanders about the course of the preparatory work.

Particular attention was devoted to questions of organizing operational and tactical cooperation between the troops. For this purpose the *front* commanders, together with a group consisting of the chief of the *front* staff's operational directorate, the commanders of artillery, armored and mechanized troops, and the commander of the air army, traveled to the headquarters of the combined-arms armies that formed part of the *fronts'* main group of forces. Here they listened to an evaluation of the armies' operational situation and confirmed the decisions and operational plans of the army commanders. Subsequently, the commanders of the *fronts'* mobile groups were summoned to the corresponding headquarters, along with their staffs, the commanders of the tank, mechanized and cavalry corps that formed a part of the the *fronts'* and armies' mobile groups, for working out questions of operational and tactical coordination, as well as the commanders of the air formations allotted for supporting the armies and mobile groups, as well as all the rifle corps commanders and the commanders of some divisions. Besides this, the *front* commanders regularly traveled to the field where, along the sectors of the forthcoming breakthrough, they checked the organization of the troops' cooperation and their readiness for the offensive.

To provide for reliable communications coordination between the combined-arms armies, each of them dispatched a communications officer, with a radio station, to its neighbor to the left.

For the practical realization of coordination between the combined-arms and artillery chiefs, their command posts were stationed together. The combined-arms, artillery, tank, and engineering chiefs had, by the start of the operation, a unified system of targets and a unified system of orientation.

A great deal of attention was devoted to the organization of a service for identifying our troops, especially tanks and aviation. For this signals were established, such as "Here are our tanks," which were transmitted from tanks by rockets or the ignition of smoke blocks, while each tank had signals on the top and sides of its turret, such as a white circle on the turret and white stripes along the sides. Daily signals were also established, such as: "Here is our plane." Recognition signals were established for our troops' front line, as well as a single system for mutual target designation.

By the start of the operation responsible representatives from the *fronts'* military councils had been dispatched to all of the *fronts'* mobile groups, along with a group of 3-4 officers, each with a radio station for controlling the fulfillment of the *fronts'* combat orders and aiding the troops. The maintenance of close and immediate coordination between aviation and the ground troops was provided for by the start of the operation by the placement of the following: the commanders of air corps and individual air divisions at the army commanders' command posts; officers from the headquarters of the air corps and divisions at the command posts of all the corps and the commanders of tank brigades; the commanders of the assault air divisions at the command posts of the corps attacking along the axes of the main blows; fighter aviation air guidance officers, with radio stations, among the troops 1.5-2 kilometers from the front.

At the moment of the mobile groups' commitment into the breach, it was planned to transfer the commanders of the supporting air formations to their command posts, along with small operational groups and radio stations.

"RSB" radio stations were mounted on tanks for guiding *shturmoviks* and fighters in the air.

For the purpose of bringing the control organs closer to the troops, in case of the *front* commanders' absence, by the start of the operation operational groups of the *fronts'* headquarters had been formed, headed by the chiefs of the operational directorates, or their deputies, and consisting of officers from the operational and reconnaissance sections, the code section, and the chief of communications or his deputy, with several officers. The commanders of the artillery, armored and mechanized troops, the commander of the air army and several officers from their staffs, were in readiness to leave with the operational group. The operational groups had their own mobile communications centers on motor vehicles.

Forward command posts were created in the armies' headquarters, headed by the deputy chiefs of the armies' staffs, and consisting of an operational group, which consisted of officers from the operational, intelligence and code sections, as well as officer-representatives of the artillery, armored and engineering troops' staffs. The operational group was accompanied by a communications center, headed by the senior assistant to the army chief of communications.

In the operation's preparatory period all the measures for organizing control and communications were worked out in detail. Communications centers for all the headquarters were prepared, and the observation posts of the *front* and army commanders were provisioned and outfitted with communications equipment, as were those of the commanders of the troop formations and units, and prearranged message codes, radio signal tables, unit codes and coded maps were drawn up and distributed to the troops.

Particular attention was paid to communications provision for the ground forces' coordination among themselves and with aviation.

Communications coordination between the *fronts* was provided directly for through special designation communications centers (USONs), or the communications centers of the representatives of the *Stavka* of the Supreme High Command.

In drawing up a communications plan, the following factors were taken into account: the large number of mobile formations in the *fronts*, the specific peculiarities of the area of combat operations, particularly in the First Belorussian Front's sector, the mobile formations' significant offensive rates, the poorly developed network of permanent telephone and telegraph lines in Belorussia, the limited number of telephone-construction communications units for restoration work and on the permanent lines.

The time allotted for communications preparation (20-25 days) was sufficient.

Command and communications in the *fronts* was organized in the following manner.

By the start of the operation the command posts in the First Baltic Front were distributed as shown in the next table.

In order to carry out cable communications in the jumping-off point, the additional development of the existing permanent communications lines was required for ensuring the communications of the operational groups of the *fronts'* and armies' headquarters, as well as for the observation posts of the *front* and army commanders.

During the operation it was planned to develop cable communications to a depth of 60-70 kilometers.

The *front* headquarter's radio communications with the General Staff was to be carried out by "RAT" radio stations along the auditory channel, and the Baudot teleprinter.[1] A special General Staff radio network no. 15 was created for communications coordination between the *fronts*, which included the radio stations of the *fronts'* headquarters, and that of the operational group of the representative of the *Stavka* of the Supreme High Command, and USON nos. 1 and 6.

The Red Army General Staff's radio network no. 16 was created for communications with the flank armies. Data for working in this network was in the hands of the *fronts* and armies, and the radio stations of the neighboring *fronts'* cooperating armies were to use this network, as necessary, for establishing radio communications.

For providing immediate radio communications between the General Staff with the headquarters of the First Baltic Front's armies, General Staff radio network no. 5 was organized.

The *front's* radio communications with the armies was organized along three channels: along separate radio axes by "RAF" radio stations; in the operational group's radio network no. 1 for communications with the army commanders at their observation posts, and; in a special radio network ("North" radio stations) for communicating with the army commanders during their trips to the front.

---

1   Editor's note. This was teleprinting apparatus widely used by the Red Army during the Second World War. It was named after its inventor, Jean Maurice Emile Baudot (1845-1903).

Table 61. The Stationing of Command Posts in the First Baltic Front

Command Posts	Distance in Kilometers			
	From the Front Line	From the *Front* Headquarters	From the *Front's* Operational Group	From the *Front* Commander's Observation Post
Front Headquarters	50	–	–	–
Front Operational Group	10	–	–	–
Front Commander's Observation Post	4	–	–	–
Front Headquarter's Second Echelon	70	20	–	–
4th Shock Army Headquarters	18	37	–	–
6th Gds Army Headquarters	11	–	10	–
6th Guards Army Commander's Observation Post	1.5	–	–	4
43rd Army's Operational Group	7	–	12	–
43rd Army Commander's Observation Post	1.5	–	–	9

It was also planned to use a Baudot teleprinter for securing the *front* headquarter's printed telegraph communications with the headquarters of the 6th Guards Army. For more reliable communications with the 1st Tank Corps, additional channels were prepared in the radio network of the *front's* directorate of armored and mechanized troops and along the radio axis through the *front* headquarters communications officer's "STsR" radio station with the tank corps.

For providing coordination radio communications between the combined-arms armies, the 3rd Air Army and the 1st Tank Corps, special radio network no. 5 was organized for coordinating with the *front*.

Besides this, the coordination of radio communications with the air formations supporting this or that combined-arms or mobile formation, was provided through air representatives.

Communications through mobile assets was planned from two positions: with the operational group and with the *front* headquarter's communications post. The *front* headquarters communications post was responsible for the exchange of correspondence with the General Staff, the neighboring *fronts*, with the operational group, and with the second echelon of the *front's* headquarters; the communications post was responsible for the armies.

All the work on preparing communications in the jumping-off position had been completed by 15 June 1944.

The Third Belorussian Front's system of command and communications in the jumping-off position was planned as follows: a) the *front's* main command post was deployed along the main axis in the 11th Guards Army's attack sector (50 kilometers from the front line); b) the *front* commander's observation post (VPU) was three kilometers from the front line along the same axis; c) the *front's* observation post no. 2 was in the 5th Army's attack zone (one kilometer from the front line; the armies' command posts were 5-10 kilometers from the front line, and; e) the army commanders' observation posts were 1-1.5 kilometers from the front line.

Cable communications in the jumping-off position was provided along permanent telephone-telegraph lines of an overall length of 1,350 kilometers. It required only an insignificant increase in the lines' volume along individual axes and the preparation of communications with the *front* commander's observation posts nos. 1 and 2 in order to ensure troop control. To do this, it was necessary to lay 106 kilometers of new lines and string 231 kilometers of cable. Upon the completion of this work, cable communications with the armies could be provided for along four channels and along one telegraph channel for the mobile formations.

Simultaneously, communications from the *front* command post with the General Staff were provided for by two telegraph channels, and with the command posts of the First Baltic, Second and First Belorussian fronts—by a telegraph channel apiece.

High-frequency telephone (governmental) communications was provided for from the *front* commander's command post and observation post with the General Staff and the headquarters of the neighboring *fronts* through the communications center of the representative of the *Stavka* of the Supreme High Command, and directly with all the *front's* armies and mobile groups.

During the operation the development of cable communications arose from the possible 100 percent destruction of the permanent lines by the enemy, while withdrawing to a depth of 20-30 kilometers, and subsequently up to 30 percent.

It was planned to restore the permanent telephone-telegraph lines on the axis of the *front's* communications (eight cables), along the axes of the army staffs' movements (five cables), and two cables of governmental high-frequency communications with each army.

Besides this, it was planned to restore four *front* lateral lines, with four cables apiece.

162 tons of iron cable and up to 3,000 poles were required to support the restoration work.

The *front* headquarter's radio communications with the General Staff was provided for along two axes by "RAT" radio stations: by an aural channel and by a Baudot teleprinter. General Staff radio network no. 5 was organized for the *fronts'* communications coordination; the radio communications of the flank armies of the adjoining *fronts* was provided for in the General Staff's radio network no. 6; the radio communications of the *front's* armies directly with the General Staff was provided for in the General Staff's radio network no. 6.

The *front's* radio communications with the armies was organized along three channels: along the axes of the Baudot teleprinter (5th, 11th and 31st armies, and the 5th Guards Tank Army); in the main no. 1 radio network, and; in the weak "RB"[2] radio stations nos. 9 and 10. As a fourth channel, the *front's* radio network no. 2 could be used for cooperation. Radio set no. 17 and radio axes nos. 17A, 19 and 22 provided for communications with the mobile formations.

For securing more reliable communications with the mobile formations, radio networks nos. 9, 10, 18, 20, and 23 were organized, consisting of weak "RB" radio stations. Also, radio communications with them could be provided for along separate axes through the radio stations of responsible representatives dispatched with a group of officers (2-3 officers from the operational directorate, an intelligence officer, a tank officer, and a code worker) to all the mobile formations.

For securing the *front* commander's communications with the army commanders, radio networks nos. 11s, 12s and 14s ("North" radio stations) were organized.

A very large amount of attention was devoted to the organization of radio communications for coordinating the mobile groups with the combined-arms formations and aviation.

The planned radio communications for the operation were provided by a comparatively limited number of radio assets, which required their extremely precise maneuver during the operation.

Communications through mobile assets was planned by axis and direction. It was planned to organize two posts for gathering reports—a main one and one in the rear—and two exchange posts.

In the Second Belorussian Front the organization of command and the stationing of command posts was approximately the same as in the First Baltic and Third Belorussian fronts.

Cable communications in the initial position required a certain increase in the volume of permanent lines along individual axes and the preparation of communications in the new areas of the *front* command post's location, the *front's* auxiliary command post and the *front* commander's observation post.

---

2   Editor's note. This stands for battalion radio station.

As a result of carrying out the planned work and the organization of ten control-measuring devices, cable communications with the command posts of the neighboring *fronts* was organized, with the operational group of the representative of the *Stavka* of the Supreme High Command, USON no. 6, and with the General Staff, and a developed network of cable communications between the command and observation posts of the *front* and armies was created.

Particular attention was devoted to the provisioning of cable communications of the *front* commander's observation post with the *front* command post, with the commander of the 49th Army's observation post, and with the *front's* forward observation posts in the combat formations of the first-echelon rifle corps' divisions (through VUS[3] no. 1 and VUS no. 2).

The organization of cable communications with the operational group of the 49th Army's army crossings along the Pronya River was planned in detail.

During the operation the construction, restoration and development of permanent telephone-telegraph lines was planned to a depth of 100 kilometers. The plan foresaw the construction of the following: a) a *front* communications axis (eight cables); b) three axes of communications in the armies, combined with the army communications axes (six cables apiece in each army), and; c) a single *front* lateral line (four cables).

Given the high offensive rates, the construction of permanent lines was planned only along the axis of the *front's* communications.

In calculating construction, the planners proceeded from the possible destruction of the permanent lines by the enemy while retreating as follows: 100 percent destruction in the area of immediate mortar and artillery fire, and a subsequent 60 percent in the depth and 25 percent along the lateral lines.

1,066 kilometers of 3mm iron cable (106.6 tons) and 5,041 kilometers of 4mm iron cable (283.4 tons) were required to provide for the construction and restoration work, for a total of 6,107 kilometers (390 tons).

Radio communications with the General Staff was provided for along two channels: aural and Baudot teleprinter. Communications for the *fronts'* coordination was provided by the General Staff's radio network no. 5; this radio network also provided for communications with the operational group of the representative of the *Stavka* of the Supreme High Command. For communications with the flank armies of the adjoining *fronts*, the General Staff's radio network no. 16 was created; radio communications of the *front's* armies directly with the General Staff was carried out through the General Staff's radio network no. 7.

The *front* headquarters's radio communications with the armies was organized along two channels: through the *front's* main radio network no. 1; and along axes nos. 9, 10 and 11 (weak radio stations). The *front's* radio network no. 3 (coordination) could be used as a third channel.

A special radio network was not created for the *front* commander.

Radio communications with the mobile group was organized along a separate axis.

Radio communications coordination between the armies was provided by the *front's* radio network no. 3, while a specially-created radio network provided for communications between the flank corps of neighboring armies.

A great deal of attention was devoted to securing the radio communications of the *front* commander's main observation post with his forward observation posts, which were situated in the combat formations of the first-echelon rifle corps' divisions. Two radio networks were organized for this: for the *front* commander and the commander of the *front's* artillery.

---

3   Editor's note. This stands for auxiliary commander center.

Communications through mobile assets was planned along axes. It was planned to carry out the exchange of correspondence at the main collection post, and reports from the *front's* command post three times per day.

In drawing up a communications plan for the First Belorussian Front, the following features were considered: the large number of armies and mobile formations comprising the *front* (ten combined-arms armies, one tank army, two air armies, and six cavalry, tank and mechanized corps); the great length of the front along the initial position (up to 760 kilometers); the poorly developed network of permanent telephone-telegraph lines; the wooded and swampy terrain, which creates difficulties in developing communications, and the near impossibility of rapidly maneuvering communications units from one wing of the *front* to another.

Besides this, in planning the organization of communications, it was necessary to draw up a communications plan for the troops of the right and left flanks, separately, taking into account the beginning of their offensive activities and different deadlines.

There was sufficient time for preparing communications in the initial position.

As a result of the additional development of the permanent lines, cable communications in the initial position was provided for the command and observation posts of the *fronts'* and armies with a sufficient number of bypass axes, which increased its reliability.

The *front's* main command post (Ovruch) had telephone and telegraph communications auxiliary command posts nos. 1 and 2, and telephone communications with the 65th and 28th armies, and the 16th Air Army (the *front's* right wing).

Besides this, the *front* command post had two telegraph communications channels with the General Staff and one telegraph channel apiece with the command posts of the Second Belorussian and First Ukrainian fronts, and USON no. 3. High frequency (governmental) communications was provided for with the General Staff, with the operational group of the representative of the *Stavka* of the Supreme High Command, with the Second Belorussian and First Ukrainian fronts, with the second echelon of the *front's* headquarters, and through auxiliary command posts' nos. 1 and 2 communications centers—with the armies' command posts.

Auxiliary command post no. 2 had telegraph-telephone and governmental high-frequency communications with the command posts of the 3rd, 48th, 65th, and 28th armies, and with the 16th Air Army, the cavalry-mechanized group, with the operational group of the representative of the *Stavka* of the Supreme High Command, with the Second Belorussian Front's command post, and the second echelon of the *front's* headquarters.

The army headquarters also had telephone-telegraph communications with the corps' (divisions') headquarters through their command and observation posts.

A great deal of attention was devoted to providing cable communications for coordinating the combined-arms armies along the boundaries of the neighboring *fronts*, with the mobile formations, and with the 16th and 6th air armies. The organization of cable communications for coordination in the initial position completely satisfied the command's requirements.

During the operation the organization of cable communications was planned in detail to a depth of 200-210 kilometers along the right wing, and to a depth of 100-130 kilometers along the *front's* left wing.

The restoration of a permanent line of the *front's* axis of communications on the right flank was planned in with six cables, and it was planned to restore the permanent army lines with a volume of four cables along certain axes. It was planned to restore the lateral line with a volume of four cables, and on the left wing it was planned to restore the permanent lines of the communications axis with eight cables and five permanent lines apiece for the armies along certain axes, with four cables apiece.

This outline of the planned cable communications network enabled us to secure troop control in the subsequent location of the *front* command post, both on the *front's* right and left flanks.

It was planned to move the *front's* command post after the *front's* right-wing forces.

It was planned to move the *front's* command post after 6-8 days, and that of the auxiliary command posts after 2-3 days.

The communications units' shortage of strength created significant difficulties in organizing cable communications during the operation, and thus the rigid planning of construction work was required, taking into account the changing situation, and the flexible maneuver of the telegraph-construction units while carrying out their work.

The organization of radio communications was planned from three of the *front's* command posts, as well as auxiliary command post no. 2 and auxiliary command post no. 1, in the following manner.

Radio communications was provided from the *front's* main command post: with the General Staff along two channels—aural and Baudot teleprinter; radio communications for cooperation of the *fronts* with the General Staff and radio communications with the operational group of the representative of the *Stavka* of the Supreme High Command through the General Staff's network no. 15; with auxiliary command posts nos. 1 and 2 in radio network no. 11; with the headquarters of the armies, the Dnepr Flotilla and the mobile formations along two channels—along radio axes nos. 122, 1, 2, 3, 9, 10, 4, 7, 8, 20, 19, 6, and 5, and through radio networks nos. 14 and 15 (weak radio stations); with the mobile formations through radio coordination network no. 16; with communications officers from *front* headquarters within the headquarters of the mobile formations—by radio axes.

It was not planned to create a special radio network for the *front* commander. As the need arose, the *front* commander's radio stations would guarantee communications by including them into the corresponding army or *front* networks.

Through auxiliary command post no. 2 radio communications was provided with: the General Staff through the General Staff's radio network no. 8 (aural reception, and with the Baudot tele-printer along the radio axis); with the *front* command post and auxiliary command post no. 1 through radio network no. 11; with the command posts of the 3rd, 48th, 65th, 28th, and 61st armies and the *front's* mobile group—through radio axes nos. 4, 10, 9, 3, 2, and 1, and through radio network no. 14 (weak radio stations); with the command post of the mobile formations (an additional communications channel) in radio network no. 16.

Radio communications between the armies' command posts and the mobile formations was planned through two radio cooperation networks: no. 12 for the forces of the *front's* right wing, and no. 13 for the left wing.

The communications coordination of the combined-arms and mobile formations with the supporting aviation would be provided for through aviation representatives, located with their communications assets, at the observation (command) posts of the commanders of the combined-arms and tank formations.

For the immediate radio communications of the armies' command posts, the *front's* auxiliary command posts nos. 1 and 2 with the General Staff, the General Staff's radio network no. 8 was organized.

The developed radio communications organization for the operation from three of the *front's* command posts did not provide for, at the time, for the precise distribution of radio assets and their maneuver during the operation.

Communications through mobile assets was planned from the main command post along axes from the 16th Air Army's command post with auxiliary command post no. 2, the 3rd Army's command post (through auxiliary command post no. 2), with the command posts of the 48th, 65th, 61st, 70th, 47th, 69th, and Polish 1st armies along an axis as far as auxiliary command post no. 1, and then along axes.

The exchange of correspondence was correspondingly conducted through report gathering posts with the main command post, the *front's* auxiliary command posts nos. 1 and 2 by planes once a day, as the great distance and the poor condition of the roads limited the use of auto transport.

Thus in preparing the Belorussian operation the command at all levels carried out a huge and useful amount of work in organizing troop control, as well as in preparing communications troops and assets for the forthcoming offensive.

11

Operational Preparation of the Command and Staffs, The Combat Training of the Troops

The operational and combat tasks given to the *fronts*, as well as the experience of the operations and battles acquired by the armies and *fronts* in the offensive operations of 1943-44, were the foundation of the troops' operational and combat training.

In all the armies comprising the *fronts'* main groups of forces, army operational command and staff exercises were carried out on maps and miniature testing grounds, which reflected the actual terrain in the area of the forthcoming combat operations.

Command-staff exercises were carried out against the background of the real operational situation and in the spirit of the decision, adopted by the *front* commander, for the forthcoming offensive operation.

The following people took part in these exercises: army commanders, members of the military councils, army chiefs of staff, commanders and chiefs of the combat arms and army services, the chiefs of operational and intelligence sections, the commanders of the mobile groups, commanders of rifle corps, and commanders of support aviation formations.

The goals of the command-staff exercises were as follows: to explain the army's place in the forthcoming *front* operation; the goals and stages of the army operation; to work out the armies' operational formation and the combat orders of the rifle corps for breaking through the enemy's previously-prepared defense in a wooded and swampy area teaming with a large number of large river barriers; to determine the methods of the artillery offensive; to work out some questions of the operation's dynamics and to study the possible variants and the order of committing into the breach the *fronts'* and armies' mobile groups according to each variant, as well as the order of their actions following their commitment into the breach, and; to work out the main questions of troop control.

According to the instructions of the *Stavka* of the Supreme High Command, these exercises were to, aside along with the working out of the main questions of the forthcoming offensive operation by stages, the most characteristic examples from the experience of the operations carried out by the armies in the preceding period.

In the army headquarters map exercises were conducted, or command-staff exercises on the spot. For example, the 65th Army's headquarters conducted a map exercise for working out a plan for the army's offensive operation. A command-staff exercise was conducted in the 48th Army, with communications assets, on the theme of "The Army Offensive Operation."

Command-staff exercises were conducted in the headquarters of the rifle corps, divisions and regiments on topics connected with the breakthrough of the enemy's previously-prepared defense and the forcing of large rivers.

In training the rifle troops' officer element, attention was mainly devoted to questions of organization and cooperation in battle, questions of troop control in battle, and while pursuing the enemy, and questions of overcoming water obstacles in a swampy area.

A huge amount of attention was devoted to the troops' combat training. For this purpose, the divisions, which were designated for breaking through the enemy's defense, were periodically moved back to the army's second echelon. But even while being on the defensive in the first echelon, the divisions would move their units and elements, in turns, into the nearby rear, where exercises were carried out on specially outfitted training grounds, involving those reinforcements with which the troops were to operate during the offensive.

The impetuousness of the attack, the rapidity and coordinated irruption of the infantry and tanks into the area of the enemy's artillery firing positions were the main requirements in the troops' combat training. Thus particular attention was paid to working out problems of cooperation between the infantry, tanks, artillery, and aviation.

The rifle troops were given the task of working out the following topics: "Attacking the Enemy's Defense to the Depth of his Artillery Positions (5-6 Kilometers)"; "The Offensive in the Depth of the Enemy's Defense after Breaking Through the Second and Third Trenches," and; "Repelling the Enemy's Counterattacks During the Development of the Battle in Depth, with the Subsequent Immediate Continuation of the Offensive." The themes, which were general for the troops of all four *fronts*, were successively worked out in the platoons and companies, and then in the battalions and regiments. Battalion exercises were conducted with the employment of artillery and tanks, as well as the laying down of smoke screens. Regimental, and a large part of the battalion, exercises were carried out with live fire. Particular attention was paid at this time to developing the ability to move behind a rolling barrage, pressing close to the explosions of one's own shells.

During the tactical exercises attention was paid to working out such questions as the organization of combat formations and the commitment of the second echelons into the battle; command in the dynamics of battle; the organization, maintenance and restoration of disrupted coordination of the infantry with its neighbors, artillery, tanks, and aviation; blocking wooden and earth pillboxes, individual fortifications and strong points; the organization of anti-tank defense the repulse of the enemy's tank counterattacks; the energetic pursuit of the retreating enemy, and; the rapid consolidation of captured targets and lines.

The training of assault and blocking groups, as well as of assault and reconnaissance battalions (one per division) was broadly conducted in all the rifle divisions.

The engineering preparation of the rifle elements and units was conducted within a program of combined-arms training. Anti-tank sections and obstacle removal groups were trained within the rifle subunits.

The rifle elements and units also studied how to overcome river obstacles using both organic equipment and materials at hand, overcoming flooded sectors using specially-prepared assets (boot attachments for wading through water, brush flooring, travois for heavy machine guns, mortars and guns). The troops also prepared various accessories from local materials for overcoming the enemy's trenches and obstacles (small bridges, mats, lengthened charges for explosive devices, etc.).

Demonstration exercises were practiced in the course of operational and combat training. For example, in the First Baltic Front a demonstration exercise was conducted, under the leadership of the *front* commander, for forcing rivers. Army commanders, commanders of corps, divisions, tank and engineer brigades, the chiefs of the combat arms and services of the *front*, armies and corps took part in this exercise. The commander of the Third Belorussian Front conducted a demonstration exercise for the commanders of tank corps and brigades on the topic of "The Commitment of the Army's Mobile Group into the Breach."

In the same *front*, beginning on 10 June, inspection battalion exercises were conducted in all the armies.

In the course of preparing for the operation, various instructions, booklets and directives on individual very important or new problems of the troops' combat activity were worked out. For example, the headquarters of the First Baltic Front drew up a directive for overcoming water obstacles and various booklets were produced, which gave bits of advice to the soldier and sergeant on activities in the offensive battle, in combating the enemy's tanks and self-propelled guns, and for forcing rivers, etc.

The preparation of the combat arms was carried out both separately and in conjunction with other arms.

Exercises on planning the artillery offensive, as applied to the conditions of the forthcoming operation, were carried out in the artillery headquarters. In the combined-arms headquarters (from regimental headquarters to army headquarters) sand table exercises were conducted involving the commanders of all the combat arms. Questions of planning the battle and the coordination of the artillery with the infantry, tanks and aviation were worked out in these exercises.

Separate and joint exercises between the rifle and artillery units and subunits were also conducted, using live fire. These exercises visually showed the order of the infantry's offensive under the cover of a rolling barrage and gave the commanders of the rifle troops practice in issuing specific assignments to the artillery in the battle, and also helped work out methods of the artillery's fire control and methods of organizing its coordination with the infantry and tanks.

The training of tank formations, units and subunits, slated for operations as part of the tank-self-propelled artillery infantry-support groups in the rifle divisions, was conducted along with the infantry, sappers and artillery. During the exercises the order and method of conducting the attack of the trenches and centers of resistance were worked out, and the place of the tanks and self-propelled artillery in the attacking troops' combat formation were determined, as was the order of maintaining coordination throughout the battle's stages.

In the tank and mechanized formations, which were slated for operations as mobile groups, command-staff exercises were conducted, involving the commanders and staffs of the cooperating formations and units of the rifle troops, aviation and artillery. Besides this, the commanders and staffs of the mobile groups were involved in exercises conducted according to the plans of the *fronts'* and combined-arms armies' headquarters.

On the basis of the decisions taking at operational games, as well as the specific tasks laid down by the commanders of the air armies and air formations with the command element of the air corps and individual divisions, as well as with their staffs, command-staff exercises were conducted under the leadership of the commanders of the air armies. The following questions were worked out at these exercises: the organization of control on the battlefield, the organization and maintenance of aviation coordination with the ground forces during the breakthrough of the enemy's defense and the order of troop support in their operations in depth; cooperation between the aviation arms in the offensive operation, and; airfield maneuver. These exercises were conducted alongside representatives from the headquarters of the armies and corps cooperating with the aviation.

Short air-tactical exercises were also conducted involving combat actions on firing ranges.

The command element of the air divisions and regiments carried out an inspection of all the forward airfields from which we planned to conduct combat operations.

The commanders of the air formations, besides taking part in various exercises, also took part in the reconnaissances carried out by the army commanders.

The units' flight personnel underwent additional training in pilot techniques and studied the area of the forthcoming combat operations.

The course of combat operations showed that a well organized and insistently conducted operational training of the command and staffs, as well as the combat training of the troops, significantly eased the fulfillment of the operational and tactical tasks assigned to the *fronts'* forces.

12

Regroupings, Concentration of the Troops and Occupying the Jumping-off Positions

Problems of the regrouping and concentration of the troops and their occupation of their jumping-off positions, in accordance with the decisions adopted, were a subject of the *front* command's particular attention while preparing for the operation. The success of the forthcoming operations depended to a great deal on their correct and timely resolution.

Regroupings of forces in the interests of the gathering operation were carried out both between *fronts* and by employing the Supreme High Command's reserves, as well as within the *fronts* for the purpose of concentrating the main efforts along the axes chosen for the main attacks.

For a multi-*front* operation, the most important thing was the *Stavka* of the Supreme High Command's correct distribution of men and materiel between the *fronts*, in accordance with the importance of the task being resolved by them.

The *Stavka* of the Supreme High Command's measures for strengthening the *fronts* with men and equipment, by the start of the operation, is shown by the data contained in table 62.

In all, during the operation's preparatory period, as a result of inter-*front* regroupings, the *Stavka* of the Supreme High Command additionally transferred to the *fronts* the following: 25 rifle divisions, eight tank and mechanized corps, two cavalry corps, one artillery corps, four artillery divisions, 17 independent artillery and mortar brigades, seven independent large-caliber and and high-power artillery battalions, 16 independent tank regiments, 22 independent self-propelled artillery regiments, one air army (five air divisions), seven independent air corps, eight independent air divisions, five independent engineer and pontoon brigades, nine independent engineer-sapper and pontoon battalions, and many other reinforcement units.

This enabled the *fronts* to sharply change the correlation of forces and equipment in their favor, to create high operational densities along the main directions, to provide for the breakthrough of the defensive structures and the development of the operation in depth at high speed.

Table 62. Measures by the *Stavka* of the Supreme High Command for Reinforcing the Troops with Military Equipment

Fronts	What and Where the *Front* Transferred on Orders by the *Stavka*	What and From Where the *Front* Received Reinforcements on Orders by the *Stavka*
1st Baltic	11th Guards Army to the Third Belorussian Front	From the High Command Reserve: 103rd Rifle Corps (29th and 270th rifle divs), 1st Tank Corps, three independent self-propelled artillery rgts, 1 flamethrower tank rgt, 1 independent tank minesweeper rgt, 4 artillery and mortar bdes, 2 guards mortar bdes, 1 air corps, 1 air div, 1 engineer-sapper bde, 2 pontoon-bridge bns
3rd Belorussian	From the First Baltic Front:	11th Gds Army. From the High Command Reserve: 5th Gds Tank Army, 2nd Gds Tank Corps, 3rd Gds Mechanized Corps, 3rd Gds Cavalry Corps, 1 breakthrough artillery corps, 2 breakthrough artillery divs, 2 high-power howitzer bdes, 5 independent large-caliber artillery bns, 2 independent tank rgts, 11 independent self-propelled artillery rgts, and 2 flamethrower tank rgts, 2 independent minesweeper tank rgts, 4 air corps, 2 independent air divs, 4 engineer-sapper bdes
2nd Belorussian		From the High Command Reserve: 4th Air Army, 81st Rifle Corps (32nd, 95th, 153rd rifle divs), 69th Rifle Corps (22nd and 42nd rifle divs), 1 corps artillery bde, 1 high-powered howitzer bde, 1 gds mortar bde, 2 anti-tank bdes, 1 anti-aircraft artillery div
1st Belorussian[1] (right wing)		From the High Command Reserve: 28th Army, 1st and 9th tank corps, 1st Mechanized Corps, 4th Gds Cavalry Corps, 1 breakthrough artillery corps, 2 breakthrough artillery divs, 6 independent artillery and mortar bdes, 2 independent high-caliber artillery bns, 4 independent tank rgts, 8 independent self-propelled artillery rgts, 2 flamethrower tank rgts, 2 independent minesweeper tank rgts, 2 air corps, and 7 independent engineer-sapper bns

Note
1 For information on the reinforcement of the *front's* left wing, which went over to the offensive during the second stage of the multi-*front* operation, see part three of this work.

For creating the main groups of forces, in accordance with the decisions of the *front* commanders, the *front* headquarters and, under their leadership, the army headquarters, as well as the commanders of the combat arms and their staffs began carrying out partial regroupings of the forces. At the same time the concentration of newly-arriving operational field forces and formations of all the combat arms and aviation was going on.

By changing the boundary line between the Second and First Baltic fronts, the *Stavka* of the Supreme High Command narrowed the First Baltic Front's sector from 214 to 160 kilometers. Thanks to this, the First Baltic Front commander had the opportunity to employ the 6th Guards Army as the *front's* main group of forces. The commander of the First Baltic Front planned to concentrate along the 25-kilometer sector of the main attack the *front's* main group of forces, which consisted of 18 rifle divisions, a tank corps, four tank brigades, and the main mass of the other reinforcements.

For this, it was necessary carry out the regrouping of forces, secretly and in strict accordance with the established deadlines. It was planned to carry out the regrouping in three stages.

During the first stage (2-10 June) it was planned to relieve the 6th Guards Army's divisions with the troops of the Second Baltic Front's 22nd Army and withdraw the relieved formations to the area southwest of Nevel', as well as relieve four of the 43rd Army divisions, which were designated for launching the main attack along the army's right flank, and to withdraw to the area southwest and east of Gorodok; the *front* was also to organize the withdrawal of one rifle division (357th) and the headquarters of the 60th Rifle Corps from the 4th Shock Army.

During the second stage (13-18 June), it was planned to move up the formations of the *front's* main group of forces to areas 12-18 kilometers from the front line.

During the third period (18-22 June), it was planned to have the troops of the *front's* main group of forces occupy their jumping-off positions.

It is necessary to note that the terrain in the 6th Guards Army's regrouping sector was wooded and swampy, with an extremely underdeveloped road network. 3-4 field roads, which mainly ran along the front, and one surfaced road, could be employed for transporting the army. We had to completely withdraw an army of six rifle divisions, two anti-aircraft artillery divisions, five artillery and mortar brigades, two artillery regiments, three tank brigades, a self-propelled artillery regiment, and two engineer-sapper brigades over these roads in the course of 7-9 days. The distance the army's formations had to travel was different and varied from 22 to 100 kilometers.

In view of the difficulty of the 6th Guards Army's regrouping, the *front* commander decided during 2-5 June to withdraw the main mass of the artillery and tanks to the concentration area. During this time the rifle divisions turned over their sectors to the formations of the Second Baltic Front's 22nd Army and prepared for moving to the concentration area.

Despite the difficulties of the regrouping and the overtaxing of the roads, the concentration of the 6th Guards Army's forces was carried out according to schedule. The army command managed to withdraw several divisions into the reserve by lengthening the defensive front of the first-echelon divisions. These divisions subsequently, along with the 357th Rifle Division arrived from the 4th Shock Army, became part of the 1st and 60th rifle corps. The movement of the 43rd Army's forces to the concentration area was carried out without particular difficulties. The large number of roads and the length of the marches, which varied from 7-20 kilometers, enabled us to regroup formations and units, which were designated for the main group of forces, completely on time; that is, by 9 June.

The movement of troops to their sectors was carried out, according to plan, during 13-18 June, in an organized and secret manner.

It was planned to carry out during 10-13 June the artillery's regrouping into the pre-positioning areas, which were 10-28 kilometers from their new positional areas. It was planned to occupy the firing positions during 13-21 June. The entire artillery's advance to its firing positions was completed by 0300 on 20 June.

In the plan for the artillery's arrival at its new firing positions, the following were indicated: the routes, the areas of the firing positions, the number of batteries and adjustment guns being moved up, the departure time for the batteries and adjustment guns occupying their firing positions, and the time they were to be ready. The artillery's arrival in the areas of the firing positions was carried out precisely according to plan. An exception was the artillery of the 4th Cannon-Artillery Brigade and the 103rd Rifle Corps, which, due to the extreme overloading of the railroad and the actions of the enemy air force, arrived late to the army.

Before 21 June the troops of the *front's* main group of forces (minus artillery) were within their sectors, in areas 12-18 kilometers from the front line. Their occupation of their jumping-off positions began on the night of 21-22 June. The rifle battalions of the first-echelon regiments moved into the first trench, while the divisions' main forces were occupied the areas located 4-6 kilometers from the front line. On the night before the offensive (23 June), the second- and third-echelon battalions reached their jumping-off positions.

As a result of the regrouping along the direction of the *front's* main attack, a group of forces was created and densities achieved, as shown in table 63.

Table 63. The Grouping and Densities of the Forces Along the Axis of the First Baltic Front's Main Attack

Armies in the Main Group of Forces	Formations and Units				
	Rifle Divs	Tank Bdes, Mechanized Bdes, Motorized Rifle Bdes	Independent Tank Rgts	Self-Propelled Artillery Rgts	Breakthrough Artillery Divs
6th Gds Army	11	2	3	2	1
43rd Army	5	2	1	2	–
1st Tank Corps and 46th Mechanized Bde	–	3/1/2	–	2	–
Total Along the Breakthrough Sector	16	10	4	6	–

Armies in the Main Group of Forces	Formations and Units				
	Cannon-Artillery Bde	Howitzer Rgt	Anti-Tank Artillery Bde	Anti-Tank Artillery Rgt	Mortar Rgt/Gds Mortar Rgt
6th Gds Army	3	3	1	1	2/2
43rd Army	2	3	1	1	1/2
1st Tank Corps and 46th Mechanized Bde	–	2	–	–	2/0
Total Along the Breakthrough Sector	5	8	2	2	5/4

Armies in the Main Group of Forces	Formations and Units			Total	
	Anti-Aircraft Divs	Anti-Aircraft Rgts	Mortar Bdes/ Gds Mortar Bdes	Battalions	Guns & Mortars	Tanks and Self-Propelled Guns
6th Gds Army	1	4	–	99	2,317	204
43rd Army	1	2	1/1	45	1,233	158
1st Tank Corps and 46th Mechanized Bde	–	2	–	–	–	297
Total Along the Breakthrough Sector	2	8	1/1	144	3,550	535

Armies in the Main Group of Forces	Width of Breakthrough Sector (in kms)	Battalions	Density Per Kilometer Along Breakthrough Sector	
			Guns and Mortars	Tanks and Self-Propelled Guns
6th Gds Army	18	about 5.5	129	20[1]
43rd Army	7	6.4	179	23
1st Tank Corps and 46th Mechanized Bde	–	–	5-6	16.5
Total Along the Breakthrough Sector	25	5.7	151	25.5

Note

1 Such a high density was the result of the fact that the tanks, according to terrain conditions, were employed only along the 10-kilometer Mazury—Sirotino sector.

In the Third Belorussian Front the operational movements began on 24 May 1944 and went on in an intense situation. The troops were transported along two railroad lines: Moscow—Vyaz'ma—Smolensk and Bryansk—Roslavl'—Smolensk. These lines were single-tracked and, furthermore, along a number of sectors they had been restored with short pieces of rails. Besides this, the western railroad was going through an extreme shortage of coal. Thus during the day trains with human reinforcements, coal and other cargoes passed through. Trains carrying artillery and shells passed through only at night. In the most intensive days rail shipments were covered by fighter aviation. By 19 June 491 operational trains and had been unloaded and the shipment of troops had been, for the most part, completed.

The *front's* main unloading area, Gusino—Smolensk—Kolodnya, was 90 kilometers from the front line. Trains with heavy equipment (tanks, self-propelled guns, artillery) were moved forward to Vydreya and Liozno stations.

Following their detraining, the troops were immediately moved to their waiting areas, from where they moved by night marches either to their concentration areas, or immediately to their intermediate positions.

The *front's* most important measure during the preparation period was the creation of two main groups of forces: northern and southern.

The essence of the *front's* measures in creating the northern group consisted in the withdrawal of the 39th and 5th armies' main forces, along with reinforcements, to the narrow front Makarovo—Yazykovo—Yul'kovo, and the cavalry-mechanized group (3rd Guards Cavalry and 3rd Guards Mechanized corps) to the intermediate area centered on Liozno. In conjunction with this, the 39th Army on 5 June receieved the 251st Rifle Division from the 5th Army, along with the division's defensive sector, and thus broadened its defensive sector to 45 kilometers. The 39th Army, in its turn, transferred to the 5th Army its 215th Rifle Division and by 18 June had regrouped its main forces, consisting of five rifle divisions, a tank brigade and other reinforcements, to the Makarovo—Yazykovo sector.

The 39th Army's artillery occupied new positional areas by the morning of 10 June.

The 5th Army, having transferred a rifle division, along with the latter's defensive sector, to the 39th Army, had thus narrowed its defensive sector to 25 kilometers. By 16 June the army's main forces, consisting of eight rifle divisions, two tank brigades and other reinforcements, had been regrouped to the sector excluding Yazykovo—Yul'kovo. The army's artillery (army and Supreme High Command reserve artillery) had occupied its new positional areas by the morning of 14 June.

The 3rd Guards Mechanized Corps had been withdrawn in march formation along the paved road through Liozno from its concentration area excluding Arkhipovka—Svetitsy—Velino in the course of two nights (11-12 June) to the intermediate area of Reuty—Krasynshchina—Karusi, where it secretly encamped until its movement to the jumping-off position. The intermediate area was 18-25 kilometers from the front line.

The 3rd Guards Cavalry Corps was withdrawn directly from the unloading areas of the Smolensk and Katyn' stations along the route Smolensk—Verkhov'e—Kasplya—Chernyany—Mikulino—Rubezhnitsa during 14-21 June to the intermediate area centered on Liozno. The 3rd Guards Cavalry Corps' intermediate area was 10-30 kilometers from the front line. The 5th Guards Cavalry Division was moved forward and stationed in the wooded area 10-12 kilometers from the front line.

Measures for creating the *front's* southern group consisted of the following: the movement of the First Baltic Front's 11th Guards Army into the 31st Army's sector, with its subsequent movement into the *front's* first echelon; the movement of the 2nd Guards Tank Corps to the intermediate area Sentyuri—Goryany—excluding Krasnoe, and the 5th Artillery Corps (2nd and 20th breakthrough artillery divisions) into its pre-position areas in the woods west of Kiseli and Gichi, and the movement of the 11th Guards and 31st armies, along with reinforcements, to a narrow front Settlement No. 7—Kirieva—Zastenok Yur'ev.

For this, the 11th Guards Army, having completed during the 27 May-9 June time period, a march from the Nevel' area, by 10 June had completely concentrated in the area southwest of Lyubavichi. During this movement, the army's various formations covered a distance of 190-250 kilometers. On 10 June the army, having received a 35-kilometer attack zone from the 31st Army along the front line Vikokorno No. 1—Kirieva, began preparing for the operation.

In order to cover the newly-concentrated army, the 152nd Fortified Area and the 31st Army's 192nd and 88th rifle divisions (minus one regiment), were left along the front line. By 0200 on 20 June the 11th Guards Army's formations had occupied the front line from the 31st Army, having relieved units of the 31st Army's 192nd and 88th rifle divisions.

The 11th Guards Army's main forces, before they occupied their jumping-off position, before 22 June had continued to remain in their concentration areas. Each first-echelon division occupied its assigned attack sector from 20 June with only 1-2 battalions.

In order to create the main group of forces, the 11th Guards Army (nine rifle divisions, one tank corps, one independent tank brigade, and other reinforcements) was not required to carry out large-scale movements, because the concentration of the army's corps in the area to the southwest of Lyubavichi was carried out by taking into account the army's operational deployment for the offensive. However, while being stationed in the intermediate area for two weeks, the army's main forces were only 12-15 kilometers from the front line, while the 16th Guards Rifle Corps was only 5-8 kilometers away. Such a close and prolonged stay by the *front's* second-echelon army from the front line during the operation's preparatory period was not justified; captured German generals testified that we had not managed to completely hide the presence of the 11th Guards Army from the enemy.

The 2nd Guards Tank Corps, which had been attached to the 11th Guards Army, had been withdrawn to the army's sector into the intermediate area Sentyuri—Goryany—Klimenki—excluding Krasnoe on 20 June.

From 7 June the 5th Breakthrough Artillery Corps moved by night marches from its concentration area (the woods north and south of Gusino) along the Moscow—Minsk highway and by 10-11 June had arrived in its pre-position area (the woods west of Kiseli and Yakimenki).

For the purpose of covering the troops' movement to their jumping-off positions, all of the 11th Guards Army's artillery occupied its firing positions by the morning of 14 June.

The 31st Army, having transferred the 152nd Fortified Area and the front it occupied to the 11th Guards Army by 12 June, and having left behind covering troops (192nd and 88th rifle divisions), had reduced its front from 70 to 35 kilometers. The 31st Army carried out its regrouping in two stages. In the 3-7 June period, in order to free up the sector being turned over to the 11th Guards Army, the 36th Rifle Corps was moved to the southern bank of the Dnepr River, and the 71st Rifle Corps' 331st Rifle Division was moved to its corps' sector. Such a preliminary regrouping enabled us to subsequently, that is; in the 18-21 June period, remove the 31st Army's main group of forces (five rifle divisions, one independent tank brigade, and other reinforcements) by short night marches to a narrow breakthrough sector: excluding Kirieva—Zastenok Yur'ev. At the same time the 192nd Rifle Division and units of the 88th Rifle Division were, upon being relieved, moved from the 11th Guards Army's sector into the 71st Rifle Corps' sector.

The 31st Army's artillery occupied new positional area by the morning of 14 June.

The 5th Guards Tank Army moved from its concentration area to the northeast of Smolensk along the Moscow—Minsk highway through Vityazi, Rogulino, Yermaki and Arkhipovka, and in the course of five nights, beginning on the night of 17-18 June to the morning of 22 June, had concentrated in the intermediate area Poteenki—Paruli—Svetitsy—Granki.

Thus by the close of 21 June the forces of the Third Belorussian Front had completed all their regroupings and in the course of two nights—22-23 June—had occupied their jumping-off positions for the offensive.

The combined-arms armies' infantry occupation of the jumping-off position for the offensive was carried out under the cover of specially allotted units and elements, and only at night in groups ranging from a company to battalion in size, depending on the terrain conditions along the front line. The tanks and self-propelled artillery took up their jumping-off positions on the night of 23 June, while some tank subunits did this under the cover of the artillery preparation. The 2nd Guards Tatsinskaya Tank Corps reached its jumping-off area 0.5 kilometers east of Novoe Selo—height 208—Red'ki—Staroe Tukhino by 0300 on 23 June.

The *front's* cavalry-mechanized group occupied its jumping-off area as follows: 3rd Guards Mechanized Corps—the area Tulovo—Ivan'kina—excluding Vydreya—Dubrovo, and the 3rd Guards Cavalry Corps—the area excluding Staraya Vydreya—Pioramont—Zhary by 0400 on 23 June.

The 5th Guards Tank Army remained in its intermediate area in readiness to operate according to two variants.

The artillery occupied new positional areas in their army sectors by 13-14 June, in order to cover the troops' regroupings and occupation of their jumping-off positions for the offensive, as well as for refining their firing data.

As a result of the regrouping along the axes of the *front's* main attacks, the main groups of forces had been created and operational densities achieved, as can be seen from table 64.

It was planned to create the Second Belorussian Front's main group of forces at the expense of the *front's* forces by means of intra-*front* regroupings. The regroupings were begun on 9 June and were completed 3-4 days before the start of the offensive. The regrouping plan called for the strengthening of the 49th Army with the newly-arrived 81st (32nd, 95th, 153rd rifle divisions) and 69th (222nd and 42nd rifle divisions) rifle corps by order of the *Stavka* of the Supreme High Command and the 369th Rifle Division from the 50th Army.

Besides this, the 49th Army was reinforced with the following units: from the 33rd Army—three howitzer regiments, one cannon-artillery brigade, one guards mortar regiment; from the 50th Army—one cannon-artillery brigade, one howitzer regiment, two guards mortar regiments, and seven anti-aircraft artillery regiments. A corps artillery brigade, a high-powered howitzer brigade, one guards mortar brigade, two anti-tank brigades, and one anti-aircraft artillery division from the *Stavka* of the Supreme High Command reserve.

The tank units and units of self-propelled artillery began to concentrate in the 49th Army's sector on 10 June and completed this on 16 June.

During 10-15 June the reinforcement artillery was concentrated in its designated areas.

As a result of the regrouping, the troops designated for operations in the main group of forces, were concentrated in the 49th Army's sector.

The occupation of the jumping-off positions by the main group of forces' formations and units began on the night of 20-21 June. At the same time, on the night of 20-21 June, four first-echelon divisions relieved the defending units, each with a single battalion, and during the night of 22-23 June all of the first-echelon units occupied their jumping-off positions. Tanks and self-propelled guns occupied their jumping-off positions on the night of 22-23 June, under the cover of night aviation.

Table 64. The Grouping and Densities of the Forces Along the Axes of the Third Belorussian Front's Main Attacks

Armies in the Main Group of Forces	Formations and Units					
	Rifle Divs	Cavalry Divs	Independent Tank Bdes/ Independent Tank Rgts	Mechanized Bdes/ Motorized Rifle Bdes	Self-Propelled Artillery Rgts	Breakthrough Artillery Divs
Northern Group:						
39th Army	5	–	1	–	2	–
5th Army	8	–	2	–	6	1
Total	13	–	3	–	8	1
Cavalry-Mechanized Group	–	3	1	3	3	–
Southern Group:						
11th Gds Army	9	–	1/2	–	3	2
31st Army	6	–	1	–	4	–
Total	15	–	2/2	–	7	2
2nd Gds Tank Corps	–	–	3	0/1	2	–
5th Gds Tank Army	–	–	6	0/2	4	–

Armies in the Main Group of Forces	Formations and Units					
	Artillery Bde/Artillery Rgt	Howitzer Bde/ Independent Artillery Div	Anti-Tank Bde	Anti-Tank Rgt	Mortar Bde/ Mortar Rgt	Gds Mortar Bde
Northern Group:						
39th Army	1	–	–	1	0/1	–
5th Army	4	1	1	1	0/1	1
Total	5	1	1	2	0/2	1
Cavalry-Mechanized Group	–	–	–	1	0/1	–
Southern Group:						
11th Gds Army	1/3	1/5	1	1	0/1	2
31st Army	2/3	–	1	1	0/1	–
Total	3/6	1/5	2	2	0/2	2
2nd Gds Tank Corps	–	–	–	–	0/1	–
5th Gds Tank Army	1	–	–	3	0/2	–

Armies in the Main Group of Forces	Formations and Units					Total	
	Gds Mortar Rgts	Anti-Aircraft Divs	Anti-Aircraft Rgts	Engineer-Sapper Bns	Battalions	Guns & Mortars	Tanks & Self-Propelled Guns
Northern Group:							
39th Army	1	1	1	1	45	724	96
5th Army	2	1	1	2	72	1,419	271
Total	3	2	2	3	117	2,143	367
Cavalry-Mechanized Group	1	–	2	–	–	463	320
Southern Group:							
11th Gds Army	3	2	1	1	81	1,778	331
31st Army	1	1	2	2	54	1,058	139
Total	4	3	3	3	135	2,836	470
2nd Gds Tank Corps	2	–	1	–	–	–	254
5th Gds Tank Army	1	1	1	–	–	298	524

Armies in the Main Group of Forces	Width of Breakthrough Sector (in kms)	Divisions per Kilometer	Density Per Kilometer Along Breakthrough Sector	
			Guns & Mortars	Tanks and Self-Propelled Guns
Northern Group:				
39th Army	6	1.21	120	16
5th Army	11.5	1.51	123	23
Total	17.5	1.4	122	21
Cavalry-Mechanized Group	–	–	26	18
Southern Group:				
11th Gds Army	10.5	1.11	169	31
31st Army	9	1.5	117	15
Total	19.5	1.3	145	26
2nd Gds Tank Corps	–	–	–	24
5th Gds Tank Army	–	–	15-17	27-30

The *front's* main group of forces and the densities achieved are shown by the following data (table 65).

The purpose of the regrouping of the First Belorussian Front's right-wing forces was to create two main groups of forces—a northern and southern one—for launching a simultaneous attack from two directions.

The point of the measures for creating the northern group of forces consisted of concentrating and deploying the 3rd and 48th armies' main forces and reinforcements along the narrow 17-kilometer Ozerane—Rogachev sector.

In connection with this, the 3rd Army, having transferred the 45-kilometer sector from Luzhki to Proskurin, along with the 115th Fortified Area and the 42nd Rifle Corps, thus shortened its front to 53 kilometers. As a result of this regrouping, the army concentrated its main forces, consisting of the 35th, 41st and 46th rifle corps (eight rifle divisions), and the 9th Tank Corps, along with reinforcements, along its left flank. Two rifle corps were deployed in the first echelon along the sector excluding Ozerane—Kostyashevo, while one corps comprised the second echelon and the 9th Tank Corps the army's breakthrough development echelon.

The 48th Army, having received the 45-kilometer sector from the 3rd Army, widened its sector to 84 kilometers. As a result of the completed regrouping, the army created its main group of forces, consisting of the 42nd and 29th rifle corps (five rifle divisions) and reinforcements along its right flank, having deployed the main forces of three of these corps' divisions along a 5-kilometer sector.

Measures for creating the southern group of forces came down to deploying the main forces of the 65th Army and the 28th Army, which was arriving at the *front* from the Supreme High Command reserve, along the 15-kilometer front marker 131—marker 142.5; the 1st Tank Corps—the 65th Army's breakthrough development echelon—was to be concentrated in the area Velikii Bor—marker 131—Setishche, and the cavalry-mechanized group (4th Cavalry and 1st Mechanized corps) in the area Zal'e—Tsidov—Lyudvinovka.

Table 65. The Grouping and Densities of the Forces Along the Axis of the Second Belorussian Front's Main Attack

Armies	Formations and Units					
	Rifle Divs	Tank Bdes	Independent Tank Rgts	Self-Propelled Artillery Rgts	Cannon-Artillery Bdes/Corps Artillery Bdes	Howitzer Bdes
49th Army	10	2	1	6	3/1	2

Armies	Formations and Units					Total	
	Howitzer Rgts/Corps Artillery Rgt	Anti-Tank Bdes	Gds Mortar Bdes/ Gds Mortar Rgts	Mortar Bdes/ Mortar Rgts	Battalions	Guns & Mortars	Tanks & Self-Propelled Guns
49th	9/3	3	1/5	1/2	90	2,239	364

Armies	Width of Main Attack Sector (in kms)	Divisions per Kilometer	Density Per Kilometer Along Main Attack Sector	
			Guns & Mortars	Tanks and Self-Propelled Guns
49th Army	12	1.2	190	30

In connection with this, the 65th Army, having turned over its left sector from the area excluding Korma to the Pripyat' River to the newly-arrived 28th Army, sharply reduced its front from 90 to 24 kilometers. As a result of the regrouping, the army created its main group of forces on its left flank, consisting of the 105th and 18th rifle corps and the 44th and 356th rifle divisions (seven rifle divisions), the 1st Tank Corps and reinforcements, having deployed four rifle divisions in the first echelon along a 6-kilometer main attack zone, marker 139.1—Korma.

The 28th Army, having received the 79-kilometer sector excluding Korma—Pripyat' River from the 65th Army, as well as the 161st, 153rd and 119th fortified areas, with their defensive sectors to the area excluding V'yunishche to the Pripyat' River, created its main group of forces on its right flank. The main group of forces included the 3rd Guards and 20th rifle corps (six rifle divisions), which had deployed four of these corps divisions in the first echelon along the 9-kilometer sector from excluding Korma to marker 142.5.

The cavalry-mechanized group concentrated in its designated area in the 65th and 28th armies' sectors.

The regroupings and concentration of men and materiel on the First Belorussian Front's right flank were completed on 22 June. During the right wing's regrouping, regroupings of the *front's* left-wing forces were also occurring.

The *front's* main groups of forces and the operational densities achieved in these groups of forces' sectors are shown by the following data (see table 66).

As a result of the regroupings carried out in the *fronts*, and the concentration of fresh forces from the Supreme High Command reserve, the First Baltic and the Second Belorussian fronts created a main group of forces apiece, and the Third and First Belorussian fronts two main groups of forces apiece, which enabled us to simultaneously inflict six powerful blows against the enemy along a 690-kilometer front. One may judge as to the power of each of these attacks by the correlation of forces achieved by our forces along the directions of the *fronts'* main blows (see table 67).

Such an overwhelming superiority in men and materiel was achieved thanks to the *Stavka* of the Supreme High Command's enormous organizational work.

Of the overall amount of men and materiel concentrated for the operation along the First Belorussian Front's right wing, the following forces came from the Supreme High Command reserve: 25 percent of the combined-arms armies and rifle divisions, 100 percent of the tank, mechanized and cavalry corps, 38 percent of the tank and self-propelled artillery regiments, 50 percent of the artillery divisions, 70 percent of the artillery brigades, 33 percent of the independent artillery regiments, 100 percent of the high-caliber artillery battalions, and 100 percent of the assault engineer-sapper brigades and battalions, etc. The same phenomenon was observed in the Third Belorussian Front.

Table 66. The Grouping and Densities of the Forces Along the Axis of the First Belorussian Front's (Right Flank) Main Attack

Front Groups and Armies	Formations and Units					
	Rifle Divs	Cavalry Divs	Tank Corps/ Mech Corps	Tank Bdes/ Mech Bdes	Motorized Rifle Bdes	Independent Tank Rgts
Northern Group:						
3rd Army and 9th Tank Corps	8	–	1	3	1	3
48th Army	5	–	–	–	–	1
Total	13	–	1	3	1	4
Southern Group:						
65th Army and 1st Gds Tank Corps	7	–	1	3	1	–
28th Army	6	–	–	–	–	3
Total	13	–	1	3	1	3
Cavalry-Mechanized Group	–	3	0/3	1/3	–	–
Total	26	3	2/3	7/3	2	7

Front Groups and Armies	Formations and Units					
	Self-Propelled Artillery Rgts	Breakthrough Artillery Divs	Artillery Bdes/Corps Artillery Rgts	Howitzer Bdes/Howitzer Rgts	Anti-Tank Bdes	Anti-Tank Rgts
Northern Group:						
3rd Army and 9th Tank Corps	1	–	0/1	2	1	–
48th Army	2	1	1	–	–	–
Total	3	1	1/1	2	1	–
Southern Group:						
65th Army and 1st Gds Tank Corps	2	1	4	–	2	–
28th Army	3	2	–	–	–	1
Total	5	3	4	–	2	1
Cavalry-Mechanized Group	–	–	–	–	–	–
Total	8	4	5/1	2	3	1

Front Groups and Armies	Formations and Units					
	Mortar Rgts	Gds Mortar Bdes/Gds Mortar Rgts	Anti-Aircraft Divs	Anti-Aircraft Rgts	Sapper Bdes	Engineer-Sapper Bdes
Northern Group:						
3rd Army and 9th Tank Corps	–	2/4	–	–	1	–
48th Army	2	–	1	–	–	1
Total	2	2/4	1	–	1	1
Southern Group:						
65th Army and 1st Gds Tank Corps	3	2	1	–	–	–
28th Army	1	0/2	2	1	–	1
Total	4	2/2	3	1	–	1
Cavalry-Mechanized Group	–	–	–	–	–	–
Total	6	4/6	4	1	1	2

Front Groups and Armies	Total					Density Per Kilometer Along Sector of Main Blow	
	Battalions	Guns & Mortars	Tanks & Self-Propelled Guns	Width of Main Attack Sector (in kms)	Divisions Per Kilometer	Guns & Mortars	Tanks & Self-Propelled Guns
Northern Group:							
3rd Army and 9th Tank Corps	72	1,742	551	12	1.5	145	46
48th Army	45	992	84	5	1.0	198	17
Total	117	2,734	635	17	–	160	37
Southern Group:							
65th Army and 1st Gds Tank Corps	63	1,312	358	6	1.2	219	60
28th Army	54	1,778	269	9	1.5	198	30
Total	117	3,090	627	15		206	40
Cavalry-Mechanized Group	–	481	274	15		32	18
Total	234	6,305	1,536	47		205	52.9

Table 67. The Correlation of Forces and Densities in the Main Groups of Forces' Sectors of the First Baltic, Third, Second and First Belorussian Fronts

Fronts	Main Groups	Men & Materiel	Our Forces[1]	
			Total	Per Kilometer of Front
1st Baltic	6th Gds and 43rd armies, 1st Tank Corps, 46th Mechanized Bde	Rifle Divs	16	1.4
		Tank Divs		
		Guns & Mortars	3,550	142
		Tanks and Self-Propelled Guns	635	25.5
3rd Belorussian	Northern Group:			
	39th and 5th armies, cavalry-mechanized group	Rifle Divs	13	1
		Tank Divs[2]	1.5	
		Cavalry Divs	3	
		Guns & Mortars	2,606/2,952	149/169
		Tanks & Self-Propelled Guns	687/1,211	40/69

Fronts	Main Groups	Men & Materiel	Our Forces[1]	
			Total	Per Kilometer of Front
	Southern Group:			
	11th Gds Army, 2nd Gds Tank Corps, 31st Army	Rifle Divs	15	1.2
		Guns & Mortars	3,052/3,396	156/174
		Tanks & Self-Propelled Guns	724/1,248	37/60
2nd Belorussian		Rifle Divs	10	1.2
		Guns & Mortars	2,239	187
		Tanks and Self-Propelled Guns	364	30
1st Belorussian	Northern Group:			
	3rd and 48th armies, 9th Tank Corps	Rifle Divs	13	1.1
		Tank Divs	1.5	
		Guns & Mortars	2,734	160
		Tanks & Self-Propelled Guns	635	37
	Southern Group:			
	65th and 28th armies, 1st Gds Tank Corps, cavalry-mechanized group	Rifle Divs	13	1.2
		Tank Divs	3	
		Cavalry Divs	3	
		Guns & Mortars	3,571	238
		Tanks & Self-Propelled Guns	911	about 61

Note
1 The number in the numerator includes the 5th Guards Tank Army.
2 One tank (mechanized) corps is considered the equivalent of 1.5 divisions.

	Main Groups	Men & Materiel	Main Group's Attack Sector (in kms)	Enemy		
				Total	Per Km	Correlation
1st Baltic	6th Gds and 43rd armies, 1st Tank Corps, 46th Mechanized Bde	Rifle Divs Tank Divs	25	5	5	3.6:1
		Guns & Mortars		970	39	3.7:1
		Tanks & Self-Propelled Guns		90	3.6	7:1
3rd Belorussian	Northern Group:					
	39th and 5th armies, cavalry-mechanized group	Rifle Divs Tank Divs Cavalry Divs	17.5	4	4.4	4.4:1
		Guns & Mortars		438	25	4.9:1-6.7:1
		Tanks & Self-Propelled Guns		118	7	6:1-10.3:1

	Main Groups	Men & Materiel	Main Group's Attack Sector (in kms)	Enemy		
				Total	Per Km	Correlation
	Southern Group:					
	11th Gds Army, 2nd Gds Tank Corps, 31st Army	Rifle Divs	19.5	4	5	4:1
		Guns & Mortars		487	25	6:1-7:1
		Tanks & Self-Propelled Guns		110	6	6.6:1-11.3:1
2nd Belorussian		Rifle Divs	12	3	4	3.3:1
		Guns & Mortars		160	13.3	14:1
		Tanks and Self-Propelled Guns		150	13	2.4:1
1st Belorussian	Northern Group:					
	3rd and 48th armies, 9th Tank Corps	Rifle Divs Tank Divs	17		4	3.6:1
		Guns & Mortars		541	32	5:1
		Tanks & Self-Propelled Guns		268	6	2.3:1
	Southern Group:					
	65th and 28th armies, 1st Gds Tank Corps, cavalry-mechanized group	Rifle Divs Tank Divs Cavalry Divs	15	4		3:8
		Guns & Mortars		390	26	9.1
		Tanks & Self-Propelled Guns		84	about 6	10.8:1

In planning and carrying out such a grandiose regroupings of forces, the command of the *fronts* devoted particular attention to concealing the processes of movement, concentration, stationing, and deployment, and occupying the jumping-off positions by the troops. The *front* commanders were instructed in the following: for concealing their forces and preserving military secrets, organizing headquarters commandant's service, for maintaining march discipline and in the troops' quartering areas. Worthy of attention were the organization of control of the regrouping by representatives of the *fronts* staffs along the route of march, in the concentration areas, and of the method of air control. Control leadership was exercised by the chiefs of the *front* staffs.

It should be noted that the regroupings went in a sufficiently organized manner and were kept secret. The troops deployed and occupied their jumping-off positions within the designated times.

On the whole, the success of such a grandiose regrouping may be explained, first of all, by our superiority over the enemy in the air.

One should further note the *front's* expedient measures for organizing the regroupings, the rigid control over carrying out these measures by the *front* headquarters, and the firm observance of the roles of troop concealment.

Conclusions to Part 2

1.   On the whole, the decisions by the *front* commanders corresponded to the plan by the *Stavka* of the Supreme High Command for conducting the Belorussian operation.

The main efforts were to be concentrated in the sectors of the Third and First Belorussian fronts. The enemy's defense was to be simultaneously pierced along two sectors in each of these *fronts*. For this purpose, the *front's* shock groups of forces were to be created, in which, aside from the first-echelon's combined-arms armies and the mobile forces and reserves, the main mass of reinforcements was also to be included.

The enemy's defense along the 690-kilometer sector was to first be broken through along only six sectors, accounting, overall, for 14.9 percent of the front. The attacks along all sectors were organized in such force that the enemy could not parry them.

The Soviet armed forces confidently held the strategic initiative in their hands. This enabled the *front* commanders to carry out the bold massing of men and materiel along the axes of the planned main attacks by the start of the operation, leaving only 10.5 percent to 29.8 percent of all their forces along the remaining 85.1 percent of the front. The resolution of this problem, to a significant degree, was made easier by seven fortified areas, which occupied broad sectors of the front and secured the shock groups of forces' flanks in their jumping-off positions.

2.   The breakthrough of the enemy's defense in the *fronts* was to be carried out along sectors not exceeding a total of 29-37 kilometers. The *fronts'* main mass of men and materiel were to be concentrated along the breakthrough sectors (see table 68). The table makes it clear that along the *front's* axis of the main blow 60-94 percent of the rifle troops, 54.1-80 percent of the guns and mortars, and 66.5-100 percent of the tanks and self-propelled guns were to be employed, which would ensure the creation of a significant superiority over the enemy along the breakthrough sectors.

A great deal of attention was devoted to the creation of the necessary operational and tactical densities in both men and materiel, in order to quickly break through the enemy's defense and achieve high rates of advance.

The densities that were to be created along the axes of the *fronts'* main attacks, spoke to the skill of the *front* and army commanders in massing men and materiel along the breakthrough sectors and were to ensure the fulfillment of the tasks laid down for the troops in this operation (see table 69).

Table 68. The Distribution of Men and Materiel in the *Fronts'* Sectors

Fronts	Overall Front (in kms)	Break-through Sectors	Distribution of Men and Materiel Along the Secondary Axes (in %)			Along the Main Axis (in %)		
			Rifle Divs	Guns & Self-Propelled Guns	Tanks & Mortars	Rifle Divs	Guns & Self-Propelled Guns	Tanks & Mortars
1st Baltic	160	25	21	21.5	3.4	79	78.5	96.6
3rd Belorussian	130	37	6	20	33.5	94	80	66.5
2nd Belorussian	160	12	40	45.9	0	60	54.1	100
1st Belorussian	240[1]	29	18	32.5	5.1	82	67.5	94.9
Total	690 (100 percent)	103 (14.9 percent)	21.2	29.8	10.5	78.8	70.2	89.5

Note
1 Counting only the *front's* right-wing armies.

Table 69. Operational Densities in the *Fronts'* Sectors and Tactical Densities Along the Breakthrough Sectors

Men & Materiel	Operational Densities per Kilometer of Front[1]				
	1st Baltic Front	3rd Belorussian Front	2nd Belorussian Front	1st Belorussian Front[2]	Average for all *Fronts*
Rifle Divisions	one div per 6.6 km	one div per 3.9 km	one div per 7.2 km	one div per 6.1 km	one div per 5.9 km
Battalions	–	–	–	–	–
Guns & Mortars (76mm and higher)	30.7	54.8	24.9	34.6	35.3
Tanks and Self-Propelled Guns	4.3	13.9	1.7	5.4	5.9

Notes
1 In order to determine the operational densities, all the men and materiel in the *front's* sector were counted.
2 Right wing.

Men & Materiel	Tactical Densities per Kilometer of Front[1]				
	1st Baltic Front	3rd Belorussian Front	2nd Belorussian Front	1st Belorussian Front	Average for all *Fronts*
Rifle Divisions	–	–	–	–	–
Battalions	5.7	6.5	6.4	6.0	6.1
Guns & Mortars (76mm and higher)	151	156	181	204.4	134.5
Tanks and Self-Propelled Guns	13.5	17.7	25.0	20.0	19.0

Note
1 In order to determine the tactical densities, only the armie's first echelons along the breakthrough sectors were counted.

The densities shown in table 69 are not very different from the operational indices of 1943. However, significant qualitative changes had taken place in the increase in the number of high-caliber guns and mortars, the improved supply of artillery shells, the further increase in the number of the latest tanks, and the growth of the troops' combat skill.

3.   The depth of the *front* and army operations was not equal and was characterized by the indices shown in table 70.

The Second Belorussian Front's operational depth, which was twice as less, is testimony to the *Stavka's* lack of desire to push the enemy out of the encirclement area being prepared for his group of forces.

Table 72 shows that the planned depth of the army operations varied. In the First Baltic and Third Belorussian fronts immediate objectives were assigned to the armies up to the moment of the mobile groups' commitment into the breach, while in the Second and First Belorussian fronts these objectives were assigned to the depth of the main tasks assigned to the *fronts*.

4.   The operational speeds in the *fronts*' and armies' planning documents did not differ greatly and were characterized by the following data (see table 72).

The planned rates of advance in the tactical and operational zones of the enemy's defense varied from five to 20 kilometers; that is, they were almost identical. The planned offensive rates in many armies proved to be too low, because they did not fully correspond to our troops' offensive capabilities and the real correlation of forces, particularly in advancing in the operational depth of the enemy's defense.

5.   The *fronts*' operational formation was in a single echelon and 1-2 echelons, given the presence of mobile groups and the armies' reserves. The corps' combat formations were organized, as a rule, in two echelons. This question was resolved, in each separate case, depending on the specifics of the situation (see table 73).

Thus if all the combined-arms armies in the *fronts* were in the first echelon, and the *fronts*' reserves, on the whole, did not exceed 2.5 percent of the overall number of divisions, then, as a whole, the organization of the troops in their jumping-off positions was echeloned in depth, which is confirmed by the presence in the second echelons and reserves of the *fronts*, armies and corps of 33 percent of the overall number of rifle divisions. The depth of the troops' echelonment in the *fronts* was also achieved by the presence of mobile groups, consisting of independent tank corps, cavalry-mechanized groups and tank armies. Besides this, it was planned to create second echelons in the *fronts* during the course of the operation by taking out part of the forces from the first echelon, and by including new reserves from the *Stavka* of the Supreme High Command in the *fronts*.

Table 70. Depth of the *Front* Operations (According to the *Stavka* Plan and the Decisions by the *Front* Commanders)

Fronts	Operational Depth According to the *Stavka* Plan (in kms)		Operational Depth According to the Front Commanders' Plan		Overall Operational Depth According to the *Front* Commanders' Plans
	Immediate	Subsequent	Immediate	Subsequent	
1st Baltic	40	95	40	150-200	Up to 200
3rd Belorussian	40-50	150-160	30-40	150	Up to 150
2nd Belorussian	45-50	65-70	45-50	65-70	Up to 70
1st Belorussian	60	130	45-50	130-140	Up to 140

Table 71. Depth of the *Front* and Army Operations (According to the Decisions of the *Front* and Army Commanders (In Kilometers)

Fronts & Armies	Operational Depth According to the Front Commanders' Plans		Operational Depth According to the Army Commanders' Plans		Overall Depth of the Army Operation
	Immediate	Subsequent	Immediate	Subsequent	
1st Baltic	40	150-200	–	–	–
6th Gds Army	–	–	12	45	Up to 45
43rd Army	–	–	17-20	30-40	Up to 40
3rd Belorussian	30-40	150	–	–	–
39th Army	–	–	16-18	50-55	Up to 55
5th Army	–	–	16	55	Up to 55
11th Gds Army	–	–	20-25	60-65	Up to 65
31st Army	–	–	12-15	45-50	Up to 50
2nd Belorussian	45-50	65-70	–	–	–
49th Army	–	–	30-35	60-65	Up to 65
1st Belorussian	60-70	130-140	–	–	–
3rd Army	–	–	60	75	Up to 75
48th Army	–	–	55	80	Up to 80
65th Army	–	–	50-60	65-75	Up to 75
28th Army	–	–	25-35	45-55	Up to 55

Table 72. Planned Operational Speeds (In Kilometers Per Day)

Fronts and Armies	Offensive Rate on First Day		Offenisive Rate in the Tactical Zone		Offensive Rate in the Operational Depth	
	Front Commander's Plan	Army Commander's Plan	Front Commander's Plan	Army Commander's Plan	Front Commander's Plan	Army Commander's Plan
1st Baltic	9-10	–	9-11	–	8-10	–
6th Gds Army	–	11	–	12-17	–	–
43rd Army	–	7-9	–	10-12	–	12-20
3rd Belorussian	10-12	–	15-20	–	12-15	–
39th Army	–	6-8	–	10-15	–	10-15
5th Army	–	16	–	10	–	10
11th Gds Army	–	10-12	–	13-15	–	13-15
31st Army	–	11-12	–	11-12	–	11-12
2nd Belorussian	15-20	–	10-12	–	8-10	–
49th Army	–	15-20	–	10-12	–	8-10
1st Belorussian	8-10	–	10-12	–	5-6	–
3rd Army	–	8-9	–	9-10	–	7.5-10

Fronts and Armies	Offensive Rate on First Day		Offenisive Rate in the Tactical Zone		Offensive Rate in the Operational Depth	
	Front Commander's Plan	Army Commander's Plan	Front Commander's Plan	Army Commander's Plan	Front Commander's Plan	Army Commander's Plan
48th Army	–	8-9	–	8-9	–	11
65th Army	–	9-15	–	16-20	–	7-11
28th Army	–	6-8	–	5-6	–	6-8

Table 73. The Number of Rifle Divisions in the First and Second Echelons and Reserves

Fronts	In the Corps' First Echelons		In the Armies and Corps' Second Echelons	In the Army Commanders' Reserves	In the *Front* Commanders' Reserves
	Total	Of These, Along the Axis of the Main Attack			
1st Baltic	15	10	7.5	1	1
3rd Belorussian	20	18	12	1	–
2nd Belorussian	18	11	2	–	2
1st Belorussian	26	19	12.5	–	–
TOTAL	79	58	34	2	3
TOTAL %	67	49	29	1.5	2.5

6. According to the plan, the forms of operational maneuver varied. All four *fronts* at first were determined to employ frontal attacks for the purpose of breaking through the enemy's previously-prepared defense.

The breakthrough of the tactical defense zone was planned at a high rate of speed, with the commitment of the corps' second echelons and the army mobile groups.

Following the breakthrough of the tactical zone, and upon reaching the operational zone of the enemy's defense, deep turning and enveloping movements were planned against the enemy's flanks, in conjunction with the frontal attacks. It was also planned to carry out the capture of large cities with only part of our forces, specially allotted for this task. It was planned to employ the main forces for the decisive pursuit of the fleeing enemy.

Thus in the *front* and army plans the following basic forms of operational maneuver were called for: a) frontal attacks for the purpose of breaking through the tactical zone of the enemy's defense; b) the envelopment, turning and encirclement of individual enemy groups of forces (Vitebsk, Orsha, Bobruisk), and; c) the envelopment of one of the flanks of the enemy group of forces (Mogilev).

There is no kind of dogmatism in the combination of all these forms. They were planned by taking into account the experience of the operations conducted during the Great Patriotic War, and depending on the specific situation that had arisen in the sector of this or that *front*.

7. It was planned to wage a struggle against the enemy's reserves at all stages of the operation.

Five rifle divisions, left in the reserves of the *front* and army commanders, were basically designated for fighting the enemy's reserves, the commitment of which into the battle was expected not only in the operational depth, but in the tactical depth as well. However, it was not the reserve divisions that were to play the main role in destroying the enemy's reserves, but the attacking troops, which were given the task of repulsing possible counterblows from one direction or another.

More than anything, the commander of the First Baltic Front feared counterblows by the enemy's reserves against his right flank and therefore ordered the 6th Guards Army to allot a corps to securely consolidate the Obol' area and prevent enemy counterblows from the Polotsk area.

The commander of the Third Belorussian Front did not plan any special measures for combating the enemy's reserves, although he devoted a great deal of attention to securing the *front's* flanks and those of the attacking armies. The 39th Army was ordered to secure the boundary with the 5th Army with a single division. The 31st Army was ordered to attack with one corps to the south, in order to cooperate with the neighboring Second Belorussian Front, an action which was to securely guarantee the *front's* left wing.

The commander of the Second Belorussian Front devoted particular attention to securing the flanks of the attacking 49th Army. He ordered this army to secure its right flank with one corps against possible enemy counterblows from the direction of Orsha, while another corps, while attacking along the left flank to the southwest, was to securely ensure the army's left flank by rolling up the combat formations of the enemy's Chausy group of forces.

The commander of the First Belorussian Front paid especial attention to securing the *front's* right flank, fearing a powerful enemy counterblow from the Minsk area. The 3rd Army, which was to attack along the *front's* right flank, was ordered, once it reached the Ol'sa and Berezina rivers, to employ part of its forces to prevent possible enemy counterblows from the direction of Minsk.

In their decisions, the army commanders also devoted a great deal of attention to securing the flanks and boundaries.

8.   The operations' planning in the *fronts* and armies was carried out in accordance with the experience of the preceding operations.

Any sort of dogmatism was absent from the planning of both *front* and army operations, and each operation was unique, while at the same time the existing situation (especially the correlation of forces and the character of the enemy's defense) was taken into account, as well as the character of the objectives assigned to the *front* by the *Stavka* of the Supreme High Command.

Front operations, as a rule, were planned by stages, of which two were usually planned. The content of these stages varied. The commander of the First Baltic Front planned only the breakthrough of the enemy's tactical defense zone during the first stage, while the commanders of the Third and First Belorussian fronts planned to resolve at this stage the immediate objective assigned them by the *Stavka* of the Supreme High Command; that is, they planned not only the breakthrough of the tactical zone, but also the development of the success in the operational depth. In the latter stage of the *front* operation it was planned to pursue the defeated enemy and seize important objectives in the operational depth.

The commanders of the First, Second and Third Belorussian fronts planned the actions of their armies by stages and by days, while the commander of the First Baltic Front planned them only by stages, although in sufficient detail. All the *front* commanders planned the offensive's first day in detail, creating a precise picture of all the attacking forces' coordination.

There were no principled differences in the planning of the army offensive operations. All the armies planned their operations by stages and by days, while the first 2-3 days of the offensive were planned in more detail, while the subsequent days were planned in general terms.

The actions of the second- and third-echelon corps were planned in sufficient detail.

The commitment of the armies' and *fronts'* mobile groups was worked out in detail in each army taking part in this, although the 5th Guards Tank Army's commitment into the breach in the sectors of the 5th and 11th Guards armies proved to have been insufficiently prepared.

It was planned to carry out the encirclement of the Vitebsk group of forces by employing part of two *fronts'* forces, while the internal front would be created by the rifle troops, and one of the Third Belorussian Front's mobile groups was supposed to create the external encirclement front. It was planned to create the internal encirclement around the Bobruisk group of forces with the forces of the 3rd and 65th armies' mobile groups, while the First Belorussian Front's mobile group was to be moved forward to create the external front. By subsequently directing the forces of three *fronts* toward Minsk, and by attacks along concentric directions, conditions would be created for encircling and destroying the enemy group of forces east of Minsk through mutual efforts.

On the whole, it should be noted that the planning of *front* and army operations was carried out with great skill, which to an enormous degree facilitated the successful resolution of the assigned objectives by the troops.

9.   The planning for employing the artillery coincided with the overall operational plan. During the preparatory period, the troops of all four *fronts* received a signficiant number of artillery formations and units from the Supreme High Command artillery reserve. Thus by the start of the operation our troops deployed 28,593 guns and mortars against the enemy's 9,635, not counting rocket-propelled artillery.

Such a significant overall superiority, as well as the expedient distribution of the artillery between the *fronts* and—within the *fronts*—between the armies of the *fronts'* main groups of forces, enabled us to achieve overwhelming artillery superiority over the enemy along the axes of the *fronts'* main attacks. This involved not only a quantitative, but also a qualitative superiority, because in the artillery groups of forces the percentage of heavy calibers had grown in comparison to their share in preceding operations. All of this would create favorable conditions for the successful breakthrough of the enemy's previously-prepared defense and the development of the operation at high speed.

However, despite the bold concentration of large masses of artillery along the axes of the *fronts'* main attacks, which was to be carried out in full accordance with the decisions by the *front* and army commanders, one cannot recognize the artillery's organization as completely expedient. At the basis of the artillery's organization lay the idea that the artillery assets should be put in the hands of the commanders of the rifle corps, divisions, regiments and battalions, and in this way provide them with the ability to exert their influence on the course of the battle. However, this idea was not realized to a sufficient degree.

The organizational scheme adopted for the artillery was characterized by the presence of numerous and powerful army artillery groups—long-range (DD), destruction (AR), guards mortars (GMCh), breakthrough and others. At the same time, quite weak regimental, divisional and corps infantry-support artillery groups (PP) were created.

In some of the Third and First Belorussian fronts' armies corps and divisional artillery groups were absent.

Thus in creating an artillery group of forces, questions concerning the amount, subordination, duration and the qualitative composition of the artillery groups were not fully resolved.

This can be explained by the absence of unity and firmness in the views relating to artillery organization.

Planning of the artillery preparation in the armies of the *fronts'* main groups of forces, as regards duration and organization, was not the same in each *front*. Besides this, each *front* enjoyed unity in the means of supporting the attack and the overall character of the artillery's actions in the depth of the enemy's defense. The duration of the artillery preparation was almost the same in all the *fronts*, while there were distinctive differences in the *fronts'* organization of the artillery preparation. In two *fronts* (First and Second Belorussian) the artillery preparation was supposed to begin with a fire onslaught of varying duration, and then the onslaughts were supposed alternate with periods of deliberate fire. In the Third Belorussian Front the artillery preparation was supposed to begin with a fire onslaught, followed only by deliberate fire. In the First Baltic Front the artillery preparation schedule called only for fire onslaughts to suppress the enemy's artillery and mortars, while only destructive fire was planned against his defense, or deliberate suppression fire.

These distinctions in the organization of the *fronts'* artillery preparation are explained by the lack of unity of views as to the role of fire onslaughts during the artillery preparation.

During the operation under review, a double rolling barrage for supporting the infantry and tank attack (in the First Belorussian Front) was planned for the first time at the operational level, which testifies as to the growing capabilities of our troops.

During the preparation period the regrouping, concentration and deployment of large masses of artillery were carried out along narrow sectors of the front. The greatest artillery regroupings took place in the *fronts*. In the armies artillery movements took place over comparatively short distances. The regrouping and concentration of the artillery were carried out during a limited time and by observing concealment measures, according to the plans of the *fronts'* artillery staffs, which had been drawn up on the basis of the troop regrouping plans, compiled by the *fronts'* headquarters.

The provision of certain types of shells was lower than planned (in the First and Third Belorussian and First Baltic fronts) by the start of the operation, but nonetheless enabled us to begin the operation, based upon the calculation of the delivery of the short items during the operation.

10.   By the start of the Belorussian operation the forces of our four *fronts* enjoyed a triple overall superiority in tanks and self-propelled guns over the enemy. At the same time among the tanks and self-propelled guns slated for inclusion in the infantry-support groups were our heavy and medium tanks and self-propelled artillery, as well as special tanks, which were the best in the world for their time. The enemy could only oppose 932 combat vehicles to our 4,070 tanks and self-propelled artillery pieces.

In the preceding period's operations, the troops of the Soviet Army did not possess such a quantity of tanks and self-propelled artillery.

Such a high concentration of tanks and self-propelled artillery among the troops enabled the *front* commanders to create powerful groups of forces from the tank and mechanized troops in the operational sectors of the *fronts'* main groups of forces.

This circumstance enabled us to allot a significantly greater number of tanks and self-propelled guns for the infantry-support groups than in previous operations, and thus create higher tactical densities of combat vehicles than before. Besides this, the high concentration of tanks and self-propelled guns in the combat formations enabled us, in some cases, to create direct infantry-support groups beforehand, not only in the first, but also in the divisions' second echelons, which had not been the case previously. Thus thanks to the multi-echelon organization of the groups of infantry-support tanks, there would be the possibility of augmenting the strength of the tank and self-propelled gun attack from the depth during the commitment of the divisions' second echelons during the breakthrough of the main zone of the enemy's defense.

The inclusion of a large number of army and *front* mobile groups in the First and Third Belorussian fronts enabled the commander of these *fronts* to augment the strength of the armored and mechanized troops' attack from the depth, both for completing the breakthrough of the enemy's tactical defense zone, as well as for carrying out and developing the operational breakthrough, while at the same time creating high operational densities of tanks and self-propelled guns.

The high concentration of direct infantry-support tanks and self-propelled artillery among the *fronts'* troops, as well as the presence of army and *front* mobile groups, enabled us to carry out the breakthrough of the defense's tactical zone along the decisive axes with rifle formations, supported by tanks and self-propelled guns, in coordination with the army mobile groups, and thus create for the *front* mobile groups favorable conditions for the immediate irruption into the enemy's operational depth, without losing time, men or equipment on completing the breakthrough of the tactical defensive zone.

Such an employment of army and *front* mobile groups, in the presence of high densities of direct infantry-support tanks, enabled us to cut down the time required to carry out the operational breakthrough of the enemy's defense and thus create, as early as possible, the conditions for carrying out maneuver for the encirclement of the enemy's operational groups of forces.

The problem of commiting the *fronts'* mobile groups into the breach was resolved, in that the responsibility for carrying out this important combat measure was entrusted to the commander of one of the field armies, in whose sector the mobile group would be committed, as well as to the commander of the *front's* air army. It would have been more expedient to have concentrated the organization for ensuring the commitment of the mobile groups subordinated to the *front* in the hands of the *front* commander.

11.   Planning the employment of the Soviet air force in the Belorussian operation was carried out in a situation of our aviation's complete air superiority, as well as a very favorable correlation of forces.

During the operation's preparatory period our aviation was significantly reinforced with formations from the Supreme High Command reserve. As a result of this, we were able to put up 5,327 combat aircraft from *front* aviation to the ememy's 1,400 combat aircraft, which worked out to a 3.8:1 superiority in our favor. If one takes into account the 1,007 aircraft from Long-Range Aviation, then the overall correlation of forces in the air was even more favorable for us. Such a high overall superiority over the enemy enabled us to create previously unheard-of air densities along the decisive directions.

The highly developed airfield network and its large capacity enabled our aviation to maneuver along the front and in depth.

Our air armies disposed of sufficient time for the all-round preparation of the *fronts'* air forces for the forthcoming operation. Thus the preparation of the *fronts'* air forces was carried out in every way without hurry and in a purposeful manner, which yielded great results.

The combat employment of our aviation was quite thoroughly organized and purposeful. However, there were also shortcomings in this regard, which may be reduced to the following:

a)   there was no unity of opinion and decision as to the problem of dividing up the zones of combat operations for the fighter air corps;

b)   the planned resubordination of a significant part of the assault and fighter aviation to the combined-arms armies (First Belorussian Front) should be viewed as precipitous: it's easier to subordinate than to again centralize the actions of the aviation that has already been subordinated to the armies;

c)   the insufficiently intensive combat schedule planned for the 1st Air Army on the operation's first day was not due to any necessity; also unjustified was the insufficiently intensive work of fighter aviation, which was planned for the operation's first day in the Third and Second Belorussian fronts;

d)   the organization of the 1st and 16th air armies' rebasing did not provide for the satisfactory resolution of this problem during the operation.

12.   The engineer support for the operation was carried out in distinctive conditions. The wooded and swampy terrain, which teemed with a large number of major rivers, in the conditions of which the Belorussian operation was prepared and conducted, placed special demands on the engineering preparation of the operation.

These requirements arose, first of all, from the fact that the existing poorly developed road network could not support our requirements in communications routes necessary for concentrating, regrouping and deploying large troop masses, equipped with a large amount of military equipment, in a limited time. Thus road and bridge work (checking the existing roads and cross-country march routes for mines, laying down new roads and cross-country march routes, the repair, improvement and strengthening of the existing roads and bridges) took up a huge portion of the overall number of engineer measures during the preparatory period.

A great deal of work was carried out in support of the concealed occupation of the jumping-off position for the offensive, the deployment of troops and large amounts of military equipment in the jumping-off area, as well as in creating conditions favorable to our forces going over to the offensive. This work consisted of preparing the jumping-off areas for the offensive by the troops of the first and subsequent echelons, particularly along the axis of the main attack (in adapting and developing the existing system of trenches and communications trenches, particularly in the jumping-off areas of the first-echelon divisions, as well as in strengthening the engineer outfitting of the terrain along the secondary axes).

A huge amount of work was carried out by the engineer troops in the engineer reconnaissance of the enemy, as well as removing mines from the terrain.

All of this demanded the concentration of the engineer troops' main efforts and the creation of high densities of these forces along the axes of the *fronts'* main attacks.

13.   Command and communications. The Belorussian operation was thoroughly prepared in all respects; however, it is particularly necessary to note the well-considered and purposeful nature of the work in preparing the command organs, communications troops and equipment.

This may be explained, first of all, by the fact that the commanders of the First Baltic, First, Second and Third Belorussian fronts had been informed by the *Stavka* of the Supreme High Command, long before the beginning of the operation, about the forthcoming operations and thus had the opportunity, in a situation of strict security, of carrying out a series of preparatory measures beforehand. Besides this, the working out of decisions by the *front* commanders, the planning of the operations and the organization of cooperation between the *fronts* was carried out under the leadership of the representatives of the *Stavka* of the Supreme High Command. Within the *fronts*, special attention was paid to the organization of operational and tactical coordination.

In drawing up a communications plan, we had to take into account the *fronts'* great number of mobile formations and technical equipment, as well as the geographical peculiarities of the theater of military activities, especially in the First Belorussian Front's sector, which had a poorly developed network of permanent telephone and telegraph lines on Belorussian territory, a certain shortage of communications troops and equipment in the Second and Third Belorussian fronts, the offensive's high rate of speed planned for the *fronts'* forces in general, and for the mobile formations in particular, and, besides this, the limited number of communications construction units necessary for carrying out restoration work.

However, the presence of a sufficient amount of time for preparing communications, and the existing number of communications troops and equipment, enabled the communications organs, on the whole, to successfully cope with the difficult tasks of organizing communications. It should also be noted that in the system of measures for organizing communications, primary attention was devoted to the organization of coordination of communications.

14.   Anti-aircraft defense. By the beginning of the Belorussian operation we had air superiority. Thus the anti-aircraft system of the *fronts* carrying out the Belorussian operation operated in conditions of a favorable air situation.

The principle of concentrating the efforts of anti-aircraft artillery and fighter aviation, first of all, on covering the operational shipment of troops and important rear targets, followed by the covering of the *fronts'* main groups of forces, was the foundation of planning the *fronts'* anti-aircraft defense.

At the basis of employing the anti-aircraft weapons lay the principle of the close coordination of two systems—the system of national air defense and the system of *front* air defense, and within each one—the principle of the close coordination of anti-aircraft artillery weapons and fighter aviation.

Anti-aircraft artillery support and the covering of troops and rear targets in the operation, both in the *fronts* as a whole, as well as in the armies, corresponded, on the whole, to the operational plans and the situation (as applicable to the conditions of the time).

All of this enabled us to repulse the enemy's air raids and facilitated the overall success of the offensive operation.

15.   Rear and materiel support.

By the beginning of the operation the provision of the *fronts* with materiel enabled us to carry out large-scale offensive operations, although not up to the norms established by the plan or the war's experience, for certain types of supplies. For example, the provisioning of the First Baltic Front with ammunition and food was close to the norm, but obviously short of the supply guidelines for fuels, oils and lubricants. In the Third Belorussian Front the supply of ammunition and gasoline was insufficient, and the 39th Army was short of diesel fuel. In the Second Belorussian Front there was a shortage of fuel and lubricants.

In the First Belorussian Front the supply of some types of ammunition and gasoline was insufficient.

By the start of the operation, in all of the *fronts*, except the Third Belorussian Front, the wounded were almost all evacuated to the rear. In the Third Belorussian Front it was impossible to completely free up the forward hospital groups, because of the large number of operational deliveries.

Thus the uninterrupted delivery of materiel, particularly of those which the *fronts* were not completely supplied with, both along railroads and dirt roads, acquired a great importance for all the *fronts*. However, it should be noted that we could not count on high rates of railroad restoration in all the *fronts*, because not all the *fronts* disposed of the necessary number of troops and equipment for restoration work. The *fronts* were sufficiently provided with the troops and equipment necessary for the restoration of the dirt roads.

Supplement:
An Operational-Tactical Description of the Terrain Covered by the Belorussian Operation 1944

The area of military operations, in the boundaries of which the Belorussian operation was conducted in June-August 1944, embraced the territories of the Belorussian SSR, a large part of the Lithuanian SSR, the northeastern part of East Prussia, and the northeastern part of Poland.

The conditional borders of this area are the lines: a) to the north—Nevel'—Dvinsk (Daugavpils)—Klaipeda; b) to the south—Chernigov—Ovruch—Kovel'—Lublin; c) to the west—Klaipeda—Warsaw—Lublin, and; d) to the east—Nevel'—Gorki—Krichev—Gomel'—Chernigov.

The strategic significance of this area was conditioned, first of all, by the fact that it included the political and administrative centers of the Belorussian and Lithuanian soviet socialist republics (Minsk, Vilnius), East Prussia (Konigsberg, now Kaliningrad) and Poland (Warsaw). The main roads from Moscow and Smolensk run to the west through this area toward Germany's and Poland's important economic and political areas.

The strategic significance of the theater was also conditioned by the fact that a large group of German-Fascist forces was deployed on its territory by the summer of 1944.

The theater's surface presents a broad and slightly hilly plain, broken by many rivers, lakes and canals, and covered to a significant degree with woods.

One may divide the surface of the area being described into two parts: a northern hilly part, and a southern lowland part.

The surface of the northern part of the area is covered with a series of uplands, which represent part of the overall watershed of the major rivers that flow into the Baltic and Black seas. This part of the area is thickly settled, and has a well developed road and airfield network.

The surface of the southern part of the theater includes the broad wooded and swampy Poles'ye lowlands, with a large number of rivers, streams, lakes, and canals, with a poorly developed road and airfield network, and with a limited number of inhabited locales.

The northern part's uplands are a component part of the Belorussian ridge and consist of individual groups of hills, usually elongated from east to west and cut by hollows and flooded river valleys.

The Belorussian ridge is a continuation of the Smolensk—Moscow uplands (the Smolensk gates) and runs to the southwest, from Orsha to Grodno, through Lepel', Minsk and Baranovichi. The ridge is divided by the broad valleys of the rivers' upper courses into the following series of uplands and groups of hills:

a) the Orsha ridge (to the west and east of Orsha). The ridge's average height is 250 meters, and its greatest height is 293 meters. Spreading to the south, this ridge of hills serves as the watershed for the Dnepr and Drut' rivers;

b) the Katarsy hills east of Lepel'. The average height is 230-240 meters;

c)   the Minsk highlands (to the north and west of Minsk). To the west of the highlands, toward Vilnius, runs a spur, forming the Oshmyany uplands, whose height is 240-340 meters;

d)   the Novogrudok heights (in the area of Novogrudok). These heights are 283-323 meters above sea level;

e)   the Nesvizh heights (east of Baranovichi), whose average height is about 226 meters;

f)   the Grodno (in the Grodno area) and Volkovysk (southeast of Grodno) heights, whose average height is 200-250 meters;

g)   the Telsiai uplands in the area of Telsiai, between the Neman, Dubissa and Venta rivers. The average height is 150-200 meters.

The lowlands in the northern part of the theater mainly extend along the river valleys. In a north-south direction one may note the following lowlands, having the greatest importance:

a)   the Polotsk lowland, formed by the valleys of the Drissa and Obol' rivers. The lowland is covered with woods and bushes and is partly swampy;

b)   the Disna River's lowland. The most convenient area for movement is the terrain immediately adjacent to the river itself. To the north and south of the river the terrain is wooded and swampy;

c)   the lowland of the Berezina River. The overall character of terrain is wooded and swampy, with a limited number of roads. This area is difficult for large formations to access;

d)   the Naroch' lowland (in the area of Lake Naroch'). The overall character of the terrain is wooded and swampy;

e)   the lowland between the Berezina River and the upper reaches of the Neman River (the so-called Nalibokskaya woods) is wooded and swampy, with a poorly developed road network.

On the whole, the surface of the northern part of this area represents a hilly plain, with a significant number of rivers and lakes. This part of the area is the most heavily settled and has a well developed road and airfield network and is the most favorable for the development of offensive operations.

The southern part of the area consists mainly of the Poles'ye lowlands, formed by the basin of the Pripyat' River and extends from the Dnepr River to the Western Bug River. It is cut by a large number of rivers, creeks, lakes, and canals.

Broad and swampy expanses are spread all over the lowland, but they are mainly grouped along the Pripyat' River and its tributaries.

In the Poles'ye there are a number of raised sectors, favorable for conducting combat operations. Among these are: a) the sector along the right bank of the Dnepr River, between the mouths of the Sozh and Berezina rivers, with a width of 20 kilometers; b) the sector between the Pripyat' and Dnepr rivers, south of the preceding one; c) the Mozyr' ridge, which extends immediately to the southwest from Mozyr'; d) the Ovruch heights, located in the headwaters of the Ubort' and Slovechna rivers; e) individual small hills, scattered along the left bank of the Pripyat' River, between its tributaries, the Sluch' and Tur'ya, and; f) the sector along the Pinsk—Brest railroad.

On the whole, the surface of the southern part of the area is cut by a large number of rivers, creeks and streams and has significant wooded and swampy expanses, lightly inhabited and with a poorly developed road and airfield network. Such terrain, to a significant degree, limited the troops' combat operations during the Belorussian operation.

To the west of the Belorussian ridge and the Poles'ye lowlands, as far as the area's western boundary, the surface represents a slightly hilly plain.

Woods occupy 25-75 percent of the area's surface. The broad area of the Poles'ye lowland is almost completely covered with woods. Large wooded areas are also located along the course of the Berezina River, to the east of Lida (the Nalibokskaya woods), along the course of the Neman River and its tributaries, in the Grodno area (the Grodno and Augustow forests), and in the Bialystok area (the Bialystok forest). With the exception of individual sectors, the woods themselves do not represent serious barriers for the movement of troops, while they make easier their concealment from the enemy in the air, and provide more than enough fuel and construction materials.

The rivers mostly flow in an east-west direction, which created favorable conditions for the organization of the enemy's defense. Soviet troops, in preparing for and during the course of the Belorussian operation, had to take into account the necessity of forcing water barriers and providing themselves with crossing means.

Below is a short description of the theater's most important rivers:

The Sozh River, a tributary of the Dnepr, is 280 kilometers long, 60 meters wide along its upper course, and with a depth of 0.5-2 meters; in its middle course (near Chechersk) it's 100 meters wide and 0.5-4 meters deep, and; in its lower course (near the mouth) it's 200 meters wide and 2-6 meters deep.

The Dnepr River along the sector Orsha—Zhlobin—the mouth of the Berezina River is 100-300 meters wide and 2-6 meters deep. The river valley extends 2-4 kilometers and more. The right bank is usually the higher one.

The Drut' River, a right-bank tributary of the Dnepr, is about 311 kilometers long, 20-70 meters wide, and 0.5-4 meters deep. The banks of the river as far as the village of Teterin are not high (up to two meters), but steep; downstream from Teterin the banks gradually grow lower.

The Berezina River, a right-bank tributary of the Dnepr, is about 280 kilometers long, 40 meters wide along its upper course, and on the average (between Borisov and Bobruisk) 120 meters wide, and 160 meters wide along its lower course. The river's depth is 2-7 meters. The river valley reaches seven kilometers and more.

The Ptich' River is the largest tributary of the Pripyat' River. The river's overall length is 324 kilometers. The river's course is very meandering and 10-30 meters wide, which increases to 40-50 meters along its middle course and 100-150 meters along its lower course. The depths are not constant and during the rainy period vary from 0.3-1.5 meters. The river's size does not present a serious obstacle, although its swampy valley (0.5-3 kilometes in width), particularly along its lower course, limited the maneuver of the attacking troops.

The Neman River is about 936 kilometers long. Its average width along the Kaunas—Grodno sector is 200-400 meters and up to 600 meters along its lower course, with a depth of 0.5-5 meters.

The Western Dvina (Daugava) River along the Vitebsk—Polotsk—Dvinsk (Daugavpils) sector was a serious obstacle for movement to the west; its width along this sector reaches 100-350 meters, and its depth 2-3 meters.

The Pripyat' River is 325 kilometers long. The river's width at the mouth of the Goryn' River is 100-200 meters, and further down 150-450 meters, with a depth of 0.5-to 10-15 meters. The river's wide and inaccessible valley divided the Soviet forces' operational sectors into two independent axes: to the north of the Pripyat' River, and south of it.

The Western Bug River, along the sector from Brest to the mouth of the Bug River, is characterized by the fact that here the Western Bug River flows through a broad and open flood plain, which is swampy, meandering and much cut up by old river beds. The banks are low and overgrown with bushes and woods. The river's width along this sector varies from 40-70 meters (in places up to 200 meters), with a depth of about two meters (in places up to ten meters). The river bottom and banks are sandy. In June-August a lot of fords open up along the shoals.

The Vistula River, along the sector from the mouth of the Western Bug River to the mouth of the San River (263 kilometers), is characterized by the following: the river's width is 400-600 meters (340 meters near Warsaw) and a depth up to two meters, with no fords. The river valley is 1-17 kilometers wide. The left bank is higher than the right, with the banks sandy and made of clay, while the flood plain is cut up and the course meandering.

On the whole, the rivers, and in many places swampy flood plains, made it easier for the enemy to create a defense and hindered the advance of our attacking troops, and various crossing materials were required for overcoming them.

A large number of lakes are located predominantly in the northern and western part of the area. Some lakes are quite large. Groups of lakes, in conjunction with the swampy and wooded terrain, sometimes form defiles and favorable defensive lines; for example, the group of lakes to the south of Dvinsk (Daugavpils) and in East Prussia (the Masurian lake district).

The climate in the area of military activities is continental. The average daily temperature during the summer of 1944 (June-July) varied from 18-20 centigrade, and on some days reached 25 degrees. During June-July the greatest number of clear days was noted—15-20 per month, and rains fell from time to time, although they were not extended and thus did not have a significant influence on the course of military operations. The winds in June-July were predominantly southern and southwestern, with a speed of 3-5 meters per second. Winds with a speed of greater than five meters per second were noted very rarely. The average number of flying days in June-July reached 20-22 per month.

On the whole, the meteorological conditions for our aviation's operations were quite favorable, particularly in July, when we had warm and dry weather.

As a result of the victory of the great October socialist revolution, the economy of the area of military activities had been quite developed. In 1940 gross industrial production in Soviet Belorussia exceeded the gross production of 1913 by 23 times, the production of electrical energy by 100 times, and the production of peat by 226 times.

As a result of the realization of the prewar five-year plans in the Belorussian SSR there was created a large-scale energy, fuel, machine-construction, chemical, and woodworking industry, based on advanced technology, various branches of light (textile, leatherworking, sewing, and glass) and food industry. The most important result of the prewar five-year plans was the creation in the republic of such new and advanced branches of industry as machine tool construction and agricultural machine tool construction, turbine construction, the production of radio equipment, phosphorous fertilizers, artificial fibers, cement, and many others.

Agriculture was also developing. In 1940 the republic contained more than 10,000 collective farms and 337 machine-tractor stations.

The German-Fascist occupiers burned 1,200,000 structures in Belorussia, laid waste to cities destroyed many factories and plants. The fascists bankrupted all the collective farms, state farms and machine-tractor stations.

The communications network was most developed in the northern and western parts of the area, and less so in the southern part—the Poles'ye.

On the average, there were up to 5-6 kilometers of railroad for 100 kilometers of territory.

The following railroads ran from east to west:

a) Nevel'—Polotsk—Vilnius—Kaunas—Konigsberg;
b) Smolensk—Orsha—Minsk—Molodechno—Lida—Grodno—Suwalki—Danzig (Gdansk);
c) Krichev—Mogilev—Baranovichi—Bialystok—Warsaw;
d) Gomel'—Kalinkovichi—Pinsk—Brest;
e) Chernigov—Ovruch—Sarny—Kovel'—Lublin, and;
f) Gomel'—Zhlobin—Bobruisk—Minsk—Vilnius—Kaunas—Konigsberg.

The most important lateral railroad was the Nevel'—Vitebsk—Mogilev—Zhlobin—Kalinkovichi—Ovruch line.

The network of dirt roads was sufficiently developed, especially in the northern and western parts of the area. The density of the automobile and horse tracks in the central part of Belorussia reached to up to 20 kilometers per 100 kilometers of territory (including more than ten kilometers of paved roads). In the western part the road density was higher. In the southern part, in the Poles'ye area, the road network was less developed. For every 100 kilometers of territory here there were only 6-8 kilometers of dirt roads and less than two kilometers of paved roads. The roads often ran through a wooded and swampy plain. Paved roads were outfitted with a large number of artificial structures (bridges, corduroy roads, embankments, etc.)

Thus it follows that the network of railroads and paved roads on the territory of the area of military operations was not equally developed—it was better in the northern and western parts and less so in the southern part. The road network in the northern and western parts enabled the conduct of the troops' broad-ranging maneuver during the operation.

In the southern part of the theater, in Poles'ye, the maneuver of forces was significantly limited.

On the whole, the physical-geographical conditions in the greater part of the area of military activities were favorable for the conduct of operations employing all the combat arms, although they required corresponding support for operations, in particular with road and crossing equipment.

Volume 2

The Conduct of the Belorussian Offensive Operation of 1944

Preface to the Russian Edition

The multi-*front* Belorussian offensive operation of 1944 may be divided into the following stages, according to the character of the military operations and the content of the tasks carried out.

The first stage (23 June-4 July) involved the defeat of the main forces of Army Group Center, the liberation of the capital of Belorussia, Minsk, and the creation of conditions for the development of the offensive along the Siauliai, Kaunas, Bialystok and Warsaw directions (see chapters 1-5).

The second stage (5 July-2 August) involved the development of the offensive, the defeat of the arriving enemy reserves and the arrival of the Soviet forces at the borders of East Prussia and at the Narew and Vistula rivers (see chapters 6-11).

During 3-29 August the forces of the First Baltic, Third, Second and First Belorussian fronts repulsed the enemy's counterblows and carried out local offensive operations to improve their operational situation (see chapter 12).

The second volume was written by an author's collective, including Major General V.N. Asafov (ret., deceased) (the Second Belorussian Front's operations), candidate of military sciences and senior lecturer Colonel A.D. Bagreev (combat operations of the First Belorussian Front's left wing, conclusions on military art, and the completion of several chapters on the combat operations of the First Baltic, Second and Third Belorussian fronts), candidate of military sciences Major General S.S. Bronevskii (the Third Belorussian Front's operations), candidate of military sciences and senior lecturer Major General F.R. Baltushis-Zhemaitis (ret., deceased) (the conduct of multi-*front* operations, the operations of the First Baltic, Second and Third Belorussian fronts), Major General A.K. Makar'ev (ret.) (the operations of the First Baltic Front), Maj. Gen. P.N. Rubtsov (ret.) (conclusions on the employment of the combat arms), and Major General Yu.I. Sokolov (ret.) (the operations of the First Belorussian Front, results of the multi-*front* operation).

The work's overall editing was carried out by candidate of military sciences and senior lecturer Colonel A.D. Bagreev.

Overall leadership was carried out by senior lecturer Lieutenant General V.G. Poznyak.

Proof readers: N.M. Burova, L.A. Subbotina.
General Staff Academy Press.

Part 1

The Operation's First Stage (23 June-4 July, 1944)

The Defeat of the Main Forces of Army Group Center and the Creation of Conditions for the Development of the Offensive

1

A Brief Review of Military Operations during the First Stage of the Multi-*Front* Belorussian Offensive Operation of 1944

The Defeat of the Main Forces of Army Group Center and the Liberation of the Capital of the Belorussian SSR, Minsk (23 June-4 July 1944)

During the first stage of the Belorussian offensive operation of 1944, the First Baltic, Third, Second and First Belorussian fronts, in conjunction with the forces of Long-Range Aviation and the partisans, and in accordance with the plan by the *Stavka* of the Supreme High Command, carried out tasks to break through the German-Fascist defense in Belorussia simultaneously along six axes, encircle and defeat the main forces of the enemy's Army Group Center, and liberate the greater part of the Belorussian Soviet Socialist Republic, along with its capital—Minsk.

In accordance with the operational plan, on 23 June 1944 the forces of the First Baltic, Third and Second Belorussian fronts went over to the offensive and those of the First Belorussian Front on 24 June.

During the course of the multi-*front* operation's first stage, the following *front* offensive operations were conducted: the First Baltic Front's Vitebsk—Polotsk operation, the Third Belorussian Front's Vitebsk—Minsk operation, the Second Belorussian Front's Mogilev—Minsk operation, and the First Belorussian Front's (right flank) Bobruisk—Slutsk operation.

The start of the overall offensive was preceded by the actions of the forward battalions, which began on 22 June.

The success of the First Baltic and Third Belorussian fronts' forward battalions, which resulted in an advance of up to eight kilometers, created favorable conditions for the beginning of the offensive by the *fronts'* main forces.

During the course of 23-28 June the *fronts* carried out tasks for breaking through the enemy's defense, the destruction of the Vitebsk and Bobruisk enemy groups of forces, and the creation of conditions for encircling the enemy's Minsk group of forces, which constituted Army Group Center's main group of forces.

On the morning of 23 June the main forces of the three *fronts* went over to the offensive.

In the course of two days the enemy's main and secondary defensive zones were pierced along almost all the sectors and the mobile groups committed into the breach. In developing the attack along the assigned axes, by the close of 28 June the *fronts* had broken through the entire depth of the enemy's army defense, surrounded and destroyed the Vitebsk and Bobruisk groups of forces and deeply outflanked the enemy's Minsk group of forces.

On the whole, the forces' successful actions, while breaking through the enemy's defense in each *front's* sector, unfolded as follows.

The forces of the First Baltic Front, in carrying out the Vitebsk—Polotsk offensive operation, successfully broke through the enemy's tactical defensive zone on the first day of the operation and, while pursuing the retreating enemy, on the offensive's second day; that is, 24 June, reached the Western Dvina River along a broad front. The Vitebsk—Polotsk lateral railroad was cut by our units in several places. At the same time, the forces of the *front's* 43rd Army not only reached the Western Dvina River, but had forced it in the Gnezdilovichi area (25 kilometers west of Vitebsk) and seized a bridgehead along its southern bank. The *front's* left-flank units had the opportunity, in conjunction with their left-wing neighbor—the Third Belorussian Front—of encircling the enemy's Vitebsk group of forces.

The unfavorable weather on the operation's first day hindered the actions of the *front's* aviation. On the second day the weather improved and the *front's* aviation could increase its support and escort of the attacking troops.

The offensive by the forces of the Third Belorussian Front, which was carrying out the Vitebsk—Minsk operation, also unfolded successfully. The right-flank 39th Army broke through the enemy's defense and on 24 June reached the eastern outskirts of Vitebsk, while part of its forces reached the Ostrovno area, thus cutting off the enemy's Vitebsk group of forces' path of retreat to the southwest and west. Thus by the close of the operation's second day the adjacent flanks of the First Baltic and Third Belorussian fronts had almost closed around the enemy's Vitebsk group of forces, which numbered five German-Fascist divisions. Only a small corridor, no more than ten kilometers wide, remained unoccupied by Soviet forces in the Ostrovno area.

During the course of 25-26 June intense fighting unfolded in the Vitebsk area. The forces of the First Baltic and Third Belorussian fronts managed to surround and split up the enemy's Vitebsk group of forces into pieces, and then to destroy it. This group of forces was completely eliminated on 27 June. During the fighting the encircled enemy group of forces tried several times to break out of the encirclement. However, only a small group of enemy troops, numbering about 5,000 men, managed to break out from the Ostrovno area, but even this group was cut off several times by our forces and, as a result, was almost completely destroyed.

During the course of the fighting around Vitebsk, Soviet forces killed about 32,000 enemy officers and men and captured more than 20,000. Thus the enemy's key Vitebsk center of resistance was eliminated and the troops of the First Baltic and Third Belorussian fronts acquired complete freedom to maneuver in the depths of the enemy's defense.

During the fighting around Vitebsk the First Baltic and Third Belorussian fronts' main forces continued their offensive to the west and southwest.

The First Baltic Front, which was attacking along a broad front, as early as 24 June began to encounter fierce resistance by the enemy's immediate reserves. In repelling these counterattacks, on 24 June the 6th Guards Army advanced nearly 30 kilometers and reached the Western Dvina River along a sector up to 60 kilometers in width. The same day the army's forward units and formations began to cross the river. By the end of 24 June three bridgeheads had been seized on the river's western bank, which on 25 June was expanded up to ten kilometers in depth. Besides this, on that day we managed to seize yet another series of bridgeheads, as a result of which the Western Dvina River was forced along a sector up to 65 kilometers in breadth, while the overall breakthrough front of the enemy's defense reached as much as 165 kilometers.

Thus a great success was achieved in the 6th Guards Army's sector. The task of capturing the line of the Western Dvina River had been accomplished by the close of the offensive's third day, instead of the close of the fourth day, as had been indicated in the operational plan.

The Third Belorussian Front's main forces, which made their main attacks on Bogushevsk and Orsha, following the breakthrough of the enemy's main defense zone, were moving forward, and by the close of 25 June had not only overcome the enemy's tactical defensive zone, but had also broken through his army zone along the Bogushevsk axis. In three days the *front's* forces advanced up to 70 kilometers.

The offensive by the *front's* formations along the Orsha axis unfolded significantly more slowly, for the enemy, having his strongest fortifications along this axis, put up stubborn resistance. However, our troops here also completely broke through the tactical defensive zone and reached the approaches to Orsha, while simultaneously outflanking it from the northwest.

The Third Belorussian Front's aviation rendered the ground troops a great deal of assistance in breaking through the enemy's defense. On the offensive's first day the aviation carried out 1,769 sorties. During the next two days the *front's* aviation assisted the *front's* forces in developing the success in the depth of the enemy's defense. It retained complete air superiority and carried out more than 2,500 sorties in the operation's first three days.

On 23 June the Second Belorussian Front, in carrying out the Mogilev—Minsk offensive operation, successfully broke through the main sector of the enemy's defense with the forces of the 49th Army and penetrated into his position to a depth of 5-8 kilometers. The army's formations encountered particular difficulty in forcing the Pronya River, which covered the front of the forward edge of the enemy's defense. It was only by the close of the operation's third day that we managed to break the enemy's resistance and advanced to a depth of 30 kilometers. The enemy's defense had been pierced along a 75-kilometer sector.

On the night of 22-23 June the *front's* aviation carried out a night air preparation along the breakthrough sector. However, on 23 June it was not very active during the first half of the day, due to the poor meteorological conditions. It was only in the second half of the day, when the weather had improved a little that the aviation could begin to make attacks on the enemy's defense. During the subsequent days the *front's* air army continued to support the actions of the ground forces.

On 24 June, following a powerful artillery preparation, the First Belorussian Front began its offensive, carrying out with its right-wing forces the Bobruisk—Slutsk operation. The *front's* forces were directed, first of all, at defeating the enemy's Bobruisk group of forces.

Following heavy fighting, the northern shock group (3rd and 48th armies) of the *front's* right-wing forces overcame the enemy's tactical defensive zone by the close of 26 June and had reached his army defensive zone. On that day the enemy began to withdraw behind the Berezina River. The *front's* forces reached the eastern bank of the Berezina River and units of the 9th Tank Corps and captured the road junction five kilometers to the east of Bobruisk.

By the close of 24 June, the southern shock group (65th and 28th armies) of the *front's* right-wing forces had broken through the enemy's defense along a 30-kilometer front to a depth of 5-10 kilometers. The 1st Guards Tank Corps, which was committed into the battle on the operation's first day, played a big role. On 24 June this corps, attacking ahead of the combined-arms formations, advanced 20 kilometers, having thus overcome the enemy tactical zone of the enemy's defense. On 25-26 June the formations of the southern shock group of the *front's* right-wing forces continued to successfully attack. General Pliev's cavalry-mechanized group, which had been committed into the breach in the 28th Army's sector during the second part of 25 June, on 26 June reached the Ptich' River and forced it in some places. Thus on the operation's third day the enemy's Bobruisk group of forces' routes of retreat to the south and southwest had been cut.

Due to the poor weather, the *front's* aviation could begin operations only during the second half of 24 June. By launching powerful blows against the enemy's combat formations, it significantly eased the breakthrough of the enemy's defense. The *front's* aviation played a particularly big role in pursuing the enemy, who was retreating toward the Berezina River. For example, on 26 June alone the *front's* aviation carried out 3,000 sorties against the enemy's retreating columns.

As a result of the four *fronts* offensive, during the period 23-26 June the main zone of the enemy's defense (the "main battlefield") had been pierced, as had been the second defensive zone (the "position of the corps reserves") along the most important axes, and not only had the enemy's forces defending the tactical zone been defeated, but his immediate reserves as well.

All of this was already creating favorable conditions for the subsequent development of the offensive in the operational zone of the German-Fascist forces' defense. Along a number of axes the army defensive zone (the "position of the army reserves") had been pierced on the march.

Thus Soviet forces successfully carried out one of the most difficult tasks, having overcome the most important previously-prepared sectors of the enemy's defense, which had been based on serious water obstacles.

The German-Fascist command sought to halt the Soviet troops' offensive at any cost along the natural lines of the Western Dvina and Berezina rivers. For this purpose, it carried out hurried regroupings of forces and began to move up significant reserves from the depth.

During 23-28 June the enemy committed up to 11 divisions (95th, 290th, and 14th infantry, the 20th, 5th and 12th *panzer*, 60th Motorized, and the 286th, 221st, 391st, and 201st security divisions) and various units of reinforcements into his corps' first echelons. All of these troops had been moved up from the depth or removed from other sectors of the Soviet-German front.

During 27-28 June the forces of the First Baltic Front, while overcoming the enemy's resistance, continued their offensive and by the close of 28 June they had captured the town of Lepel'—an important point in the enemy's defensive system. Thus the First Baltic Front fully completed the breakthrough of the enemy's defense throughout the entire depth and carried out its assigned objectives. In six days of attacking, the *front's* forces had advanced up to 80 kilometers to the west, had forced the Western Dvina River and inflicted a heavy defeat on the enemy's opposing forces.

By the close of 26 June the Third Belorussian Front's forces had broken through the enemy's defense along a front up to 140 kilometers wide and had advanced nearly 100 kilometers. A particularly great success had been achieved along the Bogushevsk axis.

The enemy continued to put up stiff resistance along the Orsha axis. On 27 June the forces of the Third Belorussian Front bypassed Orsha from the northwest and west and captured this very important defensive point by simultaneous attacks from all sides. By the close of 28 June the *front's* mobile troops had reached the Berezina River, thus securing for the *front's* main forces a rapid advance to this line.

During these days the Third Belorussian Front's aviation was very active and launched concentrated attacks to inflict heavy losses on the retreating enemy.

In six days of fighting the *front* advanced up to 150 kilometers in depth and created the real danger of turning and outflanking from the northwest and west the main forces of the German-Fascist Fourth Army, which was retreating under pressure from the Second Belorussian Front.

By the close of 27 June the forces of the Second Belorussian Front had reached the Dnepr and forced it north and south of Mogilev, and on 28 June they stormed the city and securely consolidated on the river's western bank. By the close of 28 June the forces of the Second Belorussian Front had advanced 90 kilometers and had carried out the *front's* immediate objective. During the course of the offensive the enemy suffered heavy losses along this axis.

On 27-28 June the forces of the First Belorussian Front continued their decisive offensive to the west, striving to completely encircle the enemy's Bobruisk group of forces.

The 9th Tank Corps, which had begun to pursue the retreating enemy as early as 26 June, broke into the eastern outskirts of Bobruisk on the morning of 27 June and cut off the enemy's path of retreat on Bobruisk. By this time the 1st Don Tank Corps had bypassed Bobruisk from the southwest and west and cut off the enemy's escape route from the city itself. The main forces of both the *front's* shock groups rapidly advanced behind the mobile forces and deeply outflanked the enemy's Bobruisk group of forces. Thanks to the bold actions of the 9th Tank Corps, the enemy's Bobruisk group of forces was cut up into two parts: one part was defending southeast of Bobruisk, and the other in the city itself. The elimination of these groups of forces was entrusted to the 48th and

65th armies: the 48th Army was to destroy the enemy group of forces southeast of Bobruisk, and the 65th Army the enemy in the city.

During the second half of 27 June, the enemy group of forces that had been surrounded southeast of Bobruisk attempted to break through to the north. The enemy began to concentrate his forces eight kilometers southeast of Bobruisk for the breakout. Our aviation detected this concentration and launched a powerful attack against the enemy group of forces, as a result of which the enemy suffered heavy losses. 526 Soviet aircraft were operating almost simultaneously in this area. Following this action, the forces of the 48th Army attacked and by 1300 on 28 June completely eliminated this enemy group of forces. The fighting for the Bobruisk continued two more days. It was only at 1000 on 29 June that the enemy was completely cleared out of the town. A part of the enemy's forces, which had broken out of the town, was eliminated later, along the road between Bobruisk and Osipovichi.

By taking Bobruisk, the Soviet forces carried out an objective of great operational importance, for this large enemy center of resistance was a very important link in the defensive system for all of Belorussia.

Following the elimination of the Vitebsk—Orsha and Bobruisk groups of forces, the Soviet forces had the opportunity to pursue the retreating enemy along all the main axes.

By 29 June the flanks of Army Group Center's main forces, which were retreating to the west, had been deeply outflanked by Soviet forces from two sides, which was creating favorable conditions for getting into the rear of the enemy's Minsk group of forces and encircling it.

Having reached the Berezina River (north of Borisov) and the area between the Dnepr and Berezina river, as well as the areas of Svisloch' and Osipovichi, the Soviet forces formed a 320-kilometer bulge, which outflanked the enemy's retreating forces from three sides. Our mobile formations were 100 kilometers from Minsk. The enemy's main forces, which were falling back on Minsk, were 130-150 kilometers from the city, not being able to break contact with our pursuing formations.

The Soviet forces' subsequent objectives consisted of all three Belorussian fronts attacking along concentric axes toward Minsk and completing the defeat of Army Group Center's main forces, liberating the capital of Belorussia—Minsk, and continuing to pursue the enemy to our western borders.

In accordance with the situation that had arisen in Belorussia, the *Stavka* of the Supreme High Command refined the *fronts'* objectives in operational directives of 28 June 1944.

During 29 June-4 July the *fronts'* forces were to pursue their objectives for encircling and destroying the enemy's Minsk group of forces, liberating the capital of the Belorussian SSR, and defeating the enemy's Polotsk group of forces.

Having defeated the Vitebsk—Orsha, Mogilev and Bobruisk enemy groups of forces, the troops of the Third and First Belorussian fronts, in accordance with the High Command's plan, were to reach Minsk by means of a two-sided turning movement, liberate it and simultaneously complete the encirclement of the German-Fascist forces retreating along the Mogilev—Minsk axis. The fulfillment of this mission was to be secured by the well-organized coordination of the four *fronts*.

During 29-30 June the forces of the First Baltic Front advanced 15-20 kilometers and reached the approaches to Polotsk: the 43rd Army was successfully advancing toward Glubokoe, while on 30 June the 1st Tank Corps occupied Disna and on 1 July forced the Western Dvina River and created a bridgehead along its northern bank five kilometers northwest of Disna. During 1-4 July the *front's* forces completed the encirclement of Polotsk and after stubborn fighting occupied it. The entire southern bank of the Western Dvina River from Polotsk to Drissa was now cleared of the enemy. The *front's* left-wing forces, which were successfully developing the offensive to the west, occupied Glubokoe and reached the line of the lakes northwest, west and southwest of Glubokoe.

The *front's* aviation, by carrying out 500-700 sorties per day, assisted the ground forces in carrying out their assigned objectives.

During 30 June-4 July the *front's* forces advanced to the northwest and west to a depth of 140 kilometers, and by taking Polotsk securely covered the operations of the Belorussian fronts from the north.

On 28 June the Third Belorussian Front began forcing the Berezina River. The *front's* cavalry-mechanized group crossed the river north and northwest of Borisov and thus created a real threat to Minsk.

The German-Fascist command attempted to carry out a number of measures in order to keep Minsk in its grasp. By stubbornly resisting in the area of the Borisov fortified area, it sought to delay our forces' advance and win time for organizing the defense of Minsk. However, the enemy plan was foiled. On 30 June the main forces of the Third Belorussian Front reached the Borisov area. During the night of 1 July the 11th Guards Army, by attacking from the south and southwest in conjunction with units of the 31st and 5th Guards Tank armies, occupied Borisov. By the close of 1 July the forces of the Third Belorussian Front had completed the forcing of the Berezina River and, having advanced 35 kilometers to the west and southwest began to threaten Minsk. The enemy's defensive zone along the Berezina River ("Catastrophe") had been completely cracked and had lost all significance. The German-Fascist forces, which were retreating toward Minsk, were deprived of the Moscow—Minsk highway as a result of the fall of Borisov and were now in very difficult circumstances of retreat.

By reaching the Molodechno area on 3 July, the Third Belorussian Front's cavalry-mechanized group cut the Minsk—Vilnius railroad.

During these days the forces of the Second Belorussian Front continued to pursue the retreating enemy, moving in echelon behind the Third Belorussian Front. If the forces of the Third Belorussian Front had forced the Berezina as early as 30 June, it was only on 2 July that the forces of the Second Belorussian Front reached the river. The Second Belorussian Front's echeloned position was favorable for us, for the enemy, who was falling back in front of the Second Belorussian Front, was outflanked by the Third Belorussian Front, which led to the encirclement of this enemy force in the woods southeast of Minsk.

On 29 June the 1st Guards Tank Corps, advancing on Minsk, reached the crossings over the Svisloch' River southeast of Pukhovichi, where it encountered strong resistance by the enemy's 12th Panzer Division, which had been moved to this line in order to cover Minsk from the south. Stubborn fighting along the Svisloch' River lasted until 2 July. Only on this day was the enemy's defense pierced and our forces reached Pukhovichi. The 9th Tank Corps, which was attacking to the west, on 2 July, cut the Minsk—Slutsk road. The 3rd Army's units, which had reached the Cherven' area, established direct contact with the Second Belorussian Front's 49th Army. On 2 July General Pliev's cavalry-mechanized group reached the line of the Minsk—Baranovichi railroad and occupied the towns of Stolbtsy, Gorodeya and Nesvizh.

Thus by the close of 2 July the Soviet forces, by means of attacks from three sides, had almost completely encircled the enemy's Minsk group of forces.

On the night of 3 July the Third Belorussian Front's 5th Guards Tank Army bypassed Minsk from the northwest, while the 2nd Guards Tank Corps and formations of the 31st Army broke into the city from the east at 0900 on 3 July. Within a few hours the First Belorussian Front's 1st Guards Tank Corps entered the capital of Belorussia from the south. Attacked from several directions, the enemy could not put up organized resistance and was forced to abandon the city under the blows of the Soviet forces.

Having captured the capital of Belorussia—Minsk, the Soviet forces finally closed the encirclement front around the group of German-Fascist troops that was continuing to resist southeast of Minsk.

On 4 July the Third Belorussian Front's cavalry-mechanized group occupied Molodechno; the *front's* 5th Guards Tank Army securely blocked Minsk from the west and northwest; on 4 July the combined-arms formations reached the line occupied by the mobile troops. Thus the Third Belorussian Front's forces had covered a distance of up to 170 kilometers in six days.

The Second Belorussian Front's forces were fighting the encircled enemy group of forces in the area to the south of Smolevichi, striving to break it up and destroy it in detail.

On 3-4 July the main forces of the First Belorussian Front advanced successfully to the west, encountering weak enemy resistance. With our troops' arrival at Slutsk, this resistance grew stronger. The *front's* cavalry-mechanized group, which was the first to attack Slutsk, was not able to capture it and it was only with the commitment of the *front's* new forces into the fighting that the town was captured. The enemy put up particularly powerful resistance to the Soviet forces in Baranovichi. By the close of 4 July the *front's* forces had reached the line Stolbtsy—Gorodeya—Nesvizh—Golynka, having covered about 140 kilometers in six days and thus accomplished their objectives according to the plan for the first stage of the multi-*front* Belorussian offensive operation.

The Dnepr River Flotilla, which was subordinated to the commander of the First Belorussian Front, was employed in this *front's* sector and operated along two rivers. One brigade was assisting the 65th Army's offensive over the Berezina River. The other brigade was employed along the Pripyat' River, where it was assisting the 28th Army. Both brigades assisted in occupying, with fire from their guns, the inhabited locales lying along the river. Later, while advancing, the river boats took on landing parties and landed them along the flanks or in the rear of the enemy forces, ferried our troops to the opposite shore in overcoming rivers, and, finally, dashing ahead along the river, assisted our forces in encircling individual enemy groups. The Dnepr River Flotilla rendered particularly valuable assistance to our forces in taking Bobruisk. Having boldly broken through to the town's outskirts, and waging intensive fire, our boats significantly disorganized the enemy's defense and inflicted heavy losses on him.

Thus during the course of 23 June-4 July 1944 the forces of the First Baltic Front successfully carried out the Vitebsk—Polotsk operation, and the forces of the Third Belorussian Front the Vitebsk—Minsk operation. The Second Belorussian Front was close to completing the Mogilev—Minsk operation and was successfully wrapping up the destruction of the enemy's encircled Minsk group of forces. During 24 June-4 July 1944 the First Belorussian Front completed the Bobruisk—Slutsk operation.

All the *fronts'* aviation at this stage of the multi-*front* operation were rendering active assistance to the attacking troops, attacking the enemy's retreating columns, detected enemy groups of forces, crossings, and other targets. The mobile troops, which had advanced far ahead, got particularly valuable assistance from the aviation.

It's particularly important to say something about our Long-Range Aviation, which as early as the preparatory period, on the nights of 13, 14, 15, and 18 June launched massive raids against the enemy's airfields in Orsha, Bobruisk, Minsk, Baranovichi, Pinsk, Bialystok, and Brest. In all, 1,269 sorties were conducted and 1,451 tons of bombs dropped.

On the night of 22-23 June; that is, before the start of the attack, our Long-Range Aviation launched raids against the enemy's centers of resistance in the sectors of the *fronts'* main attacks. The unfavorable meteorological conditions limited the scope of these attacks. Only 260 planes took part in these attacks, including 239 in the Third Belorussian Front's attack sector and 21 in the Second Belorussian Front's sector. In all, 369 tons of bombs were dropped.

With the beginning of all four *fronts'* attack, Long-Range Aviation continued to launch mass raids against the enemy's troops (including his encircled groups of forces), against enemy strong points and railroad junctions. These attacks, as a rule, were launched by a large number of planes (70-203).

In all, during the first stage of the Belorussian offensive operation, Long-Range Aviation carried out 2,089 sorties and dropped 2,290 tons of bombs.

The Belorussian partisans, by means of their active operations, rendered a great deal of assistance to the attacking forces throughout the entire Belorussian operation. During the operation's first stage the partisan brigades of the Eastern Minsk zone, while carrying out the orders of the Belorussian headquarters of the partisan movement and the Second Belorussian Front's military council, during 23-30 June carried out massed attacks four times against the Minsk—Borisov and Minsk—Bobruisk railroads, where they delayed rail movement for two days during a critical time for the enemy.

The partisan brigades, by means of bold and surprise raids, destroyed many paved roads, thus delaying the movement of the enemy's forces, both to the front and the rear. Many dirt roads were knocked completely out of commission and were controlled by partisans. The partisans created "traffic jams" for the enemy along the roads, which proved good targets for our aviation.

The Belorussian partisans rendered active assistance to our forces in encircling and destroying large enemy groups of forces in the Bobruisk area and east of Minsk.

The First Belorussian Front's operations were supported by the Poles'ye, South Minsk, Pinsk, South Baranovichi, Brest and Bialystok partisan formations. During the course of the Bobruisk operation, the South Baranovichi formation blew up 2,800 rails along the most important rail routes (Minsk—Baranovichi, and others), which delayed the movement of the enemy's trains by two days. Partisan brigades captured bridgeheads over large rivers in fighting and held them until the arrival of the First Belorussian Front's forces. The partisans rendered particularly valuable service to the *front's* formations during the pursuit: they led our forces through the wooded and swampy sectors, carried out deep reconnaissance, led Soviet units into the enemy's rear, and rendered assistance in overcoming water obstacles.

The first stage of the multi-*front* Belorussian offensive operation of 1944 ended with the defeat of the enemy's Minsk group of forces and the liberation of Minsk.

The enemy's defense had been broken through along a front of more than 400 kilometers, the main forces of Army Group Center had been defeated, and favorable conditions created for the subsequent development of the offensive to the west. The enemy group of forces surrounded to the east of Minsk was being successfully destroyed by Soviet forces. The task of its final destruction was entrusted to the command of the Second Belorussian Front. The *front's* forces carried out this task during 5-13 July, while at the same time the main forces of the group of Soviet *fronts* in Belorussian were already conducting a headlong offensive in accordance with the plan for the second stage of the Belorussian operation.

2

The First Baltic Front's Vitebsk—Polotsk Offensive Operation (23 June-4 July 1944)

The Vitebsk—Polotsk offensive operation may be divided into two stages, according to the actual course of events.

During the operation's first stage (23-28 June) the enemy group of forces facing the *front* was defeated northwest of Vitebsk, the enemy's entire tactical defensive zone was pierced, his army defensive zone overcome, and the enemy's Vitebsk group of forces was encircled and destroyed in cooperation with its neighbor to the left—the Third Belorussian Front. During the operation's second stage (29 June-4 July) the *front's* forces, while inflicting a defeat on the enemy's arriving operational reserves, developed the offensive along the northwestern and western directions and captured Polotsk.

The Operation's First Stage

The Breakthrough of the German-Fascist Forces' Defense Northwest of Vitebsk and the Forcing of the Western Dvina River (23-28 June 1944)

In accordance with the *front* commander's plan and the operational plan, the First Baltic Front's Vitebsk—Polotsk operation began with the breakthrough of the German-Fascist forces' defense northwest of Vitebsk.

The attack by the *front's* main forces was preceded by a reconnaissance in force, which began at 0500 on 22 June by the forces of the reconnaissance detachments (1-2 reinforced rifle companies from each first-echelon division). In all, ten reconnaissance detachments took part.

The reconnaissance in force did not achieve success in the 4th Shock Army's sector. In the 6th Guards Army's sector the reconnaissance detachments attacked their designated targets simultaneously along the entire front and by 1000 had pierced the enemy's defense in the 22nd Guards Rifle Corps's sector and captured a number of strong points in the first position. The corps commander immediately committed two forward battalions from each division (for a total of six battalions from the entire corps) to augment the blow, which, developing the success of the reconnaissance detachments, by the close of 22 June had advanced to a depth of 5-7 kilometers, having broken through the enemy's main defensive zone. On the army's left flank, along the 23rd Guards Rifle Corps's sector, the reconnaissance in force was less successful.

By the close of 22 June the enemy's main defensive position had been pierced along a 15-kilometer front in the army's attack sector.

In the 43rd Army's sector the reconnaissance detachments captured the first line of trenches along several sectors.

The 3rd Air Army supported the reconnaissance detachments' and forward battalions' combat actions from the air with groups of *shturmoviks* of 4-6 planes. In all, in the course of the day 107 *shturmovik* and 89 fighter sorties were conducted.

During the course of the reconnaissance in force, the defense's forward edge was defined more precisely, the fire system and engineering outfitting were unmasked, and the grouping of the enemy's forces was confirmed.

The reconnaissance detachments' simultaneous actions throughout the *front's* entire sector, and particularly the breakthrough of the enemy's main defensive zone along the 6th Guards Army's right flank to a depth of 5-7 kilometers, misled the enemy and gave the German-Fascist command reason to take the reconnaissance in force for our forces' general offensive.

On the whole, the effectiveness of the reconnaissance in force by the forward battalions was confirmed. Such a move enabled us to parry such enemy methods as the planned withdrawal of troops from the first position's first trench, or even from the first defensive sector to the next one, so as to force our troops to launch an attack against empty space and then encounter their organized defense in the depth. Besides this, the reconnaissance in force helped us to unearth all the changes in the fire system, in the grouping of enemy's forces, and his engineering improvements immediately before the start of the main forces' offensive. While a tactical phenomenon, the forward battalions' reconnaissance in force, when examined individually, taken together, assumed large-scale operational importance in the army's or *front's* sector.

On the night of 22-23 June a preliminary aviation preparation was carried out against the enemy's unmasked strong points and artillery.

During the course of the entire night the bombers destroyed and suppressed the enemy's men, weapons, equipment, and defensive structures along the axis of our formations' main attack.

Such a method was prompted by the war's experience and enabled us to effectively employ night bomber aviation for exhausting the enemy, suppressing his personnel and weapons, as well as destroying individual targets in the night before the infantry and tank attack.

Due to the forward battalions' successful actions, the necessary corrections were made to the plan for the artillery preparation. For example, in the 6th Guards Army the time for the artillery preparation was reduced to two hours and the amount of artillery employed cut by 50 percent. The preliminary aviation preparation, which had been called for by the plan, was not carried out. In the 43rd Army the artillery offensive did not begin with an artillery preparation along some sectors, but rather began to immediately support and accompany the attacking troops. All of these changes corresponded to the changed situation.

The offensive by the *front's* main forces unfolded in the following order.

The 6th Guards Army, having gone over to the offensive at 0600 on 23 June, was breaking through the enemy's defense along the Savchenki—Tovstyki sector and was attacking to the southwest and south. During the second part of the day units of the army's 23rd Guards Rifle Corps cut the Polotsk—Vitebsk railroad west of Shumilino and continued their successful offensive to the southwest. The enemy put up his strongest resistance along the Polotsk axis.

On this day the army's second echelon—the 103rd Rifle Corps—was committed into the battle.

By the end of the day the army had advanced 15-18 kilometers along its left flank and center, having widened the breakthrough front to 20 kilometers. On the army's right flank, the enemy had halted our troops' advance through repeated counterattacks with fresh reserves.

The 1st Tank Corps—the *front's* mobile group—which had been moving up along three routes, was advancing slowly, due to the poor condition of the roads, and was then halted, in view of the inexpediency of its commitment before the infantry could overcome the inter-lake defiles northeast of Lake Dobeevskoe.

The 43rd Army went over to the attack at 0700. Having broken through the enemy's defense along the sector Medvedi—excluding Uzhlyatino, it captured the major Shumilino center of resistance and, by the end of the day had reached the line Lake Dobeevskoe—Ladoshki—Uzhlyatino. The army had advanced up to 16 kilometers in the day's fighting along the right flank, and 8-10 kilometers along the left and had inflicted a significant defeat on the enemy's corps group "D."

Thus on the operation's first day, the *front's* forces had broken through the enemy's tactical defensive zone and inflicted a major defeat on the units of the IX Army Corps, which began to fall back to the Western Dvina River.

The German-Fascist command, for the purpose of launching a counterblow against right flank of the First Baltic Front's main group of forces, rapidly moved up the 24th Infantry Division to the breakthrough sector from the Polotsk area. Aside from this, the Third Panzer Army had been reinforced by the 290th Infantry Division, which had been transferred from Army Group Center.

However, due to the high rate of our forces' advance, the German-Fascist command did not manage to gather all these forces into a single whole and was forced to commit them into the battle in detail.

In order to deprive the enemy of the opportunity of consolidating along the line of the Western Dvina River, it was necessary to quickly develop the success in the direction of Beshenkovichi.

From the morning of the operation's second day, the *front's* forces continued to develop the offensive by pressing the enemy to the Western Dvina River.

During the second half of 24 June the 6th Guards Army's 103rd and 23rd guards rifle corps reached the Western Dvina River along the 28-30 kilometer sector Kordon—Ulla—excluding Beshenkovichi and began forcing it on the march, using materials at hand.

The forcing of the river unfolded most successfully in the 23rd Guards Rifle Corps' attack sector. By the time it had reached the river, the corps had brought up its artillery in good time to the very bank for firing over open sights, and was widely using local and crossing materials at hand. As a result, two bridgeheads were seized along a 2.5-kilometer sector in the Uzrech'e area, each with a depth of three kilometers.

The crossing was unsuccessful in the 103rd Rifle Corps' sector, because the retreating enemy had organized a solid defense along a previously-prepared line and our artillery and organic crossing equipment had fallen behind.

The 43rd Army, in overcoming the enemy's resistance, was rapidly advancing to the south. By 1800 on 24 June its forward units had forced the Western Dvina River south of Bokishevo and had seized some small bridgeheads. By the end of the day the main forces of the 1st and 60th rifle corps had reached the Western Dvina River. At the same time, formations of the 60th Rifle Corps had gotten into the rear of the enemy's Vitebsk group of forces. The 92nd Rifle Corps, in attacking toward Vitebsk, broke through the enemy's main defensive zone and captured the line Rubiny—excluding Nasalanniki—Khrapovichi.

By this time the troops of the neighboring Third Belorussian Front's 39th Army had begun fighting for the eastern outskirts of Vitebsk.

The 43rd Army faced the immediate task of linking up with the 39th Army's units as quickly as possible and, in conjunction with the army, to encircle the enemy's Vitebsk group of forces by depriving it of the opportunity of taking advantage of the corridor leading out of Vitebsk.

At 0800 on 24 June the 1st Tank Corps began its movement from the Shumilino area for the commitment into the breach in the direction of Beshenkovichi. However, this advance developed very slowly. All the roads were full of troops, equipment and wagons, as a result of which numerous traffic jams developed. By the close of 24 June the tank corps' lead brigades had reached the Western Dvina River, but because the bridge over the river near Beshenkovichi had been blown up by the enemy, and the pontoon battalions with their crossing parks had fallen behind, it proved impossible to force the river on the march.

The *front's* air army assisted the success of the ground forces' offensive by attacks against the enemy's retreating forces and concentrations of his reserves.

The *front's* forces, as a result of the two days of battle, broke through the enemy's defense along the main axes, reached the Western Dvina River along a broad front and, having captured some small bridgeheads along the western bank on the march, created favorable conditions for quickly overcoming this river by the *front's* main forces and for continuing an uninterrupted offensive toward Lepel'. The enemy, having suffered serious losses, was only able to establish an intermittent defense along the river's western bank, which was quite easily overcome by our forces.

By the close of 24 June the forces of the First Baltic Front, and those of the Third Belorussian Front attacking to the south, had deeply enveloped both flanks of the enemy's Vitebsk group of forces. It was only south of Gnezdilovichi that the enemy retained a narrow 10-kilometer escape corridor.

During the fifth through eighth days of the operation the *front's* forces continued to develop the success achieved, waging active offensive operations along all axes.

The forcing of the Western Dvina River by the *front's* main forces on 25 June, the expansion of the bridgehead on its left bank to 35 kilometers in width and 15 kilometers in depth, and the capture of the large village of Beshenkovichi, had great significance for carrying out the tasks assigned to the *front*. In the Gnezdilovichi area the 43rd Army made contact with the Third Belorussian Front's 39th Army, thus completing the encirclement of the enemy's Vitebsk group of forces.

Military operations developed in the armies' sectors as follows.

On 25 June the 6th Guards Army's right flank and center forces repelled the enemy's counterattacks, fighting along the approaches to Obol' station and along the line of the Western Dvina River. Units of the 103rd Rifle Corps' 270th Rifle Division attempted to force the river along their sectors, but had no success. Along the left flank the 23rd Guards Rifle Corps began to force the Western Dvina River on the morning of 25 June. The 67th Rifle Division, while attacking from its captured bridgeheads in the general direction of Svecha, by the end of the day had cut the Beshenkovichi—Bocheikovo paved road. The 71st Guards Rifle Division, having crossed its main forces over the to the left bank of the Western Dvina River in the area south of Uzrech'e, attacked toward Beshenkovichi from the north, although it was not able to seize the village. In order to assist it, the 2nd Guards Rifle Corps' 46th Guards Rifle Division was committed into the fighting, rapidly forced the Western Dvina River from the march northeast of Beshenkovichi and reached its southeastern outskirts in fighting. By this time the 1st Tank Corps' 44th Motorized Rifle Brigade had crossed along the 71st Guards Rifle Division's sector and had attacked Beshenkovichi from the northwest. As a result of the above-named formations' joint actions, this large village was taken by the end of the day.

Thus the 6th Guards Army's forces, having repelled the enemy's attacks, continued to expand the bridgeheads seized over the Western Dvina River. By the close of 25 June the bridgehead on the river's left bank had grown to 20 kilometers in width and ten kilometers in depth.

On 25 June the 1st Tank Corps was supporting the crossing by the 23rd Rifle Corps and its own motorized units to the opposite bank of the Western Dvina River with fire from its artillery and tanks.

The 43rd Army, without waiting for the arrival of its organic crossing equipment, began forcing the Western Dvina River on the morning of 25 June, employing the materials at hand. In the Gnezdilovichi area, units of its 60th Rifle Corps linked up with the Third Belorussian Front's 39th Army and, in conjunction with it, encircled five enemy divisions (4th and 6th *Luftwaffe* field, 246th, 206th and 197th infantry), which were defending Vitebsk.

The 1st Rifle Corps was developing the success to the southwest from the bridgeheads on the river's left bank seized the previous night. The 60th Rifle Corps, encountering the most stubborn enemy resistance and repelling fanatical counterattacks by units of the 246th Infantry Division, advanced only along the right flank during the day, where it linked up in the Gnezdilovichi area with units of the 39th Army's 19th Rifle Division. The 92nd Rifle Corps' 145th Rifle Division broke into Vitebsk and was clearing out its northwestern part.

Aviation played an important role in the successful offensive by the *front's* forces. Securely maintaining air superiority and launching powerful raids against the enemy, our aviation assisted the ground forces in capturing important enemy centers of resistance, in repelling his counterattacks, as well as in seizing and retaining bridgeheads, particularly on the Western Dvina River.

Thus in three days of fighting the *front's* forces had carried out their immediate task a day ahead of schedule: they had broken through the enemy's defense, forced the Western Dvina River with the forces of the 6th Guards and 43rd armies, captured the Beshenkovichi area, defeated the enemy's immediate reserves, and created favorable conditions for a subsequent advance to the west. As a result of the link-up of the First Baltic and Third Belorussian fronts on 25 June in the Gnezdilovichi area, five divisions of the enemy's Third Panzer Army were surrounded in the Vitebsk area.

During the 26-28 June period the main forces of the First Baltic Front continued to develop the offensive along the Lepel' axis, while part of the *front's* forces, in conjunction with the Third Belorussian Front, were fighting to eliminate the group of German-Fascist forces, surrounded in the Vitebsk area.

On 26 June the 4th Shock Army captured Rovnoe; the 6th Guards Army, attacking along the Polotsk axis, seized the previously-outfitted and powerful Obol' center of resistance. In connection with the successful development of the offensive by the army's left flank, the army was given a new task—developing the offensive to the west and northwest, to bypass the Polotsk fortified area from the south and take Polotsk.[1]

During the course of the day, the 1st Tank Corps, having completed its crossing of the Western Dvina River by the morning of 26 June, continued to pursue the enemy to the west with units of the 117th Tank and 46th Motorized brigades, in conjunction with units of the 2nd Guards Rifle Corps, and took Bocheikovo.

The 43rd Army, while pursuing the enemy along the Lepel' axis, by the close of 26 June had reached the Ulla River with the forces of its 1st Rifle Corps. The 60th Rifle Corps was fighting to destroy the enemy group of forces surrounded in the forests north of Ostrovno. However, the enemy was able to break through the 19th Guards Rifle Division's combat formations with part of his forces and began to fall back to the south and southwest. The 92nd Rifle Corps' 145th Rifle Division occupied the western part of Vitebsk by 1100 and cleared the enemy from the northern bank of the Western Dvina River.

The 43rd Army's commander, in connection with the successful advance of the 1st Rifle Corps along the Lepel' axis, made the decision, for the purpose of more quickly capturing Lepel', to create a mobile group consisting of the 10th and 39th guards tank brigades, the 1203rd Self-Propelled Artillery Regiment, the 712th Anti-Tank Artillery Regiment, and a battalion from the 5th Engineer Brigade. The mobile group was given the task of launching an impetuous attack in the direction of Lepel'; to capture Lepel' by 1500 on 27 June and to securely maintain it until the arrival of the 1st Rifle Corps' units.

By the close of 26 June the 6th Guards Army had reached the approaches to Polotsk and had begun to prepare the operation to seize the town. The 43rd Army's immediate objective was to seize Lepel'.

The further offensive by the *front's* forces was linked to overcoming the huge area of lakes and creeks stretching from Polotsk to Lepel'. This area gave the enemy great advantages in carrying out a defense. Besides this, the enemy was bringing up fresh reserves—the 201st and 221st security

---

1   Operational directive no. 0052/op, of June 26, 1944.

infantry divisions—along the Lepel' axis. The enemy's 290th Infantry Division had completed deploying its forces and had begun to put up stubborn resistance to our forces along the Polotsk axis.

The 4th Shock Army, which on 27 June had been reinforced with the fresh 100th Rifle Corps, began to press the enemy on its left flank. However, having encountered the stubborn resistance of the enemy's 205th and 24th infantry divisions, it could not advance further than the Makarov Islands Woods.

On 27-28 June the 6th Guards Army overcame the line of the lakes in heavy fighting and thus created a distinct threat to the town of Polotsk—an important center in the enemy's defensive system.

On 27 June units of the 43rd Army's 1st Rifle Corps, along with the mobile group, while overcoming the resistance of separate groups of the retreating enemy, continued to attack along the Lepel' axis.

From 1200 to 1600 an enemy force, numbering up to 2,500 men, attempted to break through to the west from the Yakubovshchina—Svitino area (eight kilometers south of Beshenkovichi). This group was located in the Ostrovno area and on the morning of 26 June broke through the 19th Rifle Division's combat formations. In the Svetogory area the group was intercepted by units of the Third Belorussian Front's 39th Army, but broke through again with great losses and, advancing to the west, ran into the headquarters of the 60th Rifle Corps in the Yakubovshchina area, as well as the operational group of the army's headquarters, which was following behind. The headquarters' and the group's personnel resisted the enemy trying the break through to Lepel'. Units of the 156th Rifle Division arrived in the Yakubovshchina area when the fighting broke out. The commander of the 60th Rifle Corps employed all the men and material at his disposal. The enemy was defeated; up to 200 of the enemy were killed and 500 officers and men taken prisoner. The remnants of this group once again broke through to the west, but in the Chashniki area they were finished off by the forces of the Third Belorussian Front's 5th Army.

At the same time, units of the 179th Rifle Division destroyed a second group of enemy forces in the Starodvortsy area, capturing 500 officers and men and seizing 1,000 motor vehicles.

At 0900 on 28 June the 1st Rifle Corps and the 43rd Army's mobile group, assisted by the 7th Mechanized Brigade of the 3rd Guards Mechanized Corps of the Third Belorussian Front's 5th Army, captured Lepel'.

The *front's* air army was covering the shock group's offensive, with the forces of the 211th and 335th air assault divisions in the interests of the 6th Guards Army, and the forces of the 332nd Assault Air Division in the interests of the 43rd Army. The efforts of the supporting *shturmoviks* were concentrated along the axes of the ground forces' main attacks. Raids against the enemy's forces were launched by small groups (4-6 *shturmoviks*) continuously throughout the day. At night single night bombers operated. Concentrated attacks by regimental groups of *shturmoviks* were launched against the enemy's men and weapons while the ground forces such major centers of resistance as Shumilino, Beshenkovichi and Lepel'.

The 1st Tank Corps' aviation support was supplied by the 335th Assault Air Division, in groups of 6-8 aircraft, as well as sorties on demand. While units of the tank corps were attacking Bocheikovo, the *shturmoviks* carried out 119 sorties.

In all, the air army carried out 2,981 sorties against the enemy's forces, which accounted for about 43 percent of the *front's* entire number of sorties. Air reconnaissance (about 500 sorties were carried out) uncovered in time the main axes of the enemy forces' retreat, as well as the arrival of his reserves from the direction of Polotsk and Lepel'. The 11th Air Corps' fighters, while covering the forces of the *front's* shock group (by constant patrolling on the operation's first day, and then by ordering sorties from the airfields), carried out 1,347 sorties. 41 enemy aircraft were shot down in 60 air battles.

Thus during the operation's first stage—from 23 June through 28 June—the *front's* forces broke through the enemy's defense in the area northwest of Vitebsk, forced the Western Dvina River, together with its neighbor to the left—the Third Belorussian Front—surrounded and destroyed the enemy's Vitebsk group of forces, and was successfully developing the success to the northwest and west.

It should be noted that the Vitebsk group of German-Fascist troops were surrounded by the forces of our rifle formations in the tactical and immediate operational depth of the enemy's defense. The destruction of this group of forces was accomplished in the course of five days, which testified to the Soviet forces' growing capabilities and high level of military art.

As a result of the rapid destruction (capture) of the encircled enemy, significant forces were freed up for developing the success in the depth.

The depth of advance amounted to 85 kilometers over six days. During this time 25,000 enemy officers and men were killed, and about 5,000 were captured.

All of this enabled the *front's* forces to reach the line Lipniki—Orekhovo—Lepel' by the close of the operation's first stage (28 June) and be in readiness to continue the offensive to the northwest and west.

The Operation's Second Stage

The Capture of Polotsk and the Development of the Offensive to the West (29 June-4 July 1944)

The changes in the situation brought about by the successful forcing of the Western Dvina River and the liberation of Lepel' demanded the amplification of the objectives assigned to the troops, which was accomplished through new directives by the *Stavka* of the Supreme High Command, which had been received by the *fronts* on 28-29 June.

The First Baltic Front was ordered to continue its offensive to the northwest and west and to capture Polotsk and Glubokoe, so as to securely guarantee from the north the operations of the Belorussian *fronts* in defeating the enemy in the Minsk area. The capture of the Polotsk area would give the *front's* armies the opportunity to further attack along the right bank of the Western Dvina River toward Dvinsk. The offensive toward Glubokoe would secure the successful advance of the *front's* forces to the west.

In order to capture the Polotsk fortified area, the commander of the First Baltic Front decided to employ two armies—the 4th Shock and 6th Guards armies. The 4th Shock Army was ordered to attack to the northwest in order to bypass Polotsk from the north. The 22nd Guards Rifle Corps, which was subordinated to the *front* commander, was to attack the town along the northern bank of the Western Dvina River. The 1st Tank Corps was ordered to seize Glubokoe on 29 June and render assistance to the 6th Guards Army, which had been ordered to launch an attack on Polotsk from the south and southwest.

On the whole, such a decision corresponded to the actual situation, which demanded the concentration of the *front's* main forces for the capture of such an important center of resistance and large city as Polotsk. The outflanking and enveloping maneuvers of the *front's* forces and the simultaneous attacks from several directions would facilitate the successful accomplishment of the task.

On the morning of 29 June the forces of the First Baltic Front began their new offensive along the entire front, having as their main assignment the capture of Polotsk. The 4th Shock Army was to outflank Polotsk from the northeast with part of its forces, while the 6th Guards Army enveloped it from the southwest. Simultaneously, the 6th Guards and 43rd armies' main forces were to attack in the direction of Braslav and Glubokoe.

The offensive unfolded in the following manner.

At 0840 the 4th Shock Army, with formations of the 83rd Rifle Corps, following a 40-minute artillery preparation, went over to the attack along the Polotsk axis, but could not advance. However, at 0300 on 30 June, the enemy, under the influence of our forces' success along the other axes, began to fall back. On the morning of 30 June the *front* commander demanded that the 4th Shock Army decisively pursue the retreating enemy units with its main forces to the northwest, outflanking Polotsk from the north.

In overcoming the enemy's resistance and repulsing his counterattacks, by the close of June 30 the army's forces had advanced 16 kilometers to the west and were 15 kilometers east of Polotsk.

Attacking along the entire front on the morning of 29 June, the 6th Guards Army encountered the greatest resistance along its right flank and in the center. The German-Fascist command strove with all its forces to hold Polotsk; it was concentrating the arriving reserves in the town and had committed the 81st and 389th infantry divisions into the battle south of Polotsk. In all, by this time six enemy infantry divisions (87th, 205th, 24th, 290th, 389th, and 81st) were operating in the Polotsk area.

The offensive developed more successfully along the 6th Guards Army's left flank.

On the morning of 30 June the 6th Guards Army continued its offensive for the capture of Polotsk.

The 103rd Rifle Division, having gone over to the offensive in the morning, was destroying the enemy with the forces of its 154th Rifle Division, along the eastern bank of the Western Dvina River, to the south of Goryany.

Under the existing conditions, the army commander considered the forces of the 22nd Guards Rifle Corps sufficient for an attack on Polotsk from the east. It was expedient to employ the 23rd Guards Rifle Corps, as the one closest to Polotsk, for attacking the city from the south.

Based on these calculations, the army commander on that day halted the 103rd Rifle Corps' offensive along the Polotsk axis and ordered it to move by forced march to the Disna area for an attack along the Dvinsk (Daugavpils) axis.

By the close of 30 June the 6th Guards Army's right-flank formations, which were attacking around Polotsk from the southwest, had advanced 18 kilometers and had reached the near approaches to the city from the south.

The 1st Tank Corps, having advanced 60 kilometers in two days along the northwest axis, captured Disna.

The *front* commander assigned the 6th Guards Army the following task for 1 July: in order to speed up the capture of Polotsk and the subsequent development of the offensive to the west and northwest, the 22nd Guards Rifle Corps was to continue to attack from the Goryany area and the 23rd Guards Rifle Corps to attack from the Lake Usomlya area and, in conjunction with the 4th Shock Army, to capture Polotsk by the close of 1 July; the 103rd Rifle Corps was to be moved to the Vetrino area for an attack to the northwest, with the task of destroying the enemy in the zone between the Western Dvina River and the Mokh Swamp and, by the close of 2 July 1944 reach the line Drissa—Ponki; the 2nd Guards Rifle Corps was to develop the offensive in the general direction of Luzhki and Germanovichi, and by the close of 1 July capture the area of Germanovichi. It was to subsequently attack toward Sharkovshchina and Iody.[2] The commander of the 1st Tank Corps was given the task of capturing Glubokoe and to subsequently continue the offensive along the railroad to the west.

---

2   Combat journal of the First Baltic Front for July 1944.

During 29-30 June the 60th and 92nd rifle corps were committed into the battle along the 43rd Army's front. The army's forces, while overcoming the enemy's resistance, including the newly-committed 212th Infantry Division, advanced 28-36 kilometers in two days.

On 1 July the 43rd Army was to leave two of the 1st Rifle Corps' divisions on the left flank and with its remaining forces attack to the northwest, outflanking Lake Sho from the north and south, in the general direction of Glubokoe.

In connection with the First Baltic Front's turn to the northwest, the *Stavka* of the Supreme High Command changed the boundary line between the First Baltic and Third Belorussian fronts and as of 1200 on 30 June established a new one: Lepel'—Pustosel'e—Paraf'yanov (all locales for the First Baltic Front).

On the morning of 1 July the 4th Shock Army's left flank, consisting of the 16th Lithuanian Rifle Division and the 100th and 83rd rifle corps, as well as the 6th Guards Army's right flank, consisting of the 22nd and 23rd guards rifle corps, attacked Polotsk. The enemy was not able to delay the 4th Shock Army's attack along the intermediate lines. By the close of the day the army reached the eastern outskirts of Polotsk. By the close of 3 July the army's forces had outflanked the city from the north, cut off the enemy's route of retreat to the north and put the roads leading from Polotsk to the northwest under threat.

On 4 July the army continued to attack. The enemy, with units of the 205th Infantry Division, the 389th Infantry Division's 544th Infantry Regiment, and the 87th Infantry Division's 185th Infantry Regiment, were putting up stubborn resistance, but by the end of the day had been thrown back to the west. The 22nd Guards Rifle Corps, which had the task of seizing Polotsk from the north, at 0200 on 1 July went over to the attack and by the close of 2 July had reached the city's northern outskirts. On 3 July the corps's units attempted to seize the northern half of Polotsk, but were unsuccessful.

The 6th Guards Army's 23rd Guards Rifle Corps attacked from the south. At dawn on 2 July the corps' units broke through the enemy's defense and broke into the southern part of the city.

By 0400 on 4 July Polotsk had been completely cleared of the enemy. In the fighting for Polotsk the enemy had suffered heavy losses and, fearing complete encirclement, began to rapidly fall back to the northwest, along the right bank of the Western Dvina River.

At the same time that the *front's* right-wing forces were fighting for Polotsk, the forces of the left wing were developing the offensive along the Svencionys axis.

During the fighting for Polotsk, the forces of the 6th Guards Army's left flank and the 43rd Army continued to attack toward Germanovichi and Glubokoe. On 1 July units of the 2nd Guards Rifle Corps, assisted by the 1st Tank Corps, liberated Germanovichi.

The 103rd Rifle Corps, because of poor march organization and the absence of route reconnaissance, advanced slowly. The army commander pointed out to the corps commander the lack of precise march organization and demanded that he complete the movement of the corps' units to the Disna area by the morning of 2 July.

On the morning of 1 July the 43rd Army continued to successfully develop the offensive to the west. In the conditions of the wooded and swampy terrain and the lack of roads, they covered up to 22 kilometers during the day.

On 2-3 July the *front's* left-wing forces continued to attack along their previous axes. On 3 July units of the 92nd Rifle Corps, in conjunction with units of the 1st Tank Corps, captured Glubokoe.

By the close of 4 July the forces of the *front's* center and left wing occupied the following position:

6th Guards Army: the 23rd Guards Rifle Corps, in connection with the transfer of the 4th Shock Army to the Second Baltic Front and the resulting wide (up to 50-55 kilometers) gap between this army and the 6th Guards Army, was moved to the southern bank of the Western Dvina River, and by the close of 4 July occupied a defensive position along a broad front from Druchany to Disna, and then to the northwest as far as Vinogrady. The 103rd Rifle Corps, while destroying individual and isolated enemy groups and his 132nd Infantry Division to the southwest of Drissa, reached the line excluding Trudy—Kislyaki—Ponki; the 2nd Guards Rifle Corps reached the area between lakes Dryvyaty and Boginskoe, where it began fighting with the enemy's newly-arrived 215th Infantry Division.

By the close of 4 July the 43rd Army had reached the line Kozyany—Kuropole—Chashkovshizna—Gruzdovo—Myadzel.

Thus the *front's* left-wing forces, while pursuing the enemy's retreating units, by the close of 4 July had reached the line Lake Dryvyaty—excluding Lake Naroch', thus securing the successful offensive by the Third Belorussian Front from the north.

The 3rd Air Army concentrated its main assault air efforts (about 80 percent of all sorties) along the Polotsk axis; parts of its forces were to assist the 43rd Army and the 1st Tank Corps. In all, during the 29 June-4 July period the 3rd Air Army conducted about 5,000 sorties. Fighter aviation (11th Fighter Corps and the 259th Fighter Division), while covering the *front's* shock group and supporting the *shturmoviks'* combat operations, carried out 2,900 sorties and shot down 63 enemy aircraft in 58 air battles.

Results and Conclusions

In the course of the operation's first six day (23 June through 28 June), the forces of the First Baltic Front successfully accomplished the task assigned by the *Stavka* of the Supreme High Command. The *front's* shock group, consisting of the 6th Guards and 43rd armies, broke through the enemy's defense and defeated the main forces of the opposing enemy.

It's necessary to note the methods of conducting the operation along the right flank of the *front's* shock group, typical of the time, where the forward battalions' initial successful actions, supported in a timely manner by the main forces and supported by the entire might of our artillery fire and aviation, grew into a breakthrough of the enemy's defense along this sector. This, to a significant degree, influenced the offensive's success along the remaining axes.

As a result of the coordinated attacks by the First Baltic Front's 43rd Army and the Third Belorussian Front's 39th Army against the base of the Vitebsk salient, the enemy group of forces in the Vitebsk area, consisting of five divisions, had as early as 25 June been surrounded and split up, and in the following days successfully destroyed. A portion of the enemy's forces, which had managed to break out of the Ostrovno area, was completely destroyed in the areas of Svetogory southeast of Starodvortsy, and Yakubovshchina. The elimination of the enemy's Vitebsk group of forces is of particular interest, for here we see an example of encircling a major enemy group of forces by the rifle formations along two *fronts'* adjoining flanks.

The Western Dvina River was forced on the march along a broad front, with the aid of materials at hand. A fierce fight was waged for the captured bridgeheads. Having successfully forced the river, our forces forced the enemy to retreat, achieved operational freedom and, not encountering in the depth continuous defensive lines and major enemy operational reserves, rapidly advanced to the west. Although the German-Fascist command committed into the fighting part of the 95th Infantry Division, units of the 201st and 221st security divisions, as well as the 64th, 335th, 340th, and 347th security battalions, the 78th, 208th, 794th, 229th, 213th, 123rd sapper-construction battalions, the 5th, 9th, 11th, and 14th punishment battalions, the Third Panzer Army's NCO school, and a number of other special subunits, none of this could change the overall course of combat operations. All of the transferred formations and units were fed into the battle piecemeal, on the march, as a result of which part of them sustained heavy losses, while many were completely destroyed.

As a result of the fighting during the first stage of the operation from 23-28 June, the *front's* forces along the direction of the main attack, in conditions of inaccessible and wooded and swampy terrain, advanced more than 80 kilometers, having a rate of advance of up to 14 kilometers per day. During this period 1,670 inhabited locales were liberated, including such large ones as Shumilino, Ulla, Beshenkovichi, and Lepel'. The German-Fascist forces lost more than 25,000 officers and men killed and wounded, 322 guns, 1,009 mortars, eight assault guns, and 51 aircraft destroyed, and more than 5,000 officers and men captured, along with 474 guns and mortars and 31 tanks captured by the enemy.

The First Baltic Front's serious success was achieved at the expense of 23,053 casualties from 21-30 June, including 4,658 men killed.[3] These losses were suffered mostly during the breakthrough of the enemy's tactical defensive zone and while forcing the Western Dvina River.

The successful breakthrough of the enemy's defense and the defeat of his troops were achieved thanks to the high level of the Soviet troops' political-morale condition, the surprise of the attack, the well-oiled coordination of the combat arms, the unbroken troop control and, what is most important, the extremely active and decisive actions of our forces. The correctly selected direction of the main blow, the adequate study of the enemy's defense and group of forces, and foreseeing the character of the enemy's actions during the operation, all had major significance.

The *front's* combat actions during the first stage are characterized by high rates of advance, the skillful destruction and capture of large enemy forces, and the energetic pursuit of the retreating enemy.

The 1st Tank Corps, as the *front's* mobile group, did not achieve the high rates of advance which one would have expected from it. During the course of six days it nevertheless was not able to break away into the open with its main forces, but rather moved behind the infantry's combat formations and was delayed at the crossings. Modern experience shows that in a tank corps' operations in wooded and swampy terrain, full of water obstacles, of particular importance is the timely arrival of crossing equipment to the crossing sites. One must count it as a serious shortcoming in employing the tank corps the fact that the *front* headquarters devoted little attention to the problems of supporting the tank corps' commitment into the breach and its subsequent actions, and instead transferred this work to the 6th Guards Army headquarters.

The 3rd Air Army, having conducted 7,000 sorties during the operation's first stage and taking advantage of our air superiority, actively supported the offensive by the *front's* shock group, conducting an average of about 1,200 sorties per day.

Characteristic of the enemy's actions were his fear of encirclement, his efforts to avoid this and to evade our troops' attack, with no regard for losses in men and materiel.

The initial operational plan called for reached the line Zelenyi Gorodok—Krulevshchizna by the tenth of eleventh day of the operation. The *front* accomplished this task significantly earlier. This was particularly the case along the center and left wing, where by the operation's eleventh day our force were already 60-90 kilometers west of the designated line.

During the operation's second stage heavy fighting took place along the Polotsk axis, where the enemy, taking advantage of the favorable terrain conditions, sought to keep Polotsk in his hands with the forces of six infantry divisions, supported by aviation. However, the Soviet forces, having employed an enveloping maneuver here, created the threat of completely encircling the entire Polotsk group of forces, which forced the enemy to rapidly begin pulling his forces back. The forces of the 4th Shock Army, in conjunction with the formations of the 6th Guards Army, inflicted heavy casualties on the enemy's Polotsk group of forces and liberated Polotsk—a major road and railroad junction. However, we were not able to encircle and completely destroy the enemy's

---

3   Ministry of Defense Archives, fond 235, opis' 2078, delo 16, pp. 76-78.

Polotsk group of forces. The reason for this was the insufficiently rapid outflanking maneuver by the 4th Shock Army from the north.

The German-Fascist troops suffered heavy casualties during the operation's second stage. In the fighting for Polotsk alone, 15,000 officers and men were killed, and 136 guns and mortars, 14 tanks and assault guns, 11 armored trains, and 52 aircraft were destroyed. Besides this, about 30,000 officers and men were captured, as well as six tanks, 14 armored trains, and 89 guns and mortars.

During the period 1-10 July the First Baltic Front suffered the following losses: 3,134 men killed, 10,617 wounded, and 109 missing in action, for a total of 13,860 casualties. These losses were sustained mainly in taking Polotsk.

On the whole, the First Baltic Front played a positive role in the first stage of the multi-*front* Belorussian operation. The *front's* forces very quickly broke through the enemy's tactical defensive zone, successfully forced a major water obstacle like the Western Dvina River, and skillfully carried out the pursuit of the retreating enemy. The capture of Polotsk, in a way, opened the gates for the subsequent advance by our forces toward the shore of the Gulf of Riga.

In 12 days of the operation the *front's* forces advanced along the center more than 200 kilometers. The rate of advance during the pursuit reached 18-23 kilometers per day.

The *front's* chief objective—the isolation of Army Group North from Army Group Center—was successfully accomplished.

3

The Third Belorussian Front's Vitebsk—Minsk Offensive Operation (23 June-4 July 1944)

The Operation's First Stage

The Breakthrough of the German-Fascist Forces' Defense, the Encirclement and Destruction of the Enemy's Vitebsk Group of Forces and the Development of the Offensive toward the Berezina River (23-28 June 1944)

The Third Belorussian Front's Vitebsk—Minsk operation began with the breakthrough of the enemy's previously-prepared and continuous defense, developed in depth, along those sectors called for by the operation's idea and plan.

The offensive by the *front's* main forces, just as was the case with the First Baltic Front's Vitebsk—Polotsk offensive, was preceded by a reconnaissance in force, which was conducted during the second half of 22 June by the forward battalions from each first-echelon division, for the purpose of uncovering the enemy's defensive system and to nail down the outlines of his forward line along the sectors of the forthcoming breakthrough.

The actions of each forward battalion were supported by the fire of 1-2 artillery battalions, carrying out a 25-minute artillery preparation.

In all, in the sector of the forthcoming breakthrough, 15 battalions and several reconnaissance detachments, from a company to a platoon in size, were operating. They achieved their greatest success in the 5th Army, where at 1600 on 22 June the rifle divisions' forward battalions pierced the enemy's defense. The forward battalions were supported in a timely manner by a part of the main forces and the entire artillery. As a result, by the close of 22 June the enemy's defense had been broken along the 5th Army's entire breakthrough sector to a depth of 2-4 kilometers. The main barriers and obstacles in the main zone of the enemy's defense were overcome, while his fire system was disrupted and the Sukhodrovka River forced. The enemy, having taken the forward battalions' actions for the start of the offensive by our main forces, committed divisional, and in places even corps, reserves into the fighting.

The 5th Army's forces captured a bridgehead on the southern bank of the Sukhodrovka River and used it for the deployment of its shock group of forces. For this purpose, during the night of 23 June sappers constructed five bridges from pre-fabricated materials, of which three could handle weights of 60 tons, and outfitted one ford. After both banks of the river were cleared of mines, the 72nd and 65th rifle corps' divisions were crossed over, along with their reinforcements.

In the 39th, 11th Guards and 31st armies' sectors the actions of the forward battalions were less successful and they (aside from the forward battalions of the 11th Guards Army's 31st and 16th guards rifle divisions) were unable to consolidate in the enemy's first trench.

The fighting by the forward battalions established that the enemy's defense in the main sector along the Bogushevsk axis was weaker than along the Orsha axis.

The enemy took the actions by our forward battalions for the beginning of the "expected great offensive along the entire front of the Third Panzer Army" and was thus disoriented, both as to the timing of the offensive, as well as to the direction of the main attack.[1]

In connection with the forward battalions' successful actions in the 5th Army's sector, changes were made in the plans for the artillery and aviation offensive.

During the night of 22-23 June a preliminary aviation preparation was carried out against the enemy's revealed strong points and artillery.

The artillery preparation of the attack on the morning of 23 June was carried out according to the changes made in the plan.

During the direct air preparation for the attack, a powerful blow was launched against the enemy's troops facing the 11th Guards Army's shock group.

Following the artillery and direct aviation preparation, the *front's* forces attacked at 0900 on 23 June with their main forces along a front from Perevoz to Zagvazdino.

The 39th Army, making its main attack with the forces of the 5th Guards Rifle Corps in the general direction of Gnezdilovichi, broke through the enemy's defense along the Perevoz—Kuzmentsy sector, forced the Luchesa River on the march, having seized three bridges, which enabled the attacking units to rapidly break into the artillery's main positional areas. By the close of the day the army's forces had broken through the enemy's main defensive zone, defeated his 197th Infantry Division and, having advanced 12 kilometers along the main axis, cut the Vitebsk—Bogushevsk road.

Combat continued at night by reinforced detachments.

The 5th Army broke through the enemy's defense along its right flank and center along the sector excluding Kuzmentsy—Yul'kovo, launching its main attack in the general direction of Bogushevsk. By the close of the day the army's forces completed the breakthrough of the enemy's main defensive zone, advanced 10-12 kilometers and, having expanded the breakthrough along the front to 25 kilometers, defeated the 299th Infantry Division, as well as the Third Panzer Army's army reserves.

As a result of the breakthrough of the enemy's defense and the forcing of the Luchesa River in the Zarech'e area, conditions were created for the commitment of the *front's* cavalry-mechanized group (3rd Guards Mechanized and 3rd Guards Cavalry corps) into the breach on the morning of 24 June.

The army's combat actions did not cease at night.

At 0900 the 11th Guards Army attacked the enemy, launching the main blow in the area of the Minsk highway. Along the sector excluding Central settlement—Kirieva sector, the 8th and 36th guards rifle corps encountered fierce resistance by units of the 78th Assault Division and other enemy units, and during the course of the day advanced two kilometers. Along the Ostrov Yur'ev—Orekhi-Vydritsa axis, on the boundary between the 16th Guards and 8th Guards rifle divisions, the enemy was forced out of Ostrov Yur'ev by 1030 and, under the attacks of our forces fell back to the regimental reserves' position (the "main battlefield"), where he continued to put up stubborn resistance by fire and counterattacks.

At 1800, following a short artillery preparation and a bombing raid by the 1st Guards Bomber Corps (162 Pe-2s), the 16th Guards Rifle Corps' second echelon (11th and 1st guards rifle divisions) was committed into the battle. As a result of the coordinated actions of the corps' attacking

---

1   The Third Panzer Army's journal of combat activities for 22 June 1944. Archive of the Military-Historical Directorate of the General Staff of the USSR Armed Forces.

divisions, as well as units of the 152nd Fortified Area, the enemy's resistance along the Orekhi-Vydritsa axis was broken.

By the close of the day the army's forces had broken through the enemy's main defensive zone along two sectors—northwest of Protasovo, and in the direction of Ostrov Yur'ev and Orekhi-Vydritsa—and had advanced 4-10 kilometers. As a result, conditions were created for enveloping the powerfully fortified enemy defensive sector along the Minsk highway from the north and for the development of the army's attack, in conjunction with the 5th Army and the cavalry-mechanized group, around Orsha from the north. In the area of the Minsk highway the enemy was holding on to the main defensive zone, as a result of which the 2nd Guards Tank Corps was not committed into the fighting and remained in its jumping-off position.

During the first half of the day the first-echelon divisions of the 31st Army's 71st and 36th rifle corps broke the enemy's defense along the front line to the north and south of the Dnepr River and advanced three kilometers into the depth of his defense. However, from 1300 the enemy's resistance grew and we were not able to develop the initial success. The enemy's defense was not pierced.

During the day the 1st Air Army supported the offensive by the 5th and 11th Guards armies, covered their combat formations on the battlefield, blocked the enemy's airfields, and carried out reconnaissance as far as the Lepel'—Borisov line (120-150 kilometers). In all, during the day our aviation carried out 1,769 sorties, of which assault air and bomber sorties accounted for 1,004. 15 enemy planes were shot down in air battles and our aviation retained complete air superiority.

By decision of the *front* commander, the cavalry-mechanized group was to move into the 5th Army's sector by the morning of 24 June.

Thus in the course of the operation's first day, the *front* achieved significant successes along the Bogushevsk axis (39th and 5th armies), where the enemy's defense was penetrated along a 25-kilometer sector to a depth of 10-13 kilometers, and by the close of the day the breach was expanded to 50 kilometers in width. The Vitebsk—Orsha rail line was cut.

The success achieved in the attack sector of the *front's* right-wing shock group was creating favorable conditions for the development of the operation's success by committing the *front's* mobile forces into the breach.

The offensive developed less successfully along the Orsha axis in the 11th Guards and 31st armies' sector, which comprised the Third Belorussian Front's left-wing shock group. These armies had to overcome the enemy's more powerful defense and, upon encountering his forces' stubborn resistance, advanced only 3-10 kilometers into the depth in a day's fighting.

Due to the unfavorable meteorological conditions, the air forces' capabilities were not fully employed on the first day of the operation.

On 24 June the most successful fighting continued along the *front's* right wing, where in the direction of Ostrovno the forces of the 39th Army were deeply enveloping the enemy's LIII Army Corps, which was defending the Vitebsk area, while the 5th Army, having overcome the Luchesa River, drove to the enemy's road junction and strong point of Bogushevsk. In order to augment the efforts of the *front's* right-wing forces in the direction of Senno, the *front's* cavalry-mechanized group was committed into the breach, and by 2400 had reached the area northwest of Bogushevsk. The 11th Guards and 31st armies were engaged in stubborn fighting to break through the enemy's defense along the Orsha axis.

Due to the fact that the enemy was holding the 11th Guards Army's offensive in the zone of the Minsk highway, the commander of the Third Belorussian Front decided to commit the 5th Guards Tank Army into the breach along the right wing in the 5th Army's sector, along the Yazykovo—Vysochany sector, in the general direction of Bogushevsk, Tolochin and Borisov.

The tank army was given the objective of capturing the Tolochin area by the close of the first day and to subsequently capture Borisov and the crossings across the Berezina River west of Borisov. Simultaneously, the army commander was instructed that the cavalry-mechanized group was to attack in the direction of Senno and Chereya, and the 2nd Guards Tank Corps in the direction of Pogost, outflanking Orsha from the north. The 5th Guards Tank Army was ordered to occupy its jumping-off position in the Krynki area during the night of 24-25 June.

Thus the tank army was to be employed not according to the first (main) variation, which had been called for by the plan (in the 11th Guards Army's sector), but according to the second (western) variation—in the 5th Army's sector, which was conditioned by the specific situation (the enemy's stubborn resistance along the Minsk highway and the 5th Army's successful advance). This example testifies to the flexibility of the *front* command. For the tank army, this meant a change of its immediate objective. As far as the subsequent objective (the arrival in the Borisov area and the capture of crossings over the Berezina River) was concerned, this remained unchanged.

The commander of the 5th Guards Tank Army decided to commit the army into the breach in a single-echelon formation (two corps side by side), having a small reserve at his disposal. The 29th Tank Corps was to attack toward Tolochin, in order that the corps' forward detachment could capture this town by the close of 25 June. The 3rd Guards Tank Corps was to attack toward Kokhanovo, with the task of seizing this village with a forward detachment by the close of 25 June.

The tank corps' forward detachments were to start their forward movement by 1000 on 25 June, behind the 5th Army's forward units, and to be ready to enter the breach at 1400. The tank corps' main forces were to remain in their jumping-off positions, ready to attack during the night of 25-26 June.[2]

The 5th Guards Tank Army, having carried out a night march, had by 0700 on 25 June, concentrated in the jumping-off area indicated by the *front* commander.

In the meantime, the combined-arms armies' combat operations developed in the following manner.

At 1900 on 24 June the 39th Army's 5th Guards Rifle Corps began fighting the enemy for Ostrovno. Simultaneously, with part of the forces of the 84th Rifle Corps, the army broke into Vitebsk and was fighting on its eastern outskirts. During the second part of the day the enemy set fire to Vitebsk. Striving to prevent an encirclement, and trying to remove its men and materiel from Vitebsk, the German-Fascist command on 24 June committed the Third Panzer Army's army reserves into the fighting and began to move the *Luftwaffe* Field 4th Division piecemeal from the Vitebsk defensive position to the Ostrovno area. Simultaneously, the enemy, under the blows of the 43rd Army and the right wing of the 39th Army, began to pull back the 246th Infantry and *Luftwaffe* 6th Field divisions to the Vitebsk area and to the west.

The troops of the 39th Army, having advanced their left wing 20 kilometers toward the First Baltic Front's 43rd Army, by the end of the day had reached the eastern outskirts of Vitebsk and the southern outskirts of Ostrovno.

The First Baltic Front's neighboring 43rd Army to the right reached the northern bank of the Western Dvina River and was forcing it.

Thus only a bottleneck, no more than ten kilometers wide, remained between the flanks of the 39th and 43rd armies in the area of Ostrovno and Gnezdilovichi. The threat of encirclement hung over the enemy's Vitebsk group of forces.

The 39th Army did not halt its offensive at night. The army, employing the forces of a rifle division and an attached tank brigade, cut the Vitebsk—Beshenkovichi paved road on the night of 25 June and captured the southern bank of the Western Dvina River north of Dobrino.

Thus the 39th Army's skillful and decisive actions enabled us to envelop the enemy's Vitebsk group of forces—the *Luftwaffe* 4th and 6th field, 206th, 246th, and 197th infantry divisions (in all, five divisions)—as early as 24 June and complete their encirclement on the morning of 25 June.

---

2   5th Guards Tank Army order no. 044, of 24 June 1944.

The 5th Army, having broken through the enemy's powerfully fortified positions around Bogushevsk (three trench lines), as a result of street fighting completely captured the town by 2100 on 24 June. The ground forces' storming of Bogushevsk was preceded by a massed aviation attack by the 1st Air Army, including 90 Pe-2s and 180 Il-2s,[3] which was launched against the enemy defending the town. During the day the 5th Army's forces defeated the 299th and 256th infantry divisions and a number of individual enemy units, inflicted heavy casualties on the newly-committed 14th and 95th infantry divisions and advanced 10-14 kilometers. With the fall of Bogushevsk, the enemy's army defensive zone was broken and conditions created for the commitment of the cavalry-mechanized group, whose routes ran through Bogushevsk, due to the wooded and swampy terrain and the string of lakes.

At 1100 on 24 June the cavalry-mechanized group began its movement to the Luchesa River for commitment into the breach in the 5th Army's sector. The crossing of the group's formations over the river was unorganized and not supported by the 5th Army.

As a result of the insufficiently organized commitment into the breach, the cavalry-mechanized group was not able to break away from the 5th Army's infantry. By the end of the day the group had begun fighting the enemy that had fallen back to the army defensive zone along the sector excluding Chudnya—excluding Bogushevsk.

At 0850 on 24 June, following a 40-minute artillery preparation, the 11th Guards Army renewed its offensive, making its main attack with the formations of the 16th and 8th guards rifle corps north of the Minsk highway. The enemy, relying on his intermediate defensive lines, was stubbornly resisting the army's offensive with units of the 260th Infantry and 78th Assault divisions, part of the 260th Infantry Division, and newly committed units from the 286th Security and 14th Infantry divisions. The fighting was particularly fierce in the area of the Minsk highway and the Smolensk—Orsha railroad.

By the close of the day the army's forces, having overcome the enemy's resistance, had completed the breakthrough of his main defensive zone along the army's entire front, as well as the second zone in individual areas; the army advanced 8-14 kilometers that day. As a result of the fierce fighting, the army had enveloped the enemy's left flank north of the Minsk highway.

The 2nd Guards Tank Corps was not committed into the fighting and remained in its jumping-off position.

On 24 June the 31st Army continued the heavy fighting to break through the enemy's main defensive zone and during the day advanced only 1-1.5 kilometers. Units of the 78th Assault Infantry and 25th Motorized divisions were defending along the 31st Army's breakthrough sector.

The 1st Air Army was supporting the 5th and 11th Guards armies' offensive and, partially, the 31st Army as well, and was reconnoitering the enemy as far as the Lepel'—Borisov line. 1,804 sorties were conducted that day, of which 816 were by assault air and bomber aviation. Our fighters shot down 17 enemy planes in air battles. The combat activities of the air army's units were limited by the unfavorable meteorological conditions.

Thus by the end of the operation's second day the Third Belorussian Front's forces along the right wing had expanded the breakthrough of the enemy's defense to 120 kilometers in width, had captured Bogushevsk and advanced from their jumping-off positions to a depth of 20-32 kilometers. As a result of the attack by the 39th Army toward Ostrovno, in conjunction with the 43rd Army, the enemy's Vitebsk group of forces had been deeply outflanked from

---

3   Editor's note. The Il-2 was a Soviet ground attack aircraft, commonly known as the "shturmovik," which first saw service in 1941. One model had a crew of two, a maximum speed of 414 km/hr and a range of 720 kilometers. It was armed with two 23mm cannons, two 7.62mm machine guns, one 12.7mm machine gun, and could carry up to 600 kilograms of bombs.

the flanks and the rear and all the conditions for completing its encirclement and destruction had been created.

In the second half of the day the *front's* cavalry-mechanized group was committed into the breach in the 5th Army's attack sector in the direction of Senno for developing the achieved success, while that same day the group's forward detachments reached the area northwest of Bogushevsk.

Along the Orsha axis, as the result of heavy fighting, the enemy's main defensive zone to the north of the Smolensk—Orsha railroad was also broken, and along some parts the second defensive zone was also overcome; to the south, the enemy was holding the attack by the 11th Guards Army's left flank and two of the 31st Army's right-flank rifle corps.

On the operation's third day the heaviest fighting unfolded along the *front's* right flank, where the 39th Army was successfully developing the attack toward Gnezdilovichi and northeast of Ostrovno, in conjunction with the First Baltic Front's 43rd Army, and had encircled the enemy's Vitebsk group of forces and was repelling his repeated attempts to break out of the encirclement.

Along the Orsha axis the 11th Guards Army's forces, having broken the enemy's resistance and completed the breakthrough of his tactical defensive zone, were decisively attacking to bypass Orsha from the north. In the center, along the Senno—Lukoml' axis, the enemy, under the blows of the cavalry-mechanized group and the 5th Army, had begun withdrawing to the west. At 1400 the 5th Guards Tank Army's main forces began their movement in the 5th Army's zone for commitment into the breach in the direction of Tolochin and Borisov.

The combat activities of the combined-arms armies and the cavalry-mechanized group developed as follows.

The 39th Army continued fighting to encircle and destroy the enemy's Vitebsk group of forces. From the morning of 25 June the success of the rifle division that had broken through to the southern bank of the Western Dvina River was consolidated, as a result of which the enemy's Vitebsk group of forces was cut up into two parts along the army's sector as early as the first half of the day. Simultaneously, part of the army's forces, attacking toward Gnezdilovichi and having thrown back the enemy to the north, by 0900 had captured that locale in conjunction with the First Baltic Front's 43rd Army.

As a result of the 39th and 43rd armies' decisive actions, the enemy' Vitebsk group of forces was surrounded in the first half of the day on 25 June, while in the 39th Army's sector it had been cut into two parts. The 206th Infantry and *Luftwaffe* 6th Field divisions and two regiments from the 246th Infantry Division were surrounded in the immediate area of Vitebsk; the *Luftwaffe* 4th Field Division, a regiment from the 246th Infantry Division, and the remains of the 197th Infantry Division were surrounded southwest and north of Ostrovno. These groups of forces also included various reinforcements from the LIII Army Corps, and rear and service units from the enemy's Third Panzer Army. The overall number of enemy troops surrounded here exceeded 40,000 men.

Immediately following the completion of the encirclement, the troops of the 39th Army carried out decisive actions toward destroying the encircled enemy. By order of the *front* commander, the 1st Air Army's bomber and assault aviation was thrown against the surrounded enemy forces and between 1530 and 1600 launched massive raids against the enemy's combat formations attempting to break out to the west. Having repelled the enemy's counterattacks, the 39th Army's forces advanced 4-6 kilometers that day and seized the northeastern and eastern part of Vitebsk along the Western Dvina River.

At 0500 on 25 June the 5th Army renewed its attack and, having expanded the breakthrough of the enemy's rear defensive line to 25 kilometers in width, the army, in conjunction with the *front's* cavalry-mechanized group began to pursue the enemy, making its main attack in the direction of Senno and Lukoml'.

The enemy, having committed fresh elements of the 14th Infantry Division into the battle, as well as several security and construction battalions, and also defeated units of the VI Army Corps, attempted during the first part of the day to hold back the army's offensive, but being thrown back, began to fall back to the west and southwest.

By the close of the day the army's forces, while destroying the enemy's rear guards in conjunction with the cavalry-mechanized group, threw him back 16-20 kilometers to the southwest and captured Senno from the march.

On the morning of 25 June the cavalry-mechanized group broke through the enemy's intermediate defensive line northwest of Bogushevsk and, having defeated part of the 299th Infantry Division, a regiment from the 14th Infantry Division, and a number of individual special units, began pursuing the enemy, making its main attack in the general direction of Senno.

The 3rd Guards Mechanized Corps, in conjunction with the 5th Army's formations, captured Senno and cut the Orsha—Lepel' railroad in the area 15 kilometers southwest of Senno.

The 3rd Guards Cavalry Corps, while pursuing the enemy in the direction of Obol'tsy, surrounded in the woods 12 kilometers southwest of Bogushevsk the remnants of two of the 299th Infantry Division's regiments and elements of the enemy's 14th Infantry Division, and was fighting to destroy them with part of its forces.

During the day the cavalry-mechanized group's formations advanced 20-45 kilometers. The cavalry-mechanized group's combat activities were supported by the 1st Air Army's 3rd Air Assault Corps.

At 1000 on 25 June the 5th Guards Tank Army's forward detachments, and at 1400 its main forces, began to move into the breach in the 5th Army's sector along the sector Vysochany—excluding Ol'kovo.

Due to the poor condition of the roads and bridges and their being full of transportation vehicles, the columns of the tank corps' main forces advanced at an average speed of only 4-5 kilometers per hour during the day. In light of this, the 5th Guards Tank Army was unable to overtake the 5th Army's infantry on 25 June and actually entered the breach only on the morning of 26 June.

The 11th Guards Army continued to attack; concentrating its main efforts in the 16th Guards Rifle Corps' sector, where as a result of the fighting on 23-24 June there appeared the opportunity of developing the army's success to bypass the enemy's Orsha group of forces from the north.

By the close of 25 June the army had thrown the enemy back 7-12 kilometers. The army's force completed the breakthrough of the enemy's defense throughout the entire tactical depth (25 kilometers), and he was faced with the fact of the complete defeat of his Orsha group of forces. The enemy was forced to begin pulling his forces back to the west on the night of 25-26 June.

The 31st Army continued its attack, concentrating its main efforts to the north of the Dnepr River, in the 71st Rifle Corps' sector, where by the end of the day it had managed to complete the breakthrough of the enemy's main defensive zone, and partially of his second.

The 1st Air Army was destroying the enemy's men and materiel through assault and bomber attacks, while concentrating its main efforts on supporting the attack by the cavalry-mechanized group and the 11th Guards Army, as well as assisting the 39th Army in destroying the enemy's Vitebsk group of forces. 1,517 sorties were carried out, of which 973 were carried out by assault and bomber aircraft. 20 enemy planes were shot down.

Thus the *front*, having reached the Senno—Orsha line by the close of the operation's third day, had fulfilled its immediate objective and, having eliminated the enemy's "Panther" defensive line within the confines of the Smolensk Gates, had created the conditions for the rapid development of the attack on Borisov, for the purpose of deeply outflanking the German Fourth Army from the north and west. The enemy's Vitebsk group of forces had been surrounded and broken up and our troops were fighting to destroy it.

In the 5th Army's sector at 1400 on 25 June, that is, according to the second variation of the operational plan, the 5th Guards Tank Army was also committed into the breach, and on that day captured Tolochin and cut the enemy's communications to the west of Orsha.

The situation of the German-Fascist forces operating in the Orsha area worsened. The enemy was forced to begin to fall back.

As early as 0600 on 25 June, thanks to the joint efforts of the 39th Army's 158th Rifle Division and the neighboring 43rd Army's (First Baltic Front) 145th Rifle Division, Vitebsk was completely cleared of the remnants of the defeated enemy.

Heavy fighting by the 39th Army's main forces continued for the destruction of the two encircled groups of enemy forces, while the largest of them was adjacent to Vitebsk in the southwest. In order to quickly eliminate this group of forces, up to four divisions were to be brought up here on the night of 25-26 June, while two divisions were to be transferred from the Ostrovno area, while leaving behind there a regiment apiece.

The enemy's group of forces surrounded in the Ostrovno area by two divisions of the 43rd Army's 60th Rifle Corps and two regiments from the 39th Army, took advantage of the weakening of the southern encirclement sector, and on the morning of 26 June more than 5,000 men of the *Luftwaffe* 4th Field Division broke out to the south, but were intercepted by two of the 39th Army's rifle divisions on the march, and after a brief battle were partially destroyed. The remnants of this group (2,500 men) broke through to the west, but were intercepted by the 43rd Army's forces and eliminated. During the second half of 26 June our forces occupied Ostrovno and by the close of the day the 43rd Army's 60th Rifle Corps had eliminated the enemy remaining in the encirclement north of Ostrovno.

The destruction of the enemy encircled to the southwest of Vitebsk proceeded in more complex conditions. The *Luftwaffe* 6th Field and 206th Infantry divisions and two regiments of the 246th Infantry Division had the objective of breaking out of the encirclement at any cost. The attempts to break out began on the night of 26 June. The enemy, having arrayed the 206th Infantry Division in several echelons of groups of 1,000-2,000 men, with tanks, broke through our combat formations by 0600, at the cost of enormous losses, along one of the 39th Army's division's sectors, and began to move into the forested area adjacent to Lake Moshno. In order to restore the situation, a single rifle division (minus one regiment) and a motorcycle regiment were committed into the battle and closed the breakthrough corridor. Simultaneously, two of the 39th Army's rifle divisions and, from 1900 units of the 5th Army's 45th Rifle Corps, blocked the enemy, who had managed to hide in the woods adjacent to Lake Moshno.

As a result of the fierce fighting on 26 June, the 39th Army's forces, in close conjunction with the First Baltic Front's 43rd Army, liberated Vitebsk and eliminated all of the enemy's attempts to break out of the encirclement.

Thus by the close of 26 June, to the southwest of Vitebsk along the southern bank of the Western Dvina River there remained in existence the main forces of the enemy's Vitebsk group of forces, firmly in the Soviet forces' pincers. Their elimination was the objective for 27 June.

At 1200 on 27 June the German-Fascist command accepted the Soviet ultimatum to surrender unconditionally. Thus on 27 June the enemy's group of forces was essentially eliminated.

The destruction of the enemy's group of forces in the woods near Lake Moshno was completed during 27-28 June.

Beginning on 23 June, as a result of the 39th Army's fighting to encircle and destroy the Vitebsk group of forces, 19,000 German officers and men were captured, including the commander of the LIII Army Corps and the commanders of the 197th, 206th and 246th infantry divisions; 348 guns, two tanks, 1,405 motor vehicles, 249 military depots, and may other prizes were captured. 18,000 officers and men were killed, and 463 guns, 54 tanks and assault guns, and 1,300 motor vehicles, etc., were destroyed. Besides this, in the fighting of 26-28 June the 45th Rifle Corps killed 1,500 German officers and men and captured 2,500 prisoners.

In connection with the defeat of the enemy's Vitebsk and Bobruisk groups of forces and the arrival of the forces of the Second Belorussian Front's 49th Army and the 50th Army's right flank at the Resta River along the Mogilev axis, all of the enemy forces defending to the east and southeast of Orsha were now threatened with encirclement. As early as 25 June, the forces of the 5th and 11th Guards armies were deeply outflanking Orsha from the north, while the 3rd Guards Mechanized Corps had cut the Orsha—Lepel' railroad. The enemy, not disposing of reserves, was forced, under the blows of the cavalry-mechanized group and 5th Army, to begin withdrawing to the west along this sector as early as 25 June. In connection with this, on the night of 26 June the German-Fascist command began the general withdrawal of its forces to the Berezina River.

On 26 June the *front's* main group of forces, consisting of the 5th Guards Tank and 11th Guards armies and the 3rd Guards Cavalry Corps attacked toward Borisov, with the task of preventing the enemy's withdrawal behind the Berezina River, while part of the 11th Guards Army, in conjunction with the 31st Army, was to capture the major Orsha center of resistance. The 5th Army and the 3rd Guards Mechanized Corps, comprising the *front's* right wing, were operating along the Lukoml'—Lake Palik axis, with the task of forcing the Berezina River to the north of Lake Palik.

It was in this situation that the 5th Guards Tank Army, which at 2100 on 25 June was located in the area to the northeast of Bogushevsk, received orders to begin moving into the breach, without waiting for the dawn. At 0120 on 26 June the tank corps' forward detachments, and at 0400 the army's main forces, entered the breach and began moving to the southwest. Having defeated the rear-guard units of the enemy's VI Army Corps, the 5th Guards Tank Army took up the rapid pursuit and by 1800 units of the 3rd Guards Tank Corps had captured Tolochin and Kokhanovo and cut the Moscow—Minsk highway along a 30-kilometer stretch, as well as the Orsha—Minsk railroad. On 26 June the army's formations advanced 50-65 kilometers in fighting. The army was faced by units of the 14th, 95th, 256th, and 299th infantry divisions and the 292nd Panzer Battalion from the High Command reserve. Aside from this, the enemy's 5th Panzer Division was being transferred here from the area west of Kovel'.

This maneuver by the 5th Guards Tank Army into the rear of the enemy's Orsha group of forces had a serious influence on the further course of the operation, because the army's tank corps on 26 June were in the rear of the enemy's XXVII Army Corps, which had been stubbornly defending the Orsha fortified area. Besides this, this maneuver forced the units of the enemy's VI Army Corps, which had been falling back from the front, to sharply turn to the south and southwest and fall back along bad roads in the direction of Starosel'e.

During the course of 26 June the cavalry-mechanized group decisively pursued the enemy in the direction of Senno and Chereya. The greatest success was achieved by the 3rd Guards Mechanized Corps, which captured the Chereya road junction. The 3rd Guards Cavalry Corps liberated Obol'tsy. During the course of the day part of the corps' forces was eliminating the enemy, surrounded in the woods northeast of Aleksinichi and, simultaneously was vigorously pursuing the German-Fascist troops in the direction of Kholopenichi, having advanced here 30-60 kilometers in a day.

The operations of the mobile forces on 26 June were quite successful: the tanks and cavalry, operating in conjunction with the aviation, by the end of the day were 20-40 kilometers ahead of the combined-arms armies.

The combined-arms armies' combat operations unfolded in the following manner.

The 5th Army continued to pursue the enemy in the direction of Senno and Lukoml' and, destroying his scattered units, advanced 25-30 kilometers in a day. By the close of the day, the army's main forces had captured the line Lake Zherinskoe—Uzdorniki—Veino.

On 26 June the 45th Rifle Corps was turned northward and by 1900 had been moved to the line Lake Skryblovo—Zadorozh'e, for covering the army's rear against the enemy's Vitebsk group of forces, a part of which broke out of its encirclement on the morning of 26 June into the wooded area near Lake Moshno.

At night the 11th Guards Army's reinforced battalions began pursuing the enemy, who had begun to fall back, while the main forces of the 16th and 8th guards rifle corps, and the 2nd Guards Tank Corps, began pursuing from dawn on 26 June, making their main attack in the general direction of Borisov.

Formations of the 16th and 8th guards rifle corps, while destroying the retiring enemy's rear guards, advanced 20-25 kilometers to the west.

The 2nd Guards Tank Corps captured Starosel'e, having routed several enemy columns, which were falling back from the Orsha area. The 36th Guards Rifle Corps, having the objective of capturing Orsha, had begun fighting the enemy in the northern and western outskirts of the town by the close of 26 June. At the same time, the 31st Army's 71st Rifle Corps was engaged in stubborn fighting with the enemy, while attempting to break into Orsha from the northeast. As a result of stubborn fighting, by 0700 on 27 June the important rail junction of Orsha had been completely cleared of the enemy. Having lost Orsha, the enemy had been deprived of the last very important strong point in his "Panther" defensive system.

The 31st Army, having established on the evening of 25 June that the enemy's rear guards had begun falling back, immediately took up the pursuit along its entire attack front.

By 0600 on 26 June the enemy's rear guards to the north of the Dnepr River had been thrown back 5-6 kilometers to the west by the formations of the 71st Rifle Corps, and the corps had reached the section of the enemy's defensive zone that ran along the line of the Vitebsk—Orsha paved road. Throughout the day the corps fought to break through this sector, but was unsuccessful. Formations of the 36th and 113th rifle corps, in throwing back the enemy's rear guards, advanced 15-27 kilometers.

On 26 June the 1st Air Army's formations unfolded their pursuit of the enemy from the air, launching attacks against his retreating columns. The air army's main forces were concentrated on supporting the 36th Guards and 71st rifle corps in taking Orsha, and the 39th Army in destroying the encircled Vitebsk group of forces; simultaneously, the air army's fighters covered our forces. In all, on 26 June our aviation carried out 2,014 sorties, of which 1,060 were by assault aircraft and bombers. 16 enemy planes were shot down in air battles.

On 27-28 June the pursuit of the retreating enemy along the *front's* sector unfolded at high speed. The Soviet troops sought to fully consolidate their victory and prevent the enemy from escaping over the Berezina River.

On 27 June the 5th Guards Tank Army pursued the enemy, who was retreating on Borisov. On that day the army advanced 30 kilometers, while its forward units reached the line excluding Chereya—Bobr.

On 28 June the army's tank corps attacked at lower rates of speed than during the preceding days. On that day enemy resistance increased, having thrown the fresh 5th Panzer Division into the battle against the army's forward units. The 5th Guards Tank Army's formations manifested slowness and indecision and an insufficient ability to maneuver in the difficult conditions of the wooded and swampy terrain. By the close of the day the army's 3rd Guards Tank Corps had captured Krupki, having advanced that day a total of ten kilometers along the highway. The 29th Tank Corps reached the Zaprud'ye area.

On 27-28 June the cavalry-mechanized group advanced rapidly, while destroying the retreating enemy units in the difficult conditions of the wooded and swampy terrain, covering 32-45 kilometers in the course of the day. Elements of the enemy's 95th, 299th and 14th infantry divisions, as well as rear and security units of the Germans' Third Panzer and Fourth armies' commanders' offices were retreating before the group. A forward detachment of the 3rd Guards Mechanized Corps' 35th Tank Brigade reached the Berezina River in the Brody area by the close of 28 June and began fighting for the crossing. By 1800 on 28 June the 3rd Guards Cavalry Corps had reached the eastern bank of the Berezina River and had begun preparing to force the river along the Zvinyaty—Bytcha sector. The corps' 32nd Cavalry Division's forward units forced the Berezina River on the march, having seized a bridgehead on its western bank in the area southwest of Zvinyaty.

On 27-28 June the 5th Army's main forces, in conjunction with the cavalry-mechanized group, rapidly advanced, pursuing the retreating enemy, who was determined to get behind the Berezina River and consolidate along a previously-prepared line. The pace of the army's formations' rate of advance reached an average of 25-30 kilometers per day.

By the close of 28 June the forces of the 5th Army had reached the line Svyaditsa—Kopachevka and were 25-30 kilometers from the Berezina River.

The 11th Guards Army, advancing with its main forces behind the mobile groups, consolidated their success and cleared the captured territory of the remnants of the enemy's scattered groups, which remained in the mobile troops' rear. By the close of 28 June the army's forces had captured the line Sokolenka—excluding Bobr—Tolochin.

The mobile group—the 2nd Guards Tank Corps—was operating in the 31st Army's sector. By 2400 on 28 June the corps captured Krucha.

During 27-28 June the 11th Guards Army advanced 50-65 kilometers and, having left the 31st Army behind by 35-40 kilometers, was now deeply enveloping, in conjunction with the 5th Guards Tank Army, the left flank of the enemy's Fourth Army, which was withdrawing to the west south of the Orsha—Borisov railroad. To the south of the railroad, along the Tolochin—Krupki sector, besides units of the Fourth Army's XXVII Army Corps, units of the enemy's divisions defeated north of Orsha had also gathered. As a result, as early as 27-28 June a major enemy group of forces began to very clearly take shape in the Third and Second Belorussian fronts' zone, and which was retreating along poor roads toward the Berezina River. This group of forces was subsequently discovered in the area to the east of Minsk.

During 27-28 June the 1st Air Army's assault and bomber actions supported the *front's* forces, concentrating their main efforts against the enemy's retreating forces; part of the army's forces assisted the 39th Army in completing the destruction of the encircled Vitebsk group of forces; the air army was destroying the enemy along the crossings over the Berezina River and was covering our forces against the enemy's aviation. In two days the 1st Air Army carried out 1,244 sorties, of which 448 were by assault air and bombers; 32 enemy planes were shot down in air battles. The great distance of a number of the army's assault and bomber formations' airfields prevented them from operating west of the Berezina River. Thus they began basing to new airfields, beginning on 23 June.

By the close of the operation's sixth day, while advancing toward Borisov, the Third Belorussian Front's right-wing mobile forces—the 3rd Guards Mechanized and 3rd Guards Cavalry corps—reached the Berezina River. The 5th Guards Tank Army, 5th and 11th Guards and 31st combined-arms armies comprised the *front's* first echelon. The 39th Army, following the elimination of the Vitebsk group of forces, concentrated in the Senno area and to the east in the *front's* second echelon.

By the close of 28 June the *front* had deeply enveloped from the north the main forces of the Fourth Army and the remnants of the Third Panzer Army's right wing, which were withdrawing in the direction of Minsk, having beaten them to the Berezina River.

Thus favorable conditions had been created for the forces of the Third Belorussian Front, for a rapid blow against Minsk and the encirclement, in conjunction with the First and Second Belorussian fronts, of the major enemy group of forces falling back on Minsk.

The Operation's Second Stage

The Forcing of the Berezina River and the Front's Operations for Capturing the Capital of Belorussia—Minsk (29 June–4 July 1944)

The *Stavka* of the Supreme High Command, taking into account the changes in the situation in Belorussia in connection with the successful advance of our forces, issued directive no. 220124, in which the Third Belorussian Front was ordered to force the Berezina River on the march and, by outflanking the enemy's strong points encountered along the way, to rapidly attack toward Minsk, and with its right wing on Molodechno, with the objective of no later than 7-8 July taking Minsk, in conjunction with the Second Belorussian Front, and Molodechno with its right wing. At the same time, it was demanded that the forces intensify their efforts, and the slowness and indecisiveness of the 5th Guards Tank Army's actions were pointed out.

This example shows once again how the *Stavka* of the Supreme High Command exercised direct control of the *fronts* during the course of the operation.

In carrying out the *Stavka* of the Supreme High Command's new directive, the commander of the Third Belorussian Front adopted the following decision.

The main attack in the general direction of Minsk would be made by the forces of the 11th Guards, 5th Guards Tank and 31st armies, along with the 2nd Guards Tank Corps, with the following task: to force the Berezina River on 30 June-1 July and no later than 5 July capture Minsk. The 5th Guards Tank and 31st armies were to move directly on Minsk, along with the 2nd Guards Tank Corps, while the 11th Guards Army would launch its attack on Radoshkovichi and secure the *front's* main group of forces from the north.

The *front's* right wing, consisting of the 5th Army and the 3rd Guards Mechanized and 3rd Guards Cavalry corps, was to force the Berezina River no later than 30 June and develop a rapid offensive on Molodechno, with the task of taking Molodechno on 2 July, with the mobile troops. The 1st Air Army's main forces were to be concentrated along the Minsk axis.

The 39th Army was to remain in the *front's* second echelon.

The troops were assigned the following objectives:

The 5th Army was to complete the forcing of the Berezina River by 1200 on 30 June and vigorously develop the offensive in the direction of Molodechno. One rifle division was to launch an attack to the south in the direction of Zembits, in order to support the 3rd Guards Cavalry Corps' crossing over the Berezina River in the area of the Veselovo State farm.[4]

On 29 June the cavalry-mechanized group was to complete the forcing of the Berezina River and by the close of 2 July capture Vileika and Molodechno.[5]

The 11th Guards Army was to complete the forcing of the Berezina River by 1200 on 1 July. As the army's units reached the Berezina River's western bank, they were to rapidly develop the offensive in the direction of Logoisk and Radoshkovichi.[6]

The 31st Army was also to complete the forcing of the Berezina River by 1200 on 1 July. As the army's units reached the river's western bank, they were to rapidly develop the offensive in the direction of Zhodino, Smolevichi and Minsk. Minsk was to be captured no later than 5 July.

The 5th Guards Tank Army was to force the Berezina River no later than 30 June along the Veselovo—Glivin sector and energetically develop the offensive along the highway's sector, with the objective of taking Minsk, by outflanking it from the north.[7]

---

4   Operational directive no. 005/op, of 30 June 1944, at 0430 hrs.
5   Coded telegram no. 10790/Sh, of 30 June 1944, at 0030 hrs.
6   Operational directive no. 006/op, of 30 June 1944, at 0430 hrs.
7   Coded telegram no. 10789/Sh, of 29 June 1944, at 2230 hrs.

Simultaneously, the *front* commander demanded that each rifle division have no less than one forward detachment, consisting of a rifle battalion mounted on motor vehicles, with artillery and sappers, and to use the for seizing favorable lines.

At the time of the river's forcing the troops had the following amount of crossing equipment:

5th Army: one division light bridge park, consisting of the 4th Assault Engineer-Sapper Brigade, six sets of flotation equipment, 95 inflatable rafts (AZ and small inflatable boats), 118 wooden sapper boats, and 582 Iolshin sacks;

11th Guards Army: one division light bridge park, consisting of the 2nd Guards Assault Engineer-Sapper Brigade, two bow half-pontoon parks in the 8th Pontoon-Bridge Brigade's 51st, 99th and 137th pontoon-bridge battalions (2/3 of a park in each battalion), seven sets of flotation equipment, 120 inflatable rafts (AZ and small inflatable boats), and 300 Iolshin sacks;

31st Army: one light inflatable pontoon park, consisting of the 31st Engineer-Sapper Brigade, one DMP-41 park, consisting of the 8th Pontoon-Bridge Brigade's 90th Pontoon-Bridge Battalion, two sets of flotation equipment, 95 inflatable rafts (AZ and small inflatable boats), 15 wooden sapper boats, and 173 Iolshin sacks;

5th Guards Tank Army: 13 small inflatable rafts;

3rd Guards Cavalry Corps: one light inflatable pontoon park;

3rd Guards Mechanized Corps: the corps had no organic crossing equipment and was supplied with a small number of inflatable rafts.

In the *front's* reserve there was a light inflatable pontoon park, consisting of the 3rd Assault Engineer-Sapper Brigade, the 66th AZ Regiment, 76 small inflatable boats, and 294 wooden sapper boats in the *front's* depots. There is no way that such an amount of organic crossing equipment can be seen as sufficient, especially when taking into account the decisive tasks to be carried out by the *front*.

The *front's* combat operations to force the Berezina River and to pursue the enemy in the general direction of Borisov developed in the following manner.

The cavalry-mechanized group: the 3rd Guards Mechanized Corps' forward units, in conjunction with the 5th Army's newly-arrived formations, was the first to force the Berezina River on 29 June in the Brody area and reached the line Babtsy—Mstizh.[8] During 29 June the 3rd Guards Cavalry Corps held the bridgehead seized on the western bank of the Berezina River, while its main forces were engaged in a firefight for the crossing with units of the enemy's 5th Panzer Division, which were occupying defensive positions along a previously-prepared line along the river's western bank along the Veselovo State Farm—Bytcha sector.

The 5th Army, while pursuing the enemy, advanced 25-30 kilometers, and in the second half of 29 June its forward detachments and vanguard reached the Berezina River. The partisans significantly assisted the rapid advance by our troops along this sector of the front. They pointed out the most convenient routes for moving through the woods and swamps of the Berezina lowlands to the 5th Army's forward units, guarded the crossings and secured the flanks of the advancing columns.

By using the materials at hand and the crossing, seized by the 3rd Guards Mechanized Corps in the Brody area, the rifle corps' first-echelon rifle divisions began forcing the Berezina River. By the close of 29 June four of the army's rifle divisions reached the eastern bank of the river along the 55-kilometer Kal'niik—Veselovo State Farm sector and crossed four rifle regiments over to

---

8   Using the wooden bridge over the river, which had been seized by the forward detachment of the 3rd Guards Mechanized Corps' 35th Tank Brigade.

the western bank. At the same time, bridges were being built and other crossings outfitted to the north of Lake Palik.

On 28-29 June the 5th Guards Tank Army inflicted a defeat on the enemy's fresh reserve—the 5th SS Panzer Division and the 286th Security Division operating with it, as well as other units, in the area to the west and northwest of Krupki. On 29 June the army threw the enemy 40-45 kilometers to the west. By the close of the day the army's forces reached the eastern bank of the Berezina River along the front Veselovo State Farm—Borisov—Bol'shie Ukholody and began fighting for Borisov. The town of Borisov and the western bank of the Berezina River were held along a previously-prepared line by units of the enemy's 5th SS Panzer Division, which had fallen back here, as well as the combat groups of the 95th, 14th, 299th, and 260th infantry, 78th Assault, and 286th Security divisions. The enemy air force, in groups of up to 20 bombers, launched raids on the army's forces.

At 0500 on 29 June the 11th Guards Army renewed the offensive toward the Berezina River, behind the 5th Guards Tank Army. During the day the army's forces, not encountering organized resistance and clearing the captured territory of small groups of the enemy, advanced 30 kilometers.

By the close of 29 June the first echelon of the army's forces was 22-28 kilometers east of the Berezina River.

On 29 June the 31st Army was also pursuing the rapidly retreating enemy, having advanced up to 40 kilometers by the end of the day.

The 1st Air Army carried out reconnaissance as far west as the Minsk meridian, while its *shturmoviks* and bombers destroyed the enemy's retreating forces along the roads and crossings over the Berezina River, and also supported the 5th Guards Tank Army along the northern approaches to Borisov. 422 sorties were carried out in a day and six enemy planes were shot down.

On 30 June the *front's* forces successfully continued crossing the Berezina River to the north of Lake Palik.

At 1200 on 30 June the *Stavka* of the Supreme High Command established a new boundary line between the First Baltic and Third Belorussian fronts: Chashniki toward Lepel'—Pustosel'e, and then to Paraf'yanov (all locales for the First Baltic Front). In connection with this move, the commander of the Third Belorussian Front on 30 June changed the direction of the 5th Army's attack, ordering it to develop the offensive on Dolginovo and Vileika.

Combat operations developed in the following manner.

The cavalry-mechanized group: the 3rd Guards Mechanized Corps, having basically completed the crossing of its main forces over bridges in the area of Brody, occupied Begoml' and Pleshchenitsy. The slowness and lack of organization in the mechanized corps' actions, which could not organize the crossing on the march, should be noted, however. The corps' crossing park fell behind and arrived at the river only on 1 July.

The 3rd Guards Cavalry Corps, employing the seized bridgehead and having broken through the enemy's defense on the river's western bank, captured Lyakhovka. Thus on 30 June the cavalry-mechanized group's main forces had been crossed over to the river's western bank.

During the course of the night and the morning of 30 June, the 5th Army's 72nd and 65th rifle corps continued crossing over to the Berezina River's western bank, while simultaneously destroying the enemy, and were widening their bridgeheads on the river's western bank. These corps' formations advanced 10-14 kilometers in depth. Up to 1500 on 30 June part of the 45th Rifle Corps was fighting in the area south of Chashniki to destroy a composite group of units from the enemy's Vitebsk group of forces, which had broken out of the encirclement in the area of Ostrovno, while the main forces continued their march to the river.

Throughout the day the 5th Guards Tank Army was engaged in stubborn and prolonged fighting for the eastern part of Borisov and the crossings over the Berezina River in the areas south of Borisov and Bol'shie Ukholody. By the end of the day only two motorized rifle battalions had been crossed over the river.

The 11th Guards Army main forces, having advanced 20-25 kilometers, arrived with its main forces during the second part of 30 June at the eastern bank of the Berezina River along the front Veselovo State Farm—Borisov—Glivin. The army's formations, in conjunction with units of the 3rd Guards Cavalry Corps and the 5th Guards Tank Army, began to force the river on the march between 1600 and 1700.

By the close of 30 June the 11th Guards Army's force, in conjunction with units of the 5th Guards Tank Army, captured Borisov and forced the river inside the town.

By 1700 the 2nd Guards Tank Corps' tank brigades had reached the Chernyavka area, where they encountered the enemy's stubborn resistance along a previously-prepared rear defensive line along the western bank of the Berezina River. At 2400 the motorized rifle battalions of all three of the corps' tank brigades, supported by the corps' artillery and tank fire from the eastern bank, crossed the river and occupied a bridgehead on the opposite bank to a depth of up to 1.5 kilometers, while at the same time a high-water wooden bridge, which the enemy had managed to partially burn, was seized.

On 1 July the forces of the Third Belorussian Front finally broke the enemy's resistance along the Berezina River and, having thrown him back to the west, forced the river with their main forces along the entire attack front. By the close of 1 July the first-echelon formations of the 5th, 11th Guards and 31st armies were 15-30 kilometers west of the Berezina River, while the 3rd Guards Mechanized Corps' forward detachment had reached the Viliya River ten kilometers southeast of Dolginovo. The 11th Guards Army operated most successfully on 1 July, and managed during the day to force, besides the Berezina River, the swampy Gaina and Tsna rivers. The army, while inflicting a decisive defeat on the opposing enemy, threw back his units 25-30 kilometers to the west of the Berezina River. As a result of these decisive actions, the army's main forces were 10-15 kilometers ahead of the 3rd Guards Cavalry Corps and the 5th Guards Tank Army, which had been held up on the crossings over the river. The 31st Army also successfully forced the Berezina River to the south of Borisov as far as Chernyavka, inclusively. Its 113th Rifle Corps, in conjunction with the Second Belorussian Front's 33rd Army, was fighting to encircle and destroy the remnants of the Ninth Army's VI and XXVII army corps, which had been pressed along the boundary between the 31st and 33rd armies in the area east and southeast of Ukhvala and which were striving to break through to the crossings over the Berezina River south of Chernyavka.

The 1st Air Army's *shturmoviks* and bombers supported the offensive by our forces on the western bank of the Berezina River and covered their combat formations and crossings against enemy air strikes. At the same time, the air army was destroying the retreating enemy's columns along the Minsk highway west of Borisov.

The enemy air force, in groups of up to 18 planes, bombed our crossings over the river and carried out reconnaissance as far as Orsha.

As a result of the three days' fighting (29 June-1 July), the *front's* main forces forced the Berezina River along the entire attack front and by the close of 1 July had seized an operational bridgehead on the western bank to a depth of 35 kilometers, which enabled us to deploy the *front's* main group of forces and organize a rapid attack on Minsk. The German-Fascist command attached a great deal of importance to holding the Berezina River, with its previously-prepared defensive line, because it was namely this line that was the most powerful along the path of our offensive on Minsk. The enemy was attempting to withdraw in an orderly fashion to this line the forces that had been defeated along the "Panther" line, and with feverish haste was throwing into its defense all available reserves, including police and SS units.

Thanks to the rapid advance of our troops and the rapidity of the forward detachments' actions, the enemy did not succeed in organizing a defense along the western bank of the Berezina River.

As a rule, the units he was bringing up from the rear were subjected to attacks along the march and suffered defeat before they managed to occupy the prepared positions along the river.

During the fighting to force the Berezina River our forces inflicted crushing attacks against the enemy's fresh reserves, such as the 5th Panzer and *Luftwaffe* 22nd Field divisions, as well as a number of individual units transferred from Poland and East Prussia.

The rear and special units of the Third Panzer and Fourth armies, which were falling back along the *front's* sector, suffered heavy losses, as did the combat groups of the previously defeated VI and XXVII army corps.

The enemy put up the most stubborn defense along the Borisov axis, although the rapid forcing of the Berezina River by units of the 3rd Guards Mechanized Corps and the 5th Army, and their arrival on 30 June in the area to the north of Zembin and Pleshchenitsy created a threat to the flank and rear of the enemy's entire Borisov group of forces. At the same time, the forcing of the river by the 11th Guards Army's formations south of Borisov, and their attacks from the south in conjunction with attacks by units of the 5th Guards Tank Army from the northeast, decided the fate of the enemy's Borisov fortified area. By 0300 on 1 July Borisov had been completed liberated from the German-Fascist occupiers.

Thus during the three-day battle to force the Berezina River from the march, the enemy suffered a serious defeat.

The Third Belorussian Front's forces had carried out their immediate objective, assigned by the *Stavka* of the Supreme High Command.[9] The opportunity now presented itself to rapidly develop the main blow by the left wing on Minsk, and the right wing on Molodechno.

Based upon the existing operational situation, on 1 July the *front's* military council issued a special directive to the troops, in which it was stated that "The enemy has suffered a major defeat and at the present time does not dispose of fresh or any kind of large-scale reserves; the enemy's rank and file are demoralized. We now have the opportunity to transform the success already achieved into the complete rout of the German-Fascist forces along our axis. For this, we need to sharply increase the speed of the offensive and immediately achieve greater forcefulness in our troops' actions. We must, without allowing the enemy to come to his senses, tirelessly inflict paralyzing blows, manifest more daring, persistence and toughness in pursuing and defeating the enemy. All the party-political work must be directed at supporting the realization of this task."

Having suffered a defeat along the Berezina River, the enemy facing the *front* was forced to fall back in disorder on Molodechno and Minsk, thus exposing even more the left flank and rear of its forces falling back in the Second Belorussian Front's sector on Minsk from the east. Striving to save its forces from encirclement, the German-Fascist command was hurriedly moving security and police units from Poland and East Prussia to the Minsk area and was putting the Minsk forti-fied area in order. In attaching great importance to the Minsk—Molodechno railroad as the most important communications route of the Minsk group of forces, on 3 July the enemy command moved the 17th Infantry Division from Army Group North (from the Narva area) to the area of Molodechno.

The enemy, in falling back from the Berezina River, clung to the natural lines, inhabited locales and road junctions. The combat activity of his aviation increased.

However, due to the Hitlerite command's miscalculations, Army Group Center did not at the present stage dispose of any kind of significant operational reserves. Reserve formations were being transferred from other sectors of the Soviet-German front and were fed into the fighting as they arrived; this gave our forces the opportunity to defeat the enemy in detail and enabled us to increase the rate of advance to the west from the Berezina River.

---

9 Operational directive no. 220124, of 28 June 1944.

After forcing the river, the Third Belorussian Front's forces, without any sort of pause and in the course of the fighting to expand the captured bridgeheads, began to carry out their subsequent task, which had been defined in the *Stavka* directive of 28 June. While breaking the resistance of the enemy's Borisov group of forces, the *front's* forces were to develop the main attack on Minsk, while the right wing would attack in the direction of Dolginovo and Vileika. Along the *front's* center, along the Molodechno—Smorgon' axis, the cavalry-mechanized group, which had the assignment of taking the Smorgon'—Molodechno—Krasnoe area by the close of 3 July, was to energetically attack.

The 11th Guards Army, which was part of the *front's* main group of forces and whose main forces were attacking from the Logoisk area in the direction of Radoshkovichi, was to support the attack on Minsk from the north.

The Third Belorussian Front's combat operations to carry out the tasks assigned by the *Stavka*, unfolded in the following manner.

Throughout 2 July the cavalry-mechanized group swiftly pursued the enemy in the direction of Smorgon', Molodechno and Krasnoe.

On 2 July the 3rd Guards Mechanized Corps forced the Viliya River on the march and at 0530 occupied Vileika, and by 1000 Kurinets, while its forward units advanced during the day 65-80 kilometers. By the close of 2 July the corps' units had reached the Minsk—Vilnius railroad between Smorgon' and Krasnoe.

In view of the commander's of the 3rd Guards Cavalry Corps' poor control of the cavalry-mechanized group, at 0300 on 2 July the 3rd Guards Mechanized Corps was subordinated directly to the *front* commander, and the cavalry-mechanized group ceased to exist as a major mobile field force for operational purposes.[10]

On 2 July the 5th Army, taking advantage of the 3rd Guards Mechanized Corps' success, was rapidly advancing in the direction of Dolginovo and Vileika. During the day its main forces advanced 32-35 kilometers.

On 2-3 July along the Minsk axis the Third Belorussian Front's decisive operations unfolded, which had the goal, in conjunction with the troops of the First and Second Belorussian fronts, of liberating the capital of Soviet Belorussia—Minsk, and encircling to the east of the city a major group of enemy forces, consisting of the Fourth, Third Panzer and Ninth armies.

By the close of 2 July the forces of the 11th Guards and 31st armies, having thrown back the remains of the enemy's Borisov group of forces to the west, captured the line excluding Lishitsy—Logoisk—Sarnatsk—Smolevichi.

The 5th Guards Tank Army, having completed the crossing over the Berezina River, during the day moved forward and by the end of the day its main forces had reached the Padoki area, while its forward detachments had advanced to Ostroshitskii Gorodok. The enemy, while putting up powerful resistance to the army's offensive, was slowly falling back along the road from Ostroshitskii Gorodok to Minsk, covered by tanks. The forward brigades of the army's tank corps did not cease fighting at night, and on the morning of 3 July began fighting the enemy on the approaches to Minsk from the north, between Ostroshitskii Gorodok and Minsk.

According to a decision by the *front* commander, adopted on the night of 3 July, the mobile forces operating along the *front's* left wing were to take Minsk, while the consolidation of their success was entrusted to the forward detachments of the 31st Army's rifle divisions. The 11th Guards Army was to support the mobile forces' attack on Minsk from the north, and its forward detachments were to assist the 3rd Guards Cavalry Corps in seizing Molodechno.

---

10 Coded telegram no. 121, of 2 July 1944.

The fighting to liberate Minsk from the German-Fascist occupiers broke out on the night of 3 July and unfolded in the following manner.

The 31st Army, having broken through the enemy's intermediate defensive line from the march on the night of 3 July, was rapidly advancing on Minsk, with the 2nd Guards Tank Corps and mobile detachments from the first-echelon divisions in front of its main forces.

On the morning of 3 July the 2nd Guards Tank Corps reached the northeastern and eastern outskirts of Minsk from the direction of the highway. Here the corps encountered an organized defense, which the enemy was conducting with the forces of two regiments of infantry, supported by tanks and assault guns. The city was defended by General Gotberg's group (the remnants of the 78th, 256th and 260th infantry divisions), units of the 5th Panzer Division, the 2nd, 24th, 25th, and 26th police regiments, and various special elements. Minsk had previously been prepared for all-round defense. Thanks to the decisive actions of the 2nd Guards Tank Corps and the 31st Army's recently-arrived forward detachments, and with the support of the 5th Guards Tank Army, the enemy's resistance was quickly broken and as early as 0730 there was already fighting in the city center. By 0930 on 3 July Minsk had been completed cleared of the German-Fascist occupiers. "The forces of the Third Belorussian Front, as the result of a rapid offensive and deep outflanking maneuver from the northwest, have occupied the enemy's very important strategic defensive center along the western direction—the capital of Soviet Belorussia, Minsk."[11]

At around 1300 on that same day the First Belorussian Front's 1st Guards Don Tank Corps reached the southeastern outskirts of Minsk. Behind it were arriving the 3rd Army's forces.

Thus on 3 July the encirclement of a major group of German forces, which had been withdrawing in the Second Belorussian Front's sector, was completed. The Third Belorussian Front's left-wing forces, in close coordination with the First Belorussian Front's right-wing forces, securely stood across the group's route of retreat. In the encirclement were the main forces of the Fourth Army and the remnants of the Third Panzer and Ninth armies, which had been thrown back by the Third and First Belorussian fronts into the Second Belorussian Front's sector.

On 3 July a *front* order placed the securing of the *front's* left wing and the boundary with the Second Belorussian Front on the 31st Army. The 113th Rifle Corps was used by the army commander for this purpose: one of the corps' rifle divisions was to advance to the Berezina River along the Bol'shie Ukholody—Chernyavka sector, with the task of taking up defensive positions facing to the west, while the other division was to move to the Plissa River, with the task of defending in the Smolevichi area, facing south.

The 5th Guards Tank Army, after capturing Minsk, pursued the enemy withdrawing to the west and, having defeated, with units of the 3rd Guards Tank Corps, two enemy columns withdrawing to Rakuv, had by the end of the day captured the Zaslavl'—Ratomka—Zabolot'e area.

On 3 July the 11th Guards Army advanced 30-35 kilometers and captured Radoshkovichi. The enemy along the army's sector was falling back rapidly to the west and putting up weak resistance.

The 5th Army, in pursuing the enemy in the direction of Smorgon', advanced 30-32 kilometers on 3 July and captured Vileika.

The mobile forces (3rd Guards Mechanized and 3rd Guards Cavalry corps) operating along the *front's* right wing were not able on 3 July to break the enemy's stubborn resistance in the areas of Smorgon', Molodechno and Krasnoe with their own forces and, while bringing up their main forces to these areas, prepared for a repeat attack on the morning of 4 July. Besides this, a serious shortage of fuel tied down our mobile troops.

The enemy, taking into account the great importance of the Minsk—Vilnius railroad, which linked army groups North and Center, stubbornly defended the indicated area. The defense of

---

11 Third Belorussian Front's combat report no. 292/OP, of 4 July 1944, at 0110.

Smorgon' and Molodechno was entrusted to the fresh 170th Infantry Division, to the commander of which were subordinated all the units that had fallen back here. Particularly active in this area was the enemy's aviation, which carried out up to 150 sorties against the 3rd Guards Mechanized Corps alone.

3 July was a great day for the *front*, because on this day the internal encirclement front was closed around the enemy's group of forces located east and southeast of Minsk, and an external encirclement front began to form with the arrival of the forces of the 5th, 11th Guards and 5th Tank armies, as well as part of the 31st Army's forces, at the line Gorodyshche—Vileika—Radoshkovichi—Zaslavl'. By 2200 on 3 July the distance between the encircled enemy group of forces east of Minsk and the line of the external front in the direction of Volma and Rakuv reached 50 kilometers.

During 2-3 July the 1st Air Army was destroying the enemy's forces in the Molodechno—Minsk area and strafing his columns, which were withdrawing along the Minsk—Rakuv and Minsk—Volma roads.

Throughout 4 July the *front's* forces continued to develop the offensive, throwing back the enemy and pushing the external front away from Minsk to the west. At the same time, part of the 31st Army's forces, in conjunction with the Second Belorussian Front's 33rd Army, were strengthening the internal encirclement front, so as to prevent the breakthrough of the enemy's encircled group of forces to Minsk from the east.

On 4 July the 5th Army advanced 24-26 kilometers and forced the Naroch' River from the march.

The *front's* right-wing mobile forces were engaged in heavy fighting with the enemy's units defending the Smorgon'—Lebedzev—Molodechno—Krasnoe area.

By 1530 on 4 July the 3rd Guards Mechanized Corps had thrown the enemy out of Smorgon'.

In the course of two day the 3rd Guards Cavalry Corps, supported by the mechanized corps' tanks, was engaged in stubborn fighting to take the enemy's fortified strong points of Lebedzev and Molodechno, which had been occupied by the 170th Infantry Division, which had arrived from the depth, and the enemy's units that had fallen back to this area, although the corps was not successful. During these days the cavalry was not supported adequately by the *front's* aviation, or by the commander of the 16th Guards Rifle Corps, one of whose rifle divisions had reached the Krasnoe area as early as 3 July.

Throughout 4 July the 11th Guards Army continued to pursue the enemy with its two first-echelon corps in the direction of Molodechno and advanced 20-35 kilometers. By the end of the day the army had captured the line Krasnoe—Petrishki.

At dawn on 4 July the 5th Guards Tank Army renewed the offensive, having the task of capturing the Rakuv—Volma—Svoboda area.

During the 25 June-4 July period the army had irretrievably lost 172 tanks and self-propelled guns and had 150 tanks and self-propelled guns remaining in service.

A difficult situation was developing in the 31st Army's sector on 4 July, which grew out of the necessity of developing the army's operation from Minsk to the west and, at the same time, to prevent the encircled enemy from breaking through to Minsk from the east, and to begin destroying him in conjunction with the Second Belorussian Front.

In order to prevent the enemy's movement to the Minsk highway in the Smolevichi area, and toward Minsk from the east, the commander of the 31st Army ordered the 113th Rifle Corps on 4 July to move into the Smolevichi area. By 1800 a part of the 36th Rifle and 2nd Guards Tank corps was to deploy for the objective of covering Minsk from the east.

As subsequent events showed, these measures for preventing the enemy's breakthrough toward Minsk were obviously insufficient and the concentration of the 113th Rifle Corps in Smolevichi was not justified by the situation. The enemy, having crossed the Berezina River on 1-2 July in the

Chernyavka area and to the south, was falling back in three groups to the west under the blows of the Second Belorussian Front, while the remnants of the VI and XXVII army corps, numbering about 10,000 men, were falling back on Volma. Units of the XXXIX Panzer and XII Army corps were falling back to the south. Many of this group of forces' units had covered 130-150 kilometers in fighting and, having felt the attacks by Soviet troops, had lost their equipment and were mixed together. All of the heavy artillery, and part of the divisional artillery, as well as a large number of tanks and assault guns were blown up due to a lack of fuel and shells, while the remaining combat equipment had a limited supply of shells. All of this sharply reduced the combat capability of the enemy's units.

The retreating enemy group of forces had the task of breaking through and linking up with its forces in the Minsk area, while the German-Fascist command, desiring to lift the troops' spirits, fooled the soldiers, telling them that several German panzer divisions had broken through the Russian front and were 10-15 kilometers away. The attack to break through the front was to be launched through Minsk and to the south. It follows that the concentration of the 113th Rifle Corps in the Smolevichi area, for exclusively defensive purposes, was not justified by the operational situation. This could be explained by the poor work of the 31st Army's intelligence and overestimating the importance of the Smolevichi area, which supposedly faced the greatest threat from the retreating enemy. However, the chief threat to Minsk was growing directly from the east and, when the commander of the 31st Army figured this out, he issued an order to the 113th Rifle Corps at 1900 on 5 July to rapidly begin a movement to the Minsk area. This took up additional time and the commander of the 31st Army could no longer gather sufficient forces for massed attacks against the surrounded enemy.

The fighting against the encircled enemy group of forces in the 31st Army's sector on 4 July unfolded in the following manner.

During the second half of the day the retreating enemy's forward units began to approach Minsk from the east and southeast. Along the Smolevichi axis it was quiet, as should have been expected.

At 1400 the 2nd Guards Tank Corps' tank brigade, reinforced with rifle troops, attacked the enemy's forward units east and southeast of Minsk and halted their movement toward the city.

During the night of 4-5 July columns containing the remnants of the Fourth Army's XXVII and other army corps began to arrive in the area southeast of Minsk.

On 4 July the German-Fascist troops continued to fall back to the west along the external front, in the 31st Army's sector.

The formations of the 71st and 36th rifle corps were pursuing the enemy, while consolidating the success of the 5th Guards Tank Army, operating ahead.

Throughout 4 July the indicated corps' rifle divisions advanced 15-25 kilometers and captured the line Petrishki—Novyi Dvor.

The events of 4 July marked the end of the Third Belorussian Front's Vitebsk—Minsk operation, which had lasted 12 days. On 5 July the *front* began the new Vilnius—Kaunas operation, with part of its forces continuing to take part in the elimination of the enemy's group of forces encircled east of Minsk.

Results and Conclusions

1.   As a result of the Vitebsk—Minsk operation, conducted by the forces of the Third Belorussian Front from 23 June through 4 July 1944, the opposing enemy had a decisive defeat inflicted upon him. Simultaneously, in conjunction with the First and Second Belorussian fronts, the enemy's retreating group of forces was surrounded in the area east of Minsk.

The encirclement east of Minsk of the main forces of the Fourth, and the remnants of the Third Panzer and Ninth German-Fascist armies, thrown back here during the Third and First Belorussian fronts' offensive, had an enormous significance for the entire subsequent course of the Soviet forces' operation in Belorussia and led to the elimination of Army Group Center's main forces. Along the Third Belorussian Front's sector, the enemy could not gather any kind of powerful group of forces from his reserves and oppose them to the *front's* forces before the line of the Neman River.

In the course of the Vitebsk—Minsk operation 12 infantry, four security, two *Luftwaffe* field, one assault, one panzer, and one mechanized divisions were defeated, as well as many security and police units and elements.

The enemy's overall losses for the entire Vitebsk—Minsk operation are shown in table 1.

The Third Belorussian Front also lost a significant number of men, weapons and equipment. See table 2.

One should pay attention to the fact that during the breakthrough of the tactical zone, that is, 23-24 June, 234 tanks and self-propelled guns were lost, and 279 in the operation's subsequent days.[12]

2.   As a result of the Vitebsk—Minsk operation, the *front* advanced 280-300 kilometers and on July 4 reached the line Mokshitsa—excluding Smorgon'—Molodechno—Krasnoe—Rakuv—Valma. The *front's* forces overcame a number of barriers on the march, among which the largest were the Luchesa, Berezina and Viliya rivers. Along the western bank of the Berezina River to the south of Zembin, our forces broke through a previously-prepared defensive line, which included in its fortification system the Borisov center of resistance.

Nor were the German-Fascist command's hopes of holding for a long time such towns as Orsha, Borisov, Minsk, and others, which had been prepared for all-round defense, justified. These towns were captured from the march by our forces. Such a success was the result of the crushing attacks by our forces, which employed enveloping maneuvers in the fight for these towns.

Despite the difficult terrain conditions, the average rate of advance during the Vitebsk—Minsk operation was 20 kilometers per day; this also includes the time spent on forcing the Berezina River. To the west of the Berezina River the operation's rate during the pursuit phase rose to 30 kilometers per day. The mobile forces covered an average of 30-35 kilometers per day.

3.   The encirclement and subsequent destruction of Army Group Center's main forces and the Third Belorussian Front's arrival at the line Smorgon'—Molodechno—Rakuv on 4 July created the conditions for the subsequent development of the offensive along the Vilnius axis for the purpose of completing the liberation of the temporarily-occupied Soviet territories, lying along the Third Belorussian Front's sector, from the German-Fascist forces.

---

12 Central Ministry of Defense Archives, fond 241, opis' 13834, delo 25, pp. 13-14.

Table 1. The German-Fascist Forces' Losses in the Vitebsk—Minsk Operation[13]

Losses	Killed and Wounded	Captured	Destroyed	Captured	Total
23-30 June					
Personnel	75,470	31,454	–	–	106,924
Tanks	–	–	95	342	437
Planes	–	–	92	–	92
Guns	–	–	1,121	709	1,830
Mortars	–	–	406	410	816
1-7 July					
Personnel	32,860	15,481	–	–	48,341
Tanks	–	–	210	85	295
Planes	–	–	43	–	43
Guns	–	–	306	503	809
Mortars	–	–	97	292	389

Table 2. The Third Belorussian Front's Losses in the Vitebsk—Minsk Operation

	Killed	Wounded	Destroyed and Damaged	Total
23-30 June				
Personnel	11,014	40,512	–	51,526
Tanks	–	–	318	
Planes	–	–	113	
Guns	–	–	28	
Mortars	–	–	31	
1-7 July				
Personnel	4,699	11,772	–	16,471
Tanks	–	–	195	
Planes	–	–	28	
Guns	–	–	15	
Mortars	–	–	17	

4.   As a result of the operation, significant territories of Soviet Belorussia were liberated from German-Fascist occupation, including the capital of Minsk, which was the enemy's center of resistance along the western direction.

5.   The Third Belorussian Front's Vitebsk—Minsk operation began with the breakthrough of the enemy's continuous defensive front simultaneously along two sectors, with the development of the attack in depth, and the encirclement of the enemy's Vitebsk group of forces in conjunction with the neighboring First Baltic Front.

During the operation's first stage, 23-28 June, the *front's* forces broke through the enemy's defense and reached the line of the Berezina River, having fulfilled the objective assigned the *front*

---

13   Central Ministry of Defense Archives, fond 241, opis' 13834 ss, delo 25, pp. 81-83.

by the *Stavka* of the Supreme High Command. During the second stage, 28 June-4 July, the *front's* forces pursued the enemy, liberated Minsk, and reached the line Smorgon'—Molodechno— Rakuv, having created favorable conditions for the liberation of Soviet Lithuania.

6.   The rapid breakthrough of the enemy's defense southeast of Vitebsk by the 39th and 5th armies had a decisive influence on the entire operation's success, as well as the skillfully conducted encirclement and destruction of his Vitebsk group of forces. The rapid pace of the breakthrough along the *front's* right wing and the arrival of the 5th Army in the Bogushevsk area on 24 June enabled us to commit the *front's* cavalry-mechanized group into the breach that day, without any particular delays, and from the morning of 26 June to augment the success by the commitment of the 5th Guards Tank Army, which by the end of the day had reached the communications of the enemy's Orsha group of forces, thus cutting off its route of retreat to the west.

The 11th Guards Army, which had taken upon itself the main weight of breaking through the enemy's most solid defense along the Orsha axis, also skillfully employed the success of the *front's* right wing by outflanking the Orsha center of resistance from the north, which enabled us to later capture Orsha by attacks from the north and west.

The breakthrough of the enemy's defense by the combined-arms armies was carried out by massive attacks along narrow sectors and conducted quickly and without significant losses. The width of the breakthrough sectors along which, on the morning of 23 June, the enemy was attacked, came to six kilometers in the 39th Army, approximately 12 kilometers in the 5th Army, 10.5 kilometers in the 11th Guards Army, and nine kilometers in the 31st Army. The overall length of the breakthrough sectors was 37 kilometers.

The success of the operational breakthrough was decided by:

- the splitting of the opposing enemy group of forces into separate and isolated centers, followed by the combined-arms armies' employment of bold maneuver of their main forces against the enemy's flanks and rear, and;
- the rapid augmentation of the success by the commitment of the *front's* mobile groups into the breach and their development of a headlong attack into the operational depth.

7.   The operation was characterized by the high rate of its conduct, which along the main axis reached up to 20 kilometers per day, and 13 kilometers on the secondary sector. By conducting the operation at such a high rate of speed, the Third Belorussian Front prevented the enemy from coming to his senses following the attack in the tactical zone, and while pursuing eliminated all his attempts to put his forces in order and restore his offensive front by means of reserves brought up from the depth. The Soviet forces, in carrying out a parallel pursuit, unfailingly preempted the enemy in occupying his intermediate lines. For example, if the enemy on 28 June was still along the Drut' River along the 11th Guards and 31st armies' attack sectors, then the *front's* cavalry-mechanized group had already reached the Berezina River by that time, while the 5th Army's infantry was located 25-30 kilometers to the east of the river.

8.   The tactical breakthrough of the enemy's heavily fortified and deeply echeloned defense was carried out by broadly outflanking and enveloping the enemy's strong points in the main defensive zone, and along the intermediary and rear defensive lines. At first the success achieved, including that along the secondary axes, was decisively developed by the commitment of the second echelons into the battle. Wide-ranging maneuver during the breakthrough and the rapid augmentation of our efforts by the second echelons prevented the enemy from winning time to bring up his reserves to the breakthrough sector. During the offensive, our forces split up the enemy's groups

of forces into separate and isolated groups, encircled and destroyed the enemy, and prevented his withdrawal from the tactical zone.

The forward battalions' battle of 22 June had great significance. As a result of this battle, the grouping of the opposing enemy was defined along the *front's* entire sector, and the forward edge of his defense along the breakthrough sectors precisely defined. Besides this, the 5th Army's forward battalions broke the enemy's defense to a depth of 2-4 kilometers. This circumstance decisively influenced the success of the offensive by the army's main forces.

9.   The encirclement of the enemy's Vitebsk group of forces was accomplished as the result of rapid and coordinated attacks by the 39th and 43rd armies' main forces in the direction of Gnezdilovichi. Characteristic of this was the fact that the encirclement was accomplished in the tactical zone of the enemy's defense at a depth of 20 kilometers, by the forces of the combined-arms formations, while in the majority of operations these tasks were resolved by the mobile forces, followed by their relief by the rifle units. It should also be noted that simultaneous with the encirclement, the enemy's Vitebsk group of forces had been split up into two parts, which speeded up the process of its elimination.

Our forces, upon completing the encirclement, immediately set about destroying the enemy. For this purpose, the offensive by the 39th and 43rd armies did not let up, and the enemy forces' encirclement area was constantly being squeezed. Individual units were broken off the enemy group of forces (for example, in the Ostrovno area). Attacks were made along the entire perimeter of the encirclement, including along the secondary axes. Along those sectors where the enemy undertook attacks for the purpose of breaking out of the encirclement, the Soviet forces held their lines and prevented the breakthrough of the internal encirclement front. A significant role in the enemy's destruction was played by the 1st Air Army's assault and bomber aviation, which in the course of 25-27 June alone carried out about 700 sorties for this purpose. The combined-arms formations' artillery carried out massive fire onslaughts, destroying the encircled enemy's personnel and equipment. All of these methods justified themselves and found broad employment in a number of subsequent operations of the Great Patriotic War.

The remnants of the enemy's routed formations that broke out of the encirclement were once again encircled and eliminated by our forces that blocked their path of retreat.

The elimination of the enemy in the Vitebsk area is an example of encircling and destroying a large enemy group of forces (five divisions) along the boundary between two *fronts*. This example is also instructive in the sense that it was replete with night battles, both while encircling the enemy and, mainly, during his destruction. A large number of battles took place in conditions of wooded and swampy terrain.

10.   The *front's* forces took up the pursuit of the enemy after having defeated his opposing group of forces and his immediate operational reserves.

The *front's* mobile groups advanced ahead during the course of the operational pursuit, and then—at a distance of 18-35 kilometers—by the combined arms armies' first echelons. The armies' operational organization and the rifle corps' combat formations during the pursuit were, as a rule, in two echelons, except for the 31st and 5th Guards Tank armies, which operated in a single-echelon formation.

Our forces pursued the enemy in the following order. Forward detachments were sent ahead from each first-echelon division, usually consisting of one reinforced rifle battalion on motor vehicles. These detachments disposed of sufficient mobility and were sent ahead for seizing road junctions and crossings over rivers, for the purpose of cutting off the enemy's retreat. A rifle division's vanguard regiment, moving 3-5 kilometers ahead of the division's main forces, independently, or in conjunction with the division's forward detachment, would destroy the enemy's rear guards.

When collisions occurred with the retreating enemy's larger columns, the rifle division's main forces would deploy for battle.

The combined-arms armies' formations carried out their pursuit 16-18 hours per day and during the hours of darkness rested and brought up their rear services and ammunition. Specially designated forward detachments operated at night.

11.   The Third Belorussian Front's role in the operation to encircle the enemy's main group of forces consisted of the deep envelopment of the retreating enemy from the north. The envelopment concluded with the rapid leap of the *front's* mobile formations toward Minsk, the capture of that city and the creation here of an internal encirclement front in conjunction with the First Belorussian Front.

12.   The *front's* cavalry-mechanized group was a powerful mobile field force, disposing of sufficient shock strength and maneuverability for operations in difficult wooded and swampy terrain. The rapid forcing of the Berezina River by the group's formations had great operational significance for the entire operation's success, as it secured the crossing of the river by the *front's* right wing on the march and enabled us to develop attacks to outflank the enemy's Borisov group of forces from the north and northwest. To the west of the Berezina, the group carried out the headlong pursuit of the enemy at a speed of 30-45 kilometers per day, defeated the German-Fascist forces in detail, disrupted their coordination, and prevented the enemy from organizing a defense along intermediary lines.

The cavalry-mechanized group's formations usually broadly employed maneuver and outflanked the enemy's strong points encountered along the way. Getting drawn into prolonged fighting (as was the case, for example, in the Smorgon' area) led to a decrease in the offensive pace.

Control of the cavalry-mechanized group was exercised by the commander of the 3rd Guards Cavalry Corps, through his headquarters, which led to overloading the corps' headquarters and negatively told on the quality of the group's control as a whole. As a result of this, the close cooperation between the corps was often lacking during the operation. The *front* commander was essentially forced to take over control of the 3rd Guards Mechanized Corps following the forcing of the Berezina River. However, despite the difficulties of troop control, the employment of the cavalry-mechanized group in a *front* offensive operation justified itself in the conditions of the wooded and swampy terrain.

13.   As regard the operation's materiel-technical support, the *front's* forces experienced significant difficulties with supply, particularly after reaching the line of the Berezina River and to the west. The shortage of fuel was particularly felt, as a result of which in the operation's final days the troop formations, particularly the motorized ones, began to become elongated and lose their mobility. For example, the 3rd Guards Mechanized Corps, which cut loose from the railroad by 180-200 kilometers, and having the most difficult supply conditions, remained without fuel on 2-3 July and was stretched out for 60 kilometers.

14.   The Vitebsk—Minsk operation is instructive in its positive experience of forcing a significant water obstacle such as the Berezina River by the *front's* forces.

The combined-arms armies' forces crossing over, aside from their organic equipment, widely employed the materials at hand, thanks to which the forcing of the Berezina was carried out along the *front's* entire sector and by the entire mass of forces that had reached the river. The success and high speed of the river's forcing were guaranteed by the bravery and decisive actions of the infantry and the troop sappers.

The forcing of the Berezina by the combined-arms armies was conducted in the following manner. The rifle corps forced the river along sectors 8-20 kilometers in width, with two rifle divisions in the first echelon and one in the second. Powerful forward detachments were allotted from each first-echelon rifle division, which, without getting involved in fighting with the retreating enemy's rear guards, quickly reached the Berezina River along a broad front and began to force it from the march. The river's forcing by the forward detachments was carried out on the materials at hand, while employing a small amount of organic inflatable rafts. The infantry, under the leadership of the troop sappers, threw together small rafts and crossed over on them, under the cover of artillery, mortar and machine gun fire.

Units of the rifle division's first echelons, just like the divisions' forward detachments, forced the river on their own, from the march. By this time the light organic equipment had been brought up to the river, from which the regimental and divisional sappers outfitted landing parties on rafts and ferries. The regimental and anti-tank artillery, mortars and ammunition, as well as the combat train, were crossed over on ferries made out of light organic equipment, or logs. Rifle subunits swam over on boards, logs, inflatable rafts and Iolshin sacks. Beside this, fords were outfitted in the 5th Army.

The crossing of the divisional artillery, reinforcement artillery and self-propelled guns, as well as the formations of the rifle corps' second echelon and the armies' second echelons was carried out over pontoon bridges.

A good deal of attention was devoted to the troops' anti-aircraft cover on the crossings over the river and anti-aircraft artillery was massively employed along the main axis. However, cover by fighter aviation was insufficient, as a result of which the enemy destroyed the crossings from the air and held up the crossing of the *front's* forces for significant amounts of time along some sectors.

While forcing the Berezina River, the anti-aircraft artillery weapons were used in the following manner (see table 3).

Such an amount of anti-aircraft equipment was insufficient, because in some cases the enemy's aviation successfully operated against the *front's* crossings.

Of the negative features present during the forcing of the Berezina River, the following should be noted:

- the 5th Guards Tank Army, having reached the Berezina River, did not search for weak spots in the enemy's defense on the opposite bank and began to cross the river in places where the enemy had his strongest defense;
- the 3rd Guards Cavalry Corps, having reached the Berezina River, did not carry out a maneuver to outflank the enemy's fortifications on the opposite bank, but rather attempted to force the river along a narrow 7-8 kilometer sector. The corps commander did not try to broaden the forcing front by employing his neighbors' success;
- the 2nd Guards Tank Corps was forced to break off crossing its tanks across the Berezina River, because the floating bridge, which had been laid down, turned out to be weak and collapsed under the weight of the tanks crossing over it:
- crossing the river by the 11th Guards Army's second-echelon corps and the 5th Guards Tank Army's tank corps took place, at times, in a disorganized fashion. The troops' consecutive arrival at their intermediate and jumping-off areas was not observed. The entire mass of troops was backing up near the crossings in the Borisov area and traffic jams were created, because the handling capacity of one pontoon bridge limited the troops' crossing over to the river's western bank, while the poorly organized traffic control system failed to prevent such a backup of forces.

A number of combined-arms and tank commanders did not only not keep order at the crossing, but themselves disrupted it, by striving to get their formations (for example, the 11th Guards Army headquarters did not call for the passage of the 5th Guards Tank Army over its crossings in the areas of Borisov and Bol'shie Ukholody) over the bridge as quickly as possible.

A major shortcoming in organizing the forcing of the Berezina River was the insufficient provisioning of the tank army and cavalry-mechanized group with crossing equipment, particularly pontoon parks for crossing tanks and self-propelled guns. Despite the fact that the operational plan called for the arrival of the *front's* mobile forces at the western bank of the Berezina on the sixth day—that is, four days before the arrival of the combined-arms armies at the river—neither the 5th Guards Tank Army nor the cavalry-mechanized group received any pontoon equipment from the *front*. This planning mistake was not fixed during the operation, when it became apparent that the cavalry-mechanized group was moving well ahead of the combined-arms armies. The situation was basically saved by the fact that the cavalry-mechanized group captured two bridges (at Brody and Studenka) over the river, although one of them (Studenka) could be used, because of damage, only after restoration.

Table 3. The Distribution of Anti-Aircraft Weapons

Armies and Targets to be Covered	PVO Formations and Units	76 & 85mm Guns	37mm Guns	20 & 25mm Guns	Heavy Machine Guns
	Army Equipment				
5th Army					
crossings over the Berezina River	33rd Anti-Aircraft Div (High Command Reserve)	13	71	–	52
the army's forces	726th Barrage Balloon Rgt	–	16	4	11
3rd Gds Mechanized Corps	1480th Anti-Aircraft Rgt (High Command Reserve)	–	15	–	16
11th Guards Army					
crossings over the Berezina River	34th Anti-Aircraft Div (High Command Reserve)	15	68	–	50
the army's forces	1280th Anti-Aircraft Rgt (High Command Reserve)	–	15	–	16
31st Army					
crossings over the Berezina River	66th Anti-Aircraft Div (High Command Reserve)	16	65	–	49
–the army's forces	1478th Barrage Balloon Rgt	–	16	–	16
Total in the Armies		44	266	4	210

Armies and Targets to be Covered	PVO Formations and Units	76 & 85mm Guns	37mm Guns	20 & 25mm Guns	Heavy Machine Guns
Front Equipment					
The crossings over the Berezina River along the Veseloe State Farm—Bytcha sector	48th and 20th anti-aircraft divs (High Command Reserve)	28	134	–	103
The crossings over the Berezina River along the Borisov—Bol'shie Ukholody sector	295th Anti-Aircraft Artillery Division (High Command Reserve)	–	–	–	12
Total *Front* Equipment		28	134	–	115

On the whole, despite the existing shortcomings, the forcing of the Berezina River was carried out successfully and the troops' operations were characterized by a high level of morale, and the commanders and staffs skillfully resolved the great and complex tasks they faced.

4

The Second Belorussian Front's Mogilev—Minsk Offensive Operation (23 June-13 July 1944)

The Operation's First Stage

The Front's Breakthrough of the German-Fascist Forces' Defense along the Pronya River, the Forcing of the Dnepr River and the Defeat of the Enemy's Mogilev Group of Forces (23-28 June 1944)

The Second Belorussian Front carried out its offensive operation along a secondary axis, which left a certain imprint on the character of its operations. The offensive was carried out with fewer forces. The breakthrough, in accordance with the operation's idea and plan, was carried out along the 49th Army's sector, where the *front's* main forces of men and materiel had been concentrated.

A reconnaissance in force was carried out before the offensive by the main forces. The goal of the reconnaissance was to determine the outline of the forward edge of the defense, and the enemy's fire system and disposition of forces. Besides this, in the 49th Army's sector the reconnaissance subunits were given tasks to seize a bridgehead along the western bank of the Pronya River.

The actions of each reconnaissance detachment, consisting of a company or battalion, were supported by 2-3 artillery battalions and 2-3 mortar batteries.

The reconnaissance in force began at 0400 on 22 June, following a 30-minute artillery preparation.

In the 33rd Army the 70th Rifle Division's reinforced rifle battalion operated the most successfully and took the enemy's second trench and consolidated there.

In the 49th Army the 330th Rifle Division's reconnaissance company was particularly successful and, having crossed the Pronya River, broke into the enemy's trenches and by 1200 had consolidated along the river's western bank.

In the 50th Army's sector the 385th and 380th rifle divisions' reinforced rifle battalions reconnoitered the enemy's defensive system and took prisoners.

As a result of the reconnaissance in force, the enemy's fire system was defined, as well as the engineer structures and obstacles along the forward edge. It was established that the first line of trenches was chiefly occupied by covering forces and that the enemy's main forces and equipment were in the second and third trenches. Prisoner interrogations enabled us to define the disposition of the enemy's forces the *front's* main attack sector. The reconnaissance in force confirmed that the Pronya River's flood plain was passable everywhere for our infantry, but only along certain sectors for artillery and tanks, without engineer outfitting.[1]

---

1 Combat report no. 794 of the 49th Army's headquarters, 22 June 1944, at 1930 hrs. Delo 3, vol. 2, p. 337.

During the night of 22-23 June the 4th Air Army carried out a night air preparation along the 49th Army's breakthrough sector. The aviation operated in three echelons. The first echelon, armed with incendiary bombs and KS combustible mixture created zones of fires in the target areas, so as to make it easier for the remaining planes to reach them. The second echelon, armed with demolition and fragmentation bombs, suppressed the enemy's anti-aircraft artillery in the target area. The third echelon launched bombing raids against the enemy's personnel and weapons.

The artillery preparation was carried out in accordance with the plan for the artillery offensive, but due to the fog and observation difficulties, began two hours later than the schedule called for.

With the first powerful artillery onslaught along the forward edge of the enemy's defense, 12 specially allotted and prepared reinforced rifle companies lunged forward along the breakthrough sector, and by 0930 had forced the Pronya River. In overcoming the mine and barbed-wire obstacles, they quickly broke into the enemy's first trench, where the enemy kept only covering forces. Not having encountered serious resistance, the rifle companies, keeping close to the explosions of our artillery shells, moved forward and captured the second and, in places the third and fourth, enemy trenches.

The sappers, taking advantage of the rifle companies' success, as well as our artillery fire, quickly laid down 78 assault walkways for the infantry and began to lay down bridges for the artillery and tanks. The main forces began crossing over to the river's western bank along assault bridges and, in part, on the materials at hand. By the end of the artillery preparation, the 49th Army's first-echelon divisions had mainly concentrated in the first and, partially in the second and even third, enemy trenches and had attacked in the general direction of Zatony, Shestaki and Ozer'e.

The infantry's vigorous advance forced our artillery to shorten the length of the attack's artillery preparation.

At 1000 tanks and self-propelled artillery, operating with the 69th and 70th rifle corps, also began to cross the Pronya River. However, by the end of the artillery preparation it became clear that only individual tanks and self-propelled artillery pieces had crossed the river, while the majority of them had gotten stuck in the river's swampy flood plain. Of the four crossings laid down to accommodate heavy loads, two crossings (for the 81st and 62nd rifle corps) were out of action. Along the approaches to the 69th and 70th corps' crossings, the soil in the river's flood plain had been ground up by vehicles and had become impassable. The laying of a path in the river's swampy flood plain was delayed and not only the crossing of tanks and self-propelled artillery was delayed, but the artillery supporting the infantry was delayed as well. Anti-tank guns were crossed over on the materials at hand. In essence, the rifle units began their attack without support tanks and guns.

The first-echelon formations, employing the fire of the artillery located along the river's eastern bank, moved forward and by 1200 had solidly consolidated along the Pronya River's western bank.

The artillery was subsequently able to accompany the infantry with its fire only after shifting its firing positions. As a result, the attacking units were temporarily without reinforcements and their advance was delayed.

The enemy, having gained a respite, was able to throw his tactical reserves into the breakthrough sector and carry out counterattacks. These counterattacks, following stubborn fighting, were repulsed, although the enemy was able to restore his fire system along the entire front and began to put up stubborn resistance.

At 1600 the corps commanders, with the exception of the commander of the 81st Rifle Corps, committed their second echelons. A sufficient quantity of artillery and tanks had still not been crossed over to the river's western bank, and the coordination that had been disrupted during the offensive had not been fully restored and thus the commitment of the corps' second echelons did not yield any effective results.

Due to the absence of organized infantry support for the offensive by the artillery and tanks, the 49th Army's shock group did not fulfill its task for the day—the arrival at the Basya River.

The unfavorable meteorological conditions on the morning of 23 June prevented our bomber aviation from carrying out its planned raid 20 minutes before the start of the attack, and supporting the attacking infantry with raids against the enemy's forces. The weather improved during the second half of the day and our aviation took part in the fighting. Its main efforts were directed at destroying the personnel and combat equipment in the immediate depth of the enemy's defense.

The 33rd and 50th armies' formations attempted to carry out an attack in small detachments, but had no significant success.

In summing up the results of the offensive's first day, the *front* commander pointed out significant shortcomings in the troops' actions. The loss of troop control in the corps, divisions and, particularly at the regiment and battalion level was noted, as was the falling behind of the tanks, self-propelled artillery, divisional artillery, and reinforcement artillery behind the infantry, which delayed its advance. The crossings for the artillery and tanks had been particularly badly prepared. The engineer units failed to cope with their task of supporting the timely advance of the tanks and artillery across the Pronya River.

The *front's* mobile group, which had not begun to operate, was subordinated to the commander of the 49th Army.[2] The *front* commander ordered that the mobile group be given the following task: upon the rifle divisions' mobile detachments reaching the Basya River, the mobile group was to leap forward and by the close of 24 June reach the Dnepr River along the sector excluding Shklov—excluding Mogilev, and by the morning of 25 June seize a bridgehead along its western bank, which it would maintain until the arrival of the 49th Army's shock group.

During the night of 23-24 June the 49th Army's shock group carried out reconnaissance and brought up reinforcements and its rear establishment.

On the morning of 24 June, following a 30-minute artillery preparation, the offensive resumed. The enemy began to fall back under our troops' blows to a previously-prepared defensive zone along the western bank of the Basya River.

In order to preempt the enemy's arriving at that line, mobile forward detachments from each rifle division began an energetic pursuit. Having defeated the enemy, they seized bridgeheads over the Basya River in the areas west of Chernevka and north of Chernovtsy.

As a result of the forward detachments' actions and the successful offensive by the 49th Army's main forces, supported by artillery, tanks and aviation, the *front's* shock group significantly expanded the depth of the breakthrough of the enemy's defense during 24 June and reached the eastern bank of the Basya River, having advanced almost 22 kilometers during the offensive's two days. The main zone of the German-Fascist troops' defense had been pierced and conditions created for the subsequent outflanking of the enemy's forces, which were defending opposite the 33rd and 50th armies.

The *front's* mobile group, as previously constituted, began crossing the Basya River at 1900 on 24 June, southeast of Bubikovo.

During the night of 24-25 June the enemy began to pull back his main forces to the Dnepr River, while attempting to delay our offensive along the Basya River with powerful rearguards.

The 49th Army's forces, without halting the offensive, forced the river during the night and by the close of 25 June had reached the Resta River.

---

2   The mobile group consisted of the 23rd Guards Tank Brigade, a rifle battalion, the 1434th Self-Propelled Artillery Regiment of 85mm guns, the 13th Anti-Tank Artillery Brigade, an independent motorized reconnaissance company, the 9th Pontoon Battalion, the 1479th Independent Anti-Aircraft Artillery Regiment, and two sapper battalions from the 1st Guards Assault Brigade. The group's actions were supported by an assault air division.

The mobile group, having lost about ten armored vehicles and up to 200 men, was located along the line of the army's first-echelon rifle divisions.

The 33rd Army's right flank was defending its line, while its left-flank units were attacking, widening the breakthrough sector and covering the 49th Army's right flank.

The 4th Air Army greatly assisted the success of the shock group's forces. During the night of 24-25 June it carried out 226 sorties. The night bombers launched raids against the enemy's retreating columns, as well as the crossings over the Dnepr River in the Mogilev area. During the daylight hours of 25 June the air formations, in conjunction with the ground forces, sought to destroy the retreating enemy units through assault and bomber raids, while at the same time tried to prevent the enemy from moving his personnel and equipment along the railroads.

Thus in the course of the first three days the *front's* forces broke through the heavily fortified enemy defense throughout its entire tactical depth. As a result of the three days' fighting, the *front's* shock group, while overcoming the enemy's resistance, advanced up to 30 kilometers and expanded the breakthrough sector to 75 kilometers in width and forced the enemy to begin a general withdrawal.

On the morning of the offensive's fourth day the offensive continued along the entire front.

The 49th Army's main forces, having in front of them the forward detachments, reinforced with tanks and artillery, had reached the Dnepr River by the close of 26 June. Attempts by the 69th, 81st and 70th rifle divisions to force the Dnepr from the march, with their main forces, were unsuccessful. The enemy tried to destroy the crossings being laid down with fire from the river's western bank. The army command was unable to organize the crossing of his forces at night in places having been seized by the forward detachments.

The aviation directed its main efforts toward supporting the 49th Army's forward detachments, which had seized a bridgehead on the western bank of the Dnepr River east of Mogilev, and operated against the enemy's crossings in the areas of Mogilev and Bykhov.

The enemy, covered by rearguards, was pulling back his main forces to the Dnepr's western bank. The enemy aviation slightly increased its activity.

On the following day the 33rd Army forced the Dnepr River from the march and, overcoming the resistance by the enemy's rearguards, advanced 36-38 kilometers that day. The towns of Kopys' and Shklov were liberated from the enemy during the course of the fighting.

The 49th Army, having brought up its artillery and engineering units during the night and, having laid down crossings, forced the Dnepr River along its entire front by the end of 27 June and had begun fighting along the western, northern and eastern outskirts of Mogilev and had cut off the enemy's retreat from Mogilev to the west. The 70th and 62nd rifle corps' formations were fighting to destroy the enemy surrounded in Mogilev.

By the morning of 27 June the 50th Army's main forces had reached the eastern bank of the Dnepr River and its forward detachments forced the river from the march. Part of these forces subsequently began fighting in Mogilev at 1900, while other units, having outflanked Mogilev, cut off the enemy's path of retreat to the southwest.

The enemy's columns retreating to the west became the objects of our air attack along the Mogilev axis, as well as his artillery, which was interfering with our forces' crossing.

Thus by the close of the offensive's fifth day the Second Belorussian Front's forces had cleared the eastern bank of the Dnepr River of the enemy and had forced the river along the right flank, having thrown the enemy back from his defensive zone that ran along the western bank. Mogilev had been surrounded and fighting had broken out on its streets with the enemy's 12th Infantry Division and various panzer and security units.

On 28 June the *front's* forces continued their pursuit, with the task of reaching the Drut' River by the end of the day with the forward detachments along the *front's* entire sector.

The 33rd Army, while successfully repelling the enemy's counterattacks, was fighting by the end of the day along the line Mal'kovo—Zelenyi—Solodovka—excluding Prudki. Fighting was simultaneously going on to destroy to destroy the enemy's Kopys' group of German-Fascist forces (the remnants of the 14th, 95th, 256th, and 259th infantry divisions) west and southwest of Kopys'.

The 49th Army's main forces continued to pursue the retreating enemy, and two of its divisions, in conjunction with the 50th Army's units, were completing the destruction of the 12th Infantry Division in Mogilev. By the close of the army's corps' rifle divisions, along with their reinforcements, were fighting along the line Prudki—Pobeda—the northern and southern outskirts of Mogilev.

By the close of 28 June, the 50th Army, having captured Bykhov, had reached the line excluding Tishovka—Dosovichi—Gorodets—Barsuki.

Thus by 28 June the Second Belorussian Front had successfully carried out its immediate and subsequent objectives, laid down by the *Stavka* of the Supreme High Command on 31 May 1944, that is, they had defeated the enemy's Mogilev group of forces and captured the town of Mogilev.

The remnants of the Fourth Army's defeated divisions (78th Assault, 260th, 110th, 31st, 267th, 57th, 337th, and 14th infantry divisions, 25th and 18th motorized divisions, and the "Feldherrnhalle" panzer group), as well as the Third Panzer and Ninth armies' divisions (299th, 95th and 256th infantry, and 707th Security divisions), which had been thrown back by the First and Third Belorussian fronts' successful offensive into the Second Belorussian Front's sector, and covered by rearguards, were hurriedly falling back behind the Berezina River.

The *front's* forces now faced another task: to tirelessly pursue the enemy and prevent him from consolidating along his prepared defensive lines, and to destroy his personnel and equipment.

The Operation's Second Stage

The Pursuit of the Enemy along the Minsk Direction, the Front's Operations to Liberate the Capital of the Belorussian SSR—Minsk, and for the Encirclement and Destruction of the Enemy's Group of Forces East of Minsk (29 June-13 July 1944)

In the *Stavka* of the Supreme High Command's directive no. 220123, of 28 June, the *front* was given the following objective: to force the Berezina River from the march and, by outflanking the enemy's strong points encountered along the way, develop a rapid offensive in the general direction of Minsk; no later than 7-8 July, in conjunction with the left flank of the Third Belorussian Front and the right flank of the First Belorussian Front, capture Minsk and reach the western bank of the Svisloch' River.[3]

The accomplishment of this objective became the basic concern of the second stage of the *front's* operation.

In order to guarantee an unremitting pursuit, the *front* commander ordered the following: to allot in each army mobile detachments, consisting of 1-2 rifle divisions and reinforcements.[4] The

---

3   Central Ministry of Defense Archives, fond Second Belorussian Front for June-July 1944.

4   The forces and composition of the mobile detachments were as follows:

    a) the 33rd Army—the 222nd Rifle Division, with the 1197th Self-Propelled Artillery Regiment, 873rd Anti-Tank Artillery Regiment, 206th Engineer-Sapper Battalion, 307th Guards Mortar Regiment, two anti-aircraft batteries, and an automobile battalion;

    b) the 49th Army—two rifle divisions (64th and 199th), an anti-tank artillery brigade, two guards mortar regiments, two engineer battalions, a tank brigade, two self-propelled artillery regiments, and two automobile battalions (one of these was from the *front* reserve);

    c) the 50th army—two rifle divisions (380th and 362nd), three anti-tank artillery regiments, two guards

mobile detachments' immediate task was to reach the Berezina River and seize a bridgehead on its western bank by the close of 29 June.

During 29-30 June the *front's* forces continued to pursue the enemy, but the mobile detachments thus created were not able to break forward and carry out their tasks.

The 33rd Army's right-flank forces were fighting to destroy the remnants of the 14th, 95th, 299th, 260th, 110th, and 256th infantry, and 25th Motorized divisions. The enemy, outflanked by the left-flank units of the Third Belorussian Front's 31st Army and the 33rd Army's right flank, was seeking to break out of the Krugloe—Krucha—Bovsevichi area to the west.

The 49th Army, following the forcing of the Drut' River, was pursuing along the Mogilev—Minsk road, while overcoming the fierce resistance of the main forces of the enemy's Fourth Army, which were retreating here. As a result, by the close of 30 June the 69th Rifle Corps' 153rd Rifle Division, employing the forest roads, covered about 50 kilometers in the course of two days. Its forward detachment, while outflanking centers of resistance along the roads and forest paths, reached the Berezina River north of Berezino on 30 June and forced it from the march. The enemy's attempts to throw the forward detachment back to the eastern bank were not successful. The detachment was stoutly holding the bridgehead until the arrival of the main forces.

By the close of 30 June, the 50th Army's forward formations had reached the eastern bank of the Berezina River along the sector Vol'nitskii Bor—excluding Svisloch'.

By this time the Third Belorussian Front's 31st Army and the First Belorussian Front's 3rd Army had outflanked the enemy's Fourth Army and completely isolated it from units of the Third Panzer and Ninth armies. The German-Fascist command, faced with the threat of encirclement, began to withdraw units of the Fourth Army behind the Berezina River along the front Ozdyatichi—Berezino.

By the close of 30 June the Second Belorussian Front's main forces were 25-30 kilometers from the Berezina River. They were to then force the river from the march and continue to pursue the enemy to the west.

On 1 July the *front's* forces along the right wing, in the area north of Bovsevichi, were destroying the units of the 260th and 110th infantry and 25th Motorized divisions, the 501st Panzer Battalion, and the 667th Assault Gun Brigade, while the center and left wing continued to pursue the enemy's forces falling back behind the Berezina River.

On that day the 33rd Army's force completely cleared the eastern bank of the Drut' River along the Teterki—Lubyany sector and captured the village of Shepelevichi.

The 49th Army's forward detachments encountered stubborn resistance in the Pogost area and were forced to wage heavy fighting to capture the crossings over the Berezina River near Berezino.

The 50th Army, while continuing to pursue the enemy, by the end of the day had forced the Berezina River in the area of Vol'nitskii Bor.

Thus the *front's* forces, having begun to pursue the enemy on 29 June, following his defeat along the Dnepr River and the Mogilev area, by the close of 1 July had reached the Berezina River and forced it in several places. During the course of three days these forces overcame the eastern part of the Berezinskoe Poles'ye, while advancing at a rate of 25 kilometers per day, and inflicted serious losses on the enemy.

The enemy, taking advantage of the terrain, which teemed with a large number of rivers, as well as swampy wooded areas and a poorly developed road net, was able to fall back behind the Berezina River.

---

mortar regiments, a mortar regiment, two sapper battalions, and two auto battalions (one of these was from the *front* reserve).

On 2 July the *front's* forces, while overcoming the enemy's stubborn resistance, by the end of the day had advanced 12-30 kilometers along the right and left flanks and reached the Berezina River in the center.

On 2 July the troops of the Third Belorussian Front attacked Minsk from the north and east and, with the active assistance of the partisans, crossed the upper reaches of the Berezina River, and by the end of the day the *front's* mobile formations had broken into the northeastern outskirts of Minsk.

To the right, the formations of the Third Belorussian Front's 31st Army had by this time reached Smolevichi.

To the left, the First Belorussian Front's 3rd Army had reached Pukhovichi.

Thus by 3 July the Third and First Belorussian fronts had created all the conditions for closing off the escape routes to the west of Army Group Center's main forces, which were located east of Minsk.

The German Fourth Army's units, following the severe defeat inflicted on them east of the Berezina River, and losing their combat steadiness, continued to fall back. The enemy's units and formations got mixed up. The retreat's central leadership was disrupted and each unit sought to break out to the west as quickly as possible.

On 3 July the Second Belorussian Front's pursuit of the enemy continued.

For 15 hours part of the 33rd Army's forces fought against the enemy group of forces pinned in the woods in the area southeast of Ozdyatichi. This group of forces consisted of the remnants of the 110th and 260th infantry and 25th Motorized divisions, the 321st Combat Group, the 56th and 663rd security battalions, and the 514th Panzer Battalion. The enemy was seeking to break through our troops' combat formations and get out of the encirclement. However, all his attempts were without result. In all, 4,000 enemy officers and men were killed in this area. The army's main forces, continuing the offensive to the west, advanced 25 kilometers.

On 3 July the 49th Army completed forcing the Berezina River along the entire front, occupied Berezino and advanced another 25-40 kilometers to the west.

The 50th Army's forward detachments reached the eastern outskirts of Minsk, while its main forces were moving to the west along the Mogilev—Minsk road.

Units of the 19th Rifle Corps, attempting to encircle the enemy falling back from the Berezina River, deployed facing northeast, north and northwest of Gorki, where they got involved in stubborn fighting. During the day they repelled six of the enemy's infantry counterattacks from a battalion to a regiment in strength.

During 3 July the forces of the Third and First Belorussian fronts, by launching joint attacks, along with the Second Belorussian Front's 50th Army, captured Minsk after fierce fighting.

As a result of the Third and First Belorussian front's deep flanking maneuver, as well as the actions of the Second Belorussian Front, which had been attacking from the Berezina River toward Minsk, not only was the capital of the Belorussian SSR liberated, but the enemy's retreat routes to the west were cut off; Army Group Center's main forces were surrounded east of Minsk.

In accordance with the *front* commander's order, 4 July was spent in regrouping the troops for the purpose of subsequently pursuing the retreating enemy and destroying the encircled group of forces.

The *front's* forces, encountering weak enemy resistance, advanced another 20-30 kilometers on 4 July.

The 33rd Army's 62nd Rifle Corps reach the line Mostishche—Mal'tsy and deployed facing south, thus cutting off the escape route north of the enemy's group of forces encircled in the area of Pekalin.

The 50th Army continued to pursue and destroy the scattered enemy groups. By the close of 4 July its 19th Rifle Corps was fighting along the line Barsuki—Velikii Bor—Volma, with its front facing north and northeast, while beating off insistent attacks by the enemy trying to break through to the south.

The 49th Army, while overcoming difficult terrain sectors, pursued the enemy throughout the day and by the close of the day was approaching Grebenka.

Following the forcing of the Dnepr River, the combat activities of the 4th Air Army's units resembled an aviation pursuit of the retreating enemy. Simultaneously, the aviation took an active part in fighting the enemy's encircled groups of forces. During the 29 June-5 July time period 2,072 sorties were carried out, of which 645 were at night.

The main stream of the enemy's retreating columns moved along the Mogilev—Minsk road, which goes through wooded and swampy terrain along almost its entire extent. Assault aviation, in observing the movement of the enemy's columns along the roads, selected those sectors, from which deployment to the sides was impossible, created traffic jams along these sectors, and then routed the enemy columns with a series of consecutive strikes.

During the pursuit phase, the 4th Air Army command accorded its assault divisions complete freedom in choosing their targets. This increased the effectiveness of the aviation's operations against the retreating columns. As a result of our aviation's ceaseless attacks against the retreating columns, the destruction of bridges and creating traffic jams on the roads, the movement of auto transport along the Mogilev—Minsk road during the day was almost completely halted and the enemy was forced to switch to the country roads or move only at night.

The aviation's actions prevented the enemy from consolidating along the previously-prepared line along the western bank of the Berezina River and also assisted in the defeat of his units in the areas south of Krugloe and southeast of Ozdyatichi.

The almost complete lack of resistance by the enemy's fighters, as well as the retreating columns' weak anti-aircraft defense, considerably facilitated the increased effectiveness of our assault aircraft.

During 3-4 July the pursuit phase was completed of the retreating enemy forces, who sought to preempt the forces of the Third and First Belorussian fronts and get through Minsk in time and thus avoid encirclement. But they did not manage to do this. Huge masses of enemy forces were cut off and surrounded east of Minsk. The forces of the Second Belorussian Front then set about to destroy them.

The Elimination of the German-Fascist Forces Surrounded in the Area East of Minsk (5-13 July 1944)

In the *Stavka* of the Supreme High Command's directive no. 220130, of 4 July, the Second Belorussian Front was assigned new objectives—the further offensive to the west and the *front's* arrival in the Bialystok area and the completion of the destruction of the enemy's group of forces surrounded to the east of Minsk.

According to directives nos. 220128 and 220129, at 2400 on 4 July the First Belorussian Front's 3rd Army was to be subordinated to the commander of the Second Belorussian Front. At 2400 on 5 July the Second Belorussian Front's 33rd Army was to be subordinated to the Third Belorussian Front.

The *Stavka* of the Supreme High Command's directives' of 4 July demanded that all four *fronts* conduct new *front* offensive operations directed at completely driving the enemy from the territory of the Soviet Union.

On 5 July the *Stavka* began carrying out its further plans, through which it was planned to realize during the second phase of the Belorussian operation.

The Second Belorussian Front's forces were faced with great and complex tasks. One the one hand, they were to complete the Mogilev—Minsk operation and eliminate the major enemy group of forces encircled east of Minsk; that is, to complete the tasks of the multi-*front* operation's first stage. On the other hand, they were to begin the new, Bialystok, operation and pursue the enemy retreating to the west.

The main mass of the Fourth Army's remnants, as well as a part of the enemy's Third Panzer and Ninth armies' formations (units of the XXVII, XII and XXXV army, and XXXIX and XLI panzer corps) had concentrated by the morning of 5 July in several groups in the woods east and southeast of Minsk. The largest group was in the wooded area southeast, east and northeast of Volma. The overall number of encircled troops reached as high as 100,000 men.

According to the testimony of the German-Fascist generals captured by the Soviet army in July 1944, and captured documents, it was established that the encircled enemy group of forces was supposed to break through to the west, bypassing Minsk from the north and south.

There were essentially no enemy units along the outer front facing our 3rd Army, which was attacking toward Minsk. Only individual units from the enemy's Fourth Army, which had not yet fallen into the encirclement, were putting up insignificant resistance to the 3rd Army. Before 5 July the enemy had not been able to bring up fresh units for closing the breaches that had formed opposite the Second Belorussian Front as a result of the encirclement of Army Group Center's main forces east of Minsk. In the beginning of July a special "blocking formation" had been created, having the task of delaying the Soviet army's offensive and gathering up the scattered remnants of the defeated German divisions. The 50th Infantry, 28th Light Infantry and 12th Panzer divisions were quickly transferred to the area west of Minsk from German and other fronts.

On 5 July the forces of the Second Belorussian Front, with the arrival of the 33rd and 50th armies' units in the area east of Minsk, completed the formation of the internal encirclement front around the enemy. The forces of the Third and First Belorussian fronts, having advanced to the west of Minsk, simultaneously created a solid external front, which was located more than 50 kilometers from the internal one.

On orders from Hitler's headquarters, the overall command of the enemy's troops encircled east of Minsk was first entrusted to the commander of the XXVII Army Corps, General Folkers. Later the commander of the XII Army Corps, Lieutenant General Mueller, was appointed temporary commander of the Fourth Army.[5] On 5 July the surrounded forces were ordered to break out of the pocket in the direction of Dzerzhinsk. The enemy's attempts to get out of the encirclement were initially more or less organized. On the night of 5 July the enemy's transport aviation dropped ammunition and food to the encircled German units. Groups of 500-2,000 and more men were formed out of remnants of the defeated divisions. These groups, having set up blocking positions, combat security and rearguards from among the most combat-capable units, began to move to the west and southwest.

Two groups were the most powerful and numerous: the first, led by the commander of the 78th Assault Division, General Traut, began to break through to the south in the direction of Smilovichi and Rudensk, and the second, led by the commander of the XII Army Corps, General Mueller, sought to break out south of Minsk, in the direction of Dzerzhinsk and Baranovichi.

The commander of the Second Belorussian Front, taking into account the developing situation, issued an order, according to which the 33rd Army was to outflank the encircled group of forces with its right flank (two divisions) from the north, with the task, in conjunction with the 50th Army's right flank, of encircling and destroying the enemy in the woods north and northeast of Volma, while the remaining forces were to reach the line Drachkovo—Smilovichi. According to this same order, the 50th Army was to rapidly advance its right flank to the Volma area and, in conjunction with the 33rd Army's formation, to destroy the encircled enemy, while its main forces

---

5   The commander of the defeated Fourth Army, General Tippelskirch, and his staff, succeeded in getting away to the west and was cut off from his forces.

would continue advancing to the Minsk area. The 49th Army was to continue the offensive in the direction of Drachkovo and Apchak.

On 5 July particularly stubborn battles broke out with General Mueller's group.

Three of the 33rd Army's rifle divisions, which were attacking north of Pekalin and Topilovo, and covered by small detachments from the south, were completing the encirclement of the enemy from the north.

The 50th Army's right-flank units were involved in stubborn fighting with the enemy's encircled units, while its left flank continued moving to the west.

The 49th Army, having organized its forces into columns, was marching to the west, destroying the scattered enemy groups of forces with part of its forces.

On the whole, on 5 July the *front's* forces, in destroying the encircled enemy group of forces, inflicted a significant defeat on it in the Pekalin—Volma—Apchak area.

The following day the encircled enemy made desperate efforts to break out of the encirclement. A group of about 2,000 officers and men, with ten guns, attempted to break through to the south. However, in the area southeast of Smilovichi the group was defeated by the forces of the 49th Army and, led by General Traut, the commander of the 78th Assault Division, surrendered.

During 6 July the group under the commander of the XII Army Corps, General Mueller, while suffering heavy losses, attempted to break through in the direction of Gatovo, but was unable to break out of the pocket in its full strength. The group was defeated and thrown back by Soviet units that had been brought up from the Minsk area. A part of this group (about 800 men) managed to force the Ptich' River near Samokhvalovichi and reach Ozero, where it ran into the headquarters of the 50th Army and was destroyed by an army mobile detachment. Another part of this group (about 1,000 men) broke through over the Ptich' River and reached Dabrynevo, but on 7 July was also destroyed.

Thus during 5-6 July the encircled enemy suffered a significant defeat and he was split up into several isolated groups, which had lost all sense of organization and control. Due to the absence of ammunition and fuel, the enemy abandoned all his combat equipment and artillery. Each group had to operate independently.

During the 7-9 July time period our units continued to defeat the enemy's scattered detachments in the area southeast of Minsk.

The *front* commander, in his directive no. 3313/Sh of 7 July pointed out the shortcomings and slowness of the troops' actions in eliminating the encircled and scattered enemy groups and demanded that the enemy's defeat be speeded up.

On 7 July in the Sinelo—Mikhailovichi—Volma area 1,500 officers and men were captured and up to 2,000 killed, and southeast of Samokhvalovichi up to 5,000 enemy officers and men were killed and captured. By the close of 7 July an enemy group of up to 8,000 men was fighting units of the 38th Rifle Corps in the Podgai area. Another group, consisting of up to 7,000 men, was attempting to break through to the northwest and by the end of 7 July was fighting with units of the 113th Rifle Corps along the Bol'shoi Trostenets—Yel'nitsa sector. A third group of up to 1,000 men broke through toward Samokhvalovichi.

On 7 July the 33rd Army organized the perimeter defense of Minsk.

On 8 July a large enemy group from the Gatovo area attempted to break through to the southwest. The enemy initially managed to press back our units and take Samokhvalovichi, but subsequently, as the result of a stubborn battle, the enemy was defeated withdrew in disorder to the northeast.

The 50th Army's 38th Rifle Corps, having left individual detachments along the Samokhvalovichi—Podgai line, concentrated its main forces by the end of the day in the area 14 kilometers east of Dzerzhinsk. The enemy, taking advantage of the weakening of our forces along the line of the Ptich' River, crossed the river and reached the Ozero area. Thus the army, as a result of the premature withdrawal of the 38th Rifle Corps, stretched out the elimination of the encircled enemy and enabled him to infiltrate to the west, southwest and south.

On 8 July the enemy attempted to simultaneously break through not only to the south and southwest, but to the north as well, through the 33rd Army's sector. The remnants of the German-Fascist 14th, 31st and 267th infantry and 25th Motorized divisions concentrated in the woods south of Smolevichi and on the morning of 8 July began to move through the Moscow—Minsk highway along the Dinarovka—Korolev Stan sector, toward the northwest. The Third Belorussian Front's formations and units, in conjunction with the partisans, completely eliminated this group during the course of 8-9 July.

Following several days of stubborn fighting, a large part of the remnants of the enemy's defeated units capitulated. On 8 July, in the area southwest of Dzerzhinsk, Lieutenant General Mueller, the commander of the XII Army Corps and temporarily commanding the Fourth Army, surrendered. In light of the hopeless situation, more than 3,000 officers and men capitulated along with him. Having agreed on the conditions of capitulation, Lieutenant General Mueller issued the following order:

> Soldiers of the Fourth Army east of the Ptich' River!
>
> Following several weeks of heavy fighting, our situation has become hopeless.... Our combat capability has fallen to a minimum and we have no hope of supply. The Russian forces, according to a report of the High Command, are near Baranovichi. The crossings over the rivers are closed to us, without hope that they can be captured by our men and equipment.
>
> We have suffered enormous losses in wounded and those who have fled.
>
> The Russian command has pledged to do the following: a) to take care of the wounded; b) to let the officers retain their swords and medals, and the soldiers their medals.
>
> They demand from us that all weapons and equipment be gathered and surrendered in good condition. Let there be an end to the senseless bloodshed!
>
> I therefore order to cease military operations from this instant. Groups numbering from 100 to 500 men, under the leadership of officers, must be created. The wounded must attach themselves to these groups.
>
> Get control of yourselves, show our discipline and help to carry out measures to realize this order as quickly as possible. It is necessary to circulate this order in written and spoken form by all means. Lieutenant General Mueller.

This order was the beginning of the organized surrender of the enemy forces that had been surrounded. However, the surrender stretched out for an entire week, for not all German commanders agreed to carry out the order and, besides, its circulation was accompanied with great difficulties, because the German-Fascist forces, which had been cut up into groups and scattered among the forests, often lacked communications with their headquarters and neighbors.

During the second half of 9 July the *front* commander gave the 49th Army commander the task of eliminating the remnants of the enemy's encircled group of forces by the close of 11 July. At 0000 hours on 10 July the army was reinforced from the *front* reserve with the 307th and 343rd rifle divisions, as well as the 50th Army's 38th Rifle Corps. The 49th Army was to transfer the 69th and 81st rifle corps to the 50th Army.[6] Aside from this, the task of eliminating the encircled enemy was refined. It was first of all required that the enemy be prevented from breaking out to

---

6 Order no. 4013/Sh of the *front* commander, 9 July 1944.

the west and southwest and it was ordered that the enemy's routes of retreat over the Ptich' River in the Samokhvalovichi area be cut off.

In accordance with the *front's* directive, the 49th Army's headquarters drew up an operational plan for eliminating the encircled enemy. The operation's goal was the elimination of the scattered enemy groups along the *front's* sector. In order to carry out the task of destroying the encircled enemy, the 38th Rifle Corps (110th and 385th rifle divisions), five independent rifle divisions (380th, 369th, 324th, 307th, and 343rd) and NKVD[7] rear security troops (218th, 87th and 219th border regiments) were committed. Each formation was assigned a sector and their arrival at their assigned lines was determined.

The operational plan described in detail the methods to be used.

For example, the elimination of individual enemy groups emerging from the encirclement was to be carried out by mobile detachments, consisting of a reinforced rifle company. Each detachment was to have auto transport for movement, or horses and wagons. Each division, which had been designated for eliminating the encircled groups, was to prepare nine mobile detachments, based upon a calculation of three detachments per rifle regiment. It was planned to throw the detachments into the battle, so as to cut off the enemy's routes of retreat, and then to destroy him. The detachments' objectives were to be first reconnoitered from the ground and air. Each division was assigned an aviation wing for carrying out air reconnaissance. The pilots were to report information on the enemy to the division commander's command post by means of pennants, or landings made in convenient areas. The divisions' main forces were to move in columns along the main axes, in readiness to fight, in case the enemy's counterattacks needed to be repelled, in order to destroy or capture him. The detachments' and main forces' actions were to be rapid and daring.

According to the plan, the attached wings of Po-2[8] aircraft were to carry out reconnaissance in the interests of the divisions they served. A regiment of Po-2s was at the disposal of the commander of the 49th Army. Besides this, the aviation was to carry out combat reconnaissance from the line of the Ptich' River to the west, for the purpose of locating enemy groups of forces that had infiltrated to the south and southwest.

During 9-13 July the 49th Army eliminated the scattered enemy groups and combed through the area.

On 9 July units of the 38th Rifle Corps eliminated an enemy group in the area of Uzlyany village numbering up to 2,000 men, along with the commander of the 260th Infantry Division, General Kliampt. In the Bol'shoi Trostenets—Yel'nitsa—Apchak area our 324th Rifle Division eliminated just such a large group, led by the commander of the 45th Infantry Division, General Engel.

On 10 July General Folkers, the commander of the XXVII Army Corps, surrendered along with part of his staff. The enemy did not put up much resistance and the majority of offices and men surrendered upon encountering units of the Soviet army.

The 4th Air Army, continuing to cooperate with the 49th Army, rendered a great deal of assistance in eliminating the scattered enemy groups roaming around the woods. Night bombers, flying singly or in pairs, carried out reconnaissance during the day and led our forces to the detected enemy groups of forces. *Shturmoviks* operated against the surrounded enemy in groups of 6-8 planes, and sometimes in hunter pairs from a height of 600-800 meters to strafing altitude,

---

7   Editor's note. The NKVD (*Narodnyi Komissariat Vnutrennykh Del*), or People's Commissariat of Internal Affairs, was the name of the Soviet secret police during these years. The NKVD disposed of its own armed formations for internal security reasons.

8   Editor's note. The Po-2 was a single-engine biplane that first entered service in 1929. It had a crew of one, a maximum speed of 152 km/hr and a range of 630 kilometers. It was armed with one 7.62mm machine gun and could carry up to 300 kilograms of bombs.

making 4-6 passes at a target. In all, 809 sorties were flown against the encircled enemy group of forces.

By the close of 13 July the army's units had cleared the area between the Ptich' and Neman rivers of the enemy and its lead divisions had reached the area Lyubcha—Vselyub—Novogrudok—Valuvka. The army's units were located in this area on 13-16 July, bringing up the rear units and putting itself in order.

Results and Conclusions

The forcing of the Dnepr River, the breakthrough of the Dnepr defensive line and the capture of the town of Mogilev marked the completion of the breakthrough of the enemy's defense by the *front's* forces throughout its entire operational depth.

In six days of attacking the *front's* forces, having broken through the enemy's defense, initially along a 12-kilometer front, advanced 90 kilometers in depth to the Drut' River and expanded the breakthrough to a 100 kilometers in width. Despite the difficulties of the offensive, which found expression in the necessity of overcoming powerfully fortified defensive zones and lines, as well as water obstacles, including the Dnepr, the *front's* forces achieved high rates of advance, moving 15-20 kilometers per day.

During the offensive not only was the enemy's defense pierced, but his opposing group of forces also suffered heavy losses. The 12th Infantry Division ceased to exist as a combat-capable formation. Heavy losses were inflicted on the 337th, 260th and 110th infantry divisions and the "Feldherrnhalle" panzer group. As a result of the offensive fighting of 23-29 June, the *front's* forces killed up to 30,000 enemy officers and men, and destroyed 60 tanks, 250 guns of various calibers, 200 mortars, 500 machine guns, and 3,150 motor vehicles, and captured 3,250 officers and men and two generals. The following items were captured: 20 tanks, 161 guns, 192 mortars, 560 machine guns, 9,100 rifles and automatic rifles, 3,000 motor vehicles, three locomotives, 120 rail cars, and 2,100 horses.

On 28 June the objective of defeating the enemy's Mogilev group of forces and capturing the town of Mogilev, assigned by the *Stavka* of the Supreme High Command, had been fulfilled.

The forward detachments, which leaped forward and penetrated the retreating enemy forces' combat formations, forced water obstacles, seized bridgeheads on the opposite banks of rivers, and held these bridgeheads until the arrival of the main forces, played a large role in overcoming defensive lines and water obstacles.

Under conditions of the pursuit, a great role was played by the 49th and 50th armies' deep reconnaissance groups. They were sent 40-50 kilometers into the rear of the enemy and, working in secret, established the time and direction of the retreat of the enemy's main forces, seized prisoners, monitored the arrival of the enemy's reserves at the front and the group of the enemy's retreating forces, and also reconnoitered the rear defensive lines, and controlled the main routes of the enemy's forces' retreat. From 10-12 scouts usually staffed these groups, armed with automatic rifles, grenades and knives; they were assigned a radio operator for communications purposes. 1-2 such groups were created in each rifle division.

Among the shortcomings of the operation's preparation and conduct must be included the troops' lack of crossing equipment for forcing the Pronya River and a shortage of materials at hand for laying down passageways through the river's broad and swampy flood plain, particularly for heavy loads, tanks and self-propelled artillery. As a result, the attacking forces were deprived of support from a significant part of our tanks and self-propelled artillery, which led to a disruption of coordination and a pause in the offensive. It was only after coordination was reestablished between the combat arms that our forces finally broke the enemy's resistance and advanced 17-18 kilometers that day.

There were also serious shortcomings in forcing the Dnepr River on 26 June. On the morning of that day the 153rd and 42nd rifle divisions' forward detachments crossed the river and seized bridgeheads on the opposite shore, although the arriving main forces did not take advantage of these bridgeheads and lost entire days in forcing the river in other places.

During the operation the *front's* mobile group did not manifest the necessary maneuverability. It was not able to break free of the *front's* main forces, did not display tenacity in collisions with the enemy and, what was most important, lacked equipment for forcing river obstacles from the march. This led to a situation in which the mobile group was almost always operating in one line with the 49th Army's main forces, thus losing its essence as a mobile group. An order by the *front* commander on 27 June disbanded the mobile group. Despite the absence of a mobile group, the Second Belorussian Front's forces, achieved high rates of advance during the pursuit of the retreating enemy, advancing 25-26 kilometers per day. A distance of 150-160 kilometers was covered in six days of pursuit. During the same period more than 10,000 German officers and men were killed and another 3,000 captured. A large amount of equipment was also destroyed or captured.

In evaluating the forces' actions during the pursuit period, one must note that it unfolded through the close coordination of three *fronts* (First, Second and Third Belorussian). If the First and Third Belorussian Front's mobile units, as well as the 31st and 3rd armies, hung over the flanks Army Group Center's main forces, then the Second Belorussian Front tied down these forces from the front and through its active operations prevented the enemy from withdrawing to the west unhindered. These mutual actions of the *fronts* enabled us to surround about 30 German-Fascist divisions east of Minsk.

The successful advance by the forces of the Second Belorussian Front's left wing was greatly aided by the First Belorussian Front's 3rd Army, which on 30 June reached the Pogost—Negonichi—Krasnaya Niva area and enabled the 50th Army's formations and the 49th Army's left flank to force the Berezina River unhindered.

The subsequent advance by the 3rd Army's units and their arrival at Minsk enabled the forces of the Second Belorussian Front's left wing to create by 4 July an internal encirclement front around the main forces of Army Group Center east of Minsk.

However, throughout the entire pursuit period, the Second Belorussian Front command did not manage to transform its frontal pursuit into a parallel one. The enemy, by taking advantage of the very broken terrain, with its large number of rivers and swampy-wooded areas, fell back as far as the Smolevichi—Rudensk line, covered by rearguards, without experiencing any sort of significant pressure along its flanks and rear from the Second Belorussian Front's units.

The armies' mobile groups, consisting of 1-2 reinforced rifle divisions, basically did not justify themselves. They carried out their assigned tasks late and were not supplied with auto transport.

During the pursuit phase, a more significant role was played by the rifle divisions' forward detachments, placed on motor vehicles, and by reinforced groups of tanks and self-propelled artillery and sapper subunits. These detachments, by dashing forward, bypassed the enemy's retreating columns and got on their routes of retreat, which created opportunities for encircling and destroying individual enemy units.

The troops' formation during the pursuit phase was as follows: reconnaissance units moved ahead, followed by the mobile forward detachments, placed on motor vehicles, and then—at a distance of 20-25 kilometers—the formations' main forces.

The experience of the operation showed that the forward detachments must dispose of a sufficient amount of sapper subunits with auto transport, for transporting materials to restore crossings and repair transportation routes.

During the course of eight days of non-stop fighting to destroy the encircled enemy group of forces, the main forces of Army Group Center surrounded east of Minsk were completely eliminated, and by 14 July the *front's* attack sector had been cleared of defeated small groups, which had been streaming to the west.

During the fighting the following enemy forces were defeated: the headquarters of the XII, XXVII and XXXV army, and XXXIX and XLI panzer corps, as well as the remnants of the 78th and 246th assault infantry, 6th, 12th, 14th, 31st, 36th, 45th, 57th, 110th, 134th, 216th, 256th, 260th, 267th, 296th, 337th, and 383rd infantry, 18th, 25th and 60th motorized, 20th Panzer, 286th and 707th security infantry, and the 18th and 10th anti-aircraft artillery divisions, the 5th Independent Panzer Battalion, the 501st Panzer Battalion ("Tiger" tanks), the 909th High Command Heavy Artillery Battalion, the 430th Artillery Battalion, the 667th Assault Gun Brigade, the 742nd Anti-Tank Battalion, the 571st Engineer and 753rd sapper battalions, and the 96th Railroad Security Regiment. In all, 72,500 enemy officers and men were killed in the Minsk "cauldron," with 950 guns and mortars and more than 1,500 motor vehicles and much other equipment destroyed. Another 35,743 officers and men were taken prisoner, and 550 guns and mortars, 900 motor vehicles and much other equipment captured. Among those taken prisoner were three corps commanders and six division commanders. Also captured were the headquarters of the XXVII and XII army corps and the 12th, 383rd and 260th infantry, and 20th Panzer divisions.

The enemy's overall losses in the Mogilev-Minsk operation during the period 23 June-4 July, are shown in table 4.

Table 4. The Enemy's Losses in the Mogilev—Minsk Operation of 1944[9]

	Killed/Destroyed	Captured
Officers and Men	54,775[1]	11,426[2]
Tanks and Self-Propelled Guns	192	345
Guns of all Types	491	561
Mortars	411	376
Machine Guns	1,243	1,137
Motor Vehicles	5,679	6,411
Armored Transports	35	115
Truck Tractors, Tractors, Full-Tracked Vehicles	278	713
Aircraft	15	–
Carts	2,959	3,802
Horses	5,448	4,965
Rifles and Automatic Rifles	–	18,033
Motorcycles	–	166
Bicycles	–	247
Radios	–	45

Notes
1 Besides this, 72,500 men were killed in the Minsk "cauldron" during 5-13 July.
2 Besides this, 35,743 men were captured in the Minsk "cauldron" during 5-13 July.

9 Central Ministry of Defense Archives, fond 237, opis' 13544ss, delo 9, p. 60.

The Second Belorussian Front's personnel losses for the 21-30 June time period are shown in table 5.

The actions of the Soviet forces around Minsk in eliminating the encircled enemy group of forces are interesting for a number of reasons. First of all, it is necessary to note that for the first time in the course of the Great Patriotic War, Soviet forces managed to completely encircle and destroy a major enemy group of forces during the pursuit to a great operational depth—at a distance of 200 kilometers from the jumping-off point. This was achieved thanks to the extremely precise organization of coordination among the three Belorussian fronts, controlled by the *Stavka* of the Supreme High Command. The headlong advance of the Third and First Belorussian fronts toward Minsk and around its flanks led to a situation whereby the enemy's main group of forces in Belorussia, which was pinned from the front by the active operations of the Second Belorussian Front, could not develop the necessary speed of retreat and pass through the Minsk area earlier than the forces of the Third and First Belorussian fronts. Having completed the encirclement of the enemy's main group of forces east of Minsk, the Soviet forces accomplished the necessary regrouping of their forces on the march and, without a prolonged pause, continued to pursue the enemy.

The Second Belorussian Front's actions in eliminating the encircled enemy may be divided into three stages. The first embraced the 5-7 July period, when the enemy still sought to break through to the west in an organized fashion, with overall troop control and the supply of food and ammunition by air. During this period our forces launched decisive attacks on the enemy in the Volma area and split him up into several isolated groups, and also forced him to abandon (mostly due to the absence of fuel) his equipment and guns.

The second stage was characterized by the defeat of the separately operating enemy detachments, which were hiding in the woods or seeking to infiltrate through our forces' combat formations. This stage lasted 2-3 days until 9 July inclusively. During this period the enemy's detachments were still attempting to put up organized resistance and, moving along backwoods roads and paths, sought to get out of the encirclement.

The third stage, during 10-13 July, essentially involved combing through the woods and sown areas and running down small enemy groups, which were no longer putting up organized resistance. In eliminating these groups, the most effective methods were the actions of small reinforced detachments (a rifle company with an anti-tank battery and a company of 88mm mortars), placed on motor vehicles. These detachments were sometimes strengthened by 2-3 tanks or self-propelled guns, with a landing force of automatic riflemen.

However, at first our forces did not create a continuous encirclement front, as a result of which individual enemy detachments managed to infiltrate to the west and southwest. In some cases, our formations and units operated insufficiently actively: they would occupy favorable defensive lines and wait for the enemy to try to leave the woods. This led to a prolongation of the elimination of the encircled enemy.

On the whole, it should be noted that the Second Belorussian Front, which was to play, according to the initial idea, a supporting role, resolved important and complex tasks during the operation, and exerted a serious influence on the entire course and outcome of the Belorussian operation.

Table 5. The Second Belorussian Front's Losses[10]

Army	Killed	Wounded	Missing in Action	Taken Prisoner	Other Losses	Total
33rd Army	759	2,041	67	–	1	2,868
49th Army	2,464	11,298	64	–	12	13,838
50th Army	681	2,121	7	–	5	2,814
4th Air Army	17	6	1	–	7	31
Units Subordinated to the *Front*	80	235	–	–	9	324
Total	4,001	15,701	139	–	34	19,875

---

10 Central Ministry of Defense Archives, fond 237, opis' 15795 ss, delo 3, p. 326.

5

The First Belorussian Front's Bobruisk—Slutsk Offensive Operation (24 June-4 July 1944)

The Operation's First Stage

The Breakthrough of the Enemy's Defense and the Encirclement and Destruction of the Enemy's Bobruisk Group of Forces (24-28 June 1944)

During the first stage of the multi-*front* Belorussian operation the First Belorussian Front sought to achieve its assigned objectives with its right-wing forces of four combined-arms armies and an air army, while at the same time the left-wing armies continued to prepare for the offensive.

During the final days before the offensive by the main forces of the First Belorussian Front's right-wing armies, a reconnaissance in force was broadly carried out along the *front's* entire sector (761 kilometers). The *front's* right-wing forces carried out a reconnaissance in force on the night of 22-23 June, in which 12 reconnaissance detachments, each consisting of a reinforced rifle battalion, took part, excluding the 48th Army's reconnaissance detachment, which included two punishment companies.

Following a 5-15 minute artillery onslaughts, all of the reconnaissance detachments attacked the German-Fascist forces' first defensive trench. In the 65th and 28th armies' sectors, the reconnaissance detachments (with the exception of the 193rd Rifle Division) managed to seize the first trench, but as a result of enemy counterattacks, supported by powerful artillery and mortar fire, they fell back to their jumping-off position, without having improved their position. The 3rd and 48th armies' reconnaissance detachments and the 65th Army's 193rd Rifle Division had no success.

As a result of the reconnaissance in force, it was established that the enemy was solidly occupying and stubbornly defending his entire defensive position. Information was confirmed as to the location of the majority of previously-reconnoitered artillery and mortar batteries, as well as machine gun firing points, reinforced concrete pillboxes and earth and timber pillboxes.

In the night before the beginning of the main forces' offensive the 16th Air Army, in conjunction with Long-Range Aviation's formations, carried out a preliminary aviation preparation against the enemy's troops, weapons, equipment, and defensive structures in the main defense zone along the main attack sectors. During the preliminary aviation preparation, our bombers carried out about 550 sorties, during which Long-Range Aviation's bombers alone dropped 310 tons of bombs.

Simultaneously, formations from Long-Range Aviation blocked the enemy's closest airfields, and the 16th Air Army's night bombers attacked an airfield located near Bobruisk.

At dawn on 24 June, immediately following the attack by night bomber aviation, the artillery preparation began, at first with a mighty salvo by a large mass of artillery and mortars along the northern breakthrough sectors of the *front's* right-wing forces, and an hour later along the southern sectors. The artillery preparation lasted two hours and five minutes.

The artillery preparation yielded the greatest results along the southern breakthrough sector of the *front's* right-wing forces (along the Glusk axis), where the enemy's fire system was suppressed, his control disrupted, and he suffered heavy losses. Along the northern breakthrough sector of the *front's* right-wing forces—along the Bobruisk axis—the enemy's defense was suppressed much more weakly, which told negatively on the unfolding of the *front's* 3rd and 48th Army's offensive. The chief reason behind the poor conduct of the artillery preparation along the northern sector lay in the limited employment of artillery for firing over open sights and the great distance of the remaining artillery's firing positions from the forward edge of the defense (5-6 kilometers and more). Besides this, artillery reconnaissance had not fully uncovered the enemy's fire system.

The meteorological conditions on the morning of 24 June did not favor the accomplishment of our aviation's first planned concentrated attacks. For this reason, the commander of the 16th Air Army cancelled the sorties by bombers and concentrated attacks by assault aircraft following the completion of the artillery preparation along the right breakthrough sector of the *front's* forces. Only small groups of *shturmoviks*, consisting of 2-6 planes, took off.

Along the left breakthrough sector of the *front's* forces the aviation immediately launched raids, following the artillery preparation, as deep as the line Gomza—Yel'tsy. The *shturmoviks* initially also operated in small groups.

Thus there was no immediate aviation preparation along the Bobruisk axis, while along the Glusk axis it was limited. All of this, together with the qualitatively weak artillery preparation, soon told on the course of combat on the operation's first day.

The main forces of the *front's* right wing attacked along both breakthrough sectors on the morning of 24 June.

The 3rd and 48th armies' shock group, while trying to break through the enemy's defense along the 15-kilometer Ozerane—Kolosy sector, attacked in the general direction of Bobruisk. The 65th and 28th armies' shock group sought to break through the German-Fascist troops' defense along the 14-kilometer Radin—marker 144.6 sector and attacked in the general direction of Glusk.

The 3rd Army's shock group (35th and 41st rifle corps), in close conjunction with the 48th Army's right-flank units, attacked in the general direction of Novoselki; by 0800 it had captured the first trench line, and the second trench line on the right flank. This group's subsequent offensive ran into the enemy's well-organized and unsuppressed defense.

In a situation where, on the one hand, a certain success was evident on the 35th Rifle Corps' right flank and, on the other hand, the rate of advance was still slow, the commander of the 3rd Army decided to commit the 9th Tank Corps, although not in the breach, as had been planned, but in order to complete the breakthrough.

Owing to the crossing's lack of repair, the tank corps was able to cross by 1800 to the bridgehead near Novaya Konoplitsa only the 108th Tank Brigade, which began to operate in the combat formations not of the 35th Rifle Corps, as had been planned, but of the 41st Rifle Corps.

The meteorological conditions improved a little bit during the second half of the day, as a result of which our *shturmoviks* significantly increased their activities over the battlefield, flying in groups 2-3 times more powerful than earlier (8-10 planes). Bomber aviation, under the secure cover of our fighters, launched two concentrated raids against the enemy's centers of resistance along the direction of the main attack: the first from 1250 to 1300, and the second from 1630 to 1700.

Taking advantage of these raids, the 3rd Army's group of forces, following a series of short but powerful artillery onslaughts, and supported by assault aviation, repeatedly sought to continue the offensive, but was not successful.

The 48th Army sought to develop the offensive by its shock group (42nd and 29th rifle corps) with great difficulty. The broad swampy flood plain of the Drut' River made the crossing, particularly of tanks, extremely difficult. Besides, the enemy constantly laid down a powerful artillery and mortar fire on the troops approaching the crossings, delaying them and inflicting casualties.

It was only after two hours of intense fighting that the army's shock group managed to force the Drut' River, knock the enemy out of the first trench line and capture it, and capture the second trench line by 1100.

Stubborn fighting then unfolded for capture of the enemy's third trench line, which continued unsuccessfully until evening.

Thus by the close of the operation's first day the troops of the *front's* right shock group (3rd and 48th armies) had penetrated into the enemy's defense along a 20-kilometer front to a depth of 2.5-3.5 kilometers.

The *front's* right-flank shock group's lack of success along the Bobruisk axis may be explained, first of all, by the qualitatively weak artillery preparation, particularly in the 3rd Army. Moreover, there were mostly 82mm mortars and 45mm guns in the infantry's combat formations on the bridgehead, as well as part of regimental artillery's guns. The remaining artillery, due to the lack of readiness and the poor work on the crossings over the Drut' River, remained on the river's eastern bank. Besides this, the low capacity of the bridgehead along the river's western bank told negatively, particularly that of the artillery positions (6 kilometers X 1.5-2 kilometers), and the absence of aviation support for the attacking troops, due to the poor meteorological conditions.

Moreover, this defensive sector contained the greatest density of enemy forces, while the defense itself was the most developed from the engineering point of view.

Besides this, an extremely insufficient number of crossings over the Drut' River had been prepared, particularly for tanks and heavy guns. Finally, this wooded and swampy area contained an extremely limited number of roads.

Also worthy of note are instances of the disruption of coordination between the rifle troops, tank units and aviation, as well as their low level of engineer support. For example, bomber aviation launched a second concentrated attack during the 1630-1700 time period, while the 108th Tank Brigade crossed over to the bridgehead by 1800. The rifle troops' offensive was conducted without sufficient coordination with the aviation and tanks. The unity of the attack was disrupted.

The 108th Tank Brigade was to have been crossed over to the bridgehead near Rumki for operations in the 35th Rifle Corps' combat formations, while the brigade was actually crossed over to the bridgehead near Novaya Konoplitsa and became part of another corps. The reason for the brigade's resubordination was the lack of repair of the bridge near Rumki.

On the whole, all of this enables us to conclude that the command and control of the fulfillment of the 3rd Army commander's decision suffered from major shortcomings.

The operation's by the *front's* left shock group developed more successfully. The 65th Army, with its 18th Rifle Corps along the main axis and the 105th Rifle Corps on the secondary axis, broke through the enemy's defense and energetically developed the offensive to the northwest and north. The army's offensive was supported by a double rolling artillery barrage to a depth of 1.5-2 kilometers and the active support of small groups of assault aviation over the battlefield. The Dnepr Flotilla's 1st Brigade of river launches supported the 105th Rifle Corps with its naval artillery.

Continuing the offensive, by 1300 the army's shock group had broken through five lines of enemy trenches, repulsed several counterattacks and penetrated into the enemy's defensive zone to a depth of 5-6 kilometers. However, the enemy's increasing resistance, as well as the difficult swampy terrain, sharply lowered the rate of advance of the army's shock group.

In this situation, the commander of the 65th Army, in order to increase his shock group's rate of advance, decided to commit the 1st Guards Tank Corps into the breach from the line Rakovichi—Petrovichi in the direction of Chernin and Moiseevka. The tank corps was reinforced with the 3rd

Anti-Tank Artillery Brigade, the 345th and 354th self-propelled artillery regiments, and an independent sapper battalion. Moreover, the 44th Guards Rifle Divisions was attached to it.

Due to the fact that the swampy terrain excluded off-road movement and that the corduroy roads and bridges had been destroyed by artillery fire and aviation bombs, the 1st Guards Tank Corps entered the breach in the 18th Rifle Corps' sector only at 1800, from the line Zabrodki—Glinishche and began to develop the offensive along two axes—toward Knyshevichi and Romanishche, into the rear of the enemy's Parichi group of forces. By the close of the day the tank corps, having captured Chernin, was fighting for Gomza and was 1.5 kilometers northwest of Glinishche.

The tank corps' offensive was supported by the 26th Breakthrough Artillery Division and the 2nd Assault Air Division, along with two fighter regiments.

The 65th Army's forces, taking advantage of the tank corps' success, sped up their advance and by the end of the day was fighting along the line Chernin—Glinishche—Zakhvatki.

The 28th Army's shock group (3rd Guards and 20th rifle corps) captured the first line of trenches in the offensive's first 2-3 hours. Breaking through to the northwest and west, by 1300 it had encountered the enemy's active resistance along the line of the wooded areas on the eastern bank of the Tremlya River. At 1700 the army commander ordered the commander of the 3rd Guards Rifle Corps to commit his second echelon into the fighting and secure the commitment of the *front's* cavalry-mechanized group into the breach on the morning of 25 June.

On the whole, in the sector of the *front's* left shock group along the Glusk axis, combat operations developed more successfully and faster on the operation's first day than in the sector of the *front's* right shock group along the Bobruisk axis. The 65th and 28th armies broke through the enemy's defense along a sector up to 30 kilometers in breadth and penetrated 5-8 kilometers there along the axis of the armies' main attacks. The 65th Army broke through the entire main zone of the enemy's defense along the axis of the army's main attack, while two brigades of the 1st Guards Tank Corps had come up right against the second zone of the enemy's defense and had begun fighting for it. The 28th Army had almost completely broken through the main zone of the enemy's defense along the axis of the main attack, while one division had broken into the second zone of the enemy's defense.

Nevertheless, the *front's* left shock group did not completely carry out its assigned objectives, which is explained not only by the enemy's stubborn defense, but chiefly by the difficult conditions of the wooded and swampy terrain, the extremely limited road network, and the great damage done to the corduroy roads and bridges during the artillery and aviation preparation. The artillery was falling behind, the troops' combat formations were strung out in depth, and the roads were crowded with troops and tanks moving up to the commitment line. Besides this, our aviation had not been able to fully assist the attacking forces (due to the unfavorable meteorological conditions) and make up for the lagging artillery. The insufficient provisioning of the attacking troops with individual and group equipment for overcoming the swampy terrain sectors deepened the offensive's lack of success.

The 16th Air Army, despite the unfavorable meteorological conditions, carried out 3,276 sorties during the day, that is, 23 times more than the enemy.

During the night of 24-25 June the *front's* shock groups along both axes continued to attack. At the same time the *front's* forces were bringing up their second echelons, reserves, tanks, and artillery, especially to the 3rd and 48th armies' bridgeheads. The 16th Air Army, in single flights of night bombers, spent all night destroying and suppressing the enemy's personnel, tanks, fire system, and positions, and together with Long-Range Aviation, launched two concentrated raids against airfields in Bobruisk and Baranovichi.

On the morning of 25 June the *front's* two shock groups broadened their offensive operations even further. These developed especially successfully, as during the previous day, along the Glusk axis.

At 1000 the 3rd and 48th armies' shock groups, following a 35- and 45-minute artillery preparation, and supported by aviation, renewed the offensive along the Bobruisk axis. Artillery support for the offensive was carried out by the method of consecutively concentrating fire.

The 3rd Army, seeking to complete the breakthrough of the main zone of the defense along the axis of the main attack and to speed up the breakthrough of the enemy's tactical zone, at 1200 committed the 9th Tank Corps' 95th and 108th tank brigades into the battle along the 35th Rifle Corps' sector.

Having crushed the enemy's stubborn resistance, by the close of the day the army's shock group had completed the breakthrough of the defense's main zone and had reached the second defensive zone of the enemy's defense.

On this day the army's second echelon—the 46th Rifle Corps—was committed into the battle in the direction of Ozerane and Pennoe, where the shock group was enjoying the greatest success. By the end of the day it was fighting along the line Bar—excluding Pennoe.

The 48th Army was engaged in heavy and intense fighting along the attack's main axis along the line Semenkovichi—excluding Berezovka.

Thus the right shock group, which was operating along the Bobruisk axis, despite the commitment of the tank corps into the fighting, had been able on the operation's second day to only complete the breakthrough of the enemy's main defensive zone and reach the second defensive zone.

The breakthrough of the enemy's defense had been broadened to a width of 40 kilometers and to a depth of 5-10 kilometers.

With the arrival of the 3rd Army at the Dobritsa River, conditions were created for the development of the success along the axis of the main attack, as well as the prerequisites for the offensive's unfolding along the right flank of the 3rd Army's breakthrough to the north, along the western bank of the Drut' River.

The slow advance by the *front's* right shock group is explained by the reasons listed above, as well as the enemy's well-developed engineer defense, and its reinforcement by the dispatch and commitment of fresh enemy units into the battle. Besides this, the most important reason behind the very unsuccessful development of the offensive along the Bobruisk axis was the crossing of the artillery over the Drut' River under enemy fire and its lagging behind our forces, particularly the 48th Army.

On the morning of 25 June the 65th and 28th armies resumed the offensive.

The 65th Army, while continuing to attack successfully, particularly with the commitment of the *front's* mobile group into the breach, had by the close of 25 June broken through the enemy's entire tactical defensive zone and reached the operational depth of his defense and was fighting along the line Pogantsy—Knyshevichi—Tumarovka—Drazhnya—Yazventsy—Moshna—Chernye Brody. With the arrival of the 1st Guards Tank Corps in the area of Drazhnya and Tumarovka, the enemy's Parichi group of forces' path of retreat on Bobruisk was cut and, in conjunction with the 105th Rifle Corps, its encirclement was completed.

One should note the loss of command and control in the 1st Guards Tank Corps, as a result of which the corps operated in an unorganized manner along a broad front, and lacking coordination between its formations.

The 28th Army, having forced the Tremlya River, captured the strong points and defensive line along its western bank.

During the second half of the day, the enemy, reeling under the army's attacks, began to withdraw to the northwest and west, putting up resistance with rearguards and broadly employing forest obstacles, while destroying embankments, corduroy roads and bridges.

The 28th Army took up the non-stop pursuit, which grew particularly strong at 1600, following the commitment of the *front's* cavalry-mechanized group into the breach.

The *front's* cavalry-mechanized group was committed into the breach in the 28th Army's sector, from the line Sekirichi—Goduny. The group's commitment into the breach was supported by the 28th Army's artillery.

In order to support the cavalry-mechanized group's operations in the depth of the enemy's defense, it had attached to it the following units: the 1st Anti-Tank Artillery Brigade, the 43rd and 46th guards mortar regiments, the 22nd Guards Mortar Brigade's 3rd Battalion, the 7th and 53rd sapper battalions, and the 274th Amphibious Automobile Battalion. Besides this, the *front's* mobile group was supported by an assault air division and two fighter regiments from the 16th Air Army's 8th Fighter Corps.

The cavalry-mechanized group deepened the 28th Army's breach to 30 kilometers, but advanced only 10-12 kilometers after passing through the army's combat formations, and by the end of the day its forward detachments had not succeeded in seizing crossings over the Ptich' River along the sector Poblin—the mouth of the Dokol'ka River.

The chief reason for the decline in the cavalry-mechanized group's rate of advance was the necessity of overcoming the terrain's swampy sectors and water obstacles.

Thus the *front's* left shock group, which was operating along the Glusk axis, had broken through the enemy's tactical defense zone on the operation's second day and had reached operational freedom, having expanded the breach in the enemy's defense to 45 kilometers in width and 15-30 kilometers in depth.

The 16th Air Army's aviation actively assisted the offensive by both of the *front's* shock groups, launching raids against strong points, centers of resistance and artillery and mortar batteries, especially along the Bobruisk axis. During the second half of the day, our aviation, having taken note of the enemy's withdrawal, began to operate with part of its forces against the enemy's vehicle columns moving to the west. The air army's aviation carried out 2,737 sorties during the operation's second day. As before, the enemy's aviation was not active. Only 77 enemy sorties were noted during the day.

Thus by the end of the offensive's second day the forces of both of the *front's* shock groups had achieved some results, particularly along the Glusk axis, where they had achieved operational freedom. The *front's* shock groups had broken through the enemy's defense along a front of 95 kilometers in width and 5-15-30 kilometers in depth. The enemy had also suffered significant casualties.

The cavalry-mechanized group's and the 1st Guards Tank Corps' arrival in the operational depth created a threat to the flank and rear of the Germans' Bobruisk group of forces, while at the same time the forces of the *front's* left shock group had the opportunity to develop the pursuit of the enemy in the direction of Glusk with the 38th Army's forces, and in the direction of Glusha with the 65th Army's forces. Particularly favorable conditions had arisen for the arrival of the *front's* mobile groups and the 65th Army in the rear of the Bobruisk group of forces and for cutting all communications leading to Bobruisk from the west.

Thus more favorable conditions had been created for the development of the offensive by the *front's* shock group in the direction of Bobruisk, and part of the 3rd Army's units to the north along the Drut' River for assisting the Second Belorussian Front's 50th Army in developing the offensive to the west. Overall, the real opportunity for encircling the enemy's Bobruisk group of forces had appeared.

The combat on 26 June was a turning point, in the sense of developing the troops' successful offensive for widening the breakthrough of the enemy's defense and his pursuit. The offensive continued in the morning with growing force, while the most intensive fighting unfolded in the sector of the *front's* left shock group along the Glusk axis. The 65th Army's combined-arms formations were successfully developing the attack toward Glusha, and the mobile group (1st Guards Tank Corps) toward Bobruisk. As a result the beginning of the encirclement of part of the enemy's Bobruisk group of forces (XXXV Army Corps) began to take shape to the southeast of Bobruisk, between the Berezina and Dobysna rivers.

To the left the enemy, attacked by the 28th Army and the *front's* cavalry-mechanized group, continued to retreat to the northwest toward the defensive line along the Ptich' River.

Along the Bobruisk axis, with the commitment of the 9th Tank and 46th Rifle corps, the main forces of the 3rd and 48th armies, having crushed the enemy's resistance and completed the breakthrough of his entire tactical depth, were decisively moving toward Bobruisk and to the north. The 3rd Army's mobile group, while cooperating with the 65th Army's mobile group, began the encirclement of the enemy group of forces to the southeast of Bobruisk by its arrival in the Titovka area.

On the night of 25-26 June the 3rd Army continued to attack the opposing enemy and by morning had reached the Dobritsa River along its entire front, and then forced it.

At 0500 air reconnaissance reported the movement of large enemy columns of artillery, motor vehicles and horse-drawn transport, which was stretched out along all the roads to the west, toward Bobruisk.

For this reason, the 3rd Army commander, without waiting for the arrival of all the 35th Rifle Division's forces at the western bank of the Dobritsa River, ordered the 9th Tank Corps to attack in the general direction of Startsy and Bobruisk, and by the end of the day to capture Startsy, thus cutting the Mogilev—Bobruisk road along this sector.

At 0900 the tank corps, having crossed to the western bank of the Dobritsa River and following a powerful attack by our aviation and artillery, launched a headlong attack along the high road toward Startsy, having two tank brigades in its first echelon. While destroying the enemy's personnel and equipment along its path and rapidly advancing to the west, the tanks soon ran into the enemy's solid columns of artillery, supply trains and motor transport. They broke into the columns at high speed, firing on the move. The enemy's burning tanks, abandoned motor vehicles, and piles of destroyed transport more and more often forced the 9th Tank Corps to halt. At 1700 one of the corps' brigades broke into Startsy from the march, captured the area and cut the Mogilev—Bobruisk road. By 2000 the tank corps' main forces reached the area of Titovka—an extremely important road junction—and firmly closed off all the routes from the southeast and east to the single Bobruisk crossing.

The army's rifle corps, in conjunction with the aviation, and the 35th and 46th rifle corps, taking advantage of the 9th Tank Corps' success, were trying to overcome the enemy's resistance and were fighting off his numerous counterattacks; they broke through his defense along the Dobritsa River, and subsequently along the Dobysna River, and were pursuing his units to the west and northwest.

Thus on 26 June the 3rd Army broke through the enemy's entire tactical defensive depth along the axis of the main attack, forced the Dobysna River from the march and widened the breach in the enemy's defense to 70 kilometers, and advanced 20-35 kilometers from its jumping-off position. As a result, the enemy's Rogachev—Zhlobin group of forces to the southeast of Bobruisk was deeply outflanked from the right, which marked the beginning of its encirclement and subsequent destruction.

The army's arrival at the Mogilev—Bobruisk paved road divided the enemy's Fourth and Ninth armies, deprived them of the capability of rapidly maneuvering personnel and equipment laterally and created a threat to the flank and rear of his Mogilev group of forces.

At 0400 on 26 June, the 48th Army, following a short but powerful fire onslaught, and in close conjunction with the 3rd Army, resumed the offensive. By 1300 the army had forced the Dnepr along the Luchin—Solonoe sector and captured the town of Zhlobin, which was a powerful strong point in the enemy's defense.

Continuing to pursue the retreating enemy to the west, by 2000 the army's shock group had reached the enemy's intermediate defensive line along the Dobysna River, along the Liskovskaya—Antushi sector and, upon forcing the river, captured it.

Thus on 26 June the 48th Army broke through the entire tactical depth of the enemy's defense along the right and center and forced the Dobysna River from the march, thus preventing the enemy from consolidating along the previously-prepared line along the river.

In three days the 48th Army's forces had completed the breakthrough of the enemy's defense along its entire 85-kilometer sector and had advanced 10-23 kilometers from its jumping-off position.

As a result of the three days' fighting (24-26 June), the forces of the *front's* right shock group widened the breach in the enemy's defense to 155 kilometers and to a depth of 10-35 kilometers.

The rapid advance of the *front's* cavalry-mechanized group significantly eased the offensive by the 65th and 28th armies' units. On 26 June the 65th Army continued its offensive along the entire front, launching its main attack with its left flank to the northwest toward Glusha and Bobruisk. The 105th Rifle Corps, with the support of the Dnepr Flotilla, broke into Parichi and, following a short period of street fighting, captured this very important enemy center of resistance along the Berezina River south of Bobruisk.

The 1st Guards Tank Corps was successfully operating to the left of the 105th Rifle Corps. Part of the tank corps' forces repelled the enemy's numerous and powerful counterattacks by elements of the 36th Infantry Division from the southeast and units of the enemy's 20th Panzer Division, which had arrived from the north from the Bobruisk area. At the same time, the corps' main forces continued to pursue the enemy to the north. At midday the army commander, in order to more rapidly encircle the enemy's Bobruisk group of forces, gave the tank corps the following assignment: "Attack toward Bobruisk with all your forces, and by the close of 26 June capture the Bobruisk area with an attack from the southwest and, by crossing the Berezina River, prevent the enemy's retreat to the west."

In carrying out this task, the corps' formations drove along the railroad in the direction of Glebova Rudnya and Bobruisk.

By the end of the day the 1st Guards Tank Corps was fighting along the line Konchany—Broshka (6-8 kilometers southwest of Bobruisk), while part of the tanks had been directed to outflank Bobruisk from the southwest, for the purpose of cutting the Bobruisk—Slutsk road near Kamenka.

On the army's left flank the 18th Rifle Corps, initially in conjunction with the 1st Guards Tank Corps and then with the 1st Mechanized Corps, was successfully operating in the direction of Glusha, with the task of cutting the Bobruisk—Glusk road.

Thus on the offensive's third day, the 65th Army, having captured the powerful strong point of Parichi and having advanced 10-30 kilometers, had widened the breakthrough of the enemy's defense to 40 kilometers and 48 kilometers in depth.

The army's attack to the northwest toward Glusha, and its 1st Guards Tank Corps' attack toward Bobruisk, in conjunction with the Dnepr Flotilla and the 1st Mechanized Corps, deeply enveloped the left flank of the enemy's Rogachev—Zhlobin group of forces.

At the same time, the arrival of the army's formations at the area 6-12 kilometers east and northeast of Glusk, signified the envelopment of the enemy group of forces in the Bobruisk area from the southwest.

During 26 June the Dnepr Flotilla carried out a landing by the 193rd Rifle Division, supported the offensive by the 65th Army's 105th Rifle Corps with its naval guns along the western bank of the Berezina River, and secured the 65th Army's right flank. Aside from this, the flotilla assisted the 48th Army's 53rd Rifle Corps' attack to the northwest along the eastern bank of the Berezina River.

By the close of the day the cavalry-mechanized group's right column, in conditions of very swampy terrain and a limited number of roads, covered 25 kilometers, and the left column 15 kilometers, and the cavalry-mechanized group reached the eastern bank of the Ptich' River in the areas of Zholvinets, Podluzh'e and Berezovka, where, having seized the crossings and forced the river with its forward detachments, it began preparing to force it with its entire group. The group encountered the enemy's increased resistance along the Ptich' River, to the north of Berezovka.

It should be noted that the partisans, cooperating with the 28th Army's shock group, had seized the crossings over the Ptich' River as early as 25 June and were holding them until the arrival of our forces.

While continuing its advance, the cavalry-mechanized group cut the Bobruisk—Glusk paved road near Vil'cha and increased the overall advance of our forces along the Glusk axis to 54 kilometers from the 28th Army's jumping-off position. However, the group failed to carry out its assignment of outflanking the enemy's Bobruisk group of forces from the west and cutting all of its communications along this axis. The group's formations were moving forward in close proximity to the rifle troops, and the mechanized corps was only 6-8 kilometers ahead, while the cavalry corps was attacking in the rifle troops' combat formations.

The slowness of the group's advance is explained, first of all, by the not quite exact troop control, which is confirmed by the delayed and imprecise information from the group's headquarters, and also the difficult wooded and swampy terrain, and the group's shortage of pontoon-bridge equipment.

The 28th Army, in conjunction with the *front's* cavalry-mechanized group and the 65th Army's left-flank corps, was successfully developing its attack along the entire front to the west and northwest toward Glusk, successively widening the breakthrough front toward the center and the left flank. On 26 June the speed of the offensive's advance increased significantly.

During the operation's third day the army's forces widened the breakthrough of the enemy's defense to 65 kilometers and pierced his defense to 30-40 kilometers from the jumping-off position.

The army's arrival at the Ptich' River, along the immediate approaches to Glusk, the weak resistance of the enemy's retreating and scattered units, and the absence of enemy reserves along this axis enabled us to more broadly carry out the pursuit of the enemy in the direction of Glusk and Starye Dorogi.

Our aviation continued to support the offensive by the *front's* forces, chiefly along the axes of the armies' main attacks, particularly along the Bobruisk axis. On the night of 26 June our night bomber aviation operated in single planes against enemy troop concentrations.

During the day, in a situation in which the enemy's withdrawal before the *front's* entire right wing had become manifest, the main mass of the air army's aviation was directed at the destruction of the enemy's retreating forces along the roads, crossings and other defiles. During this day our aviation carried out 2,943 sorties and shot down 73 enemy planes in air battles.

The partisan formations, upon the beginning of the offensive by the *front's* right-wing forces, increased their combat and diversionary work. All of their activity was subordinated to the interests of the *front*. For example, along the main rail communications of Bobruisk, Osipovichi, Minsk, Baranovichi, Luninets, and others, the partisan wrecked trains carrying ammunition and equipment, knocked out rails and trains, destroyed telegraph-telephone lines and roadbeds, and the enemy's passing auto transport, with ammunition and personnel. In this way, the partisans disorganized communications and paralyzed communications routes, making it difficult to regroup and supply the troops, as well as the evacuation of enemy stores.

Besides this, on 26 June the Poles'ye formation and part of the brigades of the Southern Minsk partisan formation, under the command of Captain Doroshko, in conjunction with the *front's* cavalry-mechanized group and the 28th Army, seized crossings over the Ptich' River near Berezovka, Kasarichi, Porech'ye, and Bubnovka and held them until our forces arrived.

The 61st Army, operating to the left of the 28th Army, continued as before to firmly hold the line along the Pripyat' River, to carry out reconnaissance in force and thus secure the combat actions of the *front's* left shock group along the Glusk axis from the south.

As a result of fighting on the offensive's third day, the forces of the First Belorussian Front's right wing achieved decisive successes. 26 June was a turning point in the course of the subsequent successful development of the *front's* offensive. The entire tactical depth of the enemy's defense had been pierced along the Bobruisk axis as well, and the Dobysna River was also forced from the march. The *front's* right wing forces widened the breach in the enemy's defense to 240 kilometers and captured the following German centers of resistance: the town and major rail junction of Zhlobin, and the town and road junction of Parichi on the Berezina River, and advanced 26-54 kilometers from their jumping-off position. In this way the *front's* forces significantly more than carried out the day's task, as called for by the *front's* operational plan, particularly along the Glusk axis.

Following the seizure of the very important road junction east of Bobruisk (in the Titovka area) by the 9th Tank Corps and the arrival of the 1st Guards Tank Corps south and southwest of Bobruisk, and following the movement of the 3rd Army's formations along the Mogilev—Bobruisk road in the Borovitsa—Startsy sector, and the advance of the 65th Army's right flank along the western bank of the Berezina River, a large part of the enemy's Bobruisk group of forces that was operating to the southeast of Bobruisk was in a catastrophic situation: five infantry divisions of the XXXV Army Corps had all their roads, going through Bobruisk to the west and north, cut.

Due to the movement of the 65th Army's units toward Bobruisk along the western bank of the Berezina River, the single remaining crossing remaining to the enemy toward the town was the rail bridge over the Berezina, which was being intensively bombarded by the 9th Tank Corps' artillery. The complete separation of the Bobruisk and Mogilev groups of forces, that is, the German Ninth and Fourth armies, had occurred. As early as the second half of 26 June the defeat of the enemy surrounded southeast of Bobruisk had begun. This marked the beginning of the creation of the Bobruisk "cauldron."

As a result of the three days of continuous fighting and the rapid advance of our forces, especially along the Glusk axis, the majority of the enemy's infantry divisions had lost direct control of their units. The enemy forces attempted to defend in scattered subunits, but under pressure from our forces they continued their general retreat along a broad front, striving to get out of the looming encirclement.

The commander of the German-Fascist Ninth Army, having expended all his reserves in these battles, was withdrawing his forces to the line of the Susha, Svisloch' and Ptich' rivers, in order to consolidate along these water obstacles and halt our forces further advance.

The German-Fascist command, having come to understand the seriousness of the Ninth Army's situation and striving to cover the Bobruisk—Minsk axis, began to transfer the 12th Panzer Division, which had arrived from the Riga area, and the 390th Special Designation Division (a former field training division) to the Pukhovichi axis from the area 5-10 kilometers northeast of Minsk.

Units of the Hungarian I Cavalry Corps were being brought up from the Luninets area to cover the Slutsk—Baranovichi axis from the northern bank of the Pripyat' River.

The forces of the First Belorussian Front's right wing, in pursuing the defeated units of the German-Fascist Ninth Army, by means of headlong attacks by the 3rd Army from the northeast and the 65th Army from the south and southwest, in conjunction with the 48th Army and the Dnepr Flotilla, and heavily supported by the 16th Air Army, in the latter half of 27 June completed the encirclement of a major enemy group of forces, consisting of formations of the XXXV Army and XLI Panzer corps, along with their headquarters, as well as part of the 20th Panzer Division, in the Bobruisk area and to the southeast.

On the morning of 27 June the 3rd Army was continuing to attack with its main forces to the northwest in the general direction of Vatsevichi, and with part of its forces and left flank to the west, in the direction of Starya Sharoevshchina, having as its main task, in conjunction with the 48th Army and the right flank of the 65th Army, the destruction of the enemy's Bobruisk group of forces to the southeast of Bobruisk.

The 41st Rifle Corps, operating along the army's left flank, while breaking the enemy's resistance, forced the Ola River from the march. The 9th Tank Corps was repulsing the enemy's counterattacks, from a battalion to 1-2 regiments in strength and supported by 16-18 tanks, as well as tank columns of 60-70 tanks and assault guns, which were attempting to break through to the northwest and to the western bank of the Berezina River to Bobruisk. During the second half of the day, both corps linked up with each other, thus forming the northern part of the internal encirclement front around the enemy by the army's left-flank forces along the Zelenka—Leitichi sector.

The army's remaining forces, by creating the external encirclement front and arriving at the flank and rear of the enemy's Mogilev group of forces, were developing the offensive to the northwest. The army's center forces (35th and 46th rifle corps), continuing to attack in the general direction of Voevichi and pursuing the defeated units of the enemy's 134th, 707th and 45th infantry divisions, forced the Ol'sa and Susha rivers from the march, cut the Bykhov—Svisloch'—Mogilev—Osipovichi communications route, and also cut the main routes to the north and northwest along the eastern bank of the Berezina River.

The right-flank 80th Rifle Corps, by securing the actions of the army's main group of forces against possible enemy counterattacks from the north, was developing its attack in the center and along the left flank to the north in the direction of Chigirinka and Chechevichi. The corps, while overcoming the resistance by elements of the 57th and 707th infantry divisions, forced the Cherobomirka River, repelled several enemy counterattacks and reached the western bank of the Drut' River along the Rezki—Shmaki sector.

Thus the troops of the army's center and right flank formed the northern part of the external encirclement ring around the enemy.

The 48th Army, in conjunction with the 3rd Army's left flank and the 65th Army's right flank, as well as the Dnepr Flotilla, while continuing to squeeze the encirclement ring from the east and southeast, forced the Ola River on the heels of the enemy, broke through his army defensive zone, and by the close of 27 June was fighting the encircled enemy group of forces along the line Barak—excluding Malinovka—Kavali—Malevo.

Thus was formed the eastern and southeastern part of the internal encirclement front around the enemy.

The 65th Army, in developing the attack along the Bobruisk axis, reached the southern and western outskirts of Bobruisk, with its mobile units on the morning of 27 June, followed by the rifle units, having cut all the roads leading out of the town to the west and northwest. The army's 105th Rifle Corps, covered by the 75th Rifle Division along the Berezina River, was developing a successful attack to the north and by the close of the day was fighting along the line of the western bank of the Berezina River, along the sector Stasevka—Novyi Poselok, cutting the Bobruisk—Glusk paved road.

The 1st Guards Tank Corps, with a headlong attack to the northwest to outflank Bobruisk from the west, reached the Berezina River along the Nazarovka—Shatkovo sector and then, covering itself from the northwest, turned its main forces to the southeast and began fighting the enemy in the northern and northwestern outskirts of Bobruisk.

The 18th Rifle Corps, continuing its further attack to the northwest, was fighting by the end of the day along the line Koritno—Bortny—Simanovichi.

Thus on 27 June the 65th Army, by its arrival at the Berezina River to the south and north of Bobruisk, as well as at the town's western and northwestern outskirts, completed the encirclement of the enemy's Bobruisk group of forces from the west, having created along the sector Stasevka—Novyi Poselok—the western and northwestern outskirts of Bobruisk a part of the internal encirclement front, and the external front along the Shatkovo—Banevka—Koritno—Bortny—Simanovichi sector.

The Dnepr Flotilla was assisting the advance of the riverine flanks of the 48th and 65th armies. The commander of the German-Fascist Ninth Army, striving to take advantage of the insufficient density of our encirclement front in the Titovka area, on 27 June issued an order to the commander of the XXXV Army Corps: "Lead the troops out of the encirclement at all costs. Lead them out either toward Bobruisk, or to the north to Pogoreloe (28 kilometers east of Pukhovichi) to link up with the Fourth Army. Operate independently." The commander of the XXXV Army Corps decided to attempt to break through to the north toward the Fourth Army. In his order to the troops, he commanded that they "immediately destroy all equipment, leaving only part of what is necessary for fighting." The breakout was set for the night of 27-28 June.

However, the adoption of this decision was delayed. By that time our forces had securely closed off all the exits from the encirclement, and on the evening of 27 June the 3rd Army's forces reached the Ol'sa River, thus cutting off all roads leading to the north.

From the middle of 27 June powerful explosions and firing from automatic rifles could be heard from the encircled enemy's position, and large fires appeared. The German soldiers were blowing up guns, truck tractors and tanks, setting fire to cars and destroying all their livestock. Units of the enemy's covering force put up resistance and counterattacked several times. However, the formations of the 3rd and 48th armies, in close coordination with the 65th Army's 105th Rifle Division, and powerful air and artillery support, were destroying the enemy and squeezing further the encirclement ring.

At 1800 the 16th Air Army's aerial reconnaissance detected a large accumulation of enemy infantry, up to 150 tanks, more than 1,000 guns of various calibers, up to 6,000 motor vehicles, 400 truck tractors, and a large number of supply trains in the Dubovka—Telusha—Savichi area. During the second half of 27 June the enemy's detachments, ranging from a battalion to 1-2 regiments of infantry, 16-18 tanks, attacked up to 15 times against the 9th Tank Corps' units in the Titovka area, trying to break through to the north.

All of this was testimony to the fact that the enemy was getting ready to take his forces out of the encirclement to the north, because it was already impossible to retreat toward Bobruisk, because of the absence of crossings over the Berezina River, as well as in connection with the arrival of the river flotilla's cutters at the southeastern outskirts of Bobruisk.

However, it was difficult to reinforce the 9th Tank Corps' defense with infantry in the short time remaining. Thus the *front* command decided to commit major aviation formations from the 16th Air Army to destroy the encircled German-Fascist forces.

At 1900 526 planes rose into the sky after the 3rd and 48th armies had precisely delineated their forward edge of the internal encirclement front. Not encountering any resistance from the enemy's aircraft, within 15 minutes our planes reached the German group of forces' encirclement area. The *shturmoviks* were the first to attack the enemy's anti-aircraft weapons and suppressed them. The bombers appeared over the battlefield after the *shturmoviks*. In groups of 6-10 planes, they began to continuously attack their targets and drop their bombs. The road and forest area in the area north of Dubovka, where a large number of enemy personnel and equipment was concentrated, was subjected to especially heavy attacks. During the next hour and a half the enemy's position was constantly under fire from the aviation's bombs, cannons and machine guns. As a result, large fires and explosions were observed in areas where the enemy's equipment was concentrated. Motor vehicles, tanks, fuel, and ammunition were burning. The enemy was seized with panic. Many motor vehicles veered off the road, fell into the swamps, ran into other cars, and blocked up the possible escape routes, while impassable traffic jams formed on the roads. Scattered enemy groups, which had survived the air strikes and having thrown away their equipment and weapons and, having no command and control, wandered through the forests. Many of these groups soon began to surrender.

Thus our aviation delivered a well-organized surprise and crushing blow against the enemy's group of forces, surrounded to the southeast of Bobruisk. The following figures show how powerful the attack had been. 159 tons of bombs, 17,880 shells and 45,380 rounds were expended.

At 2015, after the last bombers had left the battlefield, the 48th Army's infantry and tanks, supported by powerful artillery fire, went over to the attack along the entire front. The enemy once against put up stubborn resistance with those units directly adjacent to our forces and which had suffered less from the air bombardment.

Thus as a result of the fighting on the operation's fourth day, the *front's* right-wing forces along the Bobruisk axis achieved even more decisive successes than the day before. The 3rd, 48th and 65th armies, and the Dnepr Flotilla, with the intense support of the 16th Air Army, by 1800 on 27 June completed the tactical encirclement of the enemy in the Bobruisk area and to the southeast.

The encirclement ring was 25-30 kilometers from east to west and 20-25 kilometers from north to south. The densest enemy group of forces was in the east, south and west. The 9th and 1st Guards tank corps surrounded the enemy on this day from the north and northwest. Here the external encirclement front was only 8-10 kilometers away and was chiefly occupied by small covering detachments. This is why the *front* commander considered the tank corps' sector the most likely sector for an enemy attempt to break out of the encirclement.

Formations and units of the XXXV Army and XLI Panzer corps and the German-Fascist Ninth Army's 20th Panzer Division (the 296th, 6th and 83rd infantry divisions, units of the 45th, 36th and 134th infantry divisions, and a large number of independent units and elements, special services and reinforcements), with an overall strength of up to 40,000 men, were completely surrounded.

The successful encirclement of the main forces of the enemy's Bobruisk group of forces, as well as the German-Fascist command's lack of operational reserves along this axis, insistently demanded that part of the First Belorussian Front's right-wing forces destroy or capture the encircled enemy as quickly as possible, while the *front's* main forces forced the pursuit of the enemy along the Minsk and Slutsk axes.

The 3rd and 48th armies' forces forced the Ola River from the march and broke through the army defensive zone along it. Besides this, the 3rd Army's forces, having crossed the Ol'sa River, seized a bridgehead along a 10-kilometer sector, reached the rear of the enemy's Bykhov group of forces and cut off its path of retreat to the west and southwest. The army simultaneously created a threat to the chief railroad communications of the enemy's Mogilev group of forces—Mogilev—Osipovichi—Minsk.

Based upon the conditions that had arisen in the sector of the *front's* right-wing forces by the close of 27 June, the *front* commander entrusted the destruction of the enemy group of forces surrounded southeast of Bobruisk to the 48th Army, and the capture of Bobruisk to the 65th Army, with both to coordinate with each other, the 3rd Army, and the Dnepr River Flotilla, with the support of the 16th Air Army.

In carrying out this task, the 48th Army, the left flank of the 3rd Army and the right flank of the 65th Army, as well as the boats of the Dnepr River Flotilla, were involved in stubborn fighting during the night of 27-28 June and the first part of the following day to destroy the enemy group of forces encircled southeast of Bobruisk. Meanwhile, the enemy insistently sought to break out of the encirclement to the north, as the German-Fascist command had demanded. For example, the 3rd Army's left-wing forces along the northern face of the encirclement beat off 15 fierce enemy attacks of up to an infantry division in strength, supported by tanks, during the night and the first part of the day.

The enemy, while striving to break out to the north, resorted to tricks. For example, a major enemy group of forces (about 3,000 men) from the woods north of Savichi tried three times during the course of the night to break out of the encirclement to the north, but, having lost more than half of its strength, failed to achieve success. Then the remaining forces tried a trick. The group, having sent a part of its troops forward with hands raised and white flags, moved north. Having reached the forward line of the 41st Rifle Corps' left-flank units, the armed officers and men opened a heavy fire from automatic rifles in the darkness and leaped into the attack. Following the fighting, a small part of the enemy's forces managed to break through to the woods north of Dumanovshchina, but there they were soon destroyed by units of the same corps.

To the left, the 48th Army, by launching powerful concentric shattering blows with its rifle corps (the 42nd from the east toward Savichi, and the 29th and 53rd from the southeast in the general direction of Dubovka) in the first part of the night of 27-28 June, split the encircled enemy group of forces and, by destroying it in detail, advanced to the Berezina River. The German-Fascist soldiers, having lost all hope of linking up with their own forces, began to surrender in groups of 100-250 men, led by their officers and generals. Only an insignificant part of the enemy forces, having evaded defeat and captivity, hid out in Bobruisk.

Thus by 1300 on 28 June a major group of German-Fascist forces surrounded southeast of Bobruisk was completely eliminated.

Following this, the main forces of the 48th Army and the 3rd Army's left flank reached the Berezina River, while a part of their forces continued to destroy and capture the scattered and small enemy forces, which were hiding in the woods east of the river.

The *front* commander, foreseeing the rapid elimination of the encircled enemy group of forces southeast of Bobruisk, as early as 1000 on 28 June, for the purpose of employing all the 3rd and 65th armies' forces to augment the attack along their main axes, demanded of the commander of the 48th Army that he "no later than 2400 on 28 June, relieve the 3rd Army's forces along the eastern bank of the Berezina River along the Guta—Titovka sector, and those of the 65th Army along the western bank of the Berezina River and the northern, western and southern outskirts of Bobruisk, with the task of destroying the enemy's Bobruisk group of forces and capturing the town and area of Bobruisk. The commanders of the 3rd and 65th armies are to employ their freed-up (following their relief by the 48th Army's units) for operations along the main axis."

Thus, if on 27 June the destruction of the Bobruisk garrison had been entrusted by the *front* to the 65th Army, then from 2400 on 28 June this task was handed over to the 48th Army.

In connection with this, as early as 1600 on 28 June the commander of the 48th Army began to cross the 53rd and 29th rifle corps to the western bank of the Berezina River. Their crossing was carried out by the boats of the Dnepr River Flotilla.

At the same time, the commander of the 3rd Army, striving to take Osipovichi and also to speed up the offensive by the army's left-flank forces to the northwest, was moving up on the western bank of the Berezina River to these axes the 9th Tank Corps and the 40th Rifle Corps, the latter of which had been in the army's reserve up to this time. By the close of 28 June one of the rifle corps' divisions had forced the Berezina River near Shatkovo and had reached the line Shatkovo—Sychkovo—Yeloviki, having got into fighting with the enemy along the northern outskirts of Bobruisk.

The 9th Tank Corps, following its relief by the 48th Army's forces, began to cross the Berezina River at 1800 near Shtakovo, and its tank a motorized rifle brigades moved in the direction of Osipovichi.

As a result of the fighting of 27-28 June, the First Belorussian Front's 48th Army and the right flank of the 3rd Army, in conjunction with the 65th Army's 105th Rifle Corps and the Dnepr River Flotilla, and with the effective support of the 16th Air Army, completely finished the encirclement and destruction of the major enemy group of forces to the southeast of Bobruisk, while the 65th Army's 1st Guards Tank Corps and 105th Rifle Corps, with part of the 3rd and 48th armies' forces and the boats of the Dnepr River Flotilla, had not only securely surrounded the enemy's forces in Bobruisk, but had begun fighting in the city limits and had created favorable conditions for the rapid destruction of the encircled enemy.

As a result of the intense fighting of 27-28 June, our forces, which were energetically pursuing the enemy and squeezing the encirclement ring, deprived him of the opportunity of securely consolidating along any kind of line and to organize a defense in the area of Bobruisk along the Berezina River. The aviation's powerful and timely strike and the attack by the ground forces immediately afterwards, completely disorganized the encircled enemy's defense, broke him up into small and isolated pockets and in this manner ensured the complete defeat of the enemy to the southeast of Bobruisk in the shortest time possible. The idea of the German-Fascist command of the Ninth Army—to lead its forces out of the encirclement southeast of Bobruisk to the northwest, for the purpose of linking up with the German-Fascist Fourth Army—was foiled, thanks to the decisive actions of our forces.

The destruction of the German-Fascist forces surrounded southeast of Bobruisk, and the Bobruisk garrison, was begun simultaneously—on 27 June.

The town's garrison, numbering more than 10,000 men, was reinforced by the remnants of the defeated units of the XXXV Army and XLI Panzer corps and the 20th Panzer Division, which had been seeping into the town. Hiding here were units, elements, and even individual soldiers of the 296th, 6th, 45th, 134th, 36th, 383rd, and 35th infantry, 20th Panzer, and 18th Anti-Aircraft divisions, and the Ninth Army's 511th Communications Regiment, as well as several security battalions.

By conscripting the local population, the enemy constructed a powerful perimeter defense of the town, barricaded streets, adapted buildings and basements to be firing points, built barbed wire obstacles, and thickly mined the outskirts. Tanks were dug in along the crossroads and permanent stone and reinforced concrete firing points were built. Powerful anti-aircraft fire covered the town against the air.

During the second half of 27 June units of the 1st Guards Tank and 105th Rifle corps made their first attack on the city, but were unsuccessful. The enemy garrison put up stubborn resistance to our attacking forces, which was particularly powerful on the southern and northwestern outskirts of town, where the enemy organized intensive automatic rifle and machine gun fire, and fire from assault guns at close range.

In preparing for a new assault on the town, the 65th Army's right-flank forces regrouped their men on the morning of 28 June. For example, the 105th Rifle Corps relieved units of the 1st Guards Tank Corps in the Berezovichi area with its left-flank 115th Rifle Brigade and had the task of breaking into the town from the west. The 356th Rifle Division, attached to the 105th Rifle Corps from the army reserve, was moved up to the line south of Yeloviki—the southern bank of the Berezina River. The division, together with the tank corps' tanks, was to break into the town from the north. The same corps' 354th Rifle Division was to continue to attack Bobruisk from the south.

The tank corps, along with the rifle corps, was to break into the town from the northwest.

Fierce fighting continued all day on 28 June. The enemy, despite his heavy losses, fought for each building and each block. During the second part of the day the Germans increased their counterattacks from the town's northern part. At 1600 a detachment of 1,000 men, with a large number of officers, made the first attempt to break out of the encirclement to the north, but was attacked from several directions by our tanks and completely defeated. As a result of the stubborn fighting, the encirclement ring in the town was becoming tighter and by the close of 28 June units of the 105th Rifle Corps, having relieved units of the 1st Guards Tank Corps, were fighting with their 354th Rifle Division along the town's southern outskirts, the 115th Rifle Brigade in the area of the railroad station, and the 356th Rifle Division, in conjunction with part of the 129th Rifle Division—in the northwestern and northern outskirts.

At 1000 on 28 June the *front* commander, as we noted earlier, ordered the 48th Army to cross its main forces over to the western bank of the Berezina River and, no later than 2400 on 28 June, upon relieving units of the 3rd and 65th armies in the Bobruisk area, capture the town.

Upon receiving the order, the 48th Army's forces immediately began to prepare, with the assistance of the Dnepr River Flotilla, to force the river and attack the town from the east.

The 42nd Rifle Corps relieved units of the 3rd Army along the Vlasovichi—Titovka sector and on the morning of 29 June was preparing to attack Bobruisk from the northeast and east; the 29th Corps, while continuing to destroy the remnants of the enemy in the forests, during the second part of the day began a crossing in the Polovets area, with the task of relieving units of the 65th Army south of Bobruisk by the close of 28 June and being in readiness to attack the town from the south and southeast. Besides this, the river flotilla's armored cutters; having broken through to the eastern part of the city under enemy fire, by 1800 had landed a party from the 217th Rifle Division. The 53rd Corps was to relieve units of the 115th Rifle Brigade (105th Rifle Corps) during the night of 29 June and in the morning decisively attack the enemy defending the town's western outskirts.

However, the situation in the town changed sharply that night.

The enemy, having weakened his resistance on the town's outskirts, withdrew a significant part of his forces to the center under the cover of automatic riflemen. On the night of 29 June the 356th Division's reconnaissance established that the Germans had concentrated major infantry and artillery forces in the northern and northwestern parts of the town. A prisoner, who had been captured by the division's reconnaissance, said that "the garrison of Bobruisk, as the garrison commandant, General Haman, said in his order, is abandoning the town tonight and breaking out to the northwest. The shock and assault officer battalions will be the first to attack."

This information could not but arouse the concern of the 105th Rifle Corps' commander for the 356th Rifle Division's sector, because the 1st Guards Tank Corps, in carrying out the *front* commander's order, on the evening of 28 June was already moving along the road to Pukhovichi, while the 65th Army's main forces, successfully developing the offensive to the northwest, were already in the Osipovichi area. In order to strengthen the 356th Rifle Division's sector, the corps commander transferred to the northwestern outskirts a significant part of his artillery and a guards mortar battalion.

However, his most important measure was an order to immediately attack the enemy and prevent him from carrying out his plan. At 2300 on 28 June units of the 105th Rifle Corps attacked the enemy garrison, but having captured a few blocks, were forced to once again consolidate and organize in the first echelon's combat formations a dense system of guns firing over open sights (up to 15-17 barrels per kilometer of front). The detachments that were covering the escape of the garrison's main forces out of the encirclement put up desperate resistance.

The enemy, having detected the removal of the 1st Guards Tank Corps' units from the battle, became more active, particularly along the northwestern axis.

At 0130 on 29 June the German-Fascist forces, numbering up to 10-15,000 men, with 42 tanks and self-propelled guns, went over to the attack along the entire front of the 356th Rifle Division.

The artillery and guards mortar battalion, and particularly the guns firing over open sights (16 barrels per kilometer), which had been transferred in time to the 356th Rifle Division's sector, open a powerful fire on the attacking enemy. The enemy's attack did not succeed and he fell back to his jumping-off position with heavy losses. At 0200 the German-Fascist forces again attacked, but were again thrown back with heavy losses.

At 0400 on 29 June the forward units of the 48th Army's 42nd and 29th rifle corps, supported by powerful artillery fire and the Dnepr Flotilla, began crossing the Berezina River and began fighting on the eastern outskirts of Bobruisk. Units of the 105th Rifle Corps renewed their attacks from the west and south.

By 0800 the 354th Rifle Division, while destroying the enemy hunkered down in the buildings and cellars, captured the train station and the adjacent blocks. Simultaneously, the 42nd Rifle Corps' forward units were fighting in the eastern part of the town. The enemy, while holding off our forces' attack from the east and the south, once again concentrated major infantry forces in the northern part of the town, numbering up to 10,000 men, and at 0800 on 28 June made his third attempt to break out of the encirclement to the northwest.

Taking heavy losses, the German-Fascist troops managed to break through the 356th Rifle Division's defense. A German-Fascist group numbering 1,500 men managed to break through to the north along the western bank of the Berezina River toward Shatkovo through the holes in the front, which were under a constant crossfire from the division's units. The breakthrough group lost all control; a large part of its streamed toward Osipovichi, where it was destroyed by units of the 18th Rifle Corps (69th Rifle Division), while the remaining part was once again encircled in the forests west of Shatkovo, and there either captured or destroyed.

Another large enemy group, numbering 8-9,000 men, while continuing to counterattack, pushed back units of the 356th Rifle Division and, have passed through Yeloviki, scattered in the wooded areas south and east of Voskhod and Sychkovo, where it was once again surrounded by our forces.

With the abandonment of Bobruisk by the enemy's main forces, his resistance lessened significantly. It should be said that by this time the 48th Army's forces (42nd Rifle Corps), having forced the Berezina along the sector of Zelenki and to the south, broke into the eastern outskirts of the town and began to clear the enemy out, block by block. Then the 65th and 48th armies' forces (105th and 42nd rifle corps) launched a concentric attack, in conjunction with the Dnepr Flotilla, and by 1000 on 29 June had defeated the garrison and completely captured the town.

Thus the *front's* right-wing forces captured Bobruisk, an important communications center and the Germans' powerful center of resistance, which covered the axis toward Minsk, Slutsk and Baranovichi.

In the fighting for the town and the defeat of the enemy's group of forces surrounded there, the enemy lost more than 7,000 officers and men killed, and 12 trainloads of food, forage and equipment were captured, including more than 400 guns, of which more than 100 were in working order, 60 knocked-out tanks and assault guns, more than 500 motor vehicles, and six depots with other military stores. Up to 2,000 officers and men were taken prisoner.

While the 48th Army, in conjunction with the 3rd Army's left-flank forces (9th Tank and 41st Rifle corps), the 65th Army's right-flank forces (1st Guards Tank and 105th Rifle corps), and the Dnepr River Flotilla, supported by the aviation of the 16th Air Army, was successfully concluding the encirclement and destruction of the major group of German-Fascist forces to the southeast of Bobruisk and in the city itself, the main forces of the First Belorussian Front's right wing were developing the offensive to the northwest and west.

The 3rd and 65th armies' forces were developing the offensive to the northwest.[1] The 3rd Army's right flank was attacking toward Chichevichi, and the center toward Svisloch', while the left flank (9th Guards Tank and 41st Rifle corps), in conjunction with the 65th Army's right-flank forces (1st Guards Tank and 105th Rifle corps) continued, as before, to destroy the enemy's group of forces surrounded southeast of Bobruisk and in the town itself. The 65th Army's left flank was attacking in the general direction of Osipovichi and Pukhovichi.

While pursuing the scattered units of the German-Fascist Ninth Army, the 3rd Army, in conjunction with four partisan brigades from the Mogilev formation, forced the Ol'sa and Berezina rivers from the march, captured a major road junction and the towns of Svisloch' and Klichev, cut the important Mogilev—Osipovichi—Minsk rail communications route, and by the close of 28 June was fighting along the line Chechevichi—Zakut'e—Svisloch', and further along the eastern bank of the Berezina as far as the mouth of the Ol'sa River.

The 65th Army's 18th Rifle Corps, and from the latter half of 28 June—the 1st Guards Tank Corps—was developing its attack to the northwest, destroying and throwing back the scattered units of the 35th Infantry and 20th Panzer divisions.

The intelligent initiative of the 18th Rifle Corps' commander should be noted. Taking into account the enemy's weak resistance, he ordered a surprise attack by two mobile forward detachments (mounted on motor vehicles) from the 37th Guards and 69th rifle divisions to take the town of Osipovichi from the march. The enemy garrison in the town, dazed by the mobile detachment's sudden and audacious attack, lost its head and ran away in panic.

The 1st Guards Tank Corps, in developing the army's attack along the Osipovichi—Pukhovichi road, by the end of the day had reached Baranovichi-3 (ten kilometers west of Bobruisk) with its forward detachment.

Thus the 3rd and 65th armies, while developing the offensive to the northwest, moved the external front away from the encircled garrison of Bobruisk, significantly increased the speed of its advance, raising it on 28 June to 18-20 kilometers in the rifle formations, and up to 40 kilometers in the tank corps.

The 1st Guards Tank Corps, in connection with its delayed relief by units of the 105th Rifle Corps and the enemy's great activity, became scattered and could not take Pukhovichi.

The *front*'s cavalry-mechanized group and the 28th Army, while carrying out their tasks, during 27-28 June developed the offensive to the west. At the same time, the *front*'s cavalry-mechanized group was attacking in the general direction of Starye Dorogi, while the 28th Army's right flank was attacking to the northwest around the north of the swamps toward Lyuban'.

During 27-28 June the 28th Army broke through the enemy's defenses along the Ptich' River and, along the army's left flank, in the woods west of Porech'ye (28 kilometers south of Glusk), and surrounded and destroyed an enemy group numbering up to 1,000 men. In the course of two days the army significantly increased its speed of advance, especially along the right flank, and on the latter day advanced 40 kilometers. Besides this, the army captured the major road junction, district center and large town of Glusk. The crossing equipment's lagging behind the troops caused a slight delay in forcing the Ptich' River by the army's forces.

The headlong attack by the *front*'s cavalry-mechanized group along the Glusha—Gorodok axis led to the capture of the latter at 0600 on 27 June, thus cutting for the second time the

---

1   The 80th, 35th, 46th and 18th rifle corps, and the 1st Guards Tank Corps (the latter from the second half of 28 June).

Bobruisk—Slutsk road. Then, while pursuing the enemy toward Slutsk along the road and the back roads south of it, captured the major town and railroad station of Starye Dorogi along the German's important Bobruisk—Slutsk communications link, and advanced more than 50 kilometers in three days of attacking.

Besides this, with the arrival of the group's forces in the Glusha area as early as the morning of 27 June, the task of taking Bobruisk became significantly easier, and the group's arrival at the Oressa River created favorable conditions for the subsequent development of the *front's* attack in the general direction of Baranovichi.

However, the absence of crossings over the Oressa River and the lagging behind of the crossing equipment interfered with the group's carrying out in time the task laid down by the *front* commander.

The constant lagging behind of the engineering equipment testifies to our undervaluing them and shortcomings in the engineering support of the troops on the part of the group and the *front*, as well as the poor control over these services on the part of the headquarters and commanders.

The *front's* newly-created operational group of fortified areas (115th, 161st, 153rd, and 119th fortified areas), pinning down the enemy's units in the space between the 28th and 61st armies' flanks, reached the eastern bank of the Ptich' River with its right flank and center by the close of 28 June and took up defensive positions from the mouth of the Neratovka River as far as Slobodki-1, while the 119th Fortified Area continued to defend its previous defensive position along the eastern bank of the Ptich' River as far as Besedka.

The *front's* forces were greatly assisted by the Belorussian partisans in developing the offensive to the northwest and west. Moreover, if earlier this assistance had been expressed in the form of operational cooperation, here it acquired the character of tactical cooperation. For example, the forcing of the Ol'sa River near Klichev, and the Berezina River near Svisloch, the capture of these towns and the town of Osipovichi, was all carried out in our forces' close coordination with six brigades from the Mogilev partisan formation.

Besides this, the forcing of the Ptich' River along the Rylovichi—Porech'ye sector and the expansion of the bridgeheads along its western bank by the forces of the *front's* cavalry-mechanized group and the 28th Army, was also carried out in close cooperation with the Poles'ye formation's partisans and a brigade from the South Minsk formation. In assisting our forces, the partisans would seize bridges and crossings over rivers and hold them until the arrival of our forces, as well as preparing wood and other materials for laying down crossings.

At the same time, in the enemy's rear the partisans' main efforts were directed at destroying the enemy's main communications—bridges, the telegraph-telephone network, and blowing up trains along the Osipovichi—Minsk and Minsk—Baranovichi sectors, among others. In this way, the partisans not only upset the enemy's deliveries, but drew off a large number of forces to guard the roads and lowered the combat capabilities of the enemy's units.

While developing the offensive to the northwest in the direction of Osipovichi and Pukhovichi, and to the west toward Starye Dorogi and Slutsk, and Glusk and Lyuban', as a result of the decisive successes in the 65th and 28th armies' sectors, conditions had been created for the headlong attack by the First Belorussian Front's forces toward Minsk, Slutsk and Baranovichi.

Thus in the course of five days (24-28 June) the forces of the First Belorussian Front's right wing successfully accomplished their immediate objective, as laid down by the *Stavka* of the Supreme High Command. Furthermore, the objective had been achieved four days ahead of the time called for by the operational plan. The *front's* forces along the right flank advanced 14-25 kilometers further than had been called for in the plan, 15-36 kilometers further in the center, and 38-50 kilometers further along the left flank. During course of the fighting the main forces of the German-Fascist Ninth Army had been defeated, a huge amount of Belorussian territory liberated, and the necessary conditions created for the development of a headlong offensive to the northwest—toward Pukhovichi and Minsk, and to the west—toward Slutsk and Baranovichi.

Besides this, the arrival of the *front's* forces in the Svisloch'—Osipovichi area had created a serious threat to the flank and rear of the enemy's Mogilev group of forces.

The great success in carrying out the immediate objective had a decisive significance for the realization of the *front's* subsequent objective, and overall for the subsequent course of events along the First Belorussian Front's axis of advance, as well as in Belorussia as a whole. The German-Fascist Ninth Army—the bedrock of Army Group Center's right wing—had been defeated. The First Belorussian Front's right-wing forces were now able to rapidly advance, ceaselessly pursue the defeated enemy and prevent him from recovering and consolidating. Along with this, the enemy's defeat along his right wing created a favorable prospect for launching an attack along converging axes toward Minsk in conjunction with the Third Belorussian Front, in order to encircle and destroy the German-Fascist Fourth Army, which was withdrawing before the Second Belorussian Front in the direction of Minsk.

The Operation's Second Stage

The Development of the Success along the Bobruisk—Minsk and Bobruisk—Slutsk Directions (29 June-4 July 1944)

Having suffered a defeat around Bobruisk and having lost a strategically significant defensive line along the Berezina River, as well as a defensive line along the Ptich' River, the enemy opposite the *front* was forced to fall back on Pukhovichi, Minsk, Slutsk, and Baranovichi, more and more exposing the right flank and rear of the forces falling back in the Second Belorussian Front's sector toward Minsk. The German-Fascist command, striving to save its forces from being encircled around Minsk and attaching enormous significance to the Minsk—Baranovichi railroad as the most important communications route of the Minsk group of forces, was rapidly moving up the 12th Panzer Division up to Pukhovichi, and the 4th Panzer and Hungarian 4th Cavalry divisions toward Slutsk. These formations were being transferred from army groups North and South (from the areas of Ostrov and Kovel'), and from the Second Army near Pinsk.

The commander of the First Belorussian Front was striving to take advantage of the success achieved for developing the offensive along the Minsk and Slutsk axes.

At the same time, fighting continued in the area northwest of Bobruisk against a large group of German-Fascist troops, numbering more than 9,000 men, which had gotten out of the town and had been surrounded again.

At the cost of great losses, the enemy managed to break through to the northwest along the western bank of the Berezina River toward Oktyabr' (Yelizovo). A large enemy group, numbering up to 6,000 men, broke out with tanks and assault guns, under the overall command of the commander of the XXXV Army Corps, General von Lutwitz.

The enemy's forces that did not manage to break out of the encirclement were split into two parts by the *front's* forces and eliminated during the second half of 1 July. At the same time, up to 2,000 officers and men were killed, and as many captured. The main forces of the German-Fascist troops that broke out of the encirclement drove to the north along the Berezina River. In approaching the town of Oktyabr', the enemy attacked the left flank of the 46th Rifle Corps and, having pushed it back to the north, seized the town.

The 9th Tank Corps arrived at Oktyabr' and, in conjunction with the 46th Rifle Corps, encircled the enemy group of forces that had broken through here. Then an attack from the south, west and north defeated the encircled enemy and by 2030 on 30 June the tank corps captured the town and the surrounding area. As a result of the battle, up to 2,000 officers and men were killed, and 2,500 captured.

This was essentially how the large group of German-Fascist forces, which had broken out of Bobruisk and then from the encirclement north of the town, was eliminated. This required about three days or nearly twice as long as needed for the destruction of the large group of forces south-east of Bobruisk. Significant numbers of our forces were also tied down by these battles.

Naturally, all of this told negatively on the speed of developing the offensive along the main Minsk axis.

At the same time the 48th Army, the 65th Army's 105th Rifle Corps, and the 3rd Army's 40th and 41st rifle corps were finishing off the enemy encircled around Bobruisk, the main forces of the First Belorussian Front's right wing were pursuing the remains of the defeat German-Fascist forces along the Bobruisk—Minsk and Bobruisk—Slutsk axes. Besides this, the 61st Army had begun a local offensive operation along the Pinsk operational axis.

The 3rd Army was operating along the Bobruisk—Minsk axis toward Cherven' and Pukhovichi, and its 1st Guards and 9th tank corps toward Pukhovichi; the 65th Army was operating along the Bobruisk—Slutsk axis toward Slutsk, and the 28th Army toward Pogost; between them was the *front's* cavalry-mechanized group, and the 61st Army and the Dnepr Flotilla along the Pinsk axis and along the Pripyat' River.

On the morning of 29 June the 3rd Army's forces continued to develop the success, making their main attack with the left flank toward Pukhovichi, with the objective of capturing this inhabited locale, while the right flank launched a supporting attack toward Cherven', for the purpose of cutting the Mogilev—Minsk road.

On the army's main attack axis, the 1st Guards Tank Corps'[2] lead 17th Tank Brigade continued to pursue the retreating enemy along the Minsk road toward Pukhovichi; on the morning of 29 June, not having encountered serious resistance, the corps reached the Svisloch' River, where, while trying to cross the river from the march, it was hit with powerful artillery and mortar fire. Having decided to hold this line along the Bobruisk—Minsk main road and thus delay our forces' offensive along the Minsk axis, the enemy blew up all the bridges over the Svisloch' River and transformed the inhabited locales into strong points with a large number of anti-tank and assault guns, tanks and artillery.

On 30 June the 17th Tank Brigade forced the Svisloch' River, although the corps' main forces were not able to develop this success before 1 July, because each time the enemy would destroy the bridges prepared for the crossing with powerful artillery and mortar fire.

During the night of 29 June the 9th Tank Corps crossed over to the Berezina River's western bank near Shatkovo, and in the morning was following behind the 1st Guards Tank Corps along the Minsk road toward Pukhovichi.

At the same time, the 3rd Army's formations, while developing the attack along the secondary axis toward Cherven', on June 20 forced the Berezina and Kleva rivers near Kaplantsy. During the course of two days (29-30 June) the 3rd Army, following its formations' relief by the 48th Army, regrouped its forces and created a group of forces along the right flank in the direction of Cherven', consisting of three rifle corps, and on the left flank along the Pukhovichi axis, consisting of two rifle and two tank corps. Having reached the Mogilev—Minsk road, the 3rd Army's right flank successfully conducted the parallel pursuit of the Mogilev—Orsha group of forces' columns, which were retreating on Minsk, and also assisted the successful offensive by the Second Belorussian Front's left-flank forces.

---

2   On June 30 the corps was operationally subordinated to the 3rd Army.

On 29 June the 48th Army completed crossing the 29th and 53rd rifle corps over the Berezina. The crossing was carried out on the Dnepr Flotilla's boats and barges. With the arrival of these corps along the axis of the main attack, the army took up the pursuit the enemy toward Osipovichi and Pukhovichi.

In the course of two days (29-30 June) the army regrouped its forces, relieved the 3rd Army's formations and created a group of forces along the army's main attack axis toward Osipovichi and Pukhovichi, consisting of two rifle corps (29th and 53rd).

Thus in the course of two days the *front's* forces along the Bobruisk—Minsk axis carried out a major regrouping, forced the Berezina River, moved forward deeply to the northwest toward Cherven', and cut the Mogilev—Minsk highway.

All of this created favorable condition for forcing the *front's* offensive along the Minsk axis, with the objective of encircling and destroying the Minsk group of forces in conjunction with the forces of the Third and Second Belorussian fronts.

Simultaneously with the development of the attack along the Bobruisk—Minsk axis, where the 3rd Army, in conjunction with the forces of the Third and Second Belorussian fronts, was carrying out the encirclement of the enemy's Minsk group of forces, the *front's* main forces were rapidly attacking toward Slutsk and Pogost, cutting the roads to Minsk from the south.

The 65th Army, while continuing to cover Osipovichi with its 69th Rifle Division from the north along its previous line, and developing the attack toward Pukhovichi with the 1st Guards Tank Corps, and on the morning of 29 June continued to pursue the enemy at high speed to the west, toward Slutsk, with its main forces (five rifle divisions), in conjunction with the *front's* cavalry-mechanized group.

On 29 June the army forced the Ptich' River from the march and then, developing the successful offensive throughout 29-30 June, advanced 68-74 kilometers, with an average speed of 34-37 kilometers per day.

During 29-30 June the cavalry-mechanized group advanced 42-60 kilometers, at a speed of 21-30 kilometers per day, broke through the enemy's defenses along the Sluch' River and, in conjunction with the 28th Army, captured the major road and railroad junction and district center—Slutsk—and achieved the objective laid down by the *front* commander.

On 29-30 June the forces of the 28th army reached the Baranovichi axis and cut the main communications leading from Slutsk to the south, having deeply enveloped from the northwest the enemy group of forces along the Pripyat' River facing the *front's* 61st Army. In two days the army had advanced 40-54 kilometers, at a rate of 20-27 kilometers per day.

The operational group of fortified areas continued to defend the previous line along the eastern bank of the Pripyat' River in the space between the 28th and 61st armies, to tie down the enemy and cover the space between the armies.

However, at 0300 on 29 June the enemy, following a disorderly fire onslaught along the front line of the 153rd and 119th fortified areas' units, striving to avoid encirclement, began to hurriedly fall back to the west.

The fortified areas' forward detachments immediately began to pursue and, having forced the Ptich' River, captured the towns of Kopatkevichi and Ptich', and a number of other inhabited locales.

Thus over the course of two days the *front's* forces along the Bobruisk—Slutsk axis forced the Oressa and Sluch' rivers, broke through the enemy's defense along them and captured the major resistance center of Slutsk, and also foiled the enemy's attempt to halt our attack along a previously-prepared defensive line along the Minsk—Slutsk road and the Sluch' River. Besides this, the *front's* forces, having advanced far to the west, had created favorable conditions for the offensive's development on Baranovichi and to outflank the enemy's Minsk group of forces from the southwest, as well as for developing the offensive along the Pinsk axis.

On the night of 29-30 June, our Long-Range Aviation bombed the Minsk, Baranovichi and Luninets rail junctions three times.

Taking into account the favorable developing situation in Belorussia, the *Stavka* of the Supreme High Command demanded in its directive no. 220124 of the evening of 28 June, that the Third, Second and First Belorussian fronts launch a vigorous attack along concentric axes on Minsk, to encircle and defeat Army Group Center's main forces and to liberate Minsk, the capital of the Belorussian SSR.

In accordance with this, the First Belorussian Front was ordered to launch its attack on Minsk with its right flank from the south and southeast, while the cavalry-mechanized group and the 65th and 28th armies were to attack toward Baranovichi. This made the *front's* subsequent objective more specific and increased its depth. If earlier it was demanded that the *front* reach the Bobruisk—Minsk and Bobruisk—Slutsk axes in the area of Pukhovichi and Slutsk and assist with part of its forces only the Second Belorussian Front along the right flank, then now the *front's* right-flank forces along the Bobruisk—Minsk axis were, in conjunction with, first of all the Third, and then the Second Belorussian fronts, to encircle and destroy the enemy's Minsk group of forces; along the Bobruisk—Slutsk axis the *front* would not attack as far as Slutsk, but as far as Baranovichi. Thus the depth of the *front's* subsequent objective grew by 70-100 kilometers, that is, more than twice.

However, the *front's* main forces, as before, were concentrated along the Baranovichi axis.

By the close of 30 June the enemy, withdrawing to the northwest and west, was resisting along the following lines: along the Minsk axis, along the Kaplantsy—Lyady sector—with the remnants of the 14th, 12th, 337th, 57th, and 260th infantry, and 286th Security divisions from the Orsha—Minsk group of forces; from Grodzyanka to Zhernovka—with the forces of the 36th, 35th, 296th, and 283rd infantry, and 20th Panzer divisions, as well as the Ninth Army's special elements and reinforcements, and; from Zhernovka to Veselovo—by the newly-arrived 12th Panzer Division and remnants of the 134th, 383rd, 45th, 6th, and 707th infantry divisions from the Bobruisk group of forces. The enemy was especially resisting along the right flank, in the direction of Berezino, and along the left flank, in the direction of the road to Pukhovichi (12th Panzer Division). Along the Baranovichi axis the enemy was putting up resistance along the Shishitsy—Dutinki sector with scattered units of the 35th Infantry, 20th Panzer and the recently-arrived 4th Panzer divisions, and the Hungarian 4th Cavalry Brigade, as well as the remnants of separate units from the 286th and 6th infantry divisions, the Ninth Army's military school, the 1009th Security Battalion, and various rear establishments, which had early been located in Slutsk. Major Schonger's combat group was defending from Pivashi to Chizhevichi. The 52nd Special Designation Security Division—Army Group Center's reserve, was located in Baranovichi, in the operational depth.

The enemy had prepared his next defensive line along the western banks of the rivers northeast, east and southeast of Baranovichi, while the town itself was a major defensive center.

By the close of 30 June the attack front of the *front's* right-wing forces had increased from 240 to 350 kilometers. Our forces were very strung out, while many formations lagged behind.

For example, in the 3rd Army's 90-kilometer sector along the Minsk axis, by this time there were only five divisions in the first line out of 13, and in the 65th and 28th armies along the Baranovichi axis, there were, correspondingly, three and four out of nine rifle divisions in each army. The rifle divisions were located 18-30 kilometers and more from their corps, and the 105th and 128th rifle corps 45-100 kilometers from their armies.

The artillery and tanks, and particularly the rear organs, lagged behind to a significant depth. By this time the supply bases' distance from their forces was about 300 kilometers, and the troops were experiencing a great need for ammunition and fuel.

All of this was the consequence of the high rates of advance and the diversion of 12 rifle divisions for the destruction of the enemy surrounded north of Bobruisk. Moreover, the road network was extremely limited and the roads themselves were in bad condition. Besides this, the 28th Army's regrouping of its forces to its right flank was being carried out around the wooded and swampy terrain of the Poles'ye from the north.

The reason for the supply bases' lagging behind was the extremely slow rate of restoring the Kalinovichi—Bobruisk railroad, which was proceeding at the rate of 1-3 kilometers per day in the tactical depth and 5-8 kilometers per day in the operational depth. And the troops' rate of advance was much greater—20-25 kilometers per day. The first train to the Krasnyi Bereg station (40 kilometers east of Bobruisk) arrived when our forces were fighting around Baranovichi.

In this situation, the commander of the First Belorussian Front, in carrying out the directive of the *Stavka* of the Supreme High Command, decided to continue the non-stop pursuit of the enemy and launch two attacks: the first along the Minsk axis, with the forces of the 3rd and 48th armies, with the 1st Guards and 9th tank corps, with the objective, in conjunction with the forces of the Third and Second Belorussian fronts, of taking the city and area of Minsk; the second attack would be along the Baranovichi axis and involved the *front's* main forces—the cavalry-mechanized group and the 65th and 28th armies, with the objective of taking the town and area of Baranovichi and cutting off the path from Minsk to the southeast.

Moreover, the tank corps and the 3rd Army would be launching the main attack directly on Minsk along the Minsk axis, while the 48th Army, operating toward Pukhovichi and Negoreloe, would secure the main group of forces from the south and southwest.

Along the Baranovichi axis, the 1st Mechanized Corps and the 28th Army would launch the main attack on Baranovichi, while the 4th Guards Cavalry Corps and the 65th Army would attack along the secondary axis toward Bobovnya and Gorodzei, securing the main group of forces from the north.

Events developed along the Minsk axis in the following manner.

The 3rd Army, upon completing a regrouping to its right flank, was to launch its main attack on Cherven' and Minsk, while the 1st Guards Tank Corps' mobile formations would attack along the Minsk road toward Pukhovichi and then to the northwest, with the task of reaching Minsk from the south.

On 1 July the 1st Guards Tank Corps, having failed to expand its bridgehead on the western bank of the Svisloch' River in the Tsel' area (near the paved road), began to attack with its main forces around the Minsk road toward Tal'ka and crushed the enemy's resistance in a night attack and captured the town. On 2 July the corps' units broke into Mar'ina Gorka village on the heels of the retreating enemy and forced the Svisloch' River from the march, and at 2100 they captured Pukhovichi with an attack from the south and east, along with the 46th Rifle Corps' units.

The enemy, having been pushed out of Pukhovichi and Mar'ina Gorka, was putting up fierce resistance along a line 1.5 kilometers west of Pukhovichi.

At the same time, the 9th Tank Corps captured the town of Valer'yany. The corps' subsequent advance to the north on Minsk was halted, due to breakdowns in supplying the combat vehicles with oil.

Along the 3rd Army's main attack axis, at 1800 on 1 July the 35th Rifle Corps captured the district center of Cherven' and cut the Mogilev—Minsk road, and on the next day, having overcome the enemy's increasing resistance along the Minsk road, linked up with units of the Second Belorussian Front's 50th Army and reached the line Fedorovsk—Khvoiniki.

The 80th and 41st rifle corps were moving up behind the corps along the axis of the main attack toward Minsk.

The 40th Rifle Corps, which was operating along the army's left flank, was pulled back into the army's second echelon.

Thus the 3rd Army and the tank corps, having crushed the enemy's stubborn resistance, reached the near approaches to Minsk, 50-55 kilometers to the southeast and south.

The army's forces completely defeated the remnants of the enemy's group of forces that had broken out of Bobruisk to the north, and captured the important road junctions along the main Mogilev—Minsk, Bobruisk—Minsk, Slutsk—Minsk communications lines and the towns of Cherven', Pukhovichi, Mar'ina Gorka, and Valer'yany. During this time the army's rifle divisions advanced 20 kilometers along the right flank and 40 kilometers along the left, advancing at a speed of 10-20 kilometers per day, while the tank corps advanced 24-120 kilometers, having an average daily rate of advance of 12-60 kilometers.

The 48th Army, having concentrated its efforts along the right flank, had finished the elimination of the enemy's scattered units in the Solomenka area (nine kilometers northwest of Bobruisk) and in the forests east of Osipovichi, with part of its forces, while its main forces pursued the enemy in the general direction of Tal'ka, Sergeevichi and Negoreloe.

By the close of 2 July the army had reached the line Dukovka—Berezyanka (nine kilometers southeast of Pukhovichi) and Velen'—Omel'no (8-16 kilometers west of Mar'ina Gorka).

At the same time as the forces of the First Belorussian Front's right wing, which were operating along the Minsk axis, the Third Belorussian Front's tank units were approaching Minsk from the northeast. By the close of 2 July they had captured the line Pil'nitsa—Ostroshitskii Gorodok (the 5th Guards Tank Army), and Korolev Stan—Bitaya Gora (the 31st Army's 2nd Guards Tank Corps), and were 16-22 kilometers northeast of Minsk.

In this fashion, a situation arose, in which it was necessary for the First Belorussian Front to break through as quickly as possible with its tank corps toward Minsk from the south, to capture the city and, in conjunction with the Third Belorussian Front's forces, complete the encirclement of the enemy's Minsk group of forces.

At 2300 on 2 July the *front* commander issued an order to the tank corps, and an hour later to the 3rd and 48th armies, to advance as quickly as possible, day and night, and take Minsk.[3]

On 3 July even more decisive actions by the *front*, in conjunction with the Third and Second Belorussian fronts and the partisans, unfolded along the Minsk axis.

For example, the 1st Guards Tank Corps' decisive attack along the Minsk road and the railroad to Rudensk knocked the enemy out of his position, and at 1300 on 3 July the corps broke through to Minsk and reached the southeastern outskirts of the city, where it linked up with the Third Belorussian Front's 2nd Guards Tank Corps.

The 3rd Army, taking advantage of its tanks' success, crushed the enemy's resistance and by 1600 its right flank had reached the city's southeastern outskirts.

Po-2 aircraft delivered oil for the 9th Tank Corps' combat vehicles in the Valer'yany area, after which the corps, developing the offensive to the north, toward Minsk, reached the line Korma—Danilovichi by 1700.

With the liberation of Minsk by the forces of the Third Belorussian Front, the First Belorussian Front's tank forces were pulled into the *front* reserve, in readiness for further operations along the Baranovichi axis.

The *front* commander ordered the 3rd Army, without entering Minsk, to rapidly pursue the enemy in the general direction of Dzerzhinsk.[4] In carrying out this objective, by the close of 4 July the 3rd Army's lead columns had reached the line Ostrovy—Yamnoe.

Thus the *front's* forces, which were operating along the Minsk axis, carried out the tasks entrusted to them. The 1st Guards Tank Corps and the 3rd Army, quickly pursuing the enemy retreating to the northwest, in conjunction with the forces of the Third and Second Belorussian fronts, on 3 July

---

3   First Belorussian Front directive, Central Ministry of Defense Archives, opis' 20897ss, delo 1, 179, p. 182.
4   First Belorussian Front directive, Central Ministry of Defense Archives, opis' 20897aa, delo 1, 186-87, p. 214.

accomplished the encirclement of a major German group of forces east of Minsk. The 48th Army's offensive supported the shock group's successful actions on Minsk from the south. The 9th Tank Corps, due to the lack of oil for its vehicles, did not accomplish its assigned objective.

Upon completing the encirclement of the German-Fascist Minsk group of forces, a 4 July directive of the *Stavka* of the Supreme High Command transferred the 3rd Army, along with its reinforcements, to the Second Belorussian Front.

Military operations along the Baranovichi axis developed in the following manner.

In carrying out their new tasks, the *front's* right-wing forces pursued the enemy on 1-2 July. Particularly successful were the actions of the 4th Guards Cavalry Corps, whose arrival in the Stolbtsy—Mir—Gorodzei area cut all the most important communications of the enemy's Minsk group of forces to Baranovichi. The corps made a fighting advance of 73-80 kilometers, an average daily rate of 37-40 kilometers.

The 65th Army, taking advantage of the 4th Cavalry Corps' success, pursued the enemy's small and scattered groups to Bobovnya, and by the close of 2 July had reached the line Zabolot'e—Bor—Sloboda Kuchinka—Skabin.

During this time the army's forced advanced 36-40 kilometers, with a daily rate of advance of 18-20 kilometers.

On 2 July the 1st Mechanized Corps liberated Timkovichi and Semezhevo. In two days of fighting the corps advanced only 21-31 kilometers. The 1st Mechanized Corps' relatively slow rate of advance is explained by the fact that the corps' formations got drawn into frontal fighting with the enemy's units covering some axes, did not outflank them or strive to achieve the main goal—the capture of Baranovichi, and in this fashion they lost their main quality as mechanized formations—their maneuverability and mobility. The corps did not take advantage of its neighbors' success, particularly that of the 4th Guards Cavalry Corps. The corps' formations were scattered over a 40-kilometer front, road reconnaissance was conducted in an unsatisfactory manner, and the corps was not reinforced with engineer-sapper and pontoon-bridge equipment.

By the way, the *front* was very late (at about 1100 on 2 July) in attaching the 21st Guards Engineer-Sapper Battalion to the corps and the 53rd Pontoon Bridge Battalion to the cavalry corps, and then only as a result of the lowering of the rate of advance on Baranovichi.

The 28th Army, having concentrated its main group of forces along the right flank, and in conjunction with the 1st Mechanized Corps, was attacking toward Timkovichi and Kletsk, and Krasnaya Sloboda and Sinyavka. In two days of pursuing the enemy, the army, having overcome an especially swampy strip, advanced 30-32 kilometers. The army's open flank on the left grew to 100 kilometers during this time.

The enemy, while continuing to withdraw his units to the west and southwest in the space between the 28th and 61st armies, was threatening the shock group's left flank. Thus the *front* commander ordered the chief of the fortified areas' operational group to securely protect this flank with allotted detachments, in conjunction with the partisans.

Thus the *front's* right-flank forces along the Baranovichi axis achieved significant results in two days of pursuit. They cut the Minsk group of forces' main communications to the southwest and west and thus decided the latter's successful encirclement and destruction.

The armies had mainly brought up their lagging formations to the front, but the rear organs, as before, were far behind their forces. For example, in the 28th Army the army fuel depot was 250 kilometers from the troops, while the closest railroad station at Ostankovichi (40 kilometers north of Kalinkovichi) was more than 200 kilometers away.

However, the 1st Mechanized Corps' rate of advance was obviously insufficient, which threatened the *front's* ability to achieve its objective—the capture of the town of Baranovichi and the surrounding area—on time.

While striving to help the mobile formations, the *front* commander issued additional and more precise tasks to the 48th, 65th and 28th armies at 1500 on 3 July: attacking toward Shatsk and Uzda, Bobovnya and Gorodzei, and Timkovichi and Kletsk, reach by the close of 3 July (4 July for the 48th Army) the line Negoreloe—Logvishche—Mogil'no—Pogorel'tsy—Nesvizh—Kletsk—Golynka.

If before the 48th and 65th armies' attack fronts had been carved in the general direction of the northwest, now they were directed westwards. Moreover, the 48th Army main attack was shifted from the right flank to the left.

Since this time all the efforts of the *front's* right-wing forces were directed at the capture of Baranovichi.

However, the 1st Mechanized Corps failed to carry out its initial task, as did the 65th and 28th armies their additional ones during 3 July. The 1st Mechanized Corps was particularly far from achieving its objective. The corps, as before, continued in the rifle corps' combat formations, operating in scattered brigades along a front of more than 40 kilometers, and failed to exploit the success of the 4th Guards Cavalry Corps, through whose lines it could have achieved operational freedom.

On 4 July the fighting along the Baranovichi axis unfolded even more fiercely, particularly along the fronts of the 4th Guards Cavalry and 1st Mechanized corps and the 28th Army. The enemy continued to reinforce the Baranovichi group of forces by transferring to the area the Hungarian 1st Cavalry Division from the Pinsk area, as well as by bringing up all the forces of the 4th Panzer Division, as well as from units of the 12th Panzer Division, which had broken through from the Minsk axis and put into order the remnants of the defeated units of the 6th, 35th, 129th, 102nd, and 292nd and other infantry divisions, and the 183rd and 630th security regiments, and various other units.

By the close of 4 July part of the 4th Guards Cavalry Corps' forces captured a bridgehead along the western bank of the Usha River north of Khlyupichi.

At the same time, the 1st Mechanized Corps, while developing the offensive with its main forces in the direction of Baranovichi, by the close of the day had captured Senyava station (ten kilometers west of Senyavka), thus cutting the Baranovichi—Luninets railroad.

The *front's* mobile formations advanced 18-36 kilometers during the day, but due to the enemy's growing resistance and his constant air activity, they did not achieve their objectives.

It seems to us that aside from these circumstances, other reasons for the *front's* forces not fulfilling their assignments lay in the indecisiveness of the 1st Mechanized and 4th Cavalry corps' actions, which, in turn, was the consequence of their improper control. For example, the mechanized corps, instead of taking advantage of the cavalry corps' success and launching an attack as early as 2 July, against the opposing enemy's flank and rear through the cavalry corps' attack front, remained in place.

The cavalry corps, having reached its assigned area a day early, did not take advantage of its success in order to assist, with part of its forces, the mechanized corps in the direction of Baranovichi or Kletsk, although it had a cavalry division in reserve. Finally, if the control over the corps had been brought closer to them and concentrated in the hands of the mobile group's commander, and not carried out from the *front's* temporary command post at a distance of up to 280 kilometers, then the shortcomings in the corps' actions would have been uncovered in time and corrected.

Overall, the enemy gained almost two days and during this time brought up the necessary men and materiel and held Baranovichi. The possibility of launching a surprise attack by the cavalry corps from the north and northeast was missed. For this same reason the mechanized corps' axis of attack was not changed in time from the southeast to the northeast. The *front* commander was forced, although he was late by 1½-2 days, to order that Baranovichi be taken by not one, but by both corps, from the northwest, north and northeast.

The 48th Army, despite the quite swampy and forested terrain and bad roads (particularly in the center and right flank), was energetically pursuing small enemy groups and by the close of 4 July had reached the line Migdanovichi—Barsuki, and then along the Ussa River to Kukhtitsy.

By the close of 4 July the 65th Army, pushing aside the enemy's covering groups with its forward detachments, had forced the Ussa and Neman rivers and reached the line Lunino—Pogorel'tsy—Nesvizh.

By the close of 4 July the 28th Army, taking advantage of the 1st Mechanized Corps' success along the right flank, had reached the line Minkeviche—Kletsk—Rybaki.

The fortified areas' operational group (115th, 161st, 153rd, and 119th fortified areas), having gone over to the offensive on the morning of 4 July along the western axis, in the difficult conditions of the Poles'ye's lack of roads and the wooded and swampy terrain, had by 2200 advanced its right flank 20 kilometers, and the center and left flank 5-10 kilometers.

The 16th Air Army, while assisting the *front's* forces along the Baranovichi axis, covered them from the air and on the night of 3-4 July, employing single Po-2 aircraft, interfered with the withdrawal of the enemy's forces along the Sinyavka—Kobrin and Sinyavka—Baranovichi roads and launched a raid against the road junction of Stoloviche (eight kilometers north of Baranovichi). During the day the air army destroyed the enemy's men and materiel in the areas of Snuv Baranovichi, as well as trains along the Luninets—Kobrin sector.

The successful offensive by the *front's* right-wing forces along the Baranovichi—Slutsk axis created the conditions for carrying out an offensive operation along the Pinsk axis with the forces of the 61st Army (occupying the central connecting space between the *front's* right and left wings) and the Dnepr Flotilla, in conjunction with the Poles'ye and Pinsk partisan formations, with the overall goal of tying down the enemy's formations located in defensive positions along the Pripyat', Stviga, Goryn' and Styr' rivers, sharply restricting their ability to be employed along the Baranovichi axis, and to roll up the enemy's defense along the Pripyat' River and, in this way, assisting the *front's* forces in freeing up men and materiel for employment along other axes.

Before dawn on 29 June the Dnepr Flotilla's second brigade of river cutters, in tactical coordination with the 61st Army's right flank, on 29 June, landed forces from the 55th Rifle Division in the areas of Krukovichi and Belki, and in the Petrilov area a day later. The 55th Rifle Division, having forced the Pripyat' River on the flotilla's boats and overcoming the enemy's resistance, captured Petrikov, and by the close of 4 July had captured the important railroad junction of Starushki and the town of Koptsevichi.

At the same time the 23rd Rifle Division, having attacked in the direction of Ozerany and Zhitkovichi, on 30 June captured Ozerany and, having forced the Stviga River, by the close of 2 July had broadened the bridgehead as far as the line Sleptsy—Starozhevtsy, along which it was repulsing the enemy's repeated attacks.

In order to assist the division, a second cutter brigade from the flotilla was moved to its area, which at 2330 on 3 July, taking advantage of the nighttime darkness, broke through along the Pripyat' River in the Khvoensk area, landed a battalion from the 23rd Rifle Division along the river's northern bank and then supported the division with its fire.

The division's subsequent attack, as well as the attack by the 397th, 415th and 212th rifle divisions along the army's left flank, was met by the enemy's powerful artillery and mortar fire (26 batteries) and was unsuccessful. It seems as though the enemy had decided to securely hold the line.

Thus the 61st Army, having captured the rail junction of Starushki and having rolled up the enemy's defense along a 50-kilometer sector, could advance no further. Besides, the army obviously possessed insufficient men and materiel to do this, because the army was also required to hold a line of 210 kilometers.

During the 29 June-4 July time period the partisan formations, cooperating closely with the *front's* forces, took part in seizing a number of towns and inhabited locales. Besides this, they supplied the troops with guides and timely reconnaissance information as to the enemy's group of forces and defensive lines, rendered assistance in restoring bridges and crossings along such rivers as the Ol'sa, Berezina, Ptich', Svisloch', Sluch', and others.

At the same time, the partisans let loose a big combat and diversionary campaign in the enemy's rear, which was directed at paralyzing his main communications. For example, during this period 34 trains were wrecked, containing equipment, munitions, food, and troops, as were 13,464 rails, along the rail lines leading from Baranovichi to Osipovichi, Minsk, Lida, Volkobysk, Brest, and Luninets; 5,337 rails from the rail junction of Luninets to Brest and Starushki. Thanks to this, the railroads' carrying capacity was significantly reduced.

Besides this, the partisan formations in the enemy rear attacked the enemy's withdrawing forces, their headquarters, rear establishments, auto transport, and supply trains; they blew up the road bed and bridges along paved and dirt roads; they destroyed incendiarists, rescued the population from destruction and being pressed into work, saved villages and towns from destruction and burning, especially industrial establishments and government buildings.

Thus by the close of 4 July the forces of the First Belorussian Front's had successfully carried out their subsequent task, which had been assigned by the *Stavka* of the Supreme High Command, had encircled, with the forces of their right flank, in conjunction with the Third and Second Belorussian fronts and the Belorussian partisan formations, the Minsk group of German-Fascist forces and, in rapidly pursuing the enemy along the left flank, had reached the enemy's previously-prepared defensive line along the Usha, Vedzhmanka and Shara rivers, on the near approached to the center of resistance—the town of Baranovichi.

Results and Conclusions

As a result of the operation conducted by the forces of the First Belorussian Front's right wing from 24 June through 4 July 1944 (11 days), the opposing enemy suffered a decisive defeat. Major groups of German-Fascist troops were encircled and surrounded southeast of Bobruisk and, in conjunction with the Third and Second Belorussian fronts, east of Minsk.

The encirclement and destruction of the Ninth Army's main forces, the Fourth Army, and the remnants of the Third Panzer and Ninth German-Fascist armies near Minsk, had enormous significance for the further course of the entire Belorussian operation and led to the defeat of the main forces of Army Group Center. The result of this was that in the First Belorussian Front's attack sector the enemy was not able to gather up any kind of powerful group of reserves before the line of the Shara River near Baranovichi and oppose them to the Soviet troops.

During the operation the *front's* formations successfully resolved the tasks assigned to them by the *Stavka* the Supreme High Command, having advanced a distance of 220 to 245 kilometers (instead of the 130-140 called for by the plan). At the same time, our forces liberated from German-Fascist occupation an enormous part of Soviet Belorussia (more than 26,000 square kilometers) and the capital of Minsk, which was an extremely important enemy center of resistance along the western direction.

The *front's* forces routed the Ninth Army, its XXXV and LV army and XLI Panzer corps, (134th, 296th, 6th, 383rd, 45th, 292nd, 102nd, 36th, 35th, and 129th infantry divisions), the army's reserve—the 20th Panzer and 707th Infantry divisions, as well as the reserves transferred from other axes—the 12th Panzer Division and the Hungarian I Cavalry Corps' 4th Cavalry Brigade. Besides this, two artillery regiments, seven artillery and anti-tank battalions, a High Command mortar battalion, the Ninth Army's school, security regiments, and a large number of special battalions and other units and elements were defeated.

The enemy suffered enormous losses. For example, the enemy's losses for 24-30 June amounted to 21,980 men captured and 57,500 killed, for a total of 79,480 officers and men. 364 tanks and assault guns were destroyed or captured, as were 2,624 guns, 2,154 mortars, 7,362 machine guns, 22,000 rifles and automatic rifles, 7,542 truck tractors and tracked vehicles, 140 motorcycles, 624 bicycles, 15,970 motor vehicles, 11,545 horses, 7,530 vehicles, 426 depots of various types, 249 radios, and 46 planes.[5]

During this time the *front's* forces broke through seven previously-prepared defensive lines, including the particularly important and strategically significant defensive line along the Berezina River.

The *front's* forces successfully forced a large number of major water obstacles, having broad and swampy flood plains, such as the Drut', Ola, Ol'sa, Berezina, Svisloch', Ptich', Sluch', and others, and also successfully overcame very swampy areas north of the Poles'ye.

The successful achievement of the Bobruisk—Slutsk operation's objectives and the arrival of the *front's* forces at the enemy's defensive line along the Usha, Vedzhmanka and Shara rivers created the conditions for the subsequent development of the offensive along the Baranovichi—Brest axis for the purpose of liberating from the German-Fascist forces the temporarily-occupied Belorussian territory lying within the First Belorussian Front's attack zone.

The First Belorussian Front's Bobruisk—Slutsk offensive operation began with a breakthrough of the enemy's continuous defense simultaneously along two sectors. Subsequently, these blows were rapidly developed in depth, and a major enemy group of forces was encircled and destroyed southeast of Bobruisk. This was followed by no less rapid attacks to the northwest on Pukhovichi and Minsk and particularly to the west on Slutsk and Baranovichi. The encirclement of the enemy's Minsk group of forces was completed, together with the forces of the Third and Second Belorussian fronts. The *front's* formations reached the enemy's intermediate defensive line along the Shara River and the near approaches to the major defensive junction and road and rail junction of Baranovichi.

Of decisive significance for the *front's* achievement of its objective was the 65th and 28th armies' breakthrough of the enemy's defense to the southwest of Parichi and the skillful conduct by the 3rd, 48th and 65th armies of the encirclement and destruction of the enemy's major group of forces southeast of Bobruisk.

The vigorous attack by the 3rd and 65th armies' tank corps from the northeast on Titovka, and from the south on Bobruisk by the close of the third day, and that by the combined-arms formations by the close of the fourth day (27 June), brought the *front's* forces to the communications of the enemy Bobruisk group of forces, having cut off his path of retreat to the west and having split it up into three separate parts (north and south of the Rogachev—Bobruisk paved road, and west of the Berezina River), which subsequently made it easier to eliminate it.

The breakthrough of the enemy's defense was carried out by the armies' massive attacks along two breakthrough sectors, which were 80 kilometers apart and divided by the powerful water barrier of the Berezina River. The width of the breakthrough sectors, along which on the morning of 24 June the *front's* shock groups attacked the enemy, amounted to 29 kilometers, or 12 percent of the entire attack front of the *front's* right wing (240 kilometers). The overall breakthrough sector, in relation to the *front's* entire sector (761 kilometers) was about 4 percent.

The success in accomplishing the *front's* subsequent task was decisively influenced by the rapid development of the offensive and the pursuit of the enemy by the 1st Guards Tank Corps and the right flank of the 3rd Army in the direction of Minsk, and along the Slutsk—Baranovichi axis by the 4th Guards Cavalry Corps and the 65th Army.

---

5 Central Ministry of Defense Archives, fond 233, opis' 14949ss, delo 55, pp. 128-29.

A vigorous attack by the 1st Guards Tank Corps to the northwest, and by the Third Belorussian Front's 2nd Guards Tank Corps to the southwest, completed the encirclement of the enemy's Minsk group of forces at 1300 on 3 July, and three hours later the arrival of the 3rd Army's right flank at the southern outskirts of Minsk formed the internal encirclement front.

No less rapid was the advance of the 4th Guards Cavalry Corps, and behind it the forces of the 65th Army, in the direction of Baranovichi and the corps' arrival in the area Stolbtsy—Mir—Khlyupichi—Gorodzei, and the army's arrival at the line Neman River (west of Mogil'no)—Nesvizh.

One of the most important conditions that secured the operation's success was the rank and file's high morale and combat qualities. Their objective source was the Soviet social and state system, and the just and liberating character of the Great Patriotic War. Besides this, the rank and file's high morale and combat training were also the result of a great deal of work carried out among the troops for their political and military education.

The tactical breakthrough of the enemy's powerfully fortified and deeply echeloned defense was accomplished by the troops' broad employment of maneuver, the enveloping and outflanking of strong points in the defense's main zone, as well as along the enemy's subsequent defensive lines.

The mobile formations played an important role in developing the breakthrough. The experience of the Bobruisk—Slutsk operation brilliantly showed two typical methods of employing the mobile groups. An example of the first and main method is the commitment of the 1st Guards Tank Corps and the cavalry-mechanized group into the breach made by the combined-arms formations in the German-Fascist defense along the Glusk axis southwest of Parichi. Such a method, in the conditions of a developed enemy defense and the presence among our forces of powerful means of suppression, supported to the greatest extent the rapid arrival of our mobile formations in the operational depth and rear of the Bobruisk group of forces and preserved their strength.

An example of the second method of employing mobile formations is the commitment of the 9th Tank Corps into the battle along the Bobruisk axis north of Rogachev, in order to complete, in conjunction with the combined-arms formations, the breakthrough of the enemy's tactical defense zone. Such a method corresponded to the situation, but was less favorable, because it brought about premature losses, the weakening of the corps and its delay in reaching the Titovka area.

The Bobruisk—Slutsk operation was characterized by comparatively high rates of advance, the rapid completion of the encirclement and destruction of the enemy, and the rapid development of the pursuit. Thus the *front's* forces began the operation to break through the enemy's defense along a 29-kilometer sector, and by the close of the offensive's fifth day—the day for carrying out the immediate task—the width of the *front's* attack front had reached 268 kilometers, and by the close of the 11th day—the day for completing the operation—it had reached about 400 kilometers, that is, it had increased 14 times in comparison with the breakthrough sector. At the same time, the planned depth of the operation was exceeded by 100 kilometers. The planned daily rates of advance of 7-8 kilometers were significantly exceeded and reached 22-25 kilometers per day. On some days they were much greater. For example, on 3 July the rate of advance along the 3rd Army's right flank was 45-48 kilometers and 40-45 kilometers along the 48th Army's center. Such rates of advance prevented the enemy from recovering following the attack in the tactical defensive zone and during the pursuit, foiled his attempts to put his forces in order, and denied him the opportunity of employing the arriving reserves along any particular axis, by forcing him to break them up in order to restore the front.

During the pursuit, which was conducted along a broad front and without losing combat contact with the enemy, our forces, as a rule, preempted him in occupying intermediate defensive lines. This is why all the defensive lines, both before Bobruisk and then as far as the line of the Shara River, were occupied by Soviet forces from the march, although they ran along rivers.

Thus the Bobruisk—Slutsk operation is one of the biggest maneuver operations, in which the force of the attacks and the rates of advance grew during the course of the advance.

The Bobruisk—Slutsk operation represents a brilliant example of encircling a major enemy group of forces in a short time, by means of coordinated envelopment attacks along converging axes. Moreover, the encirclement around Bobruisk was carried out o the operation's third day (26 June), and the elimination of the group of forces encircled southeast of Bobruisk—on the fifth day (28 June) and on the sixth day (29 June) in the city. Thus the elimination of the major enemy group of forces southeast of Bobruisk was accomplished within a very short time (2-3 days).

In encircling the enemy's groups of forces, one may note the well organized coordination between the mobile and rifle formations. The rifle divisions and corps broke through the enemy's tactical defense zone and secured the commitment of the mobile formations into the breach, and then consolidated and exploited their success. For example, the 1st Guards and 9th tank corps were the first to close the encirclement ring near Bobruisk, and the First and Second Belorussian fronts' 2nd and 1st guards tank corps around Minsk. The rifle formations arrived behind them and securely consolidated the encirclement front around the enemy, relieving the mobile formations. After this the tank corps were directed toward carrying out new tasks.

This operation gave us the experience of a rapid and simultaneous formation of an external front and its rapid removal to a great distance (up to 30-40-85 kilometers) from the encirclement center. Moreover, the *front's* forces, having formed the external front, did not assume a defensive posture, as had been the case during the first stage at Stalingrad and during the Korsun—Shevchenkovskii operation, but rather continued to advance pushed the external front farther and farther from the internal one. The enemy's attempts to break out of the encirclement were without result.

It should especially be noted that in encircling the enemy around Bobruisk, the initial attacks were made against the weakest parts in the system of the German-Fascist defense, which significantly eased the encirclement of the large enemy group of forces as early as the operation's third day. Besides this, the well organized coordination of the *front's* four combined-arms armies and the *front's* cavalry-mechanized group, and the reduction of the operation's planned deadlines, created for the *front's* right-wing forces all the conditions for the operational pursuit of the enemy and for launching powerful attacks on Minsk, Slutsk and Baranovichi.

The operation furnishes an instructive example of non-stop conduct. Having broken through the defense, the forces of the *front's* right wing, especially the 65th and 28th armies, immediately began to vigorously pursue the enemy. Having encircled the enemy group of forces in the Bobruisk area, they did not cease advancing to the northwest and west, toward Minsk and Slutsk, and upon encircling the Minsk group of forces—on Baranovichi. The pursuit itself, as already noted, was conducted by the armies along a broad front and deprived the German-Fascist command of the opportunity to employ its reserves on any particular axis.

The examples of the 65th and 28th armies show that in breaking through the enemy's powerfully fortified defense in wooded and swampy terrain, we should have a deeper combat formation. Thus the presence of 2-3 echelons enabled the army commanders to constantly augment the attacks from the depth and achieve great results.

In the operation each of the *front's* armies attacked along a single operational axis, with the exception of the 3rd and 65th armies, which on 29-30 June were trying to destroy the enemy group of forces in the Bobruisk area, and simultaneously were pursuing the enemy to the west.

The operation's experience confirmed the effectiveness of launching massive aviation strikes against an encircled group of forces. For example, as a result of a mass attack against the enemy southwest of Bobruisk, enormous losses were inflicted and his planned breakout from the encirclement was foiled. Moreover, this attack was coordinated with the ground forces, which immediately renewed their attack and squeezed even more the encirclement ring.

According to the operation's experience, the main goal of employing fortified areas in *front* and army operations continued to remain the pinning down of the enemy along the passive sectors of the front, in order to free up rifle formations for launching a massive attack along the main axis.

For example, units of three fortified areas (161st, 153rd and 119th) occupied a sector 70 kilometers in width before the offensive, which enabled us to remove the 65th Army's forces from an 18-kilometer sector and concentrate them, as well as the 28th Army's formations, along the axis of the main attack. At the same time the 115th Fortified Area occupied an additional sector of four kilometers on the southwestern outskirts of Rogachev, having relieved units of the 48th Army.

Sometimes the fortified areas' units were employed for advancing along secondary axes, for the purpose of developing the success of the armies' shock groups and securing their open flanks. Usually in these cases the fortified areas' units advanced to a depth of 6-10 kilometers. The further independent advance by the fortified areas' units, for the purpose of pursuing the enemy, was made more difficult by the absence of transport equipment for moving the attacking infantry's own artillery and heavy firearms behind it.

The Belorussian partisans rendered significant assistance to the forces of the *front's* right wing. Their powerful group of forces, which had been created in accordance with the High Command's idea and plan, was concentrated in convenient areas for operations along the First Belorussian Front's most important attack axes. Moreover, all of the partisans' reconnaissance-diversionary and combat activity was carried out in the interests of the *front's* operation an in close coordination with our forces. For example, the partisans' actions drew off large numbers of the German-Fascist Ninth Army's men and materiel, paralyzed enemy communications and thus foiled the movement of the enemy's reserves, supplies and evacuees. The partisans disorganized, to a significant degree, the enemy's rear and communications, thanks to which the retreating enemy forces' political-morale condition and combat capability sharply worsened. Partisan formations rendered a great deal of assistance to the forces with guides, and also seized and held inhabited locales and crossings over the Ptich' and Sluch' river, and eliminating defeated forces in our rear; finally, the partisans saved many local inhabitants from being driven into slavery, as well as industrial, social and other buildings from destruction.

The Soviet forces' success was facilitated by the following: the German-Fascist command's underestimation of our forces along the Bobruisk axis; the enemy's incorrect determination of the direction of our forces' main attack; the untimely beginning of the retreat and, in connection with this, his lateness in occupying and using for defensive purposes the prepared intermediate lines, and; the enemy's untimely commitment of his operational reserves and loss of control. Besides this, the German-Fascist command disposed of obviously insufficient operational reserves. This is confirmed by the fact that when the breakthrough was accomplished and a broad breach formed along two axes, the enemy's Ninth Army command began to feverishly remove and transfer the first-echelon division's regiments and operational reserves from other axes and even bring up reserves from army groups North and Northern Ukraine. However, in view of the large losses, as well as the vigor of the offensive by the First Belorussian Front's forces, the enemy was forced to commit these forces into the battle in detail, and without the necessary preparation. Thus these forces were quickly destroyed in the fighting, not being in a condition to carry out their assigned tasks and delay our offensive.

The operation brilliantly displayed the further growth and maturity of the Soviet soldiers, sergeants, officers, and generals, who had completed mastered the techniques of breaking through a powerful, deeply-echeloned, and previously-prepared enemy defense, and by means of skillful, bold and decisive maneuver to cut his communications, encircle and split up his forces, and to destroy and capture his men and equipment.

A characteristic feature of the operation was its vigor, the bold maneuver of the mobile formations, the comparatively rapid advance by the infantry, which, while attacking on the enemy's heels, prevented him from consolidating along prepared intermediate and rear lines.

During the operation the *front's* right-wing forces lost 50,056 officers and men killed, wounded, missing in action, etc., or 11.8 percent of their strength at the start of the operation. Of this number, the killed accounted for 9,160 men, or 2.2 percent of the overall number of troops.

The greatest losses were suffered by the 65th (14.9 percent) and 48th (12.9 percent) armies. These armies had to break through the defensive sectors most prepared from the engineering point of view, and heavily occupied, while they took a greater part in the fierce fighting to surround and destroy the major group of enemy forces southeast of Bobruisk, in the city itself, and to the north.

However, if one takes into account the fact that the enemy suffered losses of more than 60 percent of his rank and file, then our losses were nearly six times less. This fact once again shows how great were the results of the First Belorussian Front's Bobruisk—Slutsk operation.

The results of the multi-*front* Belorussian operation's first stage predetermined the subsequent course of events along the entire central sector of the Soviet-German front.

The enemy's defense, so carefully prepared, was broken. An enormous breach of more than 400 kilometers was formed in the enemy's strategic front, into which poured our forces. Army Group Center's main forces were defeated.

In 12 days of fighting the maximum advance of the *fronts* reached 225-280 kilometers.

The forcing of the Berezina River by the Soviet armies denoted the enemy's loss in Belorussia of all his main prepared defensive lines.

Attempts by the German-Fascist command to close the breach by hurriedly throwing formations from other directions of the Soviet-German front here, as well as from Germany and Western Europe, did not yield any kind of significant results during the operation's first stage.

The goals and objectives, assigned by the *Stavka* of the Supreme High Command in its directives to the *fronts*, were completely carried out. More than half of the Belorussian SSR, with its capital of Minsk, was liberated.

Favorable conditions were created for our forces with the destruction of the enemy's group of forces surrounded in the area east of Minsk by part of our forces, for the main forces to closely pursue the remnants of the defeated enemy formations, and to develop a vigorous offensive to the Baltic Sea, the borders of East Prussia, and to the Vistula River.

The American-English forces, which had landed in Western Europe in June 1944, took advantage of the distraction of the German-Fascist forces and reserves to the Soviet-German front and their grounding down during the Belorussian operation, in order to expand their beachhead and prepare for an offensive from it.

Part 2

The Second Stage of the Belorussian Operation (5 July-2 August, 1944

The Development of the Offensive, the Defeat of the Enemy's Arriving Reserves and the Soviet Forces' Arrival at the Borders of East Prussia

6

A Brief Review of Military Operations during the Second Stage of the Multi-*Front* Belorussian Operation of 1944

As a result of combat activities during the first stage of the Belorussian operation and the arrival of Soviet troops at the line Polotsk—Braslav—Molodechno—Nesvizh, the armies of the First Baltic, Third and Second Belorussian fronts, and the right flank of the First Belorussian Front essentially had no continuous enemy defensive front facing them.

The liberation of Minsk on 3 July 1944 signified the accomplishment by the *fronts* of their assigned tasks. The enemy's defense in Belorussia had been penetrated throughout its entire depth and along all axes, and of the enemy's main forces defending in Belorussia, a part had been destroyed, a part had been captured, and a 100,000-man group of forces had been encircled east of Minsk and was in the process of being destroyed. The enemy's surviving forces were hurriedly falling back to the west, while putting up a certain amount of resistance along the most important axes. With the arrival of the First Baltic Front's forces at the line Braslav—Lake Naroch', Army Group North was outflanked from the south.

It was in this favorable situation that the *Stavka* of the Supreme High Command decided to continue the energetic pursuit of the retreating enemy, launching its main attacks along two main axes: with the forces of the First Baltic and Third Belorussian fronts—in the Baltic States, for the purpose of liberating the Latvian and Lithuanian Soviet Socialist republics and cutting off the remaining forces of Fascist Germany's Army Group North, and; with the forces of the Second and First Belorussian fronts—along the Warsaw direction, for the purpose of completely expelling the enemy from Soviet territory and beginning the liberation of allied Poland.

Simultaneously, the *Stavka* of the Supreme High Command decided to carry out offensive operations with the forces of the Leningrad, Third and Second Baltic fronts, for the purpose of defeating Army Group North in the Baltic States, and with the forces of the First Ukrainian Front, for the purpose of defeating Army Group North Ukraine and liberating Western Ukraine.

On 4 July the *fronts* operating in Belorussia were given new objectives.

The forces of the First Baltic Front were to develop the offensive, launching their main attack in the general direction of Kaunas, and with part of their forces toward Siauliai.

The forces of the Third Belorussian Front had the task of developing the offensive, launching their main attack in the direction of Molodechno and Vilnius, and no later than 10-12 July capturing the line Vilnius—Lida; these forces were to subsequently reach the Neman River and capture bridgeheads on its western bank.

The forces of the Second Belorussian Front, following the elimination of the enemy group of forces surrounded east of Minsk, were to develop the offensive, launching their main attack in the direction of Novogrudok, Volkovysk and Bialystok, and no later than 12-15 July capture the Novogrudok area and reach the Neman River; these forces were subsequently to take Volkovysk and attack in the direction of Bialystok.

The forces of the First Belorussian Front's right wing were tasked with developing the offensive to the southwest, making their main attack in the general direction of Baranovichi and Brest, with the immediate assignment of taking Baranovichi and no later than 10-12 July reaching the line Slonim—Pinsk; these forces were to subsequently take the town of Brest and seize bridgeheads on the western bank of the Western Bug River.

The *front's* left-wing forces (70th, 47th, 8th Guards, 69th, Polish 1st, and 2nd Tank armies, 6th Air Army, 2nd and 7th guards cavalry and 11th Tank corps) were ordered to be ready to attack in the direction of Siedlce and Lublin and with part of its forces to capture Brest, in conjunction with the *front's* right-wing forces. These forces were to be ready, at first by 15 July, and then by 17 July.

In accordance with these decisions by the *Stavka* of the Supreme High Command, the scale of the offensive in Belorussia was not only not to diminish, but quite the opposite; thanks to the offensive by the First Belorussian Front's left-wing forces—it was to be increased. The four *fronts'* attack sector was to increase even more, while the depth of the new offensive operations was defined at no less than 250 kilometers.

During the second stage of the multi-*front* Belorussian operation, the following *front* offensive operations were carried out: the First Baltic Front's Dvinsk—Siauliai operation; the Third Belorussian Front's Vilnius—Kaunas operation; the Second Belorussian Front's Bialystok operation, and; the First Belorussian Front's Baranovichi—Slonim and Brest—Siedlce operations.

In order to achieve these goals, the *Stavka* of the Supreme High Command simultaneously carried out certain changes in the disposition of men and materiel. For example, taking into account the increase in the First Baltic Front's sector and its necessity for operating to the north and west, it was decided to transfer three armies to the *front*, in exchange for the transfer of the 2nd Shock Army to the Second Baltic Front. Two armies (2nd Guards and 51st) were to arrive from the *Stavka* reserve, and one (39th) would be transferred from the Third Belorussian Front. Thus, in order to carry out his new assignment, the commander of the First Baltic Front would dispose of five armies (2nd and 6th guards, 43rd, 39th, and 51st). To be sure, of these five armies, only two were in contact with the enemy, while the remainder could only enter the fighting after a few days. The First Baltic Front also included all this time the 1st Tank Corps, which was joined on 15 July by the Third Belorussian Front's 3rd Guards Mechanized Corps.

The Third Belorussian Front, in exchange for the 39th Army, transferred to the First Baltic Front, received the Second Belorussian Front's 33rd Army, which had moved into the Minsk area. This exchange was advantageous for the Third Belorussian Front, because instead of the 39th Army, which remained in the rear, it received the 33rd Army, which was located along the *front's* left wing and closely coordinating with it.

The Second Belorussian Front, in exchange for the 33rd Army, transferred to the Third Belorussian Front, received the First Belorussian Front's 3rd Army. Such an exchange was also favorable to the Second Belorussian Front and to a significant degree made it easier for the *front* to achieve its new objective. The 3rd Army, which had moved west of Minsk, could immediately begin carrying out its new assignment. The Second Belorussian Front's 49th and 50th armies had been drawn into the fighting with the encircled enemy and could begin tackling their new assignments only after several days.

Thus the First Belorussian Front's right wing remained composed of three armies, two tank corps, and a cavalry-mechanized group. The First Belorussian Front's left wing was strengthened with the 8th Guards and 2nd Tank armies, which by this time had been regrouped to the *front's* attack sector south of the Pripyat' River, from the Third and Second Ukrainian fronts.

By 5 July the German-Fascist Army Group Center had been routed and had basically ceased to exist as a single entity. An enormous 400-kilometer breach had been created in the enemy's defensive system, in which only individual surviving enemy groups, along with reserve units and formations being transferred here, were putting up insignificant resistance.

The German-Fascist command, having understanding that the battle for Belorussia had been completely lost, gave its forces the objective for July of preventing Army Group North from being cut off in the Baltic States and restoring the front in Belorussia along the line of the Neman River, halting the offensive by the Soviet armed forces here.

In order to prevent the encirclement of Army Group North's forces, it was very important for the German-Fascist command to retain the town of Dvinsk (Daugavpils), which in the current situation, intercepted the main roads leading to the shore of the Gulf of Riga. For this purpose, 11 of Army Group North's divisions were regrouped to its right flank and included in the Sixteenth Army, which was defending in the area of Dvinsk. Aside from this, the German-Fascist command was forced to transfer men and material here from other directions, in order to stop our *fronts'* offensive between Dvinsk and Brest. Five divisions came from Army Group North, four from Army Group North Ukraine, and two from Army Group South Ukraine. Three divisions, an infantry and a cavalry brigade, and many other different units came from Norway, Germany, Poland, and Hungary. In all, during the 5-23 July time period the enemy transferred 19 infantry and six panzer divisions, and an infantry and cavalry brigade each against our *fronts* in Belorussia. These formations, along with the reserves transferred here earlier, comprised the basis of the defense, for the troops retreating from the "Belorussian balcony" no longer represented a serious military force.

By 5 July the German-Fascist armies had been thrown back to an intermediary defensive line, which had been preserved since the First World War and which ran along the line Dvinsk—Molodechno—Baranovichi, and then southwards. However, this line was in a dilapidated condition and had been only partially restored.

The enemy attached great significance to the defense of such towns as Dvinsk, Vilnius, Kaunas, Grodno, Bialystok, Baranovichi, Brest, and others, because only in this way could he count on stopping the Soviet forces and prevent them front reaching the territory of Germany itself. Each of these towns had been well prepared for perimeter defense from the engineering point of view, had large garrisons and was sufficiently well supplied with ammunition, food and other material goods. Besides this, the towns of Dvinsk, Kaunas, Grodno, and Brest were ancient fortresses.

Thus despite the defeat of Army Group Center's main forces in Belorussia, the enemy still disposed of significant forces and our troops would have to put forward great efforts, in order to throw back the enemy to the territory of Germany proper.

On 5 July 1944 all four Soviet *fronts* began carrying out the new *Stavka* directives, without having gotten any kind of significant respite, for the situation demanded the continuation of the energetic pursuit of the retreating enemy.

The First Baltic Front, having begun to carry out the Dvinsk—Siauliai operation, could only pursue the enemy with the forces of the 6th Guards and 43rd armies, because its remaining forces had not yet reached the front line. It was necessary to overcome the difficult inter-lake area stretching between Dvinsk and Podbrodze and to capture the Dvinsk fortified area, which was being defended by large enemy forces. As a result of stubborn fighting for the Polotsk fortified area, the *front's* forces were by this time highly extended, particularly the 6th Guards Army, which was operating along a 160-kilometer front.

During the 5-15 July time period the *front's* forces developed the offensive along the Dvinsk and Svencionys—Siauliai axes.

The forces of the 6th Guards Army and 1st Tank Corps were attacking along the Dvinsk axis on the *front's* right wing. The *front* commander ordered the 6th Guards Army to capture Dvinsk. The 1st Tank Corps, which had been ordered as early as July 3 to capture Dvinsk, was to operate ahead of the 6th Guards Army. However, on 4-5 July, while attempting to carry out this assignment, the tank corps was unable to overcome the enemy's resistance along the approaches to the town and, on the instructions of the *front* commander, broke off the attack and was pulled back into the reserve. The *front* commander subsequently decided to employ the 1st Tank Corps in the 43rd Army's sector for developing the success along the Siauliai axis.

The commander of the 6th Guards Army attempted to take Dvinsk with an attack by a single corps along the Western Dvina River, but this attempt failed. The corps advanced 20 kilometers on 6-7 July, but was then halted by the enemy. The 6th Guards Army commander subsequently switched his efforts to his left flank and tried to outflank Dvinsk from the southeast. The army's rifle corps, which was attacking toward Zarasai, advanced 25 kilometers in six days and reached the Dvinsk—Vilnius railroad, but was halted here. From 15 July the fighting along the Dvinsk axis became prolonged. The enemy halted the 6th Guards Army's offensive, which was operating along a broad front with only part of its forces.

The 43rd Army's offensive developed more successfully along the Svencionys axis. The army, while pursuing the retreating enemy, advanced 65 kilometers during 5-7 July and on 7 July occupied Svencionys. The 1st Tank Corps, which from 6 July had been advancing with the 43rd Army, encountered stubborn enemy resistance and was unable to break through to the Zarasai area. During 8-9 July the 43rd Army continued to push back the enemy, whose resistance continued to increase. On 9 July the 39th Army, which had deployed south of the 43rd Army, entered the fighting.

During 9-14 July the 43rd and 39th armies continued to press the enemy to the west and by the close of 14 July had deeply outflanked the Dvinsk group of enemy forces from the south and southwest, threatening to completely cut it off from East Prussia. The 2nd Guards and 51st armies (from the *Stavka* reserve) were moving along the 43rd and 39th armies' operational axis.

The Third Belorussian Front was carrying out the Vilnius—Kaunas operation. Upon capturing Minsk and Molodechno, the *front's* main forces were concentrated for the liberation of Vilnius, forcing the Neman River and seizing a bridgehead along its western bank.

The offensive was conducted along two axes: toward Vilnius and Lida. The *front* commander ordered the 5th and 5th Guards Tank armies and the 3rd Mechanized Corps to attack toward Vilnius. The 31st Army, together with the 3rd Guards Cavalry Corps, was to attack toward Lida. The 11th Guards Army was to operate in the center, between the two shock groups. The 33rd Army remained in the Minsk area to secure the *front's* left wing.

The *front's* main group of forces, which was attacking toward Vilnius, advanced 70-130 kilometers on 5-7 July and reached the approaches to Vilnius.

The German-Fascist command attached great importance to retaining Vilnius. It counted on delaying the Soviet forces here, on winning time and creating a new defensive front along the western bank of the Neman River. However, the enemy's plan was foiled by the decisive actions of the Soviet troops. On 8 July the forces of the Third Belorussian Front outflanked Vilnius from three sides and began a decisive storming of the town. The enemy, having a garrison of more than 15,000 men in the town, put up stubborn resistance, and the fighting extended to the close of 13 July. Only on that day did the Soviet forces completely clear the town of the enemy and advanced 50 kilometers toward Kaunas.

At the same time the 11th Guards Army was developing a vigorous offensive to the west, overcoming the enemy's growing resistance. The enemy tried several counterattacks to halt the army's forces and throw them back, but was unsuccessful. On 13 July a part of the 11th Guards Army's forces reached the Neman River in the Alytus area, thus threatening Kaunas. On 14 July the army's forces captured a number of bridgeheads on the left bank of the Neman River. By the close of 15 July the armies of the Third Belorussian Front had forced the Neman River along an overall front of 70 kilometers, while the depth of the captured bridgeheads reached 8-10 kilometers.

The forces of the 31st Army successfully pressed the enemy along the Lida axis, occupied Lida and reached Grodno. The 3rd Guards Cavalry Corps, having covered 210 kilometers in nine days, on 13 July reached the northeastern outskirts of Grodno and began fighting for the town.

Thus along the Baltic direction, during the course of ten days the forces of the First Baltic and Third Belorussian fronts had almost completely carried out their immediate objectives, as laid down by the *Stavka* of the Supreme High Command. They had only failed to capture the town of Dvinsk.

During 5-15 July the *front's* forces had covered about 180-200 kilometers in fighting. In connection with the arrival of major enemy reserves to the Neman River, extended fighting began for the bridgeheads.

Along the Warsaw axis, the forces of the Second and First Belorussian fronts were also successfully pressing the enemy along the western direction.

The Second Belorussian Front's forces, having begun to carry out the Bialystok operation, were pursuing the enemy, at first with the 3rd Army alone, which in five days covered a distance of 120-140 kilometers, and which by 9 July had reached the Neman River, having captured the town of Novogrudok. On 9 July the 50th Army, which had been freed up from fighting the encircled enemy east of Minsk, reached the 3rd Army's line. On this day the 50th Army forced the Neman River in the Shchuchin area and attacked toward Grodno. On 15 July the army reached Grodno from the southeast and established contact with the forces of the Third Belorussian Front, which had also reached the area of the town. On 16 July the forces of the Third and Second Belorussian fronts, having organized a close coordination, stormed the town and fortress of Grodno.

On 14 July the Second Belorussian Front's 3rd Army captured Volkovysk, which was an important enemy defensive strong point.

Thus the Second Belorussian Front advanced more than 230 kilometers during 5-16 July and was ready for a subsequent offensive into the confines of East Prussia and Poland.

In the operational sector of the First Belorussian Front's right wing, which was carrying out the Baranovichi—Slonim operation, particularly fierce fighting unfolded in the Baranovichi area. The *front's* forces, having reached the town, encountered stubborn resistance and were not able to take it from the march. The enemy decided to defend Baranovichi until he could pull back his Poles'ye group of forces, which stuck out like a wedge in the Soviet lines. Our 61st Army, which was badly stretched out along the Pripyat' River and not very big, faced the enemy's Poles'ye group of forces. The army's attempts to undertake active operations during 3-5 July were not successful.

In accordance with the *Stavka* directive, the commander of the First Belorussian Front decided to launch a powerful attack against Baranovichi with the forces of the 48th and 65th armies, and the 4th Guards Cavalry and 1st Mechanized corps. Besides this, the 28th Army was to outflank Baranovichi from the south. The 61st Army was also to begin active operations, making its main attack on Pinsk.

On 5 July the First Belorussian Front began its attack on Baranovichi, but during the first two days it developed very slowly. The enemy held up our forces with numerous counterattacks. Only on the morning of 7 July, following an artillery and powerful aviation preparation, in which up to 500 bombers participated, did our forces break through the enemy's defense and break into the town. The forces of three armies and the cavalry corps took part in storming the town. On 8 July Baranovichi had been completely cleared of enemy forces.

On 7 July the 61st Army, employing the forces of its 9th Guards Rifle Corps, attacked toward Pinsk, while the 89th Rifle Corps, together with the Dnepr Flotilla, began to press the enemy along the Pripyat' River from the east to the west. The neighboring 28th Army launched an attack with one division on Luninets, from north to south. The enemy, under our forces' pressure, began to fall back from the Poles'ye salient, hurriedly retreating to the west.

On 10 July our forces occupied Luninets, and on 14 July they occupied Pinsk. Our forces were actively assisted by the Poles'ye partisans, who knew this wooded and swampy area well, and the overcoming of which were linked to great difficulties for the attacking forces.

Thus the forces of the First Belorussian Front, while somewhat late, were nevertheless close to carrying out their immediate objective, as assigned by the *Stavka* of the Supreme High Command.

The overall results of the offensive operations during 5-15 July were highly favorable. The forces of the First Baltic Front created the real threat of encircling all of Army Group North by pinning it to the shore of the Gulf of Riga. The forces of the Third and Second Belorussian fronts covered 150-250 kilometers during this period, and by arriving at the Neman River had created the real threat of an invasion into East Prussia, to the borders of which remained no more than 70-80 kilometers. Only the First Belorussian Front was a little bit late and was a bit behind the remaining *fronts*.

During the offensive's 23 days the Soviet forces completely defeated Army Group Center, cleared out the German-Fascist occupiers from the area between the Western Dvina and Pripyat' rivers, a territory more than 400 kilometers wide and about 500 kilometers deep, and liberated almost all of Belorussia and a significant part of Lithuania.

The enemy sought at any cost to delay our forces' offensive, by transferring to the front's central sector reserves from Western Europe, as well as from other sectors of the Soviet-German front.

By the middle of July the rate of the Soviet forces' advance had slowed. It was necessary to consolidate the successes achieved, bring up ammunition and fuel, regroup our forces, and create a favorable correlation of forces along the axes of the *fronts'* main attacks. At the same time, it was necessary to take advantage of the success already achieved, in order to develop the offensive along both old and new axes.

The defeat of the enemy's Army Group Center and the liberation of Belorussia were creating favorable conditions for an advance along the adjacent strategic directions of the Soviet-German front. On 11 July the forces of the Second Baltic Front opened their offensive. On 13 July the First Ukrainian Front's L'vov—Sandomierz operation began. A little later, during the 17-24 July time period, the Leningrad and Third Baltic fronts joined in the offensive. Thus the Soviet forces' strategic offensive front expanded and stretched from the Baltic Sea to the Carpathian Mountains.

The Soviet command, in continuing to carry out the multi-*front* Belorussian operation, undertook measures to develop the success achieved into the depth and toward the flanks. The *Stavka's* strategic reserves (2nd Guards and 51st armies) were employed for this purpose, and a powerful group of forces, consisting of five combined-arms and one tank armies, which had been created on the First Belorussian Front's left wing. It was no accident that these forces were committed into the fighting almost simultaneously—during 18-20 July.

The favorable course of the offensive enabled the *Stavka* of the Supreme High Command on 14 July to carry out a new redistribution of forces, so as to create a more powerful group of forces in the Third Belorussian Front's operational sector, for an invasion of East Prussia. The 39th Army, which was located north of Vilnius, was returned to the Third Belorussian Front, in connection with which the boundary between the First Baltic and Third Belorussian fronts was shifted 120 kilometers to the north. Such a shift was supposed to ease the work of the First Baltic Front, because it was no longer responsible for the Kaunas axis and could now concentrate its entire attention on the Siauliai axis alone. In exchange for the 39th Army, the *front* received from the Third Belorussian Front the 3rd Guards Mechanized Corps, which played a major role in the First Baltic Front's subsequent offensive operations. Besides this, the First Baltic Front was significantly reinforced with aviation.

The *fronts'* objectives, as laid down by the *Stavka* of the Supreme High Command on 4 July, were further specified and broadened. The First Baltic Front was to defeat the enemy's Siauliai group of forces and, while continuing a vigorous offensive to the northwest, reach the shore of the

Gulf of Riga. The Third and Second Belorussian fronts had the goal of continuing their offensive to the west along their sectors and reaching the border of East Prussia. The First Belorussian Front was to attack with all its forces along the Brest, Siedlce and Lublin axes.

During 15-19 July the forces of the First Baltic Front continued to repulse the enemy's counterattacks and brought up equipment and carried out troop regroupings for the forthcoming offensive. At the same time, offensive actions were carried out along some axes, for the purpose of improving the *front's* operational position.

With the arrival of the First Baltic Front at the approaches to Dvinsk and Panevezys, a favorable situation developed for launching an attack along the Riga axis, for the purpose of depriving Army Group North, the main forces of which were located northeast of Riga, of its land communications with Germany.

On the morning of 20 July the First Baltic Front, having included in the first echelon the 2nd Guards and 51st armies, transferred from the *Stavka* reserve, renewed the offensive, launching the main attack along the Siauliai axis.

On the morning of 23 July the forces of the 6th Guards Army renewed their offensive. Operating in the difficult conditions of wooded and swampy lake terrain, the army's forces broke the enemy's resistance and on the attack's fifth day, together with the forces of the Second Baltic Front's left wing, captured Dvinsk.

The offensive developed most successfully along the Siauliai axis. The main attack on Siauliai was made by the 51st Army, together with the 3rd Guards Mechanized Corps. The 2nd Guards Army was to launch an attack south of Siauliai. The 3rd Guards Mechanized Corps was attacking Siauliai from the north and northwest.

On 22 July the town of Panevezys was liberated. The 3rd Guards Mechanized Corps, which was committed into the breach on 22 July, having passed through the first-echelon rifle formations' combat formations, advanced 70 kilometers that day and reached the northern and eastern approaches to Siauliai, having cut the Riga—Siauliai and Siauliai—Liepaja (Libava) roads and railroads. The 51st and 2nd armies' forces were also approaching Siauliai.

Fighting for this town began on the morning of 27 July. The enemy garrison put up stubborn resistance against the forces of the 3rd Guards Mechanized Corps. Only when units of the 51st Army arrived was the town taken, which signified the Soviet forces' capture of the enemy's last major center of resistance on Lithuanian territory, which gave them freedom of maneuver to the shore of the Gulf of Riga.

The victory at Siauliai coincided with another major victory near Dvinsk. The liberation of the towns of Dvinsk and Siauliai placed Army Group North in a very difficult situation, as it was threatened with being pressed to the Gulf of Riga and destroyed. The army group's land communications with Germany were practically cut, because it was very difficult to maintain communications along the shore of the Baltic Sea.

The successful course of the Soviet forces' offensive along the Siauliai axis enabled the commander of the First Baltic Front to immediately carry out his final attack toward the Gulf of Riga, so as to fully complete the cutting off of Army Group North from Fascist Germany's remaining forces.

On 27 July the *front* commander ordered the commander of the 3rd Guards Mechanized Corps to attack from the Siauliai area toward the Gulf of Riga. The 51st Army, having the most dense group of forces along its right flank, was to attack with its front facing north, behind the 3rd Guards Mechanized Corps.

The 6th Guards and 43rd armies were also supposed to continue their offensive to the north, while the 2nd Guards Army would cover the *front's* forces from the west.

Thus the First Baltic Front was to turn its attack front 90 degrees and deploy its main forces against Army Group North.

On the evening of 27 July the forces of the 3rd Guards Mechanized Corps began to carry out their new assignment. The corps moved to the north and by the morning of the following day its forward units had begun fighting for Jelgava, although it was not able to take the town from the march, because the enemy had concentrated up to two infantry divisions in this area, which were putting up stubborn resistance.

The arrival of Soviet forces in the Jelgava area caused a panic in the enemy's ranks, for the last land routes leading to Germany were under threat by Soviet forces. Our air reconnaissance began to report the movements of the enemy's automobile columns from the northwest toward Tukums, where the German-Fascist command had evidently decided to create a final barrier to prevent our tanks from reaching the shore of the Gulf of Riga. In this rapidly changing situation, the *front* commander issued a timely order to the commander of the 3rd Guards Mechanized Corps to launch a decisive attack with all the corps' forces from the southwest and capture Jelgava, while another part of its forces would capture Tukums and cut the maritime railroad.

The corps' forward units, having carried out a brilliant 100-kilometer march, broke into Tukums by 1100 on 30 July and, following a stubborn fight, captured the town on 1 August. A forward detachment, dispatched by the corps, reached the shore of the Gulf of Riga in the Klapkalns area and cut the last paved road running along the shore of the gulf.

The 51st Army's formations advanced 75 kilometers in four days of offensive battles and captured the town of Jelgava.

Thus the First Baltic Front's successful actions completely cut off Army Group North from Fascist Germany's remaining forces on land and pinned it against the sea. The enemy had to apply enormous efforts in order to attempt to save this group of forces. The First Baltic Front's forces now had the tasks of maintaining their favorable position and repulsing all the enemy's attempts directed at relieving the group of forces penned against the sea.

At the same time the First Baltic Front's forces were developing the offensive along the Siauliai and Riga axes, the forces of the Second, and then the Third, Baltic fronts were carrying out the Riga—Dvinsk, Pskov—Ostrov and Madona offensive operations.

At the same time fierce fighting was raging along the Neman River south of the First Baltic Front's operational sector.

The German-Fascist command, striving at all costs to delay the arrival of the Soviet forces at the East Prussian border—the citadel of the Prussian Junkers and bridgehead for aggression—dispatched more than ten divisions (including two panzer) and several independent brigades against the Third Belorussian Front.

The Third Belorussian Front's offensive during the second half of July acquired special significance, for the question immediately arose of transferring military operations to the territory of fascist Germany itself.

Heavy fighting unfolded during 16-20 July. The enemy launched fierce counterattacks in an attempt to throw our forces back across the Neman and to restore his defense along this line. However, the Soviet forces not only repulsed all of the enemy's attacks, but completed forcing the Neman and began to press the enemy back to the west. However, the final battles had revealed a correlation of forces unfavorable for us, in connection with which the *front* commander ordered all the armies to consolidate along their current lines and temporarily go over to a stubborn defense, for the purpose of inflicting maximum losses on the enemy, particularly his tanks.

During 20-28 period the Third Belorussian Front waged defensive battles. During this time the enemy suffered heavy losses. As a result, he was forced to renounce his plans and from 28 July he went over to the defensive. During the defensive fighting the Third Belorussian Front brought up its rear organs and equipment and received ammunition, and only 28 July once again went over to the offensive.

In three days our forces advanced 50 kilometers, broadened their breakthrough front of the enemy's defense to 230 kilometers, and on 1 August stormed the town and fortress of Kaunas. The 33rd Army advanced 8-10 kilometers to the East Prussian border.

By the beginning of the second half of July the enemy command along the Second Belorussian Front's attack front had managed to put its retreating forces in order, to bring up more than ten divisions from the rear and other sectors of the front to the line Grodno—Svisloch', and to organize a defense here and launch a number of counterattacks. As a result of this, and also because of the troops being stretched out, and the lagging of the artillery and rear organs, the pace of the *front's* offensive fell significantly.

The *front's* forces, having captured Grodno on 16 July, continued to attack to the west, but began to encounter the enemy's significantly increased resistance, particularly in the swampy valley of the Svisloch' River. The enemy's main efforts were aimed at halting the Soviet forces in the area west of Grodno, along the Bialystok axis, where the town of Bialystok itself was an important center of resistance along the approaches to East Prussia.

The *front* was attacking with the forces of only two armies (3rd and 50th) and one cavalry corps (3rd Guards), which had been transferred from the Third Belorussian Front. Following the elimination of the enemy grouping encircled east of Minsk, the 49th Army had been pulled into the *front's* second echelon.

During the 17-21 July period the *front's* forces were engaged in stubborn fighting, with mixed success. The enemy, having brought up fresh reserves, including a panzer division, began to carry out counterattacks and in places pressed our forces back. Only along the *front's* left wing did the 3rd Army press the enemy back toward Bialystok and in four days advanced 15-25 kilometers.

The commander of the Second Belorussian Front, upon evaluating the situation, decided to commit the 49th Army into the boundary between the 50th and 3rd armies. With the commitment of fresh forces into the fighting, the enemy's resistance was broken.

The *front's* forces fell on the enemy with all three armies and by the close of 24 July they had completely forced the Neman, advanced 20-30 kilometers and reached the eastern outskirts of Bialystok. During the 27-31 July period the *front's* forces continued to press the enemy to the west and advanced another 20-30 kilometers.

Thus during the second half of July the *front's* forces cleaned the enemy out of Bialystok and by the end of July had reached the near approaches to East Prussia.

The arrival of the two *fronts* at the East Prussian border had enormous international military-political significance, for it had become clear that the Soviet forces would soon transfer military operations to enemy territory, which, in turn, signified the rapid conclusion of the entire Second World War.

During the second half of July especially great successes were achieved along the First Belorussian Front's sector, where the Brest—Siedlce operation unfolded on 17-18 July. All the *front's* armies took part in the operation, including its left wing, which had not played an active part in the Bobruisk—Slutsk and Baranovichi—Slonim operations.

The First Belorussian Front's right-wing forces, having liberated Baranovichi, continued their attack to the southwest and by the close of 16 July had reached the line Svisloch'—Pruzhany, having liberated such major towns as Slonim and Pinsk.

The arrival of the *front's* right-wing forces at the approaches to the town and fortress of Brest created favorable conditions for the beginning of the *front's* left-wing forces' offensive, which began on 17-18 July.

The decision by the commander of the First Belorussian Front to attack with all his forces came down to the following.

The *front's* right-wing forces were ordered to continue to develop the offensive to the west, outflanking the Brest fortified area from the north with their main forces. Part of the forces would attack from the east and northwest, in conjunction with the *front's* left-wing forces and capture the town and fortress of Brest.

The *front's* left-wing forces were ordered to break through the enemy's defense west of Kovel' and develop the offensive along two axes:

a) toward Wlodawa, Lukow and Siedlce, for the purpose of linking up with the *front's* right-wing forces to the west of Brest, thus completing the encirclement of the enemy's Brest group of forces; these forces were subsequently ordered to attack to the west; part of these forces, in conjunction with the right wing, were to destroy the encircled enemy group of forces and capture the fortress of Brest;

b) in the direction of Lublin, for the purpose of capturing it and supporting the arrival of our forces at the Vistula River.

By the start of the Brest—Siedlce operation the First Belorussian Front's left wing consisted of five combined-arms armies. Of these, four combined-arms armies were to attack in the first echelon, while one (Polish) would be in the second echelon. It was planned to employ the latter after the arrival of our forces at the Western Bug River, for developing the success along the Lublin axis.

The First Belorussian Front included a large number of mobile forces, designated for operations as mobile groups. The cavalry-mechanized group, consisting of the 4th Guards Cavalry, 9th Tank and 1st Mechanized corps, was to operate along the *front's* right wing, along the Brest axis, and was given the objective of forcing the Western Bug River northwest of Brest; the 2nd Tank Army and the 2nd and 7th guards cavalry corps were designated as *front* mobile groups for developing the success along the *front's* left-wing sector; the 11th Tank Corps was to operate as the 8th Guards Army's mobile group and was designated for completing the breakthrough of the enemy's defense and developing the army's success.

In all, by the start of the Brest—Siedlce offensive operation, the First Belorussian Front had nine combined-arms, one tank and two air armies, a powerful cavalry-mechanized group, two independent cavalry corps and one tank corps. This was one of the most powerful *fronts* in the Great Patriotic War.

By the middle of July a large number of enemy reserves had been transferred from the Warsaw axis to Belorussia, although only eight infantry divisions and a ski brigade could be used in the first echelon against the First Belorussian Front. The enemy could still employ three infantry divisions, about five independently operating infantry regiments, and a panzer division as reserves along the Warsaw axis. These reserves were scattered along a sector of more than 150 kilometers. However, it should be emphasized that the wooded and swampy character of the terrain and the major water barriers enabled the enemy, even given the presence of such forces, to organize a secure defense against the forces of the First Belorussian Front.

The First Belorussian Front's Brest—Siedlce operation began along the right wing on 17 July and along the left on 18 July 1944.

On the offensive's first day the left-wing armies managed to pierce the depth of the enemy's defense along the axis of the main attack to a depth of 13 kilometers and expand the breach to 30 kilometers. On 19 July the Soviet forces completely broke through the enemy's tactical defense zone and committed into the breach a tank corps and a cavalry corps, which, supported by powerful aviation, began to pursue the retreating enemy. By the close of this day the breakthrough front grew to 120 kilometers in width and 40 kilometers in depth. By the close of 20 July our forces had advanced another 40 kilometers, had expanded the breach to 130 kilometers, and reached the Western Bug River and partially forced it. This was a brilliant success by the Soviet forces. During these days the *front's* right-wing forces were also successfully advancing, had occupied Kobrin, were approaching the Western Bug River, and had outflanked the town and fortress of Brest from the northeast.

During the first 3-4 days of the Brest—Siedlce operation eight of the enemy's divisions suffered significant losses. The Soviet forces, having thrown back the remnants of the defeated formations beyond the USSR's state boundary, entered the territory of allied Poland and threatened to encircle the enemy forces in the Brest area.

In order to hold the Brest area—an important defense center along the Warsaw direction—the German-Fascist command concentrated here a significant number of remnants of the Second Army's formations and attempted to delay our offensive on Brest for the northeast and east.

During 21-22 July a difficult struggle unfolded for the line of the Western Bug River, as a result of which Soviet forces forced the river along a sector more than 80 kilometers and advanced another 50 kilometers. A favorable situation arose for committing into the breach the 2nd Tank Army, which was given the mission of liberating Lublin.

Particularly stubborn fighting unfolded against the enemy's semi-encircled Brest group of forces, which had decided to hold the fortress, at all costs, in order to foil our forces' offensive on Warsaw. A major enemy group of forces was located in the Brest area, consisting of the remnants of the enemy Second and Ninth armies. Besides this, the enemy began to hurriedly create a group of forces northwest of Brest for launching a decisive counterattack against our forces that had arrived at the Western Bug River in this area.

During 23-27 July fierce fighting unfolded along the *front's* right wing against the enemy, who had launched a counterattack in the area northwest of Kobrin.

On 23 July the enemy managed to advance somewhat, but as a result of powerful artillery and aviation strikes, as well as a flank attack by the 28th Army, he was soon thrown back. The Soviet forces not only repulsed the enemy's counterblow, but by the close of 27 July they reached the Western Bug River and completed the two-sided envelopment of Brest, in the area of which the remains of four divisions and several independent units were located.

During this time the *front's* left-wing forces continued their offensive along the Siedlce and Lublin axes. On 25 July the mobile forces (2nd Guards Cavalry and 11th Tank corps) reached the towns of Lukow and Siedlce. The 2nd Tank Army, having been committed from the bridgehead along the western bank of the Western Bug River, occupied Lublin in a vigorous attack on 23 July, and on 25 July reached the Vistula River along the Deblin—Pulawy sector.

By the close of 27 July the *front's* left-wing forces had reached the line Siedlce—Lukow—Deblin, and then to the south along the eastern bank of the Vistula River. The 2nd Tank Army, which had been relieved along the Vistula by the recently-committed Polish 1st Army, carried out a rapid lunge along the front into the enemy's rear from the Deblin—Pulawy area to the Warsaw axis.

On 28 July the forces of the 28th, 61st and 70th armies captured the town and fortress of Brest, following heavy fighting. This was a major and important victory for the Soviet forces, because Brest, located in the center of the First Belorussian Front, linked our forces attacking north and south of the town.

The fall of the town and fortress of Brest enabled the *front* commander to direct his main forces along the Warsaw axis, where the enemy's resistance was increasing every day. The 47th Army, which was designated for deeply outflanking the Brest group of forces, was turned to the west; it was given the task of reaching the Vistula River south of Warsaw. The 69th Army, which had seized a bridgehead in the Pulawy area at the end of July, was engaged in heavy fighting to expand it. The Polish 1st Army began forcing the Vistula River northwest of Deblin. During the night of 1 August the 8th Guards Army seized a bridgehead along the western bank of the Vistula River in the Magnuszew area.

The 2nd Tank Army continued to attack along the Warsaw axis and at the end of July, having taken Minsk-Mazowiecki, reached the near approaches to Praga—a suburb of the Polish capital of Warsaw. The *front's* right-wing forces were battling the enemy along the line Bialystok—Siedlce.

With these events the First Belorussian Front's Brest—Siedlce operation came to an end, during which the Soviet forces along the Warsaw axis threw the enemy back 260 kilometers. Soviet territory along this axis had been completely cleared of the German-Fascist forces. Thus began the liberation of allied Poland, which had been occupied by the German fascists since 1939.

The joint actions of the Soviet forces and the Polish army symbolized the unity of two peoples in their struggle against German fascism.

The day of the beginning of the liberation of the eastern areas of Poland by the Soviet army and the proclamation by the Polish Committee of National Liberation of its manifesto to the Polish people was the birthday of popular and democratic Poland.

The character of the Soviet air force's activities during the second half of the Belorussian operation was the same as during the first stage, although its working conditions had become considerably more difficult, in light of its great removal from its bases and airfields.

The 3rd Air Army, which was supporting the First Baltic Front, significantly reduced the number of its sorties during the first half of July, as a result of the air forces' rebasing to new airfields lagging behind, as well as the late deliveries of fuel and ammunition. During this time only 2,419 sorties were carried out, that is, twice as few as during the first stage of the Belorussian operation. During the 13-15 July time period the 3rd Air Army was able to carry out only 128-144 sorties per day. Only 450 sorties were conducted against enemy forces. During the second half of July the 3rd Air Army's situation improved. It was reinforced with a bomber corps and an independent bomber division, and the system of basing and supply of fuel and ammunition was improved as well. All of this enabled the 3rd Air Army to carry out 12,140 sorties during the second half of July and drop 2,151.3 tons of bombs on the enemy.

The activity of the 1st Air Army, which was supporting the Third Belorussian Front, also fell noticeably during the second stage of the Belorussian operation. The air army carried out 7,254 sorties and dropped 595 tons of bombs, compared with 13,016 sorties and 2,708 tons of bombs during the first stage of the Belorussian operation.

The 4th Air Army, which was supporting the Second Belorussian Front, also reduced its activity, having carried out only about 7,000 sorties during the second stage of the Belorussian operation, compared to 8,087 during the first stage.

It was only in the First Belorussian Front, during the second stage of the Belorussian operation, that aviation support was fully realized. The *front's* 6th and 16th air armies carried out a total of 19,701 sorties during 1 July-1 August, and dropped 3,844 tons of bombs on the enemy.

A new mission arose for Long-Range Aviation during the second half of the Belorussian operation—to support the mobile forces' supply of fuel and ammunition. These measures by Long-Range Aviation were usually carried out during the day. During the night Long-Range Aviation continued to attack the enemy's operational deliveries, by launching strikes against the railroad junctions and stations along a broad front, in all four *fronts'* operational sectors. During the second stage of the Belorussian operation Long-Range Aviation launched ten raids against the following railroad junctions: Vilnius, Lida, Bialystok, Brest, Siauliai, Dvinsk, and Volkovysk. In all, 3,058 sorties were carried out and 3,424 tons of bombs dropped. 738 sorties were carried out in support of the mobile forces' supply, 469.5 tons of fuel delivered, and 539 tons of ammunition and other supplies, besides which 2,956 men were transported by air.

The enemy's air activity, in connection with our forces' approach to his main airfields during the second stage of the Belorussian operation, increased significantly. The enemy air force launched bomber raids against our forces along several axes, covered its forces and engaged in air battles with our fighters. However, overall air superiority remained in the hands of Soviet aviation.

During the second stage of the Belorussian operation the partisan formations continued to play a major role, although the character of their operations changed considerably. With the arrival of the Soviet army, many partisan detachments became organizationally part of the Soviet forces and provided excellent reinforcements for many units that had suffered losses during the non-stop offensive.

The partisans, while continuing to render all-round support to our forces, were also carrying out a new and important task, which came down to taking all measures to prevent the retreating enemy from destroying industrial enterprises, government buildings, government property, medical establishments, and communications equipment, that is, everything that might facilitate the rapid restoration of the Belorussian people's normal life and economy.

The Belorussian partisans, in their combat activity, established close tactical coordination with the attacking forces and carried out the orders of the Soviet army's commanders. The partisans' help in the wooded and swampy areas, where the conduct of reconnaissance, maintenance of communications, security and other functions demanded special skills and excellent knowledge of the terrain, remained especially effective.

Thus during the second half of the multi-*front* Belorussian operation all of our forces' objectives were completely achieved. A defeat had been inflicted on those major operational and strategic reserves that the enemy had transferred from Germany and other directions to close the more than 400-kilometer breach. The Soviet forces completed the liberation of Belorussia, liberated the Lithuanian SSR and its capital of Vilnius, liberated the greater part of the Latvian SSR and part of allied Poland, and had reached the border of East Prussia and the approaches to Praga—a suburb of Warsaw and the Vistula River.

7

The First Baltic Front's Dvinsk— Siauliai Offensive Operation (5-31 July 1944)

The Dvinsk-Siauliai operation was a consecutive offensive operation in depth by the First Baltic Front, which had arisen as a result of the realization of the *front's* preceding Vitebsk—Polotsk operation.

The *front's* successful offensive had led to the defeat of those forces facing the enemy's group of forces and had created extremely favorable conditions for the non-stop pursuit of the retreating enemy.

The *front's* combat and numerical composition by 5 July (taking into account the arriving reserves) is shown in table 6.

In all, the *front* numbered more than 350,000 officers and men, more than 8,400 guns and mortars of all types, and 588 tanks and assault guns, which made a subsequent successful offensive possible. It should be noted, however, that a significant part of the tanks (230) required repairs.

The presence of these forces enabled us to develop the success achieved toward Kaunas and then to the shore of the Baltic Sea, for the purpose of cutting off the German-Fascist group of forces in the Baltic States from Fascist Germany's main forces.

Aside from reinforcing the *front* (to five armies), it was necessary to adopt measures to ensure that its forces had everything necessary to carry out the new operation. This task was eased by the fact that there were still significant reserves at hand that had not been expended during the Vitebsk—Polotsk operation. For example, despite the fact that the *front's* forces had advanced more than 200 kilometers during the operation's 12 days and had been engaged in continuous fighting, nonetheless, by the start of the new operation (as of 1 July 1944), the *front's* provisioning of ammunition varied from 1.7 to 4.8 combat loads.

Such a high rate of provisioning with ammunition is explained by the fact that their expenditure during the Vitebsk—Polotsk operation comprised about half of the planned amount, while 2-2.5 combat loads had been delivered during this period.

The fuel situation at the start of the operation was also more or less favorable. The *front* had about ten refills at the start of the Belorussian operation. Only 0.62 of a refill was expended during the Vitebsk—Polotsk operation.

Table 6. The First Baltic Front's Combat and Numerical Composition on 5 July 1944[1]

Units	Men	Mortars		Guns	Divisional	Regimental
		120mm	82mm	122 & 203mm		
6th Guards Army	90,143	374	609	461	480	132
2nd Guards Army	70,661	197	491	136	325	168
43rd Army	59,285	302	425	230	271	76
39th Army	38,029	140	364	110	227	60
51st Army	71,547	188	464	144	380	107
Units Subordinated to the *Front*	7,231	–	–	65	21	–
1st Tank Corps	13,291	46	69	24	66	–
Total	350,187	1,247	2,422	1,170	1,770	543

Units	Guns		Tanks and Self-Propelled Guns[2]
	45mm	Anti-Aircraft[3]	
6th Guards Army	358	31/138	53/72
2nd Guards Army	324	0/46	–
43rd Army	242	16/93	9/86
39th Army	150	0/14	38/7
51st Army	306	0/17	–
Units Subordinated to the *Front*	–	36/134	62/20
1st Tank Corps	28	–	196/45
Total	1,408	83/412	358/230

Notes
1 Combat-ready tanks are shown in the numerator, and tanks in need of repair in the denominator.
2 76mm and 85mm guns are shown in the numerator, and 20mm and 37mm guns in the denominator.

However, the favorable supply situation was only at the *front* level. In view of the rapid rates of advance, transport lagged behind and did not manage to bring up everything necessary to the troops, as a result of which as early as the end of June some units and formations were experiencing a shortage of ammunition and especially fuel. Many units and formations unloaded their supplies as far back as the jumping-off position, then, having advanced over a great distance, lacked a sufficient amount of transport equipment to bring them up.

Despite a number of measures adopted, this problem was not completely resolved, which then negatively told on the course of the operation.

On 4 July the *Stavka* of the Supreme High Command issued a new directive, in which the First Baltic Front, consisting of the 6th Guards, 43rd, 39th, 2nd Guards, and 51st armies, and the 1st Tank Corps, was ordered to develop the offensive, by launching its main attack in the general

---

1   In the "anti-aircraft guns" section, the numerator shows 76mm and 85mm guns, and the denominator 20 and 37mm guns.

direction of Svencionys and Kaunas, with the immediate task of capturing the line Dvinsk—Podbrodze by no later than 10-12 July. It was further ordered that the *front*, after securing itself from the north, was to attack toward Kaunas, and with part of its forces toward Panevezys and Siauliai.

The *Stavka* ordered the *front's* neighbor to the right—the Second Baltic Front—to attack in the general direction of Riga, with the objective, in conjunction with the First Baltic Front, of cutting off the enemy's Baltic group of forces from its land communications with fascist Germany.

Of the five armies, which were designated to carry out the tasks assigned to the First Baltic Front by the *Stavka* of the Supreme High Command, only the 6th Guards and 43rd armies were in direct contact with the enemy by 5 July. The 39th Army, which was included in the First Baltic Front on 3 July, was marching, following the elimination of the enemy's Vitebsk group of forces, and by the close of 4 July was located as follows: 82nd Rifle Corps—in the Berezino—Gorodok—Osetishche area; 5th Guards Rifle Corps—in the Kal'nik—Domzheritsy—Zyaboen'ye area. Considering the 43rd Army's rapid rate of advance, it was necessary to allot 4-5 days to bring up the 39th Army and commit it into the line. The 2nd Guards and 51st armies had not yet arrived in the *front's* sector. 10-12 days would be required to unload these forces and bring them up to the front.

Thus the *front's* immediate objective—the arrival of the *front's* forces at the line Dvinsk—Podbrodze (40-70 kilometers in depth), as indicated in the *Stavka* directive, could be carried out with the forces of three armies (6th Guards, 43rd and 39th). It was planned to employ all five armies for carrying out the subsequent objective—the development of the offensive toward Panevezys and Siauliai.

The enemy decided to hold Dvinsk at all costs, in order to support the recently-begun withdrawal by Army Group North. Army Group North transferred to the Dvinsk area the 132nd, 84th, 215th, and 263rd infantry divisions, the 338th Security Division and the 226th Assault Gun Brigade. The 61st and 225th infantry divisions were also en route to the Dvinsk area. Aside from these forces, another four infantry regiments and up to seven security, sapper and punishment battalions had been brought up to the Dvinsk area.

A second serious obstacle arose before the Soviet forces, which were to attack along the Dvinsk axis—the inter-lake defile covering Dvinsk from the east, south and southwest.

The Dvinsk—Siauliai *front* offensive operation may be divided into two stages.

During the operation's first stage, the *front's* forces, while overcoming the enemy's constantly increasing resistance, reached the line of the Sventa (Sventoji) and outflanked the powerfully fortified enemy resistance center and large town of Dvinsk from the south.

During the operation's second stage, the *front's* forces developed the offensive along the Panevezys—Siauliai axis and, upon reaching the shore of the Gulf of Riga, completed cutting off Army Group North from fascist Germany's remaining forces by land.

We will now review in sequence the main military events at each of these stages.

The Operation's First Stage

The Arrival of the First Baltic Front at the Sventoji River and the Outflanking of Dvinsk from the South (5-15 July 1944)

The First Baltic Front's Dvinsk—Siauliai offensive operation began on 5 July with an offensive by the forces of the First Baltic Front along two axes—Dvinsk and Svencionys—Siauliai. On the *front's* right wing, along the Dvinsk axis, the 6th Guards Army and 1st Tank Corps were operating, while the 43rd Army and, from 10 July, the main forces of the 39th Army, were operating along the Svencionys—Siauliai axis.

In order to seize Dvinsk, it was not only important to overcome the inter-lake defile, but also to clear the entire southern bank of the Western Dvina River along the Drissa—Dvinsk sector. In doing this, the forces of the 6th Guards Army had to overcome the enemy's defense, which had been established in the numerous inter-lake defiles, as well as the wooded and swampy terrain, and then reach Dvinsk before the arrival of the enemy's new operational reserves.

The German-Fascist command, striving to delay, at any cost, the 6th Guards Army's offensive, created a powerful defense along the approaches to Dvinsk, having transferred here up to five divisions from Army Group Center.

During 5-15 July the 6th Guards Army was engaged in heavy fighting around Dvinsk. The width of the army's sector reached 160 kilometers. The army's units and formations operated along broad fronts, with significant gaps of up to 40 kilometers between them.

The increasing activity of his aviation, the growing resistance along the Dvinsk axis, and the arrival of fresh units all spoke of the enemy's desire to securely close the inter-lake defile and prevent our forces from reach the Dvinsk area.

During 5-7 July the 6th Guards Army's forces advanced slowly. This insignificant success is explained by the broad attack front and the dispersion of men and materiel.

After putting themselves in order, on 8-9 July the army's main forces resumed the offensive and launched their main attack in the direction of Opsa and Dvinsk. The enemy, taking advantage of the inter-lake defile for defense, put up a stubborn defense, employing fire and counterattacks from a battalion to a regiment in strength, and supported by artillery, tanks and aviation.

During 9-10 July the army failed to achieve success along the Dvinsk axis and only along the left flank was a breakthrough along the inter-lake defile visible. The army command decided to commit along the Zarasai axis the newly-arrived 23rd Guards Rifle Corps, with the help of which it was planned to complete the breakthrough of the enemy's defense and reach Dvinsk from the south. However, not even this maneuver was completely successful. In the wake of heavy fighting on 11-12 July, we were not able to take Dvinsk.

It should be noted that one of the reasons for the 6th Guards Army's failures was the offensive's poor organization. A sufficient superiority in men and materiel over the enemy had not been created along the axis of the main attack. The corps' and armies' second echelons and reserves were committed into the battle piecemeal and late and failed to have the desired effect. As a result of all this, the fighting along the Dvinsk axis became drawn out.

Military operations along the *front's* left flank unfolded in different conditions and more successfully. Here the 43rd Army's forces attacked, as well as the 39th Army from 9 July.

On the morning of 5 July the 43rd Army resumed the pursuit of the enemy along the Svencionys—Siauliai axis. The enemy, in order to cover the withdrawal of his forces on Vilnius, sought with the forces of the 212th Infantry Division and the remnants of the 95th, 252nd and 201st security infantry divisions, to hold on along favorable lines, with aviation support. However, under pressure from our forces, he fell back to the west.

During 5-7 July the 43rd Army's forces advanced 50-60 kilometers, and on 7 July captured the major road junction, town and railroad station of Svencionys and cut the Dvinsk—Vilnius railroad. The army achieved its objective. The enemy continued to put up stubborn resistance along the boundary with the 6th Guards Army and was holding the Vidzy area. This area, in connection with the gap that had formed between the armies' internal flanks and, which had grown to 40 kilometers by the close of 7 July, played an important role. The enemy, having transferred fresh forces against the 6th Guards Army, sharply slowed the rate of the army's advance along the left flank, while simultaneously creating a threat to the 43rd Army's right flank.

By 8 July the Third Belorussian Front's 5th Army's right flank reached the Podbrodze area. In connection with the lateral movement of the 43rd Army's units toward their right flank, by the close of 8 July a gap had also opened up, which was weakly guarded by one overextended rifle division. In order to better secure the boundary between the *fronts*, on the morning of 8 July the commander of the First Baltic Front demanded that the commander of the 39th Army move up his mobile units to cover the boundary between the *fronts*. The Third Belorussian Front's main shock group reached the Vilnius area as early as 7 July and began fighting for the town.

On 8 July, and somewhat on 9 July, the 1st Tank Corps was fighting for Vidzy with part of its forces. In connection with the delay of the 6th Guards Army's offensive, the *front* commander ordered the corps to attack toward Zarasai and support the 6th Guards Army.

On 9 July the 43rd Army continued to attack in the general direction of Utena. At 1800 its forward units cut the Dvinsk—Kaunas paved road and captured Utena.

At 1900 on 9 July the 39th Army's forward units established contact with the enemy along the line of the Zeimena River.

During 10-12 July the *front's* left-wing forces, while repulsing the enemy's fierce counterattacks, advanced 28-45 kilometers.

The 1st Tank Corps, having gone over to the attack on the morning of 11 July, for the purpose of taking Zarasai, by the close of 12 July had reached the lake area south of the town, but could advance no further and was pulled into the reserve.

By the close of 12 July the First Baltic Front's center and left wing had reached the line Utena—Vorantsy, or 25-40 kilometers farther than indicated in the *Stavka's* 4 July directive. However, the *front's* right wing, as a result of the sharply increased enemy resistance, was not able to reach Dvinsk. Despite the lagging of the right wing, the First Baltic Front's main forces had created favorable conditions for the subsequent offensive toward Panevezys and Siauliai, and for the rapid arrival at the Gulf of Riga. The enemy along this axis no longer disposed of major operational reserves, while at the same time the First Baltic Front was just committing two fresh armies (2nd Guards and 51st) into the fighting.[2] Besides this, the *Stavka* reserve was transferring independent formations (16th Lithuanian Rifle Division, 3rd Guards Mechanized Corps) to the First Baltic Front.

The German-Fascist command, fearing the First Baltic Front's breakthrough to the sea in the direction of Mitava (Jelgava) and Riga and the encirclement of Army Group North, strived to retain Dvinsk in its hands. Disposing of a bridgehead along the southern bank of the Western Dvina River, it concentrated here forces for operating against the flank of the First Baltic Front's main group of forces, which was successfully developing the offensive along the Siauliai axis. The enemy had gathered in the Dvinsk area up to eight infantry divisions, four independent regiments, up to three brigades of assault guns, and up to seven battalions of various types. There was a growing threat of an attack by the enemy's Dvinsk group of forces against the *front's* right wing.

For the purpose of supporting the successful development of the offensive along this wing, the *front* commander changed the 43rd Army's objective and ordered it to develop the offensive with its main forces on Dvinsk and, in conjunction with the 6th Guards Army, capture it, and with part of its forces to continue to pursue the enemy in the direction of Panevezys. Thus it was planned to attack Dvinsk with the forces of two armies, while the 43rd Army was to go over to the offensive on 13 July and the 6th Guards Army only on 14 July. The 1st Tank Corps did not get an independent assignment and was employed in brigade fashion for direct infantry support and as a reserve for the 43rd Army.

Having carried out these regroupings, the *front's* forces continued to attack along the new axes. The 6th Guards Army failed to advance in the course of three days.

In the 43rd Army's attack sector along the right flank, an extremely small success was achieved, but in the center and along the left flank its formations advanced 10-30 kilometers.

---

2   These armies were turned over to the *front* from the *Stavka* reserve.

On the morning of 13 July the 39th Army continued to pursue the retreating enemy and successfully advanced, without encountering significant enemy resistance. By the close of 14 July the army's forces reached the line Karolishki—Gumbeli—Keizany. From the morning of 15 July the enemy began to put up powerful resistance and the army failed to advance further that day.

The enemy's air force became increasingly active and concentrated its main efforts along the Dvinsk axis. In all, during 5-15 July 553 enemy sorties were noted.

The 3rd Air Army, while experiencing serious difficulties with fuel and ammunition, and having fallen behind in airfield basing, reduced the intensity of its combat activities. During 5-15 July the air army carried out 2,419 sorties, of which only 450 were directed against the enemy's forces. Support for the 43rd and 39th armies was expressed only in covering them from the air and carrying out aerial reconnaissance. Fighter aviation carried out about 1,500 sorties and shot down 53 enemy aircraft in 41 air battles.

On the basis of *Stavka* directive no. 220144 of 14 July, the 39th Army was transferred in full to the Third Belorussian Front as of 2400 on 15 July, while the same directive ordered the 3rd Guards Mechanized Corps to be transferred to the First Baltic Front as of 2400 on 15 July.

The 51st and 2nd Guards armies' forces, by night marching, were arriving in the 43rd Army's attack sector.

As a result of the first stage of the Dvinsk—Siauliai operation, the First Baltic Front's forces advanced 140 kilometers along the axis of the main attack. By reaching the Sventa (Sventoji) River the 43rd Army created favorable conditions for developing the success along the Panevezys and Siauliai axes, and then to the shore of the Gulf of Riga. The 6th Guards Army, which was attacking along the Dvinsk axis through inaccessible, swampy, lake, and wooded terrain and fighting off counterattacks by the enemy's reserves, which were being thrown into the battle from Army Group North, was in the most difficult situation and was not able to take Dvinsk. The 6th Guards Army's operations were influenced, in particular, by the insufficiently effective aviation support (accompaniment) for the attacking forces. The slow advance by the 3rd Air Army's rear organs and the lagging behind of airfield maneuver weakened the air army's efforts at the most critical time for the ground forces. However, it should be noted that the 6th Guards Army tied down the enemy's Dvinsk group of forces with its persistent attacks and thus eased the offensive by the 43rd and 39th armies.

The Operation's Second Stage

The Offensive's Development along the Panevezys—Siauliai Axis. The Front's Arrival at the Shore of the Gulf of Riga (16-31 July 1944)

During the first four days of the operation's second stage (16-19 July), the First Baltic Front's forces repelled the enemy's counterattacks, brought up their rear organs, fitted out their forces with the necessary supplies, and carried out regrouping for the subsequent offensive. Fighting continued along some axes, in order to improve the troops' situation.

The situation in the First Baltic Front's sector had become more complex by 16 July. The strongest 6th Guards Army was pinned down around Dvinsk and its main forces could not take the fortress. The Second Baltic Front's forces were late in reaching the Dvinsk area and were 25-40 kilometers behind the 6th Guards Army. The 43rd Army, which had received orders to launch an attack toward Dvinsk, was in need of regrouping. Both armies were attacking along a broad front, while all their corps had been committed into the battle and lacked reserves. The formations' rear organs were lagging behind the forward units, which led to a sharp reduction in the troops' provisioning with ammunition and fuel.

All of this forced the *front* command, as well as that of the 6th Guards and 43rd armies, to carry out the necessary regroupings, restore the army and corps reserves, and bring up the rear organs, which took up a certain amount of time.

At the same time, conditions had arisen for launching an attack along the Riga axis, for the purpose of cutting off the enemy's Army Group North from fascist Germany's remaining forces.

The latter circumstance was one of the reasons that forced the *Stavka* of the Supreme High Command to speed up the movement of its reserve—the 2nd Guards and 51st armies—to the First Baltic Front's sector, which had completed a nearly 300-kilometer march, so as to be able to more rapidly reach their designated areas. The necessity of forcing the Soviet forces' movement to the Baltic Sea was the reason for the transfer of the Third Belorussian Front's 3rd Mechanized Corps to the *front*. The *front's* air army was also reinforced with a bomber corps and a single bomber division.

Thus reinforced, the *front* was given the objective of attacking along the Siauliai and Riga axes. The 6th Guards Army was ordered that upon putting its forces in order, in conjunction with the 43rd Army, to destroy the enemy group of forces covering Dvinsk and occupy the Zarasai area. A part of its forces would subsequently force the Western Dvina River and capture Dvinsk, while the main forces would develop the success to the northwest.

The army was to create a shock group along its left flank along a 15-kilometer front, consisting of three rifle corps (eight rifle divisions), reinforced with tanks and artillery. It was planned to begin the artillery preparation at 0700, and the infantry attack at 0900 on 23 July. Aside from this, it was planned to carry out a reconnaissance in force between 0400 and 0700 on 23 July.

While the regroupings were taking place (17-22 July), the 6th Guards Army's forces were beating off insistent enemy counterattacks along almost the entire front.

For the subsequent development of the success along the Panevezys—Siauliai axis, the commander of the First Baltic Front on 18 July decided to commit into the fighting the 51st and 2nd Guards armies, transferred from the *Stavka* reserve, relieving part of the 43rd Army's forces with them.

With the arrival of the 51st and 2nd Guards armies at their designated sectors, the efforts of the 43rd Army shifted to the northwest axis. So that his army could reach the Dvinsk group of enemy forces' path of retreat as quickly as possible, the commander of the 43rd Army made the following decision: having securely covered his left flank, the shock group, consisting of two corps, was to attack on the morning of 19 July, with the objective of defeating the opposing enemy, cutting the Dvinsk—Panevezys railroad, and developing the attack to the northwest.

During the offensive on 19-20 July the 43rd Army's forces advanced 3-18 kilometers and cut the Dvinsk—Panevezys railroad. The enemy, concerned by the new breakthrough in his defense, began to commit in detail against the 43rd Army the SS "Nordland" Motorized and 58th Infantry divisions, with the task of preventing the advance of our units to the north and northwest.

On 21 July the 43rd Army continued attacking, but was unable to overcome the enemy's increasing resistance.

The Second Baltic Front's 4th Shock Army, while attacking along the Dvinsk axis during 18-21 July and overcoming the enemy's stubborn resistance, advanced slowly. On 20 July a turning point was reached and the *front* commander committed the 5th Tank Corps in the 4th Shock Army's sector, with orders to take Dvinsk in conjunction with the 4th Shock Army.

By the close of 21 July the 4th Shock Army was still 40 kilometers from Dvinsk.

The 51st and 2nd Guards armies, following the relief of the 43rd Army's units, established contact with the enemy. By order of the *front* commander, they attacked in the general direction of Panevezys and Siauliai and by the close of 21 July had advanced along some axes 12-40 kilometers.

At the same time, the 51st Army's forward units reached the approaches to Panevezys.

At the same time the Third Belorussian Front's 39th Army was fighting to take Ukmerge.

Thus by the beginning of 22 July a favorable situation had arisen for the subsequent offensive on Dvinsk, Panevezys and Siauliai.

By the close of 21 July there had arisen the real danger of the enemy's Dvinsk group of forces being surrounded. The enemy decided to halt at all costs the attack by the First Baltic Front's main forces in the sector between Dvinsk and Siauliai, and for this purpose launched a powerful counterblow on 22 July against the 43rd Army's forces.

During the day the 43rd Army was holding off the offensive by the SS "Nordland" Motorized, 58th and 225th infantry divisions, reinforced with the 393rd Assault Gun Brigade, the 8th Armored Company, and units of the 58th Infantry Division. The enemy tried to throw back units of the 92nd and 1st rifle corps, free up the Dvinsk—Panevezys railroad, and remove the threat to Siauliai.

At 0800 on 22 July the 51st Army launched a flanking maneuver with units of its 417th and 267th rifle divisions from the north and south, and following intense street fighting, captured Panevezys.

The enemy along the 51st Army's sector continued to defend with units of the 205th and 252nd infantry divisions and independent elements of various types. The German-Fascist command's attempts to throw against the army units and formations from Army Group North were not successful. These were pinned down by the active operations of the 43rd Army. Being thus secured along the right flank, the 51st Army successfully attacked to the west. However, the army's rear organs lagged behind, because of which the troops experienced shortages in ammunition and fuel. Due to these circumstances, the army commander, supported by the *front* commander, made the decision to securely consolidate along the army's entire front and organize the delivery of ammunition and fuel.

The 2nd Guards Army's offensive was developing successfully only along the right flank. The enemy was putting up stubborn resistance along the left flank.

From the morning of 23 July the First Baltic Front continued attacking along the entire front, making its main attacks toward Dvinsk, Siauliai and Ukmerge.

The 4th Shock Army on the right achieved a significant success and by the close of 23 July had cut the Rezekne—Dvinsk railroad.

The German-Fascist command, by putting up a stubborn resistance around Dvinsk, sought to prevent the remaining forces of Army Group North, around which the encirclement ring was tightening every day, from being cut off.

The powerful counterattacks against the 43rd Army showed that the enemy was determined to halt the offensive by the First Baltic Front's left wing and thus secure the retreat of its Dvinsk group of forces to the west.

In this developing situation, the commander of the First Baltic Front decided on 24 July to speed up the 51st Army's advance to the north and on Siauliai. With the capture of this important area, not only the enemy's Dvinsk group of forces, but all of Army Group North, would be deprived of a direct path of retreat to East Prussia.

During 24 July the *front's* forces continued to attack and advanced 2-10 kilometers.

The Third Belorussian Front's 39th Army captured Ukmerge.

By the close of 25 July the situation had become even more favorable for the First Baltic Front's forces. The Second Baltic Front's 4th Shock Army, which was attacking toward Dvinsk, was 8-10 kilometers northeast of the town by the close of 24 July, and by the close of 25 July had advanced right up to the fortress and began to prepare to storm it. The Third Belorussian Front's 39th Army to the left, upon the liberation of Ukmerge, had the opportunity to continue the offensive to the west. The enemy's counterattacks against the 43rd Army had almost completely ceased. The 51st and 2nd Guards armies along the *front's* left flank had entered the fighting in a timely manner and, without encountering serious enemy resistance along the Panevezys—Siauliai axis, advanced and created extremely favorable conditions for developing a vigorous offensive by the First Baltic Front's forces to the northwest, for the purpose of reaching the Gulf of Riga. The creation of a major group of forces along the Third Belorussian Front's right wing, for developing the offensive to the west, also aided the First Baltic Front in accomplishing the important task facing it.

In the favorable situation that had arisen, the commander of the First Baltic Front made the decision on 25 July to continue a decisive offensive, on the morning of 26 July, with his *front's* left wing, composed of the 51st and 2nd Guards armies and the 3rd Guards Mechanized Corps, with the objective of capturing Siauliai and cutting the Siauliai—Riga railroad. On the *front's* right wing, it was decided to continue the offensive with the forces of the 6th Guards Army to the northwest, for the purpose of better supporting the further development of the operation; the 43rd Army was ordered to securely maintain its present position during 26 July and be ready to attack to the northwest.

On the morning of 26 July the *front's* forces attacked, although the 6th Guards Army encountered fierce enemy resistance and by the end of the day had advanced only 2-3 kilometers.

The 4th Shock Army on the right reached the Western Dvina River and thus cut the Dvinsk group of enemy forces' path of retreat along the river's eastern bank.

During 26 July the 43rd Army's forces consolidated along their old lines, carried out reconnaissance and a partial regrouping, while readying themselves for active operations.

The 51st Army, while pursuing the enemy, advanced 40 kilometers to the north and northwest. The 3rd Guards Mechanized Corps, in conjunction with units of the 51st Army, advanced more than 70 kilometers and cut the Siauliai—Riga road and railroad. By the close of the day the corps' formations had reached the northeastern and eastern outskirts of Siauliai.

During the night of 27 July fighting continued on the approaches to Siauliai. The town's garrison, which consisted of subunits from the 640th Training Regiment, the 388th Training Division and the 677th Security Battalion, and supported by the 43rd Anti-Aircraft Regiment and an armored train, was putting up stubborn resistance. The corps commander made the decision to attack Siauliai simultaneously from all sides and set the time for a general storming at 1000 on 27 July.

The 2nd Guards Army, while overcoming the enemy's resistance, by the close of the day had advanced 4-20 kilometers to the west.

On 27 July the enemy's Dvinsk group of forces, under the threat of encirclement, began a hurried retreat to the northwest.

The enemy's stubborn resistance before the 6th Guards Army had been crushed and by the end of the day its units had advanced 10-15 kilometers, reaching the Zarasai area. By this time the Second Baltic Front's 4th Shock Army had captured the fortress of Dvinsk.

At 1300 on 27 July the 43rd Army renewed the attack, but had no particular success.

The 51st Army, in conjunction with the 3rd Guards Mechanized Corps, at 2100 on 27 July captured Siauliai, a major road junction and important link in the German defense. The army's forces advanced that day nearly 30 kilometers.

During the day the 2nd Guards Army's right flank advanced slightly to the west and southwest.

The situation that had arisen by the close of 27 July along the Siauliai axis was evidence of a new complete breakthrough of the German-Fascist forces' defense along one of the most important axes. The development of the success by the Siauliai group of Soviet forces to the west or north placed all of Army Group North's land communications with East Prussia under threat. Thus it is completely understandable that the First Baltic Front command shortly expected some sort of decisive countermeasures on the part of the enemy, who was striving to retain in his hands at least the roundabout communications routes running along the shore of the Baltic Sea. In connection with this, the commander of the First Baltic Front made a decision, which came down to repelling a possible enemy counterblow from the direction of East Prussia, while all remaining forces would be dispatched north and northwest, for the purpose of cutting off Army Group North's path of retreat.

During 28-31 July the most interesting were the actions of the 3rd Guards Mechanized Corps, which accomplished a mission of enormous importance by its leap to the north.

While carrying out the *front* commander's orders, by 0430 on 28 July the corps' forward units reached the southern outskirts of Jelgava, but were halted here. The town's garrison (the "Ostland"

15th Infantry Regiment and field *gendarme* units) put up stubborn resistance. Jelgava had been transformed into a powerful fortified locale.

Due to the arrival of the 3rd Guards Mechanized Corps' units at Jelgava, the *front* commander ordered the commander of the 51st Army to immediately launch a decisive attack to the north, in order to establish close coordination with the 3rd Guards Mechanized Corps.

Thus from 28 July a new Siauliai—Riga operational axis opened for the First Baltic Front's forces, along which the efforts of two armies (43rd and 51st), a mechanized (3rd Guards) and tank (1st) corps were concentrating. However, these forces were scattered along a 206-kilometer front.

The 6th Guards Army was operating along the Dvinsk—Riga operational axis and was attacking along the Western Dvina River, closely coordinating with the Second Baltic Front, which, in turn, was energetically pursuing the enemy toward Riga along the eastern bank of the Western Dvina River.

By mining the roads and approaches to inhabited locales, blowing up bridges and resisting along intermediate lines with rearguard units, the enemy was pulling back the Dvinsk group's main forces to the northwest. Pursuing night and day, by the close of 31 July the 6th Guards Army advanced 60 kilometers.

The 43rd Army's offensive on 28 July was unsuccessful. On 29 July the army advanced 20 kilometers. The enemy put up stubborn resistance and the situation along this axis stabilized.

The 3rd Guards Mechanized Corps was fighting in the southern outskirts of Jelgava. During the night of 28-29 July the enemy brought up units of the 388th Infantry and 281st Security divisions, the 15th Latvian SS Field Training Brigade, the 281st Independent Panzer Company, two armored trains, and three mortar batteries, and on the morning of 29 July began counterattacking, in order to throw our brigades back to the south. An attack by our forces was repulsed and by the end of the day the fighting continued along the original lines.

The fighting for Jelgava became drawn out. In order to crush the enemy's resistance, it was necessary to isolate the garrison from possible reserves and create the real possibility of encirclement.

It should be noted that despite the enemy's stubborn defense around Jelgava, there was no real continuous front. Roundabout routes west of Jelgava were open toward the Gulf of Riga.

At 0400 on 30 July the 3rd Guards Mechanized Corps' formations resumed the attack on Jelgava, while overcoming the enemy's stubborn resistance. At the same time, part of the corps' forces seized the towns of Dobele and Tukums, completely clearing the enemy out of them. The corps' forward detachment, which had been dispatched to the shore of the Gulf of Riga, had by the morning of 31 July captured Klapkalns and cut the maritime road.

The 51st Army, having gone over to the offensive in the general direction of Jelgava, was throwing back individual enemy detachments and successfully advancing during 28-29 July. The army secured Siauliai with one corps from the northwest and west. On 30 July units of the 1st Guards Rifle Corps reached the approaches to Jelgava, where they began fighting on the town's southern and southwestern outskirts, although they encountered organized resistance and had no success. The army's forward units failed to establish the necessary coordination with the 3rd Guards Mechanized Corps, which is why the joint attack on the morning of 31 July was beaten back. In order to unit all the forces in the area in the hands of a single commander, the commander of the First Baltic Front ordered the following:

> The commander of the 51st Army is to personally go to the Jelgava area and unite the army's combat activities and those of the 3rd Guards Mechanized Corps and, by attacking from the west, east and northeast, is to capture Jelgava on 31 July at all costs.[3]

---

3   Central Ministry of Defense Archives. First Baltic Front combat journal for July, pp. 79-80.

As a result of these measures, through the unified efforts of the 3rd Guards Mechanized Corps' units and the 51st Army's formations, by 1600 on 31 July Jelgava was occupied by our forces.

The 3rd Guards Mechanized Corps, following the final clearing of Jelgava of enemy forces, was no longer subordinated to the commander of the 51st Army and was concentrating in the Dobele area, having left the 8th Mechanized Brigade behind in the Tukums area.

At the same time the offensive was developing successfully along the First Baltic Front's right wing and center, a tense situation had arisen along the *front's* left wing, in the 2nd Guards Army's zone.

On the morning of 28 July the enemy in the area southwest of Siauliai launched a counterblow against the flank of our Siauliai group of forces with the forces of the 7th Panzer Division, the "Werthern" Motorized Brigade and the "Sonner" combat group.

The commander of the 2nd Guards Army made the decision to defend along the center and right flank, for the purpose of wearing out and weakening the enemy, and then to go over to the attack and destroy him.

By order of the *front* commander, the 1st Tank Corps was moved up to the 2nd Guards Army's sector. Besides this, the 20th Artillery Division from the *Stavka* reserve was subordinated to the army commander. As a result of these measures, the 2nd Guards Army successfully repulsed the counterblow by the enemy's powerful tank group during 28-31 July.

One of the main conditions for the success achieved was the skillful employment of the second-echelon formations and anti-tank reserves, their rapid maneuver, the timely creation of anti-tank centers of resistance and strong points along the likely axes of the tank attacks, and the correct employment of artillery and tanks, which played a decisive role in repelling the enemy's tank attacks.

As a result of the three-day attacks the enemy, having lost half of his active tanks and having failed to achieve visible results along a single sector, halted further attempts to carry out his plan and on the night of 1 August began to withdraw his tank units.

The 3rd Air Army's combat activities during 16-31 July were quite intense.

During this period the enemy air force covered its troops in groups of 4-14 fighters and supported the counterblow by its tank group in the area southwest of Siauliai.

The 3rd Air Army's fighter aviation, while covering the *front's* shock group and supporting the combat activities of its *shturmoviks* and bombers, carried out 6,595 sorties during this period. 440 enemy planes were shot down in air battles. The assault air formations, while facilitating the offensive by the 6th Guards and 43rd armies, launched echeloned raids against the enemy's men and materiel in these armies' sectors. The 335th Assault Air Division, supporting the 51st Army and 3rd Mechanized Corps, launched raids against enemy troops in the Siauliai and Jelgava areas. The 1st Bomber Corps and 334th Bomber Division, battled the enemy's arriving reserves, launched raids against the railroad stations in Riga and Jelgava, and against the enemy's automobile columns along the Siauliai—Jelgava sector, which eased the offensive by the 51st Army and 3rd Mechanized Corps toward Siauliai and Jelgava.

However, it should be noted that while the 3rd Mechanized Corps was moving toward Jelgava, due to the insufficient fighter aviation cover, enemy bombers launched bombing raids along the corps' columns throughout 28 July, which delayed the arrival of the corps' main units to Jelgava. As a result of these circumstances, the commander of the 3rd Mechanized Corps was forced to commit his troops piecemeal, which led to prolonged fighting in this area.

The 221st Assault Air Division, in conjunction with the 259th Fighter Division, supported the 2nd Guards Army's offensive and launched echeloned raids against the enemy's forces and interfered with the arrival of the enemy's reserves from the Kaunas area.

With the liberation of Jelgava and Tukums and the arrival at the shore of the Gulf of Riga, the First Baltic Front achieved its objective in the multi-*front* Belorussian offensive operation.

The *front*, by driving a deep wedge between the enemy's two army groups (Center and North) and breaking land communications between them, achieved an objective of enormous importance. Favorable conditions had been created for the subsequent defeat of the enemy's Army Group North, which had not managed to fall back toward East Prussia.

The German-Fascist command could not reconcile itself to the difficult situation in the Baltic States. It set itself the objective to eliminate, at all costs, the wedge driven in by the forces of the First Baltic Front, and to restore land communications between its army groups.

Results and Conclusions

As a result of the Dvinsk—Siauliai operation by the armies of the First Baltic Front, Soviet forces reached the Gulf of Riga, having sharply worsened the situation of Army Group Center. The latter was isolated in the Baltic States, deprived of land communications with Army Group Center and Germany. Thus the objectives, assigned to the *front* in the operation, were achieved.

During the Dvinsk—Siauliai offensive operation the forces of the First Baltic Front advanced up to 270 kilometers (as far as Jelgava) during 5-31 July, and the mobile formations up to 330 kilometers (as far as the Gulf of Riga).

Thus the combined-arms formations' average rate of advance was about ten kilometers per day. The mobile forces' rates of advance in this operation varied. The 1st Tank Corps advanced at the same speed as the infantry, while the 3rd Mechanized Corps moved significantly faster. The corps, which was committed into the operation on 25 July, covered 200 kilometers in seven days, for an average daily rate of advance of 30 kilometers, while on some days it moved forward 70-140 kilometers.

The objectives assigned by the *Stavka* of the Supreme High Command were achieved significantly earlier. The *front* was ordered to reach the line Dvinsk—Svencionys by 10-12 July, while it actually reached that line by the close of 7 July, although it did not take Dvinsk.

The rapid advance by the First Baltic Front's center and left wing led to a situation in which the enemy did not have time to create a reliable defense in central Lithuania and had to scatter his forces. In this manner, the realistic possibility of our forces' arrival at the shore of the Gulf of Riga arose.

The enemy's losses in the operation under study are shown in table 7.

Table 7. The German-Fascist Forces' Losses in the Dvinsk—Siauliai Operation (Rounded Out)[4]

	Killed and Wounded Personnel, Equipment Destroyed	Captured Personnel and Equipment
Officers and Men	60,000	About 7-8,000
Tanks	300	80-90
Assault Guns	7,080	7-8
Guns (all calibers)	500	35-40
Mortars	300	120-150
Machine Guns	2,000	800-900
Motor Vehicles	3-4,000	1,500
Various Depots	50-60	150-200

4   Central Ministry of Defense Archives, fond 235, opis' 20638ss, delo 16, pp. 97-98.

The serious losses suffered by the First Baltic Front in the course of the Dvinsk-Siauliai operation testify to the intensity of the fighting, as shown in table 8.

These figures show that the heaviest fighting occurred around Dvinsk, in the lake district, where the 6th Guards Army was attacking.

The First Baltic Front's Dvinsk—Siauliai offensive operation had a number of features, which distinguish it from the other operations being conducted at the same time.

The first feature of the operation under study is the fact that the *front* operated along a very broad sector throughout the entire operation. At the start of the operation the combat front reached 250 kilometers, while the neighboring Third Belorussian Front's combat front did not exceed 120 kilometers, while that of the Second Belorussian Front was only 70 kilometers. By the end of the Dvinsk—Siauliai operation the First Baltic Front's combat front nearly doubled and reached 400 kilometers along the front line, while the Third and Second Belorussian fronts continued to operate in the same sectors as at the start of the operation.

Given the presence of such a broad combat front, difficulties arose in creating sufficient operational densities, even for such a numerically large front as the First Baltic Front was in this operation. At the start of the Dvinsk—Siauliai operation the *front* had 27 rifle divisions and, at the end—38, which meant an average of one rifle division per ten kilometers of front at the beginning and end of the operation.

Table 8. The First Baltic Front's Losses in the Dvinsk—Siauliai Operation[5]

	Killed	Wounded	Missing in Action	Captured	Other Causes	Total
6th Guards Army	4,815	16,512	182	6	102	21,618
2nd Guards Army	2,180	8,360	18	–	22	10,580
43rd Army	4,367	14,735	260	–	2	19,364
51st Army	1,770	5,525	395	–	78	7,768
3rd Air Army	34	21	116	–	16	187
22nd Gds Rifle Corps	1,131	4,797	62	–	6	5,996
3rd Gds Mechanized Corps	180	539	8	4	34	765
1st Tank Corps	379	926	20	–	3	1,328
Total	14,856	51,415	1,062	10	263	67,606

A second feature of the Dvinsk—Siauliai operation was the fact that the 6th Guards and 43rd armies operated throughout against the enemy's Army Group North, attacking to the north, while the 51st and 2nd Guards armies were operating against Army Group Center, attacking from east to west and, at the very end, with part of its forces facing northwest.

A third feature of the Dvinsk—Siauliai operation is that the *front*, operating along such a broad sector, was forced to combine the offensive with short periods of defense, for the purpose of bringing up men and materiel and repelling enemy counterblows.

Thus the situation that arose during the course of the operation created additional difficulties for the First Baltic Front, which were overcome only thanks to the extremely high morale of the Soviet forces, their heroism and high degree of military skill. The commanders and staffs at all levels

---

5   Central Ministry of Defense Archives, fond 235, opis' 20638ss, delo 16, pp. 97-98.

coped with all the difficulties, skillfully controlled their forces, and maneuvered flexibly, having shown, on the whole, great skill in waging both the offensive and defensive battle.

It's particularly important to note the successful actions of the 3rd Mechanized Corps, which played an extremely important role in this operation. The corps' combat experience shows that a mechanized corps of the time was completely capable of launching deep attacks against the enemy's rear and communications, while attacking at a great remove (120-140 kilometers) from its own forces. In liberating Siauliai, the corps gave an instructive example of mobile troops' actions against a large inhabited locale. The corps, having organized the attack from several axes, felt out the weak spot in the enemy's defensive system, broke into the town and, with the assistance of the newly-arrived 417th Rifle Division, captured it. In its actions against the enemy's rear, the corps showed the ability to rapidly advance, flexibly maneuver and outflank the enemy's strong points.

On the other hand, this experience shows that the activities of a mechanized corps may be successful only given the presence of the corps' reliable fighter cover from the air. The 3rd Mechanized Corps' maneuver toward Jelgava was foiled, to a significant degree; by the fact that the air cover was insufficient the enemy's air force could launch bombing raids against the corps' columns.

In the First Baltic Front's operation under review, the offensive was conducted, as a rule, by the method of pursuing the retreating enemy. The decisive role was played by maneuver, directed at enveloping and outflanking the opposing enemy. The offensive usually began by dispatching powerful forward detachments, which, upon encountering the enemy, sought to outflank him and launch an attack from the rear. If the forward detachment could not overcome the enemy's resistance, the main forces would deploy, which would attack the enemy from the march, with artillery support. In some cases, a short artillery preparation was conducted.

In the enemy's actions one must take note of his increasingly organized resistance. If during the Vitebsk—Polotsk operation the enemy was afraid of being encircled and carried out counterattacks ranging from a company or battalion in strength, and rarely a regiment, then in the Dvinsk—Siauliai operation he manifested greater stubbornness and not only tried to hold his positions, but sought to launch decisive counterattacks and counterblows to throw back the Soviet forces. This was how it was around Dvinsk, Rokiskis, Jelgava, and Kedainiai.

Some mistakes were committed in such a large and complex *front* operation.

It was hardly expedient at the start of the operation to dispatch the 1st Tank Corps into an inter-lake area for taking Dvinsk. The issuing of such an objective to a tank corps was evidently caused by insufficient knowledge of the enemy and his plans. The corps suffered heavy losses in attempting to overcome the inter-lake defile and lost its offensive capabilities for a long time.

The 6th Guards Army initially expended a lot of strength in frontal attacks among the numerous inter-lake defiles, which it could, nonetheless, not overcome. And only when, having outflanked the numerous lakes with its left flank was it able to approach Dvinsk and assist the 4th Shock Army in taking the fortress. Evidently, it would have been more expedient from the very beginning for the 6th Guards Army to have closed the passages through the lake district with part of its forces, while its main forces deeply outflanked Dvinsk from the south, southwest and west.

8

The Third Belorussian Front's Vilnius—Kaunas Offensive Operation (5-31 July 1944)

The Vilnius—Kaunas operation was the Third Belorussian Front's consecutive offensive operation in depth, which followed after the successful completion of the same *front's* Vitebsk—Minsk operation.

The goal of the Vilnius—Kaunas operation was to inflict a defeat on the enemy group of forces along the Vilnius axis, the liberation of the capital of the Lithuanian SSR, Vilnius, and to reach the Neman River and seize bridgeheads on its western bank.

The operation was not carried out in isolation, but jointly and in conjunction with the neighboring First Baltic and Second Belorussian fronts during the multi-*front* Belorussian operation's second stage.

The Third Belorussian Front did not have a specially set aside time to prepare for the Vilnius—Kaunas operation. All the operation's preparation was conducted from the march, in conditions of pursuing the retreating enemy, who resisted only along the most important axes.

As a result of the preceding operation, the Third Belorussian Front's forces, having encircled, in conjunction with the neighboring *fronts*, a major enemy group of forces to the east of Minsk, had captured the railroad junctions of Smorgon' and Molodechno. By the close of 4 July the enemy had been thrown back along the external encirclement front to a line west of Smorgon' and Volma, and moreover lacked a continuous front. The routed German-Fascist units were falling back in disorder to the west. To the east of Minsk the *front's* forces, along with those of the Second Belorussian Front, were destroying the encircled enemy with part of their forces.

By the close of 4 July the enemy, while falling back, was putting up resistance along the *front's* sector in small pockets in the following grouping: the 221st Security Division, reinforced with tanks, was falling back in the sector west of Smorgon'; the 170th Infantry and 5th Panzer divisions were holding the area west of Molodechno; to the south, under the blows of our forces, the "Zausken," "Wergen," "Gotberg," and "Mueller" combat groups, composed of the Fourth Army's scattered units, which had been defeated along the Berezina River, were falling back, as well as independent regiments and battalions from the enemy's security and police forces.

The enemy had no reserves in the operational depth.

On 5 July the newly-arrived 7th Panzer Division from Stanislav (Ukraine) began to disembark at the Lida railroad junction.

The enemy had a single previously-prepared defensive line throughout his entire depth as far as the Neman River, along the western bank of the Oshmyanka River—Zuprany—Bogdanuv—Vishneya. He had begun building this line in 1943, with the intention of creating here fortifications that would block the route along the Oshmyanka uplands from the east to the west. By the start of the Vilnius—Kaunas operation this line was not ready and consisted of individual field fortifications. Besides this, the city of Vilnius had been prepared for all-round defense. The enemy had no previously-prepared defensive line along the western bank of the Neman River.

The Third Belorussian Front's combat and numerical strength by the start of the Vilnius—Kaunas operation is shown in table 9.

As can be seen from table 9, by this time the *front* had more than 300,000 officers and men, more than 7,800 guns and mortars of all calibers, and more than 700 tanks. This strength enabled the *front* to carry out active offensive tasks.

By the start of the Vilnius—Kaunas operation the Third Belorussian Front deployed three combined-arms armies (5th, 11th Guards and 31st) in its first echelon, and one tank army (5th Guards), while the 113th Rifle Corps, reinforced with two tank brigades, had been dispatched from the 31st Army against the encircled enemy. Besides this, the 3rd Guards Mechanized, 3rd Guards Cavalry and 2nd Guards Tank corps were also in the *front's* first echelon. The 33rd Army, transferred from the Second Belorussian Front, was tied down until 8-9 July in fighting to eliminate the enemy's encircled Minsk group of forces and, while constituting the *front's* second echelon during 9-10 July, was to moving to the Neman River behind the *front's* center.

Thanks to the rapid breakthrough of the enemy's defense in the Vitebsk—Minsk operation, ammunition expenditure in the Third Belorussian Front turned out to be less than planned. Thus as of 1 July the *front* still had the following number of combat loads: rifle rounds—1.9; mortars (82mm and 120mm)—2.7; 45mm shells—1.7; 57mm shells—2.2; 76mm regimental artillery shells—2.6; 76mm divisional artillery shells—1.8; 122mm shells—2.7; 152mm howitzer shells—16.8; 152mm gun-howitzer shells—3.1, and; anti-aircraft rounds—2.8. However, it should be noted here that despite the sufficient presence of ammunition in the *front*, as a whole, there was a shortage in the rifle divisions, for our transport failed to cope with transporting them to the troops from the army and *front* depots.

Table 9. The Third Belorussian Front's Combat and Numerical Strength by the Start of the Vilnius—Kaunas Operation[1]

Army	Men	Mortars		Guns	Divisional	Regimental	45mm
		120mm	82mm	122 & 230mm			
5th Army	76,506	306	636	360	384	14	270
31st Army	57,843	163	433	196	292	66	244
11th Guards Army	96,129	273	615	300	577	108	340
39th Army	50,717	149	437	116	232	65	161
5th Guards Tank Army	23,367	80	84	46	158	–	52
Cavalry-Mechanized group and units subordinated to the *front*	No numerical data found in the archives						
Total	304,562	971	2,205	1,018	1,643	253	1,067

---

1 Central Ministry of Defense Archives, fond 241, opis' 12938ss, delo 6, pp. 340-351.

	Anti-Aircraft Guns		Tanks and Self-Propelled Guns
	76 & 85mm	20 & 37mm	
5th Army	12	95	72
31st Army	28	110	25
11th Guards Army	32	182	294
39th Army	28	102	38
			7
5th Guards Tank	28	42	307
Army	24		
Cavalry-Mechanized group and units subordinated to the *front*	No numerical data found in the archives		
Total	128	531	736
			31

Note: Combat-ready tanks are shown in the numerator, and tanks in need of repair in the denominator.

The situation was the same with fuel. By the beginning of the Vitebsk—Minsk operation, the *front* had no less than two refills of fuels and lubricants. However, the delivery of fuel to the troops was carried out with delays. By the end of the operation the shortage of fuel among the troops was seriously influencing the course of combat activities, for in many cases, for just this reason, the tank units and formations were not in a position to support the combined-arms formations.

As regards other types of supply, the *front* had no serious problems.

On 4 July the commander of the Third Belorussian Front received *Stavka* directive no. 220126, which demanded that he develop the offensive, launching his main attack in the general direction of Molodechno and Vilnius. The *front's* immediate task was to capture the towns of Vilnius and Lida no later than 10-12 July; the *front* would subsequently reach the Neman River and seize bridgeheads on its western bank.

In accordance with this directive, the Third Belorussian Front was reinforced with one combined-arms army (the 33rd Army, consisting of seven rifle divisions and two corps headquarters) from the Second Belorussian Front.

On 4 July the *front* commander made the following decision: to launch the main attack with the forces of the 5th, 11th Guards and 5th Guards Tank armies, and the 3rd Guards Mechanized Corps, in the general direction of Vilnius, with the goal of capturing it from the march with the mobile forces by the close of 6 July. By the morning of 7 July the forces of the 31st Army and the 3rd Guards Cavalry Corps were to seize the railroad junction of Lida.

The 31st Army's 113th Rifle Corps was designated to eliminate the enemy's encircled Minsk group of forces, as was the 33rd Army, which, after completing this task, would be pulled back into the *front's* second echelon and was to advance behind the 11th Guards Army in the direction of Alytus.

The 1st Air Army had the task of supporting and covering with its main forces the *front's* forces operating along the Vilnius axis.

One may divide the Vilnius—Kaunas *front* offensive operation into two stages, according to the course of combat activities.

During the operation's first stage the *front's* forces, overcoming the enemy's resistance, attacked along the Vilnius axis and liberated the capital of the Lithuanian SSR—Vilnius.

During the operation's second stage, the *front's* forces reached the important water line of the Neman River and forced the river, having seized bridgeheads on its western bank.

We will now examine consecutively the main military events in each of these stages.

The Operation's First Stage

The Offensive along the Vilnius Direction and the Capture of Vilnius (5-13 July 1944)

During the course of the first half of July 1944 the forces of the Third Belorussian Front concentrated their main efforts at liberating Vilnius and forcing the Neman River.

The German-Fascist command, striving to prevent the loss of Vilnius and Lida, continued to hurriedly pull back its force to the previously-prepared "East Wall." Simultaneously, from 5 July it was pulling out the 7th Panzer Division and parts of the 707th Security Division to occupy this line along the Oshmyany—Bogdanuv—Vishnev sector. Police units were being transferred from Poland and East Prussia to defend the Neman's Berezina River.

The enemy was putting up stubborn resistance with the remnants of his defeated armies and forces from newly-arrived formations, which he was forced to feed into the battle piecemeal. In this situation the *front's* offensive was unfolding at a high rate of speed, both along the axis of the main attack, and along the left wing. At the same time, the fighting for the large towns along the *front's* right wing was quite fierce.

The 5th Army advanced most successfully during the offensive's first days. Having covered up to 55 kilometers in two days, by the close of 6 July it had captured the line Podvorzhizhna—Gudogai. The Zuprany area was being stubbornly held by units of the enemy's 170th Infantry Division. While pursuing the enemy during these two days, the 5th Army forced the Viliya River from the march and overcame a portion of the "East Wall" defensive line in the area of Soly and to the north, without encountering organized enemy resistance here. The "East Wall" line in the 5th Army's offensive sector ran along the western bank of the Oshmyanka River.

The 3rd Guards Mechanized Corps, which was attacking in the 5th Army's sector along the Smorgon'—Vilnius railroad, in close coordination with the formations of the 5th Army's 65th Rifle Corps, forced the Oshmyanka River in the Soly area during the second half of the day and continued its vigorous pursuit along three routes during the course of 6 July and the night of 7 July toward Vilnius.

The 5th Guards Tank Army was attacking, launching its main blow in the direction of Oshmyany and Vilnius, and with the 29th Tank Corps attacking along the Molodechno—Krevo axis along the northern bank of the Berezina River (Neman). The army's formations were pursuing the enemy and, having assisted the 11th Guards Army and 3rd Guards Cavalry Corps, with part of the 29th Tank Corps' forces, in taking Molodechno; by 1730 on 6 July they reached the line Krevo—Vishnev. With the approach of the army's units to the "East Wall," the enemy's resistance increased, particularly against the 29th Tank Corps, in connection with which the army commander decided to turn the corps to outflank the line's most powerful fortifications from the north toward Oshmyany. By the morning of 7 July the 3rd Guards Tank Corps had liberated Bogdanuv from the march.

By 1400 on 5 July units of the 11th Guards Army's 31st Guards Rifle Division, in conjunction with the 6th Guards Cavalry Division and the 2nd Tank Corps, completely liberated Molodechno. On 5-6 July the main forces of the army's 16th and 8th guards rifle corps pursued the enemy, forced the Berezina River (Neman) and, having thrown back his units 25-30 kilometers, by the close of 6 July had reached the "East Wall" defensive line. However, the poorly-organized reconnaissance uncovered this line only on the morning of 7 July and established that the enemy was determined to defend it.

The 3rd Guards Cavalry Corps, following the capture of Molodechno and Lebedzev, renewed the offensive during the second half of 5 July along the railroad to Lida, and by the close of 6 July one of its divisions had reached the Vishnev area.

The 31st Army's main forces were located in the Minsk area and were covering the *front's* rear organs, where it was simultaneously fighting the encircled enemy. The 31st Army's two-division 71st Rifle Corps was operating along the external encirclement front, as were formations from the 2nd Guards Tank Corps, which on 5 July reached the Ivenets area and to the northeast, and which remained in the area on 6 July, putting themselves in order. During 5-6 July the 71st Rifle Corps pursued the enemy to the west and, having advanced up to 40 kilometers, by the close of 6 July had reached the line of Pershaie and then to the east along the northern bank of the Isloch' River as far as Rakuv.

On the morning of 6 July part of the 33rd Army's forces continued fighting to destroy the enemy encircled in the forests east and southeast of Minsk, while the main forces were moving up to that area.

During 5-6 July the 1st Air Army strafed the columns of the enemy retreating along the Molodechno—Oshmyany—Gol'shany and Volozhin—Vishnev roads, was destroying the enemy encircled southeast of Minsk, and was carrying out reconnaissance as far as the line Vilnius—Lida. The army carried out 506 sorties on 5-6 July.

On 7-8 July the pursuit of the enemy on Vilnius and Lida continued along the *front's* entire sector, and his intermediary defensive line, which had been occupied by fresh reserves brought up from the depth, was penetrated.

On 7 July the 3rd Guards Mechanized Corps, having completed a vigorous advance of up to 45 kilometers, reached Vilnius and at 0900 on 7 July began fighting along the town's eastern and southeastern outskirts. The enemy garrison put up stubborn resistance and, going over to a counterattack, pressed the corps' units back. At 2000 the corps renewed the attack and, in conjunction with the 5th Army's forward detachments, once again broke into the town.

On 7 July the 5th Army's main forces advanced 30-35 kilometers. Its forward detachments were fighting along with units from the 3rd Guards Mechanized Corps in the northeastern and eastern outskirts of Vilnius.

The 5th Guards Tank Army, while advancing on Vilnius, encountered the enemy's "East Wall" defensive line. Units of the 29th Tank Corps outflanked it north of Zuprany and by 2100 on 7 July the army had liberated Medniki. The 3rd Guards Tank Corps broke through the enemy's "East Wall" intermediate defensive line in the area north of Bogdanuv and, while overcoming stubborn resistance by units of the enemy's 5th and 7th panzer divisions, in conjunction with the 11th Guards Army's 8th Guards Rifle Corps, advanced with its main forces on Gol'shany; by the end of the day the 3rd Guards Tank Corps captured Oshmyany.

Thus on 7 July the *front's* right-wing forces achieved major successes. Thanks to the offensive's high rate of advance, they prevented the enemy from organizing the defense of Vilnius and from the second half of the day forced him into street fighting for the city. However, in connection with the fact that the 11th Guards Army had been halted in front of the "East Wall" defensive line and that on 7 July the army was fighting to break through between the 5th Army and the *front's* main group of forces, a gap of more than 50 kilometers formed during the second half of the day. In order to improve the 5th Army's operational situation, the 29th Tank Corps was moving up on the *front* commander's instructions along the road from Medniki to Vilnius.

The "East Wall" line, which had been occupied by fresh enemy reserves from the depth, consisted of one, and in places two, fully-developed trench lines, outfitted with rifle foxholes and machine gun emplacements, and had prepared ramps for tanks; there were no anti-tank and anti-personnel obstacles. Broken trench lines had been dug in the defensive depth and the inhabited locales of Oshmyany and Gol'shany had been prepared for all-round defense. By 7 July the enemy had occupied the line with the 170th Infantry and 5th Panzer divisions, the remnants of the 337th Infantry Division, and the fresh 7th Panzer and 707th Security Infantry divisions from the reserve. With an enemy-occupied sector of 40 kilometers (Zuprany—Bogdanuv), the density of his forces reached an average of 0.8 battalions and 3-4 tanks per kilometer of front.

The organization of the breakthrough of the "East Wall" line had the following features. On 7 July the 11th Guards Army's forces were given the assignment of pursuing the enemy and did not know of the defensive line in front of them, which had been occupied by enemy forces. The contours of this line were established by our reconnaissance only on the morning of 7 July. The preparation for the breakthrough took up no more than 4-5 hours, during the course of which a final reconnaissance of the enemy's defense and fire targets was carried out, and cooperation and control were organized. During the preparation period for the attack, a group of forces was created in the rifle divisions, and the artillery, having occupied its firing positions, carried out adjustment fire. Mortars and divisional and regimental artillery took part in breaking through the defensive line. The reinforcement artillery—army and High Command reserve—arrived only by 1800, while the 2nd Guards Breakthrough Artillery Division's 114th Heavy Howitzer, 6th Howitzer and 33rd Mortar brigades could not be brought up due to a shortage of fuel.

The 16th Guards Rifle Corps was to break through the line along a 13-kilometer sector, with all three divisions in a single echelon. The 8th Guards Rifle Corps was to begin the attack along an 8-kilometer sector, with two rifle divisions in the first echelon and one in the second. The rifle divisions' breakthrough sectors, as a rule, varied from 3-4 kilometers; the 31st Guards Rifle Division was to break through the defense along a 6-kilometer front.

The offensive against the enemy, who had hurriedly taken up defensive positions along the "East Wall" line, began around 1100 on 7 July. The enemy defended stubbornly, having a large number of tank ambushes along the approaches to the line. Upon the arrival of our forces at their jumping-off positions for the attack, the enemy conducted powerful counterattacks. By 2200 the 16th and 8th guards rifle corps had advanced 4-6 kilometers and, having forced the Oshmyanka River on the right flank, broke through the enemy's defense throughout his entire depth. Combat activities subsequently began to rapidly shift into the depth, where the enemy no longer disposed of prepared positions, and only had broken trench lines in the areas of large inhabited locales and road junctions. The 8th Guards Rifle Corps' successful actions are explained by the decisive attack of the line by the 3rd Guards Tank Corps, which was breaking through the line along its sector. By 0200 on 8 July the 11th Guards Army's forces had reached the line Oshmyany—Gol'shany and securely consolidated the success by the 3rd Guards Tank Corps, which had captured these locales as early as 2100 on 7 July.

The breakthrough of the "East Wall" line by the forces of the 11th Guards Army had great operational significance: the calculations of the German-Fascist command, which assumed that, having concentrated reserves, it could hold the line Vilnius—Lida, had been disrupted. The army's and 3rd Guards Tank Corps' forces, having inflicted heavy losses on the enemy's 7th Panzer and 707th Security Infantry divisions, resumed the pursuit of the enemy on the morning of 8 July and within two days eliminated the gap with the 5th Army, having reached on 9 July a line 20 kilometers south and southwest of Vilnius.

On 7 July the 3rd Guards Cavalry Corps, taking advantage of the fact that the enemy's main forces opposing the *front's* center were tied down in fighting the 11th Guards Army along the "East Wall" line, was decisively moving on Lida. The corps, throwing back and destroying combat group "Mueller" and the enemy's security units, by 2100 had liberated Subbotniki and Iv'e, thus cutting off the path of retreat of the enemy falling back in the 31st Army's sector.

The 31st Army, with formations of its 71st Rifle Corps, continued to pursue the enemy and, not encountering resistance, by the close of 7 July had reached the Berezina River, having overcome along this axis the Nalibokskaya woods. The 36th Rifle Corps renewed its advance with a single rifle division on Ivenets and Bakshty, while its main forces, in conjunction with the 2nd Guards Tank Corps, continued to cover the army's left flank along the line excluding Ivenets—Volma.

Our forces, while passing through the Nalibokskaya woods, were greatly assisted by the Belorussian partisans, who cleared the forest roads of obstacles, and restored the bridges on the Isloch' River, etc.

On 8 July the *front's* offensive was developing throughout the entire sector. Formations of the 5th Army's 72nd and 65th rifle corps reached the area of Vilnius and, in conjunction with the 3rd Guards Mechanized Corps and the 5th Guards Tank Army, were engaged in street fighting for the city.

On that same day the 3rd Guards Cavalry Corps launched a vigorous attack from the north and northeast, and at 1630 broke into the town of Lida, having defeated the forward units of the enemy's fresh 50th Infantry Division, and on 9 July completely captured the railroad junction and town of Lida.

On 8 July the pursuit of the enemy continued successfully along the *front's* center and left wing and the first-echelon formations of the 11th Guards and 31st armies advanced 25-30 kilometers.

The 1st Air Army operated against the enemy's forces in the Vilnius and Lida area and on 8 July carried out 656 sorties. 14 enemy planes were shot down in air battles.

As a result of four days of fighting during 5-8 July, the Third Belorussian Front's forces, while vigorously pursuing the enemy, reached the line Vilnius—Lida and interfered with the enemy's organizing a defense of these locales.

During this short period of time the enemy's 7th Panzer Division, units of the 50th Infantry and 707th Security Infantry divisions, as well as a significant number of police and security units operating against the *front's* left wing, suffered heavy casualties. On 7 July the enemy moved the 761st Mountain Rifle Brigade to Vilnius by rail and unloaded the "Werthern" Armored Brigade, which was later committed into the fighting in the Maisaigala area, in Kaunas

The 100-kilometer distance from the Smorgon'—Rakuv line to the line Vilnius—Lida was covered with an average daily speed of 25 kilometers by the combined-arms armies, and 35 kilometers by the mobile forces.

The Third Belorussian Front's combat activities in taking Vilnius and advancing to the Neman River developed as follows.

The German-Fascist command attached a great deal of significance to the defense of Vilnius, both as a political center and very important strong point on the approaches to East Prussia.

The German-Fascist command had been withdrawing many formations and units from the Third Panzer Army, which had been defeated in the preceding battles.

Taking advantage of the sharply hilly terrain along the city's outskirts, and the natural line of the Viliya River, the enemy had been preparing Vilnius as a fortified area since 1943. By the start of the fighting the city's garrison consisted mainly of defeated units of the 14th, 170th, 24th, 83rd, and 299th infantry divisions, the 1065th and 1067th grenadier regiments, the 9th SS Police Regiment, and a large number of security, training and construction subunits, as well as march battalions formed out of men on leave. On 7 July the 761st Mountain Rifle Brigade was transferred to Vilnius, and on 8 July Major General Stagel, who had been appointed garrison commander, arrived by plane, with orders to hold Vilnius until the arrival of reserves. The enemy's Vilnius garrison numbered at least 15,000 men and disposed of 270 guns of various calibers, about 40 tanks and assault guns, and other equipment. The garrison was supplied with food and ammunition for a prolonged defense. The "Werthern" Armored Brigade and combat group "Tolendorf" (up to an infantry regiment, with tanks) arrived late and were subsequently employed by the enemy for organizing aid to the garrison from without.

The city's defense, from the engineering point of view, was as follows. On the outskirts and immediate approaches to the city were dug trenches, outfitted with foxholes for riflemen, machine gun emplacements, and dugouts, etc. Brick buildings, basements and other structures had been configured for defense. Artillery and mortar firing positions had been outfitted both in the outskirts of the city, as well as in the center, while the anti-aircraft artillery's positions had been configured for firing at land targets. The approaches to the city, road and street intersections, and individual sectors of squares and streets had been mines. City blocks, as a whole, represented a dense network of strong points, defended by infantry garrisons, reinforced with guns and tanks, which were also employed by the enemy as a mobile reserve during counterattacks.

The Army Group Center command, relying on Vilnius and the "East Wall" intermediate line, calculated that by moving up reserves from the depth and taking advantage of the wooded and lake terrain, and the Viliya and Merechanka and other rivers, to reestablish a continuous defensive front along the line Vilnius—Lida.

The fighting for Vilnius continued six days, during 8-13 July.

The forces of the 5th Army, along with the 3rd Guards Mechanized Corps, attack the city from the northeast, and the 5th Guards Tank Army from the southeast.

On 8 July the 5th Army's main forces reached the Vilnius area and, in conjunction with the 3rd Guards Mechanized Corps and the newly-arrived 5th Guards Tank Army from the southeast, from 0700 began street fighting for the city. Simultaneously, part of these armies' forces and those of the corps were moving up north and southwest of the city and by the end of the day cut the railroads running from Vilnius to Kaunas, Grodno and Lida.

The 1st Air Army destroyed the enemy reserves, which were arriving to Vilnius from the south, and launched bombing raids against the enemy, who was defending the northwestern and southwestern outskirts of the city.

As a result of the fighting on 7-8 July, the enemy's Vilnius garrison was surrounded from three sides and could communicate with the remaining German-Fascist forces only through the western part of the city, along the northern bank of the Viliya River, where there were no good roads.

The resulting situation in the city forced the commander of the German Third Panzer Army to take hurried measures to save the Vilnius garrison and prevent its being surrounded. For this purpose, the enemy transferred on the night of 9 July from Kaunas to Maisaigala (25 kilometers northwest of Vilnius), the "Werthern" Armored Brigade (up to 120 tanks and assault guns), just arrived from Germany and was unloading combat group "Tolendorf" at the Landvorovo railroad junction and assigning it the objective of holding Landvorovo. Having reinforced the "Werthern" brigade with infantry and artillery, taken from other sectors of the front, the enemy on 9 July made fierce attempts to break through to save the encircled garrison from the northwest. At the same time, he was reinforcing the city's garrison with the 2nd Airborne Division's 6th Parachute Regiment, having dropped up to 800 paratroopers and supplies from 100 Ju-88 100 aircraft. The majority of the paratroopers landed in our lines and were quickly destroyed.

The German-Fascist command's bringing up of new forces to the Vilnius axis required the immediate withdrawal of our mobile forces from the city and the deployment of the main forces of the *front's* right wing west of Vilnius, for the purpose of defeating the enemy's reserves and completing the encirclement of his Vilnius group of forces.

For this purpose, the *front* commander ordered the 5th Army commander, in order to destroy the Vilnius garrison and capture the city, to leave two rifle divisions in the city and, with his main forces go over to a decisive offensive and destroy the enemy's Maisaigala group of forces.

At 2400 on 9 July the 3rd Guards Mechanized Corps was subordinated to the commander of the 5th Army for attacking toward Maisaigala.

The commander of the 5th Guards Tank Army was ordered to pull his army out of Vilnius and, attacking toward Rudiskes and Alytus, take the Rudiskes area by the close of 9 July.

The 5th Guards Tank Army, having turned over its sector to the 5th Army's 144th Rifle Division, moved out of Vilnius at 1400 on 9 July, and by the close of the day had reached the area north of Rudiskes, having thrown back the enemy to the southwest of Vilnius.

The complete isolation of the encircled Vilnius garrison was completed on 10 July. The fate of the enemy defending in the city had been decided, because that day formations of the 65th Rifle and 3rd Guards Mechanized corps inflicted a decisive defeat on him. By the end of the day the Vilnius garrison had been defeated and its remnants had hidden in two groups in the area of the observatory and the old fortress's citadel, which were along the city's commanding heights. In order to prevent the Vilnius garrison's complete isolation, and to retain the woods northwest of the city, the enemy dropped 600 paratroopers from the 2nd Airborne Division into this area at 1000 and sought to withdraw his surrounded forces by means of meeting attacks from within and without the city.

The 72nd Rifle Corps, which was operating northwest of Vilnius, repulsed all the enemy's attempts to break into the city from the Maisaigala area and inflicted heavy casualties on him. To the southwest of Vilnius, the 45th Rifle Corps continued to wage a stubborn battle for Landvorovo.

The 3rd Guards Mechanized Corps, following the defeat of the Vilnius garrison, was pulled out of the city on the night of 11 July for an attack against the enemy's Maisaigala group of forces.

At dawn on 10 July the 5th Guards Tank Army renewed the attack on Alytus, but due to the fact that the enemy was continuing to bring up reserves to the Maisaigala area, the army was left there by order of the *front* commander at 1000. The army was assigned the task, upon capturing Landvorovo, to consolidate along the line Landvorovo—Rudiskes and be ready for operations toward Maisaigala; the tank corps' forward detachments were to seize crossings over the Neman River and Alytus. During 10-13 July the army was to remain in the Rudiskes area, bring up its lagging equipment, get gassed up, and conduct reconnaissance in the direction of Maisaigala and Yev'e. At 2030 on 10 July formations of the 29th Tank Corps began attacking Landvorovo and on 11 July in conjunction with the 184th Rifle Division, captured it. On 11-12 July the tank corps' forward detachments reached the Neman River and captured the eastern part of Alytus, which was located along the river's eastern bank.

At 1100 on 11 July the 5th Army's main forces resumed their offensive and, having crushed the enemy's stubborn resistance, captured Maisaigala and Landvorovo, having surrounded in the woods in the Landvorovo area part of combat group "Tolendorf," which was defending this inhabited locale. During 12 July while continuing their offensive, the 5th Army's main forces, in conjunction with the 3rd Guards Mechanized Corps, threw the enemy back 10-12 kilometers to the west and captured the road junction of Yev'e.

The 3rd Guards Mechanized Corps reached the area north of Maisaigala, where it was putting itself in order, and at 2400 on 15 July the corps was subordinated to the First Baltic Front.[2] The enemy was putting up stubborn resistance to the 45th Rifle Corps on July 12 four kilometers northwest of Landvorovo, with the forces of combat group "Tolendorf" (units of the 12th Panzer Division, the 16th Police and 1088th Grenadier regiments, and the 2nd Airborne Division's 16th Parachute Regiment, and other units), with the task of meeting the encircled garrison of Vilnius, which on 12 July received orders to break out of the encirclement on the night of 12-13 July.

In Vilnius on 11-12 July units of the 65th Rifle Corps continued intensely fighting to eliminate the enemy, who was stubbornly resisting in the area of the old citadel and observatory. During 12 July the 1st Air Army carried out two massed raids against the enemy, who had hidden in the above-mentioned areas, and carried out more than 200 sorties.

At dawn on 13 July the enemy's Vilnius garrison made a desperate attempt to break out of the encirclement. From 0400 to 0700 his units, numbering up to 3,000 men, managed to break out of the encirclement in the area of the observatory and through the western part of the city reach the woods southeast of Rykonte; here the group linked up with the surrounded units of combat

---

2   *Stavka* directive no. 220144.

group "Tolendorf." The garrison's further attempts to get out of the encirclement were foiled by the arriving Soviet forces. By 1700 on 13 July units of the 5th Army's 65th Rifle Corps had completely cleared the capital of the Lithuanian SSR of the German-Fascist occupiers.

In order to save the units of combat group "Tolendorf" and the escaped remnants of the Vilnius garrison that had reached the group's area, the Third Panzer Army command on 13 July threw in the 6th Panzer Division, which had arrived with the army on 11 July, along the Yev'e—Rykonte—Landvorovo (Northern) axis, plus a battalion of heavy tanks from the *Grossdeutschland* Panzer Regiment, the 500th SS Parachute-Jager Battalion, and two companies from the 16th Parachute Regiment, which at 1330, having broken through the 227th Rifle Division's front in the Yev'e area, reached Rykonte and linked up with its forces, which had been encircled in the woods southeast of that point. As a result of the fighting on 13-14 July and the efforts of the 72nd Rifle and 29th Tank corps, by the close of 14 July the enemy had been thrown back from the Rykonte area and squeezed from three sides in the wooded area 3-4 kilometers west of Rykonte, where he was putting up fierce resistance, trying to break out to the northwest. By this time the 184th Rifle Division and a regiment from the 215th Rifle Division had cleared the enemy out of the woods in the area southeast of Rykonte. On the night of 14-15 July a part of this group's forces fell back in fighting to the west, while the remainder was destroyed and captured. In the fighting of 13-14 July the enemy lost out of this group more than 1,000 officers and men killed, 40 tanks and assault guns, and 13 armored transports, etc. destroyed; 350 men were captured, as were one armored train, six tanks, and other prizes.

It's necessary to note that the enemy avoided being completely destroyed, to a significant degree, because the 3rd Guards Tank Corps attacked on 14 July from the Sumeliske area in the direction of Kaisiadorys, when the situation demanded the corps turn sharply away from Sumeliske to the east and Rykonte for an attack in the rear of the enemy being surrounded. By 1900 on 14 July the 3rd Guards Tank Corps reached the area 12 kilometers southeast of Kaisiadorys.

As a result of the seven days of fighting from 7-13 July, the *front's* right-wing forces defeated the Vilnius group of forces, liberated Vilnius and, by the close of 13 July had thrown the enemy 50-60 kilometers back to the west. On 13-14 July, as a result of fierce fighting, the breakthrough by the enemy's armored group of forces in the Rykonte area had been eliminated. The First Baltic Front's 39th Army on the right, while attacking to the west, by the close of 13 July had reached the area northwest of Maisaigala.

The fighting for Vilnius tied down the overwhelming part of the enemy's operational reserves, which had been transferred during this time to the *front's* sector and enabled the forces along the *front's* center and left wing to rapidly move to the Neman River.

In the immediate fighting for Vilnius, more than 7,000 enemy officers and men were killed, 121 guns, 11 tanks, and 900 motor vehicles, etc., were destroyed; more than 5,200 prisoners were taken, and 156 guns, 28 tanks, 1,100 motor vehicles, 153 supply depots, and other prizes were captured.

During the fighting for Vilnius, the forces of the *front's* center and left wing, while pursuing the enemy, during 9-13 July successfully advanced toward the Neman River.

The enemy, stubbornly clinging to the natural lines and inhabited locales, pursued the goal of winning time for organizing a defense of the Neman River. The enemy put up particularly stubborn resistance along the Alytus axis—the shortest and most convenient for reaching the border of East Prussia. For this purpose, the fresh 131st Infantry Division had been brought up from the Kovel' area to the Rudiskes area on 9-10 July and committed into the fighting against the 11th Guards Army. From 11 July the headquarters of the XXVI Army Corps, the 69th Infantry Division, the 185th and 277th assault gun brigades, the 88th Artillery Brigade from the High Command Reserve, as well as other reinforcements, began to arrive at the disposal of the Third Panzer Army for organizing the defense of Kaunas and the western bank of the Neman River.

Besides this, the enemy transferred the 201st Security Infantry Division to the Prelai area, and the combat group "Rotkirch" (up to a division in strength) to Alytus. South of Alytus, the defense of the Neman River and the Grodno area had been entrusted to the German Fourth Army, to which from 14 July the *Totenkopf* SS Panzer Division began to be transferred, as well as other small units.

On 9 July the *front's* forces captured Lida. The 3rd Guards Cavalry Corps completely cleared the town and consolidated there until the arrival of the 31st Army. On 9 July the forward detachments of the corps' cavalry divisions reached the Dzitva River and were fighting for crossings against units of the enemy's 50th Infantry Division.

At 0600 on 9 July the 11th Guards Army renewed its pursuit of the enemy along its entire front and, encountering weak resistance by the enemy's rearguards in front of the right flank, by the end of the day had advanced 30-35 kilometers. In the center and along the left flank the army was fighting the enemy's 5th and 7th panzer and 170th Infantry divisions and other units and threw them back ten kilometers to the west.

During the night and day of 9 July the 31st Army was moving by forced march to the Vilnius— Lida lateral road, in order to consolidate the Lida area. The army's divisions, not encountering resistance, advanced 40-50 kilometers by the close of the day.

During 10-11 July the 11th Guards and 31st armies continued to pursue the enemy and overcame the Merechanka and Dzitva rivers from the march.

By 2300 on 11 July the 3rd Guards Cavalry Corps liberated Nowy Dvor and Vasilishki. While located in this area, the corps received orders on 11 July to vigorously attack at dawn on 12 July in the direction of Bershty and Grodno, and by the close of 13 July to capture Grodno with an attack from the north.[3]

At 1700 on 10 July the 33rd Army began marching to the Neman River in two echelons.

On 12 July the advance by our troops to the Neman River continued. The enemy, seeking to delay the advance, committed the 131st Infantry Division and the 221st Security Infantry Division's 609th Regiment into the battle against the 11th Guards Army; to the south, relying on the natural obstacles of the Grodno forest, the enemy was seeking to prevent our forces from reaching Grodno.

By 2000 on 12 July the 3rd Guards Cavalry Corps had captured Pozheche and reached the area of Nowa-Ruda.

On 12 July the 11th Guards Army was once again involved in stubborn offensive battles and, having advanced 7-15 kilometers that day, liberated Orany. The army's 16th Guards Rifle Corps, while pursuing the enemy, by the close of 13 July had reached the Neman River in the Alytus area with part of its forces.

The 31st Army, while launching the main attack with its left flank on Grodno, during 12-13 July successfully pursued the enemy and advanced 55-60 kilometers in two days. At 1800 on 13 July the 3rd Guards Cavalry Corps reached the suburbs of Grodno. The corps' further advance was delayed by powerful enemy fire.

Thus as a result of the operation's first stage, the forces of the *front's* center and left wing, while pursuing the enemy on 9-13 July, advanced 90-130 kilometers and by the close of 13 July the 11th Guards Army's right flank reached the Neman River.

The Second Belorussian Front's 50th Army to the left also reached the eastern bank of the Neman River by the close of 13 July.

---

3   Combat order no. 643, of 11 July 1944.

The Operation's Second Stage

The Forcing of the Neman River (14-31 July 1944)

By 14 July the enemy's main group of forces opposing us had been thrown back to the line of the Neman River and the Third Belorussian Front's forces had begun to resolve the task of the operation's concluding phase, which involved the forcing of the Neman River and the fighting to liberate Kaunas.

In connection with the changing situation in the Baltic States, the 39th Army was returned to the Third Belorussian Front and continued to attack north of Kaunas and expanded the *front's* right wing as far as the area of Ukmerge.

The German-Fascist command, striving to delay the Soviet army's movement to the borders of fascist Germany and to prevent the Soviet forces' seizure of bridgeheads along the left bank of the Neman River, threw more than ten divisions (including two panzer) and several panzer brigades against the Third Belorussian Front.

The line of the Neman River was defended by the forces of Army Group Center's Third Panzer and Fourth armies, which bordered on each other in the Alytus area. The front from Kaunas to Alytus was defended by the formations of the XXVI Army Corps and combat group "Rotkirch," which together included a single infantry division, two infantry brigades, combat groups from the 24th, 83rd, 206th, and 212th infantry divisions, six independent grenadier and security regiments, three police regiments, three security battalions, two brigades of assault guns, a panzer battalion, and reinforcements. The front south of Alytus was defended by formations of the XXXIX Panzer Corps, combat group "Gotberg," and the *Totenkopf* SS Panzer Division, which formed part of the German Fourth Army. In all, there were two infantry and three panzer divisions, four combat groups, six independent grenadier and security regiments, five police regiments, three security and reserve battalions, and several units of reinforcements. Later the 6th Panzer Division was transferred for defending the sector of the river immediately south of Kaunas, and the 196th Infantry Division began to arrive from Norway and the 542nd Infantry Division from Germany, by rail. The enemy did not have a previously-prepared defensive line along the Neman River, although the river itself was a serious water obstacle.

On 14 July the forcing of the Neman River began in the 11th Guards Army's sector by units of the 16th Guards Rifle Corps, which during the night and day of 14 July crossed the river with all three of its rifle divisions along the sector in the Alytus area, and by the close of the day had captured a bridgehead along the western bank 20 kilometers in width and 2-6 kilometers in depth. The enemy put up stubborn resistance with the "Goppe" composite brigade and the 1072nd Grenadier Regiment, recently transferred to Alytus and was holding the latter town. During the second half of the day the 8th Guards Rifle Corps' 26th and 5th guards rifle divisions forced the Neman south of Merech', having seized with three regiments a bridgehead along the river's western bank in this area; on the night of 15 July these divisions' crossing continued. The enemy was stubbornly holding Merech' with units of the 131st Infantry Division, repelling the attacks by the 83rd Guards Rifle Division during the day.

To the north of the 11th Guards Army's sector, the 5th Army's rifle divisions reached the Neman River by the close of 14 July and began preparing to force it.

During 14 July the 31st Army rapidly moved toward the Neman. A forward detachment of the army's 36th Rifle Corps forced the river from the march in the area north of Grodno.

On 14 July the 3rd Guards Cavalry Corps' main forces continued fighting for the northern outskirts of Grodno, while one cavalry division forced the Neman from the march north of the town.

On 15 July the crossing front expanded considerably. As a result of two days of fighting, the forces of the 5th and 11th Guards armies seized a bridgehead along the western bank of the river, 28 kilometers long and 2-6 kilometers deep. Besides this, the 11th Guards Army was maintaining a second bridgehead up to six kilometers deep.

During 15 July the 31st Army successfully developed the offensive and, having forced the Neman with formations of its 71st Rifle Corps, by the close of the day had seized two more bridgeheads north of Grodno. By 0400 on 16 July formations of the 31st Army's 36th Rifle Corps and the 50th Army's (Second Belorussian Front) 69th Rifle Corps had completely cleared Grodno of the German-Fascist occupiers.

In connection with the transfer of the Grodno area to the Third Belorussian Front at 2400 on 15 July, the commander of the 31st Army was ordered to regroup his forces to the right flank and force the Neman along the army's entire front.

From 2400 on 15 July the 3rd Guards Cavalry Corps, in accordance with *Stavka* directive no. 220143 was subordinated to the Second Belorussian Front.

During 15 July the 1st Air Army was destroying the enemy in the Grodno area and covering our forces and the crossings over the Neman River.

During 16-17 July the *front's* forces continued to cross the river and waged intensive battles to expand their bridgeheads along the western bank of the river. On 17 July two of the 33rd Army's (the *front's* second echelon) rifle divisions were committed into the fighting along the western bank.

As a result of the four days of fighting (14-17 July), the 5th Army's left flank and the main forces of the 11th Guards and 31st armies forced the Neman along a 110-kilometer front and, having seized bridgeheads along the southwestern bank, repelled all enemy counterattacks.

On 18-20 July the *front's* forces continued fighting to expand their bridgeheads along the river's western bank.

The combat activities of the *front's* forces along the Kaunas axis developed in the following manner.

On 14-15 July the 5th Army, in conjunction with the 5th Guards Tank Army's 29th Tank Corps, completed the elimination of the enemy, who had broken through on 13 July to the Yev'e—Rykonte area, and by the close of 15 July the 72nd Rifle Corps' formations forced the Neman in the area north of Alytus.

The 5th Guards Tank Army, having received orders to attack toward Raseiniai, at 1600 on 15 July began to carry them out. By 2200 the army's main forces had reached the area of Kosedary. On 15 July the army had a total of 156 tanks and self-propelled guns in line, although many of these vehicles were worn out. For this reason, the army's further advance was temporarily halted.

At 2400 on 15 July the 39th Army was returned to the *front*, which together with the 5th and 5th Guards Tank armies took part in the fighting along the Kaunas axis. The goal of this fighting was to capture Kaunas by the close of 18 July. The 39th Army was to support the activities of the *front's* main forces from the north and northeast by an attack to the northwest.

In the following days, all the way up to 20 July, the forces of the 39th and 5th armies attacked along the Kaunas axis and, while repelling the enemy's fierce counterattacks, moved forward slightly only along the 39th Army's sector.

On 18-20 July the Third Belorussian Front's center and left-wing forces continued to attack to expand and consolidate the bridgeheads seized along the Neman River and successfully repelled the enemy's counterattacks. During the course of this fighting, the bridgeheads seized along the 11th Guards Army's left flank and along the 31st Army's sector were expanded and the troops improved their jumping-off position.

On 20 July the Third Belorussian Front, having forced the Neman along a 110-kilometer front and having seized bridgeheads along the river's western bank, accomplished their further objective, as laid down by the *Stavka* of the Supreme High Command, and went over to a temporary defense, having in its first echelon the 39th, 5th, 33rd, 11th Guards, and 31st armies, and the 5th Guards Tank Army and the 29th Guards Tank Corps in the second.

The *front's* forces had the objective of preparing an offensive on Kaunas.

The 21-28 July period is characterized by a complex operational situation, which arose in the *front's* sector.

To the right, the First Baltic Front carried out a new breakthrough of the enemy's defense and by 23-27 July had reached the area Panevezys—Siauliai. In order to parry the First Baltic Front's attack and cover the axis to Tilsit, the command of the German Third Panzer Army removed the "Werthern" Motorized Brigade and combat group "Goppe" from the Kaunas axis during this time and moved them to the First Baltic Front's sector. On 27 July the 7th Panzer Division was also transferred there.

At the same time, the enemy reinforced his group of forces facing the Third Belorussian Front, having moved the following reserves to the area: the 52nd and the 196th and 542nd infantry divisions, as well as several brigades of assault guns, the 510th Panzer Battalion from the High Command Reserve, and other reinforcements.

By 28 July the formations and units of the German Third Panzer and Fourth armies continued to defend along a 210-kilometer front against the Third Belorussian Front. In all, the *front* was faced by ten infantry and security divisions (corps group "H," corps group "D," the 201st, 221st and 52nd security divisions, the 69th, 196th, 131st, 170th, and 542nd infantry divisions), two panzer divisions (6th and 5th), two infantry brigades, six independent regiments, 22 independent battalions, two panzer battalions from the High Command Reserve, and a large number of other reinforcements, particularly artillery.

The enemy's group of forces was based on the field defensive structures, which had been built by their forces during the fighting for the line of the Neman River.

During 21-23 July the *front's* forces repelled all the enemy's counterattacks against the bridge-heads along the western bank of the Neman River. The fighting was especially fierce along the 5th and 33rd armies' bridgeheads, because here the enemy feared our attack on Kaunas. The enemy air force was very active, launching massed strikes against the crossings over the Neman River. During the nights of 20-21, 21-22 and 22-23 July the enemy air force carried out mass raids against the Molodechno, Minsk, Orsha, and Borisov railroad junctions, causing significant damage, especially in Molodechno.

On 23 July the command of the German Third Panzer Army, intending to free up a part of the Ninth Army Corps' forces for employment in the First Baltic Front's sector, pulled its forces back to the Ukmerge area, while trying to retain the town. The enemy's maneuver was foiled by the active operations of the 39th Army's formations, which, upon going over to a vigorous pursuit on 23 July, captured Ukmerge on 24 July. During 23-28 July the army's forces advanced 40 kilometers along the army's right flank. The 5th Army, having going over to the offensive on 25 July and having overcome the enemy's stubborn resistance, on 28 July reached the line of the Jonava—Kaunas railroad northeast of Kaunas, having seized a bridgehead over the Neman River in this area.

On the morning of 26 July the 5th Guards Tank Army also went over to the offensive, launching an attack on Raseiniai, having 119 tanks and self-propelled guns ready for action. The army had the objective of developing the 39th Army's success. During 26-28 July the tank army was engaged in stubborn fighting with the enemy, located in the 39th Army's infantry combat formation, and by the close of 28 July had advanced a total of 25 kilometers.

Thus the Third Belorussian Front's right-wing forces were engaged in active combat during 23-28 July, during which time they threw the enemy back 25-40 kilometers and tied down his reserves, while attempting to prevent him from throwing them against the First Baltic Front's sector. The *front's* main forces were bringing up reinforcements, troop artillery (33rd Army) and their rear organs, which had lagged behind due to a shortage of fuel. The *front's* equipment was being repaired and restored. The formations' reinforcement with personnel was carried out by calling up citizens from the liberated areas and partisans, as well as the transfer of combat-ready personnel from rear units and establishments. The commitment of these contingents was slowed down by a shortage of clothing. However, despite the difficulties, the rifle divisions were reinforced and by the beginning of the operation the *front* had: nine rifle divisions numbering 5,500-6,000 men, 23 rifle divisions numbering 4,500-5,000 men, and eight rifle divisions numbering 3,500-4,000 men.

On 28 July active operations by the 39th and 5th Guards Tank armies and part of the 5th Army continued along the *front's* right wing. On 28 July the armies of the *front's* main group of forces carried out a reconnaissance in force, while the 11th Guards Army's forward battalions broke into the enemy's defense during the first half of the day and, having committed the its first-echelon divisions into the battle, by the close of the day advanced 5-9 kilometers. On this day the 2nd Guards Tank Corps was crossing the Neman River in the 33rd Army's sector.

On 28 July the *Stavka* of the Supreme High Command issued directive no. 220160, which assigned the Third Belorussian Front commander the task of developing the offensive by the 39th and 5th armies and capturing Kaunas no later than 1-2 August, by an attack from the north and south; all of the *front's* forces were to subsequently attack toward the East Prussian border and no later than 10 August capture the line Raseiniai—Suwalki, where it was to securely consolidate and prepare for an invasion of East Prussia.

On 29 July the *front's* general offensive began. At 0840, following a 40-minute artillery preparation and air strikes, the troops went over to the attack in the 5th, 33rd and 11th Guards armies' sectors, and by the close of the day the enemy's defense had been pierced to a depth of 7-15 kilometers. The greatest success was achieved by the 11th Guards and 31st armies, which advanced 10-15 kilometers. The 5th Army's left flank and the 33rd Army broke through the enemy's defense and by the close of the day had advanced along the bridgehead on the western bank of the Neman River 5-7 kilometers in depth.

The *front's* right-wing forces continued their offensive and captured Jonava and were now 6-7 kilometers northeast of Kaunas.

On 29 July the 1st Air Army supported the offensive by the 5th, 33rd and 11th Guards armies and covered the *front's* forces. That day the air army carried out 628 sorties and shot down seven enemy planes in air battles. The enemy's aviation operated against the *front's* attacking forces in groups of up to 20 bombers, and on the night of 28-29 July again carried out a mass raid (80 He-111 planes) against the Molodechno rail junction. That day 465 enemy air sorties were registered along the *front's* sector.

On 30 July the enemy's resistance along the line of the Neman River was completely crushed and the *front's* forces began to rapidly advance toward Vilkaviskis. At 0500 the 2nd Guards Tank Corps was committed into the breach in the 33rd Army's sector. With the support of the 1st Guards Assault Air Division, the corps launched a vigorous attack and broke through 35 kilometers into the depth of the enemy defense. At 0600 on 1 August the corps began fighting for Viskaviskis. Thus the 2nd Guards Tank Corps achieved a great success during 30-31 July. The corps cut the railroad and road from Kaunas to Marijampole and Vilkaviskis, threatening the enemy's Kaunas group of forces with encirclement, and forced him to begin withdraw opposite the 5th Army's left flank, and in the 33rd Army's sector—to the East Prussian frontier defensive line.

On 30 July the 33rd Army's forces defeated the opposing enemy and, skillfully employing the tank corps' success, from the second half of the day were pursuing the enemy. By the close of 31 July the army had captured Marijampole.

On 30-31 July the 11th Guards Army continued attacking and after heavy fighting broke through the enemy's defensive line and was slowly advancing to the west.

The fighting along the *front's* left wing was drawn out. The enemy took advantage of the wooded and lake terrain in the 31st Army's sector and put up stubborn resistance. The attack by the army's 113th, 71st and 36th rifle corps on 30 July developed slowly.

Along the Kaunas axis, by the close of 30 July the 72nd and 65th rifle corps' formations reached the near approaches to Kaunas, encountering fierce resistance by the enemy, who transferred the "Werthern" Motorized Brigade, which had earlier been noted facing the First Baltic Front, to reinforce the Kaunas garrison. During the night of 31 July the 65th Rifle Corps' formations attacked the enemy in Kaunas and, having crushed his resistance along the line of the old fortress's forts, by 1900 on 31 July had cleared the enemy out of the greater part of the town. South of the Neman River, the 45th Rifle Corps pursued the retreating enemy during 30-31 July.

By 0700 on 1 August the 5th Army's forces completely cleared Kaunas, having eliminated the final pockets of resistance in the northwestern part of the town.

To the north of Kaunas, on the night of 31 July the enemy began pulling back the IX Army Corps to the northwest. The forces of the 39th and 5th Guards Tank armies continued to pursue the enemy. On 31 July the 5th Guards Tank Army had 28 tanks remaining in the line, which meant that only a motorized rifle and a composite tank brigades were operating out of each of the army's corps. All of the remaining tank brigades and other army units were concentrated in an area 3-7 kilometers north of Jonava, where until 3 August they were being reinforced with new equipment arriving from the country's rear.

During 30-31 July the 1st Air Army supported our forces along the Kaunas and Gumbinnen axes, launching strikes against the enemy's Kaunas group of forces and strafing his troops falling back on Vilkaviskis. In two days of fighting the army's aviation carried out 810 sorties and destroyed 32 enemy planes, of which six were on their airfields. During this time 242 enemy air sorties were noted along the *front's* sector.

During the course of the three days of fierce fighting (29-31 July), the forces of the Third Belorussian Front captured Kaunas along the line of the Neman River and, having inflicted heavy losses on the German-Fascist Third Panzer and Fourth armies, forced them to begin falling back to the northwest and west.

Results and Conclusions

As a result of the Vilnius—Kaunas operation, which lasted 27 days (5-31 July), the forces of the Third Belorussian Front advanced 180-300 kilometers to the west along a straight line, liberated Vilnius and Kaunas and created favorable conditions for attacking toward the border of East Prussia. During the offensive, the *front's* forces successfully overcame such difficult terrain areas as the Nalibokskaya woods, the lowland area of the Merechanka River, and the Grodno woods, and also forced a number of river lines from the march—the Neman, Viliya, Gavya, Dzitva, Merechanka, and others.

During the operation the following units were defeated or suffered heavy losses: the 6th and 7th panzer, 50th, 131st, 170th, and 212th infantry, 201st, 221st and 707th security divisions, the "Werthern" Armored Brigade, and the 765th Security Brigade, while the Vilnius garrison, numbering more than 15,000 officers and men, was surrounded and destroyed. Besides this, 22 independent grenadier, police and security regiments and a large number of various "combat groups," security, march and special battalions and other units and subunits were defeated. In all, during the operation 43,966 enemy officers and men were captured, as were 912 guns of various calibers, 67 tanks and assault guns, 3,884 motor vehicles and tows, and other prizes.

During the operation the Soviet troops, during the pursuit period from the line of the Berezina River to the forcing of the Neman River, lost 10,920 men killed, 30,700 wounded, 368 tanks and self-propelled guns, 62 planes, 63 guns of all calibers, 64 mortars, 689 machine guns, and 575 motor vehicles.[4]

The average offensive pace for the *front's* forces in the operation was equivalent to 16 kilometers per day, while this figure was higher for the *front's* center and left-wing forces, and during the July 5-13 period it reached 20-22 kilometers per day. The width of the *front's* attack sector, measured along the line where the forces met, was 150 kilometers at the beginning of the operation, and 210 kilometers at the end.

The Vilnius—Kaunas operation was the second consecutive offensive operation by the Third Belorussian Front during the multi-*front* Belorussian operation. During 23 June-31 July the *front's* forces conducted an offensive to an overall depth of more than 500 kilometers along a straight line, without any kind of extended operational pause. During the course of two consecutive *front* operations, each army carried out several consecutive army offensive operations without pauses, which is very instructive from the point of view of conducting an offensive at high speeds.

In the Vilnius operation each of the *front's* armies attacked along a single operational axis, with the exception of the 31st Army, which during 5-8 July took part in the destruction of the encircled Minsk group of forces, with its reinforced 113th Rifle Corps, and thus during these days conducted an operation along two axes—it pursued the enemy in the direction of Lida, and simultaneously was destroying the encircled enemy group of forces southeast of Minsk. Because of this, by 9 July the 113th Rifle Corps lagged 120 kilometers behind the 31st Army's first echelon and was committed into the battle along the Neman River only on 17 July, having covered 250 kilometers in forced marches (on foot, vehicles and motor vehicles) for this purpose in seven days.

During the offensive the *front's* forces showed great mobility and skill in maneuver, and skill-fully and rapidly overcame difficult terrain sectors. All the rivers in the *front's* attack sector were forced from the march, widely employing the crossing means at hand. Each army overcame during the operation 5-7 rivers of various widths, while the 31st Army overcame 12 rivers. Upon encountering such major natural obstacles as the Nalibokskaya (west of Minsk) and Grodno woods, the army's main forces moved around them from one or both sides and simultaneously combed through the woods with part of their forces, in conjunction with the partisans.

The experience of the fighting to break through the "East Wall" intermediate line is an example of a breakthrough during pursuit of an enemy, who had perrpared a line for defense and hurriedly occupied it with his reserves. Because this line was not known to the *front* headquarters while preparing for the operation and was uncovered by reconnaissance on the day of the attack, the preparation for a breakthrough was carried out over 4-5 hours of daylight. Such a limited deadline enabled us to make the necessary regroupings of men and materiel only within the bounds of the rifle divisions and the attack on the line was begun before the arrival of the reinforcement artillery; the neighboring divisions' breakthrough sectors did not border on each other. On the other hand, it was established that 4-5 hours of daylight is sufficient for preparing a breakthrough of an intermediate defensive line, hurriedly occupied by the enemy, from the march.

Worthy of attention in the experience of the fighting for Vilnius is the fact that the 5th Army was simultaneously waging street battles while outflanking the city from the north and south, which resulted in the encirclement of the defending enemy garrison and enabled us to repel all the attempts by major enemy forces to break into Vilnius from the outside. The breakthrough by the 3rd Guards Mechanized Corps and the forward detachments of the 5th Army's rifle corps into the city, through its fortifications from the march, was very important, and it immediately reduced the

---

4   Central Ministry of Defense Archives, fond 241, opis' 13834ss, delo 25, p. 83.

enemy's maneuverability and tied him down in heavy street fighting. During the street fighting the enemy garrison was defeated by splitting him up into pieces, followed by their encirclement and destruction in two isolated groups.

The Neman River was overcome by the troops along a broad front, and the enemy was deprived of time for a planned withdrawal and the organization of a defense along the western bank. The forward divisions' initial success was immediately augmented by reserves and second echelons from the corps, armies and *front*, which yielded a positive effect. The success of the forcing was guaranteed, to a significant degree, by the troops' training in overcoming rivers, as well as the timely issuing of orders to the formations upon their approach to the river at a distance of 50-70 kilometers.

Among the shortcomings of forcing the river, must be noted the troops' unsatisfactory masking and their poor air cover. For example, during 14-17 July the 1st Air Army carried out only 758 sorties, of which 99 were on 16 July, and only 57 on 17 July—the day the *front's* second echelon was committed into the battle.

By the end of the Vilnius—Kaunas operation the overall depth of the *front's* rear zone was 450-570 kilometers, of which 210-300 kilometers was for the armies' rear areas. Such a huge stretching out of the rear areas could not but tell on the troops' supply. The *front's* forces required the restoration of the mobile forces' equipment. The rifle formations were in need of significant reinforcement. For example, as of 20 July, in all of the 11th Guards Army's divisions, with the exception of the 5th and 18th guards rifle divisions, the battalions had two companies, and in some of the 26th, 83rd and 84th rifle divisions' regiments, a single company per battalion. The number of soldiers in the rifle companies did not exceed, on the average, 25-30 men, and rarely 60 men. Besides this, the artillery, particularly that of the High Command reserve, lagged behind, the rear organs were stretched out, and the supply of ammunition extremely limited. The daily expenditure of fuel, beginning on 18 July, was established by the *front's* military council at 50-65 tons for each army until the end of July.

On the whole, despite a number of shortcomings, the Vilnius—Kaunas operation was a successful consecutive offensive operation by a *front*, during the course of which Soviet forces advanced 180-300 kilometers, liberated the capital of the Lithuanian SSR—Vilnius, forced the Neman River along a broad front, reached the border of East Prussia, and inflicted significant losses on the enemy.

9

The Second Belorussian Front's Bialystok Offensive Operation (5-31 July 1944)

The Bialystok offensive operation was a consecutive operation by the Second Belorussian Front, following its conduct of the Mogilev—Minsk operation.

Upon receiving the *Stavka's* 4 July directive, the Second Belorussian Front had to conduct combat operations to eliminate the encircled enemy group of forces east of Minsk, and at the same time begin to conduct a new operation along the external encirclement front.

The *Stavka*, having resubordinated the 3rd Army, which had previously been part of the First Belorussian Front, to the Second Belorussian Front, enabled the latter to organize the immediate pursuit to the west of the remnants of the enemy's forces that had escaped encirclement around Minsk.

The resubordination of the Second Belorussian Front's 33rd Army to the Third Belorussian Front did not weaken the Second Belorussian Front, because the newly-acquired 3rd Army was very strong in men and materiel and comprised nearly half of the *front's* forces.

The composition of the Second Belorussian Front by the start of the Bialystok operation is shown in table 10.

Thus the Second Belorussian Front began the new Bialystok operation with significant forces, which were responsible for the 3rd Army's rapid advance to the west.

As can be seen from the table, the *front* numbered (including the 3rd Army) more than 185,000 officers and men, more than 5,000 guns and mortars of all calibers and designations, and 166 tanks, that is, less than in the other *fronts* taking part in the Belorussian operation. Along with this, during the new operation's first days a large part of the *front's* forces had been drawn off to fulfill the objectives of the preceding operation—the destruction of the enemy group of forces encircled east of Minsk.

The situation with the *front's* supply was, on the whole, as in all the other *fronts*. Aside from this, the delivery of ammunition, fuel and food to the troops had been highly complicated by the situation that had arisen around Minsk at the end of June and beginning of July. Large groups of the enemy—the remnants of his defeated units, were wandering around our forces' rear and made the work of our transport extremely difficult.

Table 10. The Second Belorussian Front's Combat and Numerical Strength on 5 July 1944

Army	Men	Mortars			Guns		
		120mm	82mm	107mm and more	divisional	regimental	45mm
49th	39,472	125	274	188	200	51	211
50th	50,766	17	413	123	222	77	236
Units subordinated to the *front*	35,987	210	–	308	100	91	56
Total	126,225	352	687	619	522	219	503
3rd Army[1]	59,592	216	430	192	384	116	304
Total	185,817	568	1,117	811	906	335	807

Note
1 Data for the 3rd Army is as of 15 July 1944.

Army	Anti-Aircraft Guns		Tanks and Self-Propelled Guns
	76 & 85mm	20 & 37mm	
49th	55	71	–
50th	–	16	1
Units subordinated to the *front*	53	205	69/84[1]
Total	108	292	70/84
3rd Army	16	78	12
Total	124	370	82/84

Note
1 Combat-ready tanks and self-propelled guns are shown in the numerator, and those vehicles requiring repair in the denominator.

The 3rd Army was in a particular difficult situation, as many such groups were in the army's rear. During 7-11 July the work of the 3rd Army's transport stopped completely and the troops were forced to make do with those supplies they had.

The *Stavka's* 4 July directive assigned the Second Belorussian Front the following objective: to develop the offensive to the west, making the main attack in the direction of Novogrudok, Volkovysk and Bialystok, and by no later than 12-15 July capture the Novogrudok area and reach the Neman and Molchad' rivers; the *front* would subsequently capture Volkovysk and attack in the direction of Bialystok.

In accordance with this directive, the *front* was to cover 100 kilometers to carry out its immediate assignment, and about 80 kilometers to carry out its subsequent task.

According to the way the Bialystok operation developed, it may be divided into two stages:

The first stage involved the pursuit of the retreating enemy, mainly by the 3rd Army's forces, with the arrival of the *front's* forces on 16 July at the line Volkovysk—Grodno;

The second stage involved the repulse by the *front's* forces of the enemy's powerful counterblow and the capture of Bialystok.

The Operation's First Stage

The Pursuit of the Retreating Enemy and the Front's Arrival at the Line Volkovysk— Grodno (5-16 July 1944)

The Second Belorussian Front's 5-16 July offensive in the direction of Novogrudok and Bialystok developed successfully.

The 3rd Army, having been subordinated to the Second Belorussian Front, on 5 July was located 40-50 kilometers ahead of the *front's* units along the line Dubovo—Ruzhanka—Uzda. The 3rd Army's operational situation made it possible for the *front* to continue its vigorous advance to the west, to move up the 50th and 49th armies' forward units unhindered to the west of the Minsk meridian and complete the destruction of the encircled enemy east of Minsk.

On 5 July the Third Belorussian Front's 31st Army to the right was engaged in combat north of Dubovo; the 48th Army, to the left, was emerging from the Second Belorussian Front's sector and, while moving to the southwest, was advancing in the direction of Migil'no, Gorodzei and Nes'vizh.

As a result of the encirclement of the enemy's Fourth Army east of Minsk, there were no significant enemy forces in front of the advancing 3rd Army as far as the Neman River.

During 8-9 July the 3rd Army vigorously advanced to the west and, overcoming the newly-arrived 50th Infantry Division from Germany, as well as destroying the remnants of the enemy's retreating forces, by 9 July its main forces had reached the line excluding Dokudovo—Dyatlovo, having forced the Neman and Molchad' rivers at these points.

The 50th Army (121st and 70th rifle corps), advancing to the west behind the 3rd Army, forced the Neman River on 9 July and was in the Shchors area.

Thus by the close of 9 July the Second Belorussian Front's forces carried out their immediate task, as set by the *Stavka* of the Supreme High Command in its directive no. 220130 of 4 July 1944 by forcing the Neman and Molchad' rivers and capturing the towns of Vselyub, Novogrudok, Novoel'nya, and others.

On 9 July the *front* commander assigned the 3rd and 50th armies the task of continuing to vigorously pursue the enemy in the general direction of Bialystok and by 12 July capture Grodno and reach the Svisloch' River.

The 50th Army was reinforced by the 69th and 81st rifle corps.

The 49th Army was destroying the enemy in the Minsk area and was reinforced by the 50th Army's 38th Rifle Corps.

In accordance with the task assigned by the *front* commander, the 50th Army's forces were to advance 150-160 kilometers to the west in three days (10-12 July) and capture Grodno. The 3rd Army, which was ahead, was to fight its way about 100 kilometers west at the same time and capture Volkovysk. Both armies also had the task of overcoming the Neman and Kotra rivers along the *front's* right wing, and the Shara, Zel'vyanka and Ross' rivers on the left wing.

A 55-60 kilometer daily rate of advance for the infantry, while at the same time overcoming water barriers, was obviously excessive, and the troops could not physically carry it out.

By 10 July there were no large enemy forces facing the *front's* units. In attempting to close the breach, the enemy had by this time thrown the 50th Infantry Division, in full, from Germany, and part of the 367th Infantry Division, which had been operating along the First Ukrainian Front's sector. Aside from these units, units of the 28th Light Infantry Division were still resisting, as well as the remnants of the 12th and 20th panzer divisions.

The 50th Army commander organized his army in two echelons for the offensive to the west: three rifle corps advanced in the first echelon, and one in the second.

The 3rd Army commander decided to capture Volkovysk by the close of 11 July, while on 12 July the army's main forces would reach the eastern bank of the Svisloch' River, and then capture Bialystok. The army's three corps advanced side by side. Each corps had a single rifle division in its second echelon.

During 10-12 July the *front's* forces continued to successfully advance to the west. By the close of 12 July the *front's* right-wing forces forced the Neman River for the second time, while in the center the Shara River was overcome, and the Zel'vyanka River on the left wing.

The enemy, having brought up new formations from the depth, consistently augmented his resistance. Units of the 50th Infantry and 12th Panzer divisions, a combat group from the remnants of the 20th Panzer Division, the 461st Reserve Infantry Regiment, which had been transferred from the Bialystok area, units of the 28th Light Infantry Division, the 367th Infantry Division, transferred from the L'vov area, and the 611th Security Regiment were operating in the 3rd Army's sector.

The enemy had earlier been creating a defense along a broad front in the rear with these forces along convenient natural lines, which relied on a prepared system of fire from artillery, mortars, tanks and assault guns. The remnants of the 20th Panzer, 367th Infantry, and 28th Light Infantry divisions were defending the immediate Volkovysk axis. The Zel'va—Volkovysk road was especially heavily covered, where units of the 367th Infantry and 28th Light Infantry divisions were defending.

During 13-14 July the 3rd Army's forces continued to press the stubbornly defending enemy. On the right flank these forces crossed the Ross' River from the march, while on the left flank at 1000 on 14 July, following stubborn street fighting, they liberated the town of Volkovysk, a very important road and railroad junction and a very powerful strong point along the Bialystok axis. By the close of 14 July the army's forces had reached the line excluding Lunna—Ross'—Volkovysk.

The 50th Army, having the task of capturing Grodno by the close of 14 July, in conjunction with the Third Belorussian Front's 3rd Guards Cavalry Corps, concentrated its main forces along the right flank and committed its second-echelon corps into the battle. However, the army failed to achieve a significant success, and by the close of 14 July, with all of its corps in the first line, reached the line Tobola (15 kilometers east of Grodno)—Lunna.

During 15-16 July the *front's* forces continued attacking.

Along the *front's* right wing, the 50th Army, in conjunction with the 3rd Guards Cavalry Corps and the Third Belorussian Front's left-wing units, was storming Grodno.

The enemy put up a stubborn defense with counterattacks, supported by assault guns and ceaseless air attacks, by units of the 50th Infantry Division, the remnants of the 12th Panzer Division, and of the "von Gottberg" police group, consisting of five police regiments.

At 2400 on 15 July the *Stavka* transferred the 3rd Guards Cavalry Corps, which by this time was fighting for Grodno, to the Second Belorussian Front.[1]

The 3rd Guards Cavalry Corps did not manage to capture Grodno from the march, but its seizure of the commanding heights north and east of the town, and a bridgehead on the western bank of the Neman River, created a difficult situation for the enemy in Grodno.

Besides this, the forward detachments of the Third Belorussian Front's 31st Army had arrived at the town from the northeast and east.

Besides the 31st Army's units, on the morning of 15 July the 50th Army's main forces began fighting for Grodno from the east.

The subsequent storming of the town was continued by units of the Third Belorussian Front's 31st Army, as well as formations of the Second Belorussian Front's 50th Army. At 1600 the northern

---

1   *Stavka* directive no. 220143, of 14 July 1944.

part of Grodno, located north of the Neman River, had been completely occupied by units of the Red Army. The enemy was forced to hurriedly fall back behind the Neman River.

During the night of 16 July the Second Belorussian Front, in conjunction with units of the Third Belorussian Front, stormed and captured the major road and railroad junction, the town and fortress of Grodno, which covered the approaches to the East Prussian border. After this, a *Stavka* directive ordered that the Grodno area be transferred to the Third Belorussian Front.

Thus the Second Belorussian Front, in the course of twelve days, advanced 260 kilometers to the west, at an average daily rate of 21.5 kilometers. During the offensive the following rivers were forced: the Neman, Molchad', Shara, Ross', and others. 19,240 square kilometers of the Belorussian SSR were liberated, as well as a large number of inhabited locales, including the towns of Novogrudok and Volkovysk. The *front's* forces also reached the line Grodno—Svisloch'.

The Operation's Second Stage

The Repulse of the Enemy Counterblow. The Capture of Bialystok (17-31 July 1944)

During the operation's second stage, the forces of the Second Belorussian Front continued to attack along the Bialystok axis.

After capturing the towns of Grodno and Volkovysk, the *front's* armies continued to attack in their previous formation.

Two combined-arms armies—the 50th and 3rd—were deployed in the first echelon along the Neman and Svisloch' rivers. The 3rd Guards Cavalry Corps was attacking north of Grodno along the right wing, at the junction with the Third Belorussian Front.

By the beginning of the second half of July the German-Fascist command had managed to put its retreating forces in order, and also to bring up from the rear and other sectors of the front more than ten divisions to the Grodno—Svisloch' line, organize a defense here and carry out a number of counterattacks and counterblows. The following units were defending along the Augustow axis: five police and three infantry regiments (1065th, 1068th and 1069th). The SS *Totenkopf* Panzer Division was hurriedly moving up from Romania to the line excluding Augustow—Knyszyn. The enemy's badly-battered 50th Infantry Division was putting up resistance along this axis. Along the Bialystok axis the enemy, taking advantage of the wooded and swampy terrain, was putting up stubborn resistance to the *front's* left-wing forces with units of the 12th Panzer, 367th Infantry and 28th Light Infantry divisions, the 4th Corps Artillery Brigade, and various security units.

The *front* commander's plan called for launching two attacks along the *front's* right wing with the forces of the 3rd Guards Cavalry Corps and the 50th Army, for the purpose of liberating Augustow, and along the left wing—with the forces of the 3rd Army, with the task of capturing Bialystok.[2]

The *front* commander, taking into account the enemy's increasing resistance, decided to commit the 49th Army, which following the elimination of the encircled enemy group of forces east of Minsk, was located in the second echelon, into the battle along the boundary between the 50th and 3rd armies.

The German-Fascist command decided, while holding up our units' offensive along the Bialystok axis, to launch a counterblow against the Second Belorussian Front's right wing and throw its forces back to the east behind the Neman and Svisloch'

By 17 July the 50th Army's rear organs stretched back 100-150 kilometers. The artillery lagged behind and was located in areas up to 200 kilometers from the front line. The tank units, for the

---

2   Second Belorussian Front directive no. 0034/op, of 17 July 1944.

most part, had also fallen behind. There was a shortage of ammunition. The same was true of the 3rd Army. In his report to the *front* commander, the 3rd Army commander wrote that his divisions contained no more than 350-500 infantrymen apiece. The army disposed of 0.3-0.5 combat loads and 0.3-0.5 refills of fuel and lubricants. The necessity had arisen of bringing up the artillery and tanks and supplying the troops with ammunition and fuel as quickly as possible, and of restoring the cooperation between all the combat arms and the air force, which had been lost. On the whole, the resulting situation had become unfavorable for further offensive operations.

The *front's* offensive during the operation's second stage developed in the following manner.

The 3rd Guards Cavalry Corps, having encountered the enemy's stubborn resistance, had by 1900 on 17 July advanced only 1-3 kilometers. On 18-19 July the corps, taking advantage of the success of the 31st Army's units along the right flank, captured Lipsk and attacked toward Augustow. At the same time the corps broke contact with its own forces and got into the enemy's deep rear.

On 18 July the enemy, having launched a counterblow by the *Totenkopf* SS Panzer Division from the south, reached the crossings over the Neman River and, having pushed aside the 3rd Guards Cavalry Corps' covering force here, captured Lipsk.

The 50th Army attempted to continue the offensive, but was forced to fall back to the Neman River under pressure of the enemy's counterblow.

The *front* commander made the decision to eliminate the enemy, which had launched a counterblow northwest of Grodno, after which the right-wing forces would continue the offensive to the west.

The 3rd Guards Cavalry Corps was ordered to halt its attack on Augustow and, with all its forces, attack from the Lipsk area to the south, for the purpose of cutting the enemy's path of retreat to the west and southwest.

The 49th Army received orders to prepare a breakthrough of the enemy's defense south of Indura by the close of 20 July and to attack toward Knyszyn. The 49th Army was reinforced by the 50th Army's 70th Rifle Corps.

During 19-22 July the formations of the 3rd Guards Cavalry Corps and the 50th Army were engaged in unsuccessful fighting along the *front's* right wing to eliminate the enemy in the Lipsk area.

The enemy continued to attack in the area northwest of Grodno with units of the *Totenkopf* SS Panzer Division and the 4th Police Regiment, which had been transferred from Germany, and the "Anhalt" group, which consisted of four police regiments, plus aviation support, striving to clear the Soviet forces out of the bend formed by the Neman River and the Augustow Canal.

At 2300-2400 on 20 July the 49th Army's first-echelon divisions' reinforced reconnaissance detachments carried out a reconnaissance in force. The reconnaissance detachments advanced 200-300 meters, but were met with powerful fire from all kinds of weapons, hit the dirt, and were subsequently forced to fall back to their jumping-off position. At 0630 on 21 July, following a 30-minute artillery preparation, the divisions attacked the forward edge of the enemy's defense, but were halted by organized rifle and machine gun fire and halted in front of the forward edge of his defense. The commander of the 49th Army ordered that the units be put in order and the attack repeated at 1400. At 1400 the troops renewed the attack and by 2100 on that same day reached the eastern outskirts of Indura.

On the morning of 22 July the enemy began to fall back before the 49th Army's units to the west and southwest. The 49th Army, in pursuing the enemy, threatened to encircle those enemy units operating in the Grodno area and northwest of the town.

On 23 July the enemy began to fall back from the Lipsk area to the southwest.

Thus during 17-23 July the Second Belorussian Front's forces defeated the enemy forces along its right flank, forced the Neman and Svisloch' rivers and forced the enemy to retreat along the entire front.

The enemy had organized a secure and highly-networked defense in depth along the Bialystok axis, for the purpose of securely covering Bialystok, which was a major railroad and road junction, and a major industrial site covering the Warsaw axis.

The stone buildings in Bialystok, as well as the inhabited locales adjacent to them, had been configured for defense.

In the 3rd Army's sector and along the Bialystok axis the enemy was defending with units of the 367th Infantry and 28th Light Infantry divisions, the 37th Security Regiment, the 4th Cavalry Brigade, the 5th Independent Panzer Battalion from the High Command Reserve, as well as several reinforcement battalions, which were being fed into the battle as they arrived during our offensive.

The enemy units were almost completely motorized, which ensured their flexible maneuver along the lateral and radial roads, while cooperating with the tanks, assault guns and armored transports. The enemy air force, flying in small groups, launched frequent concentrated raids against our infantry and the firing positions of our artillery and guards mortars, and attempted to disrupt our command and control with night bombing of our headquarters.

On 19 July the enemy's forces facing the army's left flank began to withdraw from the line of the Svisloch' River to the west.

During the following three days the army's forces fought to take the Bialystok woods and by the close of 24 July, having overcome the enemy's resistance and launching an attack along the Volkovysk—Bialystok road, reached the inner layer of Bialystok's defense. An attempt to capture Bialystok in a hurried attack was a failure.

Beginning on the second half of 24 July and all of 25 July, the efforts of our commanders at all levels were directed at organizing a breakthrough of the enemy's defense to Bialystok.[3]

At 0800 on 26 July the decisive fighting to take Bialystok began. Following a 10-minute fire onslaught, the army's forces attacked.

At 1000 the enemy began fierce counterattacks for the purpose of foiling our offensive. The enemy's centers of resistance changed hands several times. By 1520 the army's forward units had broken into the southeastern part of the town and had begun fighting in the streets. By 0600 on 27 July Bialystok had been completely cleared of the enemy, who had begun to fall back north and south of the town.

Results and Conclusions

During 5-31 July the *front's* forces, which were conducting the Bialystok operation, advanced 300 kilometers along a straight line. Their average daily rate of advance was 10-12 kilometers. To be sure, during the operation's first stage the advance west went significantly quicker, for the enemy here put up a very weak resistance. During the operation's second stage the enemy's resistance significantly grew and the speed of the *front's* advance fell and did not exceed six kilometers per day.

The operation's length and intensity began to tell on our force's rate of advance. The troops were experiencing exhaustion. The lagging behind or the rear organs also negatively influenced the course of combat operations. The troops experienced a shortage of ammunition, fuel and food. It was only the high moral-political *élan* among the troops that enabled them to complete the

---

3   3rd Army order no. 0034/op, of 24 July 1944.

Bialystok operation with a major success, which was expressed in the liberation of such important enemy centers of resistance as Grodno and Bialystok.

As a result our combat activities, by 1700 on 27 July 15,750 enemy officers and men had been killed, 248 guns of various caliber destroyed, along with 23 assault guns, 190 mortars, 308 machine guns, 24 armored transports, 643 motor vehicles, 38 tanks, 12 armored cars, and much other military equipment. About 1,000 officers and men were taken prisoner, while our forces captured 62 guns of different calibers, 14 assault guns, 15 armored transports, 39 mortars, 2,567 rifles and automatic rifles, 163 machine guns, 127 motor vehicles, and other equipment. 3,750 square kilometers of territory were liberated, including the towns of Bialystok and Svisloch'.

The Second Belorussian Front's losses in the Bialystok operation were 9,812 officers and men killed during 1-31 July.[4]

Many mistakes were made during the operation. Our forces acted in a scattered manner and were poorly aware of the enemy, as a result of which they suffered excessive casualties.

The numerous water barriers were forced from the march on whatever crossing materials were at hand.

The operations of the 3rd Guards Cavalry Corps were instructive in the given operation and showed a great deal of activity, flexibility of maneuver, and decisiveness and boldness. The corps, with its operations in the Augustow woods, forced the enemy to abandon further fighting for the Grodno bridgehead.

The 3rd Army's rifle formations also operated skillfully, by boldly breaking through toward Bialystok, in an act that decided the outcome of the fighting for this major town.

---

4 Central Ministry of Defense Archives, fond 237, opis' 15795ss, delo 3, p. 204.

10

The First Belorussian Front's Baranovichi—Slonim Offensive Operation (5-16 July 1944)

The Baranovichi—Slonim operation was the First Belorussian Front's consecutive operation, following the successful realization of its Bobruisk—Slutsk operation.

The preparation for the Baranovichi—Slonim offensive operation by the forces of the First Belorussian Front was conducted in conditions of a continuing offensive and growing enemy resistance. No special time was allotted for prearing the operation.

As a result of the preceding Bobruisk—Slutsk offensive operation, the *front's* right-wing forces, having independently defeated a major German-Fascist group of forces southeast of Bobruisk and having encircled, in conjunction with the Third and Second Belorussian fronts, a powerful enemy group of forces to the east of Minsk, by the close of 4 July had deeply penetrated the enemy front and reached the immediate approaches to that very important rail and road junction and powerful fortified defensive area covering the axes to Bialystok and Brest—the town of Baranovichi.

At this time the 61st Army, which was located in the center of the *front's* sector, by taking advantage of the success of the right-wing forces, had rolled up the enemy defense along the Pripyat' River along a 50-kilometers sector.

The enemy, in seeking to cover Baranovichi, halted the remnants of the Ninth Army's defeated units, as well as the 4th Panzer Division and the Hungarian 4th Cavalry Brigade, which had suffered heavy losses, along the previously-prepared defensive line along the Usha, Vedzhmanka and Shara rivers. Besides this, the German-Fascist command had brought up to this line a part of corps group "E" and the Hungarian 1st Cavalry Division from the Pinsk area,[1] and the 28th Light Infantry Division from Army Group North Ukraine.

Northeast of Baranovichi, the enemy was attempting unsuccessfully to capture Stolbtsy and the bridges over the Neman River through counterattacks by the 12th Panzer and 342nd Infantry divisions, and by launching an attack against our forces' flank, to foil their offensive on Baranovichi.

The Baranovichi garrison, which consisted of the 52nd Special Designation Security Division and a number of small units, had been reinforced by the 537th Panzer Battalion, and the 904th, 118th and 177th assault gun brigades.

In the operational depth the enemy had reserves and had prepared the Slonim defensive line along the Shara River. The operational reserves—the 5th and 23rd reserve divisions—were concentrated in the area of Bereza (Bereza-Kartuska) and Drogichin.

Furthermore, the 50th Infantry Division was concentrating in the Selets area (72 kilometers northwest of Baranovichi).

---

1   The division had arrived in the Pinsk area from Hungary.

By the start of the operation the enemy's defensive lines were not fully ready and consisted of a single line of broken trenches, with wooden and earth pillboxes along the road junctions and important sectors. The Baranovichi—Slonim—Pruzhany and Sinyavka—Kobrin paved roads had machine gun emplacements all along their length, while such towns as Baranovichi, Slonim, Pruzhany, Luninets, Pinsk, and many others, had been transformed into major centers of resistance.

The enemy had begun to construct the Baranovichi fortified area beforehand, as early as the end of 1943. It consisted of two defensive zones, four centers of resistance, two strong points, a single fully-furnished trench immediately around the town, and, finally, of reinforced and wood and earth pillboxes along the road intersections inside the town.

The first defensive zone ran along the western bank of the Vedzhmanka (Ved'ma) River, and the second along the western bank of the Shara River. They consisted of one and, in places two, lines of trenches apiece. The best outfitted, in the engineering sense, was the second defensive zone, which had been prepared along the western bank of the Shara River. Both defensive zones had been made stronger by the presence of the rivers' broad and swampy floodplains.

Centers of resistance had been created in the area of the most important of the second defensive zone's sectors, and in the depth they intercepted the railroad and road junctions, bridges and crossings and had 5-16 reinforced concrete firing points apiece. Moreover, all the centers of resistance were outfitted with trenches for infantry elements.

By covering the Bialystok and Brest axes, the enemy sought to halt or delay our offensive by means of a stubborn defense along the previously-prepared intermediate defensive line along the Usha, Vedzhmanka and Shara rivers. For this purpose, the German-Fascist command had brought up, and was continuing to bring up to this area, men and materiel from other axes, and even from Germany itself (50th Infantry Division).

All of these measures enabled the enemy to have by the close of 4 July—the start of the *front's* Baranovichi—Slonim offensive operation—the following operational densities: one division for 12 kilometers of front, and six guns and mortars and 1.6 tanks per kilometer of front.

The enemy concentrated his main efforts in the center, along the Baranovichi axis.

By the start of the operation the first echelon of the First Belorussian Front's right-wing forces north of the Pripyat' River deployed four combined-arms armies (48th, 65th, 28th, and 61st), of which three were to operate along the Baranovichi axis, and one (61st Army) along the Pinsk axis.

Moreover, the mobile forces—the 1st Mechanized Corps and the cavalry-mechanized group (4th Guards Cavalry and 9th Tank corps—were attacking along with the combined-arms armies of the *front's* first-echelon forces along the right wing, or ahead of them. The *front* commander held in reserve the 46th and 80th rifle and 1st Guards Tank corps behind the right wing.

The combat and numerical composition of the First Belorussian Front's right-wing forces on 5 July 1944 is shown in table 11.

The strength of the First Belorussian Front's right wing by 5 July had decreased compared to what it had been on 24 June. However, the *front's* offensive sector (without the fortified areas' operational group and the 61st Army) by 4 July had shrunk from 240 to 100 kilometers. All of this enabled the *front* command to create a significant superiority over the enemy in men and materiel, as can be seen from table 12.

It should be noted that the enemy's entire group of forces was mainly located in the armies' and corps' first echelons, while we had only 40 percent of the divisions of the *front's* right wing at this level. This naturally lowered our overall superiority over the enemy. Moreover, the troops along the *front's* right wing were very strung out in depth. For example, the second echelons were located as follows: in the corps—11th Corps-36 kilometers; in the armies—48th Army-62 kilometers, 28th Army-25 kilometers; army reserves—48th Army-100 kilometers, 65th Army-50-85 kilometers, and; the *front* reserves—80-100 kilometers behind the front line. The 9th Tank Corps, which was part of the *front's* cavalry-mechanized group, was at this time 40 kilometers from the 4th Guards Cavalry Corps.

Also, the 48th, 65th and 28th armies were located a corresponding 50, 35 and 12 kilometers from their designated attack sectors, which required that the *front* and army command precisely combine the uninterrupted offensive with their simultaneous regrouping to their new sectors.

Table 11. The Combat and Numerical Composition of the First Belorussian Front's Right-Wing Forces on 5 July 1944[2]

Army and Formation	Men	Mortars		Guns			
		120mm	82mm	107mm and larger	Divisional	Regimental	45 & 57mm
By the Start of the Bobruisk—Slutsk Operation—24 June 1944	426,337		3,936 total mortars	3,193 large, divisional and regimental guns			2,253
Per Kilometer of Front		1,776	16.4 mortars	13.3 large, divisional and regimental guns			9.4
By the Start of the Baranovichi—Slonim Operation, 5 July 1944 (along the Baranovichi axis)							
48th Army	57,060	188	512	141	277	99	219-0
65th Army	57,416	175	406	201	380	64	203-0
28th Army	66,897	295	472	202	341	107	336-0
Cavalry-Mechanized Group (4th Gds Cavalry and 9th Tank corps)	31,176	82	158	8	176	–	16-40
1st Mechanized Corps	16,395	54	110	–	40	–	0-40
Front Reserve: 46th and 80th rifle and 1st Gds Tank corps	34,033	103	254	48	138	23	90-0
Total	262,959	897	1,912	600	1,352	293	864-80
Per Kilometer of Front	2,629		28.1	19.5			12.4 guns

Army and Formation	Men	Mortars		Guns			
		120mm	82mm	107mm and larger	Divisional	Regimental	45 & 57mm
Pinsk Axis							
Fortified Areas' Operational Group	15,336	–	208	–	288	–	211-0
61st Army	34,580	125	249	117	150	58	143-23
Total on 5 July 1944	312,905	1,022	2,369	717	1,790	351	1,218-103
			3,391				

2   Central Ministry of Defense Archives, fond 233, opis' 11866, delo 11, 275, pp. 344-58.

Army and Formation	Men	Total Guns & Mortars	Anti-Aircraft Guns		Tanks & Self-Propelled Guns[1]	Rocket Artillery	Sector Width (in kms)
			76 & 85mm	20 & 37mm			
By the Start of the Bobruisk—Slutsk Operation—24 June 1944	9,382			566	1,351	737	240
Per Kilometer of Front	39.1			2.4	5.6	3	–
By the Start of the Baranovichi—Slonim Operation, 5 July 1944 (along the Baranovichi axis)							
48th Army		1,436	16	89	69/41	28	
65th Army		1,429	16	88	73/14	24	
28th Army		1,753	14	88	101/9	24	
Cavalry-Mechanized Group (4th Gds Cavalry and 9th Tank corps)		480	16	134	119/78	80	
1st Mechanized Corps		244	–	16	176/24	8	100
Front Reserve: 46th and 80th rifle and 1st Gds Tank corps		656	–	57	149/13	8	
Total		5,998	62	472	687/179	172	
Per Kilometer of Front		60	5.3		6.9	1.7	

Army and Formation	Total Guns & Mortars	Anti-Aircraft Guns		Tanks & Self-Propelled Guns	Rocket Artillery	Sector Width (in kms)
		76 & 85mm	20 & 37mm			
Pinsk Axis						
Fortified Area's Operational Group	707	–	–	–	–	68
61st Army	865	–	18	6/1	–	70[2]
Total on 5 July 1944	7,570	62	490	693/180	172	238

Notes

1 The numerator shows the combat-ready tanks and self-propelled guns, and the numerator those needed repairs.

2 70 kilometers is the army's attack sector, out of a total 210-kilometer front.

Table 12. The Overall Correlation of Forces and Operational Densities Along the First Belorussian Front's Right Wing on 5 July 1944 (100-Kilometer Front)[3]

Men & Materiel	Soviet Forces		Enemy Forces		Correlation
	Total	Per km of Front	Total	Per km of front	
Divisions[1]	32	3.2 per division	8	12 per division	4:1
Tank Divisions	3	–	1½	–	2:1
Battalions	221	2.2	32	0.4	6.9:1
Men	252,959	2,529	34,800	348	7.2:1
Mortars	2,809	28.1	230	2.3	12.2:1
Anti-Tank and Regimental Artillery	1,237	12.4	215	2.2	5.8:1
Divisional Artillery and higher	1,952	19.5	152	1.5	12.8:1
Total Guns and Mortars (not counting anti-aircraft artillery)	5,998	60.0	597	6	10:1
Rocket Artillery Launchers	172	1.7	Unknown	–	–
Tanks and Self-Propelled Guns	644	6.5	160	1.6	4:1

Note
1 For calculation purposes, two brigades are counted as one division.

Attention should also be paid to the lowering of the *front's* right-wing forces' strength, particularly within the tank and mechanized formations, as a result of the losses they sustained in the Bobruisk—Slutsk operation.

Table 13. Strength of the *Front's* Right-Wing Forces at the Start of the Baranovichi-Slonim Operation (as a Percentage of Their Authorized Strength)

Army and Formation	Rifle Division Personnel Strength (% of authorized strength)	Tanks and Self-Propelled Guns	
		Combat-Ready	In Repair
48th Army	76.1	55	32
65th Army	72.4	70	14
28th Army	84.7	80	7
Cavalry-Mechanized Group	–	27	18
1st Gds Tank Corps	–	44	5
1st Mechanized Corps	–	66	22
61st Army	69	–	–

The extension of the rear organs by the start of the operation was pronounced. The army bases' separation from their troops was 300-350 kilometers and the formations had a great need of ammunition and fuel. By this time the separation of railroad transport from the troops had reached 250-300 kilometers and was conducted as far as the bridge over the Dnepr River near Zhlobin.

---

3   This is the attack front of the *front's* right-wing forces, minus the fortified areas' operational group and the 61st Army.

The main obstacle to the successful restoration of the railroads was chiefly the large bridges, and on the paved roads—middle-sized bridges over rivers. Thus the army bases and the *front* depots could not move up behind the troops and the entire weight of supplying them fell on automobile transports. The dirt-road transportation link reached 250-300 kilometers by 5 July.

The *front's* forces' provisioning at the start of the operation with ammunition, fuels and lubricants is shown by the following data (see table 14)

On the whole, the First Belorussian Front, despite the overextension of its forces and rear organs, as well as the overall lowering of the troops' strength, enjoyed a favorable situation by the start of the operation, a favorable correlation of forces, and the opportunity to develop a vigorous attack along the Baranovichi—Slonim axis.

At 0400 on 4 July the commander of the First Belorussian Front received the *Stavka's* operational directive no. 220127, in which it was demanded that the 48th, 65th and 28th armies, the 1st Guards and 9th tank, 4th Guards Cavalry, and 1st Mechanized corps develop the offensive, launching their main attack in the general direction of Baranovichi and Brest. The *front* was given the immediate task of taking Baranovichi and, no later than 10-12 July to reach the line Slonim—Shara River—Pinsk, and to subsequently take Brest.[4] The Second Belorussian Front was to attack to the right, making its main attack toward Bialystok, with the immediate task of reaching the Molchad' and Neman rivers no later than 12-15 July.

The First Belorussian Front's new consecutive operation was thus planned by the *Stavka* of the Supreme High Command to a depth of up to 310 kilometers, with an immediate objective of up to 135 kilometers in depth, with an average daily rate of advance of 12-17 kilometers.

In carrying out the *Stavka* directive, the *front* commander made the following decision that same day.

The *front's* main right-wing forces (the 48th and 65th armies, the cavalry-mechanized group, and the 1st Mechanized Corps) were to, without letting up their pursuit of the enemy, to make their main attack in the direction of Baranovichi and Slonim, while part of the *front's* forces (28th Army) would launch a supporting attack in the direction of the Sinyavka—Kvatsevichi road and then to Bereza (Bereza-Kartuska), with the task of reaching the line Slonim—Shara River—Pinsk.

Table 14. The First Belorussian Front's Right-Wing Forces' Provisioning of Ammunition, Fuels and Lubricants, as of 5 July 1944[5]

Armies	Ammunition (in combat loads)							
	Rifle Rounds		Mortar Rounds		Artillery Rounds			
	Total	With the Troops	Total	With the Troops	76mm Regimental Artillery		76mm Divisional Artillery	
					Total	With the Troops	Total	With the Troops
48th Army	2.6	1.2	2.8	1.4	4.6	2.2	2.6	1.7
65th Army	2.1	1.1	2.7	1.4	3.5	1.5	3.4	1.3
28th Army	2.5	1.5	3.8	1.3	3.6	2.5	3.3	1.8
61st Army	1.4	0.8	1.4	0.9	0.8	0.5	0.7	0.6

4   Central Ministry of Defense Archives, fond 283, opis' 20897, delo 1, p. 293.
5   Central Ministry of Defense Archives, fond 233, opis' 11392, delo 4, pp. 138, 143, 146-47, and opis' 15269, delo 9, p. 4.

	Ammunition (in combat loads)					
Armies	**Artillery Rounds**			**Anti-Aircraft Rounds**		
	122mm & 155mm		**37mm**		**85mm**	
	Total	With the Troops	Total	With the Troops	Total	With the Troops
48th Army	3.4	1.0	3.3	1.8	3.4	1.1
65th Army	2.3	1.1	2.3	2.1	1.6	1.3
28th Army	1.5	0.7	2.4	2.0	2.0	2.0
61st Army	0.7	0.6	3.5	2.2	–	–

	Fuels and Lubricants (in refills)						
Army & Formation	**Tank Fuels and Lubricants**			**Auto and Tractor Fuels and Lubricants**			
	KB-70	Diesel Fuel	Aviation Oil	Auto Fuel	Nafta	Kerosine	Auto Oil
48th Army	3.2	2.2	3.0	2.39	2.6	8.1	2.4
65th Army	3.3	2.0	0.7	1.83	1.7	9.3	3.2
28th Army	0.9	1.4	0.6	2.40	7.9	5.9	2.8
4th Gds Cavalry Corps	1.6	1.9	1.5	1.9	–	–	1.9
9th Tank Corps	1.0	1.0	1.0	1.0	–	–	1.6
1st Gds Tank Corps	1.1	0.6	0.5	0.8	–	–	1.7
61st Army	6.7	6.9	3.3	4.2	7.3	10.0	5.6
In *Front* Depots	2.27	2.7	0.3	0.5	0.08	2.7	0.7

The *front* would launch attacks by its 48th and 65th armies along converging axes toward Baranovichi, while simultaneously outflanking the enemy with the 4th Guards Cavalry, 9th Tank and 1st Mechanized corps, in order to encircle and destroy the enemy's Baranovichi group of forces and capture Baranovichi. Later, by employing the two parallel paved roads Slonim—Pruzhany and Baranovichi—Brest, all forces were to develop the success in the general direction of Brest, for the purpose of deeply outflanking and encircling, together with the *front's* left wing, the German-Fascist Pinsk group of forces.

The 28th Army was to vigorously pursue the enemy in the general direction of Sinyavka and Molovidy.

The 61st Army's 89th Rifle Corps, in conjunction with the Dnepr Flotilla, was ordered to pursue the enemy along the railroad in the general direction of Zhitkovichi and Luninets.

The fortified areas' operational group was ordered to reach the line of the Sluch' River by the morning of 8 July.[6]

Long-Range Aviation, in conjunction with the 16th Air Army, was to carry out the important task of foiling the enemy's railroad deliveries, for the purpose or preventing the arrival of his reserves from the deep rear to the front.

---

6   First Belorussian Front directive. Central Ministry of Defense Archives, opis' 20897, delo 1, pp. 226-36, 249, and opis' 14949, delo 72, p. 37.

The *front's* military council demanded the following from the partisans: to continue to meet our units, show them the crossings and detours around swamps, and to supply them with guides; by a joint attack with the 61st Army from the east, and the partisans from the north and west, take the town of Luninets; the partisans were to take Starosel'e and Parokhon'sk station and hold them until the 61st Army's arrival; to deprive the enemy of the opportunity to carry out regroupings of his forces and to remove cargoes on the railroad along the Zhitkovichi—Luninets—Pinsk—Brest and Baranovichi—Brest sectors; to cut the enemy's railroad communications along the Baranovichi—Luninets and Luninets—Pinsk sectors, and blockade the town of Luninets.

Moreover, the partisans were ordered to intensify their fight to preserve industrial buildings, cities, and inhabited locales from destruction by the enemy, as well as to prevent the population from being carried off into fascist slavery.

On the whole, the decision adopted by the *front* commander for the conduct of the Baranovichi—Slonim operation, as the operational situation stood by 4 July, was the most expedient and ensured that the objectives laid down by the *Stavka* to the *front's* forces would be carried out. However, the average daily rates of advance, which the *front* laid down (24-35 kilometers per day for the combined-arms armies), were too high and issued without taking into account the degree of engineer outfitting along the Baranovichi defensive line and the enemy group of forces there, as well as the overextension of our own forces.

According to the way the Baranovichi—Slonim operation developed, it may be divided into two stages:

The first stage involved the capture of Baranovichi and the troops' arrival at the line of the Shara River near Slonim.

The second stage involved the liberation of the towns of Slonim and Pinsk, and the arrival of the *front's* right-wing armies at the far approaches to Brest.

The Operation's First Stage

The Capture of Baranovichi and the Arrival at the Line of the Shara River, Near Slonim (5-9 July 1944)

The Baranovichi—Slonim operation, as had been the case in the preceding Bobruisk—Slutsk operation, was conducted by the forces of the *front's* right wing, which continued to attack without an operational pause.

The 28th Army, due to the fact that the neighboring 65th Army was located outside and north of its designated attack sector, continued its offensive on the morning of 5 July in the direction of Kletsk and Lyakhoviche, outflanking Baranovichi from the south, and not along the Brest paved road, as it had been instructed by the *front*. By evening the army had captured Lyakhoviche.

On the morning of 5 July the 4th Guards Cavalry and 1st Mechanized corps attacked in the general direction of Baranovichi, for the purpose of capturing the town.

The 1st Mechanized Corps broke through the enemy's defense along the Vedzhmanka River and, having arrived at the second defensive line along the Shara River, was engaged in heavy fighting along the line Yushkeviche—Klompiki (northeast of Baranovichi).

The 65th Army, taking into account the presence of units of the 28th Army and 1st Mechanized Corps ahead of it in its new attack sector, deployed its forces into columns and was marching to the southwest.

The 48th Army, having lost immediate contact with the enemy, was trying to quickly reach its new attack sector.

Thus although our forces advanced 25 kilometers on 5 July along the Baranovichi axis, they failed to carry out their main objective of capturing the town of Baranovichi.

The developing situation demanded the most rapid elimination of the enemy's center of resistance in the Baranovichi area and the development of the offensive on Brest, as well as linking up with the *front's* left wing for a subsequent attack with all forces to the west tosward the Polish border. Thus at 0200 on 6 July the *front* commander ordered, without waiting for the arrival of the 48th Army, the 65th Army and right flank of the 28th Army to attack from the north, northeast, southeast, and south, and capture the town of Baranovichi by the close of 6 July.[7]

Particularly intensive fighting for Baranovichi unfolded on 6-7 July. On the morning of 6 July the enemy's defense along the Vedzhmanka River and the Shara River along the Mysloboe—Khotsyazh (5-20 kilometers south of Lyakhoviche) sector was penetrated, but the forces of the 65th and 28th armies advanced only 1-3 and 1-7 kilometers, and the cavalry-mechanized group advanced ten kilometers.[8] The day's chief objective—the capture of Baranovichi—was once again not achieved.

On 7 July the fighting in the Baranovichi area resumed with new force. The arrival of the *front's* forces immediately to Baranovichi from the east, and its planned outflanking from the north, northwest, south, and southwest, created favorable conditions for capturing the town.

The main reason for our slow actions in taking Baranovichi was the *front* commanders underestimation of the enemy's capabilities for defending the Baranovichi fortified area, particularly the defensive line along the Shara River, with its powerful centers of resistance along the key sectors of the approaches to Baranovichi, particularly as the enemy had managed to bring fresh forces up, which were sufficiently strong and well-equipped. The overall superiority was in our favor, but due to the overextension of our forces and the ongoing regrouping, this superiority actually decreased significantly, which negatively told on the pace of the *front's* advance. This can be confirmed, if only by the fact that on 5 July only 18 percent of the *front's* rifle divisions attacked in the corps' first echelons, with 30 percent on 6 July, and it was only on 7 July that 60 percent of these units attacked.

At 0300 on 8 July the 65th Army began the storming of Baranovichi by its 18th Rifle Corps from the northeast and east, and the 105th Rifle Corps from the southeast and south.

The enemy, not expecting a night storming and preparing to put up heavy resistance in the morning, could not withstand our attack and began to withdraw to the west.

By 0400 on 8 July Baranovichi had been completely occupied by our forces. By the end of the day our forces, while pursuing the enemy to the west and southwest, captured the Molchad'—Baranovichi paved road and railroad and arrived at the line: 1st Guards Tank Corps—Molchad'; 48th Army with the cavalry-mechanized group and the 1st Mechanized Corps—Molchad'—Cheshevlya—Dubishche; 65th Army—Novaya Mysh'—Nivishche, and; 28th Army—Gintsevichi—Lesnaya—Milovidy—Sel'tsy—Novoselki.

Thus as a result of the fighting, which lasted a little more than two days, the Germans' powerful Baranovichi fortified area, which covered the axes to Bialystok and Brest, fell. More than 3,000 German and Hungarian officers and men fell in the fighting, and a large amount of equipment and weapons was captured.

However, the armies' average daily rate of advance was 16 kilometers, instead of the planned 24-35 kilometers.

The Second Belorussian Front's 3rd Army, which was operating to the right, by this time, had reached the line Bitsevichi—Piserchuki—Deneiki. Units of the enemy's 12th Panzer, 342nd Infantry and 28th Light Infantry divisions were withdrawing along the army's front.

---

7   First Belorussian Front directive. Central Ministry of Defense Archives, opis' 20897, delo 1, p. 252.
8   Central Ministry of Defense Archives, opis' 20897, delo 1, p. 258.

The fortified areas' operational group, in conjunction with the partisans, was operating in the space between the flanks of the 28th and 61st armies.

The enemy, in withdrawing, blew up bridges and corduroy roads and put up insignificant resistance in the defiles between the swamps and in the inhabited locales.

Overcoming the obstacles, by the close of 6 July a group of fortified areas' forward detachments was approaching the Sluch' River, out of contact with the enemy. As this group had carried out its mission, it was pulled into the reserve on the orders of the *front* commander.

The enemy, having lost the Baranovichi fortified area and having put the 129th Infantry Division and 18th Special Designation Brigade (the first from the Pinsk area, and the second from the Kovel' area) along the line Milovidy (28 kilometers southwest of Baranovichi) and to the south, was conducting a fighting retreat to the previously-prepared Slonim defensive line along the Shara River. Moreover, the sector Kabaki—excluding Slonim had been previously occupied by the 307th Infantry Division, which had been brought up from Army Group North Ukraine.

The enemy air force became significantly more active and, in systematic raids launched attacks against road junctions and troop columns, especially of the cavalry, mechanized and tank corps, and against crossings. In striving to upset our railroad transport, the German-Fascist aviation carried out raids in groups of 160-70 planes against the important rail junctions of Korosten', Sary and Olevsk. 956 enemy air sorties were noted during these days, of which 581 were at night.

On 9 July our forces, while throwing back the enemy's covering detachments with their mobile formations, were approaching the enemy's withdrawal route and destroying his retreating units. By the close of the day, having advanced 30-35 kilometers, our forces reached the eastern bank of the Shara River along the entire front, and forced the river and seized bridgeheads along a number of sectors: the 48th Army in the Pavlovichi—Zadvor'ye area (15 and ten kilometers north of Slonim), six kilometers wide and 1-1.5 kilometers deep; the 28th Army in the area south of Ugly and in the Mogil'nitsa area, eight kilometers wide and 2.5 kilometers deep.

The tank corps achieved the greatest successes on 9 July. The 1st Guards Tank Corps forced the Shara River from the march north of Pavlovichi and, launching an attack to the south along the western bank of the Shara River, outflanked Slonim from the northwest and was fighting along the Batraki line (seven kilometers northwest of Slonim). The 9th Tank Corps broke into the eastern and southeastern outskirts of the town on the enemy's heels and began fighting for the town and the Slonim railroad station. It should be noted that the tank corps, during the course of 16 days of uninterrupted fighting, suffered heavy losses in equipment and had only the following combat-ready equipment: 1st Guards Tank Corps—31 tanks and self-propelled guns; 9th Tank Corps—62 tanks and self-propelled guns.

The Second Belorussian Front's 3rd Army forced the Molchad' River, captured the town of Novoel'nya and on 9 July reached the line Selets—Dyatlovo—Zadvor'ye, having thus carried out (on 12 July, instead of 15 July) its immediate assignment.

At the same time the *front's* right-wing forces were successfully developing the offensive on Baranovichi, Slonim and Ruzhany, the 61st Army, which was attacking in the central part of the *front's* sector along the Pinsk axis, in conjunction with the Dnepr Flotilla, the Poles'ye and Pinsk partisan formations, the fortified areas' operational group, and the 28th Army's 55th Guards Rifle Division, was rolling up the enemy's defense along the northern bank of the Pripyat', Goryn' and Styr' rivers.

The enemy, fearing encirclement, was falling back to the west before the army's right flank and center, mining the roads, clearings and inhabited locales, blowing up bridges and, along the remaining sectors was attempting through stubborn defense to cover the very important Luninets rail junction and the Pinsk axis.

The army, in conjunction with the Dnepr Flotilla and partisan formations, and having overcome numerous enemy engineering obstacles and having forced such major river barriers as the

Pripyat', Goryn', Styr', Stviga, Sluch', and others, captured the important rail and road junction of Zhitkovichi and by the close of 9 July its right flank had arrived at the approaches to Luninets, its center at the eastern bank of the Styr' River along the Gol'tse—Ovsemiruv sector, and the left flank had forced the Styr' River and seized a bridgehead in the Lopatin area.

The 61st Army, in five days of attacking and pursuing the enemy, advanced 85 kilometers, with an average daily rate of advance of 17 kilometers.

The Dnepr Flotilla's artillery fire supported the attack by units of the 61st Army and by the close of 6 July had finished putting units of the 89th Rifle Corps over to the northern bank of the Pripyat' River. Then, while moving upstream along the Pripyat' River, with the objective of seizing the railroad bridge south of Luninets, by the close of 9 July a brigade had reached the bridge, although it had been blown up by the enemy, while another brigade reached the Berez'tse area. The flotilla, having ferried a battalion of the 397th Rifle Division to the river's northern bank and the division's remaining units in the Berez'tse area, prepared to break through to Pinsk.

Simultaneous with the attack by the 61st Army's right-flank forces in the direction of Luninets from the north, the 28th Army's 55th Guards Rifle Division was also attacking. While attacking in conjunction with detachments of the Poles'ye partisans and pursuing the enemy's small and scattered groups to the south, by the close of 9 July the division had reached the approaches to Luninets from the north. In five days of attacking in the very difficult conditions of an area of impassable swamps, with scarce and unsatisfactory roads of embankment sand and pole flooring for the passage of automobile transportation, the division advanced, with a small rear establishment, to the southwest up to 90 kilometers, with an average speed of 18 kilometers per day.

The 216th "Knot" Divisional Group, along with the 544th, 244th and 129th worker battalions, and the 203rd Security and 7th Infantry divisions, part of the 3rd Cavalry Brigade, and individual security and special battalions were withdrawing in front of the 61st Army. By 8 July the remnants of the 35th Infantry Division and the 17th Special Designation Brigade, had been brought up for the defense of Pinsk.

During 5-9 July Long-Range Aviation paid particularly attention to disrupting the enemy's rail transport, particularly while transferring his reserves from the rear and other army groups. The rail sectors leading from west to east through Brest, Luninets and Bialystok, and Baranovichi were subjected to raids by long-range bombers.

During 5-6 July part of the 16th Air Army launched systematic raids against the enemy's forces, with groups of *shturmoviks*, accompanied by fighters, in the areas northeast of Baranovichi, carrying out up to 200 sorties on 5 July alone. However, the 4th Guards Cavalry Corps was not covered by fighter aviation from the air. As a result, the enemy's air force bombed and strafed the corps' combat formations without reprisal.

During 5-9 July the partisan formations continued to assist the Soviet forces' attack.

A brigade of the Baranovichi partisan formation attacked along with the 55th Guards Rifle Division to the southwest toward Luninets. Two of the Poles'ye partisan formation's brigades blew up 1,273 rails near Zhitkovichi and supported the forces of the 61st Army in taking the town and road junction of Zhitkovichi by storm. The Pinsk partisan formation was the most active. On 8 July four of its brigades began fighting for the enemy's strong center of resistance in the area of Bostyn', and the following day, in conjunction with the 55th Guards Rifle Division, captured it. At the same time another three brigades captured the rail stations of Lushcha and Lovcha, and blew up 727 rails along the Lushcha—Bostyn' sector, and blocked the departure from Lushcha station of an enemy armored train, which was later captured by Soviet forces. One of the same formation's brigades surrounded the enemy garrison in Parokhon'sk on 7 July and, together with the army's forces, destroyed it on 10 July. A brigade from the Bialystok partisan formation, while operating in the Pinsk Oblast', defeated, on orders from the 61st Army's military council, the headquarters of a combat unit in the village of Novy Dvur (25 kilometers northeast of Pinsk). During this time the

Bialystok and Brest partisan formations, which were operating in the deep rear, launched a series of powerful attacks against the enemy's communications, especially along the railroad sectors from Brest to Baranovichi and to Pinsk. The Bialystok partisans carried out several demolitions of trains along the Brest—Baranovichi railroad and blew up 19 bridges and put 15 kilometers of the enemy's telephone-telegraph line out of action. In this way the partisans basically carried out the tasks assigned by the *front's* military council.

On the whole, the *front's* right-wing forces carried out the immediate task laid down by the *Stavka* ahead of time, with an average daily raid of advance of up to 27 kilometers, as opposed to the 22.6 kilometers called for by the operational plan.

The Operation's Second Stage

The Capture of Slonim and Pinsk. The Arrival at the Far Approaches to Brest (10-16 July 1944)

On 10 July the *front's* right-wing forces began carrying out their subsequent assignment. By this time they, having broken through the enemy's Baranovichi defensive line, had reached the previously-prepared Slonim defensive line along the Shara River. At the same time, the *front's* forces had managed to seize three bridgeheads along the western bank of the Shara River, while the tank corps had begun fighting for Slonim.

The German-Fascist command attached great importance to the retention of this line, and particularly the major rail and road junction of Slonim, for with their seizure favorable opportunities would be created for developing the pursuit along the Slonim—Volkovysk, Slonim—Pruzhany—Brest and Kobrin—Brest axes. Thus the enemy put up fierce resistance to the *front's* forces along the Slonim line.

Simultaneous with this, on the morning of 10 July the German-Fascist command occupied the line along the Zel'vyanka and Grivda rivers along the Samarovichi—Ivashkovichi and Kossovo—Ivatsevichi sectors, 30 kilometers west of the line, with the 28th Light Infantry and 292nd Infantry divisions. These enemy divisions had been taken out of the fighting—the first on the night of 9 July from the Molchad' area, and the second on 2-4 July out of the fortified areas' sector. Moreover, the enemy had occupied his previously-prepared defensive line along the western bank of the Yasel'da River, along the Selets—Bereza sector and to the south, with the Hungarian 5th Reserve Division, covering the Brest road.

On 8 July the 20th Panzer Division was pulled out of the line for reinforcement.

The enemy also began to move up the SS *Totenkopf* and "Viking" panzer divisions to the northeast from the First Ukrainian Front's sector and the area west of Kovel'.

By the morning of 10 July, that is, by the beginning of the achievement of the subsequent mission, the *front's* right wing arrived in a more compact group of forces that at the beginning of the operation; that is, in a 60-kilometer sector instead of 100-kilometer one. 52 percent of the *front's* rifle divisions were attacking in the rifle corps' first echelons. Our forces were no longer so strung out and the corps' second echelons were only 5-15 kilometers from the first echelons.

However, the lagging of the artillery and rear organs had not been eliminated. The artillery mainly lagged behind because of breakdowns in the delivery of fuels and lubricants for tows. The railroad transportation sector ran, as before, along the railroad bridge over the Dnepr at Zhlobin, while the dirt road sector increased from 250-70 to 330 kilometers. Due to this, the armies moved up sections of the army bases by dirt road behind the troops. For example, the 65th Army deployed its section in Bobruisk. From the army bases' section food, fuels and lubricants and ammunition were brought up by army auto transport immediately to the divisional depots.

In this situation, while attempting to more rapidly carry out his subsequent task, the *front* commander decided to capture Slonim in a night attack and, while forcing the Shara River along a broad front, to expand the bridgeheads along its western bank, and then, having concentrated the army's main forces on the bridgeheads, and having brought up the artillery and rear organs and replenished supplies, to attack on the morning of 12 July with all the *front's* right-wing forces to the west and southwest.

In order to further this decision, on 9 July the *front* commander demanded that the 48th, 65th and 28th armies complete the crossing of their main forces over the Shara River by the morning of 11 July and move them up 10-12 kilometers to the west of the river. On the morning of 12 July the main forces, in conjunction with the mobile forces and partisans were to attack with the assignment of reaching the line Zel'va—Ruzhany—Kossovo—Nechachevo, at a depth of 28-36 kilometers, by the end of the day.[9]

While carrying out their assigned tasks, on 10 July the *front's* right-wing forces, having crushed the enemy's stubborn resistance, forced the Shara River along the entire front, captured the town and railroad station of Slonim and Byten'. In this manner the last previously-prepared enemy defensive line before the Vistula River was penetrated.

In continuing to pursue the enemy, by the close of 11 July the *front's* forces had reached the following lines: 48th Army—the eastern bank of the Zel'vyanka River along the Zel'va—Rudavka sector, having forced the river along a number of sectors with its forward detachments; the cavalry-mechanized group reached the line excluding Rudavka—Selyavichi; the 65th Army—the line Pasinichi—Sosnovka—Dubitovo, and; the 28th Army—the line Kossovo—Ivatsevichi—Gichitsy. The 1st Mechanized Corps was fighting in the 2nd Guards Rifle Corps' ranks in the Kossovo area.

Thus during 10-11 July the *front's* forces advanced 28-32 kilometers, at an average speed of 14-16 kilometers per day.

During 12-13 July the *front's* forces, while overcoming growing enemy resistance, particularly in the direction of Volkovysk and Bereza, were successfully advancing. The 48th Army and the right flank of the 28th Army achieved the greatest success.

The 48th Army, having committed its second echelon (42nd Rifle Corps) into the fighting in the direction of Mezhrech'e, crushed the enemy's fierce resistance along the Zel'vyanka River and at 0700 on 12 July, in conjunction with the 9th Tank Corps and the 40th Rifle Corps of the Second Belorussian Front's 3rd Army, captured Zel'va. Then, fighting off numerous counterattacks by the enemy's infantry and tanks, by the close of 13 July reached the line Kholstovo—Yuzefuv.

The cavalry-mechanized group, operating in the 48th Army's sector, forced the Zel'vyanka River with its cavalry corps in the Tsyganovka area (15 kilometers southeast of Zel'va) and seized a small bridgehead and began heavy fighting to expand it. At the same time, the group's tank corps forced the river in the Zel'va area and with a bold attack, in conjunction with the 29th and 40th rifle corps, captured the town and by the close of 12 July had reached the line Borodichi—Kholstovo.

On 13 July the cavalry-mechanized group, in conjunction with the 48th Army, while engaged in heavy fighting, moved slowly forward in the 29th and 42nd rifle corps' combat formations.

The 65th Army, having concentrated its main efforts in the center in the direction of Ruzhany, forced the Zel'vyanka and Ruzhanka rivers and, having captured a district center of the Brest Oblast'—the town of Ruzhany—and by the close of 13 July reached the line Dubiki—Vel'ki Ugol.

The 28th Army was making its main attack in the direction of Kossovo and Smolyanitsa, bypassing the swamps from the north. In conjunction with the 1st Mechanized Corps, the army

---

9   First Belorussian Front directive. Central Ministry of Defense Archives, opis' 20897, delo 1, pp. 305, 307-09.

moved rapidly forward and by 13 July had reached the Yasel'da River along its entire front. Here the army's forces encountered significantly increased resistance from the newly-arrived 102nd Infantry Division along the sector north of Pruzhany, and from the Hungarian 5th Reserve Division near Bereza.

The 1st Mechanized Corps, which was operating in the 28th Army's sector in the direction of Kobrin, having bypassed the swamps from the north, as early as 12 July leaped ahead, overcoming the enemy's particularly stubborn resistance and, while fighting off his unending counterattacks, forced the Yasel'da River near Selets and Bereza and began fighting along their northern and northwestern outskirts.

Thus the enemy's defense along the lines of the Zel'vyanka and Yasel'da rivers was pierced and the armies reached the far approaches to the towns of Volkovysk and Pruzhany, thus creating favorable conditions for the Second Belorussian Front's 3rd Army on the right to capture the major and important rail and road junction—the town of Volkovysk, and also for its own forces to develop the attack toward Kamenets and Kobrin.

In the two days of operations (12-13 July) our forces advanced along the greater part of the attack front 35-45 kilometers, with an average daily rate of advance of 18-22 kilometers, with the exception of the 48th Army, where the rate of advance was significantly lower (6-7 kilometers).

To the right, the Second Belorussian Front committed the 50th Army into the first echelon to the right of the 3rd Army and then, having forced the Zel'vyanka River, by the close of 13 July had reached the near approaches to the towns of Grodno and Volkovysk.

Continuing the offensive on the morning of 14 July, the 48th and 65th armies reached the Ross' River, having advanced 20 kilometers, but were not able to seize bridgeheads on its western bank. Only on 15 July were they able to crush the enemy's resistance, force the Ross' River and slightly improve their situation in the Bereza area and to the north of Pruzhany. By the close of 16 July the 48th Army had reached the line Polonka—Golobudy—Pesets, and the 65th Army the bend in the railroad (four kilometers northwest of Masevo-1)—Belovezha—Pererov and Yasen'—Stoily.

By this time the cavalry-mechanized group, in conjunction with the 65th Army's 105th Rifle Corps and the 28th Army's 3rd Guards Rifle Corps, reached the line Abramy—Chakhets, and the 1st Mechanized Corps the line excluding Chakhets—Pruzhany—Khorevo. The corps, due to delays in the delivery of fuels and lubricants, had left its equipment, auto transport and transportable ammunition in the Smolyany area (ten kilometers northeast of Bereza).

Thus in the course of three days, in conditions of the swampy terrain and difficult Belovezhskaya Woods, the *front's* right-wing forces forced the Ross' and Yasel'da rivers and, having advanced 20-45 kilometers, at a rate of 7-15 kilometers per day, reached the approaches to the important rail and road junctions along the Bialystok and Brest operational axes—Svisloch', Gainovka, Kamenets, and Kobrin, and the withdrawal route of the enemy's Pinsk group of forces.

The Second Belorussian Front, which was operating to the right, by the close of 16 July had captured, in conjunction with the Third and First Belorussian fronts, the major rail and road junctions of Grodno and Volkovysk, reached the line Kelbaski—Prokopovichi—excluding Polonka.

The 61st Army, located in the center of the *front's* sector, while taking advantage of the success of the *front's* right-wing forces along the Slonim—Pruzhany and Ivatsevichi—Kobrin axes, continued to roll up the enemy's defense along the Pripyat' River. The army was making its making attack along its right flank to the west toward Luninets and Pinsk, along the railroad, and a supporting attack along its left flank to the northwest, in the direction of Pinsk.

The army's forces, in conjunction with the 28th Army's 55th Guards Rifle Division and two partisan brigades from the Pinsk partisan formation, on 10 July took the important rail and road junction and strong point of Luninets, and the next day the town of Lunin, while the partisans took the town of Lovcha.

The Dnepr Flotilla, while supporting the attack by our units along the shore with its fire, on the night of 10 July landed the 397th Rifle Division along the northern bank of the Pripyat' River in the area of Berez'tse (19 kilometers southwest of Luninets), and then on 12-13 July landed one of the division's battalions on the eastern outskirts of Pinsk, as well as a regiment of the 415th Rifle Division.

By the close of 12 July the 61st Army had forced the Yasel'da River on its right flank and seized a bridgehead on its western bank along the sector Boyare—Vysokoe, while its left flank reached the line Gornovo—Dzikoviche Male.

Thus during 10-12 July the 61st Army, having forced such major water obstacles as the Styr', Pripyat' and Yasel'da rivers, advanced its right flank up to 50 kilometers, with a speed of 17 kilometers per day, and its left flank 8-26 kilometers, with a speed of 3-8 kilometers per day, and reached the near approaches to Pinsk.

The German-Fascist command, attaching enormous importance to Pinsk and the surrounding area along the Brest axis, had created here a strong center of resistance. Its construction had been begun by the Germans as early as May 1944.

The defensive line ran along the near approaches to the town, along the southern and western high banks of the Yasel'da and Pina rivers, and contained a continuous line of fully-equipped trenches and was covered by engineering obstacles. The inhabited locales along this line were especially heavily fortified and had wooden and earth and permanent pillboxes. The enemy had occupied this line as early as 11 July with the 216th Divisional Group and with three worker battalions, which had been pulled out of the fighting to the east of Luninets.

The town of Pinsk itself was a strongly fortified center of resistance, with an all-round defense. From the north the town was covered along its outskirts by two lines of fully-equipped trenches. There were seven concrete pillboxes along the southern outskirts. Inside the town, mainly along the intersections of the streets, wood and earthen pillboxes had been constructed, which enfiladed all of the town's main streets. From 8 July the Pinsk center of resistance had been occupied and was being prepared for defense by the remnants of the 35th Infantry Division and the 17th Special Designation Brigade.

On the night of 12-13 July the 61st Army began the decisive fight along the Pinsk axis and by the close of the day its right flank had broken through the enemy's defense on the southern bank of the Yasel'da River, and with its left forced the Pripyat' and Strumen' rivers. At the same time, the flotilla along the eastern outskirts of Pinsk landed a regiment from the 415th Rifle Division.

On the night of 13-14 July the army's forces made a turning maneuver and, attacking from the north, south and east, with the assistance of the Dnepr Flotilla, crushed the enemy's resistance and by 0600 on 14 July had captured the last heavily fortified German center of resistance along the Kobrin—Brest axis, the major rail and road junction and oblast' center of the Belorussian SSR—the town of Pinsk.

By the close of 16 July the army reached the line: the eastern outskirts of Khomsk—Ogdemer—Zhuravok, having advanced 60 kilometers to the west in four days, with an average rate of 15 kilometers per day.

On 16 July the 70th Army along the First Belorussian Front's left wing, while supporting the 61st Army's offensive west of Pinsk, forced the Pripyat' River with its reconnaissance detachments in the areas northeast and northwest of Borki and captured the inhabited locales of Grechishcha and Nevir.

While the *front's* right-wing units were carrying out their subsequent assignment (10-16 July), the 16th Air Army's formations and Long-Range Aviation supported their combat operations. The air army's formations mainly did this through strikes on the battlefield, while the latter attacked the enemy's rear targets.

During this time Long-Range Aviation launched bombing raids against the railroad junctions and stations of Brest, Bielsk, Czeremcha, and Kobrin.

It should also be noted that during 2-14 July Long-Range Aviation made daytime runs to deliver fuel, ammunition and food to those *front* units that had moved far ahead.

The partisan formations (the Baranovichi, Brest and Pinsk groups) made daily attacks along individual sectors of the Baranovichi—Brest, Luninets—Pinsk—Brest, and Baranovichi—Luninets railroads and sharply reduced their carrying capacity and thus limited the enemy's conduct of regrouping and rail deliveries along these lines.

Simultaneously, as a result of their independent activities, the partisans seized an entire series of inhabited locales and railroad stations (Losino, Lushcha, Lovcha, and others).

The partisans also took part in capturing, along with the *front's* forces, a large number of towns and inhabited locales, including Pinsk, Luninets, Bereza, Lunin, Zhitkovichi, and others.

As the *front's* formations approached the town of Bereza, the Brest partisan formation destroyed all of the bridges on the dirt roads in the enemy's rear, which sharply restricted the enemy forces' ability to maneuver.

The partisans also carried out a great deal of work to save industrial buildings, towns and villages (Baranovichi, Pinsk, Luninets, Slonim, and many others) from destruction by the enemy, and for saving a huge number of Belorussian citizens from being driven into fascist Germany.

Every day the partisans aided the *front's* forces with guides and supplying them with reconnaissance data on the enemy and terrain.

The rear organs remained greatly strung out and the troops continued to experience a desperate need of ammunition and fuel.

Troop supply was carried out both from the previous bases, which lagged almost 500 kilometers behind, as well as from the Bobruisk area (300-350 kilometers behind the troops), where the first trains (6-10 pairs per day) began to arrive from 15 July. The main reason for the rear organs lagging behind, as in the *front's* preceding operation, were the low rates of railroad restoration, and thus the great distance of the lead railroad stations form the troops. For example, when the first train arrived at the Krasnyi Bereg station (east of Bobruisk), and then at Slutsk station, the troops were by this time located along the line Baranovichi—Volkovysk—Pruzhany; that is, 350 kilometers distant. On some days this gap exceeded 400 kilometers.

All of this could not but negatively tell on the course of the troops' combat operations and on the speed of the operation's conduct.

Thus by the close of 16 July the *front's* right-wing forces had not been able to carry out their subsequent objective, as laid down by the *Stavka* of the Supreme High Command, of reaching the Western Bug River and seizing a bridgehead along its western bank. Nor was the *front* commander's idea of encircling the Baranovichi group of forces carried out.

However, the *front's* right-wing forces defeated the enemy's Baranovichi group of forces with a frontal attack, outflanked his Pinsk group of forces from the north and reached the far approaches to the city of Brest, having thus created favorable conditions for launching a powerful attack against the enemy with all the *front's* forces.

In carrying out the subsequent objective, the *front's* right-wing forces advanced 84 kilometers along their right flank, 108 kilometers in the center, and 68 kilometers along the left flank, for an average daily rate of advance of 12-15, 5-9 and seven kilometers; that is, at a rate almost twice as slow as during the fulfillment of the immediate objective and one-third lower than the offensive pace assigned by the *Stavka* of the Supreme High Command.

The reduction in the offensive pace while carrying out the subsequent assignment is explained, first of all, by the ongoing increase in enemy resistance, as a result of his committing fresh formations and divisions into the battle, which had been previously pulled out of the fighting and significantly reinforced (102nd, 292nd and 129th divisions, and others), as well as the necessity of breaking through two defensive lines along major water barriers—the Shara and Zel'vyanka rives, and overcoming a significant area of difficult wooded and swampy terrain along almost the entire attack front (more than 90 kilometers). Moreover, as the front moved to the west, the attack zone increased in width each day and by the end of the operation had reached 182 kilometers, instead of the 100 kilometers at the start of the operation; a circumstance that naturally told on the rate of attack.

Moreover, the reduction in the rates of attack occurred as the result of breakdowns in supplying the troops with ammunition and fuel, due to the significant distance between the supply bases and the troops (up to 300-50 kilometers). For example, due to a lack of fuel, the 1st Mechanized Corps was forced to abandon all the mechanized brigades' auto transport and mobile equipment eight kilometers northeast of Bereza, and from 14 July to move from the town of Bereza toward Pruzhany on foot.

The degree that the rifle divisions, tank and mechanized formations and units could be kept at strength undoubtedly had an influence on the speed of the operation, as a whole, and in carrying out the subsequent objective (see table 15).

This table shows that if by the end of the operation, the rifle divisions were at 63-85 percent of authorized personnel strength, the tank strength levels of the armies and tank and mechanized corps was significantly lower and comprised 16-55 percent of authorized strength, and only in one case reached 77 percent.

Results and Conclusions

As a result of the Baranovichi—Slonim offensive operation, which lasted 12 days (5-16 July), the forces of the First Belorussian Front advanced along their right flank to the southwest—and the 61st Army to the west—190-200 kilometers along a straight line, liberated the Belorussian SSR's oblast' centers of Baranovichi and Pinsk and reached the approaches to Brest, an important communications junction and powerfully fortified enemy defensive area along the Warsaw axis. In this way they created favorable conditions for the offensive's unfolding along a broader front with all the *front's* forces, in close coordination with the First Ukrainian Front, to the border of allied Poland.[10]

Moreover, the *front's* forces broke through two previously-prepared defensive lines near Baranovichi and Slonim and captured the major Baranovichi center of resistance and the powerful strong points of Slonim, Ruzhany, Kossovo, Luninets, and Pinsk. Along the Pinsk axis the 61st Army rolled up the enemy's defense along the Pripyat', Styr' and Goryn' rivers on a more than 200- kilometer front.

The *front's* forces defeated the opposing enemy group of forces, which he reinforced during the operation by transferring nine and one-half divisions, a Hungarian cavalry brigade, and a special designation brigade from the deep rear and other axes against the First Belorussian Front's right wing to the areas of Baranovichi, Slonim and Pruzhany.

The 102nd, 129th and 292nd infantry, 28th Light Infantry, and Hungarian 1st Cavalry divisions, the Hungarian 4th Cavalry Brigade, the 216th Divisional Group "Knot," corps group "E," and the Ninth Army's assault regiment were defeated, while the 4th Panzer, 367th and 7th infantry, 203rd Security, and Hungarian 5th Reserve divisions suffered heavy casualties.

---

10 The First Ukrainian Front began its offensive on 13 July, in accordance with the plan of the L'vov—Sandomierz operation.

Table 15. Strength of the *Front's* Forces

Army and Formations	Strength in Tanks and Self-Propelled Guns (in %)[1]				Rifle Division Personnel Strength (in %)[2]	
	5 July		16 July		5 July	16 July
	Combat-Ready	In Repair	Combat-Ready	In Repair		
48th Army	54.8	32.6	30.3	34.9	76.1	85.8
65th Army	69.5	13.4	77.1	8.6	72.4	69.4
28th Army	80.2	7.1	55.6	20.6	84.7	78.0
4th Gds Cavalry Corps	48.8	–	22.6	55.5	–	–
9th Tank Corps	31.0	31.0	16.3	47.4	–	–
1st Gds Tank Corps	43.4	5.2	39.1	0.4	–	–
1st Mechanized Corps	77.5	19.4	43.2	7.5	–	–
Total	57.7	18.1	40.6	25.0	77.7	77.7
61st Army	–	–	–	–	69.0	63.7

Notes

1 Central Ministry of Defense Archives, fond 233, opis' 11866, delo 11, 275, pp. 344-58.

2 The authorized strength of a rifle division was 7,119 men. Central Ministry of Defense Archives, fond 233, opis' 20521, delo 1, p. 145.

During the course of the offensive the *front's* forces successfully overcame the difficult wooded and swampy expanses of the Poles'ye, as well as the areas of the Ruzhanskaya woods and the greater part of the Belovezhskaya Woods, forced the Shara, Zel'vyanka, Ross',and Yasel'da rivers, and in the south the Pripyat', Goryn', Styr', Strumen', Pina, and Yasel'da rivers.

During the operation the *front's* forces cleared the German-Fascist invaders out of broad expanses of the Belorussian SSR, about 160 kilometers from north to south and up to 190-200 kilometers from east to west, for an overall territory of 28,300 square kilometers, which was 2,300 square kilometers more than during the Bobruisk—Slutsk offensive operation.

The First Belorussian Front's Baranovichi—Slonim offensive operation is an example of a consecutive *front* operation in depth, which was conducted without an operational pause, following the completion of the Bobruisk—Slutsk offensive operation.

This operation is very interesting, in that it began with a sharp change in the offensive's direction from the northwest to the west and southwest. At the same time, the offensive sector of the *front's* right-wing forces was reduced by a factor of two, while the *front's* boundary on the right was shifted nearly 50 kilometers to the south.

All of this enabled the *front's* right-wing forces to create a significant superiority in men and materiel over the enemy along the axes of their attacks during the first days of the operation.

Thanks to the shift of the armies' sectors to the south, their forces were forced to attack and arrive at their new boundaries at a 50-55 degree angle to their former sectors. This was particularly the case with the 48th and 65th armies, which were at one point 35-50 kilometers outside of their new sectors.

The Baranovichi—Slonim offensive operation's scope in depth reached 150-200 kilometers. The offensive speed of the *front's* right-wing forces along the right flank and in the center (along the axis of the main attack) was 18-19 kilometers per day, and along the left flank (the axis of the supporting attack)—13-14 kilometers. On some days the offensive speed along the axis of the main attack was significantly higher and reached 30-40 kilometers per day. For example, on 7 July the 48th Army's rate of advance, and on 7 and 9 July that of the 65th Army, reached 40 kilometers.

One should note the sharp reduction in the offensive's rate of advance while breaking through the defensive lines near Baranovichi and Slonim, as well as in breaking through the enemy's hurriedly prepared defense along the Zel'vyanka River south of Zel'va and the Yasel'da River near Selets and Bereza, where it reached only 2-6 kilometers per day.

Along the Pinsk axis, along the *front's* left-wing 61st Army's sector, the average offensive rate of advance was 16 kilometers per day.

The First Belorussian Front's offensive pace during this operation, when compared with the offensive pace of the preceding Bobruisk—Slutsk operation, was lower by 4-6 kilometers per day.

The width of the offensive sector along the line of combat contact of the *front's* right-wing forces at the start of the operation was 168 kilometers[11], and 238 kilometers with the addition of the 61st Army; at the end of the operation the distance was 182 kilometers, and 232 kilometers with the 61st Army, that is, the width of the attack sector seems to be unchanged. However, if you take only the forces of the 48th, 65th and 28th armies on the *front's* right wing, then their attack sector increased by 82 kilometers, or by 45 percent.

The operational formation of the *front's* right-wing forces was in a single echelon throughout the entire operation. There were two rifle corps (80th and 46th) in reserve.

In the armies the operational formation was, as a rule, in two echelons, except for the 28th Army, which from 13 July attacked in a single echelon, while its corps attacked in two.

In the Baranovichi—Slutsk operation each of the *front's* right wing armies attacked along a single operational direction, with the exception of the 28th Army, which attacked with part of its forces along another operational direction—toward Luninets and Pinsk, and, partly, the 65th Army in its movement from 15 July around the Belovezhskaya Woods from the north and south.

During the operation the *front's* forces displayed a great deal of mobility, skill in maneuvering, and the ability to rapidly overcome inaccessible terrain areas.

All the rivers in the attack zone of the *front's* right-wing forces were forced, as a rule, from the march; the seized bridgeheads were rapidly expanded. Such natural obstacles as the large swampy areas in the northern part of Poles'ye and in the Ruzhanskaya woods, as well as the Belovezhskaya Woods, were bypassed by the armies' and corps' main forces.

The experience of the Baranovichi—Slonim operation confirmed once again the possibility of employing such formations as field fortified areas in the offensive along supporting axes, but to a limited depth, while leaving the heavy weapons in the jumping-off areas.

The operation's experience also showed the great significance of river flotilla's actions in developing the offensive and pursuing the enemy along a river. In this operation the Dnepr Flotilla's boats carried out the crossing of the 89th Rifle Corps and part of the 397th Rifle Division to the northern bank of the Pripyat' River, and landed parties in Pinsk and other areas; it assisted with its guns the 61st Army's offensive along the Pripyat' River; it secured the flanks of the army's units along the river and, finally, cleared the enemy out of the inhabited areas adjacent to the Pripyat' River's northern bank. The successful achievement of these tasks was secured by the precise organization of cooperation between the flotilla and the ground forces.

The operation's experience shows that in a number of cases the partisans' actions created favorable conditions for achieving the *front's* tasks, as laid down by the *Stavka* of the Supreme High Command. All of the partisans' activities were conducted in operational or tactical cooperation with the *front's* forces. Assignments in the partisans' interests were issued by the *front's* military

---

11 Of this figure, three armies were attacking along a 100-kilometer sector, while the fortified areas' operational group was attacking along a 68-kilometer front.

council through the headquarters of the Belorussian staff of the partisan movement within the *front* headquarters. The presence of such a group secured both the timely issuing of tasks to the partisans by the military council, as well as their uninterrupted material-technical supply.

Partisan brigades and separate detachments, once they united with the troops, represented a large reserve of trained personnel for reinforcing the *front's* formations.

Our forces' successful advance forced the German-Fascist command to search for operational reserves and transfer them from other axes. For example, the 28th Light Infantry Division, the 18th Special Designation Brigade, and the 367th Infantry Division, were transferred from Army Group Northern Ukraine, while the Hungarian 1st Calvary Division arrived from Hungary; the 102nd, 292nd and 129th infantry divisions, which had fallen back on Luninets and taken out of the battle and, following their reinforcement with men and materiel, were once again transferred through Pinsk and Kobrin to the sector of the *front's* right-wing forces.

All of these reserves, except for the Hungarian 5th Reserve Division, were committed into the battle, as a rule, from the march, and without the necessary training. Thus they were quickly destroyed in the fighting, not being in a condition to delay our successful offensive and pursuit.

During the Baranovichi—Slonim operation the enemy lost 72,647 officers and men killed, wounded and captured. Our forces destroyed or captured 2,312 guns and mortars and 66 planes shot down, destroyed on the ground, or captured.

The Soviet forces lost 20,562 men killed, wounded and missing in action, or 6.6 percent of total personnel, of which 4,773, or 1.5 percent, were killed.[12]

The 28th Army and the 1st Mechanized Corps suffered the greatest losses (10 percent), as well as the cavalry-mechanized group (6.5 percent). This is explained by the fact that they bore the main weight of combat in breaking through the enemy's previously-prepared defense, which ran along the western bank of the Shara River near Baranovichi, and along the Yasel'da River. During this time the 48th and 65th armies were arriving at their new offensive sectors almost without fighting.

However, the losses of the *front's* right-wing forces in the operation, compared with the losses in the preceding Bobruisk—Slutsk offensive operation, were nevertheless almost twice as small—6.6 percent instead of 11.8 percent.

It should also be pointed out that the enemy's losses exceeded our losses by more than a factor of four.

These figures show how great were the results of this consecutive offensive operation by the First Belorussian Front.

The powerful attack by the *front's* right-wing forces against the German-Fascist forces, which began on 24 June near Bobruisk, was continually developed to the west, and then southwest.

---

12 Central Ministry of Defense Archives, fond 233, opis' 14780, delo 2; opis' 1478, delo 3; opis' 20519, delo 12.

11

The First Belorussian Front's Brest— Siedlce Offensive Operation (17 July–2 August 1944)

The Operation's Preparation

The First Belorussian Front's Brest—Siedlce offensive operation—the *front's* third consecutive operation—was begun on the twenty-fourth day of the multi-*front* Belorussian offensive operation of 1944.

The preparation for the operation by the *front's* forces was peculiar. For example, if the *front's* right-wing armies entered into this operation upon the completion of the Baranovichi—Slonim offensive operation without a pause, without a single day for regrouping and bringing up men and materiel, ammunition and fuel, then the *front's* left-wing armies had half a month to diligently plan for this operation. During this time, in accordance with the plan drawn up by the *front* headquarters, large forces were concentrated and all measures were carried out pertaining to the operation's preparatory stage.[1] The preparation for the *front's* left-wing armies' offensive was carried out in conditions of a rapidly-changing situation, not only along the flanks of the left wing, but in the area of the Kovel' salient.

As a result of the preceding Baranovichi—Slonim offensive operation, the *front's* right-wing forces, in throwing the enemy back to the west, had by 16 July reached the following line: excluding Polonka—Belovezha—Pruzhany—Zaluzh'e, deeply outflanking the enemy's Kobrin group of forces from the north and reaching the near approaches to the large Brest fortified area.

Simultaneously, by the close of 16 July the 61st Army, which occupied the linking position between the *front's* right and left wings, having captured Pinsk, reached the near approaches to the town of Kobrin—an important rail and road junction along the Brest axis.

The Dnepr Flotilla, while cooperating with the 61st Army's forces, by this time had concentrated in an area 8-12 kilometers west of Pinsk.

The operational group of the *front's* fortified areas—the *front* reserve—was in the area northeast of Pinsk.

In the *front's* left-wing sector the 47th and 69th armies, having detected the enemy's retreat from the area of the Kovel' salient, went over to the offensive and during 5-9 July completely cleared the Kovel' salient of the enemy, and by the close of 9 July had reached the line Les'nyaki—Yul'yanov—excluding Ruda—Tur'ya.

To the right, the Second Belorussian Front's 3rd Army, by 16 July had captured the town of Volkovysk during the Bialystok offensive operation and reached the line Kelbaski—Prokopovichi—excluding Polonka.

---

1   The operation was originally known as the Kovel' operation.

To the left, the First Ukrainian Front's 3rd Guards Army, having begun the L'vov—Sandomierz offensive operation on 13 July, broke through the enemy's defense and its right-flank 3rd Guards Army reached the line excluding Tur'ya—Volitsa—Gorokhov.

The German-Fascist command, seeking to cover the Warsaw axis and halt the offensive by the First Belorussian Front's right-wing forces, as well as to delay for a prolonged time the offensive by its left wing, was hurriedly searching for reserves and concentrating them in the Brest area and to the north, withdrew its forces from the Kovel' area by 18-25 kilometers to the west to a previously-prepared defense and was preparing a rear army defensive zone along the Western Bug River.

By the close of 16 July the following units were directly defending against the *front's* armies in the first line: in the right wing's sector—Lieutenant General Harteneck's (commander of the Hungarian I Cavalry Corps) group and the XXIII and XX army corps of Army Group Center's Second Army; in the left wing's sector—the VIII Army and LVI Panzer corps and the XLII Army Corps' 214th Infantry Division/Fourth Panzer Army/Army Group North Ukraine.

In order to create operational reserves along the Brest axis, the enemy pulled the remnants of the Hungarian 1st Cavalry Division and the 35th Infantry Division out of the fighting, as well as the Hungarian 5th Reserve Division, which were then reinforced and concentrated as follows: the first, by 16 July, in Wysokoe, and by 15-16 July the rest in the Brest area. On 16 July the Hungarian 23rd Reserve Division was transferred here from the Vysokoe area.

Moreover, by 15 July Army Group Northern Ukraine had transferred two panzer divisions: one (the 5th SS "Viking" Panzer Division—to the area of Bialystok and Bielsk-Podlaski, and the other (SS *Totenkopf*)—northeast of Bialystok. At the same time, various security regiments and special units were arriving at the *front's* right-wing sector.

Along the Kovel' axis, the German-Fascist command had shortened its front by 30 kilometers by withdrawing its forces from around the town of Kovel', had taken two divisions out of the front line—one of these into the corps' second echelon, and the other it transferred to another axis. A part of the 212th Security Division had been brought up from the depth to the area 20 kilometers south of Lyuboml'.

All of these measures enabled the enemy to have by the close of 16 July one division per 15.9 kilometers of front and 8.1 guns and mortars and 1.4 tanks per kilometer of front. On the following day (by the close of 17 July) the enemy, by straightening out his front to the east of Brest and also along the boundary with the First Ukrainian Front, shortened his front by 67 kilometers overall and thus managed to increase his operational density in guns and mortars by 57 percent, and in tanks by 25 percent.

Thus the enemy's men and materiel by the beginning of the Brest—Siedlce offensive operation against the *front*, particularly against the right wing, had not decreased, but rather had increased by means of committing into the fighting the I Reserve Corps, the 5th SS "Viking" Panzer Division, and the arrival from other axes and the deep rear of various security and special units, as well as by the significant reinforcement with men and materiel of the 35th and 7th infantry, the 1st Cavalry and 4th Panzer divisions, and corps group "E."

The enemy created his most powerful group of forces, and thus his large operational densities, against the forces of the *front's* right wing, to where, to a significant degree from the group of forces located opposite the *front's* left wing and center, during 24 June-16 July he transferred nine divisions and brigades, including two tank (4th and 5th panzer divisions), the 28th Light Infantry Division, the 102nd and 292nd infantry divisions, and the Hungarian 1st Cavalry Division and 4th Cavalry Brigade), the 203rd Security Division, and corps group "E." Moreover, the 131st Infantry Division had been regrouped to another axis from the area of the Kovel' salient. All of this led to a significant weakening of the enemy's forces facing the armies of the *front's* left wing.

By the start of the Brest—Siedlce offensive operation the enemy had along his entire front and in the operational depth a previously-prepared army defensive zone along the Western Bug River, along with the powerful Brest fortified area and its fortress. The defensive zone along the Bug River consisted of centers of resistance, connected by a fully-outfitted trench system. The centers of resistance had 4-6 permanent wooden and earth pillboxes, 1-2 concrete pillboxes, and 6-8 overhead covers and were girded with 2-3 rows of barbed wire.

In the *front's* left-wing sector this zone ran at a distance of 50-70 kilometers from the forward edge of the main defensive zone.

The town and fortress of Brest, which covered the approaches to the Western Bug River along the Warsaw axis, had been transformed into a powerful fortified area. The town was girded with three defensive zones. The first of these was located at a distance of 5-6 kilometers from the town. The second ran along the line of the external forts, left over from the First World War, while the third ran along the town's suburbs and included the forts of the internal line, with powerful reinforced-concrete structures. The inhabited locales and old reinforced-concrete forts had been configured for perimeter defense.

Along the *front's* left-wing sector the enemy had a previously-prepared defense in the entire tactical zone, which consisted of two defensive zones.

The first of these (the "main battlefield") was 3-4 kilometers deep and consisted of 1-2 positions and centers of resistance and strong points echeloned in depth and located primarily in inhabited locales and on rises, with their flanks anchored along swampy terrain sectors.

The second defensive zone (the "position of the corps reserves") was being prepared at a distance of 9-15 kilometers from the forward edge of the main defensive position, but by the start of the operation had not been fully fitted out.

From the beginning of July a defensive zone along the Lesnaya River was being prepared in the sector of the *front's* right wing.

The rear defensive position, which had strategic significance, had been under preparation for a long time along the western bank of the Vistula and Narew rivers and included the Warsaw fortified area.

The overall depth of the defense under construction reached 170-250 kilometers and more. However, the enemy's main efforts were concentrated in the tactical defensive zone, extending 10-18 kilometers.

The lines in the depth had not been occupied beforehand by the enemy's forces.

By the beginning of the operation the main axes along the *front's* sector were the Brest and Kovel'—Lublin ones. The first axis would take our forces to the important communications junction, the major oblast' center of the Belorussian SSR and the powerful fortified area and fortress of Brest and would open up the possibility of developing the offensive toward Siedlce and further toward the capital of Poland—Warsaw.

The second axis would take the *front's* forces to a major provincial and political center of Poland—Lublin, and the Vistula River south of Warsaw.

The terrain between these two axes east of Brest included the wooded and swampy Poles'ye area, which was difficult for the passage of all combat arms. West of Brest the terrain and road network were more favorable for maneuver from one axis to another, particularly for outflanking the Brest fortified area and the fortress of Brest from the south and the north.

The terrain west of the town of Kovel' allowed for, on the whole, the conduct of operations by major field forces, although here it was necessary to aid the troops' offensive operations with road and crossing equipment.

The terrain between the Brest and Bialystok operational directions consisted of large swaths of the difficult Belovezhskaya Woods.

The presence of a large number of rivers flowing east to west, including such large rivers as the Western Bug and Vistula, with very swampy and broad flood plains, made it easier for the enemy to create a defense along natural lines. On the other hand, the character of the terrain made our forces' offensive operations more difficult, as well as their materiel supply.

Thus our forces had to break through not only the enemy's deeply-echeloned defense, particularly along the *front's* left wing, but also to overcome a large number of rivers with very swampy and broad flood plains, and also the difficult expanses of the Poles'ye and Belovezhskaya Woods.

By the start of the Brest—Siedlce offensive operation, by 17 July, the First Belorussian Front had a two-echelon operational formation, as well as *front* mobile groups and reserves. Eight combined-arms armies were deployed in the first echelon (48th, 65th, 28th, 61st, 70th, 47th, 8th Guards,[2] and 69th), and the *front's* cavalry-mechanized group (4th Guards Cavalry, 1st Mechanized and 9th Tank corps).

The Polish 1st Army was concentrated in the *front's* second echelon, along the left wing's sector, and the 46th Rifle and 1st Guards Tank corps, the fortified areas' operational group and the Dnepr Flotilla were in the *front* reserve along the right flank.

Of the *front's* mobile groups, one (2nd Tank Army, 2nd and 7th guards cavalry corps) was concentrated behind the first-echelon armies along the left wing, while another (4th Guards Cavalry, 1st Mechanized and 9th Tank corps) were fighting in the right wing's first echelon.

The *front's* combat and numerical strength are shown in table 16.

The *front*, in preparing for the operation, carried out a significant reinforcement of its formations and units with both personnel and equipment, particularly along the left wing, in the zone of which the *front's* main efforts were to be switched.

Table 16. The First Belorussian Front's Combat and Numerical Strength as of 17 July 1944[1]

Armies and Formations	Right Wing			
	Men	Battalions	Mortars	
			120mm	82mm
48th Army	63,629		189	503
65th Army	55,802		173	396
28th Army	65,668		280	455
61st Army	32,616		122	341
The *front's* cavalry-mechanized group: 4th Gds Cavalry, 1st Mechanized, 9th Tank corps	44,304		125	197
Front reserve: 46th Rifle Corps, 1st Gds Tank Corps, the fortified areas' operational group	42,781		93	448
Total on 17 July	304,800	281	982	2,340
Per Kilometer of Front[2]	1,314/1,639		14.3/17.9	

Notes
1 Central Ministry of Defense Archives, fond 233, opis' 11866, delo 11, pp. 149, 390-416, 485-504.
2 The density per kilometer of front: the numerator shows the density at the start of the operation, while the denominator at the close of the operation's first day.

---

2   This army was committed into the first echelon before the start of the operation.

Right Wing

Armies and Formations	Guns				
	107mm and higher	76mm Divisional	76mm Regimental	45 & 57mm	Total Guns and Mortars
48th Army	141	274	97	222	1,426
65th Army	224	330	73	185	1,381
28th Army	272	379	102	288	1,776
61st Army	117	149	54	160	943
The *Front's* cavalry-mechanized group: 4th Gds Cavalry, 1st Mechanized, 9th Tank Corps	–	151	30	59	562
Front reserve: 46th Rifle Corps, 1st Gds Tank Corps, the fortified areas' operational group	48	399	25	296	1,309
Total on 17 July	802	1,682	381	1,210	7,397
Per Kilometer of Front		10.7/13.4		6.9/8.5	31.9/39.8

Right Wing

Armies and Formations	Anti-Aircraft Guns		Tanks and Self-Propelled Guns[2]	Rocket Artillery	Width of Attack Front[1]	
	76 & 85mm	20 & 37mm			Planned	Actual
48th Army	16	89	40/44	28	19	20/18
65th Army	16	87	82/9	24	34	68/44
28th Army	16	87	91/26	–	100	104/82
61st Army	–	12	–	–	–	40/42
The *Front's* cavalry-mechanized group: 4th Gds Cavalry, 1st Mechanized, 9th Tank Corps	16	135	151/143	95	–	–
Front reserve: 46th Rifle Corps, 1st Gds Tank Corps, the fortified areas' operational group	–	19	93/1	8	–	–
Total on 17 July	64	429	457/223	179	–	232/186
Per Kilometer of Front		2.2/2.7	2/2.5	0.8/1	–	

Notes

1 The numerator indicates situation at the start of the operation, and the denominator at the close of the operation's first day.

2 The numerator indicates combat-ready vehicles, while the denominator indicates those undergoing repairs.

Left Wing

Armies and Formations	Men	Battalions	Mortars	
			120mm	82mm
70th Army	29,054		91	176
47th Army	69,485		299	473
8th Guards Army	111,543		503	571
69th Army	65,743		315	389
2nd Tank Army	35,457		125	151
2nd Gds Cavalry Corps	19,711		82	130
7th Gds Cavalry Corps	21,814		63	110
Polish 1st Army	57,355		199	370
Total on 17 July	410,162	324	1,677	2,370
Per Kilometer of Front	2,254		22.2	
Total	714,962	605	2,659	4,710
Total per Kilometer of Front	1,727			17.8

Left Wing

Armies and Formations	Guns				Total Guns and Mortars
	107mm and higher	76mm Divisional	76mm Regimental	45 & 57mm	
70th Army	83	126	45	110	631
47th Army	312	382	59	292	1,817
8th Guards Army	607	536	128	197	2,542
69th Army	144	306	107	284	1,545
2nd Tank Army	–	60	–	54	390
2nd Gds Cavalry Corps	–	46	41	38	337
7th Gds Cavalry Corps	–	46	27	39	285
Polish 1st Army	240	136	52	198	1,195
Total on 17 July	1,386	1,638	459	1,212	8,742
Per Kilometer of Front	16.6	9.2	48		
Total	2,188	3,320	840	2,422	16,139
Total per Kilometer of Front		13.3	7.9	–	39.0

Armies and Formations	Anti-Aircraft Guns		Tanks and Self-Propelled Guns[2]	Rocket Artillery	Width of Attack Front[1]	
Left Wing						
	76 & 85mm	20 & 37mm			Planned	Actual
70th Army	–	16	–	–	120	120
47th Army	18	80	108	52	21	21
8th Guards Army	12	33	304	519	9	9
69th Army	15	86	144	48	32	32
2nd Tank Army	5	50	792	24/4	–	–
2nd Gds Cavalry Corps	–	36	80	22	–	–
7th Gds Cavalry Corps	–	34	106	17	–	–
Polish 1st Army	4	30	120	–	–	–
Total on 17 July	54	365	1,654	682	182	182
Per Kilometer of Front	2.3	9	3.9			
Total	118	794	2,111/223	861	–	414/368
Total per Kilometer of Front	2.3		5.1	2.2	–	–

Notes

1 The numerator indicates situation at the start of the operation, and the denominator at the close of the operation's first day.

2 The numerator indicates combat-ready vehicles, while the denominator indicates those undergoing repairs.

The main mass of newly-arrived reinforcements and combat equipment was dispatched to the armies of the *front's* left wing. For example, during July 40,000 reinforcements arrived at this wing's armies, including more than 26,000 from internal military districts (of 28,000 arriving at the *front*), and several hundred tanks from our industry.

The right-wing armies reinforced themselves by calling up those eligible for the draft from the territory liberated from the enemy. For example, through 14 July 40,977 men had been mobilized.[3]

The personnel strength of the rifle divisions was higher along the *front's* left wing by more than 10 percent over the right wing and by almost 40 percent in tanks.

Operational densities along the *front's* entire sector were as follows: five kilometers per rifle division, 39 guns and mortars and 5.1 tanks and self-propelled guns per kilometer of front, and in the *front's* right and left-wing sector they were, correspondingly, 5.7 and 4.5 kilometers per rifle division, 31.9 and 48 guns and mortars and 2 and 9 tanks and self-propelled guns per kilometer of front. Higher operational densities were created in the attack sector of the *front's* left-wing forces. The overall superiority over the enemy was as follows: 3.7 in divisions, 4.4 in battalions, 4.9 in guns and mortars, 3.6 in tanks and self-propelled guns, and 2.1 in aircraft, while in the *front's* right and left-wing sectors they were, correspondingly 3 and 4.8 in divisions, 3.2 and 6.2 in battalions, 4.3 and 5.8 in guns and mortars, and 1.3 and 7.7 in tanks and self-propelled guns (see table 17).

As the table shows, the presence of men and materiel and their correlation enabled the First Belorussian Front to carry out major offensive operations, especially along the *front's* left wing.

---

3   Central Ministry of Defense Archives, fond 233, opis' 14781, delo 3, p. 95.

Thus by the close of 16 July the situation, due to the defeat of the German-Fascist Army Group Center's forces in Belorussia, as well as the First Ukrainian Front's newly-begun L'vov—Sandomierz operation against Army Group North Ukraine, as well as to the arrival of the First Belorussian Front's right wing at the near approaches to Brest, was favorable for the conduct of the *front's* new consecutive offensive operation.

By shifting the *front's* main efforts to the left wing, conditions were created for increasing the forthcoming operation's scope. Moreover, the composition of the opposing enemy group of forces along the sector of the *front's* left-wing forces, compared to its strength at the start of the Belorussian offensive operation (24 June), had decreased considerably. There were no significant operational or strategic reserves of any kind along the *front's* sector.

The High Command's idea for the Brest—Siedlce offensive operation[4] was formulated and plotted on a map as early as 23-24 May 1944, when the commander of the First Belorussian Front was summoned to the *Stavka*. The idea was then refined by instructions of the *Stavka* representative of 20 June and by coded telegrams from the Supreme High Command on 2 and 7 July.[5]

Table 17. The Overall Correlation of Forces and Operational Densities in the First Belorussian Front's Sector by the Start of the Brest—Siedlce Operation of 1944

Men and Materiel	Along the Entire Front		
	Total	First Belorussian Front Per Kilometer of Front	
		By 16 July	By 17 July
Rifle, infantry, reserve, security, and cavalry divisions	82	1 division per 5 kilometers	1 division per 4.5 kilometers and cavalry divisions
Tank divisions	9.5	–	–
Manpower	714,962	1,727	1,943
Mortars	7,369	17.8	20.0
Regimental and anti-tank artillery	3,262	7.9	8.9
Divisional artillery and higher	5,508	13.3	15.0
Total guns and mortars (excluding anti-aircraft artillery)	16,139	39.0	43.9
Rocket artillery launchers	879	2.3	2.5
Tanks and self-propelled artillery	2,111	5.1	5.8
Aircraft	1,465	–	–
	Along the Right Wing		
Rifle, infantry, reserve, security, and cavalry divisions	41	1 division per 5.7 kilometers	1 division per 4.6 kilometers
Tank divisions	2.5	–	–
Battalions	281	1.2	1.5
Strength	304,800	1,314	1,639
Mortars	3,322	14.3	17.9

---

4   This was originally known as the Kovel' operation.
5   Central Ministry of Defense Archives, fond 233, opis' 20897, delo 1; opis' 17022, delo 1, coded telegram.

Men and Materiel	Total	First Belorussian Front Per Kilometer of Front	
		By 16 July	By 17 July
Regimental and anti-tank artillery	1,591	6.9	8.5
Divisional artillery and higher	2,484	10.7	13.4
Total guns and mortars (excluding anti-aircraft artillery)	7,397	31.9	39.8
Rocket artillery launchers	179	0.8	1.0
Tanks and self-propelled artillery	457	2	2.5
Along the Left Wing			
Rifle, infantry, reserve, security, and cavalry divisions	42	1 division per 4.3 kilometers	
Tank divisions	7	–	–
Battalions	324	1.8	1.8
Manpower	410,162	2,254	2,254
Mortars	4,047	22.2	22.2
Regimental and anti-tank artillery	1,671	9.2	9.2
Divisional artillery and higher	3,024	16.6	16.6
Total guns and mortars (excluding anti-aircraft artillery	8,742	48	48
Rocket artillery launchers	700	3.9	3.9
Tanks and self-propelled artillery	1,654	9	9

		Along the Entire Front		
Men and Materiel	Total	The Enemy Per Kilometer of Front		Overall Correlation of Forces
		By 16 July	By 17 July	
Rifle, infantry, reserve, security, and cavalry divisions	22.5	1 division per 18.4 kilometers	1 division per 16.4 kilometers	3.7:1
Panzer divisions	2	–	–	4.8:1
Manpower	176,150	426	479	4.1:1
Mortars	1,180	2.9	3.2	6.2:1
Regimental and anti-tank artillery	1,297	3.1	3.5	2.5:1
Divisional artillery and higher	800	1.9	2.2	6.9:1
Total guns and mortars (excluding anti-aircraft artillery)	3,277	7.9	8.9	4.9:1
Rocket artillery platforms	–	–	–	–
Tanks and self-propelled artillery	587	1.4	1.6	3.6:1
Aircraft	690	–	–	2.1:1

Men and Materiel	Total	The Enemy Per Kilometer of Front		Overall Correlation of Forces
		By 16 July	By 17 July	
The Right Wing				
Rifle, infantry, reserve, security, and cavalry divisions	14	1 division per 13 kilometers	1 division per 13.3 kilometers	3:1
Tank divisions	2	–	–	1.3:1
Battalions	88	0.4	0.5	3.2:1
Manpower	91,975	397	495	3.3:1
Mortars	658	2.8	3.5	5:1
Regimental and anti-tank artillery	682	2.9	3.7	2.4:1
Divisional artillery and higher	407	1.8	2.2	6.1:1
Total guns and mortars (excluding anti-aircraft artillery)	1,747	7.5	9.4	4.3:1
Rocket artillery launchers	–	–	–	–
Tanks and self-propelled artillery	373	1.6	2	1.3:1
The Left Wing				
Rifle, infantry, reserve, security, and cavalry divisions	8.5	1 division per 21.4 kilometers	1 division per 21.4 kilometers	5:1
Tank divisions	–	–	–	–
Battalions	58	0.4	0.4	5.6:1
Manpower	84,175	463	463	4.9:1
Mortars	522	3	3	7.8:1
Regimental and anti-tank artillery	615	3.3	3.3	2.7:1
Divisional artillery and higher	393	2.2	2.2	7.7:1
Total guns and mortars (excluding anti-aircraft artillery)	1,530	8.5	8.5	5.8:1
Rocket artillery launchers	–	–	–	–
Tanks and self-propelled artillery	214	1.2	1.2	7.7:1

Notes
1 The numerical data was taken from lists of the combat and numerical strength of Soviet and enemy forces.
2 In tallying the enemy's forces, the following units were counted: the enemy—two independent cavalry brigades, an assault gun regiment from the Ninth Army, the 37th Security Regiment, and various army units, for two divisions; our forces—five (right wing) and 14 (left wing) tank brigades, making nine and a half tank divisions, plus three motorized rifle brigades (1st Mechanized Corps), and one rifle brigade for two rifle divisions.

According to the plans's final variant, the First Belorussian Front was given the task that upon the arrival of the *front's* right-wing armies approximately at the far approaches to Brest, to carry out a consecutive offensive operation by shifting the main efforts to the *front's* left wing, for the purpose of employing the joint efforts of both the *front's* wings and, in conjunction with the First Ukrainian Front's right wing, to defeat the enemy's Brest—Lublin group of forces. Then, by developing the success to the west, on Siedlce, the *front* was to create favorable conditions for reaching the approaches to the capital of allied Poland—Warsaw and the line of the Vistula River.

According to the *Stavka* plan, the main attack would be launched by the *front's* left-wing forces on Wlodawa and Biala-Podlaska, or toward Wlodawa, Lukow and Siedlce, in the flank and rear of the enemy's Brest group of forces. A supporting attack would be made by the *front's* right-wing forces on Brest.[6]

The First Belorussian Front's overall goal in the operation consisted of independently defeating the enemy's Brest group of forces and, in conjunction with the First Ukrainian Front, the Lublin group of forces. In this way conditions would be created for the development of a subsequent offensive to the west to the capital of Poland—Warsaw and the line of the Western Bug River, and Warsaw and the Vistula River.

The *front* commander decided to launch his main attack with the *front's* left wing along the sector from Smidyn' to Dol'sk (west of Kovel') with the forces of the 47th, 8th Guards, 69th and Polish 1st armies, the 2nd Tank Army, and the 2nd and 7th guards cavalry corps in the general direction of Lyuboml' and Opalin and then toward Wlodawa and Biala-Podlaska, or toward Parczew and Siedlce, with the immediate task of defeating the opposing enemy and on the operation's fifth day reaching the line Zalesie—Osowa—Czulczice—Chelm. Subsequently, by developing the attack to the northwest and west, together with the right-wing armies, our forces were to encircle and destroy the enemy's Brest group of forces and with part of its forces, in conjunction with the First Ukrainian Front—the Lublin group of forces and by the end of July reach the line Biala-Podlaska—Lukow—Michow—Lublin.

The *front's* right-wing forces were to launch the following supporting attacks: a) with its main forces (48th and 65th armies) in the general direction of Bielsk and Podlaski, and then to the Western Bug River, for the purpose, in conjunction with the Second Belorussian Front, to split the enemy's Bialystok and Brest groups of forces and to subsequently destroy them in detail; b) the remainder of the *front's* right-wing forces (28th and 61st armies and the cavalry-mechanized group) were to attack from the north and northwest toward the *front's* left-wing forces and, in conjunction with the latter, encircle and destroy the enemy's Brest group of forces, capture the city of Brest and reach the line of the Western Bug River to the west and seize bridgeheads along its southern bank.

It was planned to commit the mobile group into the battle along the *front's* left wing on approximately the operation's third day (19 July), after breaking through the enemy's tactical defensive zone and for the 47th, 8th Guards and 69th armies to arrive at the line Skrypitsa—Skiby—Olesk, along the axis toward Siedlce and Lublin.

It was planned to commit the *front's* second echelon into the battle from the western bank of the Western Bug River along the Opalin—Bereztsy sector in the general direction of Sawin and Michow, following the arrival of the 8th Guards Army at the line excluding Osowa—Czulczice.

30 of the 42 rifle and cavalry divisions, 216 of the 324 battalions, 7,126 of 8,742 guns and mortars, and 1,633 of 1,654 tanks and self-propelled guns were concentrated along the breakthrough sector (18 kilometers out of the entire left wing's front of 182 kilometers) of the *front's* shock group. The operational and tactical densities here had been brought up to, correspondingly, 0.6 kilometers per division, 9.5 battalions per kilometer, 275-396 guns and mortars, and 30-91 tanks and self-propelled guns per kilometer of front. All of this enabled us to create an overwhelming superiority in men and materiel over the enemy along the breakthrough sector in the operational and tactical depth, namely: in infantry—9-11.4:1, in artillery and mortars—11.9-17.1:1, and in tanks and self-propelled guns—11-32:1 in favor of the Soviet troops.

---

6   Central Ministry of Defense Archives, fond 233, opis' 20897, delo 1, p. 293.

The plan for the artillery offensive[7] called for the creation of artillery groupings that would guarantee along the *front* shock group's 18-kilometer breakthrough sector (the left wing) a density of 170-220 guns and mortars per kilometer of front, not counting 45mm and 57mm guns. At the same time, army (long-range artillery, destruction artillery, breakthrough, and guards mortar units), corps and divisional artillery groups were created.

It was planned to conduct the artillery preparation for 100 minutes (20 minutes for the fire onslaught, 60 minutes for suppression and destruction, and 20 for a repeat fire onslaught).

It was planned to renew the offensive along the axes of the supporting attacks (right wing) following a short 20-30-minute artillery preparation, or following a 10-15 minute fire onslaught.

It was planned to support the infantry and tank attack along the main axis (left wing) by a double rolling barrage, in combination with a consecutive concentration of fire to a depth of up to two kilometers, and along the auxiliary axis—by the consecutive concentration of fire.

The plan for the artillery offensive called for employing the artillery upon detecting the enemy's planned withdrawal of his forces from the first position. The support of the mobile formation's commitment into the breach was also prepared.

The air offensive[8] was planned along the main axis and consisted of a preliminary air preparation and air support (escort) alone along the auxiliary axes. Given the our overwhelming superiority over the enemy in artillery and tanks along the breakthrough sector, and also for the purpose of preserving more air resources for the support (escort) period, immediate air support was not planned.

It was planned to carry out a preliminary air preparation on the night before the attack by the forces of two night bomber divisions in the 8th Guards and 47th armies' sectors, by launching raids against the enemy's headquarters, communications centers, strong points, communications lines, and airfields.

It was planned to carry out air support (escort) with the following tasks: suppressing the enemy's artillery, especially in the sector of the main forces' offensive (from H hour to H+50 minutes); disrupting the work of the enemy's headquarters and communications centers; preventing the enemy from occupying intermediate lines; destroying his personnel in concentration areas and preventing the arrival of his reserves from the depth; supporting the 47th and 69th armies with an air division apiece, and; the 8th Guards Army with an air assault corps (from H hour to H+3 hours).

It was planned to employ the 6th Air Army's main fighter and air assault forces to secure the commitment of the *front's* mobile groups into the breach. It was also planned to reliably cover them from the air, both in their jumping-off positions and at the moment of their commitment into the breach.

With the commitment of the *front's* mobile groups into the breach it was planned to support the 2nd Tank Army with a single assault air corps, and the 2nd and 7th guards cavalry corps with a single assault air division apiece.

The intensity of the air force's work was planned for each day within the falling boundaries: for fighter and assault aviation—3-3.5 sorties, for night bomber aviation—2-4, and day bombers—1-2 sorties per day.

However, the plan for the air offensive did not reflect to the necessary degree the questions of cooperation between the 16th and 6th air armies by the operation's days; nor did it call for cooperation with the neighboring Second Belorussian and First Ukrainian fronts' air armies.

---

7 Central Ministry of Defense Archives, fond 233, opis' 20992, delo 3, and opis' 21170, delo 1.
8 Central Ministry of Defense Archives, fond 233, opis' 12151, delo 4. Plans for the combat employment of the 6th Air Army.

It should be noted that during the operation Long-Range Aviation had the task of continuing to launch night raids against the enemy's forces and to subject to attack the railroad junctions and stations at Bialystok, Dragoczin, Wlodawa, Siedlce, Deblin, and Praga (Warsaw).

The partisan formations of the Brest and Bialystok oblasts had their previously-issued assignments confirmed and refined by the *front's* military council. It was demanded that they: deprive the enemy of the capability of regrouping his forces and remove freight to the west; to intensify the struggle to preserve industrial buildings, particularly in Brest, towns and inhabited locales against destruction by the enemy, as well as to prevent the extermination and expulsion of the population to Germany.

The partisans of the newly-liberated areas were assigned the task of clearing the woods and swamps of individual enemy groups that had scattered and were hiding in them.

Given the operation's overall depth of 150-170 kilometers and its planned duration of 14 days, the offensive's average daily rate of advance was set at 10.7-12.2 kilometers.

The beginning of the attack by the *front's* right-wing forces was set for 17 July, while the left wing, due to delays in moving up the artillery to their firing positions, was to attack on 18 July.

On the whole, the decision by the *front* commander corresponded to the specific situation and the task assigned to the *front*. This decision guaranteed the following: the breakthrough of the enemy's defense simultaneously along several axes, the augmentation of the attacks' strength during the operation, and the defeat of the enemy's Brest and Lublin groups of forces.

The armies' operational formation was in a single echelon, with reserves—combined arms (rifle divisions), artillery and anti-tank (from 1-2 anti-tank battalions to two anti-tank artillery brigades), engineer (1-2 engineer-sapper battalions), and others, as well as artillery groups and mobile obstacle detachments of various size. Only in the 18th and 65th armies on the *front's* right wing was the operational formation in two echelons, which was occasioned by the necessity of securing the troops against possible enemy attacks from the north.

The regrouping of the *front's* forces for conducting the Brest—Siedlce offensive operation unfolded in an original manner. While the *front* was conducting one offensive operation after another with its right-wing forces, it was carrying out complex regroupings of men and materiel along its left flank, for the purpose of creating a powerful shock group here.

All regroupings and movements of troops to their jumping-off positions were mainly carried out at night. For example, during 6-12 July the 8th Guards Army[9] reached its jumping-off position in night marches and during the nights of 12-13 and 13-14 July relieved units of the 125th and 91st guards corps (47th and 69th armies) in the sector set aside for it by the operational plan. In the remaining first-echelon armies the movement of the troops and their occupation of their jumping-off positions were carried out during 13-16 July. At the same time, the 47th Army's main forces were regrouped to its left flank, and in the 69th Army to the right flank, and in the 70th Army to the left flank and center. The 2nd Tank Army and the 2nd and 7th guards cavalry corps reached their jumping-off positions in the night of 16-17 July.

Simultaneous with these movements by the *front's* left-wing armies and formations the main mass of the *front's* reinforcement artillery was regrouped from the right to the left wing at a distance of 480-650 kilometers (see table 18).

However, the artillery's delay in getting into its firing positions caused the attack along the *front's* left wing to be moved from 17 to 18 July.

Command and control, cover, road and material support, as well as the headquarters commandant's service were carried out in a centralized fashion at the *front* and army level.

---

9   The 8th Guards and 2nd Tank armies arrived at the First Belorussian Front from the Third and Second Ukrainian fronts in the second half of June 1944.

At the same time, according to the *Stavka* plan, a regrouping of air formations and units to the 6th Air Army, which was designated to support the operations of the *front's* left-wing forces, was carried out. For example, by 5 July the 13th Fighter and 6th Assault Air Corps and the 2nd Night Bomber Division had arrived from the Odessa, Khar'kov and Kiev military districts.

The *front's* 16th Air Army transferred the 6th Mixed and 3rd Bomber corps, the 242nd Night Bomber, 299th Assault Air and 1st Guards Fighter division to the 6th Air Army.

Thanks to this measure, the 6th Air Army was transformed from a comparatively small to a powerful major air formation.

As a result of regrouping, the 8th Guards Army was inserted into the first echelon along a 9-kilometer sector in the left wing's sector along the axis of the *front's* main attack. Due to this and the rolling up of the defense along the boundary with the First Ukrainian Front, the width of this wing's other armies' sectors shrank as follows: 47th Army—to 21 kilometers, and in the 69th Army—to 32 kilometers. Both of the 70th Army's rifle corps occupied their jumping-off positions along a 56-kilometer sector of the entire army's 120-kilometer sector, while the remaining sector was covered by the 3rd Army Sniper Battalion and subunits made up of junior lieutenants' courses. However, the main forces were concentrated along the left flank and in the center along a 20-kilometer sector. The 2nd Tank Army received the 8th Guards Tank Corps from the Polish 1st Army, and the 8th Guards Army received the 11th Tank Corps.

The strength of the First Belorussian Front's forces is shown in table 19.

Table 18. Artillery Regroupings from the First Belorussian Front's Right Wing to its Left Wing, 23 June-17 July 1944

Formations and Units	To What Army or *Front* Reserve	From What Army or *Front* Reserve	Means of Movement	Distance (in kilometers)
30th Gds Corps Artillery Bde	47th Army	65th Army	Railroad	480
1091st Artillery Rgt	47th Army	3rd Army	Railroad	480
94th Rocket Artillery Rgt	47th Army	3rd Army	Own power	650
5th and 12th breakthrough artillery divs (4th Breakthrough Artillery Corps	8th Gds Army	28th Army	Railroad	480
5th Rocket Artillery Div	8th Gds Army	65th Army	Own power	560
4th Corps Artillery Bde	8th Gds Army	65th Army	Railroad	480
41st Anti-Tank Bde	8th Gds Army	3rd Army	Own power	650
122nd High Power Howitzer Bde	8th Gds Army	3rd Army	Railroad	480
43rd Gds Artillery Bde	8th Gds Army	*Front* reserve	Railroad	480
31st Anti-Aircraft Div	8th Gds Army	*Front* reserve	Railroad	480
315th and 317th high-power artillery bns	8th Gds Army	65th Army	Railroad	480
295th Gds Corps Artillery Rgt	8th Gds Army	3rd Army	Railroad	480
6th and 92nd rocket artillery rgts	8th Gds Army	*Front* reserve	Own power	650
1070th Anti-Tank Rgt	8th Gds Army	*Front* reserve	Own power	650
35th Rocket Artillery and 125th High Power Artillery bdes	69th Army	3rd Army	Railroad	480
56th Rocket Artillery Rgt (35th Rocket Artillery Bde)	69th Army	3rd Army	Own power	650
62nd Breakthrough Artillery Bde	69th Army	*Front* reserve	Railroad	480
4th and 6th Balloon bns	*Front* reserve	*Front* reserve	Railroad	480

Table 19. The First Belorussian Front's Strength by the Start of the Brest—Siedlce Operation of 1944[10]

| Armies and Formations | Right Wing | | Rifle Division Rank and File Strength (in %) |
| | Tank and Self-Propelled Gun Strength (in %) | | |
	Combat-Ready	Undergoing Repairs	
48th Army	30.3	34.9	85.8
65th Army	77.1	8.6	69.4
28th Army	55.6	20.6	78.0
61st Army	–	–	63.7
4th Gds Cavalry Corps	22.6	35.5	–
1st Mechanized Corps	43.2	7.5	–
1st Gds Tank Corps	39.1	0.4	–
9th Tank Corps	16.3	47.4	–
Total	40.6	22.1	74.2
Left Wing			
70th Army	–	–	86.3
47th Army	85.7	–	76.7
8th Gds Army	95.3	–	95.5
69th Army	75.4	–	79.6
2nd Tank Army	97.2	–	–
11th Tank Corps	71.6	–	–
11th Gds Tank Bde	12.3	–	–
2nd Gds Cavalry Corps	100	–	–
7th Gds Cavalry Corps	100	–	–
Right Wing			
Total	97.7	–	84.5
Total for the *Front*	61.5	–	79.4

The *front's* forces' level of supply with all types of material-technical equipment, particularly ammunition and fuel and lubricants, was linked to a series of difficulties. These difficulties were caused by the division in the jumping-off position in the offensive sectors of the *front's* wings by the huge wooded and swampy expanses of the Poles'ye and the Pinsk Oblast', the right wing's uninterrupted offensive, and the serious lag in the restoration of the railroad network. Thus the *front* regulating station, the army supply stations and bases for the *front's* right wing were located in areas assigned to them by the start of the Belorussian operation, while the *front* depots in the open air were located as follows: the artillery depot was in Slutsk and that for fuels and lubricants in Bobruisk.

It was only on 15 July that rail traffic was opened along the following sections: Zhlobin—Bobruisk—the 95 kilometer passing track (before the railroad bridge near Slutsk), and from Manevichi station to Kovel' station, and on 16 July from Kalinkovichi station to Korzhevka station (50 kilometers from the latter).

---

10 Central Ministry of Defense Archives, fond 233, opis' 11866, delo 11, pp. 149, 275, 344-58, 390, 416, 485-504. The authorized strength of a rifle division was 7,119 men. Fond 233, opis' 20521, delo 1, p. 145.

The restoration of these railroad sections enabled us to significantly decrease the ground transportation section. But the latter, as before, was large and reached 260 kilometers along the right wing, that is, it was the same as at the start of the Baranovichi—Slonim offensive operation. Upon the liberation of the Kovel' salient enemy the supply of the right-wing forces was additionally organized from the right wing of the Kovel' axis. For this, as early as 13-14 July trains with fuel and ammunition were transferred from Gomel' and Kalinkovichi to the Kovel' axis. A part of the *front* auto transport, which was located on the roads between Bobruisk and Baranovichi, was moved to the Kovel' area.

It should be noted that the cavalry-mechanized group, which was very short of fuel, received 270 tons of fuel at Baranovichi by plane during 15-22 July.

By the start of the operation the *front's* left-wing forces' rear organs were extended normally.

The *front* commander ordered that by the start of the operation the following supplies be created for the shock group: five combat loads of artillery shells and five refills of fuel and lubricants.

The factual presence of ammunition and fuels and lubricants in the armies by the start of the operation consisted of 2-4 combat loads and 3-4 refills of fuel, but the amount of these materials actually among the troops was significantly less in the majority of armies. However, it should be kept in mind that the shock group's armies should have received an additional 1-2 combat loads of shells from the right-wing army bases at the expense of those shells still on the way to the front, while the *front's* cavalry-mechanized group's poor state of fuel supply was to be covered by deliveries by air.

In summation, the supplies of ammunition and fuels and lubricants available with the *front*, as well as those on their way, covered the conduct of a new major *front* operation. However, the difficulty of delivering ammunition and fuel for the *front's* right-wing forces remained as before. This difficulty could have arisen in the *front's* left-wing forces as well, because the rate of restoring the railroads and railroad bridges over the rivers remained obviously insufficient.

Thus the preparation of the First Belorussian Front's Brest—Siedlce offensive operation had been fully completed by its start. The *front's* forces, having carried out a complex regrouping, occupied their jumping-off positions along the left wing and were ready on the morning of 18 July to launch a powerful attack against the enemy west of Kovel'. Along the *front's* right-wing sector, without ceasing combat and simultaneously carrying out a regrouping to arrive in their new sectors, the troops were ready to launch a supporting attack against the enemy toward the left-wing's forces.

The Operation's First Stage

The Breakthrough of the Enemy's Defense and the Arrival at the line of the Western Bug River (17-20 July)

The armies of the *front's* main shock group (along its left wing) went over to the offensive on 18 July.

The combined-arms armies' attack was preceded on the night of 17-18 July by a preliminary air preparation, for the purpose of suppressing the enemy's artillery in their firing positions, the destruction of his personnel and equipment in the defense's main zone along the breakthrough sector, and preventing the arrival of the enemy's reserves to the front line. The latter task was carried out by launching bombing raids against Lyuboml', Chelm and Wlodawa stations.

At 0530 on 18 July, following a 30-minute artillery preparation, the forward battalions' and regiments'[11] attacked, and their combat actions enabled us to determine that the enemy had with-

---

11 These forces consisted of the following: in the 47th Army, a battalion each from the 125th and 129th rifle corps and a regiment from the 77th Rifle Corps; in the 8th Guards Army, a regiment each from the 29th and

drawn his combat formations and was determined to fall back on the next defensive line on the night of 18-19 July.

Advancing successfully, the forward battalions occupied the first and, in places, the second trench line during the first 90 minutes and thus carried out their tasks and created favorable conditions for the attack by the main forces of the *front's* first echelon.

At 0700 on July 18, using and developing the success of the forward battalions, the main forces of the *front's* shock group (47th, 8th Guards and 69th armies) attacked and the planned 110-minute artillery preparation was cancelled.

The artillery support for the infantry and tank attack was carried out as planned, through a double rolling barrage in combination with successive concentrations of fire.

During the breakthrough an assault air division apiece was operationally subordinated to the commanders of the 47th and 69th armies, while an assault air corps was subordinated to the commander of the 8th Guards Army. These air formations, while closely cooperating with the infantry, launched raids against the enemy's artillery positions, troop concentrations and tanks.

Having suppressed the enemy's resistance, the 47th, 8th Guards and 69th armies broke through the enemy's main defensive zone and then, developing the offensive to the west, reached the enemy's second defensive zone along the Vyzhuvka River, and broke into this from the march in the Khvorostuv area.

The 70th Army along the *front's* left wing, employing the 61st Army's success, began attacking with its 114th Rifle Corps on the morning of 17 July in the direction of Rechitsa and Divin and, having broken the resistance of the Hungarian 12th Reserve Division, by the close of 18 July had reached the line Lelikov—Duby—Zamosh'ye.

The First Ukrainian Front on the left was engaged in heavy fighting with its right-flank 3rd Guards Army on the near approaches to the town of Vladimir-Volynskii.

Thus by the close of 18 July the *front's* main group of forces had broken through the enemy's main defensive zone, had begun fighting for the second defensive zone and had expanded the breakthrough to a width of 30 kilometers and a depth of 11-14 kilometers.

The rapid arrival of the *front's* main shock group at the enemy's second defensive zone prevented the latter from occupying it in an organized fashion and forced him to begin withdrawing parts of his forces to the army zone along the Western Bug River, which had not been previously occupied.

On 19 July the *front's* main shock group, having taken advantage of the partial piercing of the enemy's second defensive zone, upon seizing a bridgehead over the Vyzhuvka River near Khvorostuv, continued to attack. By the middle of the day it had completely broken through the second defensive zone, and by the end of the day, pursuing the retreating enemy, captured the towns of Golovno, Lyuboml' and reached the line Lyubokhiny—Gumentsy—Zapol'ye—Pisarev—Volya.

To the right, the 70th Army, by taking advantage of the *front's* shock group, attacked with its center and left flank toward Zabolot'ye and Lyubokhiny, and with its right flank pursued the enemy, who was retreating to the west along the road to Brest, with the task, in conjunction with the *front's* right-wing forces, of encircling and destroying the enemy's Brest group of forces and capturing the town of Brest. By the end of the day the army had broken through both the enemy's main and second defensive zones and captured the towns of Mokrany, Zabolot'ye, Lyubokhiny and the line Godyn'—Osowa—Draguny—Gornyaki—Zabolot'ye—Izna—Lyubokhiny.

The *front's* air force, despite the unfavorable meteorological conditions, actively supported our forces, uninterruptedly launching raids against the combat formations of the enemy's retreating forces, as well as against the crossings over the Western Bug River along the Opalin—Dubenka

---

4th guards rifle corps and a battalion from the 28th Guards Rifle Corps, and; in the 69th Army, a battalion from the 91st Rifle Corps.

sector. Long- Range Aviation continued to attack the railroad junctions and stations of Wlodawa, Siedlce and Praga (a suburb of Warsaw), disrupting the enemy's railroad shipments and preventing the arrival of his reserves from the depth.

By this time the First Ukrainian Front's 3rd Guards Army's right flank continued to attack toward Vladimir-Volynskii and reached the line Verba—Khabultov.

As a result of the fighting on 19 July, the *front's* main shock group, together with the 70th Army, having crushed the enemy's resistance, completed the breakthrough of his tactical defensive zone and then vigorously pursued the retreating enemy to the army defensive zone, which ran along the western bank of the Western Bug River, having advanced 20-25 kilometers that day. The *front's* air force carried out 1,655 sorties along the left wing alone on 18-19 July. 26 enemy planes were shot down in air battles.

Thus the forces of the *front's* left wing had broadened the breakthrough of the enemy's defense to 40 kilometers in depth and up to 120 kilometers in breadth. At the same time, the armies' daily offensive speed reached the following: 22-25 kilometers in the 47th Army; 20-23 kilometers in the 8th Guards Army; 15-23 kilometers in the 69th Army, and; 16-20 kilometers in the 70th Army, thus exceeding the planned offensive speed of 17.5 kilometers.

All of this created favorable conditions for developing the success of the *front's* left-wing forces in the operational depth.

The successful offensive by the main shock group enabled the *front* commander to refrain from committing the 2nd Tank Army into the breach on 19 July. However, for the purpose of seizing crossings over the Western Bug River from the march, it was planned to commit the 2nd Guards Cavalry Corps into the breach on the following day. It should be noted that for this purpose, on 19 July the 8th Guards Army's mobile group—the 11th Tank Corps—had been committed into the breach from the line Podgorodno—Mashev.

On 20 July the *front's* left-wing forces, particularly the *front's* shock group, while pursuing the retreating enemy and repelling his numerous counterattacks, was vigorously advancing to the enemy's army defensive zone along the Western Bug River. Moreover, the mobile formations of the 8th Guards Army (11th Tank Corps) and the *front* (2nd Guards Cavalry Corps) were used for the purpose of seizing crossings over the river from the march.

By dawn on 20 July the 2nd Guards Cavalry Corps, having entered the breach in the 47th Army's sector, by 1030 had reached the Western Bug River with its main forces, and as early as 1600 its forward detachments had forced the river on the materials at hand in the Zabuzh'ye area and seized a bridgehead. By the close of the day the corps had expanded the bridgehead to a depth of six kilometers and up to 13 kilometers in width.

At the same time, the 11th Tank Corps, having reached the Western Bug River, seized a usable crossing over the river from the march in the Opalin area, forced it and also captured a bridgehead.

The *front's* main shock group, taking advantage of the success of the mobile groups and relentlessly pursuing the retreating enemy, reached the Western Bug River, and with part of its forces forced the river from the march, seized four bridgeheads, and by the close of 20 July its armies were fighting along the following line: 47th Army—excluding Zalesie—Grabowo—Zabuzh'ye; 8th Guards Army—excluding Zabuzh'ye—excluding Volchii Perevoz, and; 69th Army—Volchii Perevoz—Gusynne—the eastern outskirts of Dubenka—Bystraki—excluding Korytnitsa.

The 70th Army, encountering insignificant enemy resistance, captured the towns of Maloryta and Krymno and Shatsk and reached the line eastern outskirts of Velikoryta—Zburazh—Pishcha—Zalesie.

The 2nd Tank Army began to move toward the west at 1700 on 20 July, in readiness to enter the breach from the seized bridgeheads along the western bank of the Western Bug River, in order to develop the success throughout the operation's entire depth.

The 6th Air Army supported our forces' combat operations, covered the commitment of the mobile groups into the breach, and launched bombing and strafing raids against the enemy along the crossings over the Western Bug River.

The First Ukrainian Front's 3rd Guards Army[12] captured the important rail and road junction and major town of Vladimir-Volynskii, and by the close of the day had reached the boundary between the USSR and Poland along the Western Bug River south of Korytnitsa.

Thus the forces of the *front's* main shock group forced the Western Bug River on 20 July along four sectors and broke through the army defensive zone along a total frontage of 25-30 kilometers. In this way the enemy was preempted in occupying a defense along the Western Bug River, and was deprived of the ability to halt our offensive along this line and was forced to fall back further to the west. The 70th Army, having opened up an offensive along its entire 106-kilometer sector, achieved no lesser results. On this day the *front's* left-wing forces expanded their breakthrough to 60 kilometers in depth and 140 in width, having advanced with its armies the following distances: 70th Army—20-28 kilometers; 47th Army—18-26 kilometers; 8th Guards Army—18-26 kilometers, and; the 69th Army—8-12 kilometers.

Thus the *front's* left-wing armies had basically carried out the *front's* immediate task a day earlier than called for.

At the same time, the advance by the *front's* main shock group to the army defensive zone along the Western Bug River had been factually begun as early as the second half of 19 July and carried out in the forces' original operational formation.

Of the *front's* mobile forces along its left wing, only the 2nd Guards Cavalry Corps was employed for developing the success after the breakthrough of the defense's tactical depth, and which was committed into the breach at the beginning of the offensive's third day by the *front's* main shock group. The task of capturing on the march bridgeheads over the Western Bug River was accomplished by this corps, in conjunction with the 8th Guards Army's mobile group (11th Tank Corps) and the mobile forward detachments of the combined-arms armies, which was justified in the given situation.

Thus the *front* commander correctly decided to commit the 2nd Tank Army and the 7th Guards Cavalry Corps into the breach from the bridgeheads along the western bank of the Western Bug River for developing the success throughout the operation's entire depth. This decision was also conditioned by the fact that the enemy's defense along the Western Bug River represented a powerful line inaccessible to tanks, and the fact that we needed to carry out major preliminary engineering measures in order to restore the roads and bridges in the liberated territory to the east of the Western Bug River.

The nearly complete absence by 18 July of enemy reserves in the immediate operational defensive depth, which could have reinforced the resistance of his first-echelon forces along the *front's* left wing and, chiefly, the catastrophic situation of the German-Fascist troops in Belorussia and western Ukraine, forced the Hitlerite command to make the decision to withdraw his group of forces to the west of Kovel' to a previously-prepared army defensive zone along the Western Bug River.

The enemy's plan for the timely withdrawal of his main forces to this line was foiled by the offensive by the *front's* main shock group along the left wing. This forced the German-Fascist command to organize the withdrawal of its forces under the direct attack of our advancing forces.

No less than a third of all his forces were set aside for rearguards. The infantry covering units and subunits were reinforced with tanks, assault guns and mortars and, where it was possible, was supported by auto transport.

---

12 Central Ministry of Defense Archives, fond First Ukrainian Front, opis' 20106, delo 1.

The enemy's main forces, in order to avoid attacks by our aviation, usually began their retreat upon the onset of darkness. Before the main forces began to retreat, the enemy would intensify his artillery fire, attempting in this fashion to create the impression that he was continuing to defend along the line being abandoned. Sometimes local counterattacks, up to a battalion in strength and with up to 25 tanks and 45 planes, were undertaken for this purpose, as was the case, for example, in the 47th Army's sector.

While retreating, intermediate lines were chosen at a distance of 10-15 kilometers from each other. For this, rivers were predominantly employed, which flowed north-south, or swampy terrain sectors.

The main mass of the artillery was usually withdrawn at the same time as the infantry formations' main forces, while fire along the intermediate lines was carried out in short 3-5-minute fire onslaughts.

The enemy, in order to cover important objectives and axes, would lay down minefields and individual mines of 5-10 mines every 40-50 meters. Roads and communications lines were put out of action.

All of this gave the enemy the opportunity to somewhat delay our forces' offensive, but it could not halt their successful advance.

In the sector of the *front's* right-wing armies along the axes of the supporting attacks, military events during the operation's first stage unfolded in the following manner.

At the same time as the First Belorussian Front's shock group (left wing) was completing its preparations for the offensive on 18 July, the armies along the *front's* right wing resumed their attack on the morning of 17 July, following a 15-20 minute fire onslaught.

The 48th Army attacked in the direction of Shimki and Narev, and the 65th Army in the direction of Velovezha, Gainovka and Bielsk-Podlaski. Having crushed the enemy's resistance and pursuing his armies in conjunction with the 2nd Belorussian Front's 3rd Army, these armies captured the important road and railroad junctions and towns of Svisloch' and Gainovka, and by the close of 18 July had reached the following lines: 48th Army—Jalowka—Cisowka—Plyanta, and the 65th Army—Kotuvka—Gainovka—Voinuvka.

The cavalry-mechanized group and the 28th Army launched their main attack around the town of Brest from the north toward Kamenets and Wysokoe, and the 61st Army toward Brest from the east and northeast.

The cavalry-mechanized group, despite strong enemy resistance, broke through with its 4th Guards Cavalry Corps toward the town of Vidomlya and on 17 July, and the next day, having forced the Lesnaya River, in a bold leap in the direction of Janow-Podlaski around the Brest fortified area from the north and northwest, reached the Western Bug River along the sector Velichkovichi—Rudavets, cutting the Bialystok—Brest railroad and begun fighting for the crossings.

The 9th Tank and 1st Mechanized corps, having encountered fierce resistance by the 102nd Infantry Division and the newly-committed (from Brest) Hungarian 5th Reserve Division, could not break through: the 9th Tank Corps to the 4th Guards Cavalry Corps, and the 1st Mechanized Corps to the Kobrin area, for the purpose of cutting off the enemy's Pinsk group of forces' path of retreat to Brest.

The 28th Army, taking advantage of the success by the 65th Army's left flank and that of the *front's* cavalry-mechanized group, continued to attack and by the close of 17 July had advanced 25 kilometers, having thus reduced the gap between it and the 65th Army to 16 kilometers.

The 61st Army had almost completely reached the 28th Army, securing its flank against enemy attacks from the south.

The 28th Army, beating off numerous enemy counterattacks, by the close of 18 July had forced the Lesnaya River east of Dmitrovichi and reached the line Pashuki—Krivlyany—excluding Zasimy.

The 61st Army, having captured the town of Antopol', advanced more than 50 kilometers and had completely reached the Mukhavets River and the Dnepr-Bug Canal and reached the front of the 28th Army and the near approaches to the important rail and road junction and strong hold on the road to Brest—Kobrin.

The Second Belorussian Front on the right, repelling with its right flank the German-Fascist *Totenkopf* Panzer Division, continued to slowly attack with its left-flank 3rd Army in the direction of Bialystok, reached the Svisloch' River and began fighting for that line.

From 19 July especially fierce fighting broke out along the First Belorussian Front's right flank along the approaches to Brest and Bielsk-Podlaski. The enemy exerted all his efforts here and continuously carried out regroupings to the most threatened sectors for the purpose, evidently, of halting our offensive, winning time for pulling back his group of forces defending west of Kovel' and Pinsk to the army defensive zone along the Western Bug River, with the powerful Brest fortified area, as well as for the purpose of bringing up reserves from the deep rear to occupying the rear defensive zone around Warsaw and the Vistula River.

As a result of these regroupings, the enemy concentrated his main efforts in the Kamenets area against the 28th Army and the *front's* cavalry-mechanized group.

In this situation, the *front* commander, while trying to support the successful offensive by the *front's* main shock group west of Kovel', decided to employ the 65th Army's growing success along the right wing in order to bring as quickly as possible the main forces of the 65th and 28th armies and the cavalry-mechanized group to the line of the Western Bug River and to encircle the enemy's Brest group of forces, in conjunction with the *front's* left-wing forces.

On 19 July the *front's* right-wing armies continued to engage in stubborn fighting with the enemy and advanced insignificantly. At the same time, they carried out a regrouping for the purpose of creating denser combat formations along the main axes.

The 4th Guards Cavalry Corps was involved in the heaviest fighting in the enemy's rear along the Western Bug River, northeast of Janow-Podlaski, 50 kilometers from its armies. The corps even managed to seize a bridgehead along the river's southern bank with two forward detachments, but under pressure from significantly superior enemy forces these detachments were pulled back to the northern bank, where fierce fighting continued. The corps was in a difficult situation, supply deliveries had ended, and a lack of ammunition and fuel began to be felt.

In trying to link up with the 4th Guards Cavalry Corps, the *front's* right-wing forces intensified their attacks.

The 65th Army achieved the greatest successes. Having committed its second echelon (80th Rifle Corps) into the battle along its left flank, the army advanced vigorously to the southwest and by the close of 21 July reached the Western Bug River in the area southwest of Siemiatycze. Having encountered the enemy's significantly increased resistance, particularly along the flanks from the direction of Bielsk-Podlaski and in the area of Czeremcha station, the army was engaged in heavy fighting. During the offensive the army captured the major road junctions—the towns of Kleszczele and Semyatiche, and the important railroad junction and town of Czeremcha. The 65th Army's forward detachments forced the Western Bug River from the march southwest of Siemiatycze and seized a bridgehead up to four kilometers deep and nine kilometers wide.

The 28th Army, with the 1st Mechanized and 9th Tank corps, launched its main attack along the right flank to the southwest in the general direction of Vidomlya, Dem'yanchitsy and Zaczopki. Having encountered the enemy's stubborn resistance and beating off unceasing counterattacks over three days (19-21 July), it advanced slowly forward. Only with the commitment of the army's second echelon (20th Rifle Corps) into the battle in the direction of the railroad to Brest along the army's left flank during the second half of 20 July, did the offensive speed up a bit and the opposing enemy units began to withdrawn toward Brest.

However, the 28th Army did not reach the Western Bug River, while the 1st Mechanized and 9th Tank corps did not break through to the 4th Guards Cavalry Corps, the condition of which worsened even more.

By this time the enemy had concentrated two groups of forces along the 65th Army's flanks and on the morning of 22 July attacked. He showed the greatest activity along the army's left flank, where the counterattacks followed one after the other, and at 1700 up to two infantry regiments from the 35th and 292nd infantry divisions and up to 85 tanks and assault guns from the "Viking" SS Panzer Division, launched an attack from the area northwest of Wysokoe in the direction of Kleszczele. Suffering heavy casualties, part of the enemy's tank forces broke through to the railroad eight kilometers southwest of Czeremcha, but were halted. The 65th Army, while beating off the counterattacks, was consolidating and improving its situation along the line Botski—Siemiatycze—Mel'nik—Bushmitsa and was pulling out formations of the 18th Rifle Corps to the Kleszczele area, along the likely axis of the enemy's counterblow.

The 28th Army, along with the 1st Mechanized and 9th Tank corps, by the close of 22 July had reached the line excluding Bushmitsa—Zamosty—Omelinka—Jamnow.

The 48th Army, which was attacking along an auxiliary axis toward Bielsk-Podlaski, crushed the opposing enemy's resistance and by the close of 22 July had reached the near approaches to that town.

The 61st Army, launching its main attack with its right flank in the general direction of Strigovo and Chernavchitsi and employing the success by the 28th Army's left flank, broke through the enemy's defense along the Mukhavets River and on July 20 captured the major rail and road junction of Kobrin.

From the second half of 20 July the army was pulled into the *Stavka* reserve.

However, due to the enemy's stubborn resistance, the commander of the First Belorussian Front was authorized to temporarily use the 61st Army's 9th Guards Rifle Corps to aid the 28th and 70th armies in capturing Brest.

The Second Belorussian Front's 3rd Army on the right forced the Svisloch' River and captured the major strong point of Krynki.

Thus the *front's* right-wing forces broke through the enemy's defensive lines along the Right Lesnaya River and the Lesnaya north of Kamenets, and along the Mukhavets River, and the Dnepr-Bug Canal; captured the important road and railroad junctions of Kleszczele, Cheremkha and Kobrin on the approaches to Brest, and a large number of such towns as Botski, Siemiatycze, and Kamenets. The 65th Army's deep penetration into the enemy's line and its arrival at the Western Bug River along the Siemiatycze—Mel'nik sector was the beginning of the encirclement of the enemy's major Brest group of forces with the formation of the internal and external encirclement fronts. The German-Fascist Second Army northwest of Brest had been split, and the Bialystok and Brest groups of forces belonging to Army Group Center had been divided. The enemy's position excluded the possibility of his reinforcing his forces in the sector of the *front's* shock group by transferring even a part of his forces from the sector of the *front's* right wing.

However, in the course of four days of heavy fighting, the *front's* right-wing forces, in light of the enemy's increased resistance, were not able to fully carry out its objectives, and the 4th Guards Cavalry Corps, as before, continued isolated in the enemy rear from our forces, engaged in heavy fighting with the enemy.

In four days of attacking the armies of the *front's* right wing advanced as follows: 48th Army—24-30 kilometers; 65th Army—20-60 kilometers; 28th Army—13-50 kilometers; 61st Army—16-20 kilometers; 1st Mechanized Corps—22 kilometers, and; the 9th Tank Corps—34 kilometers per day.

The 65th Army and the 1st Mechanized Corps advanced the fastest (from 10-30 kilometers per day). The reasons for the reduction in the rate of advance was due not only the growing enemy resistance, but and chiefly, the equal distribution of men and materiel along the front, as well as the lagging of the artillery and rear organs, because the railroad stage of delivery was the same as at the start of the operation. This means that the auto delivery leg increased another 50-70 kilometers and was 310-330 kilometers. Also, the width of the right-wing armies' front had increased as follows: in the 48th Army—from 20 to 32 kilometers; in the 65th Army—from 32 to 110 kilometers, and; in the 28th Army—from 60 to 65 kilometers.

On the whole, by the close of 20 July the forces of the First Belorussian Front had achieved their immediate task assigned them by the *Stavka* of the Supreme High Command a day earlier than planned, with an average daily rate of advance of 20 kilometers, instead of the planned 17.5 kilometers.

The *front's* forces attacked along a 340-kilometer sector and reached the USSR's boundary with allied Poland with their left flank along a 60-kilometer sector, and with their right flank along a 30-kilometer sector, and began combat operations against the German-Fascist forces on Polish territory.

The First Belorussian Front, upon reaching the Western Bug River northwest of Brest and south of Wlodawa, was now capable of beginning a maneuver to complete the encirclement of the enemy's Brest group of forces and vigorously developing the pursuit of the enemy falling back to the Vistula River.

At the same time, it should be noted that the offensive pace by the *front's* right-wing forces was less than along the left wing, but significantly less than had been planned.

The Operation's Second Stage

The Development of the Success in the Operational Depth and the Front's Arrival at the Warsaw Suburb of Praga and the Vistula River (21 July-2 August)

By the middle of July the political and strategic situation became sharply more exacerbated in allied Poland, where, in expectation of the arrival of Soviet troops on Polish territory, a fierce battle broke out between the forces of democracy, on one hand, and the forces of Polish and international reaction, on the other.

The forces of Polish reaction, led by the Polish émigré government in London, obediently carrying out the will of the Anglo-American imperialists and conducting negotiations behind the scenes with the Hitlerites, sought at any price, all the way to open provocations, to preserve the pro-fascist and anti-Soviet regime, which had existed in the country before the war. The underground Armia Kraiowa, under General Bor-Komarowski, was preparing for this goal.

The forces of democracy, which were supported by the overwhelming majority of the Polish people, were preparing to establish democratic freedoms in Poland. On 21 July 1944, at an underground session of the Kraiowa Rada Narodowa, in Warsaw, the decision was made to create the Polish Committee of National Liberation, which took upon itself the functions of a provisional government. It was then decided to unite the underground Armia Liudowa, which was supporting the forces of democracy, with the Polish 1st Army, which had been created by the Union of Polish Patriots in the USSR, into a unified Polish army. The city of Lublin, the first large Polish administrative center astride the attack route of the Soviet forces, was chosen as the seat of the Kraiowa Rada Narodowa, which had taken supreme power upon itself. Thus the liberation of this city from the Hitlerite occupiers would have major political and strategic significance.

On 21 July 1944 the Supreme Commander-in-Chief ordered the First Belorussian Front to capture Lublin no later than 26-27 July, for which purpose the 2nd Tank Army and 7th Guards

Cavalry Corps were to be chiefly employed. It was simultaneously pointed out that the political situation and interests of an independent and democratic Poland demanded this.[13]

In carrying out this directive, the *front* command formed a *front* mobile group, consisting of the 2nd Tank Army and the 7th Guards Cavalry Corps, which was given the assignment to enter the breach from the bridgeheads along the Western Bug River and, by launching an attack in the general direction of Lublin, to capture the city no later than 26 July.

The commanders of the 8th Guards and 69th armies were given the following tasks: taking advantage of the mobile group's success, the armies would attack as follows—the 8th Guards Army along the Petrikow—Wolia-Wereszinska axis, and the 69th Army along the Chelm—Siedlce axis and assist the mobile group in capturing Lublin, and by the close of 23 July reach the line: excluding Zamolodycze—Wolia-Wereszinska—Severynow and Kulik—Reewec—Selec—Busno.[14]

The *front's* second echelon—the Polish 1st Army—was to move up behind the 69th Army, simultaneously securing the flank and rear of the *front's* main shock group and its boundary with the First Ukrainian Front's 3rd Guards Army to the left.

This decision sharply altered the direction of the *front's* main shock group from Siedlce to Lublin. Instead of one army, four were now directed along the Lublin axis, including one tank army (8th Guards, 69th, 2nd Tank, and Polish 1st armies).

At the same time, the forces of the 47th Army and the newly-formed (from 22 July) cavalry-mechanized group, consisting of the 2nd Guards Cavalry and 11th Tank corps, were to launch a second attack in the general direction of Siedlce, that is, with the same strength as was originally planned against the city of Lublin. This was, in effect, a mutual shift in the power of the attacks.

The 47th Army was required to attack in the direction of Wlodawa, Czukow and Mosty over three days and by the close of 23 July capture the line Zachrukocze—Mosty—Zamolodycze.[15]

All of this gives us an extremely clear and instructive example of subordinating the operational plan to the interests of politics and strategy. The narrow operational considerations in the confines of a *front* operation, as such, demanded the launching of the *front's* attack to the northwest, which would enable us to encircle and destroy the enemy's Brest group of forces as quickly as possible. However, the political and strategic situation demanded at this stage of the operation a change in the direction of the *front's* main attack from the northwest to the west. Such a decision was the single correct and expedient one in the developing situation, all the more so as it subsequently enabled us to carry out a deeper flanking maneuver from the Lublin to the Warsaw direction.

During the night and daylight hours of 21 July the first echelon of the *front's* main shock group continued to force the Western Bug River and to broaden the bridgeheads seized the previous evening. Moreover, the formations that had been forcing the river did not stay in place, but rather moved forward, especially the mobile groups. As a result, by the close of the day the individual bridgeheads had been united into a single overall bridgehead 50-55 kilometers wide and 10-25 kilometers deep. On the following day the *front's* main shock group completed forcing the Western Bug River with all its first-echelon forces and, having expanded the bridgehead to 120 kilometers wide and 40-60 kilometers deep, was supporting the crossing of the 2nd Tank Army over the Western Bug River in the Opalin area during 21-22 July. Simultaneously, the 47th Army and the 2nd Guards Cavalry Corps, and the 69th Army and the 7th Guards Cavalry Corps, captured the important road junctions and powerful strong points and large towns of Wlodawa and Chelm.

The enemy, having lost an important and powerful defensive line along the Western Bug River, continued to retreat to the west, putting up especially stubborn resistance in the 69th Army's

---

13 Central Ministry of Defense Archives, fond 233, opis' 20897, delo 2, coded telegram no. 220149.
14 Combat orders of the First Belorussian Front headquarters, nos. 00695/op and 00690/op.
15 Combat orders of the First Belorussian Front headquarters, nos. 00695/op and 00690/op.

zone, where he committed into the fighting the newly-arrived 17th Panzer Division and the 270th Assault Gun Brigade from the rear, as well as security units.

However, our forces, overcoming the enemy's resistance and repelling numerous counterattacks, increased their rate of attack.

The successful development of the offensive enabled us to advance the deadline for taking Lublin. Thus on 22 July the *front* commander demanded that the *front's* mobile group, consisting of the 2nd Tank Army and the 7th Guards Cavalry Corps, capture Lublin three days before the deadline; that is, by the close of 23 July.

Simultaneously, the *front* commander, due to the 69th Army lagging behind somewhat, pointed out to the 8th Guards Army's commander the necessity of more closely cooperating with the 2nd Tank Army.

In order to strengthen the Siedlce axis, the *front* commander on 22 July created a *front* cavalry-mechanized group, consisting of the 2nd Guards Cavalry and 11th Tank corps.

The *front's* cavalry-mechanized group had the task of attacking toward Parczew, Radzyn and Lukow, and by the close of 23 July to take Parczew; that is, to attack along the 2nd Tank Army's original axis.[16]

The *front's* mobile group (2nd Tank Army and 7th Guards Cavalry Corps) was committed into the breach on 22 July from the bridgehead along the western bank of the Western Bug River. Its first echelon's forward units passed through the 8th Guards Army's combat formations at 1100 along the line Swerszow—Wolia (a 10-12-kilometer front) and drove toward Lublin to outflank the city from the north, northwest and southwest.

By the close of 22 July the army's 8th Guards and 3rd tank corps had reached the Wieprz River and seized a bridgehead from the march, and on the following day, 23 July, along with the 8th Guards Army's 28th Guards Rifle Corps, captured the city of Lublin—an important enemy center of resistance along the way to Warsaw from the southeast and a major rail and road junction.

At the same time, the army's 16th Tank Corps, which had been committed into the fighting along with the 4th Guards Corps, forced the Wieprz River from the march north of Lublin and reached the line Lubartow—Nowy Dwor—Rudka Kozlowecka.

The 7th Guards Cavalry Corps reached the Kremiec area six kilometers southeast of Lublin.

At the same time, the *front's* newly-created cavalry-mechanized group (2nd Guards Cavalry and 11th Tank corps), vigorously developing the attack in the general direction of Siedlce, captured the towns of Parczew and Radzyn, powerful centers of resistance along the road to Warsaw, cutting the Brest—Lublin railroad.

The 47th, 8th Guards and 69th armies, taking advantage of the *front's* mobile groups, which were operating ahead of them, were vigorously developing their attack along the axes indicated by the *front* commander. However, the 8th Guards Army, due to the 69th Army's lagging behind, had to move beyond its boundaries with its left flank (28th Guards Rifle Corps) and operate along with the 2nd Tank Army toward Lublin.

By the close of 23 July the armies reached the following lines: 47th Army—Danze—Podewucze—Pszwloka; the 8th Guards Army—Stoczek—Lubartow—Lublin, having seized from the march bridgeheads over the Wieprz River, and; 69th Army—Selisze—Spas—Woliawce—Busno.

Thus in the course of three days (21-23 July) the *front's* main shock group completely broke through the last powerful defensive line along the Western Bug before Warsaw, upon which the German command had placed great hopes. Moreover, the main shock group had captured an important political center of allied Poland—Lublin, the temporary capital, and had more than

---

16 Combat orders of the First Belorussian Front headquarters, nos. 00706/op and 00710/op, of 22 July 1944.

carried out the objectives assigned by the *front*: the 47th Army by 12-16 kilometers; the 8th Guards Army by 30-45 kilometers, and the cavalry-mechanized group by 25 kilometers. Only the 69th Army, due to the enemy's increased resistance and the slow advance of its neighbor to the left, the First Ukrainian Front's 3rd Guards Army, did not carry out its mission and failed to reach the line indicated for it.

During this time the main shock group advanced as follows: the 47th Army by 52 kilometers; the 8th Guards Army by 80 kilometers, and; the 69th Army by 50-52 kilometers, at a pace of 17-27 kilometers per day, with the exception of individual units of the 69th Army, the offensive pace of which reached 7-17 kilometers per day.

The tank army and the *front's* cavalry-mechanized group attacked with a corresponding average pace of 27 and 35 kilometers per day.

The 70th Army developed its attack; no less successfully than the *front's* main shock group, in the general direction of Slawatycze and Tuczna. By the close of 23 July the army was fighting along the line Oczkin—Tuczna—Bakinska Panska—Czuki, having advanced 25-45 kilometers, at an average daily pace of 8-15 kilometers per day.

Our aviation, supporting the main shock group, during the course of three days of the offensive, carried out 1,645 sorties, of which 185 were at night, and 28 enemy planes were shot down in 19 air battles.

The forcing of the Western Bug River was conducted, as a rule, from the march, following short but powerful artillery fire onslaughts, organized at the division level, against the enemy's trenches and centers of resistance. The infantry attack while forcing the river was mainly supported by fire from guns allotted for firing over open sights, as well as by massed reinforcement artillery fire against centers of resistance and strong point in the depth.

The crossing of the artillery and tanks to the captured bridgeheads was carried out over intact bridges, newly built or captured from the enemy, as well as on available materials, pontoons, rafts, and sometimes over fords.

It should be noted that the crossing of the 2nd Tank Army to the western bank of the Western Bug River was conducted in relatively difficult conditions, because of five crossings set aside for the army, only three proved to be operable. Besides, the corps' command and control was disrupted during the crossing, because of its headquarters lagging behind and inaccurate planning. Thus the commander of the 2nd Tank Army had to take control of the crossing into his own hands.

Nor should one pass over in silence the absence of precise order along the roads in the troop and army rears. This was all the more so, as the wooded and swampy terrain to the east and west of the Western Bug River, and thus the limited road network, required a great deal of organizational ability from the troops in moving up the artillery, second echelons and mobile groups. Because of shortcomings in the traffic regulation service, traffic jams often formed on the roads and the artillery lagged behind. For example, on 22-23 July the 2nd Guards Cavalry's artillery fell behind the cavalry's combat formations in the 47th Army's sector by up to 30 kilometers. Only interference by the *front* commander, who demanded that order be established on the roads and that the passage of, first of all, artillery on mechanized tows and transports with ammunition, be organized, eliminated their lagging.

In subsequent days in the First Belorussian Front's attack sector a battle broke out, the objective of which was the encirclement and destruction of the enemy's Brest group of forces, as well as reaching the Vistula River and the seizing of crossings over it.

The *front* commander decided the following: to repel enemy counterattacks in strength up to five divisions (of which two were panzer divisions) northwest of Wysokoe and southeast of Bielsk-Podlaski, employing formations from the 48th and 65th armies and a corps from the 28th Army; to launch attacks along converging axes toward Zaczopki from the northeast with the main forces of the 28th Army, from the southeast with the 70th Army, and from the east with the 61st Army's 9th Guards Rifle Corps, to encircle and destroy the enemy's Brest group of forces; by reaching the Western Bug River with the formations of the 65th and 47th armies, to form an external encirclement front and exclude the possibility of the encircle group of forces in the Brest area being relieved; the *front's* remaining forces (8th Guards, 69th and 2nd Tank armies) were to reach the Vistula River and seize bridgeheads along its western bank, and; the forces of the *front's* cavalry-mechanized group (11th Tank and 2nd Guards Cavalry corps) were to continue a vigorous offensive in the general direction of Lukow, and with part of their forces on Mendzizec, and to cut the Brest—Siedlce railroad and road, and to subsequently advance on Siedlce.

In carrying out these assignments, the *front's* forces began to even more intensely continue their attack. Stubborn fighting broke out in the course of carrying out the encirclement of the enemy's Brest group of forces.

At the same time, intense fighting had been going on since 23 July, at first at the base of the 65th Army's salient in the area to the southeast of Bielsk-Podlaski and to the northwest of Wysokoe, and then at the salient's tip in the area of Semiatycze and Melnik. In the middle of the day on 23 July, the enemy made major counterattacks in the direction of Kleszczele with up to two infantry regiments and 50 tanks (5th Panzer Division) from the area of Bielsk, and up to two infantry regiments from the 35th and 292nd infantry divisions and 60 tanks ("Viking" 5th SS Panzer Division) from the area northwest of Wysokoe. At the price of heavy losses, the enemy managed to press back somewhat the 65th Army's forces and break through with a group of tank and infantry and reach the Wolka area, and another the area northwest of Czeremcha. The first group of tanks was stopped and could not advance further, while the second was surrounded and destroyed on 24 July (up to two infantry battalions and 20 tanks).

During the following two days (25-26 July) the enemy sought to eliminate the 65th Army's salient in the Siemiatycze area. During these days the enemy carried out ten counterattacks toward Kleszczele from the north from the Bielsk-Podlaski area, and from the south from the area north and northwest of Wysokoe, and from the southwest from the area southeast of Siemiatycze. These counterattacks from all directions were carried out, as a rule, simultaneously from different narrow sectors, but in the same direction. The enemy's counterattacks were conducted in strength from a reinforced infantry battalion, with 20-30 tanks, to a reinforced infantry division. For example, the German-Fascist 541st Infantry Division, which had arrived on 23 July from Germany, forced the Western Bug River in the area of the railroad bridge southeast of Siemiatycze, and only 25-26 July counterattacked our troops twice along the railroad. As early as 24 July the 65th Army, having carried out a partial regrouping of its forces, strengthened its combat formations near Bielsk-Podlaski and south of Kleszczele, and with air support from the 16th Air Army, beat off all the enemy's counterattacks, and destroyed the small groups of tanks and infantry that had broken through. Nevertheless, at the cost of heavy losses, the enemy managed to press back our forces along individual sectors in the zones of the 80th and 105th rifle corps, which were experiencing ammunition shortages.

At the same time the 48th and 28th armies, the latter with the 1st Mechanized and 9th Tank corps, the 61st Army's 9th Guards Rifle Corps, and the 70th Army, while waging stubborn battles and repelling counterattacks, moved slowly forward. The 28th Army forced the Lesnaya River north of Czernawczyci, and the 9th Guards Rifle Corps along the entire front. The 70th Army's right flank broke through the first positions of the Brest fortified area.

The 48th Army was expanding its sector to the south and relieved the 65th Army's 15th Rifle Division.

The *front* commander, striving to crush the enemy's growing resistance and to increase the rate of advance, in order to more quickly complete the encirclement of the enemy's Brest group of forces, turned over his reserve—the 46th Rifle Corps—to the 28th Army and demanded that the 65th and 28th armies commit their second echelons into the battle. In order to carry this out, on 27 July the 65th Army committed its 18th Rifle Corps in the direction of Grabarka and Zurobyce, and one tank brigade in the direction of Aleksandrowka and the railroad bridge over the Western Bug River, and the 28th Army the 46th Rifle Corps along the right flank in the direction of Wysokoe, as a result of which the enemy's resistance was crushed.

On this day the 28th Army, as a result of an attack to the southwest, and the 70th Army to the north—in the general direction of Zaczopki, reached the following lines: the 28th Army the line of the Lesnaya River, and the 70th Army the Western Bug River along a broad front, and completed the encirclement of part of the enemy's forces in the Brest area. However, by dint of stubbornly resisting the 70th and 47th armies' units in the areas of Biala-Podlaska and Mendzizec areas, as well as by counterattacking with a large group of tanks and infantry in the area north of Wysokoe and southeast of Bielsk-Podlaski, the enemy managed to block the encirclement of the Brest group of forces' remaining formations and units.

By the close of 27 July the armies were fighting along the following lines: the 48th Army—Zimnochy-Swechy—Kozany—Kotly—Kozly—Czechy-Zabolotny; the 65th Army—Chanki—Zalese—Aleksandrowka—Lumno; the 28th Army—excluding Lumno—Rasno—Rakowice—Kolodno—Zadworce; the 61st Army's 9th Guards Rifle Corps—excluding Zadworce—Wulka-Zastavska, and; the 70th Army—Chutora Romanowski—Weriady—Malaszewicze-Male—Zaczopki—Rokitno and Chorbow.

The 4th Guards Cavalry Corps, following six days of heavy fighting along the Western Bug River apart from our forces, was pulled back to the rear, by order of the *front* command, to put itself in order.

The cavalry-mechanized group (11th Tank and 7th Guards Cavalry corps) on 24 July captured the important rail and road junction and town of Lukow, while a reinforced cavalry division reached Mendzizec and on 25 July broke into Siedlce, and during the following two days was engaged in heavy fighting in the town with part of the enemy's 73rd Infantry Division, which had arrived from Germany on 24 July, and the main forces of *Totenkopf* SS Panzer Division, which had been transferred from the Second Belorussian Front's sector.

On 25 July the 47th Army's right flank and center captured Biala-Podlaska station, and the following day the towns of Biala-Podlaska and Mendzizec—the latter along with a cavalry division from the cavalry-mechanized group, and by the close of 27 July was engaged in heavy fighting along the line Woskszenice-Male—Biala-Podlaska—Rogozniczka—Karcze—Zabloce.

The army's left flank, taking advantage of the success of the cavalry-mechanized group and the 2nd Tank Army, was vigorously developing the success to the west and by the close of 27 July had reached the line Welgolas—Wilchta—Gozdzik and was fighting against part of the forces of corps group "E," the 5th Jaeger and 211th divisional groups, the main forces of the Hungarian 3rd Cavalry Brigade, and the recently-committed units of the 73rd and 168th infantry divisions, the first of which had arrived from Germany, while the second had come from Army Group North Ukraine's First Panzer Army.

The army advanced up to 100 kilometers in five days.

The Second Belorussian Front on the right, having overcome the Bialystok woods with its left-flank 3rd Army, on 26 July broke into Bialystok and by morning of the next day completely cleared it of the enemy.

It should be noted that the offensive pace of the right-wing armies, compared with their speed in the preceding (19-22 July) days, fell significantly and averaged 1-5 kilometers per day, which is explained not only by the enemy's significantly increased resistance, but also by the lagging artillery, as well as shortages of ammunition and fuel. For example, on 26 July the 105th Rifle Corps fell back due to an almost complete lack of ammunition.[17] By 27 July a large part of the 28th Army's artillery had fallen behind due to a lack of fuel.[18]

The pace of advance of the 70th and 47th armies and the cavalry-mechanized group along the *front's* left wing in the first days was high and reached 15-35 kilometers per day; but subsequently, as a result of growing enemy resistance, sharply fell to 2-12 kilometers per day.

During 22-27 July the enemy put all his efforts into first holding the powerful Brest fortified area and the defensive line along the Lesnaya River, in order to exhaust our forces and win time for organizing the defense of Warsaw along the Vistula River, and then to withdraw his forces from the looming encirclement in the Wysokoe area and to the south, and later from the encirclement in the Brest area. For this purpose, as we have already noted, the enemy concentrated two groups of forces along small sectors at the base of the 65th Army's wedge: one was near Bielsk-Podlaski, consisting of the 4th Panzer Division, reinforced by the newly-committed 37th Security and the 1071st Infantry regiments (541st Infantry Division), and; the second north and northwest of Wysokoe, consisting of the "Viking" 5th SS Panzer Division, with the 292nd Infantry Division and the remnants of the 35th Infantry Division. Moreover, the enemy had transferred to the area west of Brest the 541st, 168th and 73rd infantry divisions from Germany and had committed them into the fighting as follows: the first against the 65th Army near the edge of its wedge; the second against the *front's* cavalry-mechanized group near Siedlce, and; the third near Biala-Podlaska. Besides this, the enemy had transferred from the Second Belorussian Front's sector and concentrated against our forces the *Totenkopf* Third Panzer Division, the main forces of which were putting up fierce resistance to the cavalry-mechanized group in the fighting for Siedlce.

However, the threat to the enemy was increasing along the Warsaw axis. Thus on 27 July the enemy pulled the 4th Panzer Division out of the fighting near Bielsk-Podlaski and the "Viking" 5th SS Panzer Division and the main forces of the Hungarian 3rd Cavalry Brigade out of the Wysokoe area. Part of the "Viking" 5th SS Panzer Division was thrown into the area north of Mendzizec, while the main forces of the Hungarian 3rd Cavalry Brigade had by this time been reinforced by the 168th Infantry Division near Biala-Podlaska. On this day the enemy pulled the defeated remnants of corps group "E" out of the fighting, as well as the 5th and 23rd reserve divisions and the remnants of the Hungarian 1st Cavalry Division from the defense of the southern bank of the Western Bug River, and the 12th Hungarian Reserve Division from the 70th Army's front and dispatched them to the northwest, evidently in order to occupy ahead of time the defenses along the Narew River, and with part of corps group "E" occupied defensive positions southeast of Siedlce. At the same time as this the German command was transferring, for the defense of Warsaw and the surrounding area, the "Hermann Goering" SS Panzer Division, the 73rd Infantry Division, and various security units: the first, from Italy (arrived at the Soviet-German front on 24 July), and the second, from Germany, with the rest coming from various areas. Aside from this, the enemy was bringing up the 1131st and 1132nd infantry brigades and the 174th Reserve and 137th infantry divisions from Germany to the Vistula River south of Warsaw.

For the purpose of covering the gap that had formed between army groups Center and North Ukraine, and to improve the control of the German forces on the approaches to Warsaw, the headquarters of the Ninth Army was transferred here, and on 23 July the boundary line between the army groups was shifted 50-70 kilometers southward (to the line Zberze—Markuszow—Radom).

On the night of 28 July and during the following day, the fierce fighting to destroy the enemy's encircled Brest group of forces increased further. The enemy was seeking at any price to break out

---

17   Central Ministry of Defense Archives, opis' 65th Army 213277, delo 7, p. 119.
18   Central Ministry of Defense Archives, opis' 20897, delo 6, p. 17.

of the encirclement and during 28 July he carried out more than 52 counterattacks—and 20 on 29 July—in strength from a battalion to two regiments of infantry with tanks and assault guns.

Our forces, in repelling the enemy's counterattacks, launched powerful attacks along converging axes with the 28th Army's 20th Rifle Corps from the north and the 61st Army's 9th Guards Rifle Corps from the east, and the 70th Army's main forces from the south and west and split the enemy's encircled group of forces in two, and then on 28 July captured the town and fortress of Brest, the powerful Brest fortified area and the enemy's very important communications junction along the Warsaw axis.

The enemy managed to break out of the city to the west only in small groups and link up with his forces, which were fighting in encirclement in the woods to the west of Brest, but by the morning of 29 July they had been captured or destroyed.

On 30 July the 70th Army was pulled into the *front* commander's reserve into the area excluding Janow-Podlaski—excluding Biala-Podlaska—Rokitno.

From the description above it is obvious that the destruction of the encircled enemy group of forces, which had begun during the encirclement maneuver, was carried out by the method of splitting and subsequently destroying it in detail. The single enemy group at the start was split up into two—a group of forces in the city and a group of forces in the woods to the west of Brest. Then the group in the city was split, in its turn, into two parts—a part in the city itself and a part in the fortress. The first group was destroyed and then the second. The enemy group of forces in the woods west of Brest was also split up into parts and captured or destroyed on 29 July. Overall, the process of destroying or capturing the group of forces in the Brest area was carried out quickly—in less than two days, which testifies to the growing skill of the Soviet forces.

In the Brest area various units of the 102nd and 168th infantry and 203rd Security divisions, corps group "E," and the 3rd Cavalry Brigade, as well as the 57th, 89th and 930th security regiments, the 670th Security and 642nd Fortress battalions, a battalion of men on leave, various specialized units, and a large number of reinforcement equipment were encircled and destroyed.

The enemy suffered heavy losses. In only two days' fighting (28-29 July) up to 15,000 enemy officers and men were killed in this area, 22 artillery and mortar batteries and 15 tanks destroyed, and five enemy planes shot down. During the same time 1,400 men were taken prisoner and 338 guns and mortars, 20 tanks and assault guns, 35 train cars with ammunition, 2,000 carts with freight, 8,000 horses, and much other military equipment were captured.

One should not pass over in silence the mistakes committed by our forces during the fighting for Brest, as a result of which some small enemy groups managed to break out of the encirclement. Among these mistakes is the slowness of some formations' actions during the encirclement and the insufficient coordination between the 28th and 70th armies' flank formations while completing the encirclement. Moreover, the 70th Army command did not pay sufficient attention to consolidating along the lines achieved, especially along the internal encirclement front during 27-28 July.

Meanwhile, along the *front's* left flank, the 8th Guards and 69th armies and the *front's* mobile group (2nd Tank Army and the 7th Guards Cavalry Corps) achieved significant successes. For example, the *front's* mobile group, defending the town of Lublin with a single tank corps and a rifle corps from the 8th Guards Army, on the morning of 24 July drove to the west and the Vistula River with the 2nd Tank Army's main forces and on the following day at 1100 reached it along the Deblin—Pulawy sector and by the close of the day had occupied these town-fortresses. An attempt to force the Vistula River from the march and seize a bridgehead along its western bank was unsuccessful. As a result of the 69th Army lagging behind, the 7th Guards Cavalry Corps covered Lublin as early as 24 July from the south against possible enemy counterattacks. Besides this, on 26 July the corps moved one division into the Krasnik area (40 kilometers southwest of Lublin), for the purpose of cutting off the enemy's route of retreat to the west and held it until the arrival of the 3rd Guards and 69th armies, thus rendering great assistance to its neighbor.

The *front* commander considered that the 2nd Tank Army's further planned fighting to force the Vistula River to be inexpedient in the current situation and decided, as had been noted by the plan for the *front's* further actions of 25 July, to shift the army laterally to the area of the Warsaw suburb of Praga, for the purpose of cutting off all communications running to its from the northeast and east. Thus on 27 July the tank army, having left behind one tank corps along the Vistula River near Deblin until the infantry's arrival, began to vigorously move with the remainder of its forces along the enemy's rear to the northwest, and by the close of the day had captured its assigned areas of Stoczek and Garwolin and was in readiness on the morning of 28 July to attack with the mission of capturing Praga, to cut the Bialystok—Warsaw and Siedlce—Warsaw railroads and roads and prevent the enemy from occupying defensive positions in an organized manner near Warsaw and along the Vistula River by retreating enemy forces.

The 8th Guards Army, having left one corps to defend Lublin and taking advantage of the 2nd Tank Army's and cavalry-mechanized group's success, advanced with its main forces on the morning of 24 July to the northwest. On 25 July the army's left-flank corps, following behind the 3rd Tank Corps, reached the Vistula River along the sector Golomb—the mouth of the Bystra River and, together with units of the tank corps, fought to clear the enemy out of Pulawy, and by the close of 27 July its remaining forces were fighting along the line Zofibur—Okszea—Rososz—Rycice, against the enemy's newly-committed 17th Infantry and 174th Reserve divisions, which had been transferred—the first from Army Group South Ukraine, and the second from the rear.

The 69th Army, taking advantage of the successful advance by the mobile group and the 8th Guards Army, in conjunction with the 3rd Guards Army on the left, by the close of 27 July had captured the line Paulinow—Woiceczow—Bozechow—Wilkolaz, having advanced 25-35 kilometers in the last day alone.

The *front's* second echelon (Polish 1st Army) moved up in readiness to be committed into the battle along the Vistula River behind the 8th Guards Army.

The First Ukrainian Front's 3rd Guards Army on the left reached the line excluding Wilkolaz—Sulow—Woiceczow and then to the southwest as far as Nisko.

During 22-27 July the *front's* air force continued its actions to support our forces' offensive. The air force destroyed troop columns, motor vehicles and tanks along the Biala-Podlaska—Mendzizec, Janow-Podlaski—Siedlce and Krasnik—Annopel roads in bombing and strafing raids. Besides this, our air force bombed the bridge over the Vistula near Annopel. During this time the *front's* air force carried out 932 sorties (of these six were at night) along the *front's* left wing alone. 18 enemy planes were shot down in 15 air battles.

Long-Range Aviation continued to operate against the railroad junctions and stations at Bialystok, Siedlce, Deblin, and Praga (a suburb of Warsaw).

The enemy air force bombed our forward units, especially in approaching the area of Radzyn, Lukow, Siedlce, and Deblin. In all, the enemy carried out 326 sorties, of which 96 were at night.

Thus by the close of 27 July the forces of the First Belorussian Front had completed the encirclement of the enemy group of forces in the Brest area and by the close of 29 July had defeated and captured it, completely capturing the last important communications junction on the approaches to Warsaw—the city and fortress of Brest. Moreover, the *front's* forces liberated in fighting a large number of towns, including Biala-Podlaska, Mendzizec, Radzyn, Lukow, Garwolin, Deblin, Pulawy, Krasnik, and others.

With the arrival of the 2nd Tank Army in the area of Stoczek and Garwolin, a direct threat to the Warsaw suburb of Praga arose, and to the enemy's main communications leading from the areas of Bialystok and Siedlce to Warsaw.

On the whole, the *front's* forces significantly overfulfilled their subsequent task, which had been assigned to the *front* by the *Stavka* of the Supreme High Command—to reach the line Brest—Biala-Podlaska—Lukow—Michow—Lublin—Krasnystaw, both in depth and as to the pace of the advance. During this time the *front's* combined-arms armies advanced 85-120 kilometers (instead of the planned 80-100 kilometers), and the mobile groups 130-140 kilometers, with a corresponding speed of advance of 12-16 kilometers (instead of the planned 8-10 kilometers) and 17-20 kilometers per day.

However, the enemy group of forces in the Wysokoe area was not surrounded and the enemy withdrew his main forces away from the threat of encirclement. The *front's* right-wing forces were not able to reach the Western Bug River with their main forces.

The *front* commander, in the process of completing the accomplishment of the subsequent objective, as laid down by the *Stavka*; that is, before completing the encirclement of the enemy near Brest, as early as 25 July mapped out the further actions of his forces upon their reaching the Vistula River. This plan called for the right-win combined-arms armies to reach the line Trojanow—Wolia- Starogrodska—Garwolin—Domaszew—Kobylnica—Kozenice—Zwolen— excluding Juzefow on 1 August and seizing a bridgehead on the western bank of the Vistula River along a sector up to 90 kilometers wide and up to 25 kilometers deep. The arrival of all the forces at the Vistula River was planned for 3 August. The plan called for the 2nd Tank Army, upon its arrival in the Deblin—Pulawy area, to be moved laterally to the area of the Warsaw suburb of Praga, and the 70th Army, upon capturing Brest, to be pulled back into the *front* reserve and concentrated to the wet of the city.

By the close of 28 July the First Ukrainian Front's 3rd Guards Army was to reach the Vistula River and during the night of the following day to force it.

In developing the plan for further operations, the *front* commander demanded that the 8th Guards Army attack in the general direction of Latowicz and by the close of 28 July capture the line excluding Dombrowska-Stany—Stoczek—Garwolin—Laskazew—Maceewice and then along the western bank of the Vistula River as far as Stenzica. Moreover, the army was ordered to have its main forces on the right flank, and upon reaching the indicated line to consolidate, bring up its artillery and resupply.[19]

The 69th Army was to attack in the general direction of Woiceczow and Dobre and on 28 July reach the line of the Vistula River along its entire attack front, having in reserve a rifle corps in the Weleice area (20 kilometers southwest of Lublin) for securing the *front's* left flank and developing the offensive along the bridgehead.[20]

The Polish 1st Army received orders to enter the *front's* first operational echelon on 28 July and by the close of the day to reach the Vistula River along the sector Rycice—Wlostowice, where it was to relieve units of the 2nd Tank and 8th Guards armies (16th Tank and 4th Guards Rifle corps).

Thus the *front* commander planned to carry out his task with the forces of the 69th and Polish 1st armies, and part of the forces of the 8th Guards Army to a depth of up to 45 kilometers, and with an average daily advance rate of eight kilometers, including the forcing of a river and the seizing of bridgeheads.

In carrying out these assignments, part of the forces of the 8th Guards, Polish 1st and 69th armies reached the Vistula River at the close of 28 July. However, attempts by the Polish 1st and 69th armies to force the river from the march on that day were unsuccessful.

The *Stavka* of the Supreme High Command, as early as the First Belorussian Front's movement to the Vistula and Narew rivers, issued directive no. 220162, which demanded that the *front*, after

---

19 Central Ministry of Defense Archives, fond 233. Combat orders of the First Belorussian Front headquarters no. 00743/op. of 27 July 1944.

20 Central Ministry of Defense Archives, fond 233. Combat orders of the First Belorussian Front headquarters, no. 00738/op., 25 July 1944.

capturing the area of Brest and Siedlce, was to develop the offensive with its right wing in the general direction of Warsaw, with the assignment of no later than 5-8 August of seizing a bridgehead along the western bank of the Narew River in the Pultusk—Serock area and seize the Praga suburb of the Polish capital, while the *front's* left wing would seize a bridgehead along the western bank of the Vistula River in the areas of Deblin, Ewolen and Selec.[21] It was planned to employ the seized bridgeheads for an attack to the northwest, in order to roll up the enemy's defense along the Narew and Vistula rivers and thus secure the crossing of the former by the Second Belorussian Front and the second by the First Belorussian Front's central armies. At the same time, the *front* was ordered to be ready to subsequently attack to the west toward Torun and Lodz.

The next day (29 July) the *Stavka* of the Supreme High Command, in its coded telegram no. 220168, noted that the order to seize the above-indicated bridgeheads should not be understood to mean that the other armies should not also try to force the Vistula River.[22] The *Stavka* demanded that the *front* commander maximally supply with crossing equipment those armies in whose sectors the Vistula must be forced by order of the Supreme Commander-in-Chief, but at the same time pointed out that the other armies, should the possibility arise, should also force the Vistula River. The *Stavka*, attaching great significant to forcing the Vistula River, obliged the *front* command to inform all commanders that those soldiers and commanders who distinguished themselves in forcing the Vistula River would receive special medals and orders, all the way up to the title of Hero of the Soviet Union.

In carrying out the *Stavka's* instructions, the *front* commander, having decided to force the Vistula with three armies (8th Guards, Polish 1st and 69th), demanded that the *front's* chief of engineering troops bring up his main crossing equipment to the Vistula River in their sectors.

The Vistula River in this sector is 400-600 meters across and two meters and more deep. There were no fords. The western bank rose over the eastern one. The permanent bridges over the river were put out of commission by the enemy during his retreat.

A powerful and previously-prepared rear defense area ran along the western bank of the Vistula River, and which was occupied by both enemy reserves that had by this time been brought up from the rear, as well as by his retreating forces. In all, in the operational sectors of the 8th Guards, Polish 1st and 69th armies by 29-30 July, the enemy had along the western bank, counting various security and special units, up to 7-8 divisions with 1-2 brigades of assault guns, the majority of which were in a weakened condition, although they continued to fiercely resist, particularly along the bridgeheads being seized by our forces and to where the enemy was bringing up additional forces from other sectors.

The first to force the Vistula River on 29 July were four of the 69th Army's forward detachments, which seized two small bridgeheads in the area 10-15 kilometers southwest of Pulawy, and two days later six of the 8th Guards and Polish 1st armies' forward detachments seized bridgeheads as well: the first—a bridgehead southwest of the mount of the Wilga River, ten kilometers in width and 1-3 kilometers in depth, and the second—two small bridgeheads near Pulawy and five kilometers north of the town.

During the following days the main forces of the 8th Guards and 69th armies were ferried across the Vistula River and by the close of 2 August they had expanded their bridgeheads as follows: the 8th Guards Army—up to 19 kilometers in width and six kilometers in depth, and the 69th Army—correspondingly 20 and 3-7 kilometers.

Thus was begun the seizure and formation of the Magnuszew and Pulawy bridgeheads.

---

21 Central Ministry of Defense Archives, fond 233, opis' 20897, delo 2, pp. 1-2.
22 Central Ministry of Defense Archives, fond 233, opis' 20897, delo 2, pp. 1-2.

The Polish 1st Army's attempts to cross its main forces over to the captured bridgeheads, and those of the 69th Army to seize bridgeheads south of Selec, were unsuccessful.

The enemy along the captured bridgeheads put up fierce resistance that grew with each passing day. Enemy air activity increased significantly with the arrival of our forces to the Vistula River.

By this time the First Ukrainian Front's 3rd Guards Army, having defeated the enemy group of forces in the Annopel area, reached the Vistula River and seized bridgeheads near Dorotka, west of Annopel, and near Winjary.

Thus our forces reached the Vistula River along a broad 120-kilometer front. The forcing of the river was carried out by the 69th Army on 29 July, and two days later by the 8th Guards and Polish 1st armies. Bridgeheads on the river's western bank were seized. However, the task indicated by the plan, which had been confirmed by the *front* commander, had not been fully carried out.

The dimensions of the captured bridgeheads were only 45 kilometers in width and seven in depth, instead of the planned 90-110 kilometers in width and 25-160 in depth. The pace of forcing the river and seizing bridgeheads was only 4-5 kilometers per day, which was 3-4 kilometers slower than had been planned.

The *front's* failure to entirely carry out its assignments is explained by the presence of a powerful water barrier (the Vistula River) and the previously-prepared powerful defensive line along its western bank, as well as its timely occupation by the enemy's forces.

Also, the forward detachments of both the 2nd Tank Army and the combined-arms armies, which had reached the Vistula, were not able to force the river from the march due to the lack of crossing equipment, and as a result lost the element of surprise in seizing bridgeheads. For example, the 2nd Tank Army reached the Vistula River on 25 July, while the 69th and Polish 1st armies reached it on 28 July, while the river was forced and a bridgehead seized on its western bank only on 29 July, four days after the tank army's arrival at the river and the day following the 69th Army's formations' arrival at the river. Moreover, the tank army was forced to give up trying to force the river altogether and was regrouped to another axis.

Also worthy of note is the mistake of not employing the 7th Guards Cavalry Corps for speeding up the pursuit of the enemy and the forcing of the river. Instead of this, the corps was used to defend the approaches to Lublin from the south along a broad front.

It should be especially emphasized that the forcing of the Vistula River and the battle for the capture and expansion of the bridgeheads along its western bank was carried out simultaneously along a broad front (up to 250 kilometers) by the formations of two *fronts*—the First Belorussian and First Ukrainian, which made it difficult for the enemy to maneuver his reserves and ensured the success of the river's forcing by the Soviet forces.

On the morning of 28 July the 2nd Tank Army continued its offensive to the northwest toward the Warsaw suburb of Praga. Overcoming the enemy's growing resistance, particularly along the Warsaw paved road, and bypassing strong points, the army on 29 July captured the town of Stanislawow and the line of the Swider River, and on the following day reached the line Wolomin—Radzymin—Marki—Zelenka—Mednzylese—Swider, where it encountered fierce enemy resistance. Attempts to continue the offensive in the following days were unsuccessful.

The German-Fascist command, in order to prevent our troops from reaching Warsaw, launched a powerful counterblow along the boundary of the 2nd Tank and 47th armies with a group of forces, consisting of five panzer and one infantry divisions,[23] which, relying on previously-prepared lines, sought by active operations and at any price, regardless of casualties, to defeat the 2nd Tank Army's formations, halt their advance and hold on to the Praga bridgehead fortifications.

---

23 The "Viking" 5th and *Totenkopf* 3rd panzer divisions, the "Hermann Goering" Panzer Division, the 4th and 19th panzer divisions, and the 73rd Infantry Division.

The Praga area was a modern fortress, fitted out with a system of permanent structures, consisting of several zones of concrete and earth and wood pillboxes and reinforced-concrete shelters, connected by trenches and communications trenches and outfitted with a large number of engineering obstacles, including anti-tank ditches, and post obstacles, etc. The defensive lines had already been occupied by the enemy. The positions' flanks were adjacent to the Vistula River and the stone structures had been configured for defense. It should be noted that here were the main structures of the Warsaw fortified area, which had been constructed here before the war and had been once again fitted out and strengthened since 1943.

The *front* commander demanded that the 2nd Tank Army operate in accordance with the situation and avoid the storming of the fortified areas and permanent structures.[24] As to the request by the commander of the 2nd Tank Army to reinforce the army with heavy artillery for supporting an attack on Praga, where the enemy had powerful fortifications, the *front* commander once again repeated his decision not to storm powerful fortifications with the tank army, pointing out that such is not the task of tanks and that the mission should be entrusted to the arriving 47th Army.

Carrying out these instructions and foreseeing the possibility of a counterblow by a large enemy armored group of forces, on 1 August the commander of the 2nd Tank Army decided to go over to a perimeter defense, securely holding the roads and approaches to Warsaw from the northeast and east, and upon the arrival of the 47th Army, to capture Praga. During the day and night of 2 August the army's 3rd Tank Corps repelled the beginning counterblow by the enemy's armored group, while an attack by part of the 8th Guards Tank Corps to the east toward the 47th Army facilitated its movement to the northwest and in eliminating the gap that had grown between them.

It should be noted that the 2nd Tank Army commander's decision to go over to the defense was dictated not only by the presence of the enemy's powerful fortifications and the *front* commander's instructions, but also by the serious shortage of ammunition and fuel. The army's advanced 3rd Tank Corps was actually doomed to a passive, immobile defense, because it remained without fuel and could not maneuver and thus was deprived of its chief quality—mobility.

During this period the *front's* rear, due to the lagging of the supply bases, which continued to remain in areas 60-70 kilometers east of Kovel', failed to cope with supplying the troops with fuel and ammunition. Railroad delivery during 26 July-1 August was carried out only as far as Kashary station (14 kilometers west of Kovel'), while the automobile supply leg was more than 350 kilometers.

Besides this, the closer we got to Warsaw and the enemy air force's basing areas, the activity of the latter increased, while at the same time our air force, particularly fighter and assault air, more and more felt the effects of their rebasing lagging behind the rate of the ground forces' advance. The insufficient support by the 16th and 6th air armies also played an important role in the 2nd Tank Army's forced assumption of the defense.

However, despite this, the 2nd Tank Army achieved its objective of reaching the Warsaw suburb of Praga and cutting the communications running to it from the northeast and east, and in three days advanced 72 kilometers to the northwest, at an average rate of 24 kilometers per day.

In carrying out the *Stavka's* demands, the *front* commander decided to capture the Warsaw suburb of Praga no later than 5-8 August and to seize bridgeheads along the western bank of the Narew River in the area of Pultusk and Serock, and demanded that army commanders continue their offensive in the following general directions: 48th

---

24   Central Ministry of Defense Archives, fond 233, opis' 11757, delo 43. Instructions on the 2nd Tank Army's coded telegrams, no. 51083, 30 July 1944.

Army—Bielsk-Podlaski—Bransk—Czyzewo—Ostrow-Mazowiecka; 65th Army—Ceranow—Twarogi—Sterdyn—Kosow, and; the 28th Army, with the 1st Mechanized and 9th Tank corps—Konstantynow—Losice—Mordy.[25]

The 47th Army had the objective of attacking to the north and, in conjunction with the *front's* cavalry-mechanized group's operations, to capture the town of Siedlce,[26] while one rifle corps would continue the attack to the west with the task of reaching the Vistula River on 2 August along the sector Karczew—the mouth of the Wilga River.[27]

On the night of 27-28 July and the following day stubborn fighting continued along the armies' entire front, and particular in the sectors of the 48th, 65th and 47th armies, where the fighting was actually taking place along the previous line and only the 28th Army's right flank and center, as had the left flank the evening before, reached the Western Bug River and began preparations to force it. On 29 July, in the 65th, 28th and 47th armies' sectors, and on 30 July in the 48th Army's sector, the enemy's resistance was crushed and the enemy began to slowly fall back to the west, pursued by our forces. On 30 July the 48th Army captured the powerful strong point of Bielsk-Podlaski with an attack from the northwest and south, and on 1 August the towns of Suraz and Bransk and by the close of the next day had reached the line Danilowo-Duze—Domanowo—Ciechanowiec.

During this time the 65th Army captured the towns of Bocki, Siemiatycze and Drochiczin and forced the Western Bug River along the sector Weska—Tonkele and reached the line of the Nuzec and Western Bug rivers from Ciechanowiec to Weska and then to Grudek—excluding Repki, and had begun fighting for the important road and railroad junction of Sokolow-Podlaski.

South of the Western Bug River the 28th Army, in conjunction with the 47th Army's right flank, captured Janow-Podlaski. Continuing to pursue the enemy to the west, the army captured the town of Losice and by the close of 2 August had reached the line Repki—Ruda—Broszkow, where it encountered the enemy's stubborn resistance.

The 47th Army, in conjunction with the 2nd Tank and 28th armies, having changed the axis of 129th Rifle Corps' attack from the west to the north, on 30 July outflanked Siedlce from the northeast and northwest. On the following day the *front's* cavalry-mechanized group, together with units of the 47th Army, by 1400 had captured Siedlce. By the close of 2 August two of the army's corps were engaged in heavy fighting with enemy tanks and infantry along the line Aleksandrowka—Wisnew—Wulka-Czarninywka, while another corps was moving toward the Vistula River.

The attempts by the 2nd Guards Cavalry Corps to reach the area of Sokolow-Podlaski were not successful.

The Second Belorussian Front on the left reached the Augustow Canal with its right flank, and with its left the Narew River, and was fighting to force and seize bridgeheads along their western bank.

The reasons for the slow advance by the *front's* armies were as follows: the significantly increased enemy resistance, breakdowns in supplying the armies with ammunition and fuel, due to the absence of the rear organs, as well as the troops' exhaustion following a continuous offensive over 40 days, and in the 47th Army—the dispersion of the troops along a 74-kilometer front, instead of the 21 kilometers at the start of the operation. The German-Fascist command, in order to prevent our forces from reaching Warsaw and to the north along the line of the Narew River, continued to hold the 47th and 2nd Tank armies' forward units, and the with the main forces

---

25 Central Ministry of Defense Archives, fond 233, opis' 20897, delo 6, pp. 32-35, 43.

26 Central Ministry of Defense Archives, fond 233. Combat order of the First Belorussian Front headquarters no. 00743/op, of 27 July 1944.

27 Central Ministry of Defense Archives, fond 233. Combat orders of the First Belorussian Front headquarters, nos. 00745/op., 00769/op., and 00771/op., of 31 July and 1 August 1944.

of the "Viking" 5th and *Totenkopf* 3rd SS panzer divisions and various security units. In order to occupy the line along the Western Bug River along the sector from Wiszkow to the river's mouth, in time, the German-Fascist command pulled out the following units: Hungarian 23rd, 12th and 5th reserve divisions, corps group "E," the remnants of the Hungarian 1st Cavalry Division, and the Hungarian 3rd Cavalry Brigade into the Czizow area in the 48th Army's sector.

The work of the rear. The elongation of the rear continued on a large scale, especially within the *front's* right-wing armies, and thus throughout the entire operation the *front's* forces experienced severe deficiencies in ammunition and fuel, which was one of the main reasons for the decline in the troops' offensive pace, the 2nd Tank Army's assumption of the defensive upon arriving at the Warsaw suburb of Praga, and the retreat of the 105th Rifle Corps from the Western Bug River near Siemiatycze. This was also the reason for the artillery lagging so far behind. Troop supply up to 30 July was carried out from the previous army and *front* bases, which by 23 July were located almost 530-570 kilometers from the *front's* right-wing forces, and 160-275 from the left-wing forces.

The main reason for the rear organs falling behind, as was the case in the *front's* previous operations, was the obviously slow pace of railroad repair, which was significantly less than the troops' rate of advance. For example, from the start of the operation to 23 July, 15 kilometers of railroad had been restored along the *front's* left wing (from Kovel' station to Koshary station), while the troops advanced during the same time 90-130 kilometers—that is, 6-9 times faster. On the right wing, although the railroad from Slutsk station to Timkovichi station (40 kilometers) had been restored, in light of the railroad bridge over the Sluch' River being unready, train movement continued, as before, as far as the railroad bridge near Slutsk. During this time the troops advanced 50-75 kilometers. During the following four days (24-27 July) 65 kilometers of railroad were restored along the *front's* right wing and 1.5 kilometers on the left, while the troops advanced a corresponding 20-25 and 40-50 kilometers. It follows that the automobile supply leg in the *front's* right-wing armies reached 260-340 kilometers on 23 July and 150-245 kilometers along the left wing on 27 July and still further up to the areas of the *front* depots. If one takes into account the *front* and army transport's capabilities to deliver 25 percent of a refill of fuel and lubricants up to 100 kilometers, 0.1-0.2 percent of a combat load, and a day's food ration, then it becomes clear just how serious was the problem of supplying the troops with ammunition and fuel at a greater distance. The inability to adapt a large amount of supply capacity for movement by auto transport told on the reduced supply of fuel for the troops, as a result of which it remained in its jumping-off position. With the movement of combat operations to Polish territory, additional difficulties arose in rear area organization and materiel-technical support, due to the fact that the Polish railroads are western-gauge, as well the insufficient supply of rail cars for this gauge.

The rebasing of army and *front* supply bases forward was carried out only by 30 July; that is, by the end of the operation.[28]

On the whole, the First Belorussian Front's rear, although it basically coped with the difficult tasks entrusted to it, nevertheless worked with certain breakdowns and was not able to match the volume and speed of supply delivery with the rate of the troops' advance. The latter must always be taken into account in foreseeing the pursuit at high speeds and to a great depth, especially as concerns supplying the troops with fuel and ammunition.

During the operation the partisan formations rendered a great deal of assistance to the *front*. They directed their main efforts at disrupting the enemy's regroupings, the evacuation of freight along the Kobrin—Brest railroads and then to Warsaw or Deblin, as well as along the Kovel'—Brest—Bialystok lines by blowing up rails, bridges and permanent structures. At the same time the

---

28 Central Ministry of Defense Archives, fond 233, opis' 14952, delo 7, pp. 65-70, and opis' 51100, delo 2. Red Army General Staff directives no. 333458 and 333459.

partisans intensified their struggle to preserve industrial and social government structures in the towns and large inhabited locales. The partisans carried out a major battle to prevent the extermination of the population and its removal into fascist slavery.

At the same time, the partisans cleared the woods and swamps of individual soldiers and small enemy groups that had fled and taken refuge there.

The partisans also helped our forces to restore the roads and bridges.

Aside from this, a significant portion of the partisan formations' rank and file, which was now in territory liberated from the German-Fascist occupiers, entered the *front's* formations as reinforcements.

Results and Conclusions

As a result of the Brest—Siedlce offensive operation, carried out by the forces of the First Belorussian Front during 17 July-2 August 1944, the enemy's Brest and Lublin groups of forces were defeated, and the *front's* armies reached the Warsaw suburb of Praga and an important strategic line running along the Vistula River.

During the operation the *front's* forces successfully and ahead of time carried out the tasks assigned to them by the *Stavka* of the Supreme High Command.

At the same time, our forces liberated an enormous territory (more than 41,000 square kilometers) in the Belorussian and Ukrainian SSRs, as well as allied Poland, from German-Fascist occupation.

The *front's* forces liberated a large number of important industrial, administrative and political centers and communications centers, such as the towns of Brest, Lublin, Kobrin, Czeremcha, Gainowka, Chelm, Lukow, Siedlce, and many others. The liberation of Lublin had major political significance in the conditions of the exacerbated struggle of the Polish people's democratic forces against reaction. The town of Lublin then became the location of the Polish democratic government.

Besides this, the *front's* forces also broke through several of the enemy's previously-prepared defensive zones: along the Narewka, Lesnaya Right, and Lesnaya rivers; along the line Orlanka River—Bielsk-Podlaski—Seimiatycze, and; west of Kovel' and along the Western Bug River with the powerful Brest fortified area, as well as a number of hurriedly prepared intermediate and switch positions. At the same time the *front's* armies reached the enemy's important strategic line—the Vistula River along a 120-kilometer front and seized four bridgeheads on its western bank with an overall width of up to 45 kilometers and seven kilometers in depth. These bridgeheads, as is known, later played a major role in the Soviet forces' offensive in January 1945.

During the offensive the *front's* forces successfully completed overcoming the difficult, wooded and swampy expanses to the east and southeast of Brest, as well as the Belovezhskaya Woods. They also forced the major water barrier of the Western Bug River along the *front's* entire sector, as well as a series of other rivers: Mukhavets, Lesnaya, Nuzec, Wyzewka, Kzsna, Wieprz, and others.

The *front's* forces defeated 12 infantry, reserve, cavalry, and security divisions (211th, 26th, 342nd, and 253rd infantry, 5th Jaeger, 1st Ski Jaeger, 5th, 12th and 174th reserve, 203rd and 213th security, and 1st Cavalry divisions), two cavalry brigades, one corps group ("E"), one assault gun regiment, the Merker Group, more than nine independent artillery battalions from the High Command Reserve, three brigades of assault guns, and a large number of the enemy's independent security and special units. Six infantry (7th, 35th, 73rd, 102nd, 129th, and 292nd) divisions and four panzer divisions (4th, 17th, "Viking" 5th and *Totenkopf* SS), the 18th Special Designation Brigade, and various enemy security and special units suffered heavy losses.

Thus 22-23 enemy divisions (of these, four panzer), 3-4 brigades, and a large number of independent units and groups were defeated or suffered heavy losses.

During this time the enemy suffered enormous losses. In all, he lost 224,448 officers and men (of these, 195,632 were killed), 1,209 tanks and assault guns, 3,120 guns, and 2,065 mortars. On the whole, the enemy lost more in personnel and tanks than in the *front's* two preceding operations together, and a little bit less in guns and mortars.

As a result of the First Belorussian Front's attack along the boundary between Army Group Center's Second Army and Army Group North Ukraine's Fourth Panzer Army, the German-Fascist command was forced several times to change the boundary line between these armies and search for forces to cover the tear in its front. For example, starting on 24 July the reconstituted Ninth Army[29] (including the "Hermann Goering" SS Panzer Division, 17th and 73rd infantry divisions, and the 1131st and 1132nd infantry brigades, and other units), which had earlier been defeated in the area of Bobruisk and Minsk was deployed along the boundary between the Second and Fourth Panzer armies.[30]

The successful conduct of the Brest—Siedlce offensive operation and the arrival of its forces at the Vistula River on 2 August and the seizure of bridgeheads on its western bank, and their arrival at the Warsaw suburb of Praga, created prerequisites for the preparation of a new operation to fully liberate all of Poland from German-Fascist occupation and for the development of the attack along the Berlin strategic direction.

The Brest—Siedlce operation in the multi-*front* Belorussian operation was the First Belorussian Front's third operation and represents yet another example of a *front* consecutive operation, carried out without any kind of operational pause, following the completion of the Baranovichi—Slonim offensive operation.

The First Belorussian Front's Brest—Siedlce operation began as a continuation of the offensive by the *front's* right-wing forces along the Brest axis and, a few days later, as a breakthrough by the left-wing forces of the enemy's previously-prepared and deeply echeloned defense west of Kovel', along a sector 120 kilometers removed from the *front's* right-wing attacking forces, with the subsequent development of a vigorous attack to the northwest, the forcing of the powerful water barrier of the Western Bug River from the march, and as the breakthrough of the army defensive zone on its western bank.

There then followed no less vigorous attacks along converging axes on Brest and Siedlce, with the subsequent encirclement and destruction of the enemy group of forces in the Brest area, as well as attacks to the west on Pulawy and Deblin, and to the northwest on Warsaw, which ended with the arrival of the *front's* forces at the Warsaw suburb of Praga and the Vistula River and the seizure of bridgeheads on its western bank.

The rapid breakthrough by the 8th Guards, 47th and 69th armies of the enemy's defense west of Kovel' and the defeat of the opposing enemy had a decisive influence on the success of achieving the *front's* immediate objective. This enabled the *front* command to commit the *front* mobile groups into the breach not on 19 July, but on 21 and 22 July, following the forcing of the Western Bug River and the breakthrough of the army defensive zone by the *front's* first operational echelon forces. For this reason, the *front's* second echelon was committed into the fighting not from the line of the Western Bug River, but upon the *front's* first-echelon armies reaching the Vistula River.

The breakthrough of the enemy's defense along the axis of the *front's* main attack was accomplished by a massive attack by the main forces and equipment along the *front's* left wing along a single 18-kilometer breakthrough sector, which accounted for 9.9 percent of the entire width of the attack sector of the *front's* left-wing forces (182 kilometers), and only 4.1 percent of the *front's*

---

29 During 12-23 July the headquarters of the Ninth Army was located in the OKH reserve.

30 Among the newly-arrived units, the panzer division was from Italy, the 17th Infantry Division from Army Group South Ukraine, and the rest from Germany.

entire sector (414 kilometers), that is, as much as in the *front's* Bobruisk—Slutsk offensive operation (4 percent).

The rapid development of the offensive and the pursuit of the enemy to the northwest by the *front's* cavalry-mechanized group toward Radzyn, Lukow and Siedlce had a decisive effect on the achievement of the *front's* subsequent objective, as well as that of the 2nd Tank Army, at first toward Lublin, Pulawy and Deblin, and then toward the Warsaw suburb of Praga.

One of the decisive conditions for success, as in the preceding operations, was the high morale and combat qualities of the *front's* rank and file, the objective sources of which were the Soviet social and state system, and the just and liberating character of the Great Patriotic War.

The tactical breakthrough of the heavily fortified and deeply echeloned enemy defense along the axis of the *front's* main attack west of Kovel' was accomplished by the troops' broadly employing maneuver to envelop and outflank the enemy's strong points, both in his main defensive zone, and along the subsequent defensive lines.

The mobile formations and major field forces played an important role in developing the offensive. Moreover, in this operation, as opposed to the Bobruisk—Slutsk operation, they were employed in the capacity of success development echelons (mobile groups) and committed into an already formed breach.

The Brest—Siedlce operation, as had been the Bobruisk—Slutsk operation, was characterized by the large scope and high speed with which it was conducted, the defeat of the opposing enemy group of forces and the vigorous development of the pursuit. At the same time, the speed and depth of the operation exceeded the planned indices. For example, the *front's* operation was begun along the axis of the main attack by a breakthrough of the enemy defense along an 18-kilometer sector, and by the close of the operation's third day—the day for achieving the *front's* immediate objective—the width of the main group's offensive zone reached 150 kilometers; by the close of the tenth day—the day for achieving the subsequent objective—it was 240 kilometers, and by the close of the sixteenth day—the close of the operation—it was 280 kilometers, that is, it had increased in comparison with the breakthrough sector by nearly 16 times (14 times in the Bobruisk—Slutsk operation). The overall width of the attack front of the *front's* left-wing forces grew nearly two times.

At the same time the depth of the operation called for by the plan was exceeded by 110-130 kilometers (30 kilometers more than in the Bobruisk—Slutsk operation). The planned average rates of advance for the combined-arms armies of 10.7-11.2 kilometers per day actually reached 15 kilometers. On some days they were much greater. For example, on 22, 23 and 28 July the 8th Guards Army's rate of advance was 30 kilometers, with 25 and 40 kilometers for the 69th Army on 22 and 27 July. The rates for the 2nd Tank Army's attack were an average of 22 kilometers per day, and on some days even higher. For example, during 22-25 July they averaged 32 kilometers per day, and 47 kilometers on 27 July.

Such speeds of conducting an operation along the axis of the *front's* main attack prevented the enemy, following his defeat in the tactical defense zone, from putting his forces in order, holding the army defensive zone along the Western Bug River and the major strong point of Lublin. Thanks to these speeds, the enemy was not able to halt the successful offensive by the *front's* forces before they reached the Vistula River and the Warsaw suburb of Praga.

During the pursuit, which was conducted along a broad front and without losing contact with the enemy, our forces, as a rule, preempted the enemy in occupying the intermediate lines.

The troops' rate of advance along the *front's* secondary axis (right wing) was significantly lower than along the axis of the main attack. This is understandable, for the operation's main objective, as issued to the *front* by the *Stavka* of the Supreme High Command, was to be carried out by the *front's* left-wing forces. Along the axis of the secondary attack the forces of the 48th, 65th, 62nd, and 28th armies advanced as follows: up to 100 kilometers for the first three armies, and 180 kilometers for the latter, for a corresponding rate of six and 10.6 kilometers per day. From this it follows that the *front's* right-wing forces' average daily rate of advance fell with each succeeding operation—from 22-25 kilometers in the first operation, to 18-19 kilometers per day during the second.

The reasons that led to a reduction in the rates of advance for the *front's* right-wing forces in the Brest—Siedlce operation were as follows: the enemy's significantly increased level of resistance; his commitment of fresh forces into the battle—the "Viking" 5th SS Panzer Division, the 541st Infantry Division, the Hungarian II Reserve Corps, the 4th Panzer Division, and various other units; the enemy's significantly increased density of troops, particularly tank forces; breakdowns in supplying the *front's* forces with ammunition and fuel, due to the rear organs falling far behind, and; the exhaustion of the rank and file of the *front's* right wing as a result of a 40-day uninterrupted offensive to a depth of more than 600 kilometers. Moreover, the decreasing strength of the rifle divisions' rank and file and the armies' tank forces negatively told on the rates of advance. For example, the 48th, 65th and 28th armies had 15-45 percent of their tanks combat-ready, while these armies' rifle divisions' rank and file were 64-86 percent of authorized strength.

The insufficiently high rates of advance among the *front's* right-wing forces was also due to the insufficient striving by the armies' command to create shock groups along selected axes of the main attacks. As a rule, men and materiel were distributed almost evenly along the entire front, which led to pushing the enemy back, while outflanking, enveloping and getting in the enemy's rear were rarely practiced. Cooperation between the infantry, artillery and tank formations was poorly organized. Reconnaissance, especially in the tank and mechanized formations was poorly conducted. The *front* commander directed the army commanders' attention to these shortcomings.[31]

The Brest—Siedlce offensive operation is also an example of the encirclement and destruction of an enemy group of forces in the operational depth during a successful consecutive operation by the forces of a single *front*. Moreover, the encirclement was accomplished in a powerful fortified area and town—the fortress of Brest, by the internal flanks of both of the *front's* wings on the eleventh day of the Brest—Siedlce operation, followed by the destruction of the encircled enemy in the town and fortress on the twelfth day, and southwest of Brest on the operation's thirteenth day. It follows that the elimination of the enemy's encircled group of forces in the powerful fortified area was accomplished in an extremely rapid time—2-3 days. The main means of maneuver to carry out the encirclement around Brest were the 28th and 70th armies' rifle formations.

The operation represents an instructive example of uninterruptedly conducting combat operations, from beginning to end. Having broken through the enemy's defense, the *front's* forces, particularly along the left wing, immediately took up the vigorous pursuit of the enemy. Having encircled the enemy group of forces in the Brest area, they did not halt their advance to the west on Warsaw. The pursuit itself, as we noted, was conducted by the armies along a broad front and deprived the German-Fascist command of the opportunity of employing its reserves along any particular chosen axis. For example, the attack and pursuit sectors in the 8th Guards, 47th and 69th armies increased correspondingly from nine, 21 and 32 kilometers at the start of the operation to 52, 74 and 54 kilometers at the close of the operation.

The examples of the 8th Guards, 47th and 69th armies' actions in the Brest—Siedlce operation confirm the experience of the 65th and 28th armies in the Bobruisk—Slutsk offensive operation: in both instances it was necessary to have a deep combat formation, in order to break through the enemy's heavily fortified and deeply echeloned defense in the wooded and swampy terrain. The

---

31 Central Ministry of Defense Archives, fond 233, opis' 20897, delo 1, coded telegrams.

troops' deep echelonment along a narrow sector enabled us to augment the forces of the attacks from the depth and achieve great results.

During the Brest—Siedlce operation the enemy offered the greatest resistance to our forces in the areas of Bielsk-Podlaski, Wysokoe, Brest, Biala-Podlaska, and Siedlce, and particularly upon reaching the Vistula River toward the Warsaw suburb of Praga.

This operation, like the preceding one, shows how the German-Fascist command continued to pay for its incorrect determination of our forces' main attack axis. In attempting to halt or delay the Soviet forces' successful offensive along the Warsaw strategic direction, the Hitlerite command was forced to throw in a number of formations and units here during the course of the battle, and in particular to bring up the "Viking" 5th SS Panzer Division to the area north of the Pripyat' River from the Kovel' area, and later the 541st Infantry Division from Germany and the 168th Infantry Division from Army Group North Ukraine, while simultaneously committing into the battle the Hungarian II Reserve Corps, which had previously been located in the Brest area. At the same time, the, by the start of the Brest—Siedlce operation the situation around Kovel' was obviously underestimated by the German-Fascist command. The German-Fascist command mistakenly believed that the First Belorussian Front would continue to concentrate its main efforts north of the Pripyat' River and thus decided to foil the looming offensive by the Soviet forces along the *front's* left wing by merely pulling back its forces from the area of the Kovel' salient to the second defensive zone.

It was evidently due to these considerations that the German-Fascist command lacked the necessary operational reserves along the *front's* left wing at the start of the Brest—Siedlce operation. This is confirmed if only by the fact that when the breakthrough was accomplished along the *front's* left-wing sector, the enemy was forced to hurriedly transfer various formations and units here from other axes. In all, seven divisions (of these three were panzer divisions) were transferred to the *front's* left-wing sector, as well as two infantry brigades and a large number of security and special units,[32] and with the arrival of the 2nd Tank and 47th armies at the immediate approaches to the Warsaw suburb of Praga—an additional two panzer divisions.[33]

During the Brest—Siedlce operation the enemy lost 309,990 men killed, wounded and missing in action, while the Soviet forces destroyed or captured more than 4,000 guns of all calibers and 227 planes.[34]

The First Belorussian Front lost 68,668 men killed, wounded and missing in action, or 10.5 percent of the *front's* strength at the start of the operation, of which 15,569—or 2.4 percent, were killed.[35]

The 28th, 65th and 47th armies suffered the greatest losses in the operation, as well as the 4th Guards Cavalry, 1st Mechanized, 1st Guards and 9th tank corps (10.9-17.8 percent). These losses in the 28th and 65th armies and mobile corps are explained by the fierce fighting in the Kamenec and Wysokoe area, and while encircling and destroying the enemy's group of forces in the Brest area, and those of the 69th and 47th armies in connection with the fighting: the first while forcing

32 The following units arrived here: the "Hermann Goering" SS Panzer Divisinon from Italy, the *Totenkopf* 3rd SS Panzer Division from Army Group Center's Fourth Army, the 17th Panzer Division from Army Group North Ukraine's Fourth Panzer Army, the 17th Infantry Division from Army Group South Ukraine's Eighth Army, and the 174th Reserve, 73rd and 137th infantry divisions, and the 1131st and 1132nd infantry brigades from Germany.

33 These were the 4th Panzer Division and the "Viking" 5th SS Panzer Division from the *front's* right-wing sector.

34 Central Ministry of Defense Archives, fond 233, opis' 14780, delo 2 and 3, opis' 20519, delo 12.

35 *Ibid.*

the Vistula River and along the bridgehead, and the second in the Siedlce area and to the east, while repelling a counterblow by the enemy's tank units.

The *front's* losses in this operation were a little less than in the Bobruisk—Slutsk offensive operation (10.5 perecent to 11.8 percent) and almost twice as great as in the Baranovichi—Slonim operation (10.5 percent, instead of 6.6 percent).

However, if one compares our losses with those suffered by the enemy, then they were almost three times smaller.

All of this shows how great the results were of the First Belorussian Front's Brest—Siedlce offensive operation.

The offensive, which was begun on 24 June in the Bobruisk area by the *front's* right-wing forces, was completed by an attack by all of the *front's* forces and the arrival at the Warsaw suburb of Praga and the Vistula River—an important strategic line along the Warsaw—Berlin direction.

During the second stage of the multi-*front* Belorussian offensive operation, the Soviet forces advanced to a depth of 260-400 kilometers. The offensive front was expanded to 1,000 kilometers.

All of Belorussia was cleared of the enemy, as well as a significant part of Lithuania and the eastern areas of allied Poland.

During the operation's second stage, as opposed to the first, the Soviet forces in Belorussia carried out an operation in conjunction with the armies of the Second and Third Baltic fronts to the north, and with the armies of the First Ukrainian Front to the south.

However, the enemy, at the cost of enormous efforts and by transferring major reserves to the central sector of the Soviet-German front, managed to restore his broken front and increase resistance to the Soviet forces, particularly in August 1944.

Taking advantage of the fact that the main German-Fascist forces and reserves had been drawn to the Soviet-German front, the Anglo-American armed forces launched a major offensive from their bridgehead in northern France on 25 July.

12

A Brief Review of Military Operations in August 1944

Military operations in August 1944 unfolded in a situation in which the enemy's resistance had increased significantly. As a result of these operations, the successes achieved during the course of the Belorussian operation were consolidated and the operational situation of our forces was improved. Although, these were, on the whole, offensive operations, they unfolded at a significantly slower pace than in July. The advance of the Soviet forces throughout August did not exceed 50-100 kilometers, and even this was only along certain axes.

As a result of the defeat of Army Group Center by the Soviet armed forces in June-July 1944, the German-Fascist command was forced to gather reserves from all over Europe, as well as to move forces from other directions and throw them into the central sector of the Soviet-German front, with the mission of restoring the front along the lines of the Neman and Vistula rivers, to prevent the Soviet forces from entering East Prussia, to restore Army Group North's disrupted land communications in the Baltic States, and to maintain the Warsaw fortified area and prevent the arrival of Soviet forces at the German border along the Warsaw—Berlin direction. In order to achieve these goals, the German-Fascist command planned to create two groups of forces—one along the approaches to East Prussia, and the other in the Warsaw area, with the help of which it counted on not only halting the Soviet forces, but also throwing them back to the east, thus eliminating the threat of their invasion of Germany proper.

Particularly great attention was allotted to the defense of East Prussia, to which the main mass of the enemy's arriving reserves was directed. During July the enemy concentrated against our First Baltic and Third Belorussian fronts 27 new infantry and ten panzer divisions. With the help of these reserves the enemy managed not only to restore the broken front along the line of the Neman River, but also halt the Soviet forces' offensive in Latvia and Lithuania. However, the enemy managed to do this, to a significant degree, as a result of the fact that our armies, having reached the line Tukums—Jelgava—Siauliai—Kaunas—Grodno—Bialystok—Warsaw, began to experience serious shortages of ammunition, fuel and food, and other types of supply. The main mass of our rear organs fell behind to a great distance. The depth of the *front* rear area began to reach 500 kilometers. Automobile delivery stretched out 200-350 kilometers and more. Human reinforcement became a particular problem. As a result of the non-stop fighting and serious losses, the forces in our formations, units and subunits dropped sharply. In order to understand to what degree our forces were reinforced during the offensive, it is sufficient to acquaint oneself with the figures below for the First Baltic Front.

Table 20. The First Baltic Front's Losses and Reinforcements, 23 June-20 August 1944[1]

Army & Formation	Losses	Reinforcements	Losses Covered (in %)
2nd Gds Army[2]	14,614	3,666	25.0
4th Shock Army	7,950	3,644	45.8
6th Gds Army	47,960	21,555	45.0
43rd Army	40,368	23,379	58.0
51st Army[3]	13,155	1,303	9.9
1st Tank Corps[4]	2,050	1,310	63.6
3rd Gds Mechanized Corps	1,308	1,500	115.0
46th Mechanized Bde	1,067	1,000	99.0
16th Lithuanian Rifle Div	720	3,000	416.0
Total	129,192	60,358	46.7

Notes
1 Central Ministry of Defense Archives, fond 233, opis' 20638ss, delo 16, p. 87.
2 Became part of the *front* only on 3 July.
3 Became part of the *front* only on 3 July.
4 Became part of the *front* only on 15 July.

It is clear from the table that the troops were reinforced at half the rate of their losses. If one takes into account the fact that these losses fell mainly on the combat element in the regiments, divisions and corps, then it becomes clear that in August our formations and units directly involved in combat operations were seriously short of men, which had a strong influence on the course of combat operations. For example, in the Third Belorussian Front's 11th Guards Army the rifle battalions were reduced to two companies, and in some divisions (26th, 83rd and 84th guards) these battalions had only a single rifle company, numbering 25-30 men apiece. A similar or nearly similar situation prevailed in a number of other armies in all the *fronts*.

Decisive combat operations unfolded in August along two main axes, along which the enemy not only sharply increased his resistance, but went over to active operations. These were the Riga and Warsaw axes.

During August 1944 the First Baltic Front was engaged in intense fighting west of Riga.

By the beginning of August the situation of the enemy's Army Group North had become very serious. The army group's defense along the Narva River at the end of July had been broken by the forces of the Leningrad Front, which continued to develop the offensive along the Tallinn axis. The forces of the Third Baltic Front broke through Army Group North's defense along the Pskov axis and at the end of July liberated the towns of Pskov and Ostrov. At the end of July the Second Baltic Front's forces began a new Madona offensive operation, with the goal of capturing Riga. However, the greatest threat to Army Group North was represented by the forces of the First Baltic Front, which had occupied Jelgava and Tukums and whose forward units had reached the shore of the Gulf of Riga, thus cutting off the land communications connecting the group of German-Fascist forces in the Baltic States with East Prussia. From this one can understand the fierce fighting that unfolded in August along the First Baltic Front's front.

On 31 July the commander of the First Baltic Front made a new decision, the idea of which came down to the *front's* main forces launching an attack toward Riga and liberating it. The *front* commander ordered the following: 6th Guards Army was to develop the offensive to the northwest, tying down the enemy all along its sector and preventing him front breaking contact with our forces; the 43rd Army was to continue the offensive to the north and reach the Western Dvina River south of Riga; the 51st Army's right flank (five rifle divisions) was to undertake a decisive offensive against Riga and liberate it. The 2nd Guards Army, operating along the *front's* left flank, had the mission of attacking to the west. The *front's* air army was ordered to concentrate its main forces to support the forces advancing on Riga.

On 1 August the *front's* forces, which had begun to attack in accordance with their assignments, did not manage to achieve any kind of noticeable successes. The enemy's group of forces, up to four infantry divisions (61st, 215th, 219th, and 281st) in strength, launched a counterblow that day in the area north of Birzai and pressed back units of the 43rd Army. On 2 August this enemy group of forces, further reinforced by units of the 225th Infantry Division and a motorized brigade disposing of about 80 tanks, continued to develop the success in the Birzai area and surrounded our 357th Rifle Division in the Rodziviliskis area. At the same time, the enemy's mobile detachment seized the village of Salociai. The enemy's advance in the 43rd Army's zone forced the *front* commander to halt the offensive by the neighboring 6th Guards Army and remove from the latter the 22nd Guards Rifle Corps and dispatch it to the Birzai area. Moreover, the 6th Guards Army was to relieve the 43rd Army's 1st Rifle Corps. On 3 August the enemy, continuing to develop his success, occupied Birzai. In connection with this event, the *Stavka* of the Supreme High Command handed over to the *front* from its own reserve, first the 19th Tank Corps, and then the 83rd Rifle Corps, from the Second Baltic Front.

Thanks to the *Stavka* of the Supreme High Command's measures, and those measures adopted by the *front* commander, the enemy's counterblow in the Birzai area was eliminated. The enemy did not manage to cut off the First Baltic Front's Jelgava—Tukums salient. However, the enemy did manage to foil the *front's* offensive on Riga. Stubborn fighting subsequently occurred along the Riga axis. On 5-6 August the enemy managed to seize the town of Jelgava (Mitava), but could not hold it.

On 5 August the *Stavka* of the Supreme High Command resubordinated the 4th Shock Army to the First Baltic Front, thus uniting the efforts of those forces attacking on Riga along the western bank of the Western Dvina River in the same hands.

During 5-17 August the forces of the 4th Shock and 6th Guards armies managed to advance up to 50 kilometers toward Riga and capture the enemy's important center of resistance of Jekabpils. In the areas of Birzai and Jelgava (Mitava) the forces of the 43rd and 51st armies were not able to advance and were forced to beat off the enemy's numerous counterattacks.

The enemy's counterblow in the Birzai area pursued limited aims and its main objective was evidently to foil the First Baltic Front's offensive on Riga and to eliminate our forces' breakthrough along the Jelgava—Tukums axis. At this time the enemy was preparing his main counterblow from East Prussia, on the borders of which was concentrated a powerful tank group, consisting of ten panzer divisions. The enemy's plan boiled down to launching a decisive attack with the Third Panzer Army, reinforced with six new panzer divisions, to the north and northeast, for the purpose of defeating the Soviet forces in the Siauliai and Jelgava (Mitava) areas and, as a result of the further unfolding of combat operations, restore his land communications with Army Group North in the Jelgava (Mitava) area.[1]

In accordance with this plan, the XL Panzer Corps, consisting of three panzer divisions, was to launch an attack in the direction of Kelme and Siauliai and capture Siauliai, while the XXXIX Panzer Corps, also consisting of three panzer divisions, was to attack in the direction of Telsiai and Ioniskis and capture the Ioniskis area.

Simultaneously with this counterblow, a supporting attack along the shore of the Gulf of Riga toward Tukums was being prepared. The Third Panzer Army's actions were coordinated with those

---

1   See the Military-Scientific Directorate Archives, delo 96, p. 138.

of Army Group North, which was to attack from the Riga area to the south, toward the forces of the Third Panzer Army.

The headquarters of the First Baltic Front began to receive information about the movement of the enemy's tanks from East Prussia from 12 August. On that day the movement of individual enemy tank columns was noted from the southwest toward Raseiniai and Kelme, and from the west toward Telsiai. By the morning of 13 August the concentration of the enemy's major tank forces was reliably established in the areas of Raseiniai, Uzventis and Telsiai. As early as 13 August the *front* commander began to take measures to repel a possible enemy attack from the west and southwest. He ordered the commanders of the 51st and 2nd Guards armies to reinforce their anti-tank defense along the most important axes and be ready to repel a possible counterblow. Moreover, the 17th Anti-Tank Artillery Brigade, reinforced with sappers and self-propelled artillery, was being hurriedly concentrated in the Ioniskis area.

The enemy began his counterblow on 14 August along the boundary between the 2nd Guards and 39th armies. The enemy began to press back the 24th Guards Rifle Division and before long had encircled the 25th Guards Tank Brigade and a regiment from the 158th Rifle Division in the Raseiniai area. The 18th Guards Tank Brigade and a regiment from the 164th Rifle Division were encircled in the village of Kalniai (six kilometers south of Raseiniai. Our forces continued to resist while surrounded and before long were relieved by the forces of the 84th Rifle Corps and the 5th Guards Tank Army. On 14 August *front* aviation continued to report on the movement of new enemy tank columns from East Prussia. Considering this, the *front* commander ordered the 3rd Guards Mechanized Corps to be ready to operate along the Ioniskis—Siauliai—Kelme axis. The 17th Anti-Tank Artillery Brigade was turned south into the Meskuiai area. The 103rd Rifle Corps was removed from the 6th Guards Army and was being hurriedly moved to the Siauliai area.

On 15 August the enemy was only deploying his main forces, while on the morning of 16 August he began his attack along a front approximately 70-80 kilometers broad. He launched the main attack against our 2nd Guards Army, against which on that day no less than 200 tanks and assault guns were operating. During the second half of the day attacks began against the 51st Army in the Zagare area.

On 17 August the enemy's main forces, which had launched an offensive along the entire front of our 51st and 2nd Guards armies, began to operate. Up to 400 enemy tanks and assault guns were operating on that day. However, the enemy did not manage to break through our defense. Only one group of enemy tanks, which was attacking from the Kursenai area, managed to break through toward Siauliai, where it ran into our 1st Tank Corps, which had moved up along that axis and had taken up defensive positions along the Kursenai—Siauliai road. Following three days of stubborn fighting, the enemy group of forces was defeated and thrown back toward Kursenai.

On 17 August, by order of the *Stavka* of the Supreme High Command, the Third Belorussian Front's 5th Guards Tank Army was resubordinated to the commander of the First Baltic Front. At the time the army was engaged in heavy fighting with the enemy's tank forces in the Raseiniai area, and at the time it was subordinated it had only 130 combat-ready tanks and self-propelled guns.

Having suffered a reverse near Siauliai, the enemy decided to shift his efforts north of the town and attack in the Ioniskis area, with the goal of breaking through our forces' defense between Mitava (Jelgava) and Siauliai. On 18-20 August stubborn fighting unfolded in the Zagare area between the tanks of the attacking enemy group of forces and our 3rd Guards Mechanized Corps, which was supported by the forces of the 51st Army. Nor did the enemy manage to achieve a breakthrough of our forces' defense along this axis. From 20 August he sought to outflank our forces further to the north. During 20-24 August stubborn fighting occurred along the Zagare—Bobele line, in which the 19th Tank Corps, which had been transferred from the 6th Guards Army's sector, took part on our side. The enemy's attempts to break through our defense were unsuccessful this time as well. However, he managed to push back the 3rd Guards Mechanized Corps' 8th Mechanized Brigade from the Tukums area and thus open a corridor along the shore of the Gulf of Riga.

Thus the deeply thought-out enemy counterblow by a powerful tank group, which was directed at eliminating the Siauliai and Jelgava bridgeheads, which had been formed by the forces of the First Baltic Front, ended, on the whole, unsuccessfully for him. The enemy did not manage to restore a solid defensive front between army groups Center and North. However, the enemy, thanks to this counterblow, did achieve the restoration of land communications with Army Group North along a narrow sector. Moreover, he managed to delay the First Baltic Front's offensive on Riga for an extended period of time.

The Third Belorussian Front's combat operations unfolded in August in the following manner. On 28 July the *front* received a directive from the *Stavka* of the Supreme High Command, in which it was demanded that "the *front's* entire forces attack toward the border of East Prussia and to capture the line Raseiniai—Jurbarkas—Eidkunen (Nesterov)—Suwalki no later than 10 August.[2]

Following the liberation of Kaunas, the *front's* forces in the first days of August began to carry out this assignment. The offensive was accompanied with great difficulties. Having reached the border of East Prussia, the *front's* forces ran into the well-prepared so-called East Prussian border defensive line, which had been securely occupied by the enemy's forces. During 2-6 August the *front's* forces were engaged in heavy offensive fighting, while attempting to break through the enemy's defense and carry the war onto East Prussian territory. As a result of this fighting, we managed to break through the enemy's defense only along two sectors—north of Vilkaviskis and northwest and west of Kalvarija along an overall front of 25 kilometers. However, the *front's* forces did not manage to develop this success, because the enemy continued to put up stubborn resistance. The enemy's air force was particularly active and carried out 1,500 sorties for launching raids against our forces during 2-6 August. During the same time our air force carried out 1,975 sorties. 74 enemy planes were shot down in air battles.

During 6-9 August the *front's* forces continued to engage in intensive fighting, but achieved a certain amount of success only along the *front's* right flank, where the 39th Army, supported by the 5th Guards Tank Army, forced the Dubysa River and occupied Raseiniai.

The enemy's stubborn resistance, the heavy losses, and the shortage of ammunition and fuel forced the *front's* forces to go over temporarily to the defensive in conditions in which the enemy had begun to carry out decisive counterattacks not only against the First Baltic Front, but against the Third Belorussian Front, which represented the greatest threat to the enemy with its approach to the border of Germany proper.

The enemy's counterblow against the Third Belorussian Front began on the morning of 9 August. Following a very powerful artillery and aviation preparation, one of the enemy's tank divisions, supported by various other units, broke through the defense of the 33rd Army's 222nd Rifle Division in stubborn fighting and reached the Marijampole—Vilkaviskis road, where it ran into artillery fire from the 47th Anti-Tank Artillery Brigade, and then the 2nd Guards Tank Corps' tank ambushes. Despite heavy losses, the enemy continued attacking and during the second half of the day occupied Vilkaviskis. All his subsequent attempts to advance toward Kaunas were repelled by our 2nd Guards Tank Corps and the *front's* other formations and units. Of 200 enemy tanks and assault guns, which took part in this counterblow, our forces destroyed 105 tanks and 18 assault guns. Stubborn fighting also broke out in the northern and northeastern outskirts of Vilkaviskis.

---

2   Central Ministry of Defense Archives, fond Third Belorussian Front. July-August 1944.

Having failed to achieve success around Vilkaviskis, the enemy shifted his efforts north of the town. Here, following a 30-minute artillery preparation, the enemy's 7th Panzer (130 tanks), 252nd and 212th infantry divisions, on the morning of 14 August attacked the 84th Rifle Corps and by 1700, having advanced 5-8 kilometers to the east, captured Raseiniai and Kalnuiai and encircled two of our tank brigades and two rifle regiments in this area.

On that same day, at about 2100, the commander of the 39th Army organized and carried out a counterblow with the forces of the 84th Rifle Corps and formations from the 5th Guards Tank Army, supported by the 1st Air Army's assault aviation. The enemy was thrown back to his start line and only in Raseiniai did he manage to hold on. Our units, encircled by the enemy in the area of Raseiniai and Kalnuiai, were relieved.

Having failed to achieve success around Vilkaviskis and Raseiniai, the enemy decided to reinforce his group of forces facing the First Baltic Front by transferring some forces from the Third Belorussian Front's sector. During 10-14 August the German-Fascist command transferred two panzer (5th Panzer and *Grossdeutschland* Panzer divisions) and other units to the Siauliai axis.

In order to resist these enemy transfers, as well as to reach the state border with Germany, the Third Belorussian Front on 15 August renewed the offensive in the general direction of Gumbinnen (Gusev). The *front* made its main attack with the forces of two armies (11th Guards and 33rd).

As a result of stubborn fighting with the enemy during 15-22 August, the forces of the 5th, 33rd and 11th Guards armies managed to advance 6-14 kilometers to the west and capture the town of Vilkaviskis. However, it was not possible to develop the offensive further and only the 5th Army, with a part of its forces along the right flank, reached the state boundary with Germany.

Nonetheless, with the start of our offensive the enemy was forced to quit transferring his forces from the *front's* sector to the Siauliai axis, although he committed an additional four divisions (1st, 547th and 549th infantry, and 390th Security divisions) into the fighting, plus three armored brigades (103rd, 104th and "Werthern").

The Second Belorussian Front's combat operations unfolded in August 1944 in the following manner. After the *front's* forces took the powerful Bialystok fortified area and the major railroad junction of Bialystok, they received new assignments on 30 and 31 July.

Along the *front's* right flank the 50th Army was to attack with one rifle corps on the morning of 1 August toward Augustow, and by the close of the next day capture it.

In the center the 49th Army was to continue attacking with its main forces in the direction of Jasionowka and Tzcjanne and arrive at the eastern bank of the Biebrza River along the line Osowiec—Wizna; another corps would attack south and seize a bridgehead along the southern bank of the Narew River in the Tykocin area, thus assisting the 3rd Army's advance. Along the left flank the 3rd Army was to, while continuing to attack to the west, by the close of 2 August force the Narew River, seize a bridgehead in the Lapy area and securely hold it.

In carrying out these tasks, the *front's* forces ran into the enemy's powerful and well-prepared defense along the Augustow Canal and the Bzozowka and Narew rivers. The enemy occupied this line as follows: along the 50th Army's sector—with corps group "G",[3] the 14th and 50th infantry divisions (the Fourth Army's VI Army Corps); along the 49th Army's sector—the 12th Panzer and 367th Infantry divisions (the Second Army's LV Army Corps), and; in the 3rd Army's sector— the 28th Light Infantry and 129th Infantry divisions (LV Army Corps) and the Hungarian 4th Cavalry Brigade. The enemy's army corps (VI and LV) had been reinforced with three brigades

---

3   Corps Group "G" consisted of the following: composite battalions from the 31st, 7th 337th infantry divisions, combat groups from the 237th and 260th infantry divisions, a regiment from the "East Prussia" 562nd Grenadier Division, von Gottenberg's police group (the remnants of the 2nd, 4th, 17th, 22nd, 24th, 34th police regiments), and Group "Nerkel" (1065th and 1069th infantry regiments).

of assault guns. The Lomza axis was the most densely covered. At the same time the enemy was intensively building a defensive line along the Biebrza and Narew rivers and the Augustow Canal along the Augustow—Ostroleka—Rozan sector and was rapidly reinforcing with men and materiel those units which occupied that line. The German-Fascist command sought to stop with all these measures our forces and prevent their arrival within East Prussia.

During 1-5 August the *front's* forces, while waging intensive battles with the enemy, advanced insignificantly in places, while the 3rd Army seized a small bridgehead. However, the army failed to carry out its objectives. Thus the offensive on Augustow was halted along the *front's* right flank, while the 50th and 49th armies' main efforts were switched to the Osowiec axis.[4] The armies were to attack with their main forces on the morning of 10 August toward Osowiec: the 50th Army from the line Bzozowo—Kamenka, and the 49th Army from the line Knyszyn—Krypno, and by the close of the day reach the line of the Biebrza River (from the mouth of the Bzozowka)—Goniadz—Zaiki. They were to subsequently capture the fortress of Osowiec and reach the Biebrza River along the entire front.

The 50th and 49th armies, having carried out a regrouping and concentration of forces along the main axes during 6-9 August, attacked at 1235 on 10 August, following a 35-minute artillery preparation, while the 3rd Army, to the left, continued to attack to the west.

During 10-14 August the *front's* forces completely broke through the defensive line along the Bzozowka and Narew rivers, captured the fortress of Osowiec, the towns of Goniadz, Mezenin and Wysokie-Mazowieckie, and reached the Biebrza River as far as its mouth and the intermediate defensive line three kilometers west of Mezenin and Wysokie-Mazowieckie. In this way the task, assigned to the troops on 6 August, was fulfilled, although late by three days, with an average daily rate of advance of 5-6 kilometers.

On 12 August *Stavka* directive no. 220161 assigned the *front* a new task—reach the line Augustow—Grajewo—Ostroleka—Goworowo and capture a bridgehead along the Narew River west of Ostroleka.

In carrying out this task, the *front* went over to the defensive along its right flank and center along the line of the Augustow Canal and Biebrza River along the sector Ziliny—excluding Goniadz (60 kilometers); the 3rd Guards Cavalry Corps (having relieved the 50th Army) along the sector Goniadz—Lake Maliszewskie (48 kilometers), and; the 50th Army (having relieved the 49th Army's formations from Oweczka and to the south).

Along a 30-kilometer sector on the left flank the *front* was concentrating its main efforts and planned to launch an attack on the morning of 21 August along the joint flanks of the 49th and 3rd armies: the first on Koziki, and the second on Zambrow, with the task of reaching the line Nadzeczny—Snjadowo—Kosewo by the close of 22 August.

However, on 19 August the enemy began to pull back his forces. Thus the *front's* shock group (49th and 3rd armies) was forced to go over to the offensive two days earlier than planned, without completing their regrouping.

The enemy, while striving at all costs to halt our offensive along the Narew River, put up fierce resistance, continually throwing into the fighting his reserves and formations, which had been transferred from other sectors (the 102nd, 14th and 547th infantry divisions, the 102nd Panzer Brigade, and others).

During 20-29 August the *front's* shock group was involved in intensive fighting, overcame a series of intermediate defensive lines, fitted out with permanent fortifications (concrete

---

4   *Front* directive no. 0042/op of 6 August 1944. Central Ministry of Defense Archives. Fond, Second Belorussian Front.

and wooden-earth pillboxes), which had been abandoned by us in 1941, and reached the line Wizna—Koziki—Dzerwin.

Stavka directive no. 220199, of 29 August, demanded that the *front's* forces reach the Narew River and seize a bridgehead along its western bank in the Ostroleka area, and then go over to a fixed defense. The forces of the Second Belorussian Front carried out this task by the close of 15 September.

The First Belorussian Front's combat operations in August 1944 unfolded in the following manner.

On 28 July the *Stavka* of the Supreme High Command laid down a new objective for the *front:*[5] the *front's* right wing was to develop the offensive in the general direction of Warsaw, and no later than 5-8 August capture the suburb of Praga, and seize a bridgehead along the western bank of the Narew River in the area of Pultusk and Serock, while the left flank was to seize a bridgehead along the western bank of the Vistula River in the Deblin area. Then the *front* was to launch an attack from the captured bridgeheads to the northwest and roll up the enemy's defense along the Narew and Vistula rivers and thus ease the forcing of the Narew River by the Second Belorussian Front's left wing, and the forcing of the Vistula River by its own central armies. The *front* would subsequently attack in the general direction of Torun and Lodz.

With the arrival of our forces at Praga (a suburb of Warsaw), the Western Bug and Vistula rivers, and with the seizure of two bridgeheads over the latter, the German-Fascist command concentrated the main efforts of its forces on retaining the area between the Western Bug, Narew and Vistula rivers, with the fortresses of Praga and Modlin and on eliminating our bridgeheads over the Vistula River. The enemy decided to halt our offensive to the west with these measures and block the way into Germany.

For the purpose of closing the breach that had formed as the result of the First Belorussian Front's successful offensive operations, as well as for improving its troop control around Warsaw, the German-Fascist command deployed the Ninth Army (from the Army Group Center reserve[6]) around Warsaw, between the Second and Fourth Panzer armies.

In carrying out the *Stavka's* assignment in this situation, the *front* commander decided to reach the Narew River and seize bridgeheads along its northern bank with the forces of the 48th and 65th armies, to repel the counterattacks by the enemy's tank group and capture Praga with the forces of the 2nd Tank, 28th, 47th, and 70th armies. The latter army would be committed into the battle from the *front* reserve. The *front's* remaining forces would strive to widen the bridgeheads along the western bank of the Vistula River.

Continuing to develop the offensive to the west, the *front's* forces captured the towns of Sokolow-Podlaski and Wengrow during 3-9 August and advanced 6-20 kilometers, at a pace of 0.7-2.3 kilometers per day (instead of the planned 15-25 kilometers). However, except for the 28th Army, they failed to carry out their assigned tasks. The enemy managed, by means of a powerful counterblow, in which up to five panzer and 1-2 infantry divisions took part, and at the cost of heavy losses in tanks and personnel, to halt our forces' offensive near Praga (a suburb of Warsaw) and recapture the inhabited locales of Radzymin, Wolomin and others and to press back the 2nd Tank Army,

---

5   *Stavka* directive no. 220162, of 28 July 1944. Central Ministry of Defense Archives. Fond of the First Belorussian Front.

6   The Ninth Army included the following: XXXIX Panzer Corps (17th and 73rd infantry divisions, the "Hermann Goering" SS Panzer Division, the 1131st and 1132nd infantry brigades), as well as the restored 45th and 6th infantry, and 391st Security divisions (3 and 8 August), and the following units transferred from the Second Army: the 19th and 4th panzer divisions, the "Viking" 5th SS Panzer Division and the *Totenkopf* SS Panzer Division (4 and 6 August), the Hungarian 5th, 12th and 23rd reserve divisions (8 August), and corps group "E" (16 August).

which had been weakened by several days of attacking, back to the line Okunew—Mendzylese. However, the enemy failed to achieve his main goal of defeating the army. The 2nd Tank Army, following its relief by formations of the 47th Army, had been pulled back into the *front* reserve in the Minsk-Mazowiecki area by the close of 5 August, where it was putting itself in order.

In striving to speed up the fulfillment of the *Stavka's* assignment, on 8 August the *front* commander decided to commit the 70th Army into the *front's* first echelon, to the left of the 28th Army, and ordered it, in conjunction with the latter, to launch its main attack on the morning of 10 August along the southern bank of the Liwiec River in the direction of Strachowka and reach the line Wengrow—Mendzylese.

Simultaneously, the 47th and 65th armies were to launch supporting attacks: the first toward Kossow and Wyszkow, and the second toward Radzymin, in order to arrive at the line (correspondingly) Nur—Kossow—Wengrow, and Mendzylese—Okunow.

In carrying out this task, the *front's* forces during 10-12 August broke through an intermediate defensive line, began fighting for Wysokie-Mazowieckie, Czyzew and the Western Bug River from Malkinja Gurna as far as Mlynaze (ten kilometers southwest of Wyszkow and reached the line Mlynaze—Maidan—Ossow (four kilometers east and south of Wolomin).

Our attacking forces subsequently ran into the powerful water barrier of the Western Bug River, with a powerful defensive line along its northern bank, and the powerfully-developed Warsaw fortified area, as well as the enemy's fierce resistance. The line of the Western Bug River was occupied by the 5th Light Infantry and 35th Infantry divisions, along with two brigades of assault guns, and the Warsaw fortified area was occupied by a major enemy group of forces ("Viking" 5th SS Panzer Division, a part of the 19th Panzer Division, the *Totenkopf* 3rd SS Panzer Division, the 73rd and 567th infantry divisions, and the Hungarian 1st Cavalry Division, along with two brigades of assault guns and various security and special units).

During 24-28 August the *front's* right-wing and center forces, overcoming the enemy's fierce resistance and slowly advancing, captured the important road junction of Ostrow-Mazowiecka, while an attack by two of the 65th Army's corps (moved to the northern bank of the Western Bug River) along the river rolled up the enemy's defense along a 25-kilometer sector. By the close of 28 August the *front's* forces reached the line Psziborowe—Udzin and further along the southern bank of the Western Bug River—the eastern bank of the Zondza River—Mendzylese, and the eastern bank of the Vistula River as far as the mouth of the Swider River.

During 3-28 August along the left wing the *front's* forces (8th Guards and 69th armies), while continuing to widen the Magnuszew and Pulawy bridgeheads along the western bank of the Vistula River and repelling the enemy's powerful and numerous tank and infantry counterattacks, reached the line of the mouth of the Pilica River—excluding Barcha—excluding Golowaczow—Wolnica, and Pulawy—Maszadla—Chotcza. In this way the *front's* forces broadened their bridgeheads; the Magnuszew bridgehead to 25 kilometers in width and 15-18 kilometers in depth, and the Pulawy bridgehead to a corresponding 25 and 12 kilometers.

On 29 August the *Stavka's* directive no. 220196 clarified the *front's* assignment and demanded that the left wing go over to the defensive, while the right wing would continue the offensive and during 4-5 September reach the Narew River in the Pultusk and Serock area, after which it would also go over to the defensive.[7]

By the close of 5 September the *front* had reached the Narew River in its sector and had seized bridgeheads along its western bank south of Rozan and north of Serock.

On the whole, during August 1944 the forces of the First Baltic, Third, Second and First Belorussian fronts had to wage difficult offensive battles along individual axes along a huge sector

---

7   Central Ministry of Defense Archives, opis' 20897, delo 6, p. 195.

(1,200 kilometers). As a result of these battles, the *front's* forces repelled several powerful counter-attacks by the enemy and broke through a number of his defensive lines, reached East Prussia and the capital of allied Poland—Warsaw, and also reached the river barriers of the Narew and Vistula, having expanded and consolidated the Magnuszew and Pulawy bridgeheads over the latter. This created favorable conditions for conducting offensive operations in January 1945 in East Prussia and Poland.

During August the *front's* forces liberated from German-Fascist occupation a territory of 19,180 square kilometers in the Latvian and Lithuanian SSRs and allied Poland (correspondingly 6,200, 3,100 and 9,880 square kilometers), and also inflicted heavy losses on the enemy in men and materiel. In all, eight infantry divisions and one panzer brigade were defeated.

It's typical that the enemy's losses in officers and men in August were equal to his losses for the entire first stage of the Belorussian operation, and were twice as large in tanks. This indicates just how fierce was the fighting in consolidating the successes achieved during the Belorussian operation.

The troops' advance in August was insignificant and was as follows: in the First Baltic Front—10-80 kilometers; in the Third Belorussian Front—up to 50 kilometers, and; in the Second and First Belorussian fronts—up to 80 kilometers. The pace of advance was, correspondingly, 2.6, 1.6 and 2.6 kilometers per day. Along a number of axes the troops' advance was even less. Furthermore, our formations and units were also pushed back a bit near Tukums (First Baltic Front) and near Warsaw (First Belorussian Front).

The sharp drop in the troops' offensive pace in August, compared to that of July, is primarily explained by the enemy's significantly increased resistance, his commitment into the battle of a large number of tank and infantry divisions, transferred from other sectors of the front and from the reserve,[8] the presence of a deeply-echeloned defense in a wooded and swampy area, such water obstacles as the Western Bug, Narew and Vistula rivers, the exhaustion of the troops' after an unbroken 70-day offensive, and the lagging behind of the rear organs.

Shortcomings in the offensive's organization, particularly in the First and Second Belorussian fronts, undoubtedly had a negative effect on the speed of the *fronts'* advance. For example, the operational formation of the armies and corps did not correspond to the situation, a large number of men and materiel were held in reserve, and they were allotted in a completely insufficient manner for the offensive. For example, until 16 August 49 percent of the First Belorussian Front's rifle divisions were in the first line, with only 33 percent and 37 percent in the 48th and 28th armies, 40 percent in the Second Belorussian Front's 50th Army during the offensive on Augustow, and only 28 percent along the main axis.

The supply of ammunition and fuels and lubricants was obviously insufficient, and in the majority of armies reached as follows (in combat loads): mortar rounds—0.5-0.9; 45mm shells—0.7-1; 76mm regimental artillery shells—1-1.3, 76mm divisional artillery shells—0.6-0.9, and; 122mm shells—0.4-1.

Data on the Soviet forces' losses for August testifies to the intensive fighting with the enemy and his desperate resistance.

In developing the offensive and repulsing the enemy's counterattacks in August, our forces suffered the following losses: 282,527 men killed, wounded and missing in action, or 20.5 percent of the forces available on 1 August 1944. This includes 64,258 men killed (4.7 percent). The losses

---

8   Four infantry, two panzer divisions, one panzer brigade, and one panzer corps. Moreover, three panzer brigades, four infantry and one security divisions were reformed, while 17 infantry, security and cavalry divisions and one panzer division were reconstituted.

of the German-Fascist forces in Belorussia in August were 317,091 men. Thus compared with the enemy's losses, our losses were less.[9]

The Third Belorussian and First Baltic fronts suffered the heaviest casualties (25.7 percent and 20.6 percent), and the First and Second Belorussian fronts the least (18.6 percent and 17.7 percent). The heavy losses suffered by the Third Belorussian and First Baltic fronts is explained by the fierce battles waged to repulse the enemy's powerful counterblows near Jelgava, Siauliai, Raseiniai, Vilkaviskis, and also in forcing the Memel, Dubysa and Neman rivers.

It should be noted that the *fronts* began the August offensive, having in their rifle divisions, as a rule, no more than 16 rifle companies (59 percent). For example, in the First Baltic Front 33 percent of the rifle divisions had up to 12 rifle companies and 33 percent 13-16 companies. The strength of the companies was no more than 60-70 men. This could also not but influence the speed of the *fronts'* offensive.

Thus in August 1944 the forces of the First Baltic, Third, Second and First Belorussian fronts waged combat operations to consolidate the successes achieved in the Belorussian operation and to improve their operational situation. These actions concluded with the four *fronts* going over to the defensive along these lines, for the purpose of reconstituting their expended forces and reserves and to prepare for new offensive operations.

---

9   Central Ministry of Defense Archives, fond 233, opis' 23381, delo 96; fond 237, opis' 58617, delo 10; opis' 56381, delo 10; fond 235, opis' 2078, delo 81; fond 241, opis' 45072, delo 4.

Conclusions on the Conduct of the Belorussian Operation

During the Belorussian operation all the tasks, laid down for the group of *fronts* by the *Stavka* of the Supreme High Command, were completely carried out.

During the operation's first stage the enemy's defense, which had been so scrupulously prepared during the course of an extended period, was crushed not only in the tactical zone, but in the operational depth as well, as far as the seizure by our troops of the rear defensive zone along the Berezina River, called the "catastrophe line" by the enemy. Truly, the forcing of the Berezina River by our forces was a total catastrophe for the enemy, for this signified not only the loss of half of Belorussia, but, and what is most important, the loss of the previously-prepared defensive lines, major water barriers, and almost all the major centers of resistance, which, taken together, comprised the heart of the German-Fascist army's entire defense on Belorussian territory. The enemy expected, least of all, to conduct a war of maneuver in Belorussia, hoping to repel our offensive through the stubborn defense of his defensive lines and by holding the water barriers and other natural obstacles in his hands. All of the enemy's hopes were dispelled during the course of the first days of our offensive.

The German-Fascist command placed particularly great hopes on the solidity of its tactical defense zone, considering it almost inaccessible for the Soviet forces. However, the Soviet forces required only two days to overcome this zone.

By the close of the operation's sixth day; that is by the close of 28 June, the Soviet forces, having overcome the tactical defense zone, as well as the army and rear zones, achieved operational freedom, having created for themselves favorable conditions for a subsequent offensive in the direction of Vilnius, Daugavpils, Baranovichi, Pinsk, and other major political and economic centers.

During 12 days of attacking, Soviet forces advanced 250-300 kilometers to the west. During this time the enemy's main forces, which had been defending in Belorussia, were defeated and forced to retreat toward the Baltic States and Poland. The enemy's Fourth Army, which was almost completely encircled around Minsk, suffered in particular and only managed to retreat to the west in small groups, having lost all its equipment. The enemy's Third Panzer and Ninth armies, which were partially encircled near Vitebsk, Bobruisk, near Minsk, and in other places, were also seriously mangled. These armies also lost almost all their combat equipment. Only the enemy's Second Army still maintained some sort of combat capability, but even it could no longer hold a continuous defensive front and was putting up resistance only along individual axes. The losses in military equipment, which the enemy could not evacuate in its hurried retreat, were especially heavy for the enemy, for the roads were in poor condition, were subject to systematic raids by Soviet aviation and, besides, were controlled by the Belorussian partisans.

All of this speaks to the fact that the German-Fascist forces defending in Belorussia were, to a significant degree, wiped out and that the front could only be held by those forces which had been thrown in from other strategic directions, or from Germany itself. It is known that during the period from 23 June to 4 July the enemy committed 18 new divisions into the battle, which comprised, together with the first echelon's surviving formations, the heart of the defense in Belorussia for the immediate future.

The tasks laid down by the *Stavka* of the Supreme High Command in its directives to the *fronts* of 31 May 1944, were carried out by the *fronts* in full.

The *Stavka* plan, contained in the initial directives for conducting the multi-*front* Belorussian offensive operation, was carried out by our forces during the first 12 days. The subsequent offensive was conducted according to new directives and individual orders, which were issued during the course of the operation.

The following must be considered the most important results of the Belorussian offensive operation's first stage:

1. The complete rout of a number of major enemy groups of forces (Vitebsk, Bobruisk and others) and the breakthrough of the enemy's defense along six axes and in a sector exceeding 600 kilometers.
2. The liberation of more than half of Belorussia and the overcoming of major water obstacles, such as the Western Dvina, Dnepr and Berezina rivers, and others.
3. The occupation of the capital of Belorussia—Minsk, which had enormous political significance and influenced fascist Germany's relations with many other states. The Anglo-American ruling circles appraised the events in Belorussia as the collapse of the German-Fascist defense along the Soviet-German front and began an attack with their own forces from the bridgehead captured by them in northern France. This was facilitated by the drawing off of almost all fascist Germany's reserves to the Soviet-German front, in order to seal off the 400-kilometer breach that had opened in Belorussia.
4. The encirclement, east and southeast of Minsk, of the enemy's 100,000-man group of forces, by which the Soviet forces completely deprived the enemy of the opportunity to restore his front in Belorussia and halt our offensive. The encirclement of the enemy's group of forces in the deep rear, at a remove of 200 kilometers from the forward defense line, is one of the most brilliant examples of the skillful conduct of the pursuit of a retreating enemy. By carrying out this task, the Red Army gained favorable conditions for completing the liberation of Belorussia and shifting military operations onto Latvian, Lithuanian and Polish territory.

During the second stage of the multi-*front* Belorussian operation, which lasted from 5-31 July, the Soviet forces carried out a number of tasks, which also had major significance for the subsequent course of the war.

First of all, during this stage the Soviet forces defeated a number of major enemy groups of forces, which were attempting to halt the Soviet forces' offensive, to restore the situation and to eliminate the threat of the war being carried into Germany itself. Without hoping to save the main group of forces surrounded east of Minsk, the German-Fascist command began to hurriedly create a new major group of forces in the Dvinsk area, counting on employing it to stop the First Baltic Front's offensive and thus prevent the formation of a gap between army groups Center and North. The enemy was preparing a second major group of forces in the Vilnius area and along the line of the Neman River, hoping that this group of forces would prevent an invasion by Soviet forces into East Prussia. By concentrating a part of his reserves against our Second Belorussian Front, the enemy pursued the same goal—to cover the approaches to East Prussia and, moreover, to eliminate the threat of a possible attack by Soviet forces on Warsaw from the Bialystok axis.

As early as the beginning of the operation's second stage, the *Stavka* of the Supreme High Command foresaw such a variation of the enemy's actions and, in accordance with this, carried out major troop regroupings. The reinforcement of the First Baltic Front with two armies, and then with the 3rd Guards Mechanized Corps, had a decisive influence. Five Soviet armies (2nd and 6th guards, 43rd, 39th, and 51st) and two independent corps (1st Tank and 3rd Guards Mechanized) streamed into the 150-kilometer space between Dvinsk and Vilnius and between the enemy's groups of forces being created.

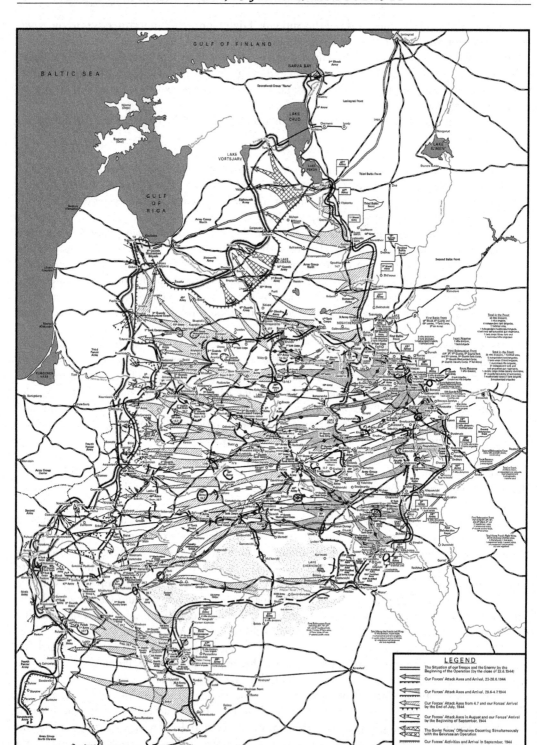

Map 4 The Rout of the German-Fascist Forces in Belorussia (June-August 1944).

Thus by the end of the multi-*front* Belorussian operation, a completely new situation had come about in the Baltic States, in which it was important for the Soviet forces to hold their positions, while the enemy had to exert enormous efforts in order to ease the developing situation.

By the end of the operation the situation for the enemy along the Warsaw axis was no less difficult. The First Belorussian Front's left-wing forces managed to break through the enemy's defense west of Kovel' and as early as the third day of the offensive force the Western Bug River along the Siedlce and Lublin axes, which enabled us to create favorable conditions for developing the offensive, both in the direction of the Brest fortress and toward the capital of Poland—Warsaw.

The German-Fascist command sought, by creating a significant reserve along the Warsaw axis, to foil the Soviet command's plans. However, the German-Fascist forces suffered just as great a defeat here as in the Baltic States. Soviet forces not only occupied Brest and cleared the space between the Western Bug, Vistula and Narew rivers, but also created bridgeheads along the Vistula and Narew, which played an extremely important role in the subsequent events of the Great Patriotic War.

The German-Fascist command also sought to prevent the arrival of Soviet troops at the borders of East Prussia and a shift in military operations to Germany itself. However, the forces of the Third and Second Belorussian fronts reached the borders of East Prussia and thus created conditions for carrying out offensive operations against this enemy citadel. However, in order to accomplish this, it was necessary to put our forces in order after the numerous offensive battles, to reinforce them with all necessary means, and to prepare a new offensive operation.

It was typical of the Belorussian operation of 1944 that during its second stage the number of operational major field forces and individual formations, committed into the operation, grew sharply (see table 21).

It is clear from the table that the augmentation of forces was carried out along the wings of the group of *fronts*—along the Baltic and Warsaw axes. Such an augmentation of forces was deeply significant, as an attack along the Siauliai axis by the forces of the First Baltic Front would greatly help the Second and Third Baltic fronts, which had begun to press the enemy's Army Group North, which, under threat of encirclement, had begun to roll back to the shore of the Gulf of Riga. The *Stavka* of the Supreme High Command sought to ensure close coordination between the First Belorussian and First Ukrainian fronts, the latter of which on 13 July had begun the L'vov—Sandomierz operation, directed at clearing western Ukraine of the enemy, by an attack by major forces along the Warsaw axis.

During August Soviet forces consolidated the successes achieved in the Belorussian operation and were carrying out combat operations to improve their operational situation.

On the whole, the multi-*front* offensive in Belorussia in June, July and August 1944 radically altered the situation along the entire Soviet-German front and created favorable conditions for future major offensive operations by Soviet forces.

Table 21. Comparative Data on the Number of Attacking Major Field Forces and Individual Formations During the First and Second Stages of the Belorussian Operation

Major Field Forces and Formations	First Stage			
	1st Baltic Front	3rd Belorussian Front	2nd Belorussian Front	1st Belorussian Front
Combined-Arms Armies	3	4	3	4
Tank Armies	–	1	–	–
Air Armies	1	1	1	1
Mechanized Corps	–	1	–	1
Tank Corps	1	1	–	2
Cavalry Corps	–	1	–	1

Major Field Forces and Formations	Second Stage			
	1st Baltic Front	3rd Belorussian Front	2nd Belorussian Front	1st Belorussian Front
Combined-Arms Armies	5-4[1]	4-5[1]	3	9
Tank Armies	–	1	–	1
Air Armies	1	1	1	2
Mechanized Corps	1	–	–	1
Tank Corps	1	1	–	3
Cavalry Corps	–	1-0[1]	0-1[1]	3

Notes
1 The first figure shows the strength at the start of the second stage, and the second at the end.

Results and Conclusions of the Belorussian Operation of 1944

Results of the Operation

The multi-*front* Belorussian offensive operation of 1944 was conducted by the forces of four *fronts*, Long-Range Aviation, the Dnepr River Flotilla, and a large number of partisan formations and units operating in the rear of the German-Fascist Army Group Center. In all, the four *fronts*, taking into account the forces transferred to them by the *Stavka* of the Supreme High Command, comprised the following: men—more than 2.5 million; guns and mortars of all calibers—more than 45,000; tanks and self-propelled guns—more than 6,000, and; aircraft (counting Long-Range Aviation)—about 8,000.[1] By the start of the operation the enemy had facing the Soviet troops attacking in Belorussia (counting only the combat element) numbered more than 426,000 officers and men, more than 9,000 guns and mortars, about 1,300 tanks and assault guns, and up to 1,400-1,500 planes. The overall number of enemy troops, which were successively fed into the Belorussian operation, reached more than 1.5 million men, up to 17,000 guns and mortars, more than 1,500 tanks and assault guns, and more than 2,100 planes.

The Belorussian operation was one of the largest offensive operations, not only of 1944, but of the entire Great Patriotic War, and exerted a great influence on its development.

The results of the multi-*front* Belorussian offensive operation of 1944 were enormous and have major military-political and strategic significance. As a result of this operation, fascist Germany's situation became even worse. Its central group of forces along the Soviet-German front—Army Group Center,[2] was routed, while Army Group North's Sixteenth and Fourth Panzer armies suffered heavy losses.

As a result of the defeat of the enemy's Vitebsk, Bobruisk and Minsk groups of forces, an enormous breach was formed, stretching more than 400 kilometers in width.

It was only in the second half of July that the enemy managed to restore a new defensive front along the line of the Neman and Vistula rivers. From 23 June through 29 August the enemy transferred against the First Baltic and the three Belorussian fronts 19 divisions and eight brigades from the Baltic States and the southern wing of the Soviet-German front. Moreover, 17 divisions from among newly-formed and reformed forces in the rear of the German-Fascist forces operating along the Soviet-German front arrived to reinforce Army Group Center.[3] Overall, during this period 36 divisions (including ten panzer), eight brigades and up to 700 enemy planes arrived in Belorussia from other axes of the Soviet-German front, and well as newly-formed ones.

The forced transfer of enemy forces to Belorussian weakened his groups of forces along other axes, which created favorable conditions for conducting new offensive operations by Soviet forces in western Ukraine, Moldavia and the Baltic States.

As a result of the crushing defeat of the enemy's major strategic group of forces by the Red Army, the German-Fascist command was also forced to transfer to the central sector of the

---

1 *Operatsii Sovetskikh Vooruzhennykh Sil v Velikoi Otechestvennoi Voine*. VNU GSh VS SSSR, vol. III, p. 292.
2 Army Group Center consisted of the Third Panzer, Fourth, Ninth and Second armies.
3 *Operatsii Sovetskikh Vooruzhennykh Sil v Velikoi Otechestvennoi Voine*. VNU GSh VS SSSR, vol. III, p. 362.

Soviet-German front 14 divisions (including 11 infantry, one motorized, and two panzer) and five brigades from Germany, Poland, Hungary, Norway, the Netherlands and other European countries,[4] which facilitated the unfolding of the Anglo-American forces' offensive in Western Europe from their captured bridgehead in northern France.

As a result of the Belorussian operation, Soviet forces advanced to a depth of 550-600 kilometers to the west along an enormous front (up to 1,200 kilometers), completely liberated the Belorussian SSR, a large part of the Lithuanian SSR, part of the Latvian and Ukrainian SSRs, and a significant part of allied Poland; forced an entire series of major water obstacles, such as the Dnepr, Berezina, Pripyat', Western Dvina, Western Bug and Neman rivers, and finally reached the Gulf of Riga, East Prussia and the Vistula River, having seized bridgeheads on its western bank.

With their arrival at the immediate approaches to Riga, our forces deeply outflanked the enemy's Army Group North from the south and southwest. Moreover, we occupied areas that enabled us to deploy our forces to defeat the German-Fascist groups of forces in East Prussia and in the central and western areas of Poland.

At the same time, the elimination of the Belorussian salient excluded the threat of the enemy's flank attack against the forces of the neighboring First Ukrainian Front and facilitated their successful offensive along the L'vov—Sandomierz axis and the defeat of Army Group North Ukraine. As a result of the defeat of major enemy forces in Belorussia, the Soviet front from the Baltic to the Carpathian Mountains began to move. From 5 August nine *fronts* were attacking.

Thus the enormous significance of the Belorussian operation of 1944 is determined, first of all, by the fact that it concluded with the defeat of a major enemy group of forces and had a decisive influence on the successful conduct of all the succeeding offensive operations of both the Soviet armed forces along an enormous front from the Gulf of Finland to the Carpathians, and the Anglo-American forces in Western Europe.

Soviet forces liberated an enormous territory of 268,300 square kilometers from German-Fascist occupation.

Simultaneously, our forces liberated a large number of towns, including the capitals of the Belorussian and Lithuanian SSRs—Minsk and Vilnius, as well as the provincial centers of Vitebsk, Vileika, Mogilev, Pinsk, Baranovichi, Brest, and Bialystok.

During the operation the enemy (not counting the August fighting) lost 986,478 officers and men killed, wounded and captured. If the August fighting is included, these losses rise to 1,303,569 officers and men. It should be noted, however, that the data on losses, although it was computed on the basis of archival documents, including captured ones, needs to be further checked and tightened up. This is especially true of the defeated German-Fascist formations and units in which the inventory of losses in the most critical days was noted conducted regularly, and thus accurate documentary data is absent.

During the course of the Belorussian operation, of the enemy's 97 divisions and 13 brigades that variously took part in the fighting against Soviet forces, 58 divisions (including six panzer) and three brigades were defeated. Of these, eight divisions were part of the Sixteenth and Fourth Panzer armies, which formed part of, respectively, army groups North and North Ukraine, while the remainder was part of Army Group Center. Of these 58 divisions, 30 were completely destroyed or captured, while the remainder suffered losses of 50-70 percent.

Moreover, in August another seven divisions and one brigade were defeated.[5]

---

4   One panzer division from Italy, one infantry division from Norway, one panzer division from the Netherlands, and ten infantry divisions and one motorized division from Germany, Poland, Hungary, and other countries, as well as five infantry brigades.

5   *Sbornik Materialov po Sostavu, Gruppirovke i Peregruppirovke Sukhoputnykh Voisk Fashistskoi Germanii i Voisk Byvshikh ee Satellitov na Sovetsko-Germanskom Fronte za Period 1941-1945 gg.* Vypusk 4, VNU GSh VS SSSR,

The figures shown above do not include a large number of the enemy's defeated special units—artillery, engineer, construction, and others.

By the end of August 44 divisions, 24 combat groups and five brigades were operating against our forces and which had also suffered losses reaching, in many cases, up to 50 percent. It should be noted that the so-called combat groups represented the remnants of German-Fascist formations.

During the operation our forces also suffered considerable losses in men and materiel. In the Belorussian operation of 1944, including the offensive operations carried out in August 1944, our forces lost 723,340 men killed, wounded and missing in action, among other reasons (or 48.8 percent of the four *fronts'* strength at the start of the operation), of which 161,490 men were killed. Not counting the August fighting, our losses amounted to 440,879 men (or 29.8 percent), of which 97,232 (or 6.6 percent) were killed.[6] However, in comparison to the enemy's losses, our losses were significantly lower. On the whole, these data testify to the fierce character of the fighting in Belorussia.

Conclusions on Military Art

Some Questions of Strategy

The Belorussian operation of 1944 was carried out along the very important Minsk—Warsaw strategic direction, which was the shortest route to the capital of fascist Germany—Berlin.

During the operation a major enemy strategic group of forces—Army Group Center, which occupied a previously-prepared defense along this direction, was defeated.

With the defeat of this group of forces, the center of the enemy's strategic front was crushed and the so-called Belorussian balcony, which hung over the Soviet forces' strategic group of forces attacking in Ukraine, was eliminated.

1.   The arrival of the Soviet armed forces in the Belorussian operation at the Soviet Union's western boundaries completed the achievement of the Soviet Union's first strategic goal along this direction—the liberation of Soviet territory and the Soviet peoples from fascist occupation. During the course of the operation, the Soviet forces began the resolution of the war's next strategic goal—aiding the peoples of Europe in their liberation from the Hitlerite yoke. The eastern part of allied Poland was liberated. Soviet forces reached the borders or East Prussia—the citadel of German militarism over an extended period and which had served as a springboard for military attacks on our country.

With the arrival of the First Baltic Front's forces at the Baltic Sea the German-Fascist strategic front was split into two parts. At the same time, Army Group North was cut off by land from fascist Germany's remaining armed forces, thus creating favorable conditions for its defeat by the forces of the Leningrad and three Baltic fronts.

2.   The success of the powerful blow, launched by the four *fronts* in Belorussia, was immediately used by the *Stavka* of the Supreme High Command for broadening the strategic offensive's front and for the assumption of the offensive by the forces of the Leningrad, Third and Second Baltic fronts to the north, and the First and then the Fourth Ukrainian fronts south of the operational area of the *fronts* taking part in the Belorussian operation.

---

pp. 88-140.
6   Data were calculated according to the *fronts'* archival documents.

If before the Belorussian operation of 1944, only the enemy's flank groups of forces along the Soviet-German front—army groups North and South—had been defeated, then with the conduct of operations in Belorussia and western Ukraine, almost the entire strategic front was enveloped by powerful successive attacks by the Soviet armed forces, which put the enemy in an extremely difficult situation as regards the conduct of maneuvering his forces and reserves from one strategic direction to another.

The defeat of the enemy's Army Group Center by Soviet forces in Belorussia, and the formation here of a more than 400-kilometer breach in the enemy's strategic defense along the most dangerous strategic direction for fascist Germany's vital centers, exerted an enormous influence on the course of military operations in Western Europe. The Hitlerite command, which threw almost all the reserves at its disposal into closing the resulting breach in Belorussia, was forced to renounce further resistance against the Anglo-American forces in France and began to withdraw its armies to the boundaries of Germany proper and the so-called Siegfried Line. As a result, the slow advance of the Anglo-American forces from the Normandy beachhead was succeeded by the high-speed pursuit of the retreating enemy in Belgium and northern France.

3.   The Belorussian operation of 1944 is an example of a multi-*front* consecutive operation in a strategic offensive by the Soviet armed forces in the summer-fall campaign of the Great Patriotic War's third period.

By this time the Soviet armed forces disposed of an overall superiority in forces over the enemy along the entire Soviet-German front. However, this superiority was not yet sufficient for simultaneously conducting an offensive along the entire front. Our strategic rear was still not in a condition to supply a series of major groups of forces in conditions of their simultaneous conduct of an offensive. Thus the Soviet Supreme High Command selected the most expedient method of operations—the launching of successive attacks against the enemy, which would come to embrace the entire Soviet-German front with offensive operations.

The Belorussian operation was carried out by the *Stavka* of the Supreme High Command after the conduct of offensive operations along the flanks of the Soviet-German front. During its conduct the direction of the main attack was shifted from Ukraine to Belorussia.

Subsequently, when the Soviet Union's capabilities had grown even further, operations began to be conducted by Soviet forces simultaneously along the greater part of the Soviet-German front, and then along the entire front.

This tendency was already visible during the course of the Belorussian operation. Even before the conclusion of the four *fronts'* offensive in Belorussia, the Leningrad, Third and Second Baltic fronts began their offensive, followed by the First and then Fourth Ukrainian fronts. In this way the offensive, which began in Belorussia, unfolded along a very broad front.

Thus the group of *fronts*, which attacked the enemy's Army Group Center in Belorussia, coordinated simultaneously with several *fronts*, which went over to the offensive against Army Group Center, and with the group of *fronts*, which was carrying out the L'vov—Sandomierz operation against Army Group North Ukraine.

The coordination of activities between the groups of *fronts* and the *fronts* operating along the other axes was carried out by the *Stavka* of the Supreme High Command directly, or through its representatives on the spot.

4.   The Belorussian operation is one of the brightest examples of carrying out precise strategic coordination of the ground forces, which played the most important role in the operation, with Long-Range Aviation, as well as with major partisan formations, in the interests of achieving a single strategic goal.

The Belorussian operation of 1944 is instructive, particularly as regards the organization and support for coordinating a group of *fronts* with Long-Range Aviation. Typical of this was the fact that Long-Range Aviation's attacks were directed by the *Stavka* of the Supreme High Command in the interests of resolving the operational tasks of a group of *fronts*. At the same time, Long-Range Aviation carried out measures for operational masking (both by its basing on Ukrainian airfields, as well as by launching demonstration attacks in the area of Kishinev and Iasi; it launched attacks against deep targets in the operational zone of the *fronts* in Belorussia and took part in the aviation preparation directly against the enemy's forces in the tactical defense zone during the first stage of the Belorussian operation.

The coordination of the ground forces with the *fronts'* air armies was chiefly carried out at the operational level, although taken as a whole, it had strategic significance. The *Stavka* of the Supreme High Command coordinated and directed the operations of the *fronts'* air armies and reinforced them with planes form its own reserve, depending on the importance of the tasks being pursued by the ground forces along this or that axis.

Coordination with the navy during this operation was almost absent, insofar as the operation was chiefly conducted in a land theater. The Dnepr River Flotilla was used by operationally subordinating it to the commander of the First Belorussian Front, which enables us to speak only of operational and not strategic cooperation, with the flotilla.

On the whole, as regards the organization of coordination of the armed services, this was a typical operation of the period under study.

5. The strategic control of the operations of a group of *fronts* on the part of the *Stavka* of the Supreme High Command was carried out along two lines, indissolubly connected between themselves: by means of issuing directives and instructions on all basic questions, and by the method of coordinating the *fronts'* activities directly on the ground through *Stavka* representatives.

In the Belorussian operation directives to the *fronts*, both before the start of the operation and during its conduct, were issued by the *Stavka* of the Supreme High Command by summoning the *front* commanders to the *Stavka* and assigning them tasks there (before the start of the operation), or by sending coded telegrams to the *fronts*. Some instructions were issued through direct high-frequency telephone, which linked the *Stavka* of the Supreme High Command directly with the *front* commanders and, when necessary, even with the army commanders. Operational ideas and plans were drawn up by the *fronts* and confirmed in the *Stavka*.

As early as April 1944 the commander of the First Belorussian Front was oriented by the *Stavka* of the Supreme High Command as to the further employment of the *front's* forces in the forthcoming summer-fall campaign of 1944. The *front* commander received more concrete instructions in the *Stavka* on 23-24 May 1944. The geographical plan of the operation was then made on a map. The assignment was received orally in the *Stavka*, followed by a *Stavka* directive confirming it. Corrections to the operational plan, which had been drawn up in the front, were made by the *Stavka* representative, after which the plan was confirmed by the Supreme Commander-in-Chief.

Strategic leadership on the part of the *Stavka* of the Supreme High Command was also manifested as concerns the all-round support of the operation. For example, for the purpose of creating in the First Belorussian Front's left-wing sector a powerful shock group, designated for operating during the second stage of the multi-*front* Belorussian operation, the *Stavka* planned and carried out ahead of time major strategic regroupings, such as the transfer of the 8th Guards and 2nd Tank armies from the Third and Second Ukrainian fronts to the First Belorussian Front, as well as the regrouping of major air formations from various military districts to the *front*, for the purpose of creating a second powerful air army within a single *front*. According to a *Stavka* plan the delivery of reinforcements, ammunition and all kinds of supplies to the *fronts* was carried out ahead of time.

Major troop regroupings were carried out according to *Stavka* orders within the *fronts* (for example, the regrouping of large masses of reinforcement artillery from the right flank of the First Belorussian Front to the left over a distance of more than 600 kilometers in July 1944). The *fronts* were presented with the necessary roads and rolling stock.

Typical of the operation was the presence of two *Stavka* representatives, of which one coordinated the operations of the group of *fronts'* right wing (First Baltic and Third Belorussian fronts), and a second the operations of the center and left wing (Second and First Belorussian fronts). At the same time the *Stavka* representatives were entrusted the task of coordinating the activities not only of the *fronts* taking part in the operation, but also of the latter with neighboring *fronts* taking part in other operations. For example, a *Stavka* representative coordinated the operations of the First Belorussian Front, which was attacking according to the plan for the Belorussian operation, with the operations of the First Ukrainian Front, which was operating according to the plan for the L'vov—Sandomierz operation.

The *Stavka* of the Supreme High Command exercised immediate and concrete control not only during the operation's preparatory phase, but during its course and throughout all its stages, both through its representatives on the ground, as well as through issuing instructions from the center at the most critical moments of the operation. For example, following the accomplishment of all missions for the first stage of the Belorussian operation, all the *fronts* were issued operational directives, in which the *fronts* were directed toward carrying out the missions of the new consecutive operations to develop the success already achieved. In a number of cases, the *Stavka* issued instructions during the course of *front* operations, when it was necessary to redirect a *front's* efforts. For example, on 21 July 1944 the *Stavka* of the Supreme High Command demanded that the First Belorussian Front redirect the 2nd Tank Army from the Siedlce to the Lublin axis and no later than 26-27 July capture the town of Lublin. It was pointed out that this was insistently demanded by the political situation and the interests of independent and democratic Poland. On 28 July 1944, following the successful accomplishment of the mission of capturing Lublin, the *Stavka* ordered the First Belorussian Front to seize bridgeheads along the western bank of the Vistula River. As is known, the capture of these bridgeheads played a very important role in creating favorable conditions for the development of the Soviet armed forces' strategic offensive in January 1945.

Upon the operation's completion, the *Stavka* of the Supreme High Command ordered the *fronts* to go over to the defensive. At the same time, the *Stavka* defined the final line and time for ending offensive operations. Thus the *Stavka* determined the date not only of the start, but also the end of the *front* operations and the multi-*front* operation as a whole. In determining the time for concluding the operations, the *Stavka* proceeded from the developing correlation of forces, the necessity to bring up the rear organs to the front line, and to need to reinforce the troops and their supplies.

Along with this, there were also certain shortcomings, which negatively affected the course of the operation. For example, the instructions on forcing the Vistula River, which were issued during the course of the operation, were issued late and were not supported in a timely manner by the necessary equipment, as a result of which the 2nd Tank Army, which was the first to reach the Vistula River, did not have the opportunity to force it from the march. Nor were the difficulties of supplying the troops with fuel and ammunition during an operation unfolding at high speed, in conditions where the existing rail net had to be reset, which was one of the reasons for the slowdown in the rate of the troops' advance at the concluding stage of the operation, taken into account in a timely manner.

On the whole, the methods of strategic control in the matter at hand justified themselves. They were based on the experience accumulated in the preceding course of the war.

Also worthy of attention is the *Stavka's* dispatch, before the start and during the course of the Belorussian operation, of major strategic reserves to Belorussia, including entire armies, which were transferred from the Second, Third and Fourth Ukrainian fronts, as well as of an enormous amount of all types of supply, being produced by the country's strategic rear.

On the whole, the multi-*front* Belorussian offensive operation of 1944, as regards its place in the strategic offensive of Soviet forces in the summer of 1944, had enormous significance, which enables us to include it, as to the importance of those missions that were resolved in its course, among the largest strategic operations of the Great Patriotic War.

Conclusions on Operational Art

The multi-*front* Belorussian offensive operation of 1944 is one of the classic examples of such a type of operation, carried out in the course of the Soviet Union's Great Patriotic War of 1941-1945.

1.   The idea of a multi-*front* operation pursued a decisive goal, because it foresaw the defeat of the main forces of the opposing enemy group of forces and the liberation of Soviet Belorussia and its capital of Minsk. At the same time, the enemy front was to be broken in simultaneously along a broad front by launching six attacks against the enemy, which would deprive him of the capability of maneuvering his forces and reserves from one axis to another. The concentration of the main efforts along the Vitebsk—Minsk and Bobruisk—Slutsk axes was to lead to the encirclement and destruction of the enemy's Vitebsk and Bobruisk groups of forces, followed by the development of the success in the flank and rear of Army Group Center's main forces. The entire course of the operation confirmed the expediency of such an idea in the given situation.

2.   The planning of the multi-*front* operation was carried out directly by the *Stavka* of the Supreme High Command; that is, it was conducted not at the operational level, but at the strategic level, which was typical for the period under study and which, on the whole, justified itself. The main forces were to be concentrated in the north with the First Baltic and Third Belorussian fronts, and in the south with the First Belorussian Front. The Second Belorussian Front was to launch a supporting attack. The overall width of the *fronts'* breakthrough sectors would not exceed 14.7 percent of the entire width of the enemy's defense. The attacks along these sectors would be organized with such forces that the enemy would be unable to parry them. For this, 4/5 of all men and materiel would be concentrated here. Along the remaining front, which accounted for 85.3 percent of the entire offensive front, only 1/5 of all the men and material were deployed. The first stage of the multi-*front* operation was prepared in detail and included the breakthrough of the enemy's defense along several axes, the defeat of the enemy's Vitebsk and Bobruisk groups of forces, followed by the encirclement and destruction of Army Group Center's main forces by attacks along converging axes. The missions of the subsequent operations would be refined, depending upon the results achieved in the course of the operation's first stage. On the whole, such methods for operational planning justified themselves.

3.   The form for conducting a multi-*front* operation was expressed in launching a series of frontal attacks for the purpose of breaking up the enemy front, followed by the development of these attacks along converging axes and the encirclement and destruction of the opposing enemy's main group of forces in the operational depth of his defense in the area to the east of Minsk.

In the present case we see how a change in the specific conditions of the situation and the growth in the Soviet forces' skill led to the further development of such a decisive form of waging an operation as encirclement.

In the first period of the Great Patriotic War, in the multi-*front* Rzhev—Vyaz'ma offensive operation, only a threat to the flanks of the enemy's Army Group Center was created by the Soviet forces' overhanging position. However, he we cannot speak here of the encirclement of the enemy group of forces. In the second period of the Great Patriotic War, in the multi-*front* Stalingrad operation, the enemy group of forces was surrounded by attacks along converging axes and then destroyed over the course of an extended period. We still lacked the men and materiel for destroying an encircled enemy group of forces in a short amount of time.

In the Belorussian operation of 1944, at first the encirclement and destruction of the enemy's Vitebsk and Bobruisk groups of forces were carried out, followed by the encirclement of the enemy's main group of forces in the operational depth of his defense, at a distance of 200 kilometers from the attack's jumping off position. The destruction of the encircled groups of forces was accomplished quickly by the method of breaking them up and eliminating them in detail. All of this was a further step forward in the development of the art of conducting a multi-*front* operation.

4.   The scale of the multi-*front* Belorussian operation, compared to the scope of other operations of the Great Patriotic War, made it one of the largest.

The troops of the First Baltic and the three Belorussian fronts, attacking along a more than 1,000-kilometer front, advanced 550-600 kilometers along a straight line, which significantly exceeded the indices called for by the operational plan. Moreover, during the operation's first stage (23 June-4 July) Soviet forces in 12 days made a fighting advance of almost 240 kilometers, at an average daily rate of more than 20 kilometers. During the operation's second stage, the *fronts'* forces advanced in 27-29 days another 300-350 kilometers in a straight line, with an average daily rate of advance of about 13 kilometers. Subsequently, while consolidating the successes achieved and creating favorable conditions for conducting new offensive operations, Soviet forces advanced in places another 50-100 kilometers.[7]

The high rates of advance in the Belorussian operation were achieved by means of a powerful initial blow, which ensured the breakup of the enemy into pieces, and then by the *fronts'* vigorous actions in developing the success to a great depth, and also through the encirclement and destruction of the enemy groups of forces in the areas of Vitebsk, Bobruisk and east of Minsk. The timely augmentation of the attacks' strength by committing into the battle the mobile groups and *front* and army second echelons and reserves, as well as the *Stavka* reserves, the latter of which were placed at the disposal of the *front* commanders during the operation, facilitated to no small degree the achievement of high rates of advance.

An important condition for achieving high rates of advance was the increased leadership skills of the commanders and staffs at all levels, as well as the skill of the entire rank and file in carrying out combat assignments.

On the whole, such an operational scope also testified to the growth in the capabilities and combat skills of the Soviet forces.

5.   The multi-*front* Belorussian offensive operation was distinguished by extremely smooth cooperation between its operational major field forces at all stages of the operation.

During the operation's first stage, the *fronts* were able to almost simultaneously break through the enemy's defense along six axes, defeat the opposing enemy groups of forces and to encircle Army Group Center's main group of forces in the area to the east of Minsk. At the same time, the defeat of the enemy groups of forces along the right wing of the attack front was accomplished through the joint operations of the First Baltic and Third Belorussian fronts, and on the left wing by the forces of the First Belorussian Front. At the same time the Second Belorussian Front launched a supporting attack in the center of the attack front. The encirclement and destruction of the enemy's main forces east of Minsk was accomplished through the joint efforts of the three

---

7   *Operatsii Sovetskikh Vooruzhennykh Sil v Velikoi Otechestvennoi Voine.* VNU GSh VS SSSR, vol. III, p. 363.

Belorussian fronts, Long-Range Aviation and the Belorussian partisans. The First Baltic Front supported these actions by means of an offensive to the northwest and west.

During the second stage of the multi-*front* operation cooperation between all the major field forces participating in the operation was expressed in the coordinated development of the success, which had been achieved during the first stage, with the inclusion into the offensive of additional forces and equipment, particularly among the forces of the First Belorussian Front's left wing south of the Pripyat' River, and the advance of the First Baltic Front toward the Baltic Sea, and that of the three Belorussian fronts to a line southwest of Dvinsk, and the Neman, Svisloch', Narew, and Vistula rivers. With the arrival of our forces at this line, of interest is the offensive cooperation between the various groups of Soviet forces deployed from the Gulf of Finland to the Carpathians.

6.   *Front* and army offensive operations were carried out within the confines of a multi-*front* operation and were subordinate to the latter. At the same time, the immediate preparation and conduct of operations were the functions of the *fronts* and armies. Only the coordination of their activities was carried out at the multi-*front* level.

On the way to achieving the goals of the multi-*front* operation, a series of consecutive and simultaneous *front* and army offensive operations was carried out. For example, during the first stage of the multi-*front* operation, four simultaneous *front* operations were conducted, after which each *front* then carried out 1-2 consecutive operations during the second stage of the multi-*front* operation. For example, the First Belorussian Front consecutively conducted the Bobruisk—Slutsk, Baranovichi—Slonim and Brest—Siedlce offensive operations.

The launching of a series of simultaneous and consecutive attacks will enable us in modern conditions to distract the enemy's attention, make it more difficult to espy our shock groups and, it follows, and enables us to inflict heavy losses on him through the employment of missile-atomic weapons.

7.   Consecutive offensive operations were widely employed during the Great Patriotic War, both on the scale of the entire Soviet-German front (consecutive blows along adjacent or separate strategic directions) and within the confines of this or that multi-*front* operation (along one or several operational directions), and also within a single *front* (consecutive army operations).

These operations were consecutive in depth, that is, they were conducted along the same axis as the preceding operation, and consecutive along the front, that is, they were conducted by switching the main efforts to a new axis.

From the point of view of the development of operational art in the Belorussian operation, which was itself one of the consecutive operations of 1944, worthy of attention are the *front* and army offensive operations, which were carried out during the course of a multi-*front* operation.

The First Belorussian Front's Brest—Siedlce offensive operation is an example of one of the most interesting *front* consecutive operations. In this operation the success of the preceding Bobruisk—Slutsk and Baranovichi—Slonim offensive operations by the same *front* developed not only in depth (along the *front's* right wing), but also along the front, by shifting the direction of the main attack from one of the *front's* wings to another, and with the commitment of additional major forces.

A feature of the given operation is the fact that it was planned and began to be prepared even before the start of the preceding planned operation, while at the same time the idea of the majority of the other such operations (for example, the Baranovichi—Slonim operation) arose in the course of the ongoing offensive.

As the experience of the Belorussian operation of 1944 shows, the success of consecutive offensive operations depends to a great degree on the correct definition of the operation's goal, the correct choice of the axis of the planned consecutive blows and the time of their launching. Each of these blows had to, aside from achieving other goals; create favorable conditions for launching the next even more powerful blow along the same or another axis.

The consecutive creation of an overwhelming superiority over the enemy along each of the planned axes was achieved by the skillful maneuver of men and materiel from one axis to another. As early as the conduct of the preceding operation, a sufficiently powerful shock group was created along the same or a new operational direction, in order to launch a consecutive operation, either without a pause, or with the pause reduced to a minimum.

The experience of the Belorussian operation shows that favorable conditions for carrying out a consecutive operation (the shape of the front line, a favorable grouping of men and materiel, etc.) must be created during the course of the preceding operation. The speed of regrouping troops from one axis of the front to another is of great importance here. The concentration of our forces along a new axis must be carried out earlier than the enemy can regroup his men and materiel there. In conducting consecutive operations like the ones that were carried out during the course of the multi-*front* Belorussian operation, one should proceed, first of all, from the organization of the enemy's forces and the character and condition of his defense. It is expedient to launch a new attack along that axis where the enemy does not expect it, where his men and materiel cannot be rapidly reinforced, and where our forces' offensive can yield the maximum effect.

The conduct of such a consecutive operation as, for example, the First Belorussian Front's Brest—Siedlce operation, was meant to unite into one the strategic offensive being conducted in Belorussia and western Ukraine, as well as to increase the scope of the multi-*front* Belorussian operation, especially its depth along its important Brest and Kovel'—Lublin, and then Warsaw, axes.

The experience of the Belorussian operation teaches that one should not confuse a consecutive *front* offensive operation with the ordinary development of the success in depth and towards the flanks following the breakthrough of the enemy's defense along the main axis, carried out in the confines of the same operation.

The experience of the Belorussian operation also shows that in conducting a consecutive operation within the confines of a single *front*, with the shift of the main efforts to another axis, it is necessary to take into account the following peculiarities:

- such an operation may be prepared along one of the axes in conditions where an offensive has begun and is being carried out along another (for example, the First Belorussian Front's Brest—Siedlce operation);
- in preparing such an operation, the necessity arises of regrouping part of the men and materiel from the former axis to a new one, in conditions of the ongoing operation along the old axis (for example, the regrouping of the reinforcement artillery from the First Belorussian Front's right wing to the left in July 1944).

Experience shows that in analogous conditions it is not expedient to halt or slow down the development of the offensive along the former axis, but rather necessary to carry out the preparation for a new operation by shifting the main efforts to another axis simultaneously with the continuance of active offensive operations along the former axis. Moreover, the success of operations along the new axis is directly dependent upon the intensity, power and decisiveness of the offensive along the former axis. On one hand, an attack along the new axis may be employed for the purpose of further activating the offensive along the former axis. This may be achieved by the following: the arrival of the forces attacking along the new axis on the enemy's flanks and communications operating against our formations attacking along the pervious axis; by the diversion of the enemy's mobile forces to oneself (for example, the diversion of five panzer divisions, transferred by the German-Fascist command to the area of the Praga fortified bridgehead along the Warsaw axis at the end of July and beginning of August 1944), as well as diverting his reserves arriving from the depth (as was the case, for example, on the bridgeheads along the line of the Vistula River at the concluding stage of the Belorussian operation).

The experience of the Belorussian operation shows that in preparing for a consecutive offensive operation that involves the shifting of the main attack to another axis, the necessity arises of shifting the *front* commander's main command and control centers to this axis.

The shift in the direction of the main attack may demand the conduct of significant operational regroupings, chiefly reinforcements, in conditions in which the sector from which these forces are being transferred, is still the scene of large-scale offensive operations. Such a regrouping requires of the *front* (army) commander not only bravery, but also precise calculation. Experience shows that the transfer of men and materiel in such cases may and should be carried out, but bearing in mind that this should not result in a sharp reduction of men and materiel along the former axis, which might result in the end, or a significant reduction, in the offensive pace.

The following may exert a decisive influence on the conduct of such consecutive offensive operations: the defeat, isolation, encirclement or destruction of the enemy's forces during the course of the preceding operation, or at least their significant weakening, so as to deny him the opportunity to then employ these forces in a new operation; the timely creation of a powerful group of forces and sufficiently powerful reserves along the axis of the main attack in the new operation, by means of decisive regrouping, as well as making good losses in men and materiel; the correct employment of mobile major field forces and formations for the purpose of rapidly developing the consecutive blows being launched throughout the enemy's entire depth; the conduct, should the situation allow, of a continuous pursuit along the previous axis (if the consecutive operation is being carried out by shifting efforts to a new axis); the securing of continuous cooperation between major field forces and formations, and also with the supporting aviation, upon completing the preceding operation and at the beginning of the consecutive operation, and; the consecutive shifting, should the situation demand it, of massed air strikes from one axis to another, if the raids against the new and important targets are in the interests of the new operation.

Thus the experience of the Belorussian operation of 1944 confirms that it is possible and expedient to prepare and conduct consecutive *front* and army consecutive operations. Undoubtedly, the increase in the mobility and shock power of modern forces increases the ability to successfully carry out such operations.

8.   The preparation of *front* and army operations was accomplished in various conditions. For example, if in the jumping-off position all operations were prepared during the course of an extended period of time—from the end of May to 22-23 June, then the consecutive *front* and army operations were usually prepared in a short period of time during the course of the preceding operation, without operational pauses. During the First Belorussian Front's Brest—Siedlce operation preparation for a consecutive operation was begun along the *front's* left wing simultaneously with the beginning of the preparation of the first (Bobruisk—Slutsk) operation by the *front's* right-wing forces. As a rule, operations were scrupulously prepared, which assured their success. The scrupulousness with which the operations were prepared is worthy of note.

The ideas of the *front* operations corresponded to the tasks laid down and the correlation of forces.

The most powerful Third and First Belorussian fronts were to break through the enemy's defense simultaneously, each along two sectors. *Front* shock groups were to be created along the breakthrough sectors, in which, aside from the first-echelon combined-arms armies, mobile groups and reserves, the main mass of reinforcement equipment was to be included.

The *fronts'* operational planning was carried out to the depth of the first (and in the course of the offensive, the next one) *front* offensive operation. Operations were planned by stages, with the first stage's plans drawn up in greatest detail—by day. The necessary corrections were made to the plans for the *front* operations by the *Stavka* representatives on the site, after which the plans were confirmed by the *Stavka* of the Supreme High Command. The plans for consecutive *front* and army operations, which arose in the course of the offensive, were usually drawn up graphically in a short amount of time (on maps with a legend). On the whole, such planning methods were widely employed and once again justified themselves in the given situation.

One should also note the circumstance that in the operation's preparatory period complex troop regroupings were carried out in all the *fronts*. For example, in the First Baltic Front the 6th Guards Army was pulled from the right flank to the axis of the main attack. No less complex regroupings were carried out in the Third Belorussian Front, in connection with the commitment of the 11th Guards Army into the first echelon, and in the First Belorussian Front, in connection with the 28th Army's commitment into the first echelon and the transfer of a large number of artillery and other combat units and formations from one of the *front's* wings to another. Moreover, the First and Third Belorussian fronts were reinforced with a large number of tank, mechanized and artillery formations and units by the start of the operation, which were included in the *fronts'* main groups of forces. Both of these *fronts* were also reinforced with a large number of aviation formations. In all the armies of the First Baltic, Third, Second and First Belorussian fronts, complex intra-army regroupings were carried out. One should note that, on the whole, all of these regroupings were carried out in secret.

To be sure, according to some indications, the German-Fascist command expected our forces' offensive operations, for example, north of Vitebsk, along the Orsha axis, and along the Zhlobin—Rogachev sector. However, while possessing certain information about the concentration of our forces along individual axes, the German-Fascist command incorrectly determined the strength of our forces along these axes and did not know along which axes we would launch the main attacks. For example, the enemy expected a local offensive from the area north of Vitebsk. At the same time, he did not expect an offensive by our forces along the Bogushevsk and Bobruisk axes.

All of this was achieved, primarily due to the fact that our troops, in preparing for the offensive, scrupulously observed all masking measures. In the First and Third Belorussian fronts the unloading of arriving trains, the movement of troops and their arrival at their jumping-off positions, were carried out, as a rule, at night. During the day only individual vehicles were allowed to move toward the front. Before the start of the offensive, tank and mechanized formations and units were concentrated in close areas, no closer than 30 kilometers from the front line. Troop masking was checked every day from the air by officers from the *fronts'* headquarters and the General Staff. The commanders of the corresponding formations were immediately informed of instances of violating masking discipline.

The conduct of radio and telephone conversations relating to the troops' preparation for the offensive was strictly forbidden. All instructions from division commander on down were authorized to be issued only orally. The troops carried out defensive works daily along their entire sector, putting up barbed-wire obstacles in front of their position, and mining the area. Reconnaissance was carried out along the entire front. Reconnaissance along the main axes was allowed only in small groups of 2-3 men. During reconnaissance efforts, officers of all combat arms put on soldiers' uniforms from the ground forces. Tank troops were forbidden to appear in the forward areas in their uniform. According to the *front* headquarters' plans, every day false rail movements were carried out, using dummy tanks and motor vehicles, as well as troop columns and artillery, from the front to the rear.

In modern conditions the demands for the secret regroupings of forces to the axes of newly planned attacks will increase. In this light the methods, with the help of which we managed to disguise from the enemy's intelligence such large-scale regroupings as the transfer of the 51st, 2nd Shock, 8th Guards, 5th Guards Tank, and 2nd Tank armies and a large number of formations to the First Baltic and the three Belorussian fronts acquire particular importance. This experience is also significant for modern conditions, when the skillful hiding of our forces' regroupings and deployment from the enemy will mean protecting them from the enemy's atomic rocket attack before the start of the operation. The surprise commitment of new formations and major field forces in the beginning of the operation and in its course acquires particular significance.

9. The *fronts'* operational organization in the jumping-off position was, as a rule, single-echelon, with the presence of powerful mobile groups along the main attack axes behind the first-echelon combined-arms armies. An exception was the First Belorussian Front, where the Polish 1st Army was concentrating in the second echelon along the *front's* left wing. The *fronts'* single-echelon organization in the jumping-off position was conditioned by the necessity of breaking through the enemy's powerful but shallow operational defense in conditions in which the enemy forces actually only occupied the tactical zone, and often only its main defensive zone. Lines in the depth were not occupied ahead of time by the enemy's forces. His reserves were few and consisted, as a rule, of individual formations.

The *front* commanders' calculation was based upon securing the first operational echelon's greatest possible superiority in men and materiel over the enemy defending in the tactical zone, so as to secure a rapid breakthrough and its subsequent development in the operational depth by the mobile groups. The breakthrough's success was to be secured by the deep array of forces in the armies and formations.

During the course of the operation, measures were adopted to create *front* second echelons and to restore reserves with the aid of the armies and formations freed up after the encirclement and destruction of the enemy's groups of forces.

In a number of cases, the augmentation of efforts during the operation was accomplished by transferring *Stavka* reserves to the *fronts*. For example, in the middle of July, when the Soviet forces reached the approaches to Dvinsk and the Neman and Svisloch' rivers, the rates of advance began to decrease. The *Stavka* reinforced the First Baltic Front with two combined-arms armies (2nd Guards and 51st), which had been transferred to Belorussia from the Fourth Ukrainian Front. This enabled us to develop a vigorous offensive along the Siauliai and Riga axes and move up part of our forces to the area of Tukums and the Gulf of Riga.

10. The massing of men and materiel along the decisive axes ensured the creation of densities of a single division per 1.5-2 kilometers of front, 151-204 guns and mortars (76mm and higher), and 22-26 direct infantry-support tanks and self-propelled guns per kilometer of front. These densities did not differ much in absolute numbers from those that had been created in the larger and successfully conducted operations in the summer-fall campaign of the second period of the Great Patriotic War, although now the troops were supported in their jumping-off positions, to a greater degree, by ammunition, which enabled us to increase the intensity of fire (to increase the time for fire assaults during the artillery preparation, and to carry out, for the first time during the Great Patriotic War, a rolling barrage in the First Belorussian Front). The percentage of high-caliber guns also rose in the overall amount of allotted artillery. The possibility of maneuvering artillery also increased, thanks to the growth of the number and power of large High Command reserve artillery formations.

11. The breakthrough of the enemy's defense occupied an important place in the *front* and army operations and was the main aspect of the operations' first stages.

The breakthrough accomplished by the Soviet forces in Belorussian in the summer of 1944 had its typical characteristics. It was accomplished along a number of axes along wooded and swampy sectors, which demanded special training of the troops.

The breakthrough in the jumping-off position was usually carried out by the *front* along 1-2 sectors by the forces of the combined-arms armies' first operational echelon.

For the breakthrough, the armies concentrated their main forces and materiel along narrow sectors, in the majority of cases less than ten kilometers for a single army. For the purpose of increasing the power of the attack and the size of the breakthrough sector, two neighboring armies launched a single overall attack along their adjacent flanks along sectors not exceeding 25 kilometers, and broadened the breakthrough in depth and along the flanks.

An important place in the breakthrough was occupied by the reconnaissance in force by forces of the forward battalions. Their actions in each individual cases were tactical in character, but, taken together, acquired operational significance at the army and *front* level. This is confirmed by the fact that in 11 armies' offensive sectors along a front of about 500 kilometers, 45 forward battalions and companies were operating almost simultaneously. Such a conduct of reconnaissance was conditioned by the character of the enemy's defense and his methods of waging the defensive battle. There were numerous instances of the German-Fascist command intentionally withdrawing its forces from the first trench, the first position, and even from the main defensive zone, before our offensive. By this method the enemy sought to force the Soviet forces to expend their efforts against an unoccupied area and then engage them with organized resistance in the defensive depth. For this purpose, we practiced the regrouping of fire weapons, the creation of a false forward edge of the battlefield, and a number of other methods. In connection with this, it was necessary to specify the shape of the enemy's forward defense line and his fire system immediately before the attack by the main forces and thus avoid the danger of expending ammunition and air bombs against a position purposely abandoned by the enemy on the eve of our attack. The Soviet forces sought to resolve this task by a reconnaissance in force by forward battalions, usually carrying it out on the eve of or the day of the attack by the main forces of the armies' first operational echelon.

The experience of the Belorussian operation showed that the greatest success was achieved where the battle by the forward battalions was better organized and where the success achieved by them was supported and developed by the main forces of the first-echelon formations (for example, in the Third Belorussian Front's 5th Army).

The breakthrough of the main defensive zone was accomplished by the combined-arms formations of the first operational echelon's armies. Mobile groups were brought in to complete the breakthrough in some cases.

Success in breaking through the enemy's defense was achieved, first of all, by concentrating large forces and materiel along the breakthrough sectors, which significantly exceeded the enemy's forces and materiel, the deep organization of the formation's combat orders, the all-round preparation of the troops taking part in the breakthrough, and the continuous cooperation of all combat arms in the offensive.

Thus the most typical methods of breaking through the enemy's tactical defense zone, according to the experience of the Belorussian operation of 1944, were as follows: the concentration of the main mass of available forces and materiel along the breakthrough sectors, with the creation of high densities and an overwhelming superiority in men and materiel over the enemy; the conduct of an aviation and artillery offensive; the broad employment of forward battalions along the entire front, particularly along the axis of the main attack; the deep organization of the formations' and units' combat orders, which enabled us to augment our efforts during the breakthrough; the presence of army and *front* mobile groups immediately behind the first operational echelon's formations, ready to be employed, should the situation require it, and to complete the breakthrough of the enemy's tactical defense zone. All of these methods justified themselves in the conditions of 1944.

12.   The development of the tactical success into an operational one usually began during the operation's first stage. The main means of developing the success was the mobile forces, which constituted the armies' and *fronts'* mobile groups. In the armies these were usually individual tank corps, and in the *fronts*—tank armies or cavalry-mechanized groups, consisting of tank, mechanized and cavalry corps. The *fronts'* mobile groups were usually committed either to complete the breakthrough and the following development of the success in depth, or into the already-formed breach.

In conditions when there was an insufficient number of direct infantry-support tanks, and when the rifle corps and divisions lacked their own tank and mechanized formations and units, the employment of mobile groups justified itself, because it enabled us to increase the rate of advance. The negative side of such a method was that the mobile formations and major field forces would break into the open, already significantly weakened. An example of such a kind of employment of mobile formations could be the employment of the 9th Tank Corps' formations for completing the breakthrough of the enemy's main defense zone, along with the 3rd Army's combined-arms formations.[8]

Alongside of this the commitment of the mobile groups into the already-formed breach also found employment. For example, in the Vitebsk—Minsk operation the 5th Guards Tank Army was committed for developing the success after the completion of the breakthrough of the enemy's entire tactical defensive depth by the formations' first operational echelon. This was achieved because the breakthrough of the tactical defense zone in the sector of the Third Belorussian Front's 5th Army had been completed by rifle forces, reinforced by tanks and self-propelled guns at a density of 23.5 vehicles per kilometer of breakthrough front, in conjunction with the cavalry-mechanized group. The 5th Guards Tank Army, which was committed into the breach behind the cavalry-mechanized group, preserved its men and materiel for carrying out its main task in the operational depth. This also guaranteed the army's high strength during the course of the entire operation and enabled it to develop the Third Belorussian Front's success to a great depth and at high speed.

The commitment of the Third and First Belorussian fronts' mobile forces (except for the 9th Tank Corps) was accomplished on the operation's second or third day. At the same time, responsibility for the commitment of the tank formations and major field forces was usually assigned to the commanders of the combined-arms armies which, as experience showed, was not always justified.

The commitment zone of the *front's* mobile group during the breakthrough was usually 12-20 kilometers wide. It was necessary to lay down 3-4 routes for the group's commitment into the breach. The commitment of the mobile group into the breach was planned according to variants in the zone of this or that army, or along the boundary of two armies. The missions laid down for the *front's* mobile group usually pursued a major operational goal. The speed at which the *front's* mobile group was committed into the breach always played a decisive role.

The redirecting of the responsibility for committing the mobile groups into battle of the combined-arms army, in the sector of which this commitment was carried out, was in a number of cases one of the reasons for the mobile groups' unsuccessful or insufficiently successful actions, as a result of which the army lacked the necessary men and materiel for this. For example, it was not possible to commit the 1st Tank Corps into the breach at the beginning of the operation, mostly because the engineer support for the corps' commitment into the breach had been insufficiently prepared. For this same reason the crossing of the 5th Guards Tank Army over the Berezina River in the 11th Guards Army's zone, and the First Belorussian Front's cavalry-mechanized group over

---

8   M.S. Tur, *Belorusskaya Operatsiya 1944 g.* VAGSh, 1956, p. 57.

the Tremlya River in the 28th Army's zone,[9] was delayed. The experience of the operation under study speaks to the fact that the *front* headquarters, and not that of the army, must be the organizer of the commitment of the *fronts'* mobile groups into the breach, because the army lacked sufficient men and materiel for this.

Once again the necessity of previously preparing the artillery support for the commitment of the armies' and *fronts'* mobile groups into the breach was made evident; the absence of such support led, for example, to the foiling of the 11th Tank Corps' commitment into the battle while clearing the enemy out of the Kovel' salient (8 July); the presence of such support enabled us to successfully commit the 2nd Tank Army from the bridgehead over the Western Bug River on 22 July 1944.

Part of the air force, which was supporting the first operational echelon's combined-arms armies, was shifted to the support (accompaniment) of the mobile group, which justified itself.

The commitment of the mobile groups usually secured the capture of the enemy's second and succeeding defensive zones from the march. On the whole, this guaranteed high rates of advance and pursuit.

It should be noted that alongside the tank armies, cavalry-mechanized groups, consisting of cavalry and mechanized or tank corps, were employed as the *fronts'* mobile groups. In these conditions, such a group was a sufficiently powerful mobile major field force, which possessed the necessary shock force and greater maneuverability in conditions of wooded and swampy terrain, than the tank armies.

Of particular interest, from the point of view of the combat employment of mobile formations, is the vigorous maneuver of the 2nd Tank Army in July 1944 from the Deblin area, along the right bank of the Vistula River along the enemy's rear, to the Warsaw axis, as well as the maneuver of the 3rd Guards Cavalry Corps from the Molodechno area to Grodno. At the same time the maintenance of uninterrupted cooperation of the tanks with the air force had great significance. The air force, through its raids against the enemy's reserves, disorganized them on the march and thus facilitated the seizure by our mobile formations of favorable lines for the subsequent repulse of major enemy counterblows.

Under conditions of the wooded and swampy terrain, some tank formations were curtailed in their maneuver and mainly operated along the roads. However, even in these conditions, given the corresponding training, many tank formations and major field forces, while maneuvering off the roads and overcoming previously flooded sectors, would unexpectedly appear in the enemy's rear (the 1st Guards Tank Corps during the attack on Bobruisk, and the 5th Guards Tank Army and the 2nd Guards Tank Corps in the attack on Minsk, etc.).

However, the actions of the mobile groups were not successful at all stages of the operation. One of the vital shortcomings in the combat employment of some mobile formations and major field forces was the fact that in a number of instances they were drawn into prolonged fighting for large inhabited areas (the 5th Guards Tank Army's formations for Vilnius, the 3rd Guards Tank Corps for Grodno, etc.), which led to heavy losses and a drop in the rate of advance. Another shortcoming was the indecisive actions of some mobile formations. For example, the 1st Mechanized Corps, which was stretched along a nearly 30-kilometer front on the approaches to Baranovichi, remained in place until the arrival of the combined-arms army. This happened because the corps did not look for detours and attempted to break through with headlong attacks. Nor did the 1st Mechanized Corps attempts to employ the success of the neighboring 4th Guards Cavalry Corps. Because of the 1st Mechanized Corps' slowness and indecisive actions during the offensive on Brest, it was not able to cut off the enemy's path of retreat to the west by an attack from the north on Kobrin. For the same reasons, the 1st Mechanized and 9th Tank corps were not able to

9   M.S. Tur, *Belorusskaya Operatsiya 1944 g.* VAGSh, 1956, p. 57.

overcome the enemy's resistance on the approaches to Brest. Nor were they able to break through to the 4th Guards Cavalry Corps, which was engaged in heavy fighting against the enemy along the Western Bug River northwest of Brest, while at the same time one of the corps' cavalry divisions had independently broken through and linked up with the corps.

In a number of cases, as a result of the untimely delivery of fuel, the tank formations were forced to temporarily halt their offensive (the 3rd Guards Mechanized Corps in the area west of Vileika, the 5th Guards Tank Army southeast of Vilnius, and the 2nd Tank Army in the Garwolin area).

In order to take the rear lines in the depth of the enemy's defense, aside from the mobile formations and major field forces, the *front's* second-echelon combined-arms armies were committed, or major field forces transferred from the *Stavka* reserve to the *front* during the operation.

Simultaneous with the development of the breakthrough of the enemy's defense into the depth, the timely widening of the breakthrough in width toward the flanks had great significance for the operation's success. For example, as early as the second day of the offensive, the First Baltic Front's forces widened the breakthrough to 85 kilometers; the forces of the Third Belorussian Front to more than 75 kilometers; the forces of the Second Belorussian Front to 20 kilometers, and; the First Belorussian Front's right-flank forces to 85 kilometers. Thus as early as the offensive's second day, the *fronts'* forces broke through the enemy's defense along a nearly 300-kilometer front, and the enemy was not in a position to plug the breach with his immediate operational reserves, and the breakthrough continued to widen. During the next two days the breakthrough of the enemy's defense was broadened to more than 400 kilometers.

It should be noted that following the defeat of the enemy's forces in the tactical defense zone and in the immediate operational depth, the forces of the attacking *fronts* did not have to break through the enemy's prepared defense all the way until their arrival at the East Prussian border and the Narew and Vistula rivers, and the Warsaw fortified area. Our forces' vigorous offensive overturned the German-Fascist command's calculations on occupying these lines in the depth with reserves and formations transferred from other axes.

Thus the development of the tactical success into an operational one was achieved by the following: the commitment of the mobile groups into the resulting breach following the overcoming of the enemy's main and second defensive zones by the first-echelon forces; the rapid taking up of the pursuit of the enemy upon discovering the beginning of his withdrawal to the army defensive zone, for the purpose of preempting his occupation of this zone; the support and accompaniment of our attacking troops by artillery and air throughout the entire operational depth of the enemy's defense; the consolidation of the mobile forces' success by moving up the combined-arms armies and formations behind them; the commitment of the *fronts'* second operational echelons in the operational depth for taking the enemy's intermediate and rear defensive lines; securing the flanks of the shock groups, developing the offensive at high speed, by turning part of the *front's* combined-arms and mobile formations toward the open flank, or by going over to the offensive along a new axis, depending on the situation and the correlation of forces, and; the broad employment of such active forms of maneuver as operational outflanking and envelopments of the enemy's major groups of forces in the operational depth of the enemy's defense.

On the whole, such methods yielded positive results in the Belorussian operation of 1944.

13.   The pursuit[10] of the enemy's defeated groups was conducted along a broad front, at full intensity and quite effectively, although in the troops' actions, as a result of their insufficiently precise control, there were certain shortcomings as, for example, in questions of reconnaissance and the

---

10 The section on pursuit is taken from the textbook by M.S. Tur, *Belorusskaya Operatsiya 1944 g.* VAGSh, 1956, pp. 58-59.

organization of security. Instances of the mixing of troops, the insufficient employment of radio communications, and the disruption of order in moving headquarters, among others, were also noticed.

The skillful combination of parallel and frontal pursuit enabled the *fronts'* forces to surround the retreating enemy's groups of forces. The necessary amount of forces was allotted in order to eliminate the encircled groups of forces, while the main forces vigorously advanced to the west. This led to high rates of pursuit, the quick conquest of space, while the enemy had no time to create a defense along intermediate lines.

The troops were arrayed in depth, which guaranteed an unbroken pursuit and the timely augmentation of efforts along the axis of the main attack. At the same time, the *fronts'* second echelons were often created in the course of the ongoing pursuit from freed-up forces or armies arriving from the *Stavka* reserve.

The broad employment in the armies and corps of mobile forward detachments, which were created from reinforced rifle units mounted on vehicles, had great significance for the success of the pursuit. These detachments, following behind the mobile groups or along independent axes, seized important lines, road junctions and crossings and held them until the arrival of our main forces.

The *fronts'* and armies' mobile groups pursued the enemy at an average remove from the combined-arms armies of 25-30 kilometers, and on certain days up to 50 kilometers. The cavalry-mechanized groups, which were employed along those axes where the employment of tank armies was made difficult by the terrain conditions, gave a good account of themselves in the pursuit in conditions of wooded and swampy terrain.

The pursuit was conducted at the following average speeds: 20-25 kilometers per day for the combined-arms formations, and 35-40 kilometers per day for the mobile forces (for example, in the Third Belorussian Front), and up to 50-70 kilometers on some days.

The continuity of the pursuit was achieved by the fact that the main forces pursued the enemy 16-18 hours per day, while at night, when they halted for rest, the pursuit was continued by the forward detachments.

While preempting the enemy in reaching intermediate and rear lines, the *fronts'* forces overcame them from the march.

14.   The encirclement and destruction of the enemy's groups of forces.[11] During the Belorussian operation the *fronts'* forces encircled and destroyed (captured) the enemy's Vitebsk, Bobruisk and Minsk groups of forces.

As to the decisive character of our forces' actions, suffice it to say that of the 43-44 enemy divisions deployed against our forces by the start of the Belorussian operation along a front stretching from Lake Neshcherdo to the mouth of the Ptich' River, more than 30 divisions, not counting individual special formations and units, were encircled and destroyed by Soviet forces. Encirclement was carried out in various ways, in accordance with the peculiarities of the situation.

The enemy's Vitebsk group of forces was encircled along the *fronts'* boundary in the tactical depth by the forces of the combined-arms formations. This was a comparatively rare instance in the Great Patriotic War, when the encirclement of a major enemy group of forces was carried out by rifle forces without the participation of large mobile formations. The following factors facilitated the success of this encirclement: the deeply outflanking position of our forces around Vitebsk; the vigorous offensive by our combined-arms formations along the converging flanks, which, in turn, was secured by the timely augmentation of these formations' efforts through the commitment of

---

11 This section is taken from the textbook by M.S. Tur, *Belorusskaya Operatsiya 1944 g.* VAGSh, 1956, p. 59.

the second echelons of the corps and armies' reserves, and; the sluggishness of the German-Fascist command, which decided too late to withdraw.

The enemy's Bobruisk group of forces was encircled in the operational depth by attacks of combined-arms and tank formations along converging axes. At the same time, the initial encirclement was achieved as the result of the 3rd and 65th armies' tank formations getting into the rear of the encircled group of forces. The combined-arms formations followed in their wake and sought to create a solid internal encirclement front.

The enemy's Minsk group of forces (the main forces of the Fourth Army) was encircled by the forces of three *fronts* during the pursuit at a depth of about 200 kilometers from the jumping-off position. Developing a vigorous attack toward Minsk and pursuing the main forces of Army Group Center along parallel routes at high speeds, the tank forces of the Third and First Belorussian fronts reached the rear of the enemy's main group of forces in the Minsk area and completed its encirclement. The leading role in the creation of an internal encirclement front and an external front belonged to the mobile formations, behind which the combined-arms formations followed.

As opposed to the Stalingrad and Korsun'—Shevchenkovskii operations, a typical feature of the encirclement and destruction of the enemy's groups of forces in the Belorussian operation was the vigorous offensive by the formations operating along the external front. This deprived the enemy of the prospect of organizing the direct coordination of the forces operating outside the encirclement with the encircled group of forces.

The most important feature of the encirclement and destruction of these major groups of forces was that they were accomplished as a unified process, which enabled us to eliminate the encircled groups of forces in a short period of time. The groups of forces being encircled were simultaneously broken up into small parts. The actions of our forces along the external encirclement front were distinguished by a high degree of activity, while the offensive was conducted uninterruptedly along all axes, which tied down the encircled forces' maneuver and prevented them from consolidating along their occupied positions.

All of this guaranteed the destruction of the encircled groups of forces around Vitebsk in the course of two days, around Bobruisk in three days, and east of Minsk in seven days.

In all these instances the tank and mechanized formations, which were operating along the external front, advanced without stopping, uninterruptedly widening the area between the encircled group of forces and the remaining enemy forces beyond the bounds of the encirclement ring, thus creating the most favorable conditions both for the isolation of the encircled enemy, as well as for his most rapid destruction.

Our aviation played a large role in the destruction of the encircled enemy groups of forces. As a result of powerful echeloned air strikes against the enemy's bunched-up combat orders, the encircled enemy group of forces suffered enormous losses and was not able to put up organized resistance.

15.   The scope of the *front* and army operations was significant. The depth of the *front* operations reached 200-250 kilometers, while the depth of the army operations varied from 30-70 kilometers. The offensive rates varied from 5-15 kilometers and more while breaking through the tactical defense zone and reached 20-25 kilometers while developing the success in the operational depth for the combined-arms formations, and up to 30-40 kilometers per day for the mobile forces.

The rates of advance could have been even higher, if not for breakdowns in the rear services' work, which were expressed in a significant lag in the rates of restoring the railroads and airfields behind that of the troops' advance. This caused great difficulties in the troops' supply, particularly of ammunition and fuel, in the operations' closing stages.

The lag in airfield maneuver led to a situation in which our fighter and assault aviation some-times lagged behind our forces, which enabled the enemy air force to strengthen his air raids against the forward units of the Soviet formations.

16.   Forcing rivers. During the *front* and army offensive operations, Soviet forces overcame numerous water obstacles, including such rivers as the Dnepr, Berezina, Western Bug, Neman, Vistula, and others.

The chief method of overcoming these rivers was that of forcing them from the march, simul-taneously along a number of sectors, thus preempting the enemy in occupying prepared defensive lines along the western banks of these rivers.

Because there was a shortage of crossing equipment and, in any case it seriously lagged behind our forces, the employment of materials at hand was very important.

The greatest difficulties arose while crossing heavy equipment, especially tanks and artillery. In those cases where there were fords or undestroyed bridges that had been captured from the march, this problem was resolved comparatively simply. In all other cases, the crossing of tanks and artil-lery was delayed until the arrival of the organic crossing equipment, which did not facilitate the rapid development of the success achieved. In individual cases the lagging behind of the organic crossing equipment excluded the opportunity of forcing a river from the march by tank formations (for example, during the arrival of the 2nd Tank Army at the Vistula River in the area to the west of Lublin in July 1944).

The combat orders of the formations and units upon arrival at a river were organized in depth, based on the calculation that their second and third echelons would be employed for the successive forcing of the river obstacles from the march, followed by the development of the success from the captured bridgeheads.

In the *front* and army attacking along the main axis (for example, the First Belorussian Front's 8th Guards Army), powerful mobile groups were created, which were assigned tasks to seize cross-ings over major river barriers (the Western Bug, Vistula, etc.) from the march.

The advancing forward detachments from the first-echelon formations attacking along the main axis were supplied with, foremost, crossing equipment. Moreover, it was planned to reinforce the mobile groups with special crossing equipment.

In order to ensure the uninterrupted forcing of a number of water obstacles from the march, the three-echelon delivery of corresponding engineer-sapper units and crossing parks was organized. In this case, while the first echelon supported the troops' crossing over the nearest water line, the second and third echelons were moving up behind the forward units, in readiness to organize the crossing over the next water lines.

The preparation of parts for wooden bridges, pontoons, boats, and other means (in addition to the limited amount of existing organic equipment) was organized as early as the jumping-off posi-tion for supporting the forcing of water barriers.

The forcing of rivers during the operation was carried out both along reconnoitered fords and bridges captured intact, as well as by employing materials at hand and organic equipment, combined with broad maneuver through neighboring units' sectors, in case they should have the necessary crossings or fords.

The forcing of a number of rivers (Western Bug, Vistula, etc.) was carried out while pursuing the retreating enemy.

It should be noted that in this case the *fronts'* forces widely employed the rich experience, acquired in preceding operations, in particular, for example, the forcing of the Dnepr River in the second half of 1943.

At the same time, it was obvious that it was absolutely necessary to increase the technical capa-bilities of the Red Army's organic crossing equipment, without which the rates of the troops' advance during the offensive, accompanied by the forcing of water barriers, could not be significantly increased.

The experience of the Belorussian operation of 1944 confirmed once again that one of the typical features of Soviet operational art in the Great Patriotic War was the ability to seize bridgeheads over major river barriers from the march and then employ these bridgeheads for launching subsequent offensive operations.

In a number of instances, particularly during the operations' concluding stages, the fight for bridgeheads became extended.

The bridgeheads seized by our forces along the western bank of the Vistula River in the areas of Magnuszew and Pulawy had particular significance for the conduct of subsequent operations.

Actions to seize bridgeheads were carried out in the following manner. Usually mobile groups, as well as the forward detachments of the combined-arms formations, moved up to the river and seized crossings from the march; then the first echelons would force the river on organic equipment and materials at hand, along captured intact bridges and fords, and seized tactical bridgeheads along a number of sectors; these bridgeheads were subsequently joined and broadened, as a result of which was formed a major operational bridgehead, and; then the main forces of the *fronts'* mobile groups crossed over to the bridgehead for developing the success from the bridgehead. For example, on 20 July the mobile group and the mobile forward detachments of the First Belorussian Front's 8th Guards Army seized a bridgehead from the march along the western bank of the Western Bug River in the Opalin area, with a width of 11-12 kilometers and 5-7 kilometers in depth. During 21-22 July the army's forces increased the bridgehead to 20-30 kilometers in depth, and at 1100 on 22 July the main forces of the *front's* mobile group—the 2nd Tank Army, which had been crossed over, were committed into the battle in the general direction of Lublin and further to the Vistula River.

The consolidation of the captured bridgeheads was carried out according to the following methods: through the immediate augmentation of men and materiel along the captured bridgeheads; by a prolonged and intensive fight, over a significant period of time, to retain and further broaden and consolidate the captured bridgeheads, and: the accumulation of men and materiel on them for a subsequent offensive according to a new operational plan.

For example, the First Belorussian Front's 69th Army's forward detachments forced the Vistula River from the march in the first half of 29 July, having initially seized two small bridgeheads southwest of Pulawy. The success achieved was immediately used to cross over the army's main forces. By the close of 2 August the size of the bridgehead had been expanded to 18-20 kilometers in width and 3-7 kilometers in depth. The same *front's* 8th Guards Army forced the Vistula River with its forward detachments on the morning of 1 August. Initially a bridgehead ten kilometers wide and 1-3 kilometers deep was seized (by 1000 on 1 August) in the Magnuszew area. By the close of 2 August the army's main forces had been crossed over to the bridgehead and its size had been increased to 18 kilometers in width and 6-8 kilometers in depth. During the course of almost all of August the formations of the 8th Guards, 69th and Polish 1st armies were engaged in intensive fighting to expand and consolidate the captured Magnuszew and Pulawy bridgeheads, overcoming the enemy's fire resistance and repelling the counterattacks of his tanks and infantry. As a result of these activities, the front line along the Magnuszew bridgehead was 46 kilometers long by the end of August (with a depth of 15-18 kilometers), while that of the Pulawy bridgehead was 29 kilometers wide and up to 12 kilometers deep. The consolidation of these bridgeheads by the Soviet forces created favorable conditions for the subsequent unfolding of a new offensive operation (the Vistula—Oder operation of 1945) from these bridgeheads.

On the whole, the experience of the Belorussian operation confirmed once again the expediency and possibility of seizing operational bridgeheads from the march in the operational depth of the enemy's defense over major river barriers, both during the development of the tactical success into an operational one, as well as in concluding the operation, for the purpose of creating favorable conditions for subsequent offensive operations.

17.   During the Belorussian operation the *fronts'* forces acquired significant experience in repelling the enemy's counterblows. The enemy's activity increased sharply from the second half of July, when he sought to eliminate the deep penetration by the First Baltic Front's forces along the Riga axis and to deprive the forces of the Third and Second Belorussian fronts of their bridgeheads along the western bank of the Neman River, as well as to halt the advance by the First Belorussian Front on Warsaw. For example, during 16-20 July the forces of the Third Belorussian Front were engaged in fierce battles to repel the counterblows by major enemy forces along the bridgeheads and did not advance. In order to more successfully resolve this mission, the forces of the Third Belorussian Front went temporarily over to the defensive. This decision fully justified itself.[12]

In modern conditions of increased troop mobility, the question of repelling counterblows by the enemy's tank group, launched in the defense's operational depth against our forces' forward mobile formations, is of particular interest.

In the Belorussian operation we have an example of repelling such a counterblow, which was launched with the forces of five enemy panzer divisions against the First Belorussian Front's 2nd Tank Army, which had moved up along the Warsaw axis.

The following are some of the troops' methods in repelling this counterblows: the assumption of the defensive by the formations of the tank army's first echelon in front of the permanent fortifications of the Warsaw fortified area; the forces' organization of an all-round defense, due to the presence of open flanks and the possibility of outflanking maneuvers by the enemy's arriving tank units; using the *front's* air force to launch raids against the enemy's formations taking part in the counterblow, and; relieving the forward tank formations with combined-arms formations and the creation by the latter of a continuous defensive front.

All of these measures were expedient in the given situation and were, in the final analysis, crowned with success. However, it should be noted that such a method as repelling the enemy's counterblow by temporarily going over to the defensive along the threatened axis, followed by a resumption of the offensive, could not be brought to completion in the given case, because the maneuver of our tanks was restricted for the following reasons. The tank army, having advanced before this to a great depth at high speed, failed to receive timely support from the combined-arms armies (the 47th Army was lagging behind). The powerfully fortified lines of the Warsaw fortified area were not favorable to the maneuver of our tank formations. The *front's* rear failed to cope with supplying the forward mobile formations with ammunition and fuel. The exhaustion of our forces after a multi-day offensive also told.

18.   The problem of consolidating the successes achieved in the offensive operation is also worthy of attention.

In the Belorussian operation this problem was resolved by the troops' arrival at favorable natural lines, particularly the Narew and Vistula rivers; by the seizure, widening and consolidation of bridgeheads along the western bank of these rivers; by the intensive fighting along the most important axes (for example, the Warsaw axis), with the repelling of the enemy's counterblows and the overcoming of the constantly increasing enemy resistance along numerous intermediate lines, which guaranteed the creation of a favorable jumping-off position for the future unfolding of offensive operations along these axes; the adoption of the defensive, according to the instructions of the *Stavka* of the Supreme High Command, for the purpose of consolidating the captured

---

12 M.S. Tur, *Belorusskaya Operatsiya 1944 g.* VAGSh, 1956, p. 61.

lines; by putting in order and reinforcing the troops; by restoring the used-up second echelons and reserves, and; by delivering all kinds of supplies and supporting the all-round preparation for new offensive operations in the future.

The extended character of the fighting for the consolidation of the successes achieved in the operation was conditioned, in the present case, by the growing enemy resistance as the Soviet forces approached Germany proper; by the presence of major previously-fortified strategic defensive lines, which ran along the border of East Prussia, as well as along the Narew and Vistula rivers; by our troops' exhaustion following a multi-day successful offensive, and; by the necessity of strengthening communications, of organizing the rear services' work, and of carrying out the reinforcement and regrouping of formations and armies.

Experience shows that the consolidation of successes achieved in an operation unfolded, as a rule, by occupying some kind of powerful and favorable natural line, which made it easier for our forces to assume the defensive. Such lines in the concluding phase of the given operation were the Narew and Vistula rivers, which had not only an important operational significance, but a strategic one as well.

However, the presence of such lines was also favorable to the enemy in organizing a new defense. Thus it proved necessary, employing all the advantages of this line for ourselves, to at the same time maximally weaken its importance for the enemy. This was achieved by the seizure of bridgeheads by our forces along the western bank of the Narew and Vistula rivers and by depriving the enemy of bridgeheads along the eastern banks of these rivers.

19.   The employment of artillery. By the start of the Belorussian operation more than 28,000 guns and mortars had been concentrated along a front from Lake Neshcherdo to the mouth of the Ptich' River, which ensured an overall superiority of 2.9:1 over the enemy's artillery. In this operation the comparative weight of heavy-caliber artillery with the *fronts* grew in comparison with operations conducted earlier. By the start of the operation the *fronts* had received a significant amount of artillery from the Supreme High Command reserve. Major artillery regroupings were carried out within the *fronts* (in the First Baltic and, in particular, within the First Belorussian fronts). The result of this movement of large artillery masses was their concentration along narrow sectors of the *fronts'* main groups. It should be noted that the regroupings, concentration and deployment of the artillery were carried out in a short amount of time and, with certain exceptions, by observing measures of secrecy and masking, which was one of the most important conditions that facilitated the achievement of operational surprise.

The principle of massing the artillery along the axes of the main attacks within the operational sectors of the *fronts'* main groups of forces lay at the base of the artillery's employment. At the same time, the main mass of artillery (up to 80 percent) was employed for breaking through the enemy's defense.

Thanks to such a massing of artillery along the breakthrough sectors, densities of 140-220 guns and mortars per kilometer of front were achieved. However, along some axes the artillery density proved to be insufficient in those conditions for the reliable suppression of the enemy's defense. The enemy's divisional and even regimental reserves and his artillery, in individual cases, were not suppressed (for example, in the attack zone of the Third Belorussian Front's 11th Guards Army).

The artillery preparation was carried out according to a schedule, while in this operation, compared to preceding operations, the percentage of time allotted for fire onslaughts rose considerably. In individual cases two schedules for the artillery preparation were drawn up, taking into account the greater or lesser success of the forward battalions' actions. Corrections were made to the plan before the beginning of the artillery preparation, depending upon the changes in the situation (for example, in the Third Belorussian Front's 5th Army).

The artillery preparation in the armies of the *fronts'* main groups of forces was organized in each *front*, as a rule, according to a single schedule. Moreover, in each *front* a single method of supporting the attack and the general character of the artillery's activities in the depth of the enemy's defense was assured. However, a comparative analysis of documents in which the artillery activities of the *fronts* were planned shows that if the length of the artillery preparation was almost the same in all the *fronts*, there were significant differences in the organization of the artillery preparation. These differences may be explained by the fact that there was no unity of views on the role of fire onslaughts during the artillery preparation. On the whole, the experience of the Belorussian operation shows that an artillery preparation, as applied to the conditions of that time, was as short as possible, so as not to give the enemy much time to bring up his reserves to the breakthrough site. At the same time, the artillery preparation's length must be sufficient to carry out all its planned fire assignments. The artillery preparation, as a rule, would begin and end with powerful fire onslaughts, mostly against the enemy's entire main defense zone and against the most important targets in the tactical depth. During the final fire onslaught the immediate depth of the enemy's defense was subjected to particularly heavy fire approximately to his third trench, from which he could fire on our infantry and tanks attacking the first trench. Between the first and last fire onslaughts there would be periods of directed fire for the suppression and destruction, from both hidden positions and over open sights, alternating with fire onslaughts. The alternation of fire onslaughts with periods of directed fire lay at the basis of the organization of the artillery preparation. In organizing the artillery preparation, a suitable place was devoted to the maneuver of fire against the depth.

In individual cases, when the forward battalions, supported by part of the first-echelon forces, managed to break through one or two positions, or the enemy's entire main defensive zone, the offensive by the main forces would begin along some sectors without an artillery preparation, following short fire onslaughts against revealed firing points.

In the Belorussian operation, as the result of the artillery preparation, the enemy's defense was suppressed to a sufficient degree along the majority of breakthrough sectors. Only along the Third Belorussian Front's Orsha axis and in the zone of the First Belorussian Front's 3rd Army did the artillery preparation for the attack fail to yield the expected results. A number of important targets remained untouched by our artillery along these axes. As a result, the infantry and tank attack during the offensive's first day failed to achieve the expected success.

The artillery support for the attack was accomplished through the method of the rolling barrage and the successive concentration of fire. A rolling barrage, as a rule, was employed against the most powerful enemy defense. As opposed to preceding operations, when only a single rolling barrage was employed, in the Belorussian operation, for the first time during the Great Patriotic War, a double rolling barrage for supporting the infantry and tank attack was employed on an operational scale. This method of supporting the attack, applied in the First Belorussian Front in the Bobruisk—Slutsk and Brest—Siedlce operations, guaranteed higher rates of crushing the main zone of the enemy's defense and, as a whole, justified itself in the conditions of the time.

In organizing the artillery offensive, all sorts of methods of artillery activity were searched for in order to deprive the enemy of the opportunity to define the time of the start of our attack by the character of our artillery fire. For this, the following was employed: shifting 1/3 of the artillery's fire to the first line of the rolling barrage 2-3 minutes before the end of the artillery preparation; increasing the density of fire during the final fire onslaught, and; continuing to suppress the defensive depth with the beginning of the attack.

A serious shortcoming committed by the Third Belorussian Front was the insufficient artillery suppression of the enemy's main defense zone. The artillery securely suppressed the enemy's defense only to a depth of three kilometers; thus his divisional and even regimental reserves remained unsuppressed. A result of this shortcoming in planning and carrying out the artillery offensive was the slow advance of the 11th Guards Army's formations in the operation's first days.

The experience of the Belorussian operation confirmed the necessity of more scrupulously organizing the forward movement of large artillery masses and the establishment of a strict priority of movement, depending on the concrete tasks which must be decided along this or that line in the depth of the enemy's defense, in close coordination with the movement of the mobile groups and second echelons of the *fronts* and armies. The artillery's movement must be particularly scrupulously regulated, given an insufficient number of roads, during the artillery's passage through a defile, and along the crossings over water lines.

One of the most complex questions that had to be resolved during the offensive was the artillery support of the infantry and tanks' operations in the depth of the enemy's defense, particularly while pursuing the enemy.

As soon as the development of the tactical success into an operational one began, particularly following the commitment of the mobile groups into the breach, the main mass of the reinforcement artillery, particularly large-caliber guns, began to lag behind the combat orders of the corps' first echelons. The artillery grouping was thus disrupted. All the difficulty of supporting the infantry and tanks' actions would fall to the regimental and divisional artillery.

The chief reasons for the reinforcement artillery's lagging behind were, first of all, the low rate of restoring the bridges capable of bearing their weight and the late delivery of fuel. Due to this, not only reinforcement artillery lagged behind, but also crossing equipment, while the delivery of ammunition for the artillery in the armies' first echelons was also delayed.

The expediency of decentralized artillery control during the pursuit was confirmed, although it should be ready for rapid centralization in the hands of the senior artillery chief in a case in which the enemy tries to organize resistance on this or that line.

The breakthrough of the enemy's defense along intermediate lines in the operational depth (along the Berezina, Ptich' and other rivers) was supported by the conduct of a short 25-35-minute artillery preparation, as well as by the broad employment of guns set up for firing over open sights.

One should also note the widespread maneuver of artillery formations during the operation, when one and the same artillery corps and divisions supported different *fronts'* armies at different periods of the operation.

The most instructive example of the skillful employment of one and the same artillery formations for the successive accomplishment of missions for breaking through the enemy's defense along two widely spaced axes is the regrouping in July 1944 of the main mass of reinforcement artillery (including the 4th Breakthrough Artillery Corps) from the First Belorussian Front's right wing to the left wing, that is, from the Bobruisk—Slutsk axis to the Kovel'—Lublin axis, which was accomplished in 4-5 days.

The regrouping of the main mass of reinforcement artillery from one wing of the *front* to the other at a distance of 600 kilometers may be typical for consecutive operations involving the shift of the main blow from one axis to another.

The organization of this regrouping is worthy of attention. The regrouping was carried out in a combined manner: the lighter and faster systems were dispatched under their own power, while the heavy systems were transported by railroad. This example indicates the possibility and desirability of regroupings for the purpose of reducing the time for transportation; the possibility of employing rail transport for transferring reinforcement equipment at the operational level within the confines of a single *front* during an operation.

During all the Belorussian operation's stages, Soviet artillery, while skillfully maneuvering by fire and wheels, ensured the uninterrupted support of the troops to a depth of more than 500 kilometers, beginning with the crushing of the enemy's tactical defense and ending with the arrival of Soviet forces at the Gulf of Riga and the Vistula River.

It should be noted, however, that in the Belorussian operation there were instances of short-comings in the employment of artillery: the insufficiently organized movement of the artillery's combat orders behind the attacking forces during the first stages of the *front* operations, which was expressed in the nearly simultaneous shift of firing positions by all the systems and which led to crowding and the formation of traffic jams on the roads and crossings, and; the lagging of the artillery (particularly the artillery of the Supreme High Command) while developing the success in the operational depth, which was caused by the lack of a sufficiently well thought out plan for supporting the artillery units with ammunition and fuel in conditions of pursuing the enemy at high speeds.

The experience of the Belorussian operation teaches us that the greatest difficulty in supplying the artillery with ammunition and fuel is reached at the conclusion of the offensive operation, carried out at a high rate of speed, when the rear organs' remove from the troops is at its greatest.

On the whole, the Soviet forces' methods of employing artillery in the Belorussian offensive operation of 1944 were typical of that time and justified themselves in practice in the situation at hand.

20.   The employment of armored and mechanized forces in this operation was at that high level for the time, which had been achieved by Soviet operational art in the middle of 1944.

The armored and mechanized forces played a major role, both in breaking through the defense as well as in completing the breakthrough and developing the success in the operational depth.

Typical of the operation under study was the diverse employment of armored and mechanized forces at all stages of the operation. Their employment was especially justified as part of the *fronts'* and armies' mobile groups, which facilitated the increase in the scope of the *front* and army operations and the achievement of decisive results in them.

The control of the mobile troops and their coordination with the rifle formations and aviation improved.

On the whole, the armored and mechanized forces put their best foot forward in the operation.

The individual shortcomings observed (shortcomings in securing the commitment of the mobile groups into the breach, in supplying them with equipment, ammunition and fuel, etc.) were elimi-nated during the course of the operation, although at the time they had not been completely eradicated.[13]

21.   The employment of aviation. A preliminary and immediate aviation preparation (the latter, not always) usually preceded the beginning of the ground forces' offensive. The preliminary avia-tion preparation was carried out, as a rule, during the night before the attack with the forces of night bomber aviation, and sometimes of Long-Range Aviation. In a number of cases, an imme-diate aviation preparation was not conducted. The reasons for this are either poor meteorological conditions, or the desire of the *front* commanders to save more aviation resources for the period of supporting (accompanying) the troops in the depth of the enemy's defense (for example, in the First Belorussian Front).

Our aviation accomplished the support (accompaniment) of the infantry and tank attack through the method of combining uninterrupted actions of small groups of *shturmoviks* over the battlefield, with concentrated raids by large forces of assault air and bomber aviation against the enemy's strong points and centers of resistance. For example, the support for the attack in the

---

13 For a fuller description of the operations of the armored and mechanized forces, see the sections on the prob-lem of breaking through the enemy's defense and its development.

Third and First Belorussian fronts was organized according to this method. In the First Baltic and Second Belorussian fronts troop support was carried out by small groups of *shturmoviks*.

During the Belorussian operation our air force fought to retain air superiority. During the operation the air force carried out about 40,000 sorties for the purpose of retaining air superiority, or more than 41 percent. The German-Fascist air force operated in a limited manner. Thus the favorable conditions of the air situation to a great extent made easier the conduct of the operation by the ground forces and facilitated the success of the operation. On the other hand, the enemy's forces, particularly during the operation's first stage, were suppressed by our air strikes to a significant degree.

Besides this, the operation's success was facilitated by the following: the secret concentration of a large mass of airplanes during the preparatory period, which ensured the surprise of our aviation's powerful attacks against the enemy's defense; the skillfully conducted aviation grouping, which enabled us to achieve heretofore unprecedented aviation densities along the decisive axes; the scrupulous operational and combat preparation of the air formations, units, commanders, and headquarters for joint activities with the ground forces in the forthcoming operations, and; the successfully conducted air reconnaissance during the preparatory period, which revealed the character of the enemy's defense, and which thus prepared the commanders at all levels, and their staffs, with the necessary data for adopting correct decisions and for the most expedient employment of the combat arms in the battle and operation.

Aviation was employed massively along the axes of the *fronts'* main attacks. For example, when the First Belorussian Front's left wing went over to the offensive, it was supported by two air armies—the 6th and 16th, which should be regarded as a special phenomenon in the operations of 1944.

The overall growth of the Soviet army's air force by the start of the Belorussian operation is characterized by the fact that the 1st and 16th air armies, which supported the forces of the Third and First Belorussian fronts, for the first time in the history of the Great Patriotic War, consisted of 18 to 20 air divisions each. It should also be noted that the 16th Air Army, also for the first time in the history of the Great Patriotic War, had on hand, aside from 2,033 planes, a significant number of reserve aircraft.

The foundation of the employment of our air force was the principle of supporting the ground forces with air power in complete accordance with the overall operational plans of the *front* commanders. In connection with this, the creation of powerful air groups for supporting the *fronts'* main groups of forces was typical of the operational employment of our aviation. About 50 percent of all sorties by bomber and assault aviation were directed toward supporting the ground forces and at attacks against the enemy's targets in his defense.

The latter circumstance, to a significant degree, facilitated the accomplishment of the breakthrough of the tactical zone of the enemy's defense at high speeds and, thanks to this, the commitment of the *fronts'* mobile groups into the breach and the achievement of an operational breakthrough to a great depth was speeded up. All of this had an immediate and decisive influence on the successful development of the operation and imparted a decisive character to it.

The air force's combat activities were not planned by the headquarters of the air armies throughout the entire depth of the operation. The air force was only assigned tasks for the first day and first stage of the operation. At the same time, on the operation's first day tasks were assigned to each air formation, according to place and time. During the first stage's subsequent days the air formations were informed of the character of their combat tasks.

Air control during the operation was centralized, which in conditions of rapid troop movement enabled us to concentrate the efforts of large masses of air power along those axes, where the success of the given stage of the operation, and the operation as a whole, was being decided.

A certain decentralization of control was allowed during the commitment of the mobile groups into the breach, when the commanders of the corresponding air formations would receive assignments personally from the commanders of the mobile groups, or through their representatives on the spot. In the First Belorussian Front it was planned to subordinate part of the assault air to the army commanders as early as the operation's first day. However, the existing control system, when the commander of the air army himself, or his deputy, commanded each aviation group, and the communications system was reliable, enabled him to take control of the temporarily subordinated aviation formations into his hands at any moment.

The air support for the ground forces enabled both the army commanders, as well as the *front* commanders, to direct the efforts of the supporting aviation formations, at the necessary moment, to any other axis for carrying out more important tasks that might have arisen during the operation.

During the organization of tactical coordination between the air force and the ground forces (the aviation preparation, the support of the troops during the operation), the commanders of the air formations were located near the aviation's area of activity and, more often, alongside the commander of the formation being supported.

During those periods when the aviation's activities were outside tactical contact with the troops, the commanders of the air formations controlled their forces from their command posts, which were located in the basing areas of the air formations.

A characteristic feature of the fight for air superiority in this operation was the fact that alongside with the fighters' covering the *fronts'* main groups of forces, our aviation also carried out raids against the enemy's air airfields at night. At the same time, the method of blockading the enemy's airfields with delayed-fuse bombs was widely practiced. However, during the operation's period of preparation and conduct only six percent of all sorties were employed in strikes against the enemy's airfields, which cannot be considered sufficient.

During the operation our air force carried out uninterrupted operational and tactical reconnaissance and observation of the battlefield. The uninterrupted character of air reconnaissance was achieved by the fact that it was conducted not only by special planes, but also by all the crews from all aviation combat arms, while at the same time carrying out their combat assignments. Air reconnaissance established in a timely manner the regroupings, transfer and concentration of the enemy's reserves, the beginning of his troops' withdrawal, the axes of withdrawal, and the enemy's attempts to remove his forces from encirclement; by this it aided our command in learning the enemy's plans.

During the operation our aviation, taking into account the difficulties being experienced by the enemy during his withdrawal along the wooded and swampy terrain, launched concentrated raids directly against crossings and his large troop columns, delaying their movement and thus facilitating the encirclement of large enemy groups of forces.

Air power participated directly in destroying the enemy's encircled groups of forces and carried out similar missions quite successfully, especially, for example, in destroying the enemy's encircled Bobruisk group of forces.

Also worthy of attention is the uninterrupted character of aviation activity, both day and night, and its uninterrupted accompaniment of the troops during the operation, as well as the skillful organization of the pursuit of the enemy from the air to a great depth, in operational cooperation with the ground forces.

The close cooperation of the air force with the ground forces and all of the aviation combat arms with each other was observed throughout the entire operation.

In the Belorussian operation Long-Range Aviation operated through concentrated and echeloned attacks. Besides airfields, its targets were railroad junctions and stations, defensive lines and the enemy's forces. In all, during the operation the air force carried out more than 10,300 sorties and dropped more than 10,000 tons of bombs. At the same time, 57 percent of all sorties were conducted to attack railroad targets, more than 17 percent against airfields, more than 18 percent against the enemy's personnel on the battlefield, and 7-8 percent for supporting the partisans.

However, our aviation's actions during the operation were not evenly spread out. Our aviation showed the greatest activity during the first stage of the operation. For example, on the operation's first day 4,000 sorties were carried out, 7,000 on the second day, and more than 7,000 on the third day. However, our aviation's activity subsequently fell sharply as a result of the lagging of the airbases and breakdowns in the delivery of fuel.

On the whole, the activities of the air force in the Belorussian operation were effective and guaranteed the successful advance of the ground forces to a great depth.

22. A great deal of significance was attached to the operational support of the troops, both during the preparatory period and during the operation.

Intelligence of all types revealed the grouping of enemy forces in their jumping-off positions and established changes in the location, forces and intentions of the enemy forces during the operation. The main types of intelligence in the *fronts* were as follows: troop reconnaissance, which was conducted by observation, battle, day and night searches, and the actions of reconnaissance groups in the enemy rear; special reconnaissance by all the combat arms, particularly the artillery, and; aviation reconnaissance with aerial photography. Besides this, data from agent reconnaissance and information received from the partisans were also employed. All intelligence data about the enemy was systematized and analyzed in the armies' and *fronts'* headquarters was displayed on intelligence maps and outline maps and passed on to the troops.

The *front* command sought to disorient the enemy as to the shock groups' concentration area and axis of attack through measures for operational masking. For example, the Second Belorussian Front imitated the creation of a major group of forces in the 33rd Army's sector. The concentration and regrouping of forces at all stages of the operation was carried out by observation concealment measures.

Long-Range Aviation, which was designated for participating in the Belorussian operation, was based on Ukrainian airfields of the purposes of masking. The demonstrative concentration of a shock group in the Third Ukrainian Front's sector along the Kishinev axis, which was carried out by order of the Red Army General Staff before the start of the Belorussian operation, deserves to be mentioned.

Boundaries and flanks were covered by specially delegated battalions from the infantry-support artillery groups, and partially from subgroups of the army artillery group, as well as by the mobile obstacle detachments. Aside from this, boundaries and flanks were covered by the corresponding location and movement of all types of reserves, as well as by the movement of formations and units in echelon.

The armored and mechanized troops (for example, the Third and First Belorussian fronts' mobile groups during the first stage of the operation) played a big role in securing the external flanks of the *fronts'* major groups of forces during the Belorussian operation. The securing of the open external flanks of the *fronts'* main groups of forces was accomplished by assigning reinforced forward detachments, which were located along previously-designated lines and maintained them until the appointed time. The forward detachments' seizure of important strong points and centers of resistance and their maintenance until the arrival of the combined-arms formations was also widely practiced.

The high rate of advance by the tank and mechanized formations had the greatest significance for securing the external flanks of the *fronts'* main groups of forces and enabled us to preempt the enemy in seizing important sites and lines.

The securing of the northern flank of the entire shock group of Soviet forces in Belorussian was achieved by turning to the north and northwest a significant portion of the First Baltic Front and the arrival of the *front's* formations at the Baltic Sea, thus turning the flank of the enemy's Army Group North.

The southern flank of the entire attacking group of Soviet forces in Belorussia was secured by the echeloned location of the First Belorussian Front's left wing, followed by its assumption of the offensive.

Anti-aircraft defense was organized and conducted in a favorable situation for Soviet forces, when by the start of the Belorussian operation air superiority was on our side.

The principle of concentrating the efforts of anti-aircraft artillery and fighter aviation for covering the troops that constituted the *fronts'* main groups formed the basis of the *fronts'* anti-aircraft defense.

One of the shortcomings of troop anti-aircraft defense during the operation was the lagging of part of the anti-aircraft artillery and fighter aviation's basing behind the attacking forces' forward units.

As for employing anti-aircraft artillery, it should be noted that its accomplishment of its tasks was made significantly easier by the fact that our aviation enjoyed air superiority.

The main anti-aircraft artillery weapons were concentrated for supporting our main groups of forces along the axes of the main attacks.

During the operation, the anti-aircraft artillery was moved in stages, and in leaps, from line to line, while pursuing the enemy at high rates of advance. The anti-aircraft divisions' small-caliber anti-aircraft artillery regiments were distributed among the columns, while the medium-caliber regiments advanced to cover crossings, gorges and defiles. During the operation, attention was mainly paid to covering the main crossings from the air, as well as troop concentrations along the most important lines. On the whole, these were expedient measures in these conditions, although they were insufficient, because they could not prevent enemy air activity against our forces and the crossings, particularly when the *front* aviation's airfield maneuver began to lag behind the rate of the ground forces' advance.

On the whole, the operational support of the forces enabled the latter to carry out their assigned objectives in the operation.

23.   The experience of the Belorussian operation once again confirmed the great significance of engineering support for the offensive by the shock group. In particular, this experience indicated the following: a) the necessity of concentrating the main engineering forces and equipment along the axis of the main attack, with the creation here of sufficiently high operational densities (6-10 sapper companies per kilometer of front); b) the necessity of paying the greatest attention to such problems of engineering support as the laying and lifting of engineering obstacles in rapid time, the repair and restoration of roads and bridges in conditions of a high rate of advance, and the support of forcing rivers from the march; c) the expediency of the timely movement of our engineering forces and equipment behind the attacking forces for the purpose of uninterruptedly supporting the first-echelon units and formations, especially while forcing the numerous river obstacles from the march; d) the necessity of having powerful mobile obstacle detachments, especially while attacking with open flanks, and also while consolidating captured bridgeheads while forcing rivers from the march, and; e) the engineering troops' large role in concluding the operation, in consolidating captured lines, and in rapidly creating a powerful and invincible defense along them.

One of the engineering troops' main tasks was providing engineering support for the breakthrough.

Passages were cleared through the enemy's minefields in the course of 2-3 nights before the offensive, based upon the following calculation: 2-3 passages, each up to ten meters wide, for each first-echelon rifle company, and; 6-8 passages, each up to 34-40 meters wide, for each direct infantry-support tank brigade. In breaking through the enemy's defense (for example, along the

Bobruisk axis), tank minesweeper and flamethrower tank regiments were employed. The mine-sweeping tanks showed their high combat qualities. Of the First Belorussian Front's 50 tank mine-sweepers, only one tank was knocked out during mine clearing duties. However, as a result of poor cooperation between combat tanks, artillery and aviation, the minesweeping tanks lost up to 50 percent of their strength from enemy artillery fire during the breakthrough of the enemy's main defense zone.

Our troops' rapid advance during the operation raised the need for echeloning the crossing equipment and the engineering units that serviced them, for the purposes of successfully supporting the forcing of rivers from the march. With the halt of the first-echelons of the engineer-sapper or pontoon units for laying down bridges, the second and third echelons would move up behind the forward units, now operating as first echelons. This method of employing crossing equipment was justified in conditions of overcoming a significant number of small water obstacles. However, upon approaching major rivers (the Western Bug, Vistula and Narew), such a dispersal of men and materiel became inexpedient; the greatest success was achieved along those sectors where all the crossing equipment advanced behind the forward units of the attacking troops. For example, as the first echelons of the First Belorussian Front's 8th Guards and 69th armies arrived at the Vistula River in July 1944, all of the crossing equipment available in these armies was following behind them. The lagging behind of the crossing equipment in the 2nd Tank Army's movement to the Vistula River forced the army command to forgo an immediate crossing of the river from the march in the Deblin area.

The experience of forcing rivers in the Belorussian operation confirmed the expediency of broadly employing mine and explosive obstacles on the bridgeheads, the use of which was most quickly and successfully accomplished by the armies' and formations' mobile obstacle detachments.

Road support for the attacking forces, especially during the pursuit, often did not satisfy the demands of the forces attacking at high speeds. Thus in a number of cases it wasn't the engineering measures that decided the success of the offensive, but the seizure of intact crossings from the march and the presence of fords, etc. (for example, along the Western Bug River).

24.   Problems of the operations' materiel and medical support were resolved with certain difficulties. As a result of the lagging of the rear services, the troops, particularly during the pursuit phase, experienced a shortage of ammunition, fuels and lubricants, and food. To a significant degree, these difficulties were overcome thanks only to the intervention of higher headquarters and the immediate delivery of all types of supplies, as well as *Stavka* reserves, to the troops.[14]

The enormous scale of the Belorussian operation and the intensive character of combat activities demanded a major expenditure of materiel resources. Ammunition expenditure for the main calibers from the beginning of the operation through July, inclusively, was 2.5-3.5 *front* combat loads, and even more for certain calibers. In all, from 23 June to the end of August 3.5-5 *front* combat loads were expended. If one takes into account that the weight of a single combat load of all four *fronts*, while counting the ammunition transferred to them from the *Stavka* reserve, reached 90,000 tons, then the overall ammunition expenditure was more than 400,000 tons.[15]

Up to 300,000 tons of fuels and lubricants were expanded during the operation, including more than 190,500 tons of automobile fuel. The expenditure of auto fuel from 23 June through the end

14 M.S. Tur, *Belorusskaya Operatsiya 1944 g.* VAGSh, 1956, p. 61.
15 *Operatsii Sovetskikh Vooruzhennykh Sil v Velikoi Otechestvennoi Voine 1941-1945 gg.* VNU GSh VS SSSR, vol. III, p. 375.

of July was 9-15 refills, that is, 2-4 times more than the *fronts'* initial supplies at the start of the operation.[16]

One of the most difficult tasks during the course of the operation was the timely delivery of materiel to the troops. The enemy, while retreating under the blows of our forces, carried out a lot of demolition work on the roads. For example, 776 kilometers of railroad were destroyed in the Second Belorussian Front's sector.

Not only was all of the available transport used to deliver ammunition and fuels and lubricants, but also part of the combat vehicles and local transportation resources.

In the jumping-off position, the outline of the railroad network, its capacity, the coincidence of the dirt road net with that of the railroads, guaranteed favorable conditions for basing the armies, with the exception of the First Belorussian Front's 3rd Army. The network of dirt roads completely satisfied the demands of the *fronts* and armies, but these roads were of poor quality. The *fronts'* and armies' auto transportation capabilities were sufficiently favorable, but only under conditions where the normal pace of restoring the railroads could be guaranteed.

However, during the operation the pace of developing the troops' offensive significantly exceeded the rate of restoring the railroads. Thus during the operation there arose a gap between the railroad supply bases and the front line. And this gap became larger the higher the troops' rate of advance. By the middle of July, following 20-25 days of the operation's successful development, the excessive lengthening of the rear delivery routes made the troops' further advance more difficult and complex.

For example, by 15 July the basing of the First Baltic Front's forces, and also those of the Second and First Belorussian fronts, remained the same as it had been at the starting point. As a result, the First Baltic Front's road delivery leg reached 270 kilometers, 250-300 kilometers in the First Belorussian Front, and 300-350 kilometers in the Second Belorussian Front, and during the latter half of July it reached 400-500 kilometers along the First Belorussian Front's right wing.

Given this extension of the road delivery leg, automobile transport worked in very difficult conditions and the delivery situation, particularly for the forces of the First Belorussian Front's right wing, was becoming critical.

Given the weight of a single refill of fuels and lubricants of 20,000 tons, and that of a single combat load at 90,000 tons, and a day's ration of food of 6,000 tons, the *fronts* had the capability of delivering by automobile transport up to 100 kilometers (counting *front* and army auto transport) only 0.25 of a refill, 0.1 of a combat load, and one day's ration of food. The delivery situation became even more complex due to the fact that the *fronts* could not employ all the vehicles at their disposal for deliveries. They had to allot part of the vehicles for transporting the wounded, deliveries to the rail brigades, road troops, and the engineer troops, and for transferring crossing parks, etc.

The restoration of the railroads was carried out along a broad front. The rate of restoration along the sectors of mass destruction was only 2.5-5 kilometers per day, 12-15 kilometers along the sectors that had suffered minor damage, and 25-30 kilometers along those sectors that only required that the gauge be changed from narrow to wide. The chief sites that delayed the restoration of the rail lines for a considerable time were bridges and railroad junctions. The average rate of restoring rail bridges was as follows: for large bridges—up to 25, medium—up to seven, and small—up to 4-5 linear meters per day. Higher rates were achieved when restoring bridges near the jumping-off point, because parts and other materials had been prepared beforehand for their restoration.

The experience of the Belorussian operation shows that in order to maintain the average rate of railroad restoration at 20 kilometers per day, it is necessary to have no less than two railroad

---

16 *Ibid*, p. 61.

brigades and special formations from the Ministry of Transportation; moreover, the restoration of the first 40-50 kilometers of railroads, which the enemy will completely destroy, must be scrupulously planned and supplied. In restoring the railroads, it is necessary to concentrate one's main efforts on restoring the railroads along the main axes, in order to guarantee the delivery from the country's rear to the *fronts'* main groups of forces. Simultaneously with the restoration of the main lines, it is necessary also to restore the station lines and stub ends, or it will be difficult to use the railroad lines being restored for delivery and supply.

The seizure of crossings from the march by mobile forces, as well as preventing the enemy from destroying the railroads and crossings is very important from the point of view of preserving high rates of developing the operation and securing normal conditions for the work of the rear. For example, practice showed that our air force was capable of preventing the destruction of the rail bed (by means of destroying the destroyers) and big bridges (for example, the railroad bridge over the Dnepr River along the Krichev—Orsha sector).

While carrying out restoration work, the establishment of railroad communications was delayed, although this may be avoided by paying attention to this problem in a timely manner.

In the conditions of the Belorussian operation's great depth and high rates of advance, which significantly exceeded the rates of restoring the railroads, and given the troops' poor supply of auto transport, particularly along the army leg, by the end of the operation the rear establishments and materiel supplies were scattered along an enormous territory from the Dnepr to the Neman.

The *fronts* and armies undertook all sorts of measures to ensure that the rear organs advanced behind the troops. However, neither the comparatively rapid restoration of the railroads after completing the restoration work in the 50-kilometer zone of complete destruction, nor the road troops' good work, could cope with this task.

Such a situation forced the *fronts* and armies to widely resort to suing local resources, especially food and forage, as well as using captured materials. Moreover, the *fronts* and armies, while striving to have their supplies closer to the troops, moved up the lead sections of their artillery depots, along with some ammunition supplies.

Nonetheless, because of the rear organs lagging behind and the stretching out of communications, by the middle of July a situation had arisen in which the armies were formally completely supplied with ammunition (up to two combat loads), but were unable to deliver them to the troops in the necessary amounts. A significant part of the ammunition was dispersed within the confines of the army's entire offensive zone, beginning with the firing positions at the jumping-off position. As a result of this, the actual level of supply of the Third and First Belorussian fronts' first-echelon forces during 17-26 July varied on the average from 0.2-0.3 to 0.5 combat loads, and in certain kinds of ammunition went down to zero.

The railroads' poor carrying capacity and the shortage of auto transport prevented us from fully employing the *fronts'* supplies, which were stranded in the deep rear. One can judge the level of supply of ammunition by the following example: on 26 July the 65th Army's 105th Rifle Corps was forced to fall back from the Western Bug River, due to the almost complete lack of ammunition.

The troops' supply of fuels and lubricants during the operation was carried out mainly by delivery from the country's rear. The supplies that had been accumulated among the troops were very quickly expended. Because of the untimely delivery of fuel, the troops became stretched out, the rates of advance fell, and weapons lagged behind the troops or could not be employed. For example, on 27 July a large part of the 28th Army's artillery fell behind the troops because of a shortage of fuel. For the same reason on 14 July a large amount of auto transport piled up northeast of Bereza (Bereza-Kartuska). The 2nd Tank Army, upon arriving at the Warsaw suburb of Praga, was deprived of the capability of waging active operations and went over to the defensive (3rd Tank Corps), because of the complete lack of fuel. Difficulties with the delivery of fuel particularly made the air force's combat operations more difficult. As a result of a shortage of fuel, in a number of situations our aviation was unable to reliably cover the ground forces against the enemy's air attacks. For example, on 29 July the 6th Air Army, disposing at this time of about 1,400 planes and having an aircraft superiority of 2-3 times over the enemy, carried out only 95 sorties, while at the same time the enemy air force carried out 286 sorties that same day. On 30 July the army carried out 232 sorties, and the enemy 300.[17]

The difficulties in supplying the troops with fuels and lubricants arose, to a significant degree, due to the fact that the armies were not able to flexibly maneuver containers from the depots. The containers in the *front* depots were not moved until almost the end of the operation, because of a lack of rolling stock and the low carrying capacity of the railroads then being restored. It was only in August that an increase in troop supply was noted, as well as the reinforcement of the supply depots with fuels and lubricants.

The operation's experience speaks of the necessity of having non-cumbersome mobile containers, good for transporting on automobiles. By the beginning of the operation the *fronts* and armies had a sufficient supply of containers, although a significant part of these were not configured for transport on automobiles.

Moreover, the troops and the depots must be supplied with a sufficient amount of pumping and refueling materiel.

The usage of pipelines will be of particular importance in the matter of continuously and reliably supplying the troops with fuels and lubricants in the *front* and army rear.

The supplies of food, which had been created by the *fronts* during the preparatory period, fully ensured the reliable supply of the troops during the operation. However, due to the rapid rates of the troops' advance and the resulting difficulties in delivering supplies, the troops encountered supply shortages of those types of food that could not be procured on the spot (tobacco, sugar, etc.). The troops experienced difficulties for a certain time in the supply of bread, because of the impossibility of processing the already procured grain into flour and groats. The enemy had put the local windmills out of commission. Due to this, the troops began to set up their own mobile windmills and hulling mills. This yielded good results: almost all the armies had their own home-made flour and groats.

The actual medical losses during the operation were less than had been assumed. This circumstance made the medical service's work on evacuating and treating the wounded and sick easier. However, the medical service experienced no little difficulties during the operation.

During the period of the operation, when the railroads had not yet been restored, or had only a limited carrying capacity, a significant portion of the *front* hospitals were carried by medical transport and on trucks, which had been allotted by the *fronts'* rear services. A portion of the *front* hospitals, burdened from the operation's first days with heavily wounded soldiers, became separated from the troops and remained in place for an extended time.

The absence of a sufficient amount of automobile transport told on the mobility not only of the *front* hospitals, but the army ones as well. The authorized amount of automobile transport could carry no more than 25 percent of the hospital rank and file and equipment. Thus, it required 4-5 round trips of authorized auto transport to move a hospital. As a rule, however, it was impossible to do this, for as soon as part of a hospital would arrive at a new site it immediately pitched into its work and its transportation was required for servicing the wounded and sick.

During the operation the system of medical service, as opposed to the plans drawn up during the preparatory period, adapted itself on the go both to the troops' supply needs that arose during the operation, but also to the *fronts'* transport capabilities.

---

17 *Operatsii Sovetskikh Vooruzhennykh Sil v Velikoi Otechestvennoi Voine 1941-1945 gg.* VNU GSh VS SSSR, vol. III, p. 376.

As a rule, first-line surgical field mobile hospitals were attached, one apiece, to each corps for the purpose of increasing their mobility, were lightened and supplied with additional auto transportation. However, they did not manage to move behind the troops, because they did not have time to evacuate their wounded. During the operation, the surgical field mobile hospitals were partially broken up, that is, they left behind part of their service personnel and equipment in their previous location, along with the wounded evacuees. The armies lacked a sufficient number of hospitals to enable them to deploy them along each new line.

The hospitals could not often maintain their specialization. The entire mass of wounded was usually directed to the first hospital that arrived.

As Soviet territory was liberated, the urgent need arose to carry out large-scale medical-epidemiological measures.

The operation's experience shows that under conditions of the troops' rapid advance, it is extremely important to preserve the necessary rates of shifting the *front* and army hospital bases. For this, all the army and *front* hospitals must be supplied with a sufficient amount of auto transportation. The *fronts* and armies must have powerful groups of surgical field mobile hospitals. They must advance behind the troops and deploy in place of those hospitals already overflowing with wounded.

The rear headquarters, with all of its subordinate directorates and sections, was usually located at a single site 20-40 kilometers from the main command post. Exceptions were the *front* and army military roads and communications directorates and sections, which were located at supply stations for direct contact with the railroads.

During the operation some rear headquarters became separated from the main command posts by a considerable distance. This led to a situation in which the deputies for the rear and their apparatuses would find themselves in a very difficult situation, because during these periods they did not know the true rear situation among the troops and could not truly control the rear units and establishments, which were scattered over a large territory.

The *fronts* and armies, in order to eliminate this shortcoming in the control of the rear, allotted during the operation 1-2 operational groups of officers—representatives of the main supply directorates and sections, under the command of either the rear chiefs' deputies, or the chief of the rear staff, or the deputy chief of staff for rear affairs.

During the operation individual instructions were the chief documents for controlling the rear. Plans for materiel supply and rear organization were drawn up only at the starting point. During the operation planning came down to the rear services' compiling individual calculations for a short period of time (usually for ten days), which were confirmed by the rear chief or the military council.

Thus the *fronts*' rear services experience significant difficulties during the operation with the delivery of supplies and the evacuation of the wounded, which arose mainly due to the varying rates of the troops' advance and the restoration of the railroads.

25. Great demands were made upon the command and control of the *fronts* and armies.

Thanks to the good organization of command and control, the flexible employment of all communications means, the rapid movement of the headquarters behind the attacking troops, and the timely issuing of instructions, the *fronts*' and armies' headquarters were able to accomplish the uninterrupted command and control of the troops and ensure the successful fulfillment of the assigned tasks.

Command and control was exercised from the command posts. The troops' rapid rate of advance demanded that the command posts be shifted often. During the operation the *fronts*' command posts moved 6-8 times, those of the armies every other day, while the formations' command posts sometimes moved several times per day. During the conduct of a single *front* operation the *fronts*' headquarters moved 1-2 times and those of the armies' 3-6 times. For example, during the 23 June-23 July time period the headquarters of the First Baltic Front shifted its command post six times and the headquarters of the First Belorussian Front four times, while an auxiliary command post in the sector of the *front's* right-wing armies moved six times. The shift in the armies' command posts was even more frequent. For example, throughout the entire period of the offensive the head-quarters of the 43rd Army changed its command post 19 times, the 48th Army 24 times, and the 65th Army 22 times, the 28th Army 17 times. During the same time the armies' forces advanced as follows: 43rd Army—about 450 kilometers, 48th and 65th armies—650-700 kilometers, and the 28th Army—650-680 kilometers. Thus the greatest distance the army command posts were from the troops during the operation varied from 24-40 kilometers.

All of this was brought about by the specific situation. Experience showed that during an offensive conducted at a high rate of advance, a particularly flexible and precise system of command and control is required, especially in the mobility of the command posts' work and their ability to uninterruptedly control their forces.

As a result of the rapid advance of the troops and the frequent changes in the command posts' locations, it was not always possible to establish permanent communications lines. Thus the main communications means were radio and mobile means, mainly Po-2 aircraft. These planes rendered an invaluable service. They were the most maneuverable and reliable means of communications at all stages of the operation, and in any conditions.

In the First Belorussian Front the broad flood plain of the Pripyat' River divided the *front's* operational sector into two independent parts. As a result, it was necessary to create, beside the main command post, an auxiliary one. One of the *front* commander's deputies was constantly at the site and sometimes the *front* commander himself travelled there.

The commander of the Third Belorussian Front had an operational group (the first echelon of the *front's* field directorate) created for him, consisting of several officers from the operational directorate and headed by its chief, as well as officers—representatives from the headquarters' other directorates and combat arms commanders.

The operation's experience confirmed that in conditions of a rapid advance, the creation of such operational groups enables the commander and staff to more firmly command their forces and not become separated from them.

The *front* commanders carried out the command and control of their forces by issuing individual combat orders and instructions, which were usually transmitted to the armies by high-frequency telephone, while the most important of these were duplicated by communications officers.

In each *front* mobile group there were representatives from the *front* operational directorate, the air force and artillery, all disposing of the necessary amount of transportation and communications means.

Of great significance was personal contact between the *front* commanders and the army commanders during the operation, as well as trips by the command's representatives to the troops and subordinate headquarters.

Headquarters at all levels, despite the difficult conditions, coped with the tasks of troop control. At the same time, a weak link during the operation was the maintenance of communications with the rear organs. The stretching out of communications in some armies reached 300-400 kilometers. Great efforts and additional means were thus required to maintain communications at such distances.

Such serious shortcomings as the loss of command and control of the mobile forces and the resulting poor knowledge of the situation in their areas by the *fronts'* headquarters, as well as the absence of the necessary control of the headquarters commandant's service along the crossings and in defiles, was noted in the command and control of the troops during the development of the offensive and pursuit of the enemy, as a result of which the timely movement of artillery and the delivery of ammunition and fuel was delayed.

On the whole, despite a number of shortcomings, the command and control of the *fronts'* and armies' forces during the preparation for the operation, as well as during its conduct, was, on the whole, uninterrupted and enabled the troops to accomplish their missions.

Thus the Belorussian operation is one of the classic examples of operations, the preparation and conduct of which became possible thanks to the high developmental level of Soviet operational art in the third period of the Great Patriotic War. The rich experience of this operation enables us to visually and concretely show the entire diversity of our troops' operational methods in carrying out major offensive operations in the conditions of the time. In this regard, particularly illustrative are the methods of carrying out the breakthrough of the enemy's prepared defense and the development of the success to a great depth and at a high rate of advance, and in conditions of close cooperation of all the combat arms and services.

Some Questions of Tactics

The Soviet troops' tactics in the Belorussian operation corresponded, on the whole, to the level achieved by Soviet military art by that time.

1. In this operation Soviet forces had to break through, in conditions of a wooded and swampy area, the enemy's powerful and deeply echeloned defense, the main sector of which had been previously occupied by his forces.

The tactical defense zone of the German-Fascist forces was, as a rule, 10-12 kilometers deep, and more. The defense had been prepared in the course of a long time. The main defense zone (the "main battlefield") was most strongly developed, in the engineering sense. Its depth reached 5-6 kilometers. At the same time the enemy skillfully took advantage of the powerful aspects of the wooded and swampy terrain.[18]

In order to overcome such a defense, it was necessary for our forces to display a high degree of skills in employing all available forces and means.

2. The experience of the recent war and, in particular, the Belorussian operation, showed that the main method of operating against a single, continuous positional defensive front, based on a system of trenches, is the breakthrough, carried out by rifle formations, in conjunction with the other combat arms, for the purpose of defeating the opposing enemy and ensuring the commitment of the mobile formations for developing the success.

The Belorussian operation of 1944 gives us numerous examples of the practical employment of the breakthrough of a prepared enemy defense.

The breakthrough was carried out in the following manner.

During the artillery preparation, the infantry and tanks were in their jumping-off positions in readiness for the attack. In those cases, when the jumping-off trench was more than 250 meters from the enemy, the infantry would move forward to the line of attack, without stopping there, during the artillery preparation. For example, units of the 65th Army's 18th Rifle Corps in the Bobruisk—Slutsk operation began to move up from their jumping-off positions 20 minutes before the end of the artillery preparation.

As opposed to the requirements of order no. 306 of 1942, the 1944 handbook for breaking through a positional defense recommended that, given the presence of the enemy's continuous deep

---

18 *Istoriya Voennogo Iskusstva. Kurs Lektsii* VA im. M.V. Frunze. Vol. VII, p. 296.

and entrenched defense, the corps and division combat orders should be echeloned in depth. The rifle troops' combat organization in the Belorussian operation was, as a rule, organized in accordance with these requirements. The rifle corps, which were breaking through the enemy's defense along 2-4-kilometer sectors, organized their combat formation, as a rule, in two and, sometimes in three, echelons. Two-thirds of all the first-echelon rifle formations and four-fifths of all the regiments had a two-echelon formation; one-tenth of all units had a three-echelon formation.[19]

In those cases in which the first-echelon divisions had a single-echelon formation, second echelons were created, on the one hand, in the regiments and, on the other hand, in the corps. The formations' and units' deep formation was conditioned by the necessity of breaking through the enemy's echeloned, entrenched and previously-occupied tactical defensive zone, as well as the conditions of the wooded and swampy terrain, which often forced us to operate along a single road and secure our flanks. On the other hand, the Red Army had begun to receive military equipment and ammunition in amounts that enabled us to not only support the creation of a sufficiently powerful first echelon, but to also allot the necessary forces and weapons to the second and third echelons.

However, the combat formations examined above did not represent a return to the combat formations that were recommended in the Soviet manuals and handbooks before the appearance of order no. 306 of 8 October 1942. The basis of the new and deeply echeloned combat formation continued to be the skirmish line, recommended by order no. 306. Only now several lines were organized, one after the other. The echeloning of combat formations in the regiment, division and corps in the new conditions transpired not at the expense of weaking the first echelons, as had been the case in the first period of the war, but by strengthening our troops' capabilities.

Following the completion of the artillery preparation, the infantry and tanks attacked the enemy, supported by artillery and aviation. Regimental guns and part of the divisional artillery fired over open sights. To ensure better communications between the artillery and infantry, forward artillery observers, with communications equipment, were moved up to the first-echelon rifle battalions. Self-propelled artillery pieces moved directly behind the infantry, accompanying it with their fire. The rifle regiments' second-echelon battalions attacked 400-500 meters behind the first echelon. They were usually committed for augmenting efforts in breaking through the second position of the enemy's main defensive zone. Sometimes the rifle divisions' second echelons were committed for this purpose.

The infantry usually attacked alongside the direct infantry-support tanks. In individual cases, when the troops could not, for whatever reason, make passages for the tanks beforehand through the enemy's anti-tank obstacles in front of his forward edge, the direct infantry-support tanks entered the battle after the infantry captured the first trench and the corresponding mine clearing of the area.

The repulse of the enemy's counterattacks, carried out by forces ranging from a company to a regiment of infantry and tanks, supported by artillery and aviation, had great significance for the successful breakthrough of the enemy's main defensive zone. The enemy's counterattacks were most often repulsed by fire on the spot, while the fire from artillery and tanks had decisive significance.

The division's second echlon was committed into the battle, as a rule, for capturing the enemy's second or third positions, during which time it was moved up from behind the flanks of the first-echelon units and, as an exception, by rolling through the first echelon's combat formations.

The corps' second echelons were usually committed into the battle in the second half of the offensive's first day, with the task of completing the breakthrough of the main defensive zone. Along the axes of the army's main blow this task was usually carried out in conjunction with the

---

19 *Istoriya Voennogo Iskusstva. Kurs Lektsii* VA im. M.V. Frunze. Vol. VII, p. 296.

forward detachments of the tank corps and army mobile groups, or the *front*. For example, the the 16th Guards Rifle Corps' 11th Guards Division (11th Guards Army/Third Belorussian Front) in the Vitebsk—Minsk operation comprised the corps' second echelon at the beginning of the offensive and was committed into the battle in the second half of the offensive's first day.

The correct determination of the second echelons' moment of commitment into the battle was one of the most important indices of troop leadership skill in carrying out the breakthrough.

The breakthrough of the enemy's main defensive zone in the Belorussian operation was carried out by the first-echelon rifle formations in conditions of high intensity and was based upon the close cooperation of all combat arms, especially of the infantry, tanks and artillery, and with aviation support.

3. The width of the attack front and the formations' and units' breakthrough sectors were determined, in each individual case, depending on the concrete situation, the operational plan, the role and place of the corps or division, the correlation of forces and the character of the enemy's defense along the given sector.

A rifle corps' offensive sector along the axis of the main attack in Belorussia varied from five to 15 kilometers and was usually 6-8 kilometers. As regards the width of the breakthrough sectors, along a corps' main attack axis it was 4-6 kilometers and 2-3 kilometers for a division, which was typical for the period under study. However, sometimes these sectors were narrower (3-4 kilometers per corps and 1.5-2.5 for a division, which was conditioned by the fact that a number of formations were not at full strength, or by actions in a narrow defile against the enemy's prepared engineering defense that had previously been occupied by the enemy's forces, and given the impossibility or great difficulty of carrying out outflanking or enveloping movements. In the wooded and swampy terrain conditions, a corps' offensive zone and breakthrough sector were twice as broad as usual. Corps operating along auxiliary axes also attacked along significantly broader zones. However, at the same time the rifle corps' breakthrough sectors were narrower than their attack fronts.

4. According to the theoretical views of the time, it was believed that in breaking through the enemy's deeply echeloned defense, the rifle regiment's immediate task was to capture the enemy's second trench; that of a rifle division—the capture of the entire first position, and; that of the rifle corps—the capture of the second position and the area of the enemy's main artillery positions. The depth of the subsequent tasks coincided with the depth of the immediate tasks of the superior formations, and that of the rifle corps with that of the army—the seizure of the second zone. In the Belorussian operation of 1944 the corps' immediate objective was usually the breakthrough of the enemy's main defensive zone and the arrival at a depth of 5-8 kilometers. The mission of the day was the breakthrough of the entire tactical defense zone and reaching a depth of 15 kilometers. In the wooded and swampy terrain conditions, the depth of the immediate mission was reduced to 3-5 kilometers, and that of the day's mission to 6-8 kilometers. The rifle divisions' immediate mission was, as a rule, the breakthrough of the first, and sometimes the second positions, while the day's mission was to overcome the main defensive zone. Sometimes the divisions were given missions of capturing the enemy's second defensive zone (the "postion of the corps reserves") by the close of the offensive's first day. In this case, the day's missions for the divisions and corps often coincided.

The axis of the formations' main attacks was chosen, depending on the concrete situation. By this time the Soviet formations and units already had a great deal of experience in the decisive concentration of men and materiel along the axes of the main attacks, which enabled us to create high tactical densities.

5.　The first-echelon formations and units attacked, as a rule, with direct infantry-support tanks, the density of which depended on the character of the terrain and the enemy's defense, while the presence of tanks in the *front* varied and could reach 22-26 armored vehicles per kilometer of front along the breakthrough sectors. However, in many cases the density of tanks was significantly less, because on a number of axes the ability to employ them was quite limited. At the same time, in those places where there was an insufficient number of direct infantry-support tanks, we often had to employ tanks from the mobile groups (for example, from the 9th Tank Corps' formations in the sector of the First Belorussian Front's 3rd Army) to complete the breakthrough.

6.　The basic principle of employing artillery at the tactical level, as was the case at the operational level, was its decisive massing along the axis of the main attack, which enabled us to create high tactical densities. The allotment of guns for firing over open sights occupied a major place in the operation. The creation of high artillery densities (151-204 guns and mortars per kilometer along the breakthrough sector), given the troops' improved supply with ammunition by that time, enabled us to increase the time for fire onslaughts in the artillery preparation and go over, for the first time during the Great Patriotic War, to the method of supporting the infantry and tank attack with a double rolling barrage.

The problem of the artillery's grouping was not fully decided. The corps and divisional artillery groups were either weak or were not created altogether. Too little artillery was at the disposal of the regimental and battalion commanders. The powerful and numerous army artillery groups were cumbersome and only existed for a short time. The main idea, which was to enable the corps, division, regimental, and battalion commanders to influence the course of the battle by artillery fire, was not put into practice everywhere.

The problem of the amount, subordination, length of existence, and qualitative composition of the artillery groups in the given operation was not fully resolved. The inexpediency of the artillery's overly complicated division into a large number of various groups and special-designation subgroups, which led to a part of the artillery weapons being idle should there be no targets corresponding to their mission, was confirmed once again. The practice of the Great Patriotic War showed the great expediency of dividing the artillery into groups not of special, but overall, designation—regimental (PAG), divisional (DAG), corps (KAG), and army (AAG), which simplified command and control and enabled us to employ more intensely all artillery and mortar systems, depending on the situation. However, some *fronts'* artillery commanders (for example, the First Belorussian Front) did not take this into account, although by this time we were already employing the "Instructions for Breaking Through a Positional Defense" of 1944, in which the problem of grouping the artillery was correctly examined, taking into account the experience of the war.

During the battle in the depth of the enemy's defense, powerful groups of accompaniment guns in the rifle battalions justified themselves. These groups, supporting with their fire the uninterrupted accompaniment of the infantry and tanks, facilitated the success of our rifle forces' offensive.

Due to the increasing practice of night actions, the artillery gained a good deal of experience in waging fire in nighttime conditions, both for supporting its forces' actions, and for repelling the enemy's night attacks.

The prior organization of artillery supporting for river forcing justified itself during the operation in forseeing the forcing of major water barriers. The forcing of rivers from the march was supported by organic artillery equipment, as well as by light artillery formations from the Supreme High Command reserve and aviation. In those places where it was possible to guarantee surprise, the forcing was carried out at night, without an artillery preparation. In a case where the enemy put up serious resistance, the artillery was brought up and the river forced with an artillery preparation.

7.   Engineering support for the offensive battle in wooded and swampy terrain conditions required enormous efforts of all formations and units. Due to the variety and large volume of engineer assignments, it was necessary to reinforce each rifle corps. Aside from its organic sapper units and subunits, a corps, as a rule, was reinforced with 2-3 engineer-sapper battalions. At the same time, a significant amount of special engineer-sapper work was entrusted to the rifle, artillery and tank subunits and units.

8.   The necessity and the effectiveness of employing in these conditions a reconnaissance in force of the forward battalions' forces were once again confirmed. Forward battalions were usually allotted from the first-echelon divisions, although this was not routine. Sometimes they were allotted from the rifle corps' second echelons. The forward battalions, having on the whole an operational designation, resolved their missions in each separate case by tactical means. They operated most effectively in the area to the norwest of Vitebsk, and then, at the second stage of the Belorussian operation, west of Kovel'. In individual cases, having supported the success of the forward battalions with the forces of the first-echelon units, Soviet forces advanced 1.5-3.5 kilometers in depth, and even as much as 6-8 kilometers. Even if the forward battalions failed to achieve major successes, then they would capture the the first trench, pinpoint the enemy's fire system, and sometimes forced him to expend part of his reserves before the beginning of the main forces' offensive.

9.   The Belorussian operation may serve as one of the examples of a successful solution to the problem of the vigorous breakthrough of the depth of the enemy's tactical defense to its completion. The main zone of the enemy's defense, as a rule, was broken through on the offensive's first day. In the majority of cases the Soviet forces advanced on the first day to a depth of 10-12 kilometers and captured the second defensive zone from the march. Along a lesser number of sectors, the tactical zone was broken through on the second or third day of the offensive.

The success of the breakthrough was achieved by the bold massing of men and materiel along the breakthrough sectors, the deep organization of the combat formations and the skillful employment of the formations' and units' second echelons, the scrupulous organization of cooperation of the combat arms and elements of the combat formation, and the skillful command and control of the troops. The high morale and combat spirit of the rank and file facilitated the success of the breakthrough.

The successful breakthrough of the enemy's defense was also facilitated, first of all, by the fact that the infantry's combat formations contained a large amount of artillery, a significant part of which was employed for firing over open sights. During the offensive, the commanders of the artillery groups were located, as a rule, alongside the commanders of the rifle formations and units, which enabled them to employ all or part of their artillery for supporting the infantry and tank attack, in a timely manner and along the necessary axis.

The infantry's and tanks' offensive actions in the wooded and swampy terrain had a number of distinguishing features. One of these was the fact that it was not always possible to carry out an attack against the defending enemy simultaneously with the infantry and tanks. In a number of cases, where due to the terrain conditions, the tanks were not able to operate alongside the infantry (for example, in the 61st and 70th armies' formations along the Pinsk and Brest axes), the rifle formations, with support from the artillery and aviation, attacked the enemy without tanks. The tanks, as a rule, attacked ahead of the infantry in the depth of the enemy defense where the terrain allowed it and, in conjunction with the latter, launched attacks against the flank and rear of the enemy defending in his strong points.

The presence of second and third echelons in the corps enabled us to augment the force of the attack from the depth by committing these echelons into the battle on the first and second days of the offensive for developing the success in depth and toward the flanks. By commiting the second echelons and reserves, the redirecting of the corps' main efforts from one axis to another was also accomplished.

The development of the breakthrough occurred at sufficiently high speeds (10-12 kilometers a day, and in individual cases up to 20 kilometers) for the time. The most important prerequisites for the development of the offensive at high rates were initiative and bold actions of the commanders at all levels, who by this stage had acquired significant combat experience.

10.   Following the breakthrough of the main defensive zone, the pursuit of the enemy began, for the purpose of capturing his second defensive zone from the march. Along the axis of the *front's* main attack, this mission was achieved by the rifle corps in close conjunction with the mobile group, the forward units of which often entered the fighting upon completing the breakthrough of the main defense zone. In this case, the combined-arms formations would arrive at the enemy's second defensive zone behind the mobile group's forces.

With the start of the pursuit the rifle corps operated in wider sectors (from 10-30 kilometers and sometimes more).

The rifle corps usually maintained a two-echelon formation during the pursuit, while the first echelons contained up to two-thirds of the rifle units, all the tanks, and a large part of the artillery. The forward detachments, which were allotted from the first-echelon divisions and which operated at times from 20-30 kilometers from the main forces, played a major role, as did the vanguards, which moved ahead of the main forces at a distance of 4-6 kilometers.

The composition of the forward detachments usually varied from a company, reinforced with a battery from an anti-tank battalion, 2-3 guns from regimental artillery, a sapper platoon, up to two battalions, reinforced by a cannon artillery regiment, an anti-tank artillery battalion, a battalion of rocket artillery, tanks, and sappers.

The mission of the forward detachments consisted of, while avoiding getting drawn into fighting with the retreating enemy forces, bypassing them along parallel roads, getting into the enemy's flank and rear, occupying bridges and crossings, seizing defiles and bridgeheads, and holding them until the arrival of the main forces. In the overwhelming majority of cases, the forward detachments were supplied with auto transport.

The divisions' main forces, as a rule, moved in column formation during the pursuit and, as was necessary, they would deploy for battle, mainly in front of the enemy's intermediate lines.

In the majority of cases the corps' forward detachments were made up of a reinforced rifle regiment.

During the pursuit, night actions were widely employed, while sometimes entire formations operated at night. The main goal of the nighttime offensive was to prevent the enemy from consolidating along his occupied lines, keep him in a tense state for entire days, and to capture lines and locales supporting a more successful development of the battle during the daylight hours. The pursuit of the enemy at night was often conducted by the forces of separate battalions, more rarely regiments, which had been moved up by the close of the day from the second echelons and reserves.

Along certain axes, where the possibility of pursuing the enemy was made more difficult by the terrain conditions, a frontal pursuit was predominantly carried out (for example, in the wooded and swampy areas of the Poles'ye).

11.   Methods of forcing water lines by formations and units from the march were further developed. It should be noted that not one of the *front* operations carried out in Belorussia in June-July 1944 did not pass without forcing water obstacles, and that our forces forced the majority of them not as the result of planned preparation, but directly from the march. Closely pursuing the enemy,

our formations and units forced river barriers from the march with the forces of the forward detachments, which were moved up on auto transport, widely employing materials at hand. The boldness and decisiveness of the forward detachments' actions meant the successful overcoming of the water obstacles and the seizure of bridgeheads along the opposite bank which, in turn, created favorable conditions for forcing the rivers by the main forces. It was by using such methods that in June 1944, for example, the formations of the Second Belorussian Front forced in the course of three days of attacking the Pronya, Resta and Dnepr rivers. In July 1944 the formations of the First Belorussian Front forced the Western Bug and Vistula rivers from the march. The experience of the Belorussian operation once again confirmed that such a method of forcing had become the chief method of overcoming rivers by the Soviet forces. Along with this, the operation's experience showed that one must prevent the organic crossing equipment from falling behind, for without this the crossing of tanks and artillery is made more difficult and thus the augmentation of men and materiel on the bridgeheads is slowed down.

On the whole, the art of the offensive battle in the Belorussian operation was characterized by a more scrupulous and all-round preparation, the most important question of which was the organization of cooperation between the combat arms. The breakthrough of the enemy's prepared positional defense occupied the main place in the offensive battle.

The experience that was gathered in the multi-*front* Belorussian operation of 1944, of organizing a powerful initial attack and the skillful augmentation of its power in the enemy's operational depth, which ensured the Soviet forces' high rates of advance, had enormous significance both for the further conduct of the war, and for the elaboration of many problems in the theory of military art in the postwar period.

Supplement

A List of Front and Army Commanders in the Belorussian Operation of 1944

Front	*Front* Commander	Army	Army Commander
First Baltic	General I.Kh. Bagramyan	4th Shock	Lieutenant General P.F. Malyshev
		6th Guards	Lieutenant General I.M. Chistyakov
		43rd	Lieutenant General A.P. Beloborodov
		3rd Air	Colonel General of Aviation N.F. Papivin
		2nd Guards (from 2 July 1944)	Lieutenant General P.G. Chanchibadze
		51st (from 4 July 1944)	Lieutenant General Ya.G. Kreizer
Third Belorussian	Colonel General I.D. Chernyakhovskii (General from the operation's second stage)	39th	Lieutenant General I.I. Lyudnikov
		5th	Lieutenant General N.I. Krylov
		11th Guards	Lieutenant General K.N. Galitskii
		31st	Lieutenant General V.A. Glagolev
		5th Guards Tank	Marshal of Armored Troops P.A. Rotmistrov/ Lieutenant General of Tank Troops M.D. Solomatin
		1st Air	Colonel General of Aviation M.M. Gromov/ Colonel General of Aviation T.T. Khryukin
Second Belorussian	Colonel General G.F. Zakharov	33rd	Lieutenanat General V.D. Kryuchenkin/ Lieutenant General V.I. Morozov (from 10 July 1944)
		49th	Lieutenant General I.T. Grishin
		50th	Lieutenant General I.V. Boldin
		4th Air	Colonel General of Aviation K.A. Vershinin
First Belorussian	Marshal K.K. Rokossovskii	3rd	Lieutenant General A.V. Gorbatov
		48th	Lieutenant General P.L. Romanenko
		65th	Colonel General P.I. Batov
		28th	Lieutenant General A.A. Luchinskii
		61st	Lieutenant General P.A. Belov
		70th	Lieutenant General V.S. Popov
		47th	Lieutenant General N.I. Gusev

Front	*Front* Commander	Army	Army Commander
		8th Guards	Lieutenant General V.I. Chuikov
		69th	Lieutenant General V.Ya. Kolpakchi
		Polish 1st	Lieutenant General S.M. Berling
		2nd Tank	Colonel General of Tank Troops S.I. Bogdanov
		16th Air	Colonel General of Aviation S.I. Rudenko
		6th Air	Lieutenant General of Aviation P.F. Polynin
		Dnepr Flotilla	Captain First Class V.G. Grigor'ev

Index

INDEX OF PLACES

INDEX OF GERMAN MILITARY FORMATIONS & UNITS

INDEX OF HUNGARIAN MILITARY FORMATIONS & UNITS

INDEX OF SOVIET MILITARY FORMATIONS & UNITS

INDEX OF GENERAL & MISCELLANEOUS TERMS

CPSIA information can be obtained
at www.ICGtesting.com
Printed in the USA
LVOW04*0349010617

536553LV00006B/33/P